BOOKS BY JOHN H. WALLER

Gordon of Khartoum:
The Saga of a Victorian Hero

Tibet: A Chronicle of Exploration
(Written under the pseudonym John MacGregor)

Princep portrait of Charles George Gordon in Chinese Mandarin dress, 1866.
Printed by permission of the officers of the Corps of Royal Engineers.

Gordon of Khartoum

THE SAGA OF A
VICTORIAN HERO

JOHN H. WALLER

ATHENEUM · NEW YORK

1988

FOR BOBBY

Atheneum
Macmillan Publishing Company
866 Third Avenue, New York
N.Y. 10022
Collier Macmillan Canada, Inc.

Library of Congress Cataloging-in-Publication Data
Waller, John H.
  Gordon of Khartoum : the sage of a Victorian hero / John H. Waller.
    p. cm.
  Bibliography: p.
  Includes index.
  ISBN 0-689-11812-0
  1. Gordon, Charles George, 1833–1885.   2. Generals—Great Britain—Biography.   3. Great Britain. Army—Biography.
4. Colonial administrators—Sudan—Biography.
5. Sudan—History—1862–1899.
I. Title.
DA68.32.G6W33 1988
941.081′092′4—dc19   88-16987   CIP
[B]

Macmillan books are available at special discounts for bulk purchases for sales promotions, premiums, fund-raising, or educational use. For details contact:
Special Sales Director
Macmillan Publishing Company
866 Third Avenue
New York, N.Y. 10022

Designed by Jerry Kelly

10   9   8   7   6   5   4   3   2   1

Printed in the United States of America

ACKNOWLEDGMENTS

I am grateful for the assistance given me by the U.S. Library of Congress. Dr. Julian Witherell, head of the library's African Department; Ms. Joanne M. Zellers, Area Specialist in the African Section; and Mr. Ibrahim V. Pourhadi of the library's African and Middle East Division were particularly kind and helpful.

The British Library manuscript department has the most extensive collection of Gordon correspondence, and without the efficient help of this magnificent institution, adequate research on Gordon would have been impossible.

The Boston Public Library collection of Gordon's letters was invaluable; Mrs. Zonghi kindly assisted me. The library of the Royal Commonwealth Society in London was also most helpful.

I am especially indebted to Mr. and Mrs. John Brinton and their daughter, Alice, who made available to me a fascinating and unrecorded collection of Gordon's letters written while Gordon was Governor General of the Sudan. Mr. E. J. Applewhite also has my thanks for his help and good advice.

I wish to thank Ms. Judith Prendergast of the British National Portrait Gallery. Fresh from her organization of the gallery's centenary exhibition, *Gordon of Khartoum*, she was generous in advising me on the availability and location of photographs and illustrations for this book.

The Gordon Boys' School of Woking, Surrey, and its Museum Trustees were most accommodating in the matter of illustrations and for granting me permission to quote from Gordon's childhood diary, a rare addition to Gordon material recently acquired by the school. I would like to thank particularly Colonel J. R. M. Hill, OBE.

I am very grateful to Mrs. Martin Bergin, on whose friendship I imposed to translate a series of Gordon letters written in French. Other friends who made important contributions to my research include the

ACKNOWLEDGMENTS

Honorable Robert Gordon, former U.S. Ambassador to Mauritius; Dr. Jack Mower, the distinguished Africanist; Mr. Archibald Roosevelt; Mr. Dan Wages; and Mr. Vladimir Kabes.

Lieutenant Colonel R. R. Beringer and the Regimental Headquarters of the Royal Engineers at Chatham were very cooperative with photo reproductions, as was Lieutenant Colonel R. B. Merton, Regimental Secretary of the Home Headquarters of the Royal Hussars. I also wish to express my appreciation to the Leeds City Art Galleries for permission to reproduce G. W. Joy's well-known painting *Death of Gordon*.

I thank Mr. Robert Gottlieb, Vice President of the William Morris Agency, who, as my literary agent, encouraged me to write this book and was very supportive during the course of its gestation. Mr. C. Brian Kelly, Managing Editor of *Military History* magazine, also deserves my gratitude. Mr. Thomas A. Stewart, Atheneum's Publisher, and Mr. Lawrence McIntyre, associate editor, have my thanks for the indispensable help and encouragement they have given me.

Finally, I want to express gratitude to my wife, Bobby, who helped enormously in my research, ruthlessly proofread my typescript, and cheerfully endured the continual clatter of my word processor.

CONTENTS

CONTENTS
PART IV
SLAVERS AND BRIGANDS

PART V
ODD JOBS AND REFLECTION

PART VI
THE MOSLEM MESSIAH AND THE CHRISTIAN MARTYR

CONTENTS

ILLUSTRATIONS

ILLUSTRATIONS

ILLUSTRATIONS

MAPS

PREFACE

What manner of man was Charles George Gordon? The evidence is strangely contradictory, though it says something about Gordon that he evoked such a range of emotions in those who knew him. But was he judged so differently by his contemporaries because they saw him through different lenses or because, in fact, he was a welter of inconsistencies? Perhaps Cecil Rhodes was right when he concluded that Gordon was an unknowable "fanatical enigma."

Field Marshal Viscount Wolseley, Commander in Chief of the British Army and lifelong friend of Gordon, described him as "the most remarkable man he ever knew—a Christian hero." Charles Gordon and Robert E. Lee were, in Wolseley's opinion, the two most outstanding men of their time. The *Times* thought of him as a "knight of romance," who "wanders through space, and has seldom been without dragons to subdue and victims of outrage to succour." Lord Cairns, in a burst of hyperbole, announced in the House of Lords that Gordon was "one of our national treasures." Lord Northbrook, First Lord of the Admiralty, called him "an extraordinary man with an enormous power over uncivilized people." With "civilized" people, however, he was not always so successful.

George Bernard Shaw, with an acid-coated tongue, called Gordon "a most infernal scoundrel according to any workable standard of human morality." Evelyn Baring, the Earl of Cromer, Britain's proconsul in Egypt for many years and the person most responsible for supporting Gordon in his final assignment in Khartoum, was more balanced in his public judgment: He referred to him as "a curious creature." That muted opinion, however, did not begin to convey Baring's private disapproval of the man whom he only reluctantly accepted as would-be rescuer of Egypt's Sudan garrisons—and was sorry he did. Yet Baring in his memoir *Modern Egypt*[1] made some effort to be fair to Gordon's memory when he wrote: "It may be that the Gordon of real life did not always act quite up to the standard of the idealized hero who was present to the public mind, but, after all, this is merely to say that he was human and fallible."[2]

Prime Minister Disraeli was crisp and unequivocal in his appraisal of Gordon as a "lunatic"—this, after reading a memorandum Gordon wrote on "The Eastern Question." In the same vein, an acquaintance and biographer, Wilfrid Scawen Blunt, alleged that Gordon while fighting slavers in the southern Sudan was considered "mad" in some Foreign Office circles. Blunt himself thought Gordon "less than fully sane" during his "religious debauch" in the Holy Land.[3] (Of course, a century ago the word "insane" was often confused with "neurotic.") Prime Minister Gladstone's biographer, Lord Morley, was marginally kinder when he wrote that Gordon was "the creature, almost the sport, of impulse."[4]

Was Gordon, in fact, an entirely rational man? The British people, who idolized him, certainly thought so. So did the press for the most part. England's popular magazine *Vanity Fair* went so far as to blame accusations of madness on the "limited capacity of the bureaucratic mind."[5]

Gordon's admirers were staunch in his defense and delighted in seeing him pitted as a brave David against the bureaucratic Goliath. W. T. Stead, the aggressive, crusading editor of the *Pall Mall Gazette*, for example, was always a great promoter of Gordon, doing much to sway public opinion by such puffery as: "Gordon was a man, who on more than one occasion has proved himself more valuable than an entire army." Lord Kitchener, the cold, brittle hero of the Battle of Omdurman who avenged Gordon's murder in 1898, sobbed unashamedly on the occasion of a special memorial service held for Gordon in Khartoum after the British Army's triumphal entry. Lord Tennyson used his poet's talents to claim "this earth has never borne a nobler man." The *London Quarterly Review* referred to Gordon after his death as "the Galahad who rode through life in the strength of God." And Lucas Malet in the *Fortnightly Review* wrote an article canonizing him as "the Great Warrior Saint."[6] Even a symphony might have helped to preserve his saintly image if the well-known Victorian composer Edward Elgar had gotten around to writing it as he had planned.

People are often kinder to the dead than the living, but well before Gordon died, *Vanity Fair* favored him with one of its famous cartoons by

"Ape," describing him in the caption as "a fair, noble, knightly gentleman such as is found but once in many generations," yet it cautioned that his boundless enthusiasm "often leads him to interfere in matters which he does not understand and make in haste statements he has to correct at leisure."[7]

Queen Victoria, overcome by the tragedy of Gordon's death, wrote his sister Augusta a moving condolence, referring to him as a "noble" man "who served his country and his Queen so truly heroically." Victoria's uncle, Leopold, King of the Belgians, thought enough of Gordon to try repeatedly to hire him to help administer his private fiefdoms in the Congo. Farther afield, Li Hung-chang, the influential Chinese mandarin under whose authority Gordon fought the Taiping rebels, called him "a direct blessing from heaven."

Sir Richard Burton, the famous but erratic explorer who was one of Gordon's many correspondents, thought him "more fatalistic than a Moslem"[8] and generally did not approve of what he considered his excessive piety. Even one of Gordon's closest friends, Octavia Freese, who helped mold many of his religious convictions, criticized his obsession with death and some of his religious fantasizing in the Holy Land. Annie Besant, founder of the Theosophical Society, predictably disapproved of his highly personalized brand of Christian fundamentalism and was critical of his "fanatical impudence and self will." Yet it seems these very qualities enabled him to face down Chinese revolutionaries, American freebooters, British bureaucrats, mad Ethiopian princes, slave barons and Sudanese religious crusaders.

Some of Gordon's fellow officers were disapproving of him, but most who knew him liked him and some were mesmerized by him. Lieutenant Chippendall, who served briefly with Gordon in Equatoria, admired him but thought him a "fearful egotist," who seemed "always to think that nobody but his blessed self can even screw a box-lid on." Another fellow officer in Equatoria, the American Chaille-Long, was disgruntled because Gordon had maligned him and ultimately gotten rid of him, so for reasons of spite accused him by innuendo of being a drunkard. Lytton Strachey picked up this unwarranted accusation and used it in a catty assault on Gordon's reputation in his popular book *Eminent Victorians*,[9] doing grievous damage to the general's heroic image. Sir Redvers Buller is remembered for saying that "Gordon is not worth the camels" needed to rescue him.

Early in Gordon's career, while he was commanding the engineering detachment at Gravesend, England, his officers frowned at his self-isolation and his absorption by charitable works; he showed little of the worldly camaraderie customary among fellow officers. But he had a faithful and admiring constituency in the many homeless young boys—the "scuttlers," as he called them—whom he helped. They paid tribute to him by scrawling admiring graffiti on the walls of Gravesend, such as "God bless the Kernel." General Gerald Graham, the last friend Gordon would see before he went to his death in the Sudan, summed up his devotion to young people when he described him as "a man whom all children intuitively worship for he loves them so."[10]

Perhaps closest to the mark in summing up Gordon in a phrase was Winston Churchill, who fought in the Battle of Omdurman, fourteen years after the martyr's apotheosis. Churchill, with his usual inspired rhetoric and historical insight, considered Gordon a commander of the same stature as Peterborough, Wolfe and Clive. In his *River War*, he wrote of Gordon: "He was a man of stainless honour and enduring courage, who in varied capacities displayed a fertile and abundant genius. . . ." Churchill added in an accurate and well-crafted line: "The uncertainty of his moods may have frequently affected the soundness of his opinions, but not often the justice of his actions."[11]

It is significant that those who knew Gordon well usually loved and admired him. The jaundiced view was held, in most instances, either by those who distrusted mavericks daring to be different, or by those who found themselves the butt of his contempt.

But if Gordon's contemporaries were not agreed on his character, did his physical appearance provide a key to the inner man? Gordon would not have thought so; he was always contemptuous of his body, or "sheath," as he referred to it, and spent most of his life denigrating it as an instrument of the Devil. Nonetheless, his mien, if not his body, was revealing, and in a strange way one of his most effective weapons. His height was only medium, although his physique well knit and trim, and his gait sprightly rather than dignified. He had a boyish way about him and spoke gently, with a slight lisp. But if this seemed unprepossessing, hypnotic blue-gray eyes quickly trapped his viewers and radiated an inner power not easily ignored.

General Wolseley described Gordon's eyes as "light and fearless." One of his friends at Gravesend remembered them as having "a magical power over all who came within their influence," making it "impossible for you to tell him anything but the truth." Another Gravesend friend compared Gordon's eyes to "the sky on a bitter March morning," while his religious confidante Octavia Freese was convinced that his "intensely penetrating eyes . . . could see through a millstone."

Richard Burton, whose satanic-looking visage could cast a different kind of spell, was struck by Gordon's eyes when he first met him; he saw them as "calm and benevolent." General Graham wrote: "The steady, truthful gaze of the blue-gray eyes seemed a direct appeal from the upright spirit within." Perhaps the most revealing comment on Gordon's eyes, however, came from Capsune, a Sudanese boy whom Gordon had rescued from a slave train and sent to England to be educated. Capsune remembered that he had at first been terribly frightened by his rescuer's eyes. With the intuitive wisdom of childish innocence he had been convinced that Gordon could see in the dark because "he had the light inside him!" While Gordon's eyes arrested those who looked upon him, they provided no window through which to see him.

Despite the pendulum of judgments about Gordon made since his death more than a century ago, no consensus has been reached. An insightful comment once made by Gordon himself to his beloved sister, Augusta, perhaps came as close as is possible to explaining this. "Talk of two natures in one," he complained, "I have a hundred and they none think alike and all want to rule." As his life suggests, he was a man of contradictions.

Gordon was a nonconformist even though in many ways he embodied the spirit of his times. He not only did not conform to many of the mores of his society, but more profoundly he rejected the superstructures of church and state. As a fundamentalist he could not accept many of the rituals and doctrines of the "Established Church" of England, but neither could he accept the creeds of Dissenters such as John Wesley's Methodists or Evangelical reformers with fundamentalist leanings within the Presbyterian and Baptist sects. Gordon had a personal, unadorned faith based on the Bible as he understood it, and this served as his lodestar in life. But at least, like a growing number of his Protestant countrymen, he searched for a better path to the Christian God rather than turn toward the new gods of the Enlightenment.

Gordon ran with no pack, but he embodied many of the attributes common to the Victorian subspecies of his genus. He believed in a benign and responsible British Empire, he could not abide man's inhumanity toward his fellow man, and while God-worshiping, he was irreverent toward his secular masters and intolerant of their follies. He was thrilled by fighting—in a righteous cause—but compassionate toward the needy wherever they might be found.

Another contradiction which characterized Gordon was his longing for death and ascension to the better world of the hereafter in apparent conflict with a rage for life. The side of him which wanted to meet his Maker would bow to his instinct for winning when faced with sufficient challenge.

Gordon's supreme self-confidence, the confidence of one who walked with God, would soon dissolve when depression struck. Yet a period of solitude, the immutable words of the Bible always by his side, and, perhaps more than anything else, an urgent need to perform his duty would release him from the baleful grip of the "doles," as he nicknamed these attacks. He was also torn between a craving for public recognition and shame in succumbing to such vanity, or "Agag," to use his pet name for another mischievous genie lurking in his psyche. Similarly, he spent a lifetime concerned by the temptations of the flesh, which he felt were manifestations of the Devil within all beings. His sex drive seemed to be totally repressed or sublimated; while he gloried in the home life of his friends and seemed to need the warmth of family life, he ruled out marriage for himself early.

Gordon was an infinitely compassionate man who helped the elderly and befriended homeless boys, yet in battle he did not shrink from having a mutinous soldier shot on the spot to set a vital example. And within him there was a bully who could occasionally emerge to savage someone who had fallen short of his expectations.

This then is the saga of a remarkable but fallible man whose enigmas and contradictions made him the more interesting, and who by his genius found a place in Great Britain's pantheon of public heroes. This inevitably is also the story of British imperial dramas that provided him the arenas in which he became a hero in life and martyr in death.

The deeds of his life and his thoughts as he revealed them are what must best define Gordon. A believer in predestination, Gordon made frequent reference to the "unrolling of the scroll" in his correspondence. He was convinced that all had been written. But if his remarkable life had not been foreordained—and Gordon himself finally compromised and accepted some degree of free will in human existence—it was well documented as it came to pass. Gordon was a prolific letter-writer and through his candid, almost stream-of-consciousness style revealed himself more than most—probably more than he realized. The record of his extraordinary life and times tells the rest.

GORDON OF KHARTOUM

The Saga of a Victorian Hero

PROLOGUE

A public hero in life, martyr in death, Charles George Gordon made a significant impact on the progress of the British Empire. Preceded in his family by three generations of professional army officers, he was destined to be a soldier, but his life as an officer in the Royal Engineers was anything but typical. Gordon's extraordinary career took him to the Crimea, the Caucasus, the Balkans, China, Equatorial Africa, the Sudan, Mauritius, Cape Colony, Palestine and finally the Sudan again where his death in Khartoum at the hands of Moslem holy warriors would shock his nation and shatter Prime Minister Gladstone's government. But before retracing Gordon's tumultuous life and discovering the nature of the man, it is worth looking at the England that nurtured him and the arenas abroad where he would earn his place in Britain's imperial pantheon.

Only fifteen years before Gordon was commissioned as an officer in the Royal Engineers, Victoria ascended the throne at age eighteen. Having sustained the loss of the American colonies half a century earlier, the British were now more interested in matters at home than abroad, more interested in peace and prosperity than colonial acquisition. Colonies were, as the eighteenth-century French statesman Turgot claimed, "fruits which cling to the tree only till they ripen." Moreover, with free trade, industrial pre-eminence, supremacy at sea and the continent no longer in thrall to Napoleon Bonaparte, there seemed no reason why Great Britain could not prosper as it was. After a quarter century of war and revolution, the British were eager for internal stability and harmony with Europe.

That the British Empire did, in fact, expand during the nineteenth century was not, therefore, the result of any conscious sense of territorial aggrandizement. More likely, events were driven by motives of power, profit and pride, sometimes garnished with Christian duty. It is a moot question whether the empire bred intrepid souls such as Gordon, whose exploits aroused public imagination and pride, or whether such extraordinary individuals instead sired the empire.

1

PROLOGUE

After the Duke of Wellington defeated Napoleon in 1815, the British could feel pride as well as relief. Waterloo had proved Britain a continental land power just as Trafalgar had made it supreme at sea. Yet there were reasons to be uneasy. Russia was stirring, restless from its own imperial urges in view of the power vacuum created by Napoleon's defeat. Since Peter the Great, Russia, for all its backwardness, had loomed as a menacing colossus of the East, and the Czar now began to sound dissonant notes in the European concert. With France cut down to size, the sheer bulk of Russia weighed heavily in Europe's balance of power. But the more immediate fear was that Russia's nearness to the decaying Ottoman Empire posed a threat to the Mediterranean, and Russia's inevitable eastward expansion would bring it perilously close to Persian and Afghan approaches to India.

To preserve the rewards of its victory at Waterloo, Britain was willing to use its power to contain Russia even if it meant war. And war it meant, when a wave of jingoism swept the British into a contest with Russia for which it was unprepared. The events setting off the Crimean War may have been trivial, but there was an underlying British conviction that Russian ambition had to be curbed.

In 1852, the year Gordon was commissioned, the Sultan made substantial concessions to Napoleon III's demands that Turkey reaffirm its 1740 treaty which made France custodian of Jerusalem's Christian shrines in behalf of the Roman Catholic Church. But Czar Nicholas I, who considered himself protector of the Greek Orthodox Church, was determined to keep control of the shrines, which for all practical purposes he had already assumed. He insisted, moreover, on the right to protect members of the Greek church in the Turkish Ottoman Empire, a clear affront to the Sultan's sovereignty. With encouragement from the British government, which suspected Nicholas's deeper expansionist motives, Turkey refused the Czar's requests. In 1853 Russia moved to occupy the Balkan provinces of Moldavia and Wallachia, exactly what Britain feared. Turkey retaliated by announcing hostilities, and the Crimean War was on.

When Russia committed the further outrage of sinking the Turkish fleet in its Black Sea port at Sinope, war fever raged through England. "The massacre of Sinope," as the British press stridently referred to the incident, caused both Great Britain and France to declare war on Russia in 1854 and rush troops to Turkey's defense. European stability was at stake. The

PROLOGUE

"Eastern Question," a euphemism for Balkan tensions and Turkish fragility, would plague Europe for years to come. And as Russia moved into the Caucasus and Central Asia, the British began to fear for India as well. For Charles Gordon this was an exciting time to emerge from the cocoon of the Royal Military Academy.

Prestige was a fragile commodity which had to be defended on a wide front. While Britain's attention was riveted on the Crimean War, sore spots festered farther afield in the empire. India, administered by the Honorable East India Company, was nearer to disaster than anyone realized. The "Great Mutiny" of 1857, while not far in the future when Gordon entered on active duty five years before, was not anticipated even though British military fallibility had been painfully revealed in 1842 when a British army had been annihilated in Afghanistan.

If the East India Company, cutting edge of Britain's eastern empire, had fostered an aggressive policy on India's northwest frontier out of fear for the subcontinent's security, it showed the same aggressiveness in China for more parochial reasons of profit. Power and profit were, after all, different sides of the same coin.

The xenophobic Manchu rulers of China had traditionally refused foreigners entrance to the "Celestial Realm," except as tribute bearers. An effort in 1793 to establish a presence in China failed when Lord Macartney's mission to Emperor Ch'ien Lung's court was soundly rebuffed. The "Son of Heaven" would permit limited, highly controlled trade through the port of Canton, but British access to other ports or the Chinese interior was forbidden.

So the rewards of China trade remained minimal, the one notable exception being the illicit opium trade, which had been filling the coffers of the East India company since the eighteenth century. Legitimate foreign traders, British included, were confined to a cramped zone along the Pearl River outside the walls of Canton. They were required to trade through authorized Chinese "hongs," or merchant guilds, which extorted outrageous profits in their middlemen roles.

Exasperated by the opium trade, the Emperor sent a special imperial high commissioner to Canton in 1839 to stamp out the odious traffic in "foreign mud," as the Chinese referred to the drug. Lin Tse-hsu, a portly mandarin with a luxuriant black beard, took himself and his high-ranking commission

3

in the Chinese service seriously. After seizing some two hundred British traders in Canton and holding them hostage, he confiscated twenty thousand chests of opium. He then wrote Queen Victoria, to whom he referred in his journal as "that young girl," complaining about foreigners who sell opium for profit, "tempting fools to destroy themselves."

In England there were some who were conscience-stricken by the opium trade. Gladstone, for one, called it "an infamous and atrocious business." But Parliament, under pressure from China traders and free-trade advocates, voted in April 1840 to punish the Chinese, and the Whig Prime Minister, Lord Palmerston, with the clearest of conscience ordered an expeditionary force to China. Thus began the Opium War.

Antique Chinese shore batteries, and an antique Chinese mind for war, proved no match for the attacking British ships. A Chinese officer bewailed: "The barbarians' guns are bobbing up and down on the water, yet they hit us and we miss them." He blamed it on witchcraft and ordered the local populace to hang out their chamberpots to exorcise the witches. A scheme to ignite British ships by throwing aboard monkeys strapped with fireworks was no more effective. Nor was the strategy of embargoing the export of rhubarb to England on the grounds that the English susceptibility to constipation would be fatally aggravated.

English power prevailed. In August 1841, a British fleet occupied Amoy, Tinghai and Ningpo. By the following summer Shanghai was in British hands, and on August 29, 1842, the Emperor sued for peace. Under the harshly punitive agreement signed in Nanking, China was forced to acknowledge Great Britain's diplomatic presence, open five major port cities to foreign trade, pay a large indemnity and turn over Hong Kong to the British.

British victory in the Opium War began nearly a century of foreign domination of China, accelerating the processes of profound change in that ancient but ailing empire. An early symptom—and cause—of change was the Taiping Rebellion. Farmers and villagers, restive under Manchu rule, flocked to the banner of a mystical "Christian" zealot, who called himself T'ien Wang, or Heavenly King, and claimed to be Christ's younger brother. It began as a lightly regarded local nuisance in 1850, but it was destined to engulf China in the bloodiest civil war the world has known. During the almost fifteen years it raged, the rebellion exacted a terrible toll in human life—thirty million Chinese are estimated to have died.

4

PROLOGUE

Halfway around the world, the British public received only vague, distorted news of the early rebellion. Heartened by the professed Christianity of the movement, the *Times* in August 1853 reported that progress of the "patriotic army . . . continues as wonderful as ever." Not so easily beguiled, the *Quarterly Review* saw the rebellion more political than religious, but it badly underestimated the rebellion's potential when it predicted "all ordinary experience is against their [the Chinese] throwing up their ancient superstitions at the mere bidding of any army who are but a handful of the vast population."[1] However successful the Taiping Rebellion was in jarring a tottering, corrupt dynasty and alarming foreign concessionaires, it proved to be anything but a noble movement. Karl Marx may have seen in the Taiping uprising the inspiration for Communist revolution in China, but rather than curing the Chinese disease, the rebellion proved nearly fatal. The violent excesses of the Taiping rebels exceeded even those of the Manchus; fanaticism made their swords sharper and their compassion duller.

If the imperatives of trade with China calloused the British conscience, moral revulsion to the trafficking in human beings provided the first stimulus for Britain's involvement in sub-Saharan Africa. In the eighteenth century, the British colonial West Indies had enjoyed the benefits of slave labor on the sugar plantations, as had the United States' old south in the cotton fields, but the nineteenth century brought a profound change in British attitudes. A national conscience decried slavery, bringing about its abolition in 1834, long before the Civil War settled the issue across the Atlantic. Christian duty would be done; downtrodden natives, wherever they might be, not only would be freed but would have salvation as well. Thanks to powerful evangelical movements in England, the empire was now expected to protect Christian standards no less than the Union Jack.

Africa, once described as the greatest geographical secret after America had been discovered, was ripe for exploration by mid-nineteenth century. Little more was known about "darkest Africa"—the heart of the great continent—than had been known in Herodotus' day, and strangely, by the time Gordon received his officer's commission, Nile exploration had progressed no farther than the southern Sudan.

Egyptian efforts to explore the southern Sudan, begun in 1839, brought the Egyptians in contact with the tall Nilotic nomads so different from themselves, but unnavigable rapids in the Nile and vast swamplands made settlement difficult. Khedive Mohammed Ali's agents brought back reports of abundant ivory but only dubious rumors of mineral wealth. When Egypt opened the southern Sudan for trading in 1853, a few hardy and enterprising Europeans braved the hardships of that inhospitable land to deal in ivory to supply European and American billiard tables. But it soon became obvious that the biggest profits were to be made in trading human beings. In this commodity Arab traders monopolized the market in Egypt and the Sudan.

Motives other than profit initially attracted Englishmen to Central Africa. The search for the headwaters of the Nile had captured public imagination by midcentury, and the saga of intrepid explorers who vied for the glory of finding the source of that mighty river is perhaps unequaled for drama in the annals of exploration. But the Christian Evangelical movement would have an even more profound effect on British imperial progress in Africa.

The Church of England, the Established Church, had long filled a comfortable niche in British society. John Stuart Mill in the mid-nineteenth century called the church "a bulwark against fanaticism, a sedative to the religious spirit, to prevent this from disturbing the harmony of society or the tranquillity of the State." But the Church of England was slow to respond to the threats and challenges implicit in the age of Enlightenment, and the antireligion permeating this new devotion to reason would counterbreed a religious intensity outside the Established Church, particularly among the lower middle classes, giving rise to a less stylized fundamentalism. The Dissenters, especially John Wesley and the Methodists, but also reformers among the Baptists, Presbyterians, Congregationalists and Quakers of the eighteenth century, became the hosts for the growing movement. John Wesley's promise of instant salvation for those who embraced Christ and committed themselves to a demanding moral code was an antidote to unbridled reason.

The Dissenters also served to prod the Church of England to emerge from its old ways. The Evangelical movement, which came into being in the latter part of the eighteenth century, fostered a new breed of Anglican cleric who sought to revitalize the church, give it a new sense of social consciousness and serve the spiritual needs of the more common man.

PROLOGUE

A heightened morality was also part of the Evangelical movement, especially within the middle class, and would serve as a protective barrier against an urban, industrialized class of society—the morally depraved who inhabited William Blake's "dark, satanic mills." In insisting that nude statues have their private parts covered with fig leaves, the lower middle class was doing more than expressing moral concern; it was defending its social ramparts from working-class depravity.

William Wilberforce, a Conservative member of Parliament from the prestigious constituency of Yorkshire, was important in broadening the Evangelical movement to include some of the upper classes, thereby providing it political power. Using social occasions as well as Parliament's lobbies for Evangelical casting, he could fish for souls in very privileged ponds. But Wilberforce was a truly saintly person, genuinely dedicated to the welfare of his fellow man. He worried about factory working conditions, Royal Navy press gangs, prison conditions and a variety of other social ills. It was not surprising that Wilberforce led the charge against the African slave traffic going to the British West Indies, but when he first spoke out in the House of Commons against slavery in 1787, he gave the abolitionist movement a new momentum.

The antislavery movement was something unique in British history. While having strong Evangelical undertones, it spread far beyond the parishes to become a nationwide agitation. Propaganda, heretofore never so well marshaled, aroused public opinion. Demonstrations, petitions and street-corner canvasing as well as the pulpit spread the message. English thinkers such as John Locke, Alexander Pope, William Cowper and Thomas Clarkson were articulate spokesmen for the antislavery campaign, while groups such as the Anti-Slavery Society, the African Association, the Aborigines Protection Society and Exeter Hall provided the organizational machinery.

In 1807, after some eleven million African slaves had been shipped to the Western Hemisphere, with perhaps as many dying en route, a bill was passed outlawing the transportation of slaves on British ships and the involvement of British merchants in the evil traffic. Then on August 28, 1833, just before Wilberforce's death, all slaves in British territories were emancipated, the historic parliamentary act decreeing that slavery would

7

cease altogether in 1834. The economic consequences were significant, but England had finally put morality over money.

The Evangelical movement was also manifested in an increase of missionary work in Africa. These newly discovered African peoples, denied "civilization" in their isolation, were not to be deprived of Christian salvation. But in African mission work, there may also have been the need to expiate guilt, to atone for the many years in which Africans had been enslaved by Christian white men.

The work of one such missionary, David Livingstone, did much to dramatize the plight of the impoverished, exploited Africans. Livingstone, who was also a physician, joined a mission in what is now Bechuanaland in 1841. He walked the breadth of Central Africa, from the Atlantic to the Indian Ocean, exploring places where no white man had trod before. He followed long stretches of the Congo and Zambezi rivers, dreaming of a day when the slave trade would no longer exist and European colonists would settle, build churches and bring the fruits of civilization and Christian faith to the native Africans.

In 1856 Livingstone visited England, where he fascinated people with his tales of Africa. At a gathering of Cambridge University students he promised he would "go back to Africa; to try to make an open path for commerce and Christianity," and he did, apparently believing that there was no reason why God and mammon could not happily exist side by side.

Livingstone's story, known to every British schoolboy, tells of the great missionary's "disappearance" in the heart of Africa and his dramatic, though unwanted, rescue by Henry Stanley, who greeted him with the now-famous statement "Dr. Livingstone, I presume."

Explorers as well as missionaries played a role in making the British public aware of the human tragedies in Africa. Richard Burton and John Hanning Speke, two early explorers who undertook the search for the source of the White Nile in 1856, were witness to awful scenes of human mistreatment in Zanzibar as they began their African journey. Under British pressure, Sultan Barghash of Zanzibar had in 1848 barred the export of slaves, although not the practice of slavery itself in his own country. While English and French naval vessels idled off the coast to intercept Arab dhows that tried to run the blockade with their human cargoes bound for Arabia, slaves were bought and sold freely by Arab dealers in the Zanzibar marketplaces.

Burton's vivid account of events here aroused a distant British public. Despite efforts by the British Navy, the flow of human cargo from Zanzibar went on uninterrupted. Burton wrote: "Lines of negroes stood like beasts. . . . All were horribly thin with ribs protruding like the circles of a cask." They were packed tightly between eighteen-inch tiers; some 30 percent of them died before reaching their destination. Ironically, Burton, who developed an untoward contempt for blacks and a preference for the Arabs in East Africa, probably did not mean to stir up public indignation, intending simply to inform, or titillate, with his dispatches.

Another Nile explorer of the time, Samuel Baker, was an early witness to the slave traffic moving northward to Khartoum and Egypt from Equatorial Africa. His descriptions, like Burton's, had an important impact on the British people. He told of victims rushing from their burning dwellings and men "shot down like pheasants in a battue."[2] Slavery was a "trade so hideous that every heart of slave and owner becomes deformed and shrinks like a withered limb incapable of action."[3] Baker was outspoken in his criticism of English official apathy, wondering "whether the English government will take active notice of the White Nile trade, or whether diplomacy will confine them to simple protest and correspondence, to be silenced by a promise from the Egyptian Government to put a stop to the present atrocities."[4]

Royal Navy patrols did stop slave ships of every nationality on the high seas and did raid West African slave depots along the coast, but the overland movement of slaves from Equatorial Africa and the southern Sudan was more difficult to arrest. Powerful Arab slave barons had become virtually autonomous, and corrupt Egyptian administrators in the Sudan were usually in league with them. While the search for the source of the White Nile in mid-nineteenth century thrilled the British, the outrage of a cruel and blatant slave trade, reported by missionaries and explorers alike, stirred public emotions even more.

The world known to Gordon and his contemporaries as they entered it from the Royal Military Academy in 1852 was thus not a tranquil one.

PROLOGUE

Despite visions of enduring peace following the Napoleonic wars, European conflict would soon erupt again in the Crimea, and a succession of little wars in defense of trade or empire would characterize Victoria's long reign. As a soldier Gordon would have his share of fighting, first in the Crimean War and then in some of the "savage wars of peace," as Kipling euphemistically called Britain's many quarrels with the "natives" farther afield. In the Crimea Gordon would see his only service as an orthodox regimental officer in a European-style war, but he would see much combat afterward leading mercenaries against revolutionary hordes in China and fighting slavers in the Sudan. In the Sudan as Governor General, Gordon found his greatest fulfillment; for all his frustrations, he loved the Sudan, but as his comrade-in-arms Romolo Gessi said, "Africa is like the beautiful siren that often kills her lovers."[5]

Gordon's greatest challenge seemed to be in his continual efforts to commune with God in his own way. A product of Evangelical England, he wanted to share his faith and help those less fortunate than himself. And he was a Christian soldier in a British age when battles for "good" causes could also be justified as doing God's will. Yet despite his own intense faith and devotion, he would strangely underestimate the religious force of revolt led by the Mahdi, the "Divine Guide," who in 1881 sprang from the desert to prominence in the Sudan. That God's "unrolling of the scroll," to use a favorite expression of the fatalistic Gordon, ultimately pitted him against the Mahdi is the stuff of fictional romances. This Christian gladiator faced a Moslem crusader—whose troops were known to wear ancient chain-mail armor taken from fallen Christian Crusaders—to rescue Egyptian soldiers garrisoning the Sudan whose rule he abhorred as much as the Mahdi did. But the real irony is how much the two adversaries had in common. Both worshiped with a burning zeal the God of the Old Testament, both possessed charismatic military leadership qualities, both hated tyranny, and neither feared death. In the end both became heroes of their people.

Gordon met a violent death, although perhaps he welcomed joining his God more than most. This, however, is a story of life, an extraordinary life led by an uncommon man.

PART I

The Molding and Annealing

1

WOOLWICH

While he is in the Academy, I feel I am like one sitting on a powder barrel.
—Lieutenant General H. W. Gordon, referring to his son, Charles

Charles George Gordon was one of several boisterous cadets waiting impatiently to leave the dining hall of the Royal Military Academy at Woolwich. The senior cadet-corporal, trying to prevent a stampede, stood at the top of a long staircase, arms akimbo, blocking the exit. Late for his next class, Charlie Gordon was furious. He lowered his head and charged, butting the hapless corporal in the pit of his stomach, catapulting him down the stairs and through a glass door. Miraculously, the boy was not hurt, but this spectacular exhibition of defiance put Gordon in confinement and almost caused his expulsion from the academy.

This early incident in Charlie Gordon's life was symbolic of his enduring intolerance of what he considered injustice and a willingness to flout authority if it was being misused, no matter what the consequences. Academy Commandant General Parker, a Waterloo veteran who had sacrificed one leg to Wellington's victory, was lenient in his punishment of Cadet Gordon, considering him guilty of nothing more than an excess of high spirits. High-spirited he was, but this trait portended something more. He would become an officer of uncommon initiative and strong will, inspiring both awe and exasperation on the part of his superiors—though usually it was the latter.

Such rebelliousness earned Charlie Gordon a reputation as a loner, different from his peers, who were more willing to accommodate to the military mold. Because of this trait, Cadet-Captain Eardly Wilmot bluntly told him he "would never make an officer," provoking an outraged Charlie to tear off his cadet-corporal's epaulettes and announce: "If I am not fit to become an officer, I am not fit to wear these."

13

THE MOLDING AND ANNEALING

Charlie resented cadet officers who, in his opinion, took unfair advantage of their rank. In general, he respected authority at Woolwich if based on just rules and fair administration, but authority was not to be abused. His pronouncements, however, lacked a certain fairness. Regarding General Parker, who had disciplined him, Charlie later stated flatly: "Never employ anyone minus a limb to be in authority over boys—he is apt to be irritable and unjust."

For his rebelliousness, Charlie received no hero's status from his fellow cadets. He found himself an outsider, a role that would always be his. His early-developed defense against opposition and rejection was to project an indomitable will, using his penetrating gray-blue eyes as its enforcer, or, if defied, to retreat into solitary depression. Gordon would refer throughout his life to this latter trait as the "doles." Related to this was a tendency toward morbidity. After his religious reawakening, this morbidity would take the form of longing to join his Maker, but even at an early age death concerned him, as demonstrated by this couplet he wrote at age fourteen:

> Laugh not, laugh not, it may be your turn next.
> Where others lay, it may be your turn next.[1]

Yet it would be misleading to suggest that Gordon's youth was unhappy. Born at Woolwich on January 28, 1833, Charlie spent his early boyhood in that garrison town, where his father, Henry William Gordon, destined to become a lieutenant general in the Royal Artillery, served as Inspector of the Carriage Department at the military academy. Theirs was a large family, six children who survived childbirth or death in infancy. Henry Gordon was a Victorian patriarch to whom laughter came easily, but who believed earnestly in duty to God, country, and the Army. His wife, Elizabeth Enderby Gordon, from an English middle-class Puritan background, was a cheerful, graceful woman. She lavished especial love on Charlie, who, as a child, had not been robust and likely needed more of her attention.

The Gordon children indulged in many a childish prank. Having coaxed the toolmakers at the Royal Arsenal into making crossbows which shot near-lethal screw projectiles, young Charlie and his brothers would delight in shooting out windowpanes at the academy. They were also known to catch mice and infiltrate them into the commanding officer's front hall. Charlie's irreverent attitude toward the military establishment, it would seem, began early.

Nonetheless, it was little wonder that Charlie entered the Royal Military Academy and chose to pursue a military career, as his paternal forebears had all been soldiers. His great-grandfather David Gordon, born in 1712, forsook his Scottish Highland kin to join the Hanoverians, where he served in the 47th Regiment of the English Army under Sir John Cope in Lascelles's Foot. In the Rebellion of 1745, David was captured at Prestonpans by soldiers of his own clan who were fighting for the Pretender. As the tide of Hanoverian retribution swept over the Highlands in 1746, the Duke of Cumberland, known thereafter to dissident Jacobean Scots as "Stinking Willie, the butcher of Culloden," managed to secure Gordon's release. Out of gratitude and friendship, David named his son William Augustus after the Duke, who had agreed to stand sponsor for the baby.

In 1751, David Gordon died while serving in Halifax, Nova Scotia, leaving his son, William Augustus, an orphan. The dying man's hope that William be raised by his nearest kin, Sir William Gordon of Park, was not realized; unknown to David, Sir William had long since died. But the boy survived to enter military service at age sixteen as an ensign in the 40th Foot, rising to the rank of captain in the English Army before he finally retired. Among his friends he could include the influential Lord Chatham as well as his namesake, the Duke of Cumberland, both of whom were instrumental in seeing that he prospered in his early career.

William Augustus saw combat in the Seven Years War against the French at Minorca. He also fought with General Wolfe on the Plains of Abraham and took part in the capture of Quebec from the French in 1759. Then in 1762 he served as Assistant Quartermaster in the campaigns in Martinique and Cuba. An officer's pension was a meager thing, however, and William Augustus found it difficult to live on half pay when he was retired after the Seven Years War, particularly as he was about to be married. With remarkable imagination and initiative, he wrote Prime Minister William Pitt (the elder), asking for reinstatement and complaining: "The inactive life I at present lead is irksome to me." His appeal was successful and he was taken back into the Army, at least until he could retire as captain.

William Augustus's marriage to Anna Maria Clarke, sister of the prominent Evangelical clergyman the Reverend Slaughter Clarke, was a happy one. But the untimely deaths of Anna Maria and their third son, also named William Augustus, when he was serving as captain in the 95th Foot in Cape Colony, left the old warrior saddened and lonely. He spent his last years as a part-time soldier in the Devonshire Militia, taking consolation in the fact that his other two sons were enjoying honorable military careers. The elder, Charlie Gordon's father, Henry William, named after George II's grandson, the Duke of Gloucester, was destined to serve with distinction in the Royal Artillery, eventually rising to the rank of lieutenant general. To his own sons, Henry William set a fine example of soldierly devotion to duty, and it was rather in keeping with tradition that three of them, including Charlie, chose to follow in his career.

Lieutenant General Gordon was an imposing man with a face radiant with geniality. "In his company it was not possible to be dull," recalled one of his contemporaries. Yet in his determination to have them lead upright Christian lives, he was sometimes severe with his children.

Charlie's mother, Elizabeth, was the God-fearing daughter of Samuel Enderby, a prominent shipowner whose whalers, registered both in London and Boston, roamed the seas. Enderby's ships rounded the ferocious Cape Horn with impunity, proving that the route was feasible for commercial shipping. A pioneer in trading with South America's western coast—often running contraband to the Spanish colonies—Enderby provoked protests from Madrid. Prime Minister William Pitt (the younger) himself defended Enderby when the Spanish threatened to confiscate any ship found within fifty miles of their South American coasts. Enderby had petitioned the British to hold fast to a twenty-mile limit, and Pitt is alleged to have answered: "Make it five, and if you are caught within that limit, say you are short of water and need a supply."

Enderby's ships plied the Pacific, opening Australia to trade and taking the first prisoners to Botany Bay. His whalers ranged as far south as the Antarctic Ocean and, under the command of Briscoe and Bellamy, discovered the Auckland Islands. Boston was home port for some of Enderby's ships; it was one of them, in fact, that had the distinction of being the scene of the Boston Tea Party.

The Enderby family never strayed from an unquestioning belief in the

16

Bible. If Charlie Gordon's paternal heritage was responsible for his soldier's bent, it was his mother's side that contributed much to his faith. Elizabeth Gordon read the Bible to her children for long hours each day, and Sundays saw the children in church squirming in the family pew as an Evangelical minister droned on.

Charlie was born too soon to have been exposed during his impressionable years to Darwin's theory of evolution, nor was he otherwise touched by eighteenth-century skepticism. Earlier theories of evolution, such as Robert Chambers's *Vestiges of Creation* in 1844, would never have been allowed in the Gordon household. The Bible contained all truth and was the only guide for the family.

Even in religion, however, Charles would not run with the pack. Church bored and annoyed him. "What husks the Evangelical religion is," he observed; a useless ritual, he thought. Charlie's God was a very personal one, and from an early age he was disdainful of the rites and biblical interpretations adopted by established religions. Why were churches necessary if one read the Bible?

Later in life when Charlie found himself excluded from the easy camaraderie of his fellow officers, he took solace in writing his sister Augusta, twelve years his senior. Their steady correspondence, which would last his lifetime, was a way for him to share his thoughts and seek her advice. As a child, he asked her opinion of Garibaldi before admitting the great Italian patriot to his personal pantheon. And he would always discuss with her religious matters, receiving detailed doctrinal essays which dissected the Bible in her own search for truth. A humorless maiden lady, Augusta was a fountainhead of Christian commentary. How could two people so different in temperament be so close? To him, she may have served as an extension of his mother, but whatever the case, it is clear this dour puritan woman exerted an undeniable influence on Charlie from an early age, imbuing him to a great degree with the conviction that the spiritual world should be every Christian's goal while flesh is the dominion of the Devil.

Charlie's father's military postings took the family to various countries overseas in adventures which they all enjoyed. But at the Pigeon House Fort in the Bay of Dublin, where Henry was in charge of relining the cannons, the military environment was at times upsetting to young Charlie. He particularly disliked the roar of nearby gunfire during practice. And the mustering of troops to control Irish street mobs, angered by overbearing English rule, also left an impression on the five-year-old boy.

After Ireland, the family moved to Leith Fort near Edinburgh, not far from Prestonpans, where great-grandfather David had been taken prisoner. Charlie noted in his boyhood diary that his father, then a lieutenant colonel, was "obliged to go out every morning and practice with the soldiers on the sands," as though this were onerous duty.

The next assignment was in the idyllic British protectorate of Corfu in the Greek islands of the Ionian Sea. Charlie's father commanded the island's artillery. These were carefree, happy days. At age nine, before he could swim, Charlie delighted in leaping into Corfu's clear, deep waters, confident that someone would rescue him. But impressions of Corfu jotted down in his diary betrayed more somberly a fascination with the twin themes of death and religious faith, themes that would permeate much of his thinking for the rest of his life.

In Corfu Charlie was struck by the peculiar people there who wore jackets "made of velvet, generally purple, embroidered with gold thread." But the saga of Saint Spirodon seemed to intrigue him the most. In wonderment he related how one day a buried coffin had been unearthed, containing an old man "who moved." The Senate declared the man to be alive, so "they worshipped him ever since."[2] Charlie interrupted his diary entry to comment: "They [the Greeks] worship Jesus Christ, as well as him, and they say their Saint is equal with him."

How long Saint Spirodon, through this obvious miracle risen from the grave, lived on, Charlie Gordon did not explain, but now "he is kept in a coffin, or rather seat, with all sorts of jewels on it, and glass windows around his seat are most splendid with all the gold on them. . . . He wears a crown as good as our Queen wears. . . . " Charlie added vividly: "One of his legs and one of his arms are cut off and preserved in a bottle; his head is hanging on one side and his teeth are as white as yours or mine and they are quite perfect."

Life in Corfu also had its high drama: "There was a fuss in Corfu a little time ago caused by an Englishman throwing a brick at the Saint" while he was being carried in a procession. The Greeks "would have killed the Englishman had not the English soldiers ran out and protected him and took him into the citadel—he was very much bruised with the stones that had been flung at him." Charlie concluded authoritatively that "the Greeks are considered to be very savage; you can also tell by their countenance for they have very thick moustaches."

Charlie found the ornate religious rites and relics in Corfu fascinating, so at odds were they with the stark fundamentalist customs he was used to. He wrote of a colorful Good Friday procession in which little children were dressed up as angels. He described with awe the relics of the local Catholic Church: " . . . the nails that they say were thrust in the hands of our Saviour . . . the sponge that the Jews gave our Saviour, the vinegar to drink, the dice that the Jews tossed up for our Saviour's garments . . . the cross on which our blessed Saviour suffered."[3] The Catholic sacraments, too, seemed strange to him: "Instead of bread . . . they used wafers with J. H. S., that is 'Jesus the Saviour of men,' and they call it 'Holy wafer.' "

And on the macabre: "They were digging for a foundation for a house and they dug into a subterranian cavern where they found a great many bones of men that had been taking [sic] a long time ago and pulled joint from joint." Gordon discovered that according to custom, Greeks "always broke a person's bones" before burial.[4]

Charlie's happy days in Corfu had to come to an end when his father was transferred to England. "You may be sure," Charlie wrote in his journal, "We were very sorry to leave such a nice place as Corfu."[5]

The journey home included a stop in Venice, "built on 72 small islands," with streets of water on which you must "go in a goundalor [sic]." Charlie considered the Italian language "remarkable for its mouthness, and . . . easily mastered by a classical scholar."

The Gordons visited Padua, Milan and Lake Como as well, arousing in Charlie awe of the countryside: "The happy soil of Italy" which produces "the luxuries of life in great abundance." He also developed a taste for Italian cheeses, particularly Parmesan, and olive oil.

After Italy there were the sights of Switzerland, "a small, romantic country lying upon the Alps"; Cologne, in Germany, where "eau de cologne" comes from; and Belgium, where "omelets are made." Impressionable Charlie was taken on a grand tour of Waterloo, where the great battle was fought that "terminated in the total defeat of Bonaparte."

After returning home from Corfu, Charlie attended Fulland's grammar school in Taunton, chosen by his parents because it was properly Evangelical and run by George Rogers, related to a governess of the Gordons. It was dedicated to what Thomas Arnold, founder of the reformed Rugby School, referred to as "Godliness and good learning." Godliness in Victorian England emphasized morality as well as Christian doctrine; boys were taught to be serious, proud of hard work, ascetic, and resolute in resisting sexual impulses. Athletics, too, were important, and at Fulland's cricket was the primary sport. Even so, Charlie found irksome his duties helping to maintain the manicured cricket field.

Charlie's five years in Taunton were not particularly happy. He was often teased by the other boys, mostly about his name. A Lord Gordon had just achieved popularity as a fictional character in the Charles Dickens novel *Barnaby Rudge*, and Charlie was kidded mercilessly by the other boys as being his kin. After this Charlie refused ever to read Dickens.

In a cryptic but emotional letter written many years later in 1883 from Palestine to his friend and religious mentor, the Reverend Reginald H. Barnes, Gordon reminisced about an experience at Fulland's school which, despite Charlie's young age of "only 10 or 12," changed his life "humanly speaking, so it was never the same since." "Writing in hurt" about his memories, Gordon in a near-scrawl recalled that the headmaster of Fulland's, George Rogers, had threatened him with a bad end in life if he did not behave. And, indeed, behavior may have been a problem, judging from a reference made to young Charlie as a "difficult" young gentleman many years later in the *Aluredian*, school magazine of King's College, which succeeded Fulland's school.[6]

In his letter to Barnes, Gordon suggested that the miseries at Fulland's were somehow responsible for his lifelong compassion for children. "I love children so very much," he wrote, adding enigmatically, "to know this thing can rest this hurt much."[7]

"I will never come this way again," a miserable Charlie declared as he left Fulland's. Nor did he. One can only imagine the reasons for Charlie's unhappiness, but many years later, towards the end of his life, he confided in another letter to the Reverend Mr. Barnes: "I wished I was a eunuch at fourteen."[8]

Now, after a few months at Mr. Jeffery's preparatory school, Charlie would begin serious training for his inevitable career in the Army. The Royal

WOOLWICH

Military Academy was the Army's best effort in the development of professionalism, training artillerymen and engineers, positions more specialized but generally considered less prestigious than cavalry and infantry with their dash, color, glory and bought commissions.

Charlie Gordon's attendance, at age fifteen, at the academy happened also to coincide with a golden age of English industrial supremacy. The Great Exhibition of 1851, inaugurated with pomp by Queen Victoria, was a glittering symbol of an age of prosperity. Lord Macaulay said it went beyond the dreams of "Arabian romances." Crowds thronged the new Crystal Palace, looking in awe at the wondrous new machines which promised to keep England preeminent in world trade, and gawking at the great Indian Koh-i-noor ("Mountain of Light") diamond, on exhibit for the first time, an undeniable emblem of colonial riches and natural resources. The repeal of the Corn Laws in 1846 and the Navigation Acts three years later guaranteed that free trade would everlastingly preserve England's prosperity. And, somehow, the Victorian climate was such that the underprivileged proletariat were kept at bay, in contrast to elsewhere in Europe, where lower-class stirrings threatened an old way of life.

The Evangelical Gordons, no special beneficiaries of England's national prosperity, were more concerned about the issuance of a papal rescript in 1850 which divided England into dioceses so as to strengthen the Roman Catholic Church, and an announcement by the Pope that the English people were ready to rejoin the Holy Roman Church. These were steps going beyond the missionary status to which the Roman Church had heretofore confined itself; they seemed to claim status on a par with the Church of England. Prime Minister John Russell denounced the papal decree as an insult to the Queen, while the public at large grew restive over the apparent Anglican complacency toward the Pope's new aggressiveness.

In these heady times, Charlie commenced his military training, but the academy offered little in the way of a liberal-arts education to broaden the cadets. Even if their personal fates, as well as that of England, would be vitally affected by the exigencies of national and world affairs, the boys at Woolwich were served up only a technical diet of mathematics, map-drawing, fortifications and gunnery basics, although French was included in the curriculum in deference to France's still-preeminent role on the continent and the use of French as a *lingua franca*.

THE MOLDING AND ANNEALING

There was much happening across the Channel. Eighteen forty-eight, Charlie's first year as a cadet, saw startling changes in Europe with its revolutions and social upheavals. In that year Queen Victoria wrote with distress in her journal: "It seems as if the whole face of Europe were changing. I maintain that Revolutions are always bad for the country and the cause of untold misery to the people."[9]

Notwithstanding Victoria's pronouncements, the Second French Republic was born of revolution in 1848 when Louis Philippe was forced to abdicate and Socialists clamored for power. Armed workmen demonstrated at the Hôtel de Ville in Paris, demanding that the red flag of Socialism replace the tricolor. More traumatic was the terrible street war in Paris which erupted on June 23, 1848. Proletariat insurgents manned barricades in a revolution which raged four days before being put down. The cost of this uprising was ten thousand dead or wounded; another eleven thousand workers were deported from the city. But in the long run even more costly was the widened gulf between the poor and the bourgeoisie, a situation which would long be the bane of France.

Inspired by the 1848 uprisings in Paris, the Italian nationalist Giuseppe Garibaldi rushed back to Italy from exile in South America, where he had fought in various battles of liberation. The Hero of Montevideo attracted thousands in his struggle against Austria that year. The movement foundered and Garibaldi was forced to flee back to South America, but his heroism had lit fires of nationalist fervor among the Italians which would not be extinguished. At the Royal Military Academy young Charlie Gordon thrilled to the brave exploits of Garibaldi, whom he would always hold up as a hero.

Nearer by, the Irish too were seething with the spirit of revolt in 1848. A terrible potato famine drove many dispirited, hungry Irish to America, and those who remained grew impatient with the exploitive landlord system. The Young Ireland extremists plotted a rebellion, which was·nipped in the bud, but the unhappy Irish were not to be silenced for good.

England in 1848 could feel satisfaction that it had escaped European radicalism and, insulated from Europe's wicked winds of change, was prospering in relative tranquillity. Yet the adventurous Palmerston, Foreign Secretary to Lord John Russell, could not leave well enough alone. Without consultation, he undertook the action of shipping arms to Sicilian insurgents. Palmerston subsequently apologized to the King of Naples, causing Victoria to write indignantly to the Prime Minister: "The partiality of Lord Palmerston in this Italian question really surpasses all conceptions, and makes the Queen very uneasy on account of the character and honour of England, and on account of the danger to which the peace of Europe will be exposed."

In the same fateful year, Palmerston instructed the English Ambassador in Madrid to advise the Queen of Spain to liberalize her government. This succeeded only in getting the presumptuous envoy expelled from the country. Three years later, Victoria rose again in indignation when the "dreadful Lord Palmerston" agreed to receive the Hungarian nationalist Lajos Kossuth. Continental conservatives, enraged by Palmerston's adventures in liberalism, coined the couplet:

> If the Devil has a son,
> He surely is Palmerston.[10]

Charlie Gordon found confirmation for his own rebelliousness and sense of justice in the actions of his hero Garibaldi, however much these traits were fundamentally products of Christian compassion instilled by his mother. Another hero with whom he identified was Lord Byron, self-appointed martyr to tyranny, who gave his life fighting for Greek independence in 1824.[11] Gordon's father was distressed by Charlie's independent spirit, which, while good in principle, interfered with the obvious need for conformity in an Army career. Charlie's radical social and political opinions needed to be tempered by duty and discipline, he lectured, once driving the young man to the sanctuary of his room.

For all his father's concern, Charlie was not a bad student. While weak in math, he excelled at mapmaking and received a medal for his mastery of French. But a propensity for getting into trouble persisted and was not looked upon kindly in an institution demanding obedience.

In his last year at the academy, Charlie, like all senior cadets, was given disciplinary responsibilities toward underclassmen. He soon gained a reputation for being tough and intemperate in the punishment he meted out. The system lent itself to abuse, about which Charlie himself had complained when he was at the other end of the flogging stick. When one cadet accused Charlie of hitting him with a clothesbrush and bruising his back—a rare piece of evidence to come forth from the usually closemouthed cadet corps—a commission of inquiry recommended that Cadet Gordon be dismissed. The lieutenant governor of the academy intervened to reduce the punishment, instead requiring only that his graduation be delayed by six months—back-terming, as it was called—during which time he would be on probation. Charlie was incensed, but he did settle down enough to finish the course, even winning first prize in "fortifications." Charlie's military schooling had not been easy; if his father felt as if he were sitting on a powder barrel,[12] Charlie considered Woolwich an ordeal and was haunted by it from time to time for the rest of his life. He complained years later that he had awakened from a fearful dream that he was "back at the Academy and had to pass an examination."

Gordon passed out of the academy on June 22, 1852, but, by not being graduated with his class, he missed selection for the Royal Artillery, his father's and brothers' service. Instead, he was commissioned in the Royal Engineers, an apt situation, after all, given his talent for mapmaking and sketching.

As Gordon's academy schooling drew to a close nearly five years after it began, another ominous European development loomed to dwarf all others in scope and importance. Untouched by significant liberal eruptions around him, the Russian Czar began to cast covetous eyes on his Balkan neighbors still ruled by the Turkish Sultan. Imperial Russian expansionism, aggravating the "Eastern Question," would soon provoke European armies into war after the long respite following Waterloo. In anticipation of the brewing conflict, Gordon would dream of combat, but in the meantime he had to content himself with advanced training.

Gordon spent the next nineteen months studying at Chatham, headquarters of the Royal Engineers, before being ordered to Pembroke Dock in Wales in February 1854 for his first duty assignment. The place and the work, concerned with the construction of defensive forts of dubious strategic value, were not inspiring.

What made the tour of duty at Pembroke significant, however, was a new sense of religion which he gained. Both his mother and his sister Augusta had been important in giving young Charlie a faith in God, although he had rejected form, but now came his true "awakening," his Christian rebirth. His previous unquestioning acceptance of the Bible as the true gospel now became a deep emotional commitment to Christianity that would guide and solace him for the rest of his life.

The intermediary for this sudden rebirth was Captain Drew, a fellow officer at Pembroke. Drew of the 11th Regiment, an intensely religious man with an Evangelical calling, supplied religious tracts to Gordon, who devoured them eagerly. Because of Drew's influence, Gordon took Communion for the first time in his life one Easter Sunday. This was a major leap forward toward embracing the church, something which he had always resisted. In a letter home he reminded his sister Augusta that when he was a cadet he thought Confirmation was "a useless sin" (Gordon was in fact never confirmed), but he announced proudly, "I took my first Sacrament on Easter Day," and he now felt "much happier and more contented." His religious revival even gave him new lenses through which to see dreary Pembroke Dock. "I did not like Pembroke," he wrote home, "but now I would not wish for any prettier place." In his euphoria he also found Drew's wife attractive, describing her as a "very stylish person with luxuriant auburn hair," a rare compliment paid to feminine beauty. The books in Drew's house inspired him. On the mantelpiece was a religious tome called *Priceless Diamond*, which he read, then sent off to his sister so that she might share his discovery. He pored over the sermons of the Reverend Robert M'Cheyne and sent his favorite, *The Remains of the Reverend M'Cheyne*, to her as well.[13] And there was Thomas Scott's *Commentaries*, which moved him deeply.[14]

A whole new world appeared to Gordon, thanks to the pious Captain Drew. The two would drive "all about the country," deep in religious discussion. His new cup of faith was running over: He wanted to share it, to evangelize. He even felt compelled to spread the word to his already deeply religious parents, writing to Augusta: "I hope my dear father and mother [now at Gibraltar, where the general commanded the artillery] think of eternal things. . . . Can I do or say anything to either to do good?"

But aside from his frequent visits with the Drews, Gordon still kept to himself. He was grateful that his assignment permitted him to go about his work without any obligation to join in the camaraderie commonly expected in a line regiment. The kind of off-duty revels typical of exuberant young British Army officers had no place in Gordon's life. "Where sin aboundeth, grace aboundeth more fully," he observed piously. "I am such a miserable wretch, that I would be sure to be led away."

Another side of Gordon, however, was growing restless for action. He was, after all, a soldier, and a new war raging in the Crimea tugged at him. His older brothers, Henry and Enderby, were already there. The conflict had become a righteous crusade against the "Eastern tyrant," Czar Nicholas, and Gordon did not want to be left out of it. He was, therefore, disappointed to receive orders for Corfu instead. Remembering the island from childhood, he knew service there would be pleasant enough, but it was far from center stage. The only good thing about this dreary prospect was that duty in the West Indies or New Zealand would be even duller. In a letter to his mother he complained: "I suspect you used your interest to have me sent there instead of to the Crimea." Later in his career it would perturb Gordon to see officers using influence to get preferred assignments, but now he was so eager to join the war that he cajoled his family into presuming on an old friendship with Sir John Burgoyne, Inspector General of Fortifications, to have him assigned to the Crimea.

Public enthusiasm for the war was running high. There were, of course, voices in Parliament that spoke out against the conflict, but the majority supported this "noble" struggle. The Queen, who had hoped for peace, was critical of the Cabinet for having taken on "the risks of a European war without having bound Turkey to any conditions with respect to provoking it." Particularly reprehensible were Lord Stratford's efforts to "drag" England into war from his position as British Ambassador in Constantinople. "When he speaks of the sword which will have to be drawn, but the scabbard thrown away," she wrote, "it becomes a serious question whether we are justified in allowing Lord Stratford any longer to remain in a situation which gives him the means of frustrating all our efforts for peace."[15]

When war became inevitable and the plunge was made, the Queen too was swept along by the wave of English pride. She wrote her uncle, King Leopold of Belgium, on February 24, 1854: "The last battalion of the Guards [Scots Fusiliers] embarked today. They passed through the courtyard here [Buckingham Palace] at seven o'clock this morning . . . an immense crowd collected to see these fine men, cheering them immensely. . . . It was a touching and beautiful sight."[16]

The *Times* had its own ideas regarding what was important as England prepared for the first European war in forty years. An editorial found the glorious uniform of the 11th Hussars, which it compared to the costume of the female hussars in the ballet of *Gustavus*, unfit for modern combat: "the shortness of their jackets and the tightness of their cherry-coloured pants." While this was admittedly trivial, the *Times* was not alone in recognizing that England's war machine was still mired in outdated concepts and, under Wellington's leadership, had not progressed since Waterloo.

It could not have been easy for Gordon's mother to see still another son exposed to the dangers of war when Burgoyne finally arranged a Crimean assignment for Charlie. In fact, engineers were badly needed at the front, where the ill-equipped troops were making do in shockingly primitive circumstances. Adequate shelter was nonexistent and supply services hopelessly snarled. Charlie Gordon was put in charge of collecting and shipping wooden huts, which he would erect in the Crimea. He would soon be at the front and discover what it meant to be a soldier.

2

THE CRIMEA

. . . something indescribably exciting in war.
—Charles Gordon in the Crimea

The great battles of Alma, Balaklava and Inkerman had already taken place by the time Gordon was ready to leave for the Crimean War, but at Sevastopol, where the Russians were dug in behind well-fortified positions, the prospects for early Allied victory now seemed dim. There was plenty of fighting left.

Gordon's orders arrived on December 4, 1854. Within two days he was at Portsmouth supervising the loading of huts for the troops in the Crimea and preparing for his own journey to the front. "I have taken out a good supply of tea," he wrote his mother, "because I knew you would scold me if I did not." Gordon traveled overland as far as Marseilles rather than embark at Portsmouth on a collier or cargo transport. Being a bad sailor, he was grateful for this privilege, except that it required him to prepay his passage against later reimbursement. When it came to finances, he always lived close to the line.

The six-day trip from Marseilles to Constantinople was exactly the kind of sea voyage Gordon dreaded. Since childhood, ship travel had always made him seasick.[1] For all his own misery, however, Gordon felt sorrier for the 320 French soldiers on board, who had to sleep on deck, without shelter of any kind, in unusually wet and cold weather. He went ashore at Messina in Sicily to see the town and was shocked to learn that 22,000 people out of a total population of 66,000 had recently died in a cholera epidemic. It was the same scourge that was taking a terrible toll of British soldiers' lives in Turkey and the Crimea, but it had now spread to the Mediterranean.

The next stop was Piraeus in Greece. The Acropolis was "a beautiful ruin," but Athens "very ugly and dirty." On Christmas Day the ship reached the Dardanelles, giving Gordon his first glimpse of Asia. Here he was more

28

concerned with logistic matters than seeing the sights: The famous strait was not well fortified, he observed. As for Constantinople, Gordon was interested only by the British hospital at Scutari, the Sultan's seraglio palace and the Russian embassy. Otherwise this fascinating and historic city, overlooking the Sea of Marmara and the Bosporus, was memorable merely for its "filth and bad drainage." He had little time to explore further, having discovered that four of the ships carrying his huts had already passed through the Bosporus on their way to the Crimea.

At the British hospital at Scutari, Gordon saw that the wounded at least "have everything they want and all comforts." Disease was the Allies' principal enemy, and the appalling medical services that disgraced the early months of the campaign had cost an estimated eighteen thousand British lives. Cholera was the worst killer, although typhus, dysentery, malaria and the cold of winter had also taken their toll. Death was so common that the British stopped holding military funerals: They were all too depressing and bad for morale. In the case of cholera victims, it was thought advisable to bury them at night without bystanders who might become infected. The Guards Division was so weakened by disease that its men were able to march only five miles a day and could scarcely lift their packs.

The outrage at home in England, fanned by gruesome reports from war correspondents, helped speed an overhaul of the army's medical services, but Florence Nightingale and her small but dedicated corps of volunteer nurses were eventually given most of the credit for the almost miraculous improvement in medical care. Florence Nightingale's contribution to nursing in the Crimea revolutionized the profession in general, giving it a dignity and prestige it neither had nor deserved before. During the first nine months of the war, eighteen thousand British soldiers lost their lives to sickness and inadequate care of wounds. The figure dropped to two thousand in the next nine months after Florence Nightingale's reforms in management and procedure had had a chance to show results. When she first arrived—two months before Gordon—she was met by an appalling situation. Seemingly endless ranks of beds were jammed together in the barracks near a row of foul-smelling cesspools. Never had she seen anything to compare with the horrors of the barrack hospital at night, with its tragic neglect of patients and total lack of concern for hygiene.

Gordon's initial task in the Crimea was a critical one. The year was 1855, and a vicious winter had taken its toll. A hurricane had wreaked havoc with French and British ships as they bobbed helplessly in the narrow harbor of Balaklava and had devastated jerry-built tent camps, leaving troops shelterless in its wake. An assault on the Russian positions had to be postponed, while the troops dug in as best they could to get through the bitter cold. The Russians suffered just as much. Leo Tolstoy, who was among the Russian troops, recounts the season in *Tales of Sebastopol*, published after the war.

Buoyed by the thrill of war, Gordon took the hardships of winter in his stride. He compared the British soldiers to children who, unlike the French, could not look after themselves: "I hope you will not believe all the atrocious fibs which are told in the papers of our misery. No one seems to interest himself about the siege, all appear to be engaged in foraging expeditions for grub." Yet the struggle for survival against the elements was very real. Officers froze to death in the night, others were smothered from the smoke of charcoal fires started for warmth. There was palpable need, Gordon recognized, to put the huts up in a hurry.

As if these problems were not bad enough, the British suffered from poor military leadership. Lord Raglan, the commander, was a staff officer who had never commanded as much as a company in the field. He had splendid personal qualities, he was kind, courteous and conscientious, but he found it difficult to act resolutely. When he did, his orders were often unclear or confusing. "A very good man," Florence Nightingale said, "but not a very great general."

After the first British engagement, the bloody attack against Alma on September 20, 1854, Queen Victoria had commended Lord Raglan on a performance worthy of Wellington: "Such coolness in the midst of the hottest fire,"[2] she wrote. But the reality was different. Casualties had been so numerous that they attracted the first vultures ever seen in the Crimea, the birds mysteriously appearing from distant North Africa to attend the battlefield feast. When Raglan suddenly died after an abortive and much-criticized assault on Sevastopol in June 1855, Gordon was convinced he "died of tear, wear and general debility," and hoped that the general had been "prepared."

Gordon himself was prepared. In a letter written retrospectively in 1883 to his friend the Reverend Mr. Barnes, he confessed: "I went to the Crimea, hoping without having a hand in it, to be killed." His exhibitions of bravery in the Crimea, which drew praise from his superiors, might well have been considered sheer recklessness, but it probably bespoke an underlying readiness to join his God if that was what was ordained. Yet Gordon's lust for battle and his competitive spirit, which made failure in combat unacceptable, warred with his passive fatalism and deep desire to be relieved of the emotional burdens of life. It was a dualism that would persist throughout Gordon's lifetime; he was impatient to go on to the next, better world but could not resist the challenges of this one, which in turn gave him the will to live.

Raglan's replacement, General James Simpson, was a weak commander despite experience in India. Nobody put it better than he himself did: "They must indeed be hard up when they appointed an old man like me."[3] The French commander, Marshal Saint-Arnaud, died of cholera soon after he arrived. His successor, Canrobert, who was a timid commander for all his posturing, resigned in May 1855 over disagreements with the British over the conduct of the war. Gordon cryptically commented: "General Canrobert moves about in great state; he always has a great banner with him and an escort of Spahis." The third French commander was as reckless as Canrobert had been cautious, and earned a reputation for needlessly incurring heavy casualties.

What saved the Allies despite their mediocre commanders was the even more inept leadership on the Russian side. General Menshikov was a catastrophe, a victim of severe neurosis. Gorchakov relieved Menshikov but was only marginally better. A bright spot among the imperial defenders was the Russian engineering officer, Colonel Todleben, a fortifications genius whose defenses around Sevastopol made the Russian positions almost impregnable. Gordon learned much about siege defenses by observing Todleben's artistry from the other side of the ramparts as he helped plot the final assault on Sevastopol.

Sevastopol was to make up for Gordon's missed battles at Alma, Inkerman and Balaklava. His first combat assignment called for him to lead a party of eight men to dig rifle pits linking the French and English sentry positions in front of the main Allied trench network. His own account of this hazardous mission gives some of the flavor of front-line action, the human foibles and fears at the muddy trench level:

THE MOLDING AND ANNEALING

I never had [seen combat action] although I kept that to myself. I led forward the sentries, going at the head of the party, and found the sentries of the advance had not held the caves, which they ought to have done after dark, so there was just a chance of the Russians being in them. I went on, however, and though I did not like it, explored the caves almost alone. We left two sentries on the hill above the caves, and went back to get round and post two sentries below the caves. However, just as soon as we showed ourselves outside the caves and below them, bang! bang! went two rifles, the bullets hitting the ground close to us. The sentries with me retired in a rare state of mind, and my working party bolted, and were stopped with great difficulty. What had really happened was this. It was not a Russian attack, but the two sentries whom I had placed above the caves *had fired on us*, lost their caps, and bolted to the trench. Nothing after this would induce the sentries to go out, so I got the working party to go forward with me.[4]

Regarding another close call, one of Gordon's friends recounted: "Charlie has had a miraculous escape. The day before yesterday he saw smoke from an embrasure on his left, and heard a shell coming but did not see it." Those were the days of "bobbing," as Gordon put it, when one could actually dodge shells if they were spotted in time. But on this occasion the shell struck the ground five yards in front of him, exploding, but not harming him—"If it had not burst, it would have taken his head off!"

For the Allies the Sevastopol siege was a frustrating proposition, as the city was never completely encircled and supplies continued to filter through. But the Russians' extended supply line, which required transport and troop movement over endless, almost impassable roads ravaged by winter ice and snow, exacted a heavy price. It was estimated that one out of ten Russian soldiers sent south to the Crimea died during the terrible three-month march. In all, the Russians lost about a half million men, two-thirds of whom were stricken down by disease.[5]

Gordon saw his brothers Henry and Enderby whenever he could. He reported home that they were well. "Enderby's hut was a comfortable one," he reassured his parents, and war "certainly suits him." His two older brothers' well-being seemed to concern him more than his own. If their mother insisted on sending packages to the front with food and clothing, Charlie urged that they be sent to Henry and Enderby, not to himself. This may have reflected his tendency toward asceticism but it was also genuine concern for his brothers. In a letter to his mother, he confided that Enderby "has not been properly taken care of" and is in need of "warm things."

Many of Gordon's lifelong friends date from the Crimea. It was there that he met Garnet Wolseley, who would eventually become one of England's most esteemed officers and rise to Commander in Chief of the British Army. In the Crimea Wolseley was an infantry captain, but because he was attached to the Royal Engineers, he found himself subordinate to Gordon despite his higher rank. This anomaly, however, did not prevent them from forming an enduring friendship. Not only were they comrades-in-arms, but they shared a deep faith in God. In Wolseley's opinion, Gordon was one of the few persons who qualified as a truly "Christian hero."[6]

Sir Garnet later recalled: "When I first met him in the Crimea, he was a good looking, curley-headed young man of my own age. His full, clear and bright blue eyes seemed to court scrutiny, while at the same time they searched into your inner soul."[7] But he was cognizant as well of Gordon's curious death desire: "An indifference to danger of all sorts . . . bespoke a want of the sense which generally warns man of its presence. Life was to him but a Pilgrim's Progress between the years of manhood and the Heaven he now dwells in, the home he always longed for,"[8] Wolseley wrote after his friend's tragic death.

Gordon also made a good friend of Lieutenant Colonel Sir Charles Staveley. Staveley would later be Gordon's commanding officer in China and eventually become his brother-in-law. In the Crimea, Staveley was impressed with Gordon's valor: "He took me outside our most advanced trench, the bouquets [volleys of small shells from the mortars] and other missiles flying about us in, to me, a very unpleasant manner, he taking the matter remarkably coolly."[9]

Then there was Romolo Gessi, the Levantine, part Italian and part Armenian, who was serving as an interpreter for the British Army in the Crimea when he and Gordon met. Of all Gordon's military friends, perhaps no one was closer to him than Gessi. Gordon believed their fates were intertwined: Gessi would figure prominently with Gordon both in Galatz on the Danube and in the Sudan.

Events in the Crimea continued at an impasse. British assaults on the Redan fortifications were repeatedly unsuccessful—so much so that Gordon, after a failed attack, with more contempt than sorrow, noted that the Russians hurled "a fire of grape, mowed down our men in dozens, and the trenches, being confined, were crowded with men who foolishly kept in them instead of rushing over the parapet." Had the men charged, they would soon have outrun the effective range of the artillery and "we could have moved up our supports and carried the place." The engagement had begun with an artillery duel in which some thousand guns hurled their shot across the lines. Gordon, who spent sixteen hours in the trenches, was slightly hurt when a stone ricocheting about in the upheaval struck him in the head and momentarily stunned him. He was carried from the field, but his brother Henry promptly assured their parents that "Charlie is all right, and has escaped amidst a terrific shower of grape and shells of every description. You may imagine the suspense I was kept in until assured of his safety."[10]

Another assault on the Redan occurred September 8. Again Gordon blamed the men for not pressing their advance. Some 150 officers and 2,400 men were killed and wounded in this engagement before the British were forced to retire. It had been a heartbreaking rush as the city-bred recruits wavered and fell back despite the efforts of seasoned noncommissioned officers urging them on. The French fared better, however, and managed to take a key bastion known as the Malakoff, making the Russian positions at Sevastopol indefensible. The entire Russian garrison slipped out that night after destroying the fortifications they had so tenaciously fought to hold. Gordon wrote: "During the night I heard terrible explosions and, going down to the trenches at 4:00 A.M., I saw a splendid sight—the whole town in flames and every now and then a terrific explosion. The rising sun shining on the scene of destruction produced a beautiful effect." On September 10, he wrote home jubilantly: "We are at last in possession of the vile place."

The end of the fighting was a time for rewarding those who had served with distinction in this enormously popular though mismanaged war. The Queen approved a design for a new medal, the Victoria Cross, intended to be Britain's highest honor for valor in combat, but rejected the motto in the citation, "For the Brave," since this would imply that only Victoria Cross recipients were brave. Lesser awards were passed out with reckless frequency, based more on seniority than merit, causing Gordon to scoff at such debasing of the medals.

For her efforts, Florence Nightingale received a warm letter of praise from the Queen as well as a brooch commemorating her "great and blessed work." The Queen added that she looked forward to making "the acquaintance of one who has set so bright an example to our sex."[11]

Gordon had to be satisfied with inclusion in a long and indiscriminating list of engineer junior officers who had "distinguished" themselves. Awards meant little to him, or so he claimed, and he could take pride that he had acquitted himself well in the Crimea and that he had been promoted to the acting rank of captain. One of his commanders, Colonel C. C. Chesney, later wrote of him: "Gordon had first seen war in the hard school of the 'black winter' of the Crimea," and had "attracted the notice of his superiors, not merely by his energy and activity, but by a special aptitude for war, a personal knowledge of the enemy's movements such as no other officer attained."[12] The French, more generous than his own army in honoring his performance, awarded him the Legion of Honor.

After the shooting stopped, Gordon for the first time could explore the countryside. He wandered far afield with his friend Romolo Gessi. They explored the now-abandoned Sevastopol defenses. This was an engineering officer's postmortem, a lesson in siege defenses more valuable than anything learned at Woolwich or Chatham. They visited the cathedrals along the Crimean coast, Gessi salvaging icons to add to his already remarkable collection. War booty was scarce in the ravaged Crimea, but Gessi had rare instinct and unerring skill in searching treasures out.

Gessi was a hybrid Italian, a colorful man with an aura of dash and daring about him. After being trained as a soldier in Wiener Neustadt outside of Vienna and Halle in Germany, he had fought with Garibaldi in Italy. This in itself was enough to commend him to Gordon. The idea of guerrilla partisans fighting for the righteous cause of social justice fired Gordon's imagination.

Gessi was a consummate survivor in the uncertain world of Mittel Europe. His father had been British Consul in Bucharest, but despite this claim to British nationality, Gessi was a mongrel. To make matters more complicated, his mother had given birth to him on a boat, further clouding his citizenship. Finding himself ineligible to serve the Queen, he joined the army of the King of Piedmont instead. But his mastery of most of the languages used in the polyglot alliance that fought the Russians made him invaluable as an interpreter for British field forces.

Gordon's religious feelings drew him close to such persons as Captain Drew, but his soldier's soul was attracted to adventurers like Gessi. Later in China and the Sudan there would be others of this type—some reprehensible—whom Gordon would include among his friends. Just as a yearning to die—part of his Christian ecstasy—existed in stark conflict with a strong sense of survival and a good soldier's compulsion to win, his choice of friends throughout life also suggested a duality of personality.

Gordon spent four more months in the Crimea toward the end of 1855. This was a time of diplomatic maneuvering in the chanceries of Europe, well beyond the view of Gordon, whose humble part in the peace process consisted of destroying the abandoned Russian defenses in the Crimea. Years later he would occasionally reminisce about this time with a fellow engineering subaltern, Gerald Graham. They had been friends as cadets at Woolwich, and their paths would cross again many times, including in Egypt, where Graham watched Gordon ride off on camelback into the desert to Khartoum and his last mission.

Prime Minister Palmerston had visions of carrying on the war so that the Czar would be more completely humbled, but Napoleon III feared that prolonging and widening the conflict would prove too costly to France. Weary of war and conscious of revolutionary rumblings in his empire, the Czar too wanted peace. After much backstage intrigue, including artful foot-dragging by Palmerston, a peace conference finally opened in Paris on February 25, 1856, to bring the Crimean War formally to an end. Gordon's duty in Asia Minor, however, was by no means over.

3

FROM PEACEMAKER
TO WARRIOR

I am pretty tired of my post of peacemaker, for which I am naturally
not well suited.
—Charles Gordon with the Boundary Commission, 1858

For Gordon the 1856 Treaty of Paris, which marked the formal end of
the Crimean War, meant new duty. In May he was sent to the frontier
that divided Russia from the states of Moldavia and Wallachia—soon
to become Rumania. There for the next year he served on the Boundary
Commission, surveying the region in implementation of the provisions of the
peace treaty.

The areas under survey were sometimes interesting, but the work was
dull and the diplomatic bickering annoying. While the Turks and Russians
maneuvered for advantage, the British and French argued interminably. The
Russians, whose fighting qualities Gordon had admired during the war, did
not endear themselves to him in peace. In Bessarabia they muddied the
negotiations with their incessant intrigues, attempting to retrieve by guile
what they had lost by war. The Governor of Bessarabia offered no gesture of
hospitality toward the boundary commissioners, and the general population
seemed only interested in fleecing the uninvited foreigners in their midst.
Gordon could not even find merit in Russian music or Russian wine. As for
Black Sea caviar, he could only say it was cheap.

Gordon felt that he was in a backwater, although he at least had a change of
scenery when he was shifted by the Boundary Commission from Bessarabia
to the Turkish-Russian frontier of Armenia. He considered this new
semidiplomatic assignment equally uninspiring and tried to wiggle out of
it, but his protest were met with an unequivocating: "Lieutenant Gordon
must go."

Elsewhere, the British situation in India had grown precarious, and as

37

Gordon took up his new assignment in Erzurum, a mutiny of Indian sepoys threatened the loss of the empire's most lustrous jewel. Gordon's brother Enderby drew India duty and gained distinction in action against the mutineers, but Charlie had to reconcile himself to missing the latest main show.

Asia Minor, however, was not without its charms—at least for someone like Gordon. The assignment gave him a taste for working on his own among tribal people. In stark contrast to cosmopolitan, decadent Constantinople, he found in eastern Turkey an exhilarating primitiveness. It was nature unadorned, though the people were poor and backward, particularly in the rural areas where Gordon spent most of the time. "There is no such thing as a wheeled carriage," he noted in wonder.

Gordon traveled widely in Armenia, visiting out-of-the-way spots, including the ancient capital of Ani. In his travels he was usually accompanied by a half-Turkish major whom Gordon called Robert and who functioned as interpreter and somehow managed to produce food and lodging on demand, even if he had to confiscate it. A Bible-reading Russian servant named Ivan was also part of his entourage. As the little party wandered about the countryside, Gordon found that he liked the rugged Kurdish tribesmen: "a fine-looking people, armed to the teeth," whom he could trust. He mingled with them easily and was fond of squatting on the ground alongside the taciturn hillsmen, sharing with them rice from huge flaps of unleavened bread. This he enjoyed more than dining with diplomats in the salons of Constantinople.

With the help of Kurdish guides, Gordon climbed Mount Ararat, where legend says Noah's Ark came to rest after the Flood subsided. A bottle stuffed with a piece of paper with Gordon's name on it was left on the slopes of the mountain by one of the party to memorialize the ascent. (Gordon, in fact, never actually reached the summit, having been turned back by bad weather.) Gordon was nonetheless skeptical about Ararat being the true site of the Ark, arguing that nothing in Scripture suggested that Armenia was the place. Scripture, as far as Gordon was concerned, was the only valid authority, and believing that, he much later would find a more likely place.

In the Caucasus region known as Lazistan, Gordon was appalled to find a thriving slave trade. Traders kidnapped Gourelian peasants from the Russian side of the border and sent them to Constantinople to be sold as servants for the seraglios of the wealthy. Gordon was so upset by this that he complained repeatedly to the British embassy in Constantinople, alerting the Anti-Slavery Society in London as well. But the slave trade, which in Africa so outraged the British, did not arouse much interest in its Caucasian form.

The winter of 1857–58 was a homecoming for Gordon. His family was delighted to see him and eager to hear about his adventures. Gordon brought home with him his servant, Ivan, who regularly read the Bible, so even though he was a foreigner and a Lutheran, he fitted well in the Gordon household. The other servants liked Ivan, too, particularly Emma, the maid, to whom he paid special attention.

Gordon's sister Helen was charmed by her brother's description of Caucasian princesses. Gordon thought them beautiful but with "dirty habits, taking a bone and gnawing it." Less-worldly Augusta encouraged him in his new hobby, begun during his wanderings in Asia Minor: mapping the sites of biblical history. Ararat had set him thinking and had whetted his appetite for further exploration. A family friend, Colonel Simmons, obligingly put him up for membership in the Royal Geographical Society so that he could have access to existing maps of the Holy Land and Asia Minor.

Talk in England that winter was dominated by the Sepoy Mutiny. The unspeakable atrocities of Cawnpore chilled British hearts as few events in the empire ever had. Some 240 British wives and children had been seized and "barbarously slaughtered."[1] Eyewitnesses described the tragedy in gruesome detail.[2] September 1857 had seen the British trying desperately to put down the Indian uprising. Soldiers were mustered from all over India, and some were diverted while en route to China. Major reinforcements were also on their way from England, provoking the *Illustrated London News* to wonder if they would arrive too late, as they usually do at "the beginning of military undertakings."[3]

The front pages of all the newspapers were full of the mutiny, so the long-ongoing uprising in China, called the Taiping Rebellion, was relegated to the back pages. Civil war in China had been raging for seven years and was horrible in its despoliation, but it had not aroused the emotions of Englishmen remote from the scene. News dispatches reported in September: "The Hakkas of Komeng and six other districts have united and are burning and destroying wherever they go. Canton is the great point of escape to [where] the poor starving wretches of the surrounding districts are congregating by the thousands."[4] But this was obviously not as important to the British public as news that Lucknow had been relieved at last by General Colin Campbell.

Gordon looked forward to his return to Asia Minor despite its disagreeable aspects. Protracted idleness never appealed to him, much less the niceties of English society. Better to shake the "sticky" hands of minor Caucasian princes and visit the barely habitable huts of the hill people than endure the small talk of well-meaning English matrons or hopeful virgins. According to R. H. Barnes, Gordon was much less at ease in talking to women than men: "His sympathy, geniality and attractiveness became veiled, and he was 'himself again' only with the restraint removed."[5]

On the ship home Gordon was still not rid of English feminine company. One lady he met on board "chattered" too much, while he could escape from another only because she retreated to her cabin with an attack of seasickness. Some ladies he described more generously, "lively, volatile and very fascinating." But Gordon knew by now that marriage was not for him. Years later he observed to a friend: "You have wives and families; I thank God I have none of them and am free." Wilfrid Blunt, friend and biographer, noted: "He seems never to have been in love or indulged, even for a moment, in any dream of earthly happiness to be found in domestic joy. These he regarded as not intended for him, and he was as far from the thought of marriage as though he had renounced the possibilities of it by a vow."[6] It seemed Gordon's self-imposed renunciation of sex and family was in many ways not unlike a Roman Catholic priest's vow of chastity, but to Gordon fleshly temptations were the work of the Devil and for this reason had to be resisted.

Traveling through the Black Sea en route to Odessa, Gordon's ship called briefly at Sevastopol, giving him an opportunity to revisit the scene of the fighting. In Odessa, Gordon's Turkish aide, Robert, met him when he arrived, but another assistant, the Russian Colonel Khleb, had also joined the mission in his absence. Robert and Khleb, strong partisans each, continually quarreled, much to Gordon's annoyance.

Gordon's work was frustrating for other reasons. Lack of local cooperation, vandalism—carefully erected boundary cairns were often destroyed— and bickering between the Russians and the Turks sapped his enthusiasm for the job. When in the autumn he finally headed for home, his assignment completed, he found a somewhat cynical attitude toward the whole matter on the part of British officialdom in Constantinople. Gordon could only conclude that no one was interested in the boundary demarcation, much less his own work, which he admitted was "anomalous" in nature.

In Constantinople, Gordon renewed an earlier acquaintance with the French engineer Ferdinand de Lesseps, who had become president of the Suez Canal Company. The Egyptian Khedive had provided thousands of *fellahin,* or Egyptian farmers, as laborers, and they were now busy digging the big ditch between the Mediterranean and the Red Sea, an enterprise which must have seemed as ambitious as the great pyramids. It was an awesome project, and an unexpected offer of employment from de Lesseps was tempting to Gordon. He was flattered, but as a fledgling officer he thought it no time to leave the Queen's service.

Gordon arrived back in England in time for Christmas 1858. This holiday, with its festiveness and heavy eating, never appealed to Gordon, but he was glad to see his family. In April he was promoted to captain, a quick progression for a twenty-six-year-old officer, and was stationed at Chatham as Second Adjutant and Field Works instructor.

The year at Chatham was uneventful compared to war in the Crimea and the exotic duty in the wilds of the Caucasus. He complained that at Chatham one needed at least eighteen pairs of spurs, as they were required on all occasions. "Sleeping in them is a nuisance," he joked to a friend, although it was very stylish to have them "clank as you walk." By now, fighting had broken out again in China, and Gordon was determined to be part of it. He volunteered and was accepted.

While Gordon would eventually develop respect and affection for the Chinese, he understood little about them as he prepared to depart. He shared the preconceptions and prejudices held by most Englishmen, and he was too excited by the prospects of active service to consider either the upheavals in the ancient kingdom or the validity of British intervention.

There was British opposition to Palmerston's "filibustering" in the Far East, but by and large the English were inclined to dismiss the Chinese as heathens led by an arrogant and xenophobic Emperor who needed to be taught a lesson. Even the British statesman Richard Cobden, who championed the causes of the downtrodden—he had fought against taxing "the poor man's loaf" in England and objected to imperial adventures abroad as a prop to domestic prosperity—asserted in the House of Commons: "You cannot like a people who do not like you." China's authoritarian government more critically was severely restrictive of foreign commerce. The 1842 Treaty of Nanking, which ended the Opium War, had liberalized trade, but the Emperor was not fully living up to its terms. Equally annoying to the British, he still refused to permit normal diplomatic relations and would not accept a resident British ambassador in the capital, Peking.

The new crisis in British-Chinese relations again began in the port city of Canton. Since the Opium War, the Cantonese had endured an increasing Western presence at the same time they chafed under oppressive Manchu misrule. The economy was also depressed. This gave rise to insurgency throughout the city of Canton and the surrounding province of Kwangtung. The Emperor sought to regain control by appointing a ferocious Imperial commissioner named Yeh Ming-ch'en. Yeh's solution was uncomplicated; by his own account he ordered some seventy thousand suspected rebels slaughtered!

Yeh disliked Western traders as much as he did Cantonese rebels, concomitantly subjecting the "foreign devils" to all kinds of petty harassment. Relations grew tense when he refused to meet with British and French representatives seeking to discuss a revision of the Treaty of Nanking. Then in October 1856 Canton police boarded the sailing ship *Arrow*, which was flying the Union Jack, and arrested its Chinese crew on charges of smuggling opium. The ship's owner was a Chinese pirate and the ship's British registration had expired, but the doughty British Consul, Harry Parkes, seized on the incident as an excuse to confront the strong-armed commissioner.

Yeh refused to apologize. The British shelled the city, which led to mobs sacking foreign trading stations, and quickly controversy was beyond quiet negotiations. Yeh was resolute even as the British pushed to redress a decade-long situation in which China had flouted the 1842 treaty. The British, moreover, saw in this an opportunity to extract from the Chinese even more favorable trading terms.

While the end of the Crimean War had freed the British to take a more aggressive approach to their interests in the Far East, Parliament had qualms about involvement in another imbroglio with China. By the margin of 263 to 247, it voted to censure Prime Minister Palmerston for approving Parkes's belligerent initiatives. But Palmerston was adamant. Anyone who sided with a Chinese "barbarian" against a British colonial official, he ranted, was no true Englishman, and he called for a general election to test public sentiment on the issue.

While serving in Bessarabia on the Frontier Commission as these events were unfolding, Gordon had written home expressing his hope that the Prime Minister would win the election. In a stunning victory Palmerston did triumph, interpreting the vote as a mandate to chastise the Chinese militarily. The French, too, were dissatisfied with Chinese behavior and joined the British in this punitive campaign, which came to be known as the Second Opium War. It was for this war that Gordon had volunteered.

After traveling across France, Gordon boarded the P & O steamer *Valleta* in Marseilles for Egypt, the first leg of his long journey to the Orient. For Gordon it was an exhilarating time to be in the Mediterranean. Garibaldi was about to invade the Italian peninsula from the toehold he had won in Sicily, the *Times* reporting that it would be hard for any new hero "to surpass the reputation which the Italian general has acquired." All Europe had followed Garibaldi's exploits in Sicily—his victory at Calatafimi and capture of Palermo—and now watched intently to see if the mainland would also become his prize. But there was another reason for Gordon's interest in these developments: Fighting with Garibaldi's forces was Gordon's close friend Romolo Gessi, who had in fact invited Gordon to join in the struggle for Italian independence.

On shipboard there was drama too. When a ship's steward named Kirkham was accused of stealing money from the stateroom of a passenger, Gordon pleaded the young man's case and made up the loss to the irate victim. Rather than see Kirkham thrown off the ship, Gordon engaged the steward as a personal servant. This charitable act would prove fortuitous, as Kirkham, whom Gordon later made a soldier, fought loyally and well throughout the China campaign.

The overland trip across the narrow strip of desert between Cairo and Suez had to be made by train. A hot, dusty and monotonous ride was slightly enlivened by the sight of Egyptian labor battalions digging de Lesseps's canal. With every shovelful Egypt came closer to gaining a new strategic importance. Now, however, the focus was on China, where Gordon would arrive after a nearly two-month journey.

PART II

Mandarins, Mercenaries, and Heavenly Rebels

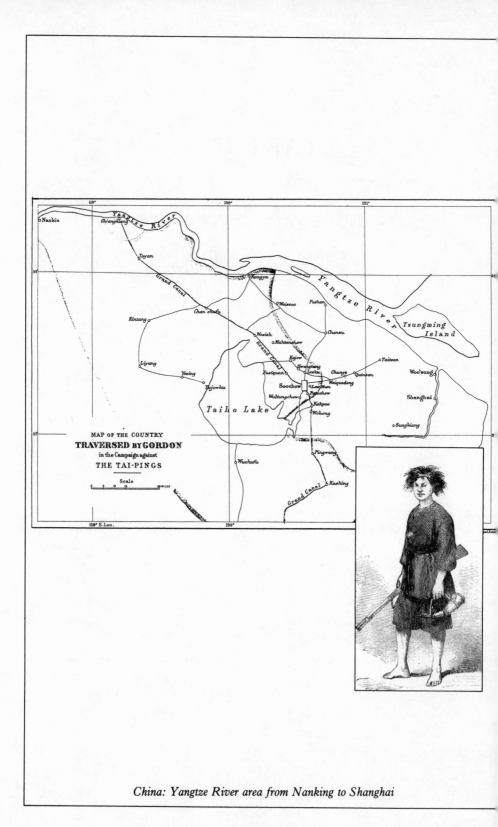

China: Yangtze River area from Nanking to Shanghai

4

THE HEAVENLY KINGDOM

No matter how the devils fly,
They are many times surrounded
By nets above in Heaven, and the snares below on earth.
Under the sword there is no forgiveness.
It is better that they find their way easily to Hell.
　　　　　—T'ien Wang, "Ten-fold Perfect Auspicious Poems"

In mid-September 1860, Gordon reached Hong Kong. It had been a long voyage, and he feared he would be "rather late for the amusement" as the news was that the Anglo-French expeditionary force had already opened the approach to Tientsin and Peking. Led by British Commissioner James Bruce, Earl of Elgin, and Military Commander Sir Hope Grant, an Allied flotilla of two hundred warships had landed at Taku with ten thousand British soldiers; they were joined by a French contingent six thousand strong, led by Commissioner Montauban and General Gros. Together, the combined forces had succeeded in seizing Taku, the Chinese forts that guarded the mouth of the Pehho River.

This was a welcome victory after the several earlier frustrations in trying to bring the Chinese Emperor to heel. The *Arrow* incident had been resolved to the Britons' satisfaction when, in collaboration with the French, they occupied Canton in November 1857. Commissioner Yeh, the Chinese antagonist, who in fact had done nothing to defend Canton except consult a mystical poet, was captured and exiled to Calcutta. But Canton's capture was not sufficient persuasion for the Emperor Hsien-feng to meet the Allies' demand for a new treaty.

On the first attempt in 1858 to obtain an acceptable treaty from the Emperor—before Gordon's arrival in China—an Anglo-French expedition had easily captured the wooden forts of Taku and sailed upriver to Tientsin. British Commissioner Lord Elgin, leading the expedition, wrote wistfully in his journal: "The night was lovely." Having watched the gunboats "cutting ruthlessly and recklessly through the water of that glancing and startled river, which . . . no stranger keel had ever furrowed," he pondered: "Whose work are we engaged in, when we burst thus with hideous violence and brutal energy into these darkest and most mysterious recesses of the traditions of the past?"[1] But despite any reservations he may have had about upsetting ancient ways, he dutifully and forcefully presented the Allies' demands in Tientsin.

The Anglo-French force provided whatever persuasion the Chinese commissioners needed to sign draft treaties with each power. But the treaties would yet have to be ratified by the Emperor, who was sure to balk at one of the most important provisions: the right to accredit minister plenipotentiaries at the court, resident in Peking. (Foreign envoys had traditionally been received in Peking only as vassals and tribute-bearers, kowtowing before the Emperor not as ambassadors from equal powers, but as lesser supplicants.)

The British treaty draft also specified that ten additional ports would be open to trade; that British naval vessels would be allowed entry to all treaty ports, including the four ports located up the Yangtze River deep inside the country; that missionary evangelism would be permitted; and that British subjects would enjoy a degree of extraterritoriality as far as Chinese courts were concerned. Because of damage inflicted on the British, the Chinese would pay a $4 million indemnity. (France, the United States and Russia extracted from the Chinese similar terms before the force left Tientsin.) It was understood that Great Britain and France would return the following year to ratify the treaties after the Emperor had had an opportunity to "study" them.

When the Allies returned in June 1859 and attempted to force their way past the Taku garrisons to Tientsin, they had been met by unexpected opposition. Reinforced Chinese garrisons inflicted such losses that the British troops had to retreat to their ships under fire. Three United States men-of-war accompanying the expedition in a naval operation permitted by Washington as an exception to its policy of nonintervention entered the fray despite orders not to take part in actual combat. Later arguing that "blood is thicker than water," the American commander justified this breach of his instructions on the grounds that the battered British forces urgently needed help. Rather than suffer further indignities the British and French retired to consider their next move.

The successful July 1860 offensive, in process as Gordon arrived in China, redressed the defeat suffered the year before, although Lord Elgin noted

48

wearily in his journal: "I am at war again! My idiotical Chinamen have taken to playing tricks. I am sure that we must get nearer to Peking before the Government there comes to its senses."

He was right. A Chinese army under its tough Mongol commander in chief, Seng-ko-lin-ch'in, unexpectedly withdrew rather than engage the Allies. He had been instructed not to risk his person "in combat with ugly barbarians," although it was probably Chinese strategy to draw the Allies inland and preserve the Imperial army for the crucial defense of Peking.

Gordon's disappointment that he had missed out on the action at Taku was short-lived, as he received orders to join the Anglo-French force now marching on Peking. On his way there he passed through Shanghai, where on September 17 he was treated to the sight of baskets suspended from the walls filled with the heads of unlucky Taiping rebels.

Only a month before, the British garrison had rallied to the defense of this important international trading port as it was threatened by these rebels. The paradoxical situation was not lost on Gordon: British troops, under Sir Frederick Bruce's command, had gone to the aid of Imperial forces defending Shanghai against the long-feared attack at almost the same moment that Lord Elgin, Bruce's brother, and Sir Hope Grant were leading British soldiers in an assault against the Emperor's forts at Taku. While trying to remain neutral in China's civil war, Britain's first priority was to defend British trade and protect British nationals.

In Shanghai, Gordon gained his first insights into the long and debilitating Taiping Rebellion. When he arrived in this key city, he, like many Englishmen, believed that the Taipings as professed Christians had good in them. Gordon was soon disabused of that notion, viewing them as a malign movement, guilty of untold atrocities as well as systematic despoliation of the countryside.

The rebels, who wore their hair long and straggly in symbolic defiance of the neat queues of the traditional Chinese, were camped only fifteen miles out of Shanghai. An earlier attempt to capture Shanghai had failed, but led by their most capable general, Li Hsiu-ch'eng—known as Chung Wang, "Faithful King"—they were not to be so easily deterred. Before Gordon arrived, they had taken the important city of Soochow, and they had not given up on Shanghai. Li sent Bruce a letter threatening harm to British trade on the Yangtze River if Bruce sided with the Manchus in the civil war. And, unknown to the British and the Imperialist Chinese alike, Li had gone to the rebels' capital at Nanking to draw up plans for a new winter offensive against Shanghai.

While Gordon soon began to understand the Taiping threat from a tactical point of view, neither he nor most other foreigners knew much about the beginnings of this movement and its astonishing success. It seems the inspiration for the rebellion, so long in progress, was a curious half-mad native of Kwangtung Province named Hung Hsiu-ch'uan who in 1851 had proclaimed himself T'ien Wang, "Heavenly King"; a man from modest beginnings, he attracted a zealous following which would fight to the death to change China. Gordon, devoted to the word of the Bible, could only have loathing for a man who blasphemed Christ, frolicking in his harem while his armies marauded about the countryside spreading terror among the peasantry.

Despite his own evangelical propensities, Gordon had misgivings about Protestant missionaries who still hoped that the Heavenly King might be persuaded to embrace true Christianity. He felt sympathy for the peasants, whom he had seen displaced and ravaged by the Taipings near Shanghai. Many of the peasants, he could see, blamed the Western missionaries—who sometimes were referred to as the "spawn of the Devil"—for encouraging, if not instigating, the Taiping movement.

Who was this self-styled messiah and Heavenly King? Hung Hsiu-ch'uan began his extraordinary life on January 1, 1814, with nothing then to suggest that he would prove more remarkable than any other child born of humble Kwangtung farmers. Revolutionary leaders often emerge from obscurity to shake the foundations of their societies, but few have had the shattering impact of Hung as leader of the bloodiest civil war the world has known. In the many years the Taiping Rebellion raged—slaughtering some thirty million people[2] and laying waste vast areas of the country—China was wrenched from its centuries-old ways. Modern China was born, it is said, of the Taiping upheaval, a cataclysm second only to World War II in death and destruction. All the more startling, Hung convinced his myriad followers that he was Jesus Christ's younger brother, and led them to war under the banner of an aberrant Christianity.

Hung's family belonged to the Hakka people, Taoist by religion, whose ancestors had migrated to Kwangtung from the north centuries before when

China was overrun by Tartar invaders. With their different dialect and customs, the Hakkas were easily distinguishable from the more numerous Punti people who had settled the land at an even earlier time and considered the Hakkas inferior. Communal clashes between the Taoist Hakkas and Confucian Puntis were common and troublesome.

The Chinese peasants' lot in general also suffered from the exploitation and corruption of Manchu rule. Rents and taxes were unreasonably high, causing widespread abandonment of the land. In order to survive, roaming gangs of the dispossessed turned to banditry, making life worse for others, while government troops proved more a menace than protection. As Imperial rule atrophied, local self-defense organizations and "secret societies" assumed the burden of their own defense. But there was little security to be had. Lawlessness became a way of life as bandits, secret societies and ill-controlled militia brawled in the chaos of the decaying Manchu dynasty.[3]

Administration, too, had by now become more a local affair than a function of the Imperial government. The gentry, or provincial educated elite, while sometimes holding titular government posts, drew real power from its local landholdings and deep roots in the community. Most matters were locally decided, the Emperor's writ being reserved for matters transcending parochial concern. The gentry had thus provided continuity and a modicum of order. Imperial dynasties waxed and waned, each destined eventually to lose its "Mandate of Heaven"—as the Chinese referred to an emperor's authority—and to be replaced by a new, more virile power. But this historical rondo was soon to be tested by new forces at work. An astonishing population increase throughout much of China placed new strains on an old land, but it was the impact of Western traders that would cause more immediate changes in the ancient civilization.

While foreign trade was rigidly regulated and confined to Canton, the illicit opium trade drained China's supply of silver, the principal medium of exchange, producing inflationary conditions disastrous for the peasantry. And the opium trade, having led to war with the British, led subsequently to the trauma of alien Western influences. Traders, missionaries, soldiers and vagabonds arrived in ever-increasing numbers to leave their mark on this long-cloistered empire.

In this turn of events, Hung grew up. His parents recognized him as a gifted child and sought for him the opportunities provided by the Imperial civil service. Examinations offered the lucky few who passed some hope of a relatively prosperous career—a sinecure from which to extract at least a small share of the graft that oiled the machinery of government. But at age fifteen Hung failed the test for the civil service, and he had to content himself with teaching school in local villages. In 1837 the stress and frustration of once again failing the civil service examination proved too much for Hung, and he collapsed in Canton with a severe mental breakdown. For forty days he lay delirious and feverish, hovering on the verge of death. He survived, but even after he was well enough to return home, he was tortured by fits of rage, often requiring physical restraint. In fact, he seemed quite mad.

Gradually Hung improved, but his family and friends were astonished at a transformation that had taken place within him. He now assumed the air of a man with a mission, entertaining strange ideas of grandeur. He now walked tall, with a stride suggesting self-assurance. Politics interested him, and he began to write odes and treatises on affairs of the day. He attracted people to him, his new charisma impressing the simple townsfolk, who looked to him for leadership. He harangued them on the horrors of the foreign opium trade and crusaded for morality in the community, sometimes taking it upon himself, personally, to beat transgressors.

In 1843 Hung discovered among his papers a Christian missionary tract entitled *Good Words to Admonish the Age*. Hung had ignored it for a decade, ever since it had been given him by a Chinese Christian named Liang A-fang. But now Hung read it with new interest. It was as if the feverish visions that had visited him during his breakdown suddenly had significance, and the tract inspired him to reinterpret their meaning. He became convinced that he had undergone a religious experience, that in his delirium he had been transported to Heaven to talk with a venerable elder—God Himself—about the sinful plight of the world, and there he had met Jesus Christ, whose teachings he eagerly embraced. Hung, who had been shamed by his irrational outbursts while ill, now gloried in them. The violence he had felt within him was the result, he believed, of battles undertaken at God's bidding with dark demons of evil. His forty days of sickness were like unto Moses' wanderings in the wilderness.

Returning to earth from his odyssey to Heaven, Hung converted his best friend and fellow schoolteacher Feng Yun-shan. Because of their unorthodox beliefs, Hung and Feng were then dismissed as teachers, whereupon they roamed Kwangsi Province as itinerant evangelists preaching a new faith. The year was 1844.

In 1847, back in Canton, Hung sought further Christian instruction from Issachar T. Roberts, an American Southern Baptist missionary. But after only two months and before he could be baptized, Hung left Roberts. His strange, mystical ways had offended some of his fellow novitiates and had troubled the missionary as well.

Undaunted, Hung devised his own "Christian" doctrine—the product of a hallucinated mind, which invented more details of his sojourn to Heaven, including his amazing discovery that he was Jesus Christ's younger brother. God the Father was an impressive figure with a golden beard who sat on a throne in a black dragon robe and high brimmed hat, railing against the evil in the world. Despite His wrath, sinners still served the Devil. God, therefore, ordered Hung to go forth and destroy the demons that undermined His kingdom on earth.

Hung's demons resembled, more than anything found in Christian doctrine, those in Chinese folklore, and his writings revealed more than a trace of Chinese influence. Even in Heaven terrible demons lurked, especially the powerful "serpent god," who seemed identical with the snake that tempted Eve with the forbidden fruit from the Tree of Knowledge. Hung's account of living with a wife provided by God and being surrounded by beautiful angels in Heaven was his own creation, however, and when he returned to earth he was never without women, angelic or otherwise, whatever other asceticism he practiced.

Hung believed Buddhism and Taoism were teachings of the Devil. Confucianism, whose moral values he felt had some virtue, was nonetheless distracting, and Hung finally rejected it. Later Hung embroidered his heavenly lore with anecdotes, including one which described an angry encounter between God and Confucius, God thrashing the great philosopher for his lack of faith. The Manchu dynasty, primarily, was the essence of evil, and Hung saw the need to destroy it. His teachings, which constituted a "New Testament," relegating Christ's teachings to the status of "Former Testament," were simple. Mankind must worship God, the Creator, and fight Satan's demons, who undermined God's kingdom. Believers were graced on earth and would be received into Heaven after death regardless of the kind of lives they had lived. Finally, human nature was fundamentally good.

In referring to this God, Hung preferred the term "Lord of Heaven"—as opposed to "Spirit"—for reasons of semantics. A deity who bestowed the "Mandate of Heaven" on a ruling dynasty could, in the same fashion, withdraw it when the dynasty proved no longer worthy of power. Dedicated to destroying the Manchus, Hung needed a God with the authority—and the persona—to bless his crusade.

Particularly in south and central China, secret societies began to flourish at this time. They appealed primarily to the many who had never fully reconciled themselves to Manchu rule. Usually local in membership, these societies privately favored a return of the Ming dynasty and had conjoined in a loose confederation called the Triad, or the Heaven and Earth Society.[4] By shrewd maneuvering, Hung was able to achieve loose coordination with this dissident confederation, further enhancing his power. He formed four armies, commands prepared for combat in the north, east, south and west.

By the beginning of 1851 Hung Hsiu-ch'uan was ready to launch his revolt. At its Kwangtung redoubt on Thistle Mountain, Hung's followers, some two thousand strong, called itself Pai-Shang-ti-hui, "Society of God Worshipers." It was organized much like the secret societies, but its doctrines, based on Hung's teachings, represented a sharp break with the Chinese tradition by calling for a basically different structure of society. Consisting mainly of Hakkas, the society assumed a militant nature, often doing battle with the rival Puntis. This intercommunal conflict proved to be the nucleus of a movement that would go far beyond religious evangelism and local dissidence to become a revolution such as China had never experienced before.

In a historic January 1851 meeting, Hung, now thirty-eight years old, formally declared himself founder of a new Chinese dynasty, the T'ai-ping T'ien-kuo,* "Heavenly Kingdom of Great Peace," and took the exalted title Tien Wang, "Heavenly King." He donned a resplendent yellow satin robe in defiance of the Manchu Emperor's ban on common men wearing Imperial

---

* Hereafter, this will be shortened for convenience to "Taiping," the name commonly used in the Victorian period.

yellow, and decked himself with gold and lapis lazuli in further contempt of royal prerogative.

The apex of the Taiping military organization was an army corps consisting of five battalions, roughly thirteen thousand men. Women as well as men were enlisted, although the two sexes were completely segregated. Since God demanded chastity during this holy war, sexual relations were banned—even between married couples. Violators could be beheaded. In practice, this rule was relaxed when the troops were not in the field, although Hung promised a truly normal sex environment only when China became "free of its demons."

The Taiping leaders, however, blatantly exempted themselves from this strict sexual prohibition and, in fact, kept lavish harems. Hung set the example; at first he seemed satisfied with fifteen beauties he collected during his campaigns, but later he indulged in a vast seraglio on his Nanking palace grounds.

Not only did the Taiping leaders luxuriate in the pleasures of their harems but they were ordained by Hung as "Brothers"—which gave them semi-divine status. Two especially ambitious leaders, Yang Hsiu-ch'ing and Hsiao Ch'ao-kuei, as self-proclaimed mediums for God's and Christ's voices, had carved high positions in the hierarchy for themselves, but the others who had risen to prominence also enjoyed great power in the movement. Lesser leaders who had only allied themselves with the Taiping, such as pirate chiefs, bandits and Triad leaders, had authority commensurate with the size of their following. In this feudal setting, they were auxiliaries for as long as it suited them to be—usually as long as they were winning.

The Taiping army of the Heavenly Kingdom, exhorted to "fight like tigers," descended into the rich Yangtze River Valley in early 1852. Nanking was its first major objective, but the troops were badly beaten in Hunan Province, the Taipings' first defeat. Despite heavy casualties, however, their momentum went unslowed. New recruits flocked to their banner; the rebel force swelled to over half a million. In January 1853, they captured Wu-ch'ang, the capital of Hupeh Province. Moving down the Yangtze River, the Taipings took Kiukiang next, on February 9. Within a week, the Taiping tide reached Anking, capital of Anwei, with nothing between them and Nanking.[5]

In its wake, the rebel march left behind burned villages, destroyed countryside, and heaps of mutilated corpses. This was civil war in no uncertain terms.

Nanking, the old Ming capital, fell easily. The city's inhabitants, petrified of the advancing horde of now over a million, gave up without a struggle. But the rebels were without mercy. The massacre was so great that the Yangtze River choked with corpses. More than 28,000 Manchus were killed in the city's capture. The Taipings boasted: "We killed them all, to the infant in arms, . . . we left not a root to sprout from."[6]

The Taipings renamed the city[7] T'ien-ching, "Heavenly Capital," and made it seat of the rebellion. From here the Taiping armies could strike out in all directions in their drive to conquer China. But first, Peking itself had to be reduced, and in May 1853 an army moved swiftly northward toward the Manchu capital. The Taipings rallied more recruits along the way. Their propaganda, which had ready appeal to the dissatisfied peasants and workers, called the Manchus "stinking Tartars," usurpers who had enslaved the Chinese and ravaged their women. The Emperor Hsien-feng, a dissolute, debauched man who had mounted the throne in 1850, was accused of maintaining a harem of "small-footed" concubines. It was not so much the harem which provoked the outcry—rather it was the custom of female foot-binding from childhood, which was strongly opposed by the reformist Taipings. The Taipings charged the Emperor with encouraging promiscuous behavior with "stolen women." "A million rouged faces share pillows with the lustful foxes" was typical of Taiping epithets hurled at the Imperial court.

The Taiping offensive against Peking failed. Hastily called reinforcements from Central Asia, led by Imperial General Seng-ko-lin-ch'in, stopped the Taiping advance 150 miles south of the capital and inflicted terrible casualties. Had the Taipings marched on Peking directly, without pausing to establish a capital in Nanking, they might have caught the Manchus unprepared and taken the country. But their opportunity was lost. The defeat of the Taipings before Peking was a watershed. Rebel momentum had finally been checked by this setback; while the Taipings would continue to be troublesome for years, they would never again pose the same threat.

As the Taipings were rebuffed, Imperial resistance grew stronger. At the urging of his shrewd concubine, the legendary woman who would rise to power and rule China herself as Empress Tz'u-hsi, the Emperor called out of retirement Tseng Kuo-fan, a Hunan grandee who had once been a minister at court. Tseng quickly formed a new army known in China as the Hunan Braves, and imbued it with the urgency of defending the empire and Confucianism. Under Tseng's leadership, these hardy Hunan peasant soldiers proved to be the empire's saving grace, deserving much of the credit for ultimately rescuing the tottering Manchu throne.

The phenomenon of the Taiping Rebellion was carefully watched by European governments and traders. In contrast to the Imperial government, which was corrupt and, more important, unwilling to carry out the agreements reached with European and American trading powers in the treaties of 1842–44, the Taipings were viewed as uncommonly well disciplined, abiding by a spartan life-style rarely seen in China. Above all, the Taipings professed to be Christian; missionaries were tantalized by the evangelistic opportunities the Taiping Rebellion might present. Only belatedly did the Protestant missionaries become disenchanted by the aberrant doctrines and the ruthless behavior of the Taipings—even as Roman Catholics had never been taken in. For sympathetic Protestants in Europe, the horrors committed when the Taipings captured Nanking were particularly difficult to overlook, even in China, where gratuitous brutality in war was commonplace.

In April 1853, Sir George Bonham, a British emissary, attempted to open lines of communication with the Taiping government in Nanking. While willing to accept Western trade (though not opium), the Taipings, he dicovered, were no better than the Manchus in their attitude toward foreigners. He was told, in effect, that Britain must recognize Hung as the Heavenly King if it wanted the friendship and trade of the Taipings. Despairing of getting better treatment from Hung, Bonham recommended that Britain follow a policy of strict neutrality in the struggle between the Manchus and the Taipings. Neither group had much to commend itself over the other.

The French Minister, de Bourboulon, was equally distressed by the treatment he received in Nanking in December 1853, and Robert McLane, the American commissioner, was dismayed by Taiping arrogance when he viewed the situation five months later. The English *North China Herald* of June 17, 1854, concluded: "Whatever mingling of Christianity there might be among the leaders of the great insurrectionary movement, they would be found to be veritably Chinese in their relations with foreigners." While many missionaries continued to see religious good in the Taiping movement, Western governments no longer had any illusions and would soon look with apprehension as the "heavenly" horde threatened their trading colonies.

The important treaty port of Shanghai was suddenly vulnerable when a rebel group calling itself the Small Sword Society took over the city in 1854. Loosely affiliated with the Triad confederation, the Small Swords claimed a vague relationship with the Taipings. While the Taipings denied the connection, normal trade through Shanghai was nonetheless disrupted. The inability of the customs system to function properly while the Small Swords were in control of the city deprived the Emperor of badly needed revenue—which may have rankled more than the loss of political control of Shanghai. In June 1854 the consuls of the three principal trading powers, Great Britain, the United States and France, made an arrangement with the Customs Administrator, Wu Chien-chang, in which foreigners would administer Shanghai's maritime customs and pay the collected receipts directly to Peking.

It was an extraordinary feat of tightrope walking for the Western powers to remain neutral between the rebels within the city walls and the besieging Imperial forces encamped nearby. Harassment from government forces was, in fact, more onerous than the Small Swords' occupation of the city. Western powers also feared that the Taiping army itself would march against Shanghai and impose a far more ruthless occupation. Finally, in February 1855 a French naval unit spearheaded an Imperial assault on the city, defeating the Small Swords in a short but bloody engagement.

In the meantime, the Taipings were having difficulties. Not only had the Taiping offensive failed to take Peking, but a campaign westward up the Yangtze Valley had been blocked. But even more damaging to the Taipings' fortune was a debilitating leadership struggle that weakened the movement. The problem was provoked by the growing ambitions of the semidivine Yang Hsiu-ch'ing, the vaunted Tung Wang, who sought to outshine the Heavenly King and arrogate to himself spiritual as well as military leadership. No longer satisfied as the medium for the "golden voice" of God, he began to claim divine authority in his own right.

As Hung luxuriated in the pretentious palace and disported himself in his ever-growing harem, Yang plotted against him. When Yang's spies in Hung's seraglio told tales of debauchery, Yang, "in the name of God," accused Hung of abusing the heavenly concubines and had the temerity to demand that Hung be punished by forty lashes. This infuriated Hung, but in it he saw the more grave portent of Yang's bid for power. In secret collaboration with Wei Ch'ang-hui, the North King, Hung plotted his would-be usurper's assassination. Wei murdered Yang on September 2, 1856, but that was not the end of it; some twenty thousand followers of Yang were beheaded before vengeance was complete.

This set off a bewildering, protracted struggle for power which would plague the movement for the next four years. Hung had rid himself of a dangerous rival but also a talented military commander. Now he was faced with a more powerful Wei, who nursed ambitious plans of his own. Alarmed by the massacres, Shih Ta-k'ai, one of Hung's loyal princes and military commanders, hurried back from Hupeh Province to Nanking to defend his master in the power struggle. But he was nearly murdered by Wei. Shih was able to escape alive, but many of those known to be his partisans were killed. Shih returned—this time at the head of his army. Emboldened by his ally's show of strength, Hung assassinated Wei.

Now only Hung and Shih Ta-k'ai, among the Heavenly Leaders, remained. Shih, for his loyalty, was made Chief of Staff, but differences with the Heavenly King soon soured the relationship and Shih defected with his own troops to the Imperialists.

With Yang's death, Hung had lost a military genius; with Shih's defection, Hung had lost his most articulate theoretician and doctrinal spokesman, in addition to a well-trained army. Just as internecine power struggles were weakening the Taipings, the Imperial government found itself distracted by new threats from the "foreign devils." The British-French expeditionary force had landed at Taku and begun its march to Peking.

5

A BARBARIAN INTRUSION

The shortest, most brilliant and most successful [war] of all we have
waged with that country.
—Lieutenant Colonel Garnet J. Wolseley,
on the 1860 British war with China

After his brief stop in Shanghai, Gordon was off to Tientsin to join
Lord Elgin's force, now poised to attack Peking. To spare the
Emperor the ignominy of full-scale foreign occupation of the
celestial capital, a lower-level conference was mutually agreed upon to work
out a peace agreement outside the city limits and the Allies were prepared to
limit their occupation force in Peking to only a thousand soldiers to ensure
that the Chinese surrender their arms. But despite the Allies' white flag of
truce, the emissaries led by Harry Parkes and their small escort of Indian
Sikh troops were seized and thrown into jail in Peking.[1]

Incensed by this provocation, the Allied forces moved against Peking on
October 6, 1860. Gordon, who had been promoted to captain with the brevet
rank of major and made second in command of an engineering unit, was in
the forefront of the assault. The Allies planned to enter the city at Anting
Gate. "We made a lot of batteries, and everything was ready for the assault on
the [forty-foot] wall," recalled Gordon disappointedly, but "at 11:30 P.M. the
gate was opened and we took possession, so our work was of no avail." Angry
Chinese satisfied themselves by hurling epithets from the top of the wall but
resistance was nil. The surrender occurred on October 13, although the
Emperor and his household, it was discovered, had fled to the northern city
of Jehol, leaving the fugitive's brother, Prince Kung, temporarily in charge.

When the Allies learned that some of the imprisoned emissaries had been
tortured and that four had died, they were enraged. Harry Parkes was one of
the survivors, and on the day following his rescue he wrote home about the
fate of his companions: "They were foully murdered. Hands and feet tied
together, they were exposed in that state in an open court for three days and

nights, very little food and water given to them, but blows in abundance." The ropes binding them cut into the flesh of the delirious men, causing it to mortify; the horrified Parkes concluded, "I cannot go on with the description. . . ."[2]

In retaliation, Lord Elgin ordered the Emperor's Summer Palace, just outside the city, burned to the ground. It was felt that this punishment, aimed particularly at the Emperor, fitted the crime, and that such "a solemn action of retribution" was required to shock the Manchu leaders into ratifying the Treaty of Tientsin.

As an engineer attached to Major General Sir John Michel's First Division, Gordon found himself detailed to carry out Lord Elgin's orders. Like all British soldiers in Peking, he shared Elgin's outrage at the brutal deaths and torture of their comrades—Gordon perhaps more so as one of the victims, an officer named de Norman, had been a good friend—but Gordon still found the task of destroying the magnificent, historic Summer Palace repugnant. "It made one's heart sore," he wrote to his sister Augusta—"wretchedly demoralizing work for an army." Garnet Wolseley, another witness to the burning of the palace, wrote a vivid description of the scene: "A gentle wind, blowing from the northwest carried the mass of smoke directly over our camp into the very capital itself, to which distance even large quantities of the burnt embers were wafted, falling about the street in showers as silent but unmistakable evidences of the work of destruction and retribution going on in the palace of the Emperor."[3] The smoking ruins darkened Peking for two days. Nothing had done more to shatter the myth of the invincibility of the "Celestial Empire" of China than this act of destruction by Lord Elgin. The French, however, had refused to be party to this act of artistic sacrilege.

Only a few days before the palace was razed, Gordon had gazed in awe at "the garden of perpetual brightness" and marveled at the priceless objects housed in it. In an area covering twelve square miles the Chinese with the help of Jesuit architects had built their Versailles in the eighteenth century to be one of the wonders of the world. The exquisite landscape, which included lakes, artificial cascades, delicately crafted pagodas, woodlands and finely sculpted formal gardens, was a masterpiece, exciting the senses of those fortunate enough to see it. Gordon was transfixed when he saw the throne "lined with ebony" with its "huge mirrors of all shapes and kinds . . . as much splendor as you would see at Windsor [Castle]."

61

But with the Chinese guard down, the grandeur of the palace was jarred by French soldiers looting its treasures. Silver, jewels, rare porcelains and priceless textiles were carried off to be peddled on the streets with no regard for their real worth. Gordon wrote in disgust: "The French have smashed everything in the most wanton way. . . . There were carts after carts full of silks taken away. . . . There was also a history of China for the last 2,000 years kept by the Emperor."[4] Amid this pillage, Gordon himself came away with a handsome throne chair, which he donated to the Royal Engineers.

Here were the differences between the French and the British. While looting was common practice in the British Army, it was modest compared to this plunder by the French. The French, on the other hand, viewed the torching of the Summer Palace as "vandals' work" and would not participate in it. Each pointed the finger, each was responsible. Wolseley, in his memoir of China, defended Elgin's act, contending that it hastened the Chinese capitulation. Besides, destroying the palace was simply the *coup de grâce* to the looting of the French.[5]

Lord Elgin would long be criticized for his action. His justification was that it was proper punishment for the Emperor, and that any indemnity levied on China for the atrocity committed by the court would unfairly harm the common man whose taxes would have to pay it. Yet as Gordon's early biographer, William Butler, wrote: "It is difficult to believe that the perpetration of such an act of vandalism could be possible in these later days of the worldly men who were supposed to represent the most advanced civilization."[6] Others saw similarity between this act and the vandalism committed by Elgin's father, who carted off the ancient sculptures, now famous as the Elgin Marbles, from Athens's Parthenon in 1806.[7]

By today's standards, the Allies' insistence on free and unfettered trade with China, including the importation of opium, as a natural right heedless of the Emperor's sovereign wishes was arrogant. But then it was a day when the strong imposed their will on the weak. Fair or unfair, the Treaty of Tientsin would determine British-Chinese relations for the next forty years.

There was the comforting conviction held by many in England that a "superior" culture had the license to discipline the heathen of the East. War was a classroom to teach British justice and manners to "backward" natives. Free trader Richard Cobden's cry, "Cheapness and not the cannon and the sword is the weapon through which we alone possess, and can hope to defend our commerce,"[8] could scarcely be heard for the din of imperial jingoism.

Wolseley, in what today sounds fatuous, wrote solemnly in 1862: "Before the Asiatic world can be led to believe in the justice of our polity, or before it will be applicable to Eastern nations, it will be necessary first to raise them up to our standard of knowledge, and enable them to reason in the same logical manner with ourselves."[9] And Thomas Meadows, a British China scholar, marveled that the Chinese could not see that "a country where such an enormous, yet beautiful fabric as a large English ship is constructed . . . must be inhabited by a people not only energetic but rich and free to enjoy the fruits of its own labour; that such a country *must*, in short . . . be altogether in a high state of civilization."[10] Gordon was not immune to such sentiments and referred once to opening China "to civilization."

Gordon's initiation to Peking, particularly the disagreeable task of razing the Summer Palace, was a lesson in international politics. The broken Emperor died soon after fleeing the city, leaving his seven-year-old son as the new Emperor of China, although the boy's uncle, Prince Kung, acting as Regent, was made to host the ratification ceremony. To the strains of the British national anthem, played by a British military band, Lord Elgin dismounted from a state palanquin carried by sixteen elegantly attired Chinese to join Prince Kung in affixing their signatures to the Treaty of Tientsin. British will had been done.

In November, Gordon, as commanding officer of the Royal Engineers, was detailed to a three-thousand-man force stationed in Tientsin to enforce treaty provisions. His job, as in the Crimea, was to provide quarters for the garrison troops. Command had its virtues, and Gordon admitted, "It is a grand thing being one's own master"—something he always aspired to. There were positive diversions as well; Gordon managed a charitable fund collected in Tientsin to care for poor Chinese children. During a ceremony to disburse funds to the needy, however, the crush of three thousand trampled eight people to death.

The eighteen months of garrison duty in Tientsin were basically dull. To relieve the tedium, Gordon traveled about as much as time would allow, sometimes visiting places never before seen by Europeans. On one occasion, traveling with a Lieutenant Cardew, he saw the outer Great Wall of China, a construction marvel which he, as a trained engineer and student of fortifications, could fully appreciate. He saw the Taku forts, 140 miles from Tientsin, the scene of much British military action.

Of British troops posted in Tientsin, Gordon had little good to say. "The 31st and 60th are in a very bad state. They are much demoralized, drunkenness on duty being common." Gordon added: "What a brute the ordinary British linesman is; the lash is going constantly . . . without avail." His own engineers were also a nuisance, and his senior sergeant was "so cracked" he had to be transferred.

Major General Charles Staveley, Gordon's brother-in-law, was commander of all British forces garrisoned in Tientsin. This coincidence was a source of annoyance to Gordon, who never approved of any officer taking advantage from special relationships—and wanted no one to think he did. He considered Staveley an "essentially selfish man," but they seemed to get on after Gordon told him straightaway that he expected no special treatment. "It is the bother of one's life to be trying after the honours of the profession," he wrote, "and it has grown in late years into a regular trade—everyone uses private interests." Gordon was especially perturbed that his brother Henry, also serving with British forces in China at the time, tried to put in a good word for him at headquarters.

At least garrison duty gave Gordon an opportunity to see friends. When new wars erupted in or around the edges of empire, British officers would invariably scramble for billets at the front. Some sought glory, others simply saw it as a route to promotion. In the tightly knit military fraternity few wanted to be left out. Not to be posted to the war of the year was like not being invited to the party of the year—either was a social deprivation. In addition to Charles Staveley and his brother Henry, several friends of Gordon's—many of them veterans of the Crimean War as well—had tours of duty in China. Gerald Graham, a friend from Woolwich, and Garnet Wolseley, fated to play an important role in the last few months of Gordon's life, were both there. Even officers from other armies were attracted to China. Prince Wittgenstein, a Russian Cossack colonel of distinguished family, whom Gordon had met after the Crimean War during service with the Boundary Commission at Jassy, also appeared in China. A good soldier who had made a name for himself in battle at Kars, the Prince would soon serve under Gordon.

A BARBARIAN INTRUSION

In the spring of 1861 Gordon contracted smallpox, which provided him with a short period of enforced leisure. Signs of growing intensity in his Christian faith thereafter appeared in his correspondence. Gordon considered this illness, curiously similar to Hung's forty days of delirium during which he claimed heavenly transformation, an important milestone in his religious maturity. He wrote his sister Augusta: "This disease has brought me back to my Saviour, and I trust in future to be a better Christian than I have been hitherto." It was also at this time that he began more frequently to use in his correspondence the punctuation "D. V."—*Deo Volente,* "if God wills." He also befriended the chaplain, Mr. Beech, whom he described as "excessively kind."

As soon as he was well, Gordon was relieved to be included in a nine-hundred-man contingent sent to reinforce the British garrison in Shanghai, again threatened by the Taiping rebels.

The leap from Christian reflection to thoughts of war posed no problem for Gordon. For all his piety and compassion, he was also a soldier. In this he was not unlike the Taiping zealots—or later, the Sudan's Mahdi, the Messiah of Allah—who also saw the spear and sword as weapons with which to do God's will. Gordon the soldier was exhilarated by combat just as Gordon the devout was inspired by religious faith.

6

EVER VICTORIOUS ARMY

I can assure you and my father that I will not be rash.
—Gordon in a letter to his mother as he assumed
command of the Ever Victorious Army

The Taiping juggernaut had begun its advance toward Shanghai in early 1860 under its ablest commander, Li Hsiu-ch'eng, the Chung Wang or Faithful King. His objective was to divert the Imperialist army under Tseng Kuo-fan away from Anking, key to Nanking's defense. Shanghai's vulnerability to the Taiping offensive increased as the Imperialist army began to make progress in pushing the Taiping back down the Yangtze, eastward toward that vital port city.

The tempo of British Army involvement picked up when General Sir Charles Staveley took over command from Sir John Michel in April 1862. While the British naval brigade had earlier plunged into combat because of Admiral Hope's initiative and sense of urgency, the Army had held back pending higher authority and the arrival of reinforcements. Staveley, however, arrived with the authority he needed and was determined to commit his troops to battle as soon as possible.

Gordon and his engineers arrived in Shanghai on May 3 in time to see action at Tsingpu. He and Staveley first conducted a reconnaissance of the rebel stronghold by boat, wending their way through the confusing web of waterways, which Gordon was learning to use to his advantage. On one occasion Staveley watched horror-stricken as Gordon advanced on foot to within range of rebel fire. Gordon ignored him while he sketched in meticulous detail the twenty-foot-high town walls which would have to be breached. Gordon's efforts were in large part responsible for a successful attack a few days later.

Gordon's initiation into war Chinese-style otherwise began tamely. He watched 250 small Chinese boats bobbing along, making their way toward Tsingpu, as one might watch matchstick boats launched by small children playing in a drainage ditch. Steamers mounting guns plowed through a clutter of two-man boats which reminded Gordon of "little chips like coffins." British officers returned to camp early to enjoy a leisurely roast pork dinner washed down with Indian ale. The next day Tsingpu's walls obligingly crumbled under bombardment from the Armstrong guns. It was like a picnic in the country. But it was thanks to the accurate plotting by Gordon and his intimate knowledge of the rebels' deployment that very few casualties were suffered in the town's capture.

The harsher realities of war in China came afterward. Gordon moved through the countryside mopping up after the rebels. Dead were strewn everywhere, mutilated reminders of Taiping brutality toward the peasants. Decapitation was common, but one English soldier reported with undisguised horror that he had come upon a long-haired rebel earnestly trying to sever a dead peasant's head with a dull pocket knife. Any peasant lucky enough to escape the knives of the rebels and reach Shanghai was then subject to starvation as the city swelled with hundreds of thousands of refugees. Nor were children exempt from the brutality, the rebels often carrying off small boys to be raised as janissaries to fight with the Taipings.

This, more than most other atrocities of war, was disturbing to Gordon, who saved one abandoned little boy and arranged for his upbringing. But no less disturbing to him was the sympathy many back home in England retained for the rebels. It was the Taipings' apparent claim to be Christian reformers, however spurious, that generated the sympathy, and Gordon grew to feel great contempt for such ignorance.

While most of the British in China, having felt the rebel threat at close hand, were quick to reject the Taipings, it took longer for British public opinion at home to face up to reality. By 1862, however, most people in England had accepted government policy of limited intervention to stem the Taiping advance. As more detailed information reached England about Taiping atrocities, missionary groups were beginning to abandon wishful hopes that the Taiping movement heralded a Christian reformation in China. They rationalized that for all the excesses, the Manchu Imperialists had, after all, signed the Treaty of Tientsin, which promised freedom to evangelize.

The London Missionary Society finally admitted that its earlier hopes had not been warranted and found comfort that "God has now answered our supplication by other means . . ."[1] British merchants and traders were for a while also ambivalent on this issue. The pacesetter, Jardine-Matheson, held no brief for the rebels but was disturbed by the British Government's half measures, and thought it should reach a *modus vivendi* with the Taipings, at least in the Shanghai area, rather than see trade disrupted. But there were also merchants who had seen enough Taiping earth-scorching and favored limited intervention to stop it.

Parliament, too, was divided on the matter, but when the House voted on a resolution to restrain British officials in China from intervening in the civil war, the resolution was soundly defeated, 197 to 88. Prime Minister Palmerston favored intervention and had little patience for those who did not. With subtle levity, he said: "We have interfered with great success in the affairs of other countries, and with great benefit to the countries concerned."[2] And with strained logic he argued that, having weakened the Manchus by invading China and having unwittingly improved the environment for rebellion, ". . . we are bound now to do everything in our power to make amends to the Imperial Government for the injury they have sustained."[3]

By 1862 few were willing to defend the Taipings, but those who opposed intervention, for the most part, did not want Britain to become enmeshed in the morass. Some, like Lord Naas, feared that China might become another India, another vast land with uncounted hordes which would become a prohibitively expensive ward. "What has happened repeatedly in India is certain to happen in China if we persist in our present course," he warned.[4]

Press and public opinion still reflected some of the earlier missionary attitude of sympathy for the Taiping movement. But the *Times* had come around to referring to the Taipings as "bloodthirsty and rapacious"; several other newspapers now supported government policy. The *Daily News*, however, was typical of newspapers which opposed "Lord Palmerston's clandestine war," and took delight in printing atrocity stories about the Imperial government. And the *Morning Herald* criticized Palmerston for keeping "the Yellow Dwarf of modern times on his goblin throne."

Events in China grew more ominous from a British point of view. News that a Chinese Imperial force, six thousand strong, had been mauled at Taitsang by a Taiping army under Li Hsiu-ch'eng, the Faithful King, caused Staveley to draw his troops back to defend Shanghai. In May the British representative in Shanghai, Frederick Bruce, jointly with the French representative, General de Bourboulon, declared that the Allied forces would defend Shanghai against Taiping attack. Gordon was put in charge of planning the city's defenses, and within two weeks he had produced a blueprint for new defense construction.[5]

Shanghai was crawling with Taiping spies preparing the ground for invasion. But as the invasion seemed imminent, the Taipings suddenly withdrew from the area. It was later learned that Hung, the Heavenly King, besieged by a large Imperial army, recalled Li to help defend Nanking. For the moment, at least, Shanghai was safe.

Shanghai's Chinese merchants, however, felt far from comfortable. They knew the Taiping threat would likely return and thought it wise to look to their own defenses rather than rely on either the inept Imperialist troops—or the "foreign devils" who might one day have a change in policy and abandon Shanghai. So in June 1860, the prominent Shanghai merchant Yang Fang, known by the Europeans as Taki, joined with the top Imperial official in Shanghai, Wu-hsu, to raise a mercenary force for the defense of the city. The man they chose to head the unit was an American adventurer from Massachusetts named Frederick Townsend Ward.

Ward came from a respected Salem family and had been a Yankee Clipper first officer before arriving in Shanghai in 1859.[6] The force he gathered together was a disreputable one whose raw courage was not matched by discipline, although Ward, who led his troops into battle dressed in a black frock coat and armed with only a bamboo swagger stick, commanded their respect and affection. He was an exceptional leader who well understood the art of guerrilla warfare.

Ward's first campaign ended in dismal defeat. Yet he profited by his mistakes, and in July captured the rebel-controlled town of Sunkiang, near Shanghai, which he used to garrison his troops. To the annoyance of some Chinese, he made the municipality his personal fiefdom, ignoring its normal administration. Nonetheless, the American's army was now a force to be reckoned with. Despite all its drunken brawling between battles, wanton looting after battles, and incorrigible arrogance, it had become an effective fighting machine. But the force was beset by troubles. Late payrolls drove many of Ward's men to desert, creating a chronic staffing problem and forcing him to lure sailors from British ships. This infuriated Admiral Hope, who had Ward arrested. Only by claiming Chinese citizenship, hastily conferred on him by his Chinese patrons, did the American adventurer avoid imprisonment and repatriation to the United States.

Ward's problems with the British caused a suspension of the mercenary operation. But by September, Shanghai's Chinese merchants, still alarmed by the specter of a Taiping advance, again approached the American and asked him to raise a new force. This time he recruited Chinese soldiers and named the unit Ever Victorious Army, with perhaps more hope than conviction. Trained in Western drill procedures, the troops began to show promise. Ward, now a general in the Chinese army, then led his large force of mercenaries to retake Tsingpu from the Taipings. Wearing his frock coat as usual, he directed his men over the city walls under heavy fire, inspiring the Chinese, oddly, to praise his bravery in "urging his soldiers on to slaughter."[7]

Ward's luck ran out in September 1862 when a bullet, fired by a deserter from a British regiment who was fighting with the rebels, claimed his life near Ningpo. During his two years of command, the able American had fought some seventy battles and had been wounded innumerable times. Ambitious and unscrupulous as he was, he faithfully served his Chinese masters with valor. He was a Yankee freebooter in the best tradition of that breed and, following World War II, would be memorialized by the American colony in Shanghai, raised on the same pedestal as Claire Chennault, who had commanded the Flying Tigers mercenary air squadron in defense of Nationalist China. Most important, Ward had proved the usefulness of the Ever Victorious Army.

While the British at first resented the mercenary army as a haven for deserters, General Staveley, Captain Borlase (temporarily substituting for Admiral Hope as commander of the British naval squadron), and British Consul Medhurst now agreed that the strange but effective force should be retained—but under the command of a British officer. Permission had to be sought in London for this further involvement in the China civil war. In the meantime Ward's American Chief of Staff, Henry Burgevine, assumed command of the mercenary force.

The Ever Victorious Army fought well. But Staveley and Hope, who still nursed a prejudice against the ruffians in the force, were appalled by the looting carried on by the mercenaries in the wake of battle. It revealed a serious lack of discipline for which they blamed Burgevine. The American mercenary was, indeed, an unsavory character whose concept of the rules of war was shocking. When he had some of his Taiping prisoners blown out of cannons, it was clear to the British command that he was not the man to lead the Ever Victorious. Captain Holland of the Royal Marines was, therefore, attached to the force as Burgevine's deputy, a stopgap measure to control the American until London approved the assignment of a permanent British commander.

Burgevine also fell afoul of the Chinese establishment which Ward had so carefully cultivated. Li Hung-chang, made Governor of Kiangsu Province in 1861, and a rising star in Chinese politics destined to become one of China's great statesmen, would be the cause of his downfall. With Machiavellian cunning Li set about unseating the American mercenary. He also managed to break the grip on Shanghai held so long by Yang Fang and Wu-hsu so that their patronage of the Ever Victorious Army could no longer protect Burgevine. Financing of the force was, in fact, transferred from the Shanghai merchants to the Imperial Governor's treasury so that Li now held the purse strings.

Burgevine tried local lobbying to protect his position. In an interview with the *North China Herald* he explained that because his men had not been paid, they had become mutinous and were threatening to "lop off the heads" of all Chinese officials in the area. This kind of bombast was not helpful in winning the goodwill of Chinese officials.

Li then provoked the American by accusing him of not being willing to join the siege of Nanking with his troops, and, in a move calculated to infuriate any mercenary, he continued to withhold the army's payroll. Enraged by this, and falling into Li's trap, Burgevine with a band of his toughest mercenaries descended upon the bank responsible for disbursing the funds and arbitrarily seized the money owed his troops. But worse, in anger he slapped Yang Fang, the bank's director and original patron of the mercenary force—an unforgivable affront. This provided Li Hung-chang with the excuse he needed to dismiss Burgevine. It also opened the way to appoint a British commander to the position right away, which the shrewd Governor saw as a way to involve more deeply the British military forces in the government's struggle against the Taipings.

With Burgevine's removal, command devolved upon Captain Holland.

Disaster followed, however, when Holland failed to judge correctly the width of the moat defending the city walls of Taitsan and led his men to one of the Ever Victorious Army's greatest defeats. Sixteen officers and 450 men were killed or wounded in this unfortunate engagement. The rebels gloried in their victory and ridiculed Holland in his defeat: "Oh, how we laughed on the morning of the assault as they advanced nearer to the creek which they brought no bridges to throw over. How we laughed when we saw their ladder getting weaker and weaker beneath them and at last crashing into the creek!" Soon afterward a battle for Shao-hsing also failed miserably, making Holland's position untenable in the eyes of the near-mutinous troops clamoring for Bourgevine's reinstatement.

So it was that Charles Gordon, only thirty years old, found himself launched into fourteen months of fierce action destined to make him England's hero of the moment. General Staveley had proposed his candidacy as commander of the Ever Victorious to London because he genuinely admired him. While Gordon did not at the time have any particularly obvious qualifications for the command, Staveley had been impressed with his performance in the field thus far and his demonstrated ability to get along with the Chinese. There had been others suggested, however. In his memoirs many years later,[8] Field Marshal Viscount Wolseley recalled: "It was a question whether Colonel Charlie Gordon or I should.be sent to help China in dealing with the Taiping rebellion; he was most wisely selected. How much loftier and noble were the objects he sought after than the part I aspired to play there."

Minister Frederick Bruce in Peking, as senior British official in China, did not approve of involving a British officer in this mercenary venture.[9] Suspicions would be stirred up among the other treaty powers that Britain was seeking primacy, he feared. The Americans, specifically, might resent Bourgevine's removal and believe that the British were responsible for it. More fundamentally, however, Bruce was trying to break down provincial Chinese power, which had arisen at the expense of central control. He believed that British involvement at the Chinese provincial army level—Gordon would come under Li Hung-chang, Governor of Kiangsu and commander of the province's armed forces—would undercut his strategy of strengthening the entire Imperial army structure with military aid and training in Peking. Bruce also believed that it was more fitting for British officers to help the Chinese as trainers rather than lead them in combat. The Minister's objections were delayed in the mail when the S.S. *Colombo* foundered in a cyclone off Ceylon, but this may not have mattered. London was more realistic than Bruce on the issue of central versus provincial power in China, realizing the impracticality of trying to change a system which was firmly entrenched, however at odds it was with British logic.

London's approval arrived forthwith, and on March 24, 1863, Gordon received his appointment as Commanding Officer of the Ever Victorious Army. The British Foreign Office approved a formula by which other British officers could also serve the Chinese—even beyond the Shanghai area—without giving up their regimental status, although they would have to serve on half pay.

Gordon was promoted to the British brevet rank of major, but in the Chinese hierarchy he would have the exalted rank of general. Most impressive of all, he was made a mandarin to ensure that he had maximum prestige when dealing with the Chinese.

The agreement reached between General Staveley and Governor Li Hung-chang[10] placed the Ever Victorious Army under joint British-Chinese control. The army would be commanded jointly by an English and a Chinese officer (although the Chinese officer inevitably played only a passive, titular role), but be under the overall orders of the Futai, as the Chinese referred to Li's title. It was not to operate outside a thirty-mile radius around Shanghai without the permission of the British and French, and the force's size was to be no greater than three thousand men. No longer would the Ever Victorious be a quasi-independent creature of Shanghai merchants, beyond any real government control. Unlike Ward, Gordon would have to use political and diplomatic wiles with both the Chinese and the British, as well as exercise skill in guerrilla tactics, if he was to succeed.

Typical of Gordon's thoroughness, he asked Staveley to permit him to finish his detailed survey of the thirty-mile radius around Shanghai. Gordon's project proved invaluable in the coming campaigns when his intimate familiarity with the intricate waterways contributed significantly to his victories over the Taipings.

Gordon had firm ideas of how he wanted to run things. He made it clear in a letter to Li Hung-chang that he insisted on having full control of the Ever Victorious Army and expected no Chinese interference. Li grumbled, but accepted these terms. British friendship was important to him at this point, and anyway, he had taken a liking to Gordon at their first meeting. Li had been impressed with Gordon's frankness, however blunt. He thought Gordon's bearing "had the stamp of an excellent soldier" and that he was "direct and businesslike."

The prospect of having his own command was appealing to Gordon, particularly a command which promised heavy combat. To fight blaspheming false Christians made the challenge even more attractive to the pious Gordon.

Gordon's family were not enthusiastic about Charlie's new command. His father did not believe it right for an officer of the Queen to fight for a foreign government, and his mother was afraid for his life. To allay his mother's fears he promised not to be "rash" and asked her in a letter to reassure his father on this score as well. (It is interesting that he most often corresponded with his mother, not his father.) Rash he would not be, according to his concept of how a soldier should conduct himself in battle, but for Gordon the next fourteen months were notable for his almost constant courtship with death as he struggled with the Taipings.

7

BATTLE FOR QUINSAN

What a sight for tired eyes and elixir for a heavy heart to see this
splendid Englishman fight!
—Chinese Governor Li Hung-chang on Charles Gordon

When Gordon took command of the Ever Victorious Army in March 1863, he saw the rebel stronghold of Soochow as key to his strategy. The Taiping rebels dominated most of the region between the Yangtze River and the Grand Canal west of Shanghai, but if Soochow could be taken by the Ever Victorious and used as its base, the pressure on Shanghai would be relieved. Imperialist troops could then concentrate on their siege of Nanking without distraction from rebel attacks along the lower Yangtze. It was important to defend Shanghai, not only because the Imperial government needed customs receipts collected at this important port, but to deny it to the rebels, who would use it to import supplies from foreign gunrunners. The safety of Shanghai, however, depended on securing Soochow.

Rather than again attack Taitsan as the nearest stepping-stone toward Soochow and risk another devastating defeat by the strongly entrenched rebels, Gordon and Li Hung-chang agreed to go up the Yangtze estuary by boat and strike Chanzu first. This meant landing at a place along the river called Ushan, then moving ten miles inland to attack the Chanzu fort. By thus planting the Imperial flag well within rebel territory, Gordon could block Taiping access to the Yangtze, by way of which Western arms were being smuggled by various profiteers.

Governor Li Hung-chang had another reason to find a new base for the Ever Victorious Army. The mercenary stronghold of Sunkiang with its three thousand well-trained troops was for the moment serving a vital function as sentinel, standing guard over nearby Shanghai; but Li shrewdly reasoned that one day, with a twist in British policy, or if the force should fall under the control of ambitious soldiers of fortune such as Burgevine in the chaotic conditions that characterized China, it could become a threat rather than a guardian to this important gateway to China.

Gordon, with a thousand-man force, disembarked from two steamers at Fushan as planned and attacked Chanzu, sending its long-haired defenders fleeing toward Soochow thirty miles to the southwest. Effective bombardment at close range by the steamers anchored in the canal had opened a large hole for the storming party. Only two men were killed and six wounded in what had been a nearly flawless operation. Leaving a garrison of three hundred to hold this strategic fort, Gordon returned to the Sunkiang garrision to face a more threatening enemy: dissension in his ranks.

Gordon had wanted to march immediately to Quinsan from Chanzu and attack the important Taiping garrison there with its large arsenal. By doing this, he could divide the rebel force and gain the key to Soochow, but his undisciplined mercenary officers were restive under their new British commander. Most of the Americans, at least, preferred to fight under their fellow countryman Burgevine—fifty soldiers having signed a petition to this effect when Gordon took command—and most of them wished to return quickly to their base, where they had connections to sell the loot captured at Chanzu. Then suddenly, complicating the problem, Burgevine appeared to reclaim his command.

Burgevine had tried to outmaneuver his nemesis, Governor Li Hung-chang, by appealing to the American Minister, Anson Burlingame, in Peking. Burlingame in turn went to Sir Frederick Bruce, who had never favored having Her Majesty's officers involved with the unruly and unpredictable mercenaries anyway. Bruce pinned his argument for restoring Burgevine rather flimsily on "a policy of seeing justice done to foreigners in the Chinese service," whatever their nationality.[1] Bruce also realized that Burlingame must be handled diplomatically. The Americans were still angry at the British over Britain's assistance to the Confederate Army in the Civil War, so Bruce did not want to exacerbate the situation. Bruce appealed to Prince Kung, who finally permitted the matter to be decided by Li Hung-chang at the provincial level, but Li predictably said no. Burgevine had insulted a mandarin—an unforgivable sin, particularly on the part of a "barbarian"—and Li did not want to see the strong mercenary force in the hands of someone he neither trusted nor controlled. Moreover, he had taken a liking to Gordon, as his journal entry of March 27 revealed: "It is a direct blessing from Heaven, I believe, the coming of the British Gordon. . . . He is superior in manner and bearing to any of the foreigners I have come into contact with and does not show outwardly that conceit which makes most of them repugnant in my sight."[2]

General W. G. Brown, who had replaced Staveley as head of British forces, refused to intervene in this matter despite explicit instruction from Bruce to do so. And Li, to make his point clearer, promoted Gordon to *tsung-ping*, or general of division, the second-highest rank in the Imperial army. Gordon, standing on the sidelines, referred to the whole affair in his journal only cryptically: "Burgevine comes from Peking to take force. Local authorities will not have it."

Burgevine's influences was still pervasive among the American officers, who were quick to criticize Gordon. Some of the more intransigent had to be fired, and Gordon took advantage of the new authority that permitted British officers to fight in the Chinese army to call for some of this own country-men. As professional soldiers, they could be expected to be more sympathetic to him.

He secured a commitment from the Chinese to place his three-thousand-man force on an established and predictable payroll. In return, he banned looting, which not only had given the troops a bad name but had interfered with rapid redeployment as well. To give the troops a sense of pride-in-unit, he issued new uniforms. The Zouave-like dark serge jackets with knickerbocker trousers and bright green turbans looked very smart, although the Chinese soldiers had to endure the derision of being called "imitation foreign devils" by their countrymen.

Gordon emphasized training. The troops were both rigorously drilled, as in the British Army, and trained specifically for the job at hand. They learned how to scale the walled fortresses guarding Chinese towns, and they learned the art of precision artillery firing—critical if walls were to be properly breached before attack. Taking a lesson from Ward, Gordon augmented his force with a flotilla of steamers, as amphibious assault was the key to conducting warfare in the maze of waterways that crisscrossed the Yangtze delta. Overland movement was difficult, the crucial element of military surprise almost impossible to achieve. Gordon's greatest genius, however, was realized in his strategic planning and thorough reconnaissance. His battle plans were meticulously wrought masterpieces. This was Gordon, the engineer and master mapmaker, at his best.

Gordon's schedule for attacking Quinsan had again to be postponed when news of a debacle at Taitsan reached him toward the end of April. Imperial Chinese troops—"Imps," as Gordon called them—had suffered a defeat. Just as Holland and the Ever Victorious Army had lost at Taitsan, the Imperial troops were badly mauled as they tried to take the city. This had been a typical case of rebel treachery. In a secret agreement, Taitsan's commander, Tsah, had promised Li Hung-chang that he and his troops would surrender. Trusting that Tsah would throw down his arms, Li's brother, commanding the operation, confidently entered Taitsan to accept the surrender only to discover that this was a trap. Furious, Li ordered Gordon to march on Taitsan.

Gordon immediately set out to avenge the humiliation of the Imperial army. Avoiding the mistake Holland had made by approaching Taitsan from the south, Gordon launched his attack from the west, where his steamers could more easily maneuver. After two and a half hours of bombardment by howitzers and 32-pounders, a yawning gap in the wall seemed to invite a storming party. But after bitter hand-to-hand fighting, the first assault failed. So did the second. Met by telling artillery fire from European mercenaries fighting with the rebels, a curtain of spears, and stink bombs hurled by the Taipings, the attack was stalled.

Gordon led a third effort, coolly directing his men with a short rattan cane. This time he succeeded, although casualties were high. "It really was a tremendous fight and I never hope to see another like it," Gordon commented afterward. The cane, called the "wand of victory," became Gordon's trademark. It symbolized his courage and contempt for enemy fire and marked the beginning of the legend of Gordon's invincibility. With cigar in mouth and "wand" in hand, Gordon led his troops forward, apparently immune to the hail of bullets around him. This was unnerving to the Taipings, who believed he had magical powers.

One of the mercenaries on the rebel side was captured and brought before Gordon. The frightened soldier identified himself as British Private Hargreaves, a deserter from the 31st Regiment, and begged for mercy. Gordon ordered him shot, but as the wretched man was dragged off, Gordon whispered counterorders that he be spared and sent back to Shanghai for medical attention. Several other foreign mercenaries found with the rebel defenders were not as lucky and were shot out of hand by the attackers.

The Ever Victorious Army, intoxicated by its victory, went on a looting and shooting spree after the battle was over. Gordon was dismayed but did not then choose to make an issue of it. His army was marched back to Sunkiang to prepare for the Quinsan campaign. There was much to be done.

Discipline was a problem, but for the sake of morale, Gordon issued a general order commending his troops for their valor. He generously thanked them for "gallant exertions during the late operations" and noted that "in spite of a most determined and desperate resistance they carried the city, which had a garrison of five times their number, and have done what could not have been surpassed by any troops in the world."

As a way to improve the force, Gordon upgraded the quality of rations. He appointed a British lieutenant colonel to run a centralized commissariat rather than have this vital service handled unevenly by the regimental commanders. The commanders resented this and sulked in anger. Some of them went so far as to threaten mutiny if they were not at least promoted one grade to make them equal to the newcomer.

A showdown came on the morning the Ever Victorious was supposed to muster for the march on Quinsan. The disgruntled officers kept their troops in their barracks, and so only Gordon's own loyal bodyguard fell in for duty. Determined to face down his challengers, Gordon announced before he set out that he would give everyone until the following evening to join him midway to Quinsan. Those who failed to appear for the roll call could consider themselves dismissed. This was a gamble, but most of the troops straggled leaderless to the rendezvous point and reported for duty. The crisis had passed.

Gordon fired from service all but two of the regimental officers who had defied his orders, and was glad to be rid of them so he could recruit more reliable replacements. While he had admired Ward, the first leader of the Ever Victorious, he thought the American guilty of spoiling his officers and letting them drift into bad habits. Ward's leadership had relied on the respect and affection his officers felt for him. Gordon had their respect but demanded unquestioning discipline—something easier to find in professional officers on loan from the British Army than in mercenaries. The camaraderie Ward shared with his officers was not Gordon's style, although he did make some good friends among his officers, including the surgeon, Moffitt. He also had the personal loyalty of Kirkham, his adjutant, to whom he had entrusted command of his bodyguard. Kirkham, it will be remembered, had been the thieving servant whom Gordon rescued from arrest on the sea voyage to China.[3]

With a depleted officer corps, the Ever Victorious Army at brigade strength went off to face its greatest challenge. Gordon's problems, however, were not over; he was about to hear still another discordant note.

The Imperial army, under the command of General Ching, a rebel leader before defecting to the Imperial side, was already besieging Quinsan. It became immediately apparent that Gordon and the Chinese general disagreed profoundly on tactics. Although a defector from the unorthodox Taiping army, Ching was traditional in his approach and had little imagination. He had planned an impossible frontal assault against the Quinsan fort, but before he could attempt it he found himself on the defensive, attacked by rebel reinforcements sent from Soochow. The Ever Victorious drove back the rebels from their advance stockades to relieve the pressure, but Gordon had no intention of helping Ching court disaster again by trying to break through the heavily defended east gate.

Quinsan stood high on a hill from which the rebels could see every move an attacker from the east could make. Twenty-foot ramparts protected by a wide moat made the city virtually invulnerable from that direction. Moreover, the city's ten thousand defenders were commanded by General Li Hsiu-ch'eng, the Chung Wang, whom Gordon described as "the bravest, most talented and enterprising leader the rebels had."

Gordon had an inspired idea: He would come around by boat behind Quinsan and cut off the road to Soochow west of Quinsan, the rebels' only line of retreat. The road was a narrow causeway running between a canal and a lake, thus was particularly assailable by water. The paddle wheeler *Hyson*, piloted by an American sailor named Davidson, would serve as Gordon's flagship in this amphibious campaign. The boat was worth ten thousand men, Gordon claimed, and he made it the centerpiece of his plan. By detouring around Quinsan some twenty miles, the steamer could reach Chunye, about a third of the way to Soochow, and by attacking there easily cut off the road. This would bottle up the Taipings in Quinsan fort with no hope of retreat or rescue. Rebel surrender would be inevitable.

On May 29, Gordon, accompanied by an angry General Ching—and by Governor Li Hung-chang himself to keep peace between the rival commanders—reconnoitered on board the *Hyson*. What Li saw convinced him of the soundness of Gordon's plan, so Ching's frontal-attack plan was abandoned and General Ching, "surly as a bear," was left to sulk. Out of spite he spread the rumor that Gordon had taken a bribe from the rebels not to attack the fort itself.

An Imperial flotilla of gunboats under cover of night followed a circuitous waterway to the west of Quinsan with instructions to pull up the stakes driven into the channel by the Taipings to block hostile traffic. This would prepare the way for the *Hyson* and a fleet of sailboats transporting Gordon's troops. As Gordon's attack force left at dawn on May 31, Li Hung-chang, eager to share in the laurels of victory, joined Gordon on deck of the *Hyson*. They surveyed a picturesque tableau of billowing sails and colored flags fluttering in the breeze as the fleet neared its objective.

Unfortunately, the Imperial flotilla, having been intimidated by the rebels, failed to get close enough to fulfill its mission, so Gordon had no choice but to put his infantry regiment ashore and attack. The *Hyson*, pulling out barrier stakes as it went, kept pace, its 32-pounder, in fact, providing artillery support for the troops. With its devastating fire it cleared the rebel stockades at Chunye, west of Quinsan. According to Samuel Mossman of the *North China Herald*, "The consternation caused by the unexpected attack completely paralyzed the rebels. To their superstitious imagination the armed steamer appeared like some demon in their mythology, belching forth fire and vapor and destroying every human being on land or water who could not get beyond the reach of its death-dealing shot."[4]

While the Ever Victorious infantry chased rebels fleeing toward Quinsan, Gordon on the *Hyson* steamed westward on the main canal, harassing those retreating toward Soochow. The intrepid paddle wheeler came within a mile or two of Soochow itself before turning back, causing momentary panic in the rebel stronghold. It raked the retreating rebels along the way, and captured a small fort, taking its 150 defenders prisoner. It had been a good afternoon's work.

MANDARINS, MERCENARIES, AND HEAVENLY REBELS

It was 3:00 A.M. on June 1 when the *Hyson* returned to Chunye, only to find a very dangerous situation. The Imperial troops and their supporting craft had suddenly been faced by eight thousand rebels, nearly the full strength of the Quinsan garrison, now desperate to break out of the trap and retreat to Soochow. With Captain Davidson at the helm, the fire-belching *Hyson* saved the day. Gordon described it vividly:

> The *Hyson* blew her whistle and was received with deafening cheers from the [other] gunboats which were on the eve of bolting. She steamed up the creek toward Quinsan and at a distance of 200 yards we saw a confused mass near a high bridge. It was too dark to distinguish very clearly but as the steamer was blowing the whistle the mass wavered, yelled and turned back. . . . Matters were in too critical a state to hesitate, as the mass of rebels, goaded into desperation, would have swept our small force away. We were therefore forced to fire into them and pursue them.

General Ching entered the defeated city by way of the east gate, which he had been watching like a cat at a mousehole. The mice had fled, however, and he had a difficult time trying to convince his masters that he deserved the credit for the Quinsan victory.

Here along the banks of the canal, in the midst of the fighting that day, Gordon had spotted an abandoned Chinese boy. He swept the boy into his arms and held him as he led his troops forward. Gordon named him Quincey, British Army slang for Quinsan, and sent him off to Shanghai. The little lad was adopted by a British regiment and later taken home with it to England, although Gordon continued to contribute generously to his support.*

The carnage at Quinsan was terrible. It was estimated that between four thousand and five thousand of the Taipings were killed in the battle, either by gunfire, drowning as the mass of retreating rebels jostled one another into the canal, or murder as the peasants saw their chance to take revenge. More than two thousand prisoners were taken and fifteen hundred boats captured. Only two members of the Ever Victorious Army lost their lives in this stunning victory for Gordon. It was the high point of his China campaign.

---

* Gordon later found Quincey a job with the Chinese Customs Service and once had an opportunity to have a fond reunion with him in Hong Kong, where he met his wife and three children. Quincey prospered, ultimately becoming head of the Shanghai Railway police.

Li Hung-chang was ecstatic with joy and wrote in his journal after the battle: "What a sight for tired eyes and elixir for a heavy heart to see this splendid Englishman fight! . . . Fight—move—fight again—move again—landing his men—planning by night and executing by day— planning by day and executing by night! He is a glorious fellow!"[5] The Governor told Gordon that he must now consider himself his brother and fulfill the role of his real brother, who had been killed by the rebels. Li, however, was puzzled by his friend's reaction to such praise. "The Englishman's face first filled with deep pleasure," he recalled, but then "he seemed to be thinking of something depressing and sad; for the smile went from his mouth and there were tears in his eyes. . . ." In recollecting this incident, Li wondered, "Can it be that he has, or has had, some great trouble in his life and that he fights recklessly to forget it, or that death has no terrors for him?"[6]

Not everyone was willing to praise Gordon, however. From various quarters he was criticized for the slaughter he had inflicted on the Taipings. There was still enough sympathy for the rebel cause among missionaries and certain foreign business circles to raise questions about the wisdom of England's favoring the corrupt Manchus in China's civil war. Explanations that much of the killing had been perpetrated by vengeful peasants, not by the Ever Victorious Army, did little to quiet Gordon's critics.

Gordon abhorred gratuitous killing, so the barbs of criticism cut deeply. He was responsible enough to hope that the Taipings could be induced to make peace rather than endure more needless bloodletting. But feelers he put out came to nothing, and he made plans for the next bloody offensive.

8

CROSS AND DOUBLE CROSS

> . . . in this officer are combined so many dashing qualities, let alone skill and judgement, to make him invaluable to command such a force.
> —General Brown, British Army Commander in China, on Gordon

An ominous threat faced Gordon in late May. A letter was delivered to him unsigned, making clear the intentions of his artillerymen not to follow Gordon's orders to move the home base for the Ever Victorious Army from Sunkiang to Quinsan. With a macabre sense of protocol, the letter threatened death to the European officers with the large artillery and death to the Chinese troops with smaller guns. However naive this insubordination, it was mutiny, and mutiny could not be allowed to go unchallenged.

With Quinsan in his grip, Gordon had made the decision to establish the Ever Victorious Army there. It made tactical sense to move the force within closer striking distance of the next target, Soochow. Gordon, besides, never liked Sunkiang. With its fleshpots and thriving black market for battle loot, it was a cesspool of corruption, breeding indiscipline among his mercenaries. It depressed and angered him to think about the "passion pen," a compound where captured Chinese girls between the ages of fourteen and twenty-four were kept for the pleasures of his officers.

Although everyone was unhappy about having to give up this comfortable home base, it was only the artillerymen who dared to defy Gordon. The crisis occurred when the enlisted men refused to fall into formation for parade. While the rebellious gunners loitered sullenly in the background, their noncommissioned officers appeared innocently in the line. This struck Gordon as odd, and he correctly suspected that the noncoms were the real villains in the drama. Confronting them on the parade ground, Gordon demanded to know who had drafted the mutinous letter. Met with mute response, he warned the group that he would shoot one in every five men on parade until the guilty party stepped forward. There were hostile groans, but no one confessed.

The flash point was near, and Gordon knew he must act first. Without hesitation, he grabbed the loudest groaner from the ranks and ordered him shot immediately. As his comrades watched, too stunned to react, the hapless corporal was escorted out the west gate and, within earshot, killed behind a tombstone.

The other artillery noncoms were disarmed, placed under arrest, and taken off the parade ground. They were given an hour to produce the name of their ringleader. As Gordon anticipated, they soon returned the name of the corporal who had been executed. Guilty or not, the corporal was beyond saving and made a convenient scapegoat.

So the crisis passed, although discontent continued to simmer under the surface. In the next few days some two thousand men deserted. Gordon was not dismayed. He proceeded to enlist the Taiping prisoners seized at Quinsan, who, he was convinced, would make better soldiers anyway. Gordon had already filled his bodyguard with young rebels captured in battle and had found them completely loyal, but this was the first time he pressed into duty his erstwhile enemy on a mass scale—a tactic that he would use again with good success. Clearly, the Taiping zealots, who had formed the cutting edge of the army during the early years of the rebellion, were now outnumbered by simple peasants they had made homeless. While good fighters if well led, these rebels had but faint ideological attachment to the Taipings and, it seems, found paid duty in the Ever Victorious Army under Gordon more congenial.

Trouble came from another quarter. General Ching, smarting from being upstaged by Gordon during the battle for Quinsan, was enraged when Gordon decided to make that town his headquarters. Ching wanted to occupy Quinsan himself, and had his troops deliberately fire on a detachment of the Ever Victorious under Major Kirkham as they returned from a sortie. Ching's excuse—that he had mistaken them for the enemy—was unconvincing, as Gordon's distinctively dressed mercenaries were flying the Imperial colors when the incident occurred.

Gordon was set to confront Ching when an emissary from Governor Li arranged a reconciliation. Li's peacemaker, Halliday Macartney, had been a surgeon with the British 99th Regiment when he was loaned to Li as the

Governor's military secretary. It was he whom Li had appointed to the Ever Victorious Army during Burgevine's short stewardship to control the American's headstrong behavior. Well acquainted with Gordon, Macartney smoothed his hackles by promising an apology from Ching, and the crisis passed.

Li wearily noted the incident in his journal: "General Ching threatens to resign if some curb is not put upon General Gordon. Both are quick to say hot words—like myself." But Gordon, he hoped, would at least learn to hold his tongue even "if he could not control his mind."[1]

Hot words were one thing, poor support was another. Gordon became furious when Li suddenly failed to meet the payroll for the Ever Victorious and was behind schedule in delivering new river craft vital to amphibious warfare. Li, for his part, was also annoyed. In his journal he complained: "Gordon thinks of nothing but money . . . and demands coin of me as if I were the god of gold and silver. I tell him that as soon as Soochow is in our hands there will be funds sufficient to pay all arrears and some good bounty. This is the word that I have from the Viceroy [Tseng Kuo-fan] . . . and his promises came from the throne!"[2]

Tseng's objective was to push the rebels as far as possible toward the coast, where he knew the British and French could be relied upon to engage them in the interest of defending Shanghai. It was important to this strategy that Gordon and the Ever Victorious take Soochow as soon as possible. Not understanding mercenary psychology—money before action—and much less Gordon's stubbornness, Tseng mistakenly believed that by withholding their pay, the mercenaries could be goaded into moving more quickly against Soochow.

By late July, Gordon felt beleaguered on all sides. Even some of the British were undercutting his position. Horatio Nelson Lay, British Director of Chinese Customs, had brought from England a fleet of seven craft, justified to protect custom revenues by suppressing river piracy and rebel harassment. Lay and Bruce intended to include them in a reorganized Chinese fleet under central Imperial authority rather than under provincial control. Accordingly, Lay would report only to the Emperor and would direct the fleet's operations through British Navy Commander Captain Sherard Osborne. In effect, this would be a triumph for central control of military operations at the expense of provincial power, not to mention a triumph for Lay's own inflated ambition.

As the principle of central control was compromised by Gordon's command of the Ever Victorious Army under a provincial governor's authority, Lay recommended that Gordon be relieved. His plan envisioned a foreign-staffed, centrally administered Imperial army in any case, which would render Gordon's force redundant. Bruce favored central control versus provincial power, on the argument that a strengthened central executive in China provided the British with a more efficient lever to enforce their treaties than periodic gunboat diplomacy in the ports.

But China simply did not work that way; provincial power was too entrenched and the central government too weak. Lay and his boats were sent back to England by the Chinese in what was an embarrassing episode for Bruce, and effective power remained very much in the grip of the provincial governors.

Gordon survived in his command, but uncomfortably. Considered by Bruce and Lay an aberration of British policy, he had been a centerpiece in this diplomatic skirmish. Gordon was also still hurt by accusations that he had committed atrocities in taking Quinsan—the Bishop of Victoria in Australia had written to the British Foreign Secretary condemning Gordon's action at Quinsan.

Dispirited, Gordon submitted a formal resignation to Governor Li, in July 1863, claiming that the present unfortunate circumstances were "derogatory to my position as a British officer, who cannot be a suppliant for what Your Excellency know to be necessities." Not wanting to leave Li in the lurch, however, he planned to attack the rebel stockades around Soochow as a farewell gesture. As in the case of Quinsan, Gordon's strategy called for blockading Soochow rather than trying to force entry into the well-defended city. By taking Wokong, fifteen miles west of Soochow on the Grand Canal, and Woosieh, thirty miles northwest of Soochow, he could cut off communications of the rebel stronghold, thereby strangling it.

Toward the end of July 1863, disconcerting rumors began to drift about that Burgevine was hiring European mercenaries in Shanghai. As early as July 15, Macartney warned Gordon that Burgevine was "for certain enlisting men for some service or other."[3]

MANDARINS, MERCENARIES, AND HEAVENLY REBELS

Despite all the drama of Burgevine's efforts to keep command of the Ever Victorious Army, he and Gordon were on good terms. Gordon from the beginning seemed to like the man, for all his rascality, and see qualities in him which most others could not. (Gordon admitted that the American was overbearing and could not "brook advice," but considered him, like Ward, to have been "a gallant soldier whom he was fond of.") So when Burgevine wrote Gordon a friendly letter urging him to ignore the rumors, saying that "he could explain everything," Gordon naively took him at his word. Gordon then assured Governor Li that there was nothing to worry about and gave his personal guarantee that Burgevine would not join the rebels. But on August 2, as Gordon and Li were meeting in Shanghai, definite news of Burgevine's flight to the rebel camp at Soochow with more than one hundred newly recruited mercenaries made a mockery of these assurances. Burgevine had clearly lied.

Burgevine's new force changed the whole strategic position. The rebels now posed a formidable threat to Shanghai, and the Ever Victorious Army suddenly found itself on the defensive. In good conscience Gordon could not resign, particularly since he had gone out on a limb to vouch for Burgevine. He hurried back to Quinsan to meet the new threat.

Henry Andrea Burgevine was an American southerner of good education and quick wit. Born in 1836, he lived through the tumultuous period culminating in the American Civil War, and from early youth he seemed to have dreams of empire. He also had an incurable wanderlust, which took him around the world—the South Sea islands, Australia, India, and Arabia, among other places. The driving force behind his unscrupulous adventures in China was romantic ambition—including an obsession to rule the ancient empire. Unscrupulous he was, but not mad. Burgevine had a free-swinging, daredevil way about him which appealed to Gordon despite the threat he now posed.

Not only had Burgevine joined the rebels but he had audaciously stolen the steamer *Kajow* from under Li's nose at Sunkiang, using it to transport his mercenaries to Soochow. Sir Frederick Bruce was alarmed. The situation placed Gordon and Ching on the defensive and set back the timetable for taking Soochow. But, strangely, he placed the blame on Li for antagonizing Burgevine rather than on Burgevine for his crass opportunism. "A man who could have been a useful friend has been thus converted to a dangerous enemy," he wrote Foreign Secretary Lord John Russell on September 9. He feared nothing would "compensate for the injury done to the Imperialist cause by the accession of Burgevine to the insurgents' ranks."[4]

The British also worried that Burgevine would serve as a magnet for some of Gordon's officers who still preferred their former leader. Colonel Hough, commanding the British garrison in Shanghai, feared that Gordon might be taken prisoner by some of his officers or have his artillery seized by Burgevine sympathizers. Guarding against this possibility, Gordon sent some of his heavier guns to Taitsan for safekeeping. He also moved his troops up to Waiquidong, only six miles from Soochow, so they could be kept occupied in a state of combat alert. At Quinsan, where the men were easily distracted, Gordon noted that there had been "too much talk about Burgevine."[5] As a precaution, General Brown, now commander of British forces, transferred three hundred Indian Baluchi troops to Quinsan to hold that garrison while Gordon and the Ever Victorious moved to the more advanced position.

The Ever Victorious had no difficulty in taking Wokong, the first target in Gordon's original plan. On July 30, the garrison surrendered and thousands of rebels were taken prisoner, seven hundred of whom Gordon recruited for his force. But with Burgevine's arrival in Soochow with three hundred mercenary reinforcements he had recruited, the Taipings were able to seize the offensive. Only with great difficulty were Imperial troops able to drive off an attack against their positions at Kahpoo, and then only with the help of Gordon and 150 men who rushed to their rescue on the *Hyson*—that fearsome "dragon of the water."

Patachiao on the Grand Canal now took its place as the next target for the Ever Victorious. If Kahpoo was to be held and if the rebels were to be prevented from spilling out into the lake district near Shanghai, Patachiao had to be held. Li, however, desperately wanted Gordon to go straight for Soochow, to get the campaign over with before the British, who still persisted in talking about a centralized command, could undercut his power in the Shanghai area. Gordon had, in fact, received a letter from British Navy Commander Captain Osborne, on September 3, saying: "I shall advocate at Peking our having joint naval and military powers over all Europeans under arms in China . . . in no way to be interfered with by *Footais*, *Tootais* and birds of that feather."[6]

To attack the forty-thousand-man garrison of Soochow, particularly with

Burgevine's men lending muscle to its defenses, would be foolhardy, Gordon realized. Instead, quietly he hatched another strategy: He would try to talk Burgevine and his men into returning to the fold. Perhaps he could even cause dissension in the ranks of the rebels themselves.

On September 29, Gordon, with two Ever Victorious regiments, a small French-Chinese force which had been brought up to the line at British urging, an Imperial contingent under General Ching, and the steamships *Hyson* and *Firefly*, launched a surprise attack on Patachiao. It was pouring rain at the time, which Gordon credited for causing the rebels to retreat so quickly. "Rain," he declaimed on some authority not identified, "depresses Asiatics!"[7]

Burgevine had missed the first action, because he was in Shanghai trying to find more ammunition. Nearly captured by a river patrol, he arrived back in Patachiao two days later, in time to take part in an almost successful counterattack. According to Gordon's account of the battle, "the rebel artillery was very accurate and the affair looked doubtful when the *Hyson* came around the point."[8] Once again the ubiquitous steamer under Captain Davidson made the difference between defeat and victory.

Burgevine took advantage of his nearness to the Ever Victorious force and met with Gordon on a bridge near Patachiao to negotiate his defection from the rebels. Secret overtures to the American made by Gordon seemed to be bearing fruit. Burgevine passed along word of his disillusionment with the rebels, expressing his intention to come over with his foreign contingent, the stolen steamer *Kajow*, and all his artillery if Gordon would arrange amnesty and pay his men for their service with the Taipings. Gordon agreed to these terms and left it to Burgevine to fix the time. The plan was going well.

Burgevine, like many foreigners in China, had contempt for both the government and the rebels in this unending civil war. "I am perfectly aware," he wrote to Gordon on October 3, "that both sides are equally rotten. . . . I am suffering very much from old wounds, and I shall avail myself of your kind offer. . . . I should like to see and converse with you very much." But even at this stage of his disillusionment the American seemed to favor the rebels, whom he praised, at least, for their "disregard for many of the frivolous and idolatrous customs of the Manchus."[9] He also had good words for the rebel commander, Lin Shao-chang, the Chang Wang.

On October 8, Burgevine and his trusted deputy, former U.S. Navy

Captain Charles F. Jones, met with Gordon and agreed to surrender on the following day, bringing with them the *Kajow*. Gordon was of course gratified but totally unprepared for the astonishing proposal which Burgevine now made to him, one which revealed a more complex motive for leaving the rebels than Gordon had imagined. The American renegade, misjudging his friendship with Gordon, audaciously suggested that the two join forces to seize Peking and rule China! It was a wild scheme but one which might even have worked amid the chaos of China—except for the intervention of British, French or Russian forces. Even Wolseley reflected, half seriously, that had he been chosen to lead the Ever Victorious instead of Gordon, he might have exploited it to aggrandize himself. "I should have gone there with the determination of wiping out the rebellion and of becoming, myself, the Emperor of China!"[10]

The Imperial government was at that moment extremely fragile, and almost anything could have toppled it. It was just the kind of situation that would whet the power appetite of a freebooter like Burgevine. Bruce noted the situation in a dispatch to Lord John Russell: ". . . there is a feeling at Shanghai that he [Burgevine] will endeavour to organize an expedition and strike a blow at Pekin . . . and success at Pekin would certainly overthrow the present dynasty, whether it led to the establishment of the Taiping or not."[11]

Gordon, however, harbored no illusions of grandeur. Dismayed that Burgevine thought him capable of abusing his position and deceiving his Chinese masters, not to mention Her Majesty's government, he rejected the proposition forthwith.

Although Gordon's negative response made Burgevine angry and relations between the two men cooled precipitously, plans for the American's surrender proceeded. Burgevine, under cover of a false attack scheduled for the following day, would desert the rebels and bring his men over to Gordon. But as General Ching chose that day to launch an unauthorized offensive, Burgevine had to postpone his surrender and continue for the time being to defend the side he intended to betray.

Jones, Burgevine's deputy, and forty of his comrades found an occasion to give themselves up on October 14. In a deposition filed with the American Consul, he told a strange and harrowing story of his last encounter with Burgevine. On October 12 Jones had found Burgevine sleeping off a drunk on the deck of a gunboat. Jones roused him to warn of men complaining about his condition under these perilous circumstances. Two disasters had just occurred. Careless firing from the *Kajow* had ignited a powder keg and blown the bow off the steamer, badly injuring two men. Then an ammunition barge on which battle wounded had been placed blew up, killing almost half of the men.[12] When Jones refused to tell the still-drunk Burgevine who the complainers were, the mercenary leader pulled out his pistol and shot Jones in the cheek. As blood spurted from his grazed face, Jones screamed: "You have shot your best friend!" Unmoved, Burgevine growled, "I wish I had killed you."

But there was another reason for the strained relations: Burgevine had confided in Jones a plot to double-cross Gordon. Under pretense of surrender, he would seize Gordon and hold him prisoner. When Jones, who respected Gordon, protested and refused to be a party to the scheme, Burgevine became furious.

Gordon had suspected treachery when Burgevine, during a clandestine rendezvous to discuss his surrender, had turned the tables and instead encouraged him "to rat out." Sensing some deeper plot, Gordon escaped during the night, later admitting that "Burgevine could have bagged me."

However much Gordon may have been disillusioned by Burgevine, it was vital that the American freebooter and all his men be taken out of action if Soochow was to be captured. After Ching had upset the surrender plan, another unanticipated occurrence complicated matters further. One of Burgevine's officers, an American named Morton, convinced that the Taiping leaders were on to the plot, fled to Gordon's camp without waiting for his commander. Fearing that this irresponsible act would tip the hands of the mercenaries and place Burgevine and his remaining men in jeopardy, Gordon gambled. He wrote the Taiping commanders, T'an Shao-kuang (the Moh Wang) and Li Hsiu-ch'eng (the Chung Wang): "If there are many Europeans left in Soochow, I would ask your Excellencies if it does not seem to you much better to let these men quietly leave your service if they wish it; you would thereby get rid of a continual source of suspicion and gain the sympathy of the whole of the foreign nations." As an incentive, Gordon offered guns to the rebels if they would release the mercenaries from service. Then, adding stick to carrot, he added: "Should you behead the Europeans . . . you will eventually regret it."[13]

In response to Gordon the rebel commanders wrote: "We have just received your letter and learned of your desire for us to release the wounded . . . and also of your desire to do business with us in guns and cannons." The wounded would be released; as for the others, "each may follow his own preference." On the matter of guns, the rebels put it on a business basis: "Your side seeks profit, and we shall buy . . . if at present you have guns, cannons or other foreign commodities please come and trade with us as usual." Then in a sly overture, beckoning Gordon to defect, they wrote: "And if your Excellency should be willing to come to our side, we shall be delighted to work together with you."[14]

It was a strange war in this twilight of the Taiping Rebellion: Chinese allegiances were becoming as mercurial as those of the European mercenaries. And the British, not wholly sure of how to proceed, were still feeling their way. Gordon, however, instinctively played a Machiavellian game with sureness and skill, somehow weaving his way through the maze.

The next message from Burgevine reported disaster after Morton's premature flight from Soochow. Gordon's letter to the rebel chiefs had "upset everything . . . almost caused all of the mercenaries to be beheaded."[15] Burgevine pleaded for Gordon to return the horses and arms Morton had brought with him. But neither Burgevine nor Gordon realized that it had been the troublesome General Ching behind the problems. Only later would it be learned that Ching was carrying on a secret correspondence with the rebel leader, the Moh Wang. In contradiction of Gordon's pleas for mercy, Ching was inciting the Taipings to lop off the mercenaries' heads.

Despite the confusion and conflicting signals, the Moh Wang finally released Burgevine and gave him safe conduct to Gordon's camp on October 17. He was transported to Shanghai on the *Hyson,* preparatory to being expelled from China. Gordon was relieved; his negotiations with the rebel chiefs, sweetened by bribes of arms, had worked. The Moh Wang acknowledged receipt of the guns and cannon, thanking him for the present of a horse which he "found very good." The horse had been an added flourish, part of Gordon's strategy of winning over the Moh Wang to his side.

The tenor of the rebel leader's letters was in fact becoming quite cordial. The Moh Wang wrote: "Our country is fighting for the territory against Ch'ing [the Manchus]; we do not have any grudge against foreign countries. Please come to us as much as you like and trade with us as usual." Then, mysteriously, he added, "What has not been said will be transmitted to you through the messenger."[16]

Although the American Consul in Shanghai had promised Governor Li that he would deport Burgevine, he had not been prompt enough to prevent the renegade from masterminding the theft of another steamer, the *Firefly*, and selling it to the rebels. Li, who hated Burgevine and suspected him of faking his defection in order to steal the *Firefly*, would have liked to have Burgevine's head for this latest outrage, but he satisfied himself with an irate letter to the American Consul, who still had custody of him. The Consul, indulgent of his charge, let Burgevine leave China for Yokohama, Japan, rather than repatriate him to the United States for prosecution. If Li was suspicious of the British and American roles in this sordid affair, he could hardly be blamed.

The problem was over, and Bruce praised Gordon in a letter to the Foreign Office for "tact in dealing with the difficulties arising from the jealousy and suspicion of the Chinese authorities in rescuing Burgevine and the misguided foreigners who served in the Taiping ranks, and thereby obviating the risk of this foreign adventurer element uniting with them."[17] Gordon had, in fact, not escaped Governor Li's suspicion for his role in the Burgevine saga. Even by Chinese standards of the day, the intrigues of the Burgevine affair were labyrinthine. Although Gordon and the Ever Victorious Army had been seriously menaced by Burgevine's mercenary force, jealous officials such as General Ching saw to it that dark rumors accusing Gordon of complicity with the rebels reached the Governor's ears. Not until later would it become apparent to Li that Gordon's secret relationship with the rebels, established during the Burgevine negotiations, had provided the key to Soochow's surrender.

Why the Taiping commanders were so accommodating with Gordon may seem puzzling, but it was not illogical. Soochow's fall was conceded—it was only a matter of time—and they wanted to stay in the good graces of the foreign powers. Better they be at Gordon's mercy than that of the Imperial government. Moreover, Gordon appeared honorable. "The rebel chiefs would come to terms if they had fair ones offered to them," he believed.

Gordon wanted peace. It would be "a greater victory than any capture of cities would be."

9

SOOCHOW MASSACRE

The Destiny of China is at present moment in the hands of Gordon
more than any other man. . . .
—Robert Hart, Inspector of Chinese Customs

The capture of Soochow was a more realistic expectation now that Burgevine's mercenary force had been vacated, although the Chung Wang, Commander in Chief of the Taiping army, had personally taken command of eighteen thousand new troops and moved them up to a nearby town to defend the Taiping stronghold. Gordon still sought surrender of the forty-thousand-man Soochow garrison rather than risk direct attack, believing that once surrounded and cut off, the rebels would give up. Intelligence that rivalries existed among the Wangs, the princely commanders of Soochow, made surrender even more likely.

Gordon moved the Ever Victorious forces, supported by the *Hyson*, closer to Soochow's south gate, subduing rebel stockades as he went. Territory gained by the 2,100-strong Ever Victorious was held by units of General Ching's Imperial forces, which numbered 7,500, or by an independent Chinese unit of a thousand, commanded by Macartney. A Franco-Chinese detachment of four hundred, under the French officer Bonnefoi, was also involved so that Gordon could continue to tighten the ring around the city.

Gordon was in his element. Always in front of his troops, brandishing his "magic wand of victory" and chewing on his cigar, he had become the personification of success—a favored one of God—in the eyes of the Chinese. Officers and soldiers around him might fall in battle, but Gordon seemed impervious to bullets.

During the attack on the Leeku stockades the American officer George Perry, standing beside Gordon, was killed instantly by a bullet through his mouth. He fell backward into a horrified Gordon's arms.

A few days earlier, Gordon had learned that the officer had in correspondence revealed the Ever Victorious positions to a friend in the mercenary rebel army. Gordon had forgiven this treachery, but told Perry he would have to lead the next attack as penance. While Gordon had forgotten this order, Perry had not, and joined him in the van only to be killed moments later. Whatever poetic justice there may have been in the incident, Gordon blamed himself for a brave, if not always reliable, officer's death.

But otherwise, Gordon remained untouched by the bullets—and other calamities—around him. When he descended from his exposed position atop a bridge to board his steamer, the arched span on which he had seconds before stood suddenly collapsed, missing him by inches. Wearing his bright red coat, he recklessly dashed around in the thick of battle from one sector to another without fear—almost as though he were inviting death.

In a daring night attack on a rebel stockade near Soochow's east gate, the Ever Victorious suffered its first defeat under Gordon on November 28, 1863. More than three hundred men were killed in the abortive effort. Gordon himself came close to death as the rebels let loose with their artillery against the attacking force. The superstitious soldiers blamed their defeat on an eclipse of the moon which had occurred just before the attack. The eclipse, in fact, was more than just an evil omen, as the loss of moonlight added to the fatal confusion. Gordon was forced to retire, but a few days later was encouraged to try again after receiving intelligence from General Ching that all the rebel leaders in Soochow except the Moh Wang himself were on the verge of surrender.

Gordon and his men struck on the 29th. The key stockade was taken this time, though casualties were high. Major Kirkham, who had more than once distinguished himself in battle, was wounded, while several other valuable Ever Victorious officers were killed in the assault. It had been a hotly contested battle, with the Chung Wang personally commanding the defenses. Now at first hand Gordon knew that the vaunted rebel commander was worthy of his reputation. But realizing the hopelessness of the situation in Soochow, the Chung Wang escaped to safety to plot the next rebel move.

Gordon congratulated his men for their gallantry in a General Order: "The loss of the whole of the stockade on the east side of the city, up to the walls, has already had its effect, and dissension is now rife in the garrison."

General Ching and Gordon met secretly with the rebel Wangs on December 1 to discuss the surrender of Soochow. Ching followed this up with more detailed discussion with the Wangs, while Gordon extracted a commitment from Governor Li Hung-chang, the Futai, extending mercy to the defeated enemy, sparing Soochow the massacres that usually accompanied Imperialist victories.

T'an Shao-kuang, the Moh Wang, suspected that his subordinate Wangs were negotiating with the Imperialists without his knowing. There had been telltale signs of treason during the recent battle. The Lar Wang, for one, had failed to come to his aid when Gordon broke into the stockade. But now the Moh Wang was probably making his own plans. The respectful, almost friendly, correspondence he had carried on with Gordon over the Burgevine affair had given him confidence in the British officer—certainly more than he had in the Imperialists. Gordon, moreover, owed him a favor in return for his cooperation in the release of Burgevine's mercenaries. Through a French mercenary, the Moh Wang sent word to Gordon for a clandestine meeting which he would attend in disguise. The rendezvous never took place, however, and Gordon could only speculate that the Moh Wang had defection in mind.

The tempo of intrigue quickened as the inevitable rebel collapse at Soochow drew closer. The Moh Wang, now highly suspicious of the other officers, invited them to a rather surreal, formal banquet where he would confront them. Everyone wore his official robes of rank and crown. After a fine meal, discussion began. The Moh Wang accused his guests of plotting with the Imperialists behind his back. As he went on, he became more abusive. Finally, as he rose from his chair in fury, one of the Wangs plunged a knife into his back and another chopped off his head. This grisly souvenir of the banquet was sent to General Ching as a signal that the surrender could now proceed without opposition.

The headless trunk of the Moh Wang was left sprawled grotesquely on the floor in a pool of blood. Gordon's letter to him of October 16, asking for the release of Burgevine and his men, was found in the Moh Wang's clothing, and returned to the Ever Victorious leader. It was a poignant clue that the Moh Wang may have planned to appeal to Gordon for asylum.

The Lar Wang replaced the Moh Wang as leader of the rebel force, and prepared to hand over the city to the Imperialists. He and General Ching, it seems, had once been "blood brothers" as comrades in the Taiping army. That, combined with Governor Li's assurances that the surrendering Wangs would be pardoned, gave Gordon confidence that the transition of authority in Soochow would be orderly. Ching marched his victorious troops to the east gate on December 5.

Gordon did not permit the Ever Victorious Army to share in the town's occupation, because he feared that they would go on a looting spree. To make up for this loss, he asked Li to grant them two extra months' pay. When the parsimonious Futai granted them only half that amount, the men were furious. Gordon tendered his resignation to Li in protest, but with tempers running so high, Gordon decided to withdraw his troops before violence broke out. As it was, the irate soldiers shouted angrily in front of the Futai's headquarters as they marched by. Any spark could have ignited the smoldering Ever Victorious, but Gordon managed to maintain discipline and get his men back to Quinsan. His brief absence from Soochow, however, would have tragic consequences.

Sunday, December 6, was a day Gordon would never forget. As victor of the Soochow campaign, he had reason for satisfaction, but the day brought him only rage and profound grief. An instinct of unease prompted him to visit the Lar Wang twice that morning. Gordon offered his steamer as sanctuary if the new rebel leader felt he was in danger. All seemed well, as the Lar Wang and the other rebel officers prepared to capitulate formally at noon, when they would meet with Governor Li. Gordon had elected not to be present at the ceremony, believing that it should be an all-Chinese event. Moreover, he expected to be busy supervising the capture of the stolen steamship *Firefly* on Taihu Lake.

Stopping by the house of the late Moh Wang to see if the burial of the murdered leader had taken place, Gordon encountered Macartney. Together they rode toward the east gate, where Gordon expected to board his boat. From the height of the town wall, they could see the Futai's barge moored on the canal a mile away, and noticed a large crowd gathering, presumably to watch the defeated Wangs as they arrived for the ceremony. Soon Imperial soldiers could be seen approaching the town from the direction of the Futai's boat. They were exultant, shouting and prancing about uncontrolledly as they poured through the town gate. Some were firing guns at random in celebration of their victory; others were looting.

Gordon was alarmed. The "Imps," contrary to Li's assurances, seemed bent on exactly the kind of rape and pillage that Gordon had sought to end. General Ching rode by—it was now 1:00 P.M. and the surrender ceremony should have been over—agitated as well by the worsening state of affairs. When Gordon hailed him, Ching was noticeably uncomfortable. From Ching's semicoherent account, Gordon was given to understand that the Wangs had not met Governor Li after all—even though Gordon had seen them on their way to the Futai's barge in high spirits. Ching alleged that at the last minute the rebel chiefs had set new terms of surrender which were totally unacceptable, including a demand that they be permitted to rule half the city with twenty thousand of their men armed. When Li rejected the demands, according to Ching's unconvincing story, the rebel leaders fled the town.

At 5:00 P.M. Gordon rode on horseback to the Lar Wang's house. It was burned to the ground, with some five hundred armed rebels still there and in imminent danger of colliding with the marauding Imps. In the confusion, Gordon found himself taken prisoner by Taiping troops, a hostage for the Lar Wang's safe return. As night fell, Gordon could hear the sounds of rioting in town. Soochow was by now totally out of control, and Gordon was in mortal jeopardy. His emotions were not of fear, however; they were of anger and frustration as he remained under guard unable to act. If Li was holding the rebel leaders prisoner, Gordon vowed to himself that he would personally seize the Futai and demand an accounting for this betrayal of the terms of surrender.

Not until 3:00 A.M. the next day was Gordon able to talk his way out of rebel custody—not a moment too soon. For had the rebels known what had happened, they surely would have killed him in revenge. As Gordon made his way through the chaos in the streets toward the south gate, he was captured again—this time by the Imperialists. After a maddening delay of more than an hour, he finally satisfied the Imps as to his identity and was released. Gordon was so consumed by anger that he never realized the jeopardy he had been in during that terrible night.

Soon after dawn, Gordon, now seething, again encountered General Ching. Gordon erupted in uncontrollable anger. Heaping vituperation upon Ching, he blamed him for the orgy of rioting, looting and wanton killing—a disgrace to the Imperial army. The transformation of Gordon from mild-mannered officer to ogre filled with fury sent Ching scuttling for cover. According to Major Bailey, an American officer, who met Ching inside the east gate, the shaken general had dissolved in tears as soon as he was out of

Gordon's range. Then, in a mindless effort to bring order out of chaos, Ching shot dead twenty Imperialist soldiers whom he suspected of looting.

Not until the Lar Wang's son told Gordon the grim truth did he know that all the Wangs had been executed. When Gordon sent his aide, Prince Wittgenstein, to verify the story, the officer found the headless bodies of the victims lying in a ditch, some horribly mutilated. A shocked Gordon went to see the gruesome evidence himself. He leaped to the conclusion that Governor Li was the culprit and set out to find him, clutching the Lar Wang's severed head as though he needed it as evidence. Fortunately for all concerned, the Futai could not be found; he had been tipped off by Ching that Gordon was after him and went into the city.

Gordon, instead, vented his rage in a letter to Li, threatening to charge him with treachery. If Li would not step down as Governor, Gordon promised to return all the captured towns to the rebels, a rashly seditious threat which Macartney as messenger fortunately chose not to deliver. Gordon retreated to Quinsan on his steamer with the Lar Wang's now-orphaned sixteen-year-old son, whom he took pity on and promised to adopt. The Lar Wang's head, not improving with time, was still in Gordon's custody.

The truth of what happened that bloody Sunday in Soochow was not easy to discover. Li's own version, as recorded in his journal and later expanded as a kind of apology to an outraged British public, put an entirely new light on what occurred:

> Last night, to please the Wangs, I invited them to a council of peace and a banquet, and it was interesting the way we settled old scores in words. I spent a large sum upon the foods, and the table was well set. There was much merriment and good-nature, and I too enjoyed meeting with these men—Long-hairs though they were. But I made a serious mistake in not having a strong guard about the east gate, at which my boat was lying, and before the banquet was ended a great horde of lawless fellows, some of them Imperialists, but a majority of them drunken fellows of the Wang's army, poured through the gate, killing and assaulting. I was one of the first to hear the great uproar, and, believing the marauders might be intent on dispatching me—for threats had been made in many quarters—I made my escape from the barge and hurriedly entered the city. Ching also managed to escape from the hands of the rioters and followed me to the landing and into the town. Immediately, I sent orders by officers we met to get troops as soon as possible and arrest all the rioters; but the orders were not quickly obeyed and a scene of wholesale slaughter occurred upon the barge. I must make report of this to Peking; but it is not likely that great sorrow will be felt.[1]

SOOCHOW MASSACRE

In a later statement, Li described how Imperial soldiers, crazed with the urge for revenge, boarded his boat and "began cutting down every one they met." The Lar Wang was killed, he said, as he stood by his side. Li and Ching escaped, so were not present when the rest of the rebel leaders were beheaded. Li blamed Gordon for having sent the Ever Victorious back to Quinsan at this critical time, when they might have kept the Imperialist soldiers under better control.

British press accounts had a wildness of their own. They were irresponsibly inaccurate, exacerbating the situation by stirring up British public opinion against the Futai. The first *Times* account, which appeared on January 29, 1864, accused him of commanding a wholesale massacre—men, women and children. In a highly imaginary episode, which the *Times* attributed to Prince Wittgenstein's testimony, Gordon and a few men he had with him witnessed a scene so revolting that "they all fired and loaded and fired again on every mandarin they met." Gordon was given credit for having shot thirty-five "buttons"—the derogatory term for mandarins—himself. Other newspapers had Gordon stalking the Governor, pistols strapped to his waist, with every intent to kill. Unable to contain its outrage, the *Times* added that there was universal feeling of regret that "Gordon did not succeed in capturing the Futai and hanging him."[2] A later article in the *Times* corrected this sensational and erroneous article, but like all corrections it mattered little after public opinion had turned. A myth was born.

Knowing the hysterical tenor of Gordon's letter to Li, Macartney refused to translate it into Chinese. Li did not insist, relieved that he did not have to be faced with an intemperate letter the contents of which he could imagine. On the grounds he could not read it he refused to accept it, and sent Macartney to make peace with his old friend. This was not the first time Gordon's temper had exasperated the Futai, but he still liked the volatile Scotsman and wanted to keep his services. He could forgive Gordon for not accepting the Chinese way of dealing with problems.

In Quinsan, Macartney found Gordon in his room, sobbing on the bed. When he entered, Gordon reached under his bed and produced the bloody bundle he had brought from Soochow. Convulsed with a new onslaught of tears, Gordon held up the macabre reminder of Imperialist treachery and murmured: "Do you see this? Do you see this? It is the head of the Lar Wang: foully murdered!"

This was obviously no time to reason with Gordon, so Macartney withdrew and waited until breakfast. The officers' mess was crowded when the two men sat down at a long common table. Macartney was reticent, given the openness of the room, but Gordon, still in a foul mood, barked at him, "You have come on a mission from the Futai. What is it?" When Macartney suggested they get off alone to talk, Gordon insisted they do their business then and there. "There are only friends here," he said. "I have no secrets—speak out."

Macartney did his best, but despaired of influencing the distraught man. Intent on punishing the Futai, Gordon told Macartney that he would have none of his "mild counsel." As Macartney rode back to warn Li of his failure, Gordon in a belligerent mood set out for Soochow on the *Hyson*. But somewhere between Quinsan and Soochow, Macartney's logic got through to him—or his own better judgment prevailed—and he abandoned any idea of seizing the Governor. He paused in Soochow only long enough to retrieve the Lar Wang's body so it could be joined with his head and given a decent burial. When Gordon returned to Quinsan he transferred command of the Ever Victorious to General Brown.

Gordon was a man of honor, and faithlessness was in his opinion a serious crime. His fury was understandable in such terms, but the extent and duration of his grief seemed inordinate. A. Egmont Hake, a contemporary biographer, visited Gordon five days after the distraught man had returned to Quinsan, finding him in "a truly sorrowful state. He could not speak from emotion, his eyes were full of tears, he did nothing but walk about the room in a distracted manner."[3] The Lar Wang's son was with him at the time, and Gordon mentioned that he had adopted him.

Reconstructing the events attendant to Li's meeting with the Wangs in Soochow was not as simple as Gordon imagined it. In an independent investigation, Prince Kung satisfied himself that the Wangs had, in fact, been menacing. They had not disarmed their men and were making demands which could not be tolerated. They insisted, for example, on holding three of the fortified city gates. The Prince concluded that had the Wangs not been beheaded, the Imperial soldiers would have been massacred by the rebels, and thus "violence would have been done to the beneficent principle of Heaven and Earth, which delights to create, and is opposed to destruction."[4]

102

Once before, in Taitsan, the rebels had used the ruse of surrender to turn on the Imperialists and defeat them.

Another possibility, which was not aired but must have occurred to Gordon, was that General Ching, without Li's complicity, provoked the whole affair. Burgevine had written Gordon from Japan that Ching had secretly discussed his possible redefection to the rebels with the Wangs. If this were the case, Ching had reason to fear leakage of this highly compromising intelligence if the Wangs were allowed to live.

Gordon's near-breakdown over this matter might also have been due to a sense of his own culpability. His absence at the fateful meeting and his choice to keep the Ever Victorious out of Soochow had, as Li contended, contributed to the trouble. Moreover, Gordon condemned himself for turning the problem over to General Brown rather than trying to resolve it himself.

Brown's protests to Li, it turns out, were clumsy and unhelpful. He told the Futai of his recommendation to disband Gordon's Quinsan force, and to have Gordon himself recalled. And, in fact, Brown did make such a recommendation to Bruce in Peking.

Li, despite his differences with Gordon, genuinely wanted a reconciliation with the man and wanted the Ever Victorious to continue fighting under him. Throughout the month of December, Li sent various mandarins to Gordon with peace feelers. On New Year's Day an emissary brought Gordon a military decoration and ten thousand taels as a present from the Emperor. Gordon rejected it all, however, and scrawled a disrespectful reply to the Emperor: ". . . owing to the circumstances which occurred since the capture of Soochow, he [Gordon] is unable to receive any mark of His Majesty's recognitions. . . ." He also rejected two rebel battle flags which Li sent him as his personal peace offering. Gordon's price of reconciliation could not be measured in personal honors or money; he wanted the Futai to take full responsibility for the massacres and to give his troops the battle bonuses they deserved.

Robert Hart, now head of the Imperial Maritime Customs Service, also tried to convince Gordon to return to duty. According to Hart: "The destiny of China is at the present moment in the hands of Gordon more than any other man, and if he be encouraged to act vigorously, the knotty questions of

Taipingdom versus 'union in the cause of law and order' will be solved before the end of May."[5] Hart, who understood the Chinese better than most foreigners, made his own investigation of the Soochow incident and concluded that there had not been premeditated treachery on the part of the Imperialists. Governor Li had feared for the safety of his forces in Soochow and saw the beheading of the rebel chiefs as an act of prudence. The Futai, furthermore, credited the Taiping offer of surrender in the first place to General Ching's negotiations, not to Gordon's. Thus, this had been a Chinese affair and Gordon had no need to burden himself with it.

By February, Gordon was willing to make peace with Li. The Futai publicly took full responsibility for the affair, absolving Gordon of any blame or complicity, granting the Ever Victorious a handsome bonus for valor. Gordon realized that his own intransigence was only helping the Taipings, and a life of idleness in the barracks was badly hurting his troops' morale; already several officers had resigned. As for Li, Gordon now admitted in a letter to Bruce: "The Futai has some extenuating circumstances in his favour for his action. . . . I think we can scarcely expect the same discernment that we should from an European governor." With Bruce's permission, Gordon made peace with Li—even reestablished their old friendship—and resumed his command. Another storm had passed.

Gordon's letter to Bruce, explaining his reasons for returning to the Ever Victorious, was significant in another respect. Gordon revealed: "I know of a certainty that Burgevine meditates a return to the rebels; that there are upwards of 300 Europeans ready to join him, and that the Futai will not accept another British officer if I leave the service. . . ."[6] Gordon's intelligence was good, but it was also likely that he was in correspondence with Burgevine while the American bided his time in Japan; what he knew about Burgevine probably came from Burgevine himself. Despite all that had occurred, the two men were still friendly adversaries.

By repairing his relationship with Li Hung-chang, Gordon knew he would offend those in England who still had sympathy for the rebels. Reflecting the jaundiced view of several members of Parliament, Lord Naas attacked Gordon for "condoning" the Futai's act of "treachery" against the rebels. Even Lord Palmerston referred to Gordon as an "unwilling instrument to lure these people [the Taipings] into the power of the Futai—and instrument to their barbarous execution."[7]

SOOCHOW MASSACRE

Parliamentary attacks did not concern Gordon as much as the need to end the chaotic death throes of the Taiping movement. Having convinced himself that he alone could end the rebellion within six months—without him it might take "six years"—he returned to the contest. For Bruce's benefit, Gordon sketched his strategy: ". . . to cut through the heart of the rebellion, and to divide it into two parts by the capture of Yesing and Liyang." He knew that his force would not be used in the final attack on Nanking—General Tseng Kuo-fan wanted that honor for himself—but he saw the fall of the rebel capital as the inevitable denouement once he had succeeded in his next campaign.

10

VICTORY

The disasters at Soochow and Hangchow were occasioned by the
mischief of the foreign devils. . . .
—Li Hsiu-ch'eng, the Taiping Faithful King

As February's cold gripped the countryside, Gordon and the Ever
Victorious Army moved against Yesing on the western side of Lake
Taiho. Gordon had received Bruce's blessing for the new campaign, and he was back on good terms with Li. And Li, having received the
British Minister's backing, had survived pressure from the British community in Shanghai and British public opinion back home to have him removed
because of his role in the Soochow massacre.

Still worrisome, however, was Burgevine's potential for causing trouble
even though he had been deported from China and was now in Japan. But at
least the British Minister, who probably had been too solicitous of his
American colleague Anson Burlingame in trying to restore Burgevine's
command of the Ever Victorious Army, finally realized that the mercenary
had in fact been, and continued to be, a threat to British interests. Bruce
specifically feared the possibility that the Confederate side in the American
Civil War might back him in some adventure aimed at U.S. Northern
commercial interests in China. In a letter to Gordon of March 3, Bruce wrote:
"Burgevine is a Southerner; the trading interests in America are Northern,
and Burgevine attributes his treatment to the British authorities at Shanghai.
It would not surprise me if he and the *Alabama* [a ship which the British had
sold to the Confederacy despite loud protests from Washington] were to
make common cause with the insurgents. . . . you may depend upon it they
would directly attack the foreign settlements, where most of the plunder is to
be had."[1] Bruce even envisioned the possibility that Burgevine with

106

Confederate support might try to raise the Imperialist siege of the rebel capital at Nanking.*

Yesing fell easily to the Ever Victorious on March 2, the rebels putting up little resistance before taking flight. The greater problem for Gordon was his own troops, who resented being kept out of the town and deprived of loot. To enforce discipline among the angry men, Gordon found it necessary to have one man shot for defying his order.

Liyang, too, was given up without a struggle. Rebels who felt so inclined were permitted to leave the town, although about a thousand men of the Liyang garrison elected to shave their heads and join the Ever Victorious Army. Gordon also profited by the addition of twenty-five gunboats, appropriated from the defeated rebels.

But Gordon was sickened by the sights he saw in the city. Everywhere people were starving, scavenging about for food. They were too weak to bury their dead, leaving them to sink in the mud, "trodden quite flat by the passers-by." In the words of one officer, "Hundreds of dead bodies were strewn along the roads—people who died from starvation; and even the few who were yet alive watched one of their comrades dying, so as to obtain some food off his dead body."[2] How far from the reality of life in rural China was the foreign community in Shanghai, Gordon bewailed. "They do not *see* things, and to *read* that there are human beings eating human flesh produces less effect than if they saw the corpses from which that flesh is cut." He opened the Liyang granaries to the surviving peasants.

Kitang, the next objective on the march toward Nanking, proved to be more formidable. Despite three hours of heavy bombardment, Gordon could

---

* In early 1865 the irrepressible Burgevine did, in fact, appear briefly in Shanghai before taking a ship to Amoy, where a fragment of the Taiping movement still survived. Burgevine's fate was shrouded in mystery from that point on. The Chinese government seems to have caught up with him on May 15, 1865, in Changchow, where he was arrested, and then sent him to Foochow. The American Minister in Peking, D. C. Williams, was formally informed that Burgevine would be tried in a Chinese court and risked execution if found guilty. But before Williams could take action, Burgevine's body was found on June 26 drowned in Chekiang. The Chinese blamed the death on a boat accident, but the foreign community in Shanghai assumed Governor Li Hung-chang had finally got his revenge.

not wear down the rebels. They responded to Gordon's attack with a murderous fusillade and a shower of "stinkpots"—with the accompaniment of clashing cymbals and screeching horns. Intimidated, many of the Ever Victorious refused to leave the relative safety of their landing boats to join the charge when the wall was finally breached.

Clutching his Chinese battle standard, Gordon found himself alone and exposed, an inviting target. His "magic wand" failed him this time, and he received a bad leg wound. But not until he felt faint for lack of blood would he permit himself to be carried off the field and back to the safety of the *Hyson*. Without his presence the attack faltered even more, and Gordon had no choice but to withdraw his troops. In this abortive attack, the Ever Victorious sustained a hundred casualties.

His wound notwithstanding, Gordon refused to slow his pace, and he set off to defend the Quinsan area, which suddenly was being menaced again by the Taipings. At a town called Waisso, Gordon's force suffered another serious setback. Immobilized by his wound, Gordon yielded command to a less experienced assault officer who made the mistake of launching his troops too soon against the strongly entrenched enemy. More than 250 men were killed in what was the army's worst defeat.

The wounding of the "invulnerable" Gordon was a signal event; a myth had been shaken. Governor Li Hung-chang solicitously called on him daily with orders from the Celestial Throne itself cautioning Gordon to exercise care until he regained his strength. Even Lord Palmerston, who had been scathing in his criticism of Gordon's reconciliation with the Futai after Soochow, now had warm words of praise. On the floor of Parliament the British statesman lauded him as "a distinguished officer . . . who has performed great services for the Imperial Government."[3]

On the same day that Gordon was hurt, General Ching received a bad head wound in a neighboring battlefield. He died on April 15, 1864. No one had exasperated Gordon more than Ching, but when Gordon heard the news, he was genuinely saddened. Ching had been a brave man, and Gordon eulogized Ching as "by far the best mandarin the Imperialists had." Whatever their differences, whatever their incompatibility, they shared the bond that comrades-in-arms often experience after long campaigns facing the ever-present prospect of death. Although it was unclear if Ching seriously considered returning to the rebel side, as Burgevine—who was not always a reliable informant—claimed, Ching had given his life for the Emperor.

If the rebel cause was fast fading, one of its commanders, a south Chinese known as "Cock-eye," did not act as though he knew it. He was determined to hold the fort at Ch'ang-chou[4] on the Grand Canal with his twenty thousand veteran fighters despite an Imperialist siege which had lasted for weeks. When a rejuvenated Gordon and 3,500 Ever Victorious troops arrived, the outlying stockades south of Ch'ang-chou were quickly reduced, enabling the force to move up to the southeastern corner of the city wall. As Gordon's artillery pounded this sector, the Imperialists bombarded the southwestern wall.

By noon the next day, the Ever Victorious artillery had smashed a gaping hole in the wall, and after laying pontoon bridges across a sixty-foot moat under heavy Taiping fire, a storming party attacked. Two attempts failed, however, causing heavy casualties and forcing Gordon to withdraw. The Imperialists fared no better.

Gordon now looked to his engineering skills. Because of the enemy's firepower, Gordon had trenches dug and breastworks erected at the edge of the moat, offering attackers some measure of protection. The pontoon bridge crossing the moat was replaced by a barrel bridge to provide additional cover from heavy rebel fire from the wall top. Still, at best, attack would be a risky venture. On the eve of the new assault Gordon wrote his mother: Earlier losses had been severe—forty-eight officers out of a hundred killed, a thousand men out of 3,500 killed or wounded—but "six months will see the end of the rebellion."

It was May 11 when a new attack, the third effort, was launched, spearheaded by Imperialist troops because the Futai wanted them to have credit for taking this strategic city. As Governor Li and Gordon's friend Robert Hart, China's chief Maritime Customs Service officer, watched anxiously from a hilltop, the Imperialists charged. When the charge faltered, they saw Gordon leading his 1st Regiment forward in an effort to rally the Chinese. He scrambled through the breach directly in the face of a 32-pounder which had been taken from the stolen *Firefly*. Miraculously, the gun failed to fire—its powder apparently damp—and Gordon with the Ever Victorious regiment swarmed over the enemy before the big gun could be reloaded. Once again Gordon had exhibited his "magic" invincibility, and Ch'ang-chou was taken—in what was Gordon's last battle in China.

From a military point of view, the Taipings, after nearly fifteen years of spreading death and destruction, had been defeated. In a deposition, Li Hsiu-cheng, the rebels' Faithful King, just before his execution, wrote: "The disasters at Soochow and Hangchow were occasioned by the mischief of the foreign devils in the pay of Governor Li. . . . It was not [Governor] Li Hung-chang, but the foreign devils who were capable of capturing Soochow and other districts. . . . the sight of money made the devils reckless of their lives."[5]

Gordon made a quick visit to the Nanking environs to help plot the Imperialists' final blow against the rebel capital. But it had been decided that the Ever Victorious would not take part in the assault. The glory would go to the Imperialists—appropriately so in view of the long years they had borne the brunt of fighting.

On July 19, 1864, the rebel capital at Nanking fell. As the Imperial army led by General Tseng Kuo-fan's brother, Tseng Kuo-ch'uan, poured through a sixty-yard breach blown in the city wall by sappers, the Taiping cause was lost. Most of Nanking's rebel defenders died in the fighting. Of the survivors, some 100,000 died either at the hands of the Imperialists or by suicide. Witnesses of the carnage reported that large groups of Taipings huddled together as they immolated themselves. Others drowned themselves rather than be captured. The fires in the city burned for three days, leaving only desolation as the Imperialists' price. A few escaped—including the son of Hung Hsiu-ch'uan, the T'ien Wang, to be later hunted down and beheaded. Thus ended one of the world's worst wars.

Hung Hsiu-ch'uan, the Heavenly King himself, had vowed he would never be taken alive, and before the Imperialists entered Nanking, the heart of his doomed realm, had ended his own life as the most honorable way to atone for failure. During his last days, the prospect of defeat had made him more erratic than usual. His acts were even more cruel and capricious; subjects who offended him were skinned alive or pounded to death. His last testament, in which he reaffirmed his faith in the Christian God, bequeathed with more symbolism than hope his crumbling kingdom to his sixteen-year-old son—a meaningless gesture. On June 1, in the long tradition of emperors who have lost their Mandate from Heaven, he drank a lethal brew of pulverized gold leaf in a chalice of wine, and in terrible agony returned to the God who had dispatched him to fight sin on earth.

After the fall of Nanking, the late Heavenly King's body was exhumed and his head sent to Peking, where it was mounted on a pole for all who entered the Celestial City to see. The Faithful King, Li Hsiu-ch'eng, was also beheaded after writing a proud memoir of the rebellion, and his head likewise was exhibited at Peking's city gate. While the Heavenly King committed unspeakable excesses and degenerated into a madman during the waning years of the Taipings, the stature of the Faithful King—or Chung Wang— steadily grew as he proved himself a brave warrior and compassionate victor. It was the Chung Wang, not the T'ien Wang or Heavenly King, who thus entered China's pantheon of folk heroes. His memory survived to become an inspiration for future, more successful revolutions China would undergo: Sun Yat-sen's overthrow of the Manchu dynasty in 1911, and Mao Tse-tung's Communist revolution in 1949.

It had been Gordon's intention that the Ever Victorious Army would be disbanded when its mission was completed. As early as May 10, 1864, on the eve of his final assault on Ch'ang-chou, he wrote his family that as soon as the attack was over, he would return to Quinsan and break up the force. "On these subjects, I act for myself and judge for myself," he declared. It was a credo that would guide him for the rest of his career, but in this case, the unilateral decision was made without the consultation of either the British Minister or the Commander of British Forces in China—a fact that neither appreciated. Gordon knew, however, that he had Governor's Li's approval. First of all, the Futai was anxious to end this drain on his treasury, and second, he feared that such a mercenary force under the wrong kind of leadership could turn on him, or become a menace to the general public. Moreover, because of British public outcries following the massacres of the rebels at Soochow, Her Majesty's government had canceled the Order-in-Council allowing Gordon and other British regulars to serve under the Chinese flag. Thus there could no longer be the responsible leadership of British officers. It had been fortunate that the Ch'ang-chou campaign had ended before the ruling was applied.

On Gordon's recommendation, Governor Li approved generous severance bonuses to the Ever Victorious, and by June the strange foreign-led army which had shed so much blood for China was no more. Gordon himself was handsomely honored by the Chinese, although he steadfastly refused to accept monetary reward. He wrote home: "I know I shall leave China as poor as I entered it." His greatest reward was the satisfaction that through his efforts, "upwards of 80,000 to 100,000 lives [by his estimate] have been spared." He was given the exalted Chinese rank of *ti-tu*, or provincial commander in chief, and became the first "foreign devil" to receive the "Yellow Jacket" and the right to wear a peacock feather in his hat.* Two special gold medals were also struck in his honor.

Gordon's new rank and status brought a glorious wardrobe of honor which took Gordon five hours to model before an audience of admiring mandarins. The sartorial trimmings pleased Gordon, although some of the buttons on the mandarin hat, he noted, "are worth 30 or 40 pounds," a sum he felt the Chinese "cannot afford over well." On one occasion, a portly old mandarin, who kowtowed before Gordon and respectfully backed away from him, tumbled ingloriously into a water vat used to cool the wine for the officers' mess.

The Regent, Prince Kung, took it upon himself to write British Minister Bruce in praise of Gordon and to recommend that the British government pay this gallant officer due honor as well: "General Gordon's title, *Ti-Tu*, gives him the highest rank in the Chinese army; but the Prince trusts that if, on his return home, it be possible for the British Government to bestow promotion or reward on General Gordon, the British Minister will bring the matter forward that all may know that his achievement and his character are equally deserving of praise."[6]

Bruce added his praise in forwarding the Prince Regent's letter to the British government, pointing out that Gordon had not only "refused any

---

* The origin of the Yellow Jacket order dates from the Ming dynasty, not the Manchu. As the last Ming Emperor fled from the invading Manchus, he dressed his forty-man bodyguard in yellow jackets, identical to the one he wore, in the hope that he could not be identified and singled out for death when his pursuers caught up with him. The new Manchu dynasty adopted the Yellow Jacket as the highest decoration of the empire, to be awarded only to those rendering great service in the defense of the Emperor. In memory of the Ming bodyguards who were willing to die for their Emperor, it was decreed that no more than forty honorees could hold this rank at one time.

pecuniary reward, but has spent more than his pay in contributing to the comfort of the officers who served under him, and in assuaging the distress of the starving population whom he relieved from the yoke of their oppressors."[7]

Gordon received a British promotion to brevet lieutenant colonel in recognition of his performance in China, although his basic rank in the Royal Engineers would remain captain for eight years more. A grateful government, but a less demonstrative one than Imperial China's, took note of Gordon's achievement by bestowing on the thirty-one-year-old hero the modest accolade of Companion of the Bath.

Shanghai's foreign business community, including such establishments as Jardine-Matheson and Dent & Co., whose approval of the Ever Victorious Army ebbed and flowed depending on how close the rebels approached Shanghai, also saw fit to express its gratitude. The somewhat ornate citation read: "In a position of unequaled difficulty, and surrounded by complications of every possible nature, you have succeeded in offering to the eyes of the Chinese nation, no less by your loyal and, throughout, disinterested line of action, than by your conspicuous gallantry and talent for organization and command, the example of a foreign officer serving the Government of this country with honourable fidelity and undeviating self-respect."[8]

A *Times* editorial of August 5, 1864, was typical of English press praise now that Gordon was the man of the hour: "Never did a soldier of fortune deport himself with a nicer sense of military honour, with more gallantry against the resisting, with more disinterested neglect of opportunities of personal advantage, or with more devotion to the objects and desires of his own Government, than this officer who, after all his victories, has just laid down his sword."

If Gordon laid down his own sword, figuratively speaking, he appropriated another physically from his adversary, the Faithful King, and sent it back to England as a trophy for the Duke of Cambridge, then Commander in Chief of all British ground forces. Gordon described the sword as having been personally presented to the Chung Wang by the Heavenly King.[9]

Governor Li was generous in his praise of Gordon, who, despite their rift over events at Soochow, remained a good friend for life and would once again come to Li's and China's rescue. Li called him "valiant, daring, industrious and able."

Although Li would not admit it, Gordon had done much to lessen the Governor's distaste for foreigners. The pious British officer had perhaps also given Li a more balanced opinion of Christianity. The Futai had been convinced that Western missionaries in China bore a heavy responsibility for the Taiping uprising. While he could never be completely disabused of this, he at least had found in Gordon one Christian whom he could respect. He had to conclude that there were things to admire in "foreign devils" with their strange religious convictions besides their talent for war.

For all Gordon's experience in China, his observations and views on Britain's China policy received a remarkably deaf ear. His thoughts were, however, memorialized in letters home. Regarding Great Britain's eagerness to impose rapid reforms on China: "If we try to drive the Chinese into sudden reforms they will strike and resist with all the obstinacy of a pig, and will lapse back again into old habits when the pressure is removed." Regarding British arrogance: "They [the Chinese] like to have an option, and hate having a course struck out for them as if they were of no account." Regarding military reforms and the fallacy of central control: "Change should be made gradually, on a small scale at first, and through the [provincial] futais, not through the Peking government, who are a helpless lot."

During his last summer and autumn in China, Gordon kept occupied by planning a new Chinese army, one which would place more emphasis on guerrilla warfare tactics and training. He also found time to perfect his comprehensive survey of the area around Shanghai.

With his usual abhorrence of lionization, Gordon was determined to leave China quietly. It may be a moot point whether he genuinely was embarrassed by the spectacle of public praise or whether he liked it too much and, therefore, feared it as a sinful indulgence. Whatever the case, Gordon's efforts to slip out of China unnoticed were unsuccessful. He dined normally at his officers' mess without announcing his departure, much less making a ceremony of it. He then boarded the faithful *Hyson*, his battle steed, and prepared to relax in his cabin. Then suddenly on the banks of the canal there erupted a cacophony of fireworks and artillery salutes. For more than a mile the Chinese had strung festive lanterns along the banks, and brass bands hooted a raucous accompaniment to the cannonading. What no one could see, fortunately, was a bundle of brand-new clothes trailing in the water behind the *Hyson*. Gordon knew that convention demanded he have a decent outfit to wear on the elegant P&O steamer which would take him home, so he bought the essentials, but he chose this curious method to rough up the new clothes lest the sheen of newness make him conspicuous.

After years of ugly conflict with casualties greater than in any other civil war in history, Imperialist Commander Tseng Kuo-fan had finally bested the Taiping rebels. For all their brutality, the Hunan Braves had acquitted themselves well. But it was Gordon who administered the *coup de grâce*. His strategic concept, better developed than Ward's, and his ability to thread his way through the labyrinth of Chinese intrigues, mercenary plots, and British bureaucracy made him deserving of praise. Gordon's personal bravery, as he daily courted death armed only with his "wand of victory," was the stuff of legend. In a time when Great Britain found its heroes in the service of empire, Gordon was for a moment a star—if perhaps an eccentric one.

PART III

Contentment on the Thames, Boredom on the Danube

11

GRAVESEND

God bless the Kernel.
—Graffiti in Gravesend in praise of Gordon, 1869

Gordon returned to England in January 1865 a hero publicly acclaimed for his defeat of the Taiping rebels, but he was unable to bask contentedly in his sudden fame. The praise which followed Gordon home from China released within him stirrings more discomfiting than exhilarating. He feared that an evil genie, whom he gave the nickname "Agag,"* dwelled within him, inciting his craving for recognition. Agag would have to be suppressed if Christian puritanism and proper humility before God were to survive. Gordon's friend and biographer Wilfrid Scawen Blunt described this inner conflict as Gordon's only serious failing and a source of continuous torment to him.[1] Gordon himself viewed this craving as a "snare," to proper humility, and frequently he accused himself of "hailing the tram of the world"—playing to the gallery.

In addition to offending a puritan conscience, fame brought Gordon unwanted lionization. Never one to enjoy social niceties, he became an artful dodger of all manner of invitations and secluded himself in his parents' home on Rockford Place, Southampton. Even there, fawning matrons and hopeful spinsters would try to capture him as a social prize. He would sometimes decline an invitation on the excuse he had to visit London, and when he actually found himself in London, he would avoid social entrapment there by pleading an obligation to return to his parents in Southampton. This strategy was costly in time, since his conscience always forced him actually to make the trip he had invented as an excuse. Both his brother Henry, who had a more keenly developed instinct for prospering in a traditional Army career,

---

* Biblical reference: Numbers 24:7. In a letter to his sister Augusta, Gordon wrote once: "I have not yet seen where Agag was hewn in pieces before the Lord, but I expect to find it. (He, Agag, is still alive in all of us.)"

and Augusta, his puritanical spinster sister, encouraged him to take advantage of his popularity to find a place in their society—even to find a suitable wife. But loath to exploit his position for military advancement and terrified by the thought of marriage, Gordon wanted only to hide in his Southampton refuge until a new Army assignment could take him back to the world he knew—the sooner the better.

Gordon also had to fend off the wishes of a loving and proud mother to brag about him. Even before his return home he had written to warn his family against sharing his diary with others. "It would be better for everyone," he said, if his exploits sank into oblivion. When he discovered after his return that his doting family had circulated his war diary among friends, he destroyed it in pique, forgetting that he had promised to lend it to his comrade-in-arms Moffitt, surgeon with the Ever Victorious Army (and soon-to-be brother-in-law), who planned to write a history of the campaign. Gordon's China adventures, nonetheless, became part of the lore of the family as well as the nation. Louis, his brother Henry's young son, remembered vividly the awe he felt hearing about his uncle's exploits in China. Gordon, for that matter, was always happier relating his stories to children, in whose world of innocence he felt most comfortable.

Coming home also meant seeing his friend Romolo Gessi again. Gessi was now with Garibaldi's forces, and since the Italian leader had left his exile in England to return and fight for freedom, Gessi would soon follow. In the meantime, he and Gordon enjoyed each other's company, and he was a frequent guest at the Gordon household. Always charming with women, Gessi attracted the stern, pious Augusta with almost as much ease as he did the more worldly mistress of the Southampton inn where he stayed. Gessi did his best to recruit Gordon to Garibaldi's cause, but as much as the thought of fighting with Garibaldi for Italian liberty may have thrilled him, Gordon was a British officer with obligations to his own country.

Gordon's father had always had reservations about his son's experience. As an officer proud to serve his monarch, he did not wholly approve of Charlie's risking his life for an alien, dubious cause. He had disapproved when Gordon resigned his appointment at Chatham and went to China, feeling that this was not a useful or justifiable war. Gordon's service with the Ever Victorious Army had been sponsored by the British Army in China and approved by Whitehall, but the old general never thought it the proper service for a regular officer to distinguish himself. As Gordon's contemporary biographer A. Egmont Hake wrote: "So deeply did General Gordon revere the ideal of the British officer . . . that Charles Gordon's acceptance of a foreign command gave him no pleasure; he was proud of his son, but he did not like to think he was serving among foreigners. . . ."[2] In this particular case, the general also believed that the Chinese should deal with their internal affairs without British involvement.

What his father thought of him was very important to Charlie Gordon. From China, he had written propitiatory letters even as he pursued his own course. When he returned home, he was pained to see his father dying. When the ailing general expired after considerable suffering on September 19, 1865, it made a deep and lasting impact on him. The sad event marked an important stage in his religious development. In a soul-searching "memorandum" entitled "My experience showing the order in which God revealed himself to me," written to himself three years later, he noted that the period of his "captivity," between his service in the Crimean War and 1864, firmly established his devotion to Christianity. Then, "At my father's death," he wrote, "I was brought to think how vain the world was to give satisfaction." Later, remembering this grief, he confided to a friend, "I used to walk out to Chalk [near Gravesend] in the afternoon and go into the churchyard and think about my father, and kick the stones about and walk back again."[3] Such lonely introspection was a large part of Gordon's "long, dreary struggle" for eight or nine months following his father's death.

Although by Army regulation Gordon could have taken a generously long furlough, the life of inactivity did not suit him. In September he applied for and was given a new posting as Commanding Officer of the Royal Engineers at Gravesend, charged with the construction of five new forts to guard the Thames approach to London. Two of the fortifications were to be placed on the Essex shore at East Tilbury and Coalhouse, while the other three would stand guard along the Kentish shore. It was a disappointment: a radical change of pace from leading four thousand Chinese mercenaries against the Taiping rebels.

Nonetheless, as a brevet lieutenant colonel, Gordon approached his new assignment with typical vigor, driving his personnel as though they were fighting in the front lines. But the whole project, the inevitable product of a jittery Parliament which had voted extravagant appropriations in a moment of alarm when France once again seemed threatening, was a useless waste of time and money (£12 million, to be exact).

No stranger to fortifications, Gordon saw immediately the fallacy of the Gravesend defenses. Any invader would only have to land farther down the river, flanking the forts along the Essex marshes. Although the *Gravesend Reporter* assured the townsfolk that with Gordon's arrival they could rest easily, Gordon, as usual, was not reticent about his disapproval. Memos on the subject had obviously been ignored in headquarters; so on one rare occasion when Gravesend was visited by the Army Commander in Chief, the venerable Duke of Cambridge, Gordon took the opportunity to describe the folly of the project. As an implicit denunciation of his superiors responsible for this costly misjudgment, his remarks could have been interpreted as insubordination, but the incident went unnoticed. It was such outspoken comments, however, that gave Gordon his reputation in the service as a prickly nettle—a trait which did not endear him to many of his fellow officers.

Gordon not only worked his men hard but drove himself on the job as well. That there was no particular urgency did not prevent him from imposing his own stringent deadlines. One of Gordon's clerks, who worked closely with him, attributed his drive to a horror of letting work accumulate.

Time was always important to Gordon. He was compulsively restless and gloried in self-discipline. He replaced his boat carrying a single pair of oars with a gig with two pairs, for example, so that he could make better time traveling from one work site to another. Visions of coxswains exhorting their crewmen at the Henley Regatta could be conjured up as he shouted to his Thames watermen: "A little faster, boys, a little faster!" The work day always found Gordon dashing about the construction sites, issuing orders and pushing for quicker progress. He was known to glance at his pocket watch and say, "Another five minutes gone . . . we shall never have them again."

Gordon rose early and began his day with a cold-water bath, that symbol of Christian asceticism which still endures in a few British public schools. Prayers and Scripture reading, of course, followed. His monklike regime never permitted anything but the most minimal breakfast. Food was not to be made a ritual. It was meant to assuage hunger and sustain life, not to provide a pleasurable pastime or even promote bread-breaking camaraderie among friends. To find pleasure in eating was antireligious, a catering to the flesh. Much later, even when death seemed near, Gordon found time to wonder philosophically "why men cannot be friends without bringing their wretched stomachs in." As in China, he would gulp down raw eggs from the larder to give himself energy, or munch on bread crusts swilled about in tea to soften their stale crustiness. He also believed that eating aggravated his angina pectoris, a condition which worried him early in life.[4] Later he suffered from liverish flare-ups which must have made food even more unappetizing.

Gordon's official duties ended at 2:00 P.M., leaving him a long afternoon. Sometimes he indulged himself in his hobby of photography, which he had taken up during the Crimean War. The camera, still a novelty, appealed to his engineering mind because of its accuracy: "It tells the truth better than any letter." Soon, however, he would banish photography from his life as frivolous and time-consuming when there were more worthy things to do. He devoured the daily newspapers, which he had sorely missed in remote corners of the globe. And there would be more Bible reading before the day ended. He did little reading of other books, although he did occasionally pick up a classic. More often he would thumb through his favorite religious books: Bishop Joseph Hall's *Christ Mystical* (1654), Thomas à Kempis's *The Imitation of Christ*, and Cardinal Newman's *Dream of Gerontius*.

Two years after his arrival in Gravesend, in July 1867, Gordon met the Freeses, a fervently Christian couple and their three small children, who were to become especially dear to him. Octavia Freese, particularly, was a friend with whom he could discuss Christianity in all its doctrinal intricacy; they exchanged serious thoughts by correspondence for the rest of his life. The Freese relationship was an important one to Gordon, alleviating much of his loneliness. It offered to him the comfort and pleasure of family life which he chose never to recreate himself. He gave their young children special nicknames and played with them as a doting father would.

Mr. Freese, although genuinely fond of Gordon, was much less close to him than was his wife, Octavia. It was she, not her husband, with whom Gordon later corresponded. Even while in Gravesend, Gordon would frequently dash off notes to her. For all their close friendship, however, he always addressed her as "Mrs. Freese," and concluded his letters with the very proper salutation "Sincerely yours, C. G. Gordon." While their relationship had begun with their common interest in Christianity, Octavia

Freese seemed also to have fulfilled a need for feminine companionship which he was unable to gratify otherwise.

Octavia Freese preserved in her writing a vivid picture of Gordon's life at Gravesend. Her insights are important in knowing him as a person. Fortunately for latter-day biographers, she left a collection of unpublished letters and recorded some of her impressions in a slim volume entitled *More About Gordon*,[5] published anonymously in 1894, a decade after his death. Having been withdrawn soon after publication—perhaps under pressure from Gordon's family—the valuable little book attracted scant attention.

Mrs. Freese first met Gordon as a result of his frequent purchase of religious pamphlets from the Religious Tract Society, a missionary endeavor which she had been instrumental in founding. This led to an afternoon at Home Mead, the Freeses' residence in Milton-next-Gravesend. Gordon was "difficult-to-label," Mrs. Freese remembered; she was struck immediately by his "almost boyish looks and some of his utterances, . . . an eye and expression that might have been a thousand years old."[6]

The Freeses and Gordon would often go walking together. "We rejoiced in his companionship," and "his superior mind, striking out as it did, a truth here, suggesting a deep thought there." To the Freeses he projected an aura of fascinating mysticism—and those eyes!—"light gray and fine in shape . . . intensely penetrating and clear. . . . [They] could see through a millstone. He saw through everybody in a most wonderful way."[7]

When, a few weeks after their meeting, Gordon chanced on the topic of China, Mr. Freese asked ingenuously if he had seen anything of the Taiping Rebellion. While the Freeses knew Gordon as Commanding Officer of the Gravesend engineering detachment, they were quite oblivious to the fact that he was the Gordon of China fame. They were startled when he blurted out: "I should think I did; why it was I who put an end to it!"[8] It was typical of Gordon's modesty not to have raised the subject before, but the tenor of his impulsive reply, once triggered, betrayed the genie, Agag, who always lurked within him waiting to confound his Christian humility.

With the Freese children, Gordon would invent little games to delight them. He would dash upstairs to the nursery when they were slow to bed, shouting "Naughty, naughty!" with mock fury. Then in tenderness he would call the children "angels" and ask, "Where are your wings?" For treats, he buried silver coins in his garden, then gave them clues to guide them in their glorious treasure hunt. Gordon had named his garden "Paradise" and gave the Freeses a key to it. And paradise it was to the children, who would romp there and watch the ships glide along the Thames, bound for adventures in their imaginations. Gordon became particularly close to the Freeses' four-year-old son as the boy convalesced from a severely burned hand. Gordon wrote to him for years afterward.

The world of adults was more complicated for Gordon. When Mrs. Freese chided him for not eating properly and blamed this on his excessive smoking, he huffily told her that he would not take that kind of criticism even from his own mother. And Gordon seemed disconcerted when the Freeses at first—before they knew better—tried to invite him over at specific times. He had a horror of formal social engagements, preferring to drop by as the spirit urged him. In like spirit, he reminded them that his door was always open to them, although they learned that if Gordon did not feel in the mood to receive friends, he would seclude himself in the far reaches of his spacious residence, known as the Fort House.

With the Freeses he could discuss religion to his heart's content and plan charitable projects, but he avoided the usual social events at Gravesend lest he have to endure forced conversation. Even in his last days in Khartoum, feeling depressed and betrayed by his country, he still railed about dinner parties in his correspondence. In one letter he wrote: "I dwell on the joy of never seeing Great Britain again with its horrid, wearisome dinner parties. . . . At those dinner parties we are all masks, saying what we do not believe, eating and drinking things we do not want. . . ."

Yet more frightening to him were the widows and spinsters of Gravesend, for whom he was "eligible." One widow of an officer killed fighting with Gordon in China misinterpreted his several compassionate visits and asked him hopefully what his intentions were. Gordon retreated quickly, shattering her dream with assurances that he had no intentions whatsoever. Then there was the good Miss Surridge, who asked Gordon to think of her at Christmas when she would be "all alone." Ignoring the hint, Gordon replied, "I will," adding that he hoped he would be "alone" as well. Another widow, grossly overweight, could only arouse in him the sentiment: "I should be very sorry if she trod on my toe."

While in Gravesend in 1867, Gordon closely followed the news that General Sir Robert Napier, Commander in Chief of the Bombay Army, was preparing to lead an expeditionary campaign to the mysterious country of Abyssinia. Mad King Theodore, Christian monarch of the untamed highlands, was holding a small colony of Europeans, including British Consul Captain Charles Duncan Cameron, in squalid and cruel captivity. Despite four years of patient negotiations, the King refused to release them. The trouble stemmed from a slight the unbalanced King felt after Queen Victoria failed to respond to a letter from him complaining that Moslem Turks were oppressing Christians in their realm and asking that Her Majesty please "arrange for the safe passage of his ambassadors abroad" through the Turkish-dominated Red Sea. It seems that the Foreign Office had misplaced the letter, and it was never received. When the Queen tried to make amends by sending a special emissary, a courageous Christian Arab from the British consulate in Aden named Hormuzd Rassam, Theodore seized him as well.

By August 1867, when Theodore ignored a final demand to free the hostages, the British had reached the end of their patience. The decision for war was made by the new Conservative government under Lord Derby. Units of the Indian Army, including forty-four elephants to carry the heavy mountain guns, were assembled by Napier for what promised to be a difficult campaign.

Gordon eagerly volunteered for duty in Abyssinia, but on what seemed to him the flimsy excuse that the force was being drawn only from the Indian Army, his application was rejected. He was bitterly disappointed. In his gloom "he shut himself up for a whole day before he could get over it—and went through something."[9] The "something" was apparently an attack of depression, or the "doles," as he called it.

The 1868 Abyssinian campaign, which involved transporting 32,000 soldiers to the Red Sea from Bombay by a fleet of 280 ships, was probably not Gordon's kind of war anyway. The orderliness and efficiency of the campaign reflected the good leadership of Napier. Gordon's approach would probably have been to beard the Abyssinian ogre in his den at Magdala and try through sheer force of will to convince him to release the hostages. But just as Gordon risked his life eleven years later by visiting Theodore's successor, King Johannes, to negotiate in vain a territorial dispute, such an attempt at personal diplomacy would probably not have succeeded with mad Theodore.

Napier led his army up the steep mountain trail to the high, isolated plateau of Magdala only to find that Theodore, while defending his stronghold, had shot himself in the mouth rather than face defeat. The victorious general returned to England in triumph. He had earned a peerage and was given a vote of thanks by Parliament. Great Britain had won a timely victory—proof that the empire was not to be trifled with.

Gordon, who usually detested official functions, attended a military levee in honor of Napier in July 1868 and found it "not unenjoyable": "It was a glorious sight," he admitted. In his usual original style, tinged with his faith, he wrote Mrs. Freese: "The event is over and all are a day's march nearer home." Obsessed with death, he added: "Napier, feted and honoured, toils on that march to the haven of rest." As for Theodore, he was at home . . . with "his upturned face, eyes staring up into the blue expanse of heaven, into which we may trust his bright and glorious soul has entered."

Gordon would always remember Gravesend as the place where he experienced a revelation, another milestone on his road to salvation. He learned "the secret," and immediately wrote the good news to Mrs. Freese. "While dressing rather listlessly before dinner," she wrote in her book about him, "his eye fell on an opened Bible . . . and on these words: 'Whosoever confesseth that Jesus is the Son of God, God dwelleth in him and he is God.'[10] . . . It flashed upon him that he had found a jewel of priceless value—he had found what alone could satisfy him, oneness with God."[11]

Just as a Christian missionary tract, piously entitled *Good Words to Admonish the Age*, ignited the spark which drove Hung Hsiu-ch'uan to launch a cataclysmic revolution in China, Gordon's glance at a page in the Bible nourished his Christian rebirth and guided him in his own crusades— happily more constructive ones. This curious coincidence was never noted by Gordon, if indeed he ever knew how Hung had first been attracted to Christianity. But perhaps both men's minds had at least one thing in common: a special craving for a faith which could provide solace for inner torments.

Gordon was a compassionate man, and, once introduced by Mr. Freese to a Gravesend social worker, he threw himself into local charities. Once a week, at least, he devoted his afternoon to visiting the sick and aged poor at the Workhome Infirmary, handing out a "bit o' baccy" to the old men and a "screw o' tea" to the women.[12] To one old man, too weak to do anything but read, he sent a life subscription to the daily newspaper. Gordon's dedication to the poor may be judged also by his act of donating the gold medal, especially struck for him by the Emperor of China, to Canon Miller's campaign to raise money for the victims of the Coventry "cotton famine," whose jobs had been lost when the U.S. Civil War interfered with cotton shipments from the southern states.

This was a time of great need in England. The Industrial Revolution had left a legacy of poverty and squalor in the cities. One of those good souls moved to help the poor was William Booth, whose Christian "Whitechapel Mission" in London's East End was opened just before Gordon arrived in Gravesend. Gordon visited the mission and was clearly inspired by Booth's work. Gordon came to enjoy working similarly with homeless or deprived boys, particularly those who hung about the fishing docks. (The Whitechapel Mission endures to this day as the Salvation Army.)

W. E. Lilley, a clerk at the Royal Engineers office, joined Gordon in his charity work, and after Gordon's death published a monograph entitled *The Life and Work of General Gordon at Gravesend*. With sentiment approaching hero worship, Lilley wrote: "It had fallen to the lot of a few to enjoy a closer intimacy with Colonel Gordon than he accorded to his ordinary acquaintances. . . . they humbly tried to help him in some of his philanthropic work, and they were rewarded by the affectionate interest which he took in their welfare and that of their families."[13]

"Kings" and "lambs"* were terms Gordon used for the homeless boys whom he rescued from poverty, gave food and clothing, taught to be literate and in some cases provided shelter at his Fort House residence. Biographers have written at length about this, but there is no more eloquent testimony than a letter scrawled by one of the "kings" and sent to Lilley after Gordon's death:

> During the time I went to General Gordon's house, I met several other lads who, like myself, were ailing, and whose parents were unable to provide the nourishment they required. To prevent our suffering thus, the General invited us every day to dinner and tea, when we would eat from the same joint as himself. He paid 16s or 18s per week for the admission of three of us, a little boy and girl and myself, into the Royal Sea Bathing Infirmary at Margate.

---

* For "kings," Gordon would sometimes use the Chinese *wang*. The appellation was inspired by Revelations 1.6: "And hath made us kings and priests unto God." "Lambs" refers to Christ's "flock" of followers.

. . . I thank God that I was one of the three, for it was there that I was cured; and not only did he pay for our being there, but for the riding to and fro.

. . . Every evening there would be a dozen or more boys, mostly fisher-boys, who did not go to school, at an evening class, held in a room adjoining the General's sitting room, when the reading and writing was over, they would play at chess or draughts, and in the summer, at cricket.

When the boys were old enough to go to work the General would procure them a situation in some ship and sometimes in a War Department vessel at Woolwich. . . .[14]

Gordon's Christian compassion was interesting for the fact of the violence that surrounded his military career. Gordon once confessed to Octavia Freese that he had wept over his wounded soldiers in China. "It was this sympathy for the harshness in the lives of others that made him get the boys together to teach them, feed them, sit up all night mending their clothes [Gordon begged her not to mention that], then find them situations and follow the career of each of them. . . ."[15]

Gordon derived deep personal satisfaction from his work with the boys. In a letter written to Mrs. Freese after a visit to Warwick and Kenilworth castles, he mused: "Would you have cared whether you were Guy, Earl of Warwick, or the shoemaker of the village *now?* . . . all are in ruins. . . . How far better it is to be allowed to be kind to a little lamb than to govern kingdoms."[16] He was rewarded with the boys' responses. At the end of the school day in Fort House, the "scuttlers"—another pet name for them— would shout at the top of their voices his favorite hymn, "A Day's March Nearer Home." On the walls near Fort House, anonymous youthful admirers scratched "God Bless the Kernel," and similar adulatory graffiti.

Consumed by his own Christian faith, Gordon became an ardent evangelist for the rest of his life. The boys he befriended had to listen to his Christian lessons, his entreaties to accept "the secret"—the essence of Christianity. But his efforts went well beyond his own flock of "scuttlers"; he would scour the countryside for unwary subjects to whom he could hand Christian tracts which he had composed himself, sometimes with the help of Mrs. Freese. Irreverent junior officers delighted in watching, through telescopes, their commanding officer as he flagged down farmers in the field and pressed his tracts upon them.

Gordon visited a prodigious number of schools and churches on his charitable rounds. The Ragged School was his most frequent port of call, but there were also the schools at Perry Street and Princess Street and the variety of Sunday schools where he conducted Bible classes.

Holy Trinity Church Night School in Gravesend was the first school at which Gordon taught. He issued his young charges a card admitting them to class, and he set forth stern rules of behavior. The boys were admonished to be punctual and well scrubbed, to be "quiet and orderly," and to "pay proper respect to the teachers." Each boy was required to pay a halfpenny each night he attended, but if he observed the rules of conduct, the accumulated pennies would be credited to his account and refunded at Christmas and Easter with a bonus.

According to Lilley, Gordon's life at Gravesend was the "most peaceful and happy of his life," yet even there he was not free from those attacks of depression he called the "doles." Mrs. Freese noted the periods of "imaginary woes or fits of low spirits," but was impressed that he did not succumb to his melancholy or engage in self-pity. He would only become angry with himself, and immerse himself in religious contemplation. To a lady of Gravesend similarly afflicted, he prescribed a remedy of simple hard work. He told her to stand for a day at a washtub. Gordon observed: "Kitchen maids and warehousemen never get it [the doles]—if they did they would soon be driven out of them by their lords and masters. [Doles] are confined to those who are more or less idle and who have time to have them."[17]

Mr. and Mrs. Freese were privy to a strange drama involving the neurotic Sir William Gordon, member of the Gordon clan, with whom he had served in the Crimea. Gordon frequently complained to Mrs. Freese that Sir William "was strongly and, to his mind, strangely attached to himself." Sir William pressed upon him expensive presents and threatened to bestow upon him a very handsome inheritance. Only by accepting a silver tea service, which Gordon justified because it would pay for his own burial service, could he talk his friend out of the embarrassing gesture. Gordon considered Sir William "a sore trial," but he did not want to hurt his feelings.

During a visit to Sir William in Scotland, Gordon became alarmed at what he considered Sir William's suicidal frame of mind—so much so that he hid Sir William's shaving razor. Because this upset the depressed man even more, he returned it. The very next day Sir William committed suicide, slashing his throat with the razor. It was a tragedy that troubled Gordon for the rest of his life.

Regarding members of his family, Gordon was usually reticent, but he would be quite candid with Mrs. Freese. He indicated that while he adored his sister Augusta, she could be trying. "[She] comes next Monday, and the place is to become a hermitage. I cannot help it; she likes it, so I shall tell my friends I am in New Zealand till she goes." He was also fond of his mother, but as she aged she clung to him oppressively. He visited her often in Southampton, but complained that on such occasions he could not leave her sight without being asked where he was going. And she insisted on being taken out for frequent drives. A high point for his mother on one of these outings was when Gordon saved her from a bolting horse.

The glory days of China receded gradually into the past, but on one occasion Gordon opened the front door of the Fort House to find a group of Chinese men with whom he had served in the Ever Victorious Army. There was delight on both sides, and the day was spent in fond reminiscences. In London, they passed a shop window cluttered with orientalia, and Gordon, spotting a mandarin yellow jacket, casually noted that he had been given a similar one by the Emperor. Suddenly his Chinese friends fell to their knees and kowtowed to him. It was the realization that they were in the presence of a man who held China's highest accolade that had set them banging their heads on the muddy pavement. A much chagrined Gordon ordered them to their feet.

Memories of China intruded on his Gravesend world another time when Gordon received a letter from Li Hung-chang, his old friend and onetime nemesis. The Futai wanted to express his best wishes for the marriage of Gordon's sister Helen and Dr. Moffitt, Gordon's friend and comrade-in-arms throughout the Ever Victorious campaigns. Foreshadowing things to come, Li added: " . . . if an appeal to arms should at any time become necessary, I shall . . . still be inclined to look to you for aid."[18] It pleased Gordon very much.

A military career consists of a succession of farewells, and Gordon's long assignment in Gravesend drew inevitably to a close. For all its official dreariness, it had been an enriching time. He had come closer to God and had found his charitable work fulfilling. Gordon the soldier had metamorphized into Gordon the champion of Gravesend's poor. The town would never forget him.

It was Easter Sunday when he first received an intimation of his next assignment—a further "unrolling of the scroll," as he referred to it. He received an invitation from the Gladstone government to fill a newly vacated position as British representative on the multinational Danubian Commission, a body formed after the Crimean War to oversee navigation on the Danube River. Gordon considered the offer carefully. The commission seat was a quasi-diplomatic assignment controlled by the Foreign Office, and so it would take him away from the Army for a while; despite his experience in the Crimea and his extraordinary service in China, the War Office did not seem able or willing to provide an active duty post abroad. Even though the commission job carried with it a handsome salary of £2,000 per year, Gordon viewed the Danube as backwater and accepted the post with a distinct lack of enthusiasm.

Before leaving Gravesend, Gordon presented to Mrs. Freese his Crimean diary as a memento of their friendship. At least it was almost all of his diary—he had torn out a few pages, leaving her to guess that the missing parts described some episodes of derring-do which he was too modest to let her read. He had, after all, to keep Agag in his place. He also promised his furniture to the Freeses, although the couple watched good-naturedly as he impulsively gave much of it away, bit by bit, to needy people in Gravesend.

To the Ragged School, in whose service he had devoted much time, Gordon left his Taiping battle flags. A yearly raising of the flags in fond memory of Gordon became a ritual for many years.

In Gravesend Gordon had found a happiness he would never know again. It was a difficult leave-taking. "Goodbye!" he told his friend W. E. Lilley. "I have all my anchors up, and wish it were a start for the better land."[19]

The Freeses accompanied Gordon to Dover to see him off. At their last lunch together, in the warmth of their friendship, Gordon rambled on. Mrs. Freese particularly remembered his philosophizing about marriage: "He said he felt so glad he was not married, for the pain of parting with a wife would be too great."[20]

Soon after arriving at his post at Galatz, still weary from his long journey, Gordon wrote Mrs. Freese: "I look forward to a terminus where there will be no more tickets or baggage or differences of language, where there will be one kingdom, that of Christ, and no more wars."[21]

12

GALATZ

. . . it is semi-civilized and therefore, worse than if thoroughly barbarian.

—Gordon on Galatz

Gordon felt isolated, and the small British community was of little comfort, even sometimes trying. "There is no bond of union yet between me and them," he complained.[1] His intense devotion to Christianity had caused a resentment of Jews, and he railed against the large Jewish population in Galatz. He thought them "an evil looking lot." In an unworthy burst of bigotry, he wrote: "You would certainly wonder that they should have been and are now the chosen people of God, and that our Saviour was one of their nation."[2]

Soon after reaching Galatz, Gordon received the distressing news that Mr. Freese had suffered a serious illness and had been forced to give up his business. Gordon wrote to express his sadness and concern, suggesting that Mr. Freese join him in Galatz as his secretary—with no duties beyond what he could handle—and take the occasion to rest, while Mrs. Freese and the children would be welcome to stay in Southampton, where Gordon's family could look after them. Gordon also suggested that Mr. Freese bring with him one of the Gravesend "laddies." Apparently he wanted to recreate his happy life of Gravesend, but the plan was impractical. Mr. Freese was too ill to be moved.

Gordon tried to immerse himself in his work—not that his duties were that demanding or interesting. The Commission was something between "the Thames Conservancy and the Elder Brethren of Trinity House." With time on his hands, he browsed through Byron, that "melancholy man." Although Gordon wrote the Freeses that he was "quite happy," his letters betrayed his nostalgia for Gravesend and the ones dear to him there. "I want you to do something for me," he wrote his friend Lilley, "vis. look in *now and then* at

133

Mrs. Patrick . . . and ask after Martin. . . . If you see the lads, Bowen, Birls, Ridley, let me know how they get on—also the Palmers."

Gordon found some pleasure in traveling about, seeing new places and new people. Sulina and St. George, the two southern mouths of the Danube, were desolate, dreary marshes, but at least it was a change from Galatz. "The inhabitants, mostly Russian, are happy and contented," he noted, then added fatalistically, "It will matter little in a few years where they (or we) have pitched their tents."[3]

Still, Gordon's opinion of the Russians, tarnished by his earlier experiences in Bessarabia, was not improved by his stay in the Danube delta. A visit to Kilia and Ismail, two fortresses blown up by the Russians in contravention of the Treaty of 1865, convinced him that the people there were far from happy. "They lament the Russians, who foment all troubles. Russia will soon make a move to get the strip of Bessarabia back again."[4]

Gordon was appalled by Russia's neglect and abuse of the Allied gravesites in the Crimea. The Russians were defensive about this and were barely civil to him when he inspected the British cemetery. But there was no denying the bodies dug up, apparently for their rings and buttons. Fearing such a fate, the French had reburied all their dead in seventeen large mausoleums.

Galatz offered Gordon little religious stimulation. An Italian sometimes talked to him about spiritual matters, but Gordon could not find much in common with a Roman Catholic. As far as Russian priests were concerned, Gordon thought them simply "agents of the government," interested only in manipulating the peasants.

Then came the news of the death of his youngest brother, Freddie. As a child, Freddie had cheerfully fallen in with his older brothers' pranks— sometimes at his expense. But Freddie never grew very strong and was always "anxious-minded," and Gordon felt guilty for not having seen more of him. In February 1872, Gordon wrote to Octavia Freese with sorrow:

> Eight years ago, one bright Sunday morning, I went out to a hilltop [in China] in this same month to read a letter from home which told me that God had gathered of our flock one brother. Two years ago, the same month, with snow on the ground, I sat with the dying Sir William Gordon, and today finds me in much the same weather with a telegram announcing the death of my youngest brother. All repining is rebellion and can do no good. Would you have events altered? If we would, we put ourselves in the

position of Alphonso X of Spain, who said if he had been with God at the creation of the world, he would have advised him better.[5]

Freddie had died, leaving a wife, Frances, destitute with six very young children. While Gordon had not approved of Freddie's marriage to Frances in the first place ("she has a hard-looking jaw which promises a very acidulated old age"), and disapproved of their having such a large family, he now took out £2,000 of life insurance with Frances as beneficiary. Gradually he paid Frances the £2,000 so she would not have to wait until he died to receive the nest egg.

One bright spot in Gordon's stay in Galatz was his reunion with Romolo Gessi. Having left Garibaldi's army to marry a Rumanian woman in Bucharest, Gessi had embarked on a new business venture, a steam-driven mill at Tulcea which he was building. There were many occasions to visit the Gessi household from Gordon's *pied-à-terre* in the Rumanian capital—even though he preferred the simpler life of Galatz.

In time, Gordon became absorbed in his vision of a Danube–Black Sea canal linking Cernavoda and Medgidia, thereby saving four hundred navigational kilometers. His efforts to interest the British government in this ambitious project were unsuccessful, however, leaving him frustrated by the bureaucrats' lack of vision.*

While in Constantinople to discuss the canal idea with the British Ambassador—and bring him up to date on Danubian Commission affairs— Gordon by chance met Nubar Pasha, a shrewd Armenian who was Egypt's Prime Minister under the Khedive Ismail. Aware of Gordon's illustrious career in China, Nubar coyly asked Gordon if he might recommend a qualified military engineer to replace Sir Samuel Baker as Governor of the Sudan's Equatorial provinces. This was a scarcely veiled circumlocution, as Nubar wanted Gordon, himself, for the job.

Equatoria was the key to the slave trade moving northward from Central Africa. Slaving was of increasing concern to conscience-stricken Europe. The Khedive, debt-ridden and beholden to European bondholders, wanted a successor for Baker who would suppress the insidious trade. Nubar was

---

* Although a route different than the one proposed by Gordon was selected, a canal ultimately was constructed to speed Danube river traffic to the Black Sea.

quickly convinced that Gordon was the man, and Gordon was intrigued. Although he could not commit himself without permission from the British government, Nubar had planted a seed Gordon began to dream of. It offered escape from Galatz.

In December 1872 Gordon spent two months on leave in Southampton, visiting his ailing mother. He wrote Mrs. Freese, whom he was eager to see again: "I am an aide de camp in close attendance—no chance of getting away for a month." But in January he took the time to visit the Freeses in Chislehurst. "He was all joke and geniality," Octavia Freese noted, despite his being out to pasture in Galatz. She tried to console him by comparing him with Moses: "You are being prepared in solitude and loneliness for some great work."[6] He was clearly upset that the War Office showed little interest in him.

Before returning to Galatz, Gordon went with the Freeses and his brother Henry to pay homage to the just-deceased Napoleon III, lying in state at Camden House. Louis Napoleon, whose reign as Emperor of France had ended in exile after the Franco-Prussian War, had always appealed to him. "I think the Emperor was a kind-hearted, unprincipled man, a man who in the respectable world was a bad man," he wrote Mrs. Freese later, although the unflattering obituary did not detract from his admiration for Napoleon III. For all his own high principles, Gordon always seemed to be attracted to men of destiny and men who dared, whatever their failings.

Passing through Berlin, Gordon by chance caught a glimpse of the Kaiser in the Unter den Linden, doffed his hat, and received a gracious nod in return. Viewing the Kaiser's "old face," Gordon thought of "the Herald who will turn it to wax." Life is a "little stage, and the part is soon acted," he philosophized on death, his favorite theme.

When Gordon returned to Galatz, in February 1873, he found letters reporting the sad fate of his little "kings." One, who had gone to sea, died falling from the rigging, days before he was to marry. Another died from fever, while two others, merchant mariners, fell overboard in a storm and drowned. Gordon kept a list—apparently a very long list—of those for whom he prayed every night. Though he felt the loss of these boys, surely there was Divine reason for all things. And indeed, death's sting had to be less for those who knew that God dwelled within them.

Perhaps less easy to accept was his exclusion from a military expedition against the King of Ashanti in West Africa. The campaign, planned in the summer of 1873, would involve the kind of warfare Gordon understood well. The little genie Agag which lurked in Gordon's soul, waiting for an opportunity to prod his ego, must have danced a jig when the *Daily News* on July 24, 1873, referring to the Ashanti campaign, asked: "Can we account for that systematic neglect on the part of the Horse Guards of the high, we might say the transcendent, claims of 'Chinese Godron'?" The *News* hailed Gordon as "the best leader of irregulars that the world contains," and took the War Office to task for ignoring Gordon and perhaps even hoping "that his services may be forgotten by his country as well as lost to its army."

Gordon's more puritanical side subdued this spasm of Agag and resisted the impulse to leap aboard the "tram of the world." He was, in fact, embarrassed by the *Daily News* article, which he feared might be attributed to backstairs lobbying on his part. Moreover, Wolseley was being considered for command of the expedition, and Gordon did not want to be in competition with one of his closest friends. He made amends by writing an open letter to the paper, saying that he did not feel in any way "ungrateful" for the treatment he had received in the service.

Wolseley did get the appointment and sailed for Africa on September 11, 1873, leading British troops successfully in another of England's little wars. If Gordon wondered why his friend did not invite him to take part in the campaign, he may have reasoned it only fair, as Gordon had beat out Wolseley for command of the Ever Victorious Army in China.

In October, Gordon's mother suffered a paralytic stroke, and Gordon hurried home to Southampton. She could barely recognize him, and it was with some relief to Gordon that she died within a few days. He wrote to the Freeses: "I left my mother happily without suffering, but evidently on *her route to the better land*."

The leaden atmosphere of Galatz made Nubar Pasha's overtures seem more attractive with every day that passed. Later in October 1873, Gordon was exhilarated to receive a telegram from Nubar, formalizing the offer. He asked—and received—the government's permission for a leave of absence from the Army, and accepted Nubar's offer of the position in Equatoria. He convinced himself that he wanted the job, not for self-glory, but because he could accomplish something good for the world. He wrote his sister Augusta somewhat self-righteously: "After a study of Sir Samuel Baker's expedition,

137

gathered from his letters in the papers, I think he was guided by a wish to glorify himself." Gordon's own professed motives—to govern Equatoria well and to suppress the vile slave traffic—were reflected in his wish to "keep clear of any who might consider that they can claim from me any particular course of action." It was typical of him to insist on being free of compromising constraints, as taking orders was not easy for him. But another line in his letter to Augusta revealed the other Charles Gordon, eager for action: "To be happy is to be like a well-broken horse, ready for any event."

Gordon was back in England in January 1874, having gladly left Galatz to a successor. There were friends to bid farewell, and there was research to do on the virtually unknown area of Equatoria.

As in China's Yangtze Valley, the key to control in the southern Sudan was clearly the waterways. He was reminded of the valiant steamer *Hyson,* but on the Nile and its tributaries he would need boats that could survive the cataracts and brave the tangled marshlands of Equatoria. Alfred Yarrow, expert shipbuilder, counseled him to avoid screw drives, which could be easily bent by rocks in the cataracts, and instead to rely on stern-driven paddle wheelers. It proved to be good advice.

In his rounds of farewell, he described to Augusta a Miss Dykes, calling her "the nicest girl I ever knew," but added hastily, "do not be alarmed; the dead marry not." And in a note to his dear friends the Freeses, he referred to his journey as a hegira. Hejira, Arabic for flight from danger, hallowed by Mohammed's flight from Mecca to Medina, which began the rise of Islam, was vintage Gordon. For him, it was escape from the perils of English society to the safety of untamed Equatoria—a new odyssey.

Gordon talked over his new assignment with Gessi, of course. The adventurous Italian had been enthusiastic about Nubar's offer when it was first made, and had not hesitated a moment when Gordon offered to take him along. His wife would handle his new mill venture while he was gone. However much he had enjoyed his entrepreneurial venture, the lure of a new exotic adventure tugged more strongly.

Sir Samuel Baker's experience in Equatoria was important to analyze. The great explorer had been a trailblazer, and Gordon realized he could learn from the eminent explorer—certainly from his mistakes—but he was determined to do things his own way. In considering a plan to overlap with Baker, Gordon said no, observing: "I can do better without Baker; in a month I would know more than he does, whereas if I take him and do not follow his advice, he would be vexed." Moreover, Gordon did not believe Baker's assertions that slavery had been suppressed: "Born in the people, it needs more than an expedition to eradicate it."

Gordon believed that if the south could be opened to normal commerce, slavery would fall of itself, and he was determined to take a peaceful approach. He was "averse to the loss of a single life." If at this stage he presumed too much and rushed to hasty judgments, it was because his confidence flowed from his conviction that he had an ally, someone "richer than the Khedive and more knowledgeable of the country than Baker. I trust *Him* to help me out of every difficulty."

Gordon left for Cairo and the Sudan on January 28, 1874, his forty-first birthday. It was on this same date, as Gordon prepared to enter the African stage, that news of the death of David Livingstone, the dark continent's greatest pioneer, reached London. The famous missionary died by his bedside, evidently in a posture of prayer, deep in the heart of the Africa he loved. Also on this day, as Gordon was to depart, he sent a poignant postcard to Mrs. Freese. "He had drawn a lonely desert path which led up higher and higher to the sun, which was rather low on the horizon; one solitary traveller was walking on the lonely path, his eyes fixed upon the distant sun."[7] The only words he wrote on the card were "Isaiah 35, Goodbye."[8]

PART IV

Slavers and Brigands

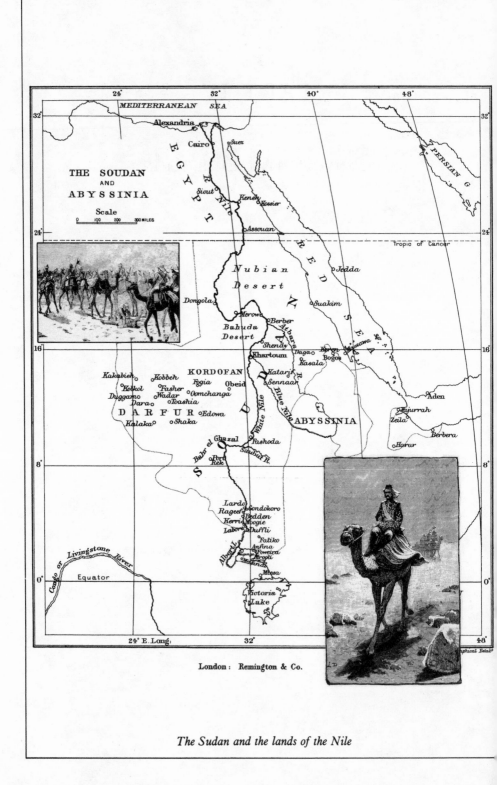

The Sudan and the lands of the Nile

13

EQUATORIAL BACKDROP

Egyptian society without slaves would be like a carriage devoid of
wheels . . . it could not proceed.
—Sir Samuel Baker, Governor of Equatoria

The Nile River, the longest river in the world, flows 4,145 miles from the center of Africa before escaping into the Mediterranean. Surprising though it may seem, the true source of the Nile was never found until 1937, when a virtually unknown German explorer, Dr. Burkhart Waldecker, found a small spring trickling down a hillside about one hundred miles from Burundi's capital, Bujumbura. The ever-growing trickle becomes a stream as it flows northward, joining with another near Kigali, capital of Rwanda, to form the Kagera River, whose waters debouch into Lake Victoria and nourish the Nile's great reservoir.

Europe's fascination in the mid-nineteenth century with Nile exploration and the then newly discovered Central Africa was soon tempered as the degradation of the Africans, cruelly exploited by slave traders, became known. Following in Sir Samuel Baker's footsteps in Egypt's Equatoria Province, Gordon would find himself the instrument of Khedive Ismail's efforts to combat slave trading and—more important to Ismail—to stake out his claim to the headwaters of the Nile.

To understand the history and dynamics of the Central African slave trade, Gordon had first to understand the role of Egypt in the scheme of things, particularly as he would find himself in a somewhat anomalous position as a British officer in the employ of the Khedive. It was a circumstance not unlike his role as leader of the Ever Victorious Army in China. With the opening of the Suez Canal in 1869, Egypt became a centerpiece of French-British rivalry. For Britain it was vital for its strategic position astride the shortest route to India, and for France it was an important link between its interests in the Levant and North Africa. As both prime mover and pawn in events along the Nile and Red Sea, Egypt would be important to Gordon as well.

SLAVERS AND BRIGANDS

The inauguration of the Suez Canal in 1869 had been an international gala event. The glitter of the occasion, however, was a small gesture to the accomplishment it honored. If Vasco da Gama's feat of reaching the Indies in 1499 by rounding the Cape of Africa was a signal triumph in the age of exploration, then Ferdinand de Lesseps's engineering accomplishment of digging a navigable canal across the narrow neck of the Sinai Peninsula, thereby diminishing the route from Europe to India by thousands of miles, was a triumph of technology in the industrial age.

The canal project had long fascinated Gordon. He had known de Lesseps in Constantinople, where he had also met Luigi Negrelli, who in 1837 was the first man in modern times to conceive the idea of a canal. Before he died, Negrelli told Gordon of his dream: to link the Mediterranean and the Red Sea with a navigable waterway. Now it was a reality.

For the thirty-nine-year-old Khedive Ismail, the opening of the canal was an occasion for basking in the glow of international attention. While still a tributary viceroy of the Ottoman Turkish Sultan Abd ul Aziz, he enjoyed virtual autonomy. The position of Khedive of Egypt had in fact been hereditary since the rule of his powerful Albanian grandfather, Mohammed Ali. Had it not been for the restraints of the European powers—particularly of France, which feared that Russia would benefit from any further weakening of Turkey—Mohammed Ali might well have seized the "Sublime Porte" and reversed the relationship with Turkey by making the Sultan his vassal. The Khedive Ismail was enormously wealthy and enjoyed the power and prestige that went with this happy state. Still ahead were the consequences of his financial profligacy, but for the moment he was spared the pressure of European creditors. On November 17, 1869, as the celebrations began, Ismail was content.

The Khedive had imported a small army of chefs from Europe to cook for the six thousand distinguished foreign guests invited. An opera house had been built in Cairo to be inaugurated by the premiere performance of Verdi's new opera, *Aïda*, written especially for the occasion by the great Italian composer. The Khedive's entire harem, occupying three large boxes, graced opening night. The pyramids of Giza and the Great Sphinx, crouching beside them as an enigmatic sentinel, were rigged with magnesium flares so they could be illuminated at night. A new town, Ismailia, named after the Khedive, was completed midway between the Mediterranean and Red Sea entrances to the canal and handsomely decorated to receive the Khedive's guests in splendor.

The canal was a monument to de Lesseps's genius and patience. The engineering challenge alone had been enough to make skeptics of most when the project was begun. The cost, which would ultimately amount to 287 million gold francs, was frightening, disease took a terrible toll of workers' lives and, of course, there were inevitable international complications. Even in de Lesseps's hour of triumph, he had to endure last-minute problems which, coming at this crescendo of celebration, must have been demoralizing. A warehouse of fireworks in Suez blew up, providing an unscheduled display of pyrotechnics which shook the town. And if that wasn't enough, one of the inaugural vessels ran aground, blocking the canal just as the parade of ships was about to make the epic voyage between the seas. De Lesseps, personally, had to rush to the rescue and detonate the obstructing vessel so that the show could go on.

Empress Eugénie of France led the parade of ships in the royal yacht, *Aigle*. The Khedive and a bejeweled entourage followed on his yacht, *Mahrousa*. The British, however, were represented by lesser notables. The Royal Family did not attend, perhaps because it did not want to be outshone by the French, but the Union Jack was flown from five British warships in the parade—a not-too-subtle reminder that Britannia ruled the waves even though the French were principal keepers of this critical gateway. The Russians, not to be forgotten, were represented by a sloop in the long line of ships, seventy in all, which graced the canal.

To celebrate the linking of two seas, the passengers disembarked at Ismailia to feast at a magnificent banquet and dance at a grand ball hosted by the Khedive. With full decorations and Paris gowns, the glittering gathering of Europe's elite danced under ten thousand lanterns as fireworks lit the clear Egyptian night. Africa was physically separated from Asia in a spectacle worthy of emperors, kings, and assorted potentates from all over the world.

The four-day celebration, however, was more than a recognition of a great technical achievement; it heralded Europe's new awareness of Africa and its intention to unlock the dark continent's secrets. Thanks to the canal, the East African coast would now be relatively accessible to Europe. Empress Eugénie's ride on a camel during the festivities presented a fetching tableau of Egyptian exotica, but the Suez celebration was anything but a frivolous outing. The revels of royalty could not obscure the significance of the event. Black Africa had lost its pristine isolation. Earlier exploration had tentatively lifted the veil, but the short sea passage to Africa's east coast offered by the canal now made serious European penetration possible. Commercial exploitation was only a matter of time.

When de Lesseps vowed to build a canal, and acquired from the Khedive Said not only a concession to do so but a promise to provide labor to the project, the British were unenthusiastic. From an engineering point of view, they were skeptical, and from a political point of view, apprehensive. While London could see the advantages of an uninterrupted short sea route to the East, the canal might one day provide a predatory enemy—one with the ambitions of Napoleon Bonaparte—with easier access to India. The prospect of French control over this vital link in Britain's imperial lifeline was discomfiting. Not only was de Lesseps, as a Frenchman, presumed to favor his homeland, but, more important, predominantly French capitalization of the canal gave France an important stake in Egypt. France and Great Britain seemed headed for imperial competition, if not collision.

Russia, too, was perceived by the British as a threat to India. The Czar's ambitions toward Turkey had not been satisfied by his defeat in the Crimean War. The so-called Eastern Question was still very much alive (and destined to erupt in another Russian-Turkish war in 1877). Were Turkey to fall to Russian aggression, Egypt, Turkey's vassal, would be in grave jeopardy, threatening Britain's access to India through the Suez Canal. The Russian shadow was also lengthening in the direction of Persia and Afghanistan, making Great Britain's rationale for keeping Egypt neutral and open as a transit route all the more convincing.

The Khedive knew that it was inadvisable to ignore the strong abolitionist movements in Europe, particularly in England, where antislavery organizations had found a powerful political voice. Europe was the principal source of the capital he must borrow to support his extravagances. The Khedive also had territorial ambitions beyond the Sudan. Egypt, whose existence depends on the Nile waters, had long had proprietary instincts about the great river's headwaters, as though some malign neighbor to the south or east might shut off the life-giving flow.[1] This fortuitous confluence of motives called for sending an expeditionary force to the Upper Nile to appease European antislaving pressures while at the same time extending Egypt's sphere of control farther south to the region of the great lakes.

A few months before the opening of the Suez Canal, the Prince and Princess of Wales had been treated to a private tour of the nearly finished project, and had watched the opening of the Bitter Lake segment near the Red Sea exit of the canal. Accompanying them as companion and interpreter was the great Nile explorer Samuel Baker and his charming new Transylvanian wife, both of whom had recently earned fame by their extraordinary adventures in discovering Lake Albert as they searched for the source of the Nile.[2]

The Khedive, perhaps with a sense of the theater, chose the occasion of a masquerade ball to offer Baker command of the expedition to conquer the Upper Nile. One wonders what costume Baker was wearing when he received this exciting proposition; he was not in any case concerned by the Khedive's complex motives. This was the opportunity of a lifetime for the Nile explorer; he could continue his explorations, indulge his passion for big-game hunting, and wield the kind of power the job demanded. He would lead an army of seventeen hundred men and receive a salary of £40,000 during the course of a four-year contract.

The expedition was to be escorted by two regiments of soldiers, one Sudanese, the other consisting of ex-prisoners recently released from Cairo jails, and a cavalry troop of two hundred horses. Sir Samuel Baker and Lady Florence farsightedly hired a personal bodyguard of forty-eight soldiers, whom they fitted out smartly in scarlet tunics and jaunty red fezzes. These stalwarts were given the sobriquet "The Forty Thieves," although they not only proved honest but on at least one occasion saved their employers' lives.

By February 1870, after a year of careful preparations, the Bakers and their small army were in Khartoum ready to set sail for Gondokoro, some thousand miles to the south. It was none too soon to leave as far as Baker and his wife were concerned. Both had taken an instant dislike to Khartoum when they first saw it in 1863, and it appealed to them no more now.

Settled by the Egyptian occupying authorities in 1821 because it was strategically located at the confluence of the White and Blue Niles, Khartoum had flourished more as a slave depot than as an administrative seat. Egyptian bureaucrats were generally oppressive as well as corrupt, and most of them were involved somehow in the slave trade, which the Khedive was pledged to stamp out. The unruly garrison troops, particularly the "Bimbashis," a polyglot collection of mercenaries recruited by the Turks to police their far-flung empire, made themselves unwelcome by extorting taxes and raiding the farmers' stores.

Nor was nature kind to Khartoum. Insufferable heat, flies and periodic dust storms which blackened the skies and coated everything with yellow grit for days on end made the townsfolk irritable. As a caravan crossroads, Khartoum perhaps held some excitement because of goings and comings of busy traders, and the relatively cooler, clear desert nights permitted one to forget for the moment the mud hovels that cluttered the crooked alleyways. At least the stars had beauty. But Khartoum's joys were few and miseries many. The Bakers found more appealing the prospects of the expedition, the certain promise of adventure, however harrowing it might prove.

Khartoum's small European colony was what might be expected in a frontier town not wholly tamed. It consisted mainly of a few hardy ivory traders, slave traders, and adventurers. One of the more interesting Europeans was a Welsh mining engineer, John Petherick. He had been sent to the Sudan by Mohammed Ali in the 1840s to look into rumors of coal deposits. When the great Egyptian ruler died, Petherick remained in the Sudan as a gum and ivory trader. He ultimately was made British Consul, but became controversial in the Foreign Office for maintaining a private army and spending more time in private trading than performing official duties.[3]

Baker understood the imperial objectives of the expedition. Simply put, "after crushing the slave trade," he would secure the Equatorial Nile Basin for Egypt. More specifically, he would install a strong government to control the warring tribes and, after establishing a system of steam navigation on the lakes, would erect a chain of trading stations. Telling the Khedive what he already believed, Baker wrote: "As the prosperity of all Egypt depends on the Nile, it has become indispensable to annex for Egypt the two lakes [Victoria and Albert] from which it takes its source."[4]

Baker understood less well the complexities involved in suddenly freeing the slaves—even if this were possible. Once freed, all that the slaves needed to survive, he imagined, was work. "I shall insist upon their working for themselves," he wrote to his friend Lord Wharncliffe. And betraying a racist sentiment typical of his times, he added: "Unless by a vigorous authority compelled to work, they would quickly relapse into hopeless apathy and indolence. It is hopeless to think of elevating the Africans spiritually, culturally or economically to [the level] of the European."[5]

Florence Baker, Sir Samuel's courageous and beautiful bride, whom he had not long before bought at a Turkish slave market in the Balkans to prevent her from being purchased as a slave, was always by his side. She was a remarkable woman for her times, willing to share equally the hardships of her husband. In England gossips questioned whether the couple had the benefit of a Christian marriage, and there was much tongue-wagging about a woman traveling about in a heathen land. Even the practical Gordon expressed disapproval of unladylike behavior when he heard she had worn bloomers on her African trip so she could more easily ride on camels.

After nearly a year of preparation in Khartoum, Baker's formidable expeditionary force, more than a thousand strong, started up river for Gondokoro on February 8, 1870. The expedition was a difficult one. Their boats were trapped for two months in the Sudd, a vast marshland which began choking the river some one hundred miles into the Sudan and did not release its grip for another four hundred miles downstream. Finally reaching the post of Gondokoro, Baker renamed his primitive headquarters Ismailia in honor of his patron, the Khedive (a name, however, which never caught on), who would not have been flattered if he had seen the sad state to which the post had degenerated. The powerful slave trader Abu Sa'ud treated Baker with undisguised hostility and raised the neighboring tribes against him. By the time Baker felt ready to march southward to Bunyoro, Chief Kamrasi's kingdom, in fulfillment of Ismail's ambition of annexing the lake regions, Baker had only five hundred troops left beside his bodyguard, the "Forty Thieves."

The climax of Baker's mission was his southern campaign, which began on January 22, 1872. By April he had arrived at the tribal capital, a sprawling town of circular straw huts looking like haystacks, located near the present-day site of Masindi in Uganda. He found that Chief Kamrasi of Bunyoro had died and been buried in a long trench filled with his harem favorites while they were still alive. Baker now had to deal with Kamrasi's debauched and treacherous young son, Kabarega. When Baker gracelessly announced his annexation of Bunyoro, he not surprisingly enraged the new king, who had no intention of donating his realm to Egypt.

The young chieftain attacked ferociously and was driven back only because of the stout defense put up by the Forty Thieves. Baker's assertion that Kabarega had poisoned the soldiers with adulterated beer was disputed by an Egyptian officer who had been with the expedition. The officer later told Gordon that much of Baker's report had, in fact, been inaccurate.[6] Baker's rocket fire ignited the tribe's straw-hut village, which erupted in plumes of flame, but whatever hopes Baker may have had for winning Bunyoro as a peaceful vassal of Egypt also went up in smoke in what became known as the Battle of Masindi. Baker's mission had been frustrated, and Gordon would inherit Kabarega's hostility. When his contract expired in March 1873, Sir Samuel Baker was not sorry to leave.

Baker's claim that he had ended all opposition and had replaced hatred and insubordination with discipline and order was an exaggeration. And it was preposterous for him to write: "The White Nile, for a distance of 1,600 miles from Khartoum to Central Africa, was cleansed from the abomination of a traffic which had hitherto sullied its waters."

When he took command, Gordon described Equatoria as considerably less cleansed than his predecessor had claimed. Moreover, he would find misleading Baker's assertion that his term of office "expired in peace and sunshine." While Baker succeeded somewhat in policing the Nile as an avenue for slave movement and had clipped Abu Sa'ud's wings, he had done little to prevent slave trading from prospering in the hinterland out of range of the Nile. The natives in fact resented his high-handed rule, and Egyptian officials suspected that Baker was more interested in laying the groundwork for British rule in the Sudan than serving the Khedive's wishes. There was much left for Gordon to do—and undo.

14

ON TO GONDOKORO

The lesson must be clearly taught that even in those remote parts a
mere difference in color does not turn men into chattels, and life
and liberty are sacred things.

—Charles Gordon

Following in Baker's footsteps, Gordon would police the Nile. A
religious man of human compassion, he could sympathize with the
"natives." And, although a soldier, he could bear arms in defense of
Christian values as well as fight in traditional battles for Queen and empire.
While the British government on more than one occasion saw Gordon as a
hazard to official policy, he nevertheless seemed to be the man for the job.
There were those, however, who saw his appointment as a cynical effort by
Ismail to appease British public sentiment and mollify the bondholders on
whom the Khedive relied.

The Egyptian Khedive, of course, had his own motives for employing
Gordon—motives not entirely altruistic and not quite in the British
interest. The Egyptian bureaucracy had its reservations. Officials resented
an Englishman wielding such power: Gordon's zeal in prosecuting the war
against slaving could disrupt a practical, established order.

Gordon's approach to his Equatoria mission was different from Baker's.
Instead of devising grand schemes to stamp out slavery and institute
ambitious economic development, Gordon approached the job pragmatically,
not as a crusade or "mission of humanity."[1] He concentrated on stopping the
slave traffic at its origins. He was not ready, as Baker had been, to rely on
force of arms, and he was not eager, as Baker had been, to cater to Khedive
Ismail's imperial ambitions in Central Africa.

Gordon's style was also very different from Baker's. Just as Gordon had
refused high reward from the Emperor of China, he rejected the £10,000
annual salary from the Khedive which Baker had enjoyed. He settled instead
for minimum subsistence of £2,000. He wrote Augusta: "My object is to

151

show the Khedive and his people that gold and silver are not worshipped by all the world."[2] It was the Egyptian peasant who bore the brunt of the Khedive's bloated expenses, and Gordon wanted to lessen their burden, if only symbolically.

While Baker had devoted a year to assembling an elaborate logistical apparatus before beginning his Equatoria mission, Gordon gave little thought to such housekeeping. He hurried through two weeks in Cairo—just long enough to reach a meeting of the minds with the Khedive and recruit a small staff—before heading for his post. Gordon could benefit from Baker's experience, but it was typical of Gordon to want to operate without pomp and panoply. He had intended to take only one assistant with him and had to be convinced that more were needed.

Gordon, the sometime idealist, conceived an eminently pragmatic strategy. He saw the hopelessness of trying to outlaw slavery, a system deeply imbedded in the culture and economics of the land, and believed that it was the slave traders who first had to be put out of business. If their slaving could be stopped, the institution of domestic slavery would eventually die of malnourishment. To fight the slavers, he had to control the waterways—not only the Nile itself, but the big lakes, Albert and Victoria, as well. He also had to conquer the slave barons who plied the desert caravan routes remote from the waterways.

Baker had also believed in the need for curbing the slavers, but he saw his operations more as a way of promoting legitimate commerce.[3] Christian missionaries could, in his opinion, take care of the humanitarian objectives.

From the beginning, Gordon recognized that the problem had to be approached practically in Egypt, where British control was not yet established and there was no way to dictate what would be done. He wrote his sister: "When in 1834, His Majesty's Government abolished slavery, they had an irresistible force with troops at their disposal. In my case I have nothing of the sort. His Majesty gives a proclamation, and it is over. Needless to say, that's not the case in these lands." In confidence he confessed: "Egypt cannot exist without slaves, its economy would collapse."[4] In this matter, Gordon grew contemptuous of the Anti-Slavery Society, which wanted to see slavery disappear instantly with the flourish of a pen: "I do not wish to be hard on individuals, but on the class who are bigots [the Anti-Slavery Society] . . . who do not consider the other [practical] side."[5]

152

ON TO GONDOKORO

The Khedive gave Gordon an impressive title, "His Excellence, General Colonel Gordon, the Governor General of the Equator," and, more useful, a free hand. Gordon would be operationally independent of the Governor General in Khartoum and enjoy the privilege of corresponding directly with the Khedive. Pleased, Gordon thought the Khedive "an honest fellow."

The two shared similar views on the problems of Equatoria, and set these views down in a memorandum, dated February 16, 1874, on the eve of Gordon's departure from Cairo: "The Egyptian Government, in the hope of putting an end to this inhuman trade, has taken the factories [slave camps and caravans] into its own hands, paying owners an indemnity. . . . [It is resolved to] claim the whole of the trade with the outside world as a monopoly of the state. . . . If the men who have been in the pay of these adventurers are willing to enter the service of the Government, Colonel Gordon is to make all the use of them he can." If not, the terms of the memorandum would be enforced "with the utmost rigour of martial law."[6]

The memorandum wisely included a resolution that government troops would not raid the southern tribes for their stores of corn as they had traditionally done, but would grow their own corn and be otherwise self-sufficient. Government outposts, once established throughout the province, would cultivate the goodwill and confidence of tribal chieftains so that they could be persuaded not to wage war with one another as they had been doing. Going beyond practical mechanics, Gordon inserted a denunciation of race discrimination. "The lesson must be clearly taught that, even in those remote parts, a mere difference of color does not turn men into chattels and that life and liberty are sacred things."[7]

While he sensed that the Khedive was really quite sincere in his motives, Gordon was depressed by what he perceived to be the hypocrisy of the Egyptian bureaucracy in its attitude toward his mission. "I think I can see the true motive now of the expedition, and believe it to be a sham to catch the attention of the English people. . . . you have no idea of the intrigues here; . . . things cannot last long like this." Gordon was convinced that Prime Minister Nubar Pasha, the architect of the deception, had "humbugged" him, and not the Khedive, "an honest fellow."

Events in Egypt were in many instances determined by the rivalry between Britain and France for imperial advantage in Africa. Each country was alert to plots and ulterior motives on the part of the other. The French assumed that Gordon was a British secret agent, operating under cover as an Egyptian official, not an unwarranted assumption, given Gordon's unorthodox Army career. Gordon did, in fact, keep his compatriots informed; he regularly wrote to Stanton, a fellow Royal Engineer serving in Cairo as the British Consul. But that was expected of any British officer. Had the French realized Gordon's independence of mind they might not have been so suspicious that he was primarily serving British interests.

Gordon was not always a good judge of men, and this gave rise to problems later. Of the men he enlisted in Cairo, some were good, some were not. The one who would later prove the most troublesome, though able, was Colonel Charles Chaille-Long, an American veteran of the Civil War who had found a position in the Khedive's army. As the American described his recruitment in Cairo, Gordon sent him a note in Cairo one evening, informing him that the Khedive had agreed to lend him to the Equatoria mission. "You will command the soldiery," Gordon told him when they met, "I don't want the bother."[8] Then to Chaille-Long's astonishment Gordon mentioned abruptly that they would leave the next night. When the American protested that he could not get his kit together on such short notice, Gordon tossed him some clothes and a pair of shoes. After making Chaille-Long try on one of the shoes, he triumphantly asserted: "It fits perfectly," as though that was all that mattered.

Chaille-Long claimed to have had a confidential talk alone with the Khedive the next day. He quoted Ismail as saying: "You have been chosen as his [Gordon's] Chief of Staff for many reasons, chief of these is to guard the interests of the Egyptian Government. An expedition is being organized in London under command of a pseudo-American, named Stanley, ostensibly to succour Dr. Livingstone, but in reality to plant the British flag in Uganda." The Khedive ordered Chaille-Long to reach Uganda first and "make a treaty with the King," promising "a debt of everlasting gratitude."[9]

Chaille-Long's account of his meeting with the Khedive may well be exaggerated, as the American tended to inflate his own importance, but it would not have been surprising that the Khedive wanted a spy to watch Gordon. While he liked the Englishman and would soon come to trust and rely on him, he was very conscious that Egyptian ambitions in Central Africa could conflict with those of the British. Already Britain was casting covetous glances toward Uganda and the lake region from their mission to the Sultan's court in Zanzibar.

Chaille-Long brought along as secretary and interpreter for the mission Auguste Linant de Bellefonds, a French Arabist whom Gordon came to distrust. And so Gordon's Equatorial expedition was assembled in an atmosphere of intrigue in which British, Egyptian and French interests quietly stalked each other.

The expedition was a curious mix. In addition to Chaille-Long, who had served in the Union Army in the American Civil War, Major William Campbell, a veteran of the Confederate side, was seconded to Gordon's staff by the Khedive. Romolo Gessi, described by Gordon as a "most determined man with the disposition of Francis Drake," was entrusted with the important task of managing logistics from Khartoum. Gessi's assistants were Gordon's nephew Willy Anson and two other Englishmen, Frederick Russell, nephew of Lord Russell, and J. Kemp, whose specialty was steamboats. A German botanist named de Witt accompanied the group at his own expense so that he could pursue his professional research. Happy for the opportunity to explore this virgin territory, two German naturalists, Friedrich Bohndorff and Joseph Menges, were hired at modest pay as Gordon's personal servants.

Consistent with his strategy of winning over the slavers (it takes one to catch one), Gordon freed the infamous Abu Sa'ud from the Cairo jail where Samuel Baker had put him and made him his "Deputy for the East Bank of the Nile." Baker was aghast at this appointment, and complained in a letter to the *Times:* "It is useless to shut the eyes to the support openly given to the greatest slave hunter of the White Nile."[10] The Austrian Consul in Khartoum, Martin Hansal, however, thought Gordon shrewd in this choice, referring to Sa'ud's assignment as providing an "African foot" to a "European head."[11] As it would turn out, Sa'ud was a disastrous choice. Another Egyptian, Hassan Ibrahim, was named "Deputy for the Western Bank of the Nile." The appointment of two Egyptians, Gordon hoped, would dilute the impression that the mission was an all-European affair.

Getting to Gondokoro was not a simple matter: first Suez by train, then Suakin on the Red Sea coast of the Sudan by steamer, Berber on the Nile by camel, Khartoum by riverboat, and finally the thousand-mile ordeal paddle-wheeling up the Nile and through the dread Sudd swamps to Gondokoro. Arriving at Suakin on February 26, Gordon was clapped into quarantine for the night, probably because the Governor was not yet prepared to receive him.

With due ceremony, Gordon was officially greeted the next day in Suakin. He quickly set out for Berber, a dusty town trying to survive near the confluence of the Nile and Atbara rivers, with his 220-man camel-mounted military escort. This two-week, 250-mile journey across eastern Sudan's blistering desert was Gordon's first experience atop the perpetually bad-tempered but indispensable camel. He survived the experience, however, and in the years ahead he would often find himself covering very great distances on one of these incredible beasts of burden, and enjoying it. A four-day trip by steamer up the Nile brought Gordon's party to Khartoum on March 13, 1874. Obstructions in the Nile slowed the trip, and Gordon once had to shed his trousers to help pull the boat—despite the presence of crocodiles. "Crocodiles never touch you if you're moving," he observed.

Upon Gordon's arrival in Khartoum with his advance party, consisting of Chaille-Long and his Egyptian aide-de-camp Lieutenant Hassan Wassif—described by Gordon as "sallow and more trouble than worth"—he was met by the Egyptian Governor General of the Sudan, a sophisticated Circassian named Ismail Ayyub Pasha. The occasion was celebrated with a noisy brass band, which made each tune sound like the one before, and an artillery salute. Gordon thought it a "fine sight." Even finer was the good news which awaited him: Egyptian soldiers had finally been successful in clearing a passage through the Sudd so that Gordon would not be delayed in reaching Gondokoro as Baker had been.

Gordon found the people of Khartoum agreeable and hospitable. They greeted him with an odd shrill noise "like a jingle of bells and somewhat musical." He was struck by the air—so dry that a dead camel did not decay or smell but swelled up like a drum—and by the rats at night "circusing about everywhere." Gordon feared that "the older ones would eat the younger members of their families, for there are great outcries at night with lamentations and woe."

Even in primitive Khartoum, Gordon could not escape the social formalities he dreaded. At the banquet given in his honor by the Governor General, he stomped out in disgust when a shuffling line of naked women, clucking and chirping in native fashion, seductively beckoned a line of leering soldiers to join them in an orgy of dancing. Austrian Consul Hansal flung himself in the midst of the revels, earning Gordon's everlasting contempt; as the Governor General himself was on the verge of doing the same, Gordon beat his hasty retreat.

Protocol demanded that Gordon respond to the Governor General's banquet by hosting one himself. Chaille-Long claimed that he found Gordon in the kitchen washing some cheap plates he had hurriedly bought in the bazaar for the occasion. He was boiling up a quantity of tapioca for his guests. Coming to Gordon's rescue, the American unearthed a treasure of rich tinned victuals and splendid china left behind by Baker. The banquet tables with "snow-white table linen of finest damask, the service of Sèvres, the glassware from Bohemia" impressed even Gordon, and the party seemed to be a success as the officials made short work of the bottles of Veuve Clicquot, also from Baker's stores.[12]

During his week in Khartoum, Gordon issued a decree declaring ivory trading to be a government monopoly and outlawing armed marauders and gunpowder in Equatoria. Obliquely but effectively, Gordon was addressing the slaving problem. Without guns and private armies there could be no slave roundups. And if ivory was to be the exclusive province of the government, there could be no private traders using this as a cover for clandestine slaving.

As Gordon prepared for his onward Nile voyage, he learned that it had taken hundreds of men many months to conquer the choking grasses of the Sudd, where no one stranded can long survive—except for the mysterious pygmies called "Thoonies" who made the cruel marshes their home. When the soldiers clearing a channel had finally made a breakthrough, shortly before Gordon's arrival, it was as though a dam had broken. The released waters swept everything before it; bellowing hippos and thrashing crocodiles were jumbled up with careering boats.

The vast marsh barrier had consisted of aquatic plants, some with roots extending five feet into the water. The natives regularly burned off these grasses, the ash matting into the marsh until hard and damming up the channels.

The Nile steamer, struggling against the current, was frustrating with its slow pace. Gordon was anxious to get on and berated the captain for not making better time. But in more serene moments he enjoyed the panorama of exotic wildlife surrounding them. With the awe of a child he described crocodiles with open mouths, "garnished with teeth"; hippopotamuses, ungainly on land but as graceful as ballet dancers in the water; "monkeys with very long tails stuck up straight like swords over their backs"; and a herd of ferocious wild buffaloes "looking as black as coals" careering toward the riverbank.

Farther upstream, Gordon viewed the tribes who lived along the river: the stately Shilluks, the Nuers, the Dinkas, and other Nilotic tribes. Standing naked and ramrod-straight, often on one leg, the Dinkas had tall, polelike bodies that glistened like polished ebony, except when smeared with white wood ash to keep off the flies and mosquitoes. The Shilluks could be easily identified by the line of bubblelike scar tissue across their foreheads, like a black pearl headband and done for cosmetic effect by rubbing ash into deep incisions in the forehead. The Shilluks were also conspicuous by their hairstyles: matted disks of hair jauntily arranged like a high-fashion woman's hat that were also useful in keeping rain off the neck. There was a wraithlike quality to these magnificent tribesmen as they loped along the shore, spears in hand.

As he passed Aba Island, some 160 miles south of Khartoum, Gordon noted in a letter to his sister: "We were going along slowly in the moonlight . . . all of a sudden from a large bush came peals of laughter." The raucous chorus, it was discovered, came from migrating Danube storks, "highly amused at anybody thinking of going up to Gondokoro with the hope of doing anything."

Gordon had no idea that near this same spot, an ascetic by the name of Mohammed Ahmad ibn Abdullah, claiming to be a descendant of the Prophet, lived humbly in a cave by the river. Gordon and Mohammed Ahmad would never meet, but their destinies would eventually collide and change the course of both British and Sudanese history dramatically. As Gordon embarked on an African career which would one day make him a Victorian hero in life and martyr in death, Mohammed Ahmad was starting out on his own odyssey to become a Moslem Messiah, the long-awaited Mahdi of Allah. Each was a zealous servant of the same God of the Book, and each had a magnetism that attracted followers willing to die for his cause.

Absorbed in his own mission, Gordon in 1874 concentrated on the problem of the slave barons of the south and on the native kingdoms of Bunyoro and Buganda (the area of Uganda today), between Lake Albert and Lake Victoria—objects of the Khedive's territorial ambition. Gordon was not even to know about this obscure dervish zealot for another ten years, and before then it was inconceivable for him to believe that Mohammed Ahmad would ever pose serious problems for the Khedive's imperial plans, much less affect the British Empire.

Upon reaching Fashoda, Gordon's party changed to a faster steamboat, the *Bordein*, which had come up from Gondokoro. From the crew Gordon learned that the garrison at his future post had no idea of his arrival. More problems. Gordon anticipated a not too pleasant reception by the Governor when he appeared suddenly to take command.

As the *Bordein* stopped at the entrance to the Sobat River, a tributary of the White Nile, so that wood could be cut for the boat's boilers, Gordon saw a tribe of Dinkas terrified by the invasion of the smoke-puffing monster. He was reminded of his fire-breathing dragon the *Hyson*, which struck terror in the hearts of the Taipings at Quinsan. Here the naked Dinka chief approached tentatively, and as Gordon described it, grabbed each of his hands and "gave a good soft lick to the backs of them." Then the chief held Gordon's face and "made the motion of spitting in it," apparently his form of greeting. The chief was hungry as well; when offered food, he devoured it quickly, then grabbed the food before the tribesman beside him and ate it as well.

The steamer trip up the Nile was anything but idyllic. Restless as usual, Gordon became testy. In his memoir, *My Life in Four Continents*, Chaille-Long reported that Gordon slapped the ship captain's face in a fit of temper over a delay in repairing the engine. He yelled at his aide-de-camp, Lieutenant Hassan, and called him a "baboon." He kicked his German servant, Kellerman.[13] Was this another example of Gordon's temper on the same order as his hitting a fellow cadet with a hairbrush at Woolwich? Or were these incidents exaggerated—possibly fabricated—by Chaille-Long after many years of nursing a grudge against Gordon? It was on this journey that Gordon developed an enduring dislike for Chaille-Long. In a letter to his sister, Gordon confided: "[Chaille-Long]* is a regular failure. He is so feeble, he can do nothing at all. He lives on what he *has done*, and of course that does not help what *has to be done* now."

When, after Gordon's death,[14] many of his letters to Augusta were published, Gordon's estimation of Chaille-Long became public knowledge. Of course, the American was angered, reciprocating by maligning Gordon in reminiscence. Relations between the two men never got any better. In the meantime, Gordon and his Chief of Staff had no choice but to get along.

---

* In his letters, even to his sister, Gordon often left spaces blank rather than identify persons whom he maligned. But the context of his statements often revealed whom he had in mind. They certainly did in Chaille-Long's case.

15

EQUATORIA

Love cannot exist with slavery. . . .

—Sir Samuel Baker

On April 16, 1874, Gordon disembarked from the steamer *Bordein* at Gondokoro. As he expected, no one knew he was arriving. The garrison was a dismal place, consisting of a meager collection of straw huts. The three hundred or so dispirited Egyptian and Sudanese troops under Mohammed Ra'uf Bey exerted no authority beyond a half-mile radius; they were useless in maintaining security, much less exercising Egypt's sovereignty. The same was true of the other garrison established by Samuel Baker farther south at Fatiko.

Gordon was dismayed. Things had not progressed since Baker's departure, and it was clear the Baker had greatly exaggerated his accomplishments. The great Nile explorer had, moreover, antagonized most of the southern tribes whom he was supposed to defend from slavers and whose confidence he should have gained. Thus where Gordon should have found allies, he found hostility.

Baker's campaigns to secure Bunyoro, led mainly by the friendly chieftain Rionga, had succeeded for a while, but by the time Gordon reached Gondokoro, Kabarega had reinstated himself as King of the Bunyoro and showed no inclination of friendliness. Gordon did not want to do battle and so turned his attention to Buganda, southeast of Bunyoro on the northern shore of Lake Victoria.

Buganda's King, the shrewd Mutesa, was, unlike Kabarega, pretending friendliness. Having prospered by trading ivory and slaves to powerful Sudan slavers since the 1840s, Mutesa understood how pretense could sometimes work better than spears. All the same, he was building a strong army in the event force was required. And with a sense of diplomacy, he sent feelers to the Sultan of Zanzibar, who he hoped would provide a counterbalance to Egyptian expansion in Central Africa.

161

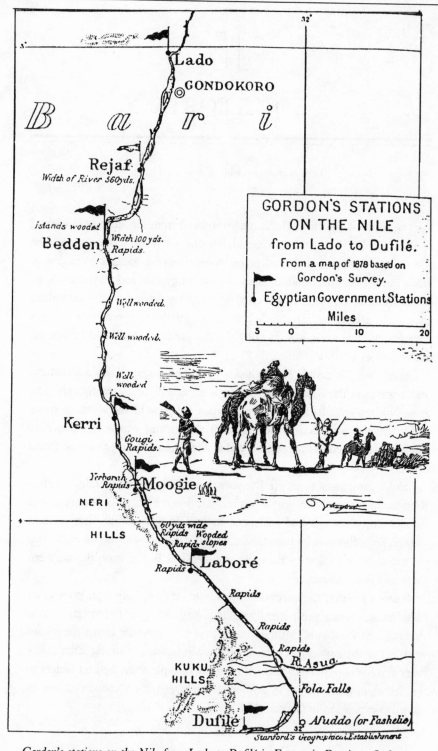

Gordon's stations on the Nile from Lado to Dufilé in Equatoria Province, Sudan

EQUATORIA

When Gordon arrived in Gondokoro, emissaries from Mutesa met him. They were probably spies scouting out the situation in Gondokoro, but Gordon took Mutesa's gesture of friendship at face value, hoping to gain the King's goodwill. He sent Chaille-Long off to the capital with gifts and conciliatory messages. Considering the state of the Gondokoro garrison, seen in all its weakness by Mutesa's envoys, Gordon had very few bargaining chips.

In his memoir, however, Chaille-Long recounted an entirely different version of how his mission to Mutesa came about. The veracity of his version is suspect, but it is interesting for the light it sheds on Chaille-Long's character. According to him, Gordon had no sooner arrived in Gondokoro than he announced his return to Khartoum to deal with supply and pay problems. "The Governor General knew nothing of my private instructions [to explore and annex Buganda] from the Khedive, and these were sufficient to prevent me from returning with Gordon. What if Gordon should insist upon my return to Khartoum?"[1] On the side, Chaille-Long took into his confidence Lieutenant Hassan Wassif, Captain Ali of the *Bordein*, and Ra'uf Bey, commander of troops at Gondokoro, and under cover of darkness secretly arranged to have his bags removed from the *Bordein*. "In the early morning I repaired to the steamer, arranged that Lieutenant Hassan was not within Gordon's call and, when the order was given to cast off, I stepped ashore. I waved my hand adieu, and finally it must have dawned upon Gordon that I had purposely remained, and the *Bordein* proceeded on her way without me."[2]

That Gordon never related this insubordination, even in his confidential correspondence with his sister, casts doubt on the truthfulness of the account. Chaille-Long may have found such embroidery necessary to substantiate his claim that the genesis of his Buganda mission was the secret agreement with the Khedive and that it did not involve Gordon; Chaille-Long would thus be the sole hero of exploration in Buganda. The absurdity of this implication can be seen in the memorandum written jointly by the Khedive and Gordon in Cairo: "In dealing with the chieftains of the tribes which dwell on the shores of the lakes, the Governor [Gordon] is above all to try to win their confidence. He must respect their territory, and conciliate them by presents. . . . Their obedience must be secured by making them dread his power."[3]

Chaille-Long set out for Mutesa's court laden with presents for the African leader: cottons, fancy silks, flannels, jewelry, precious stones and, best of all, a horse—which would be a startling novelty, as the people of Buganda had never seen one before.

In the meantime, Gordon—who, it must be presumed, had been the one to dispatch Chaille-Long to Buganda—retraced his steps to Khartoum. Learning that the baggage had been held up in Berber, he went on there to expedite matters. "The Governor General would have done nothing for months had I not arrived," complained Gordon. He consulted with his staff in Berber, then was back to Khartoum before long. Such dashing about in a land where travel was arduous and dangerous astonished the Governor General. He had not expected to see Gordon again so soon, and did not want to.

Gordon was imperious, and the two men argued over finances, division of authority, and reinforcements for the southern garrisons. In a letter home, Gordon admitted that he had been very undiplomatic to the Sudan's ruler, accusing him of "telling stories," but seemed to have gained satisfaction from the confrontation: "I think I have crushed him." Ismail Ayyub was not pleased, and it was disconcerting that the acerbic foreigner had the Khedive's confidence.

The main point of contention concerned payment of the Gondokoro troops. Gordon was outraged at the system, which frequently compensated the soldiers with slave girls and liquor rather than money. The Governor General was forced to provide the mission with an abundant supply of Austrian currency with which to meet expenses and to back down on the issue of Gordon's autonomy. An appeal to the Khedive had settled the issue promptly in Gordon's favor.

Before returning to Gondokoro, Gordon spent ten weeks establishing a new post at the mouth of the Sobat River, where it joins the White Nile—the northern boundary of his authority. Here he could intercept slave traffic plying the Sobat tributaries, and the west bank of the Nile at this point was Shilluk territory, where Gordon could repair relations with the warlike tribesmen, whose friendship he needed. But there were other problems.

The new garrison immediately attracted several Shilluk families who wanted to settle nearby for the security it provided. The first couple to build their straw hut outside the stockade was fleeing the wrath of a neighbor whose cow they had stolen. The aggrieved cow owner caught up with the culprits and after remonstrating with them, accepted their twelve-year-old child in payment. Gordon was aghast. "If the mother had expressed the slightest wish, I would have rescued the child again, but it was evidently a matter of rejoicing, and she did not care as much as if she had lost a handful of *ahura* [grain]." Apparently, to have feasted on beef was worth the loss of their child.

After that, a Shilluk tribesman brought him two children, ages twelve and nine, explaining that they were too great a burden. Rather than see them sold into the slave market, Gordon bought them for a small basket of *dhoora*— sorghum cereal—and gave them both away to staff members as servants. Here was Gordon, the antislavery crusader, buying slaves himself, though the circumstances were extenuating. It was a rude lesson in Gordon's education on the slave issue.

The low value placed on human life shocked Gordon. It was a testimony to the brutalization of the African as a consequence of slaving, and it reinforced Gordon's view that the ending of slavery depended no less upon civilizing equatorial Africa and introducing European values. His predecessor, Baker, had observed: "Love cannot exist with slavery—the mind becomes brutalized to an extent that freezes all those tender feelings that Nature has implanted in the human heart to separate it from the beast."[4] While Gordon was more sympathetic, he was no more optimistic: "It will be a very long time before much can be done to civilize them. The climate is against it; and there can be no trade for they have nothing to exchange for goods. Poor creatures; they would like to be left alone." He tried to institute the rudiments of capitalism. Rather than rely on a primitive and inefficient system of barter, he experimented with a currency system permitting savings. It was not a great success.

When two nuggers (native-made Nile boats) stopped at Sobat loaded with ivory and ebony, Gordon suspected trickery. He had the floorboards ripped up and found ninety-six ill-fated prisoners. The miserable men were freed, but none wanted to be sent home. "Home" was a concept that slaves did not understand. Even if a slave's village had not been burned to the ground in the course of the raid, the slave would only be captured the next time a slaver came through. As an expedient, Gordon settled this group as farmers around the Sobat garrison, but the experience made him wonder if there was no solution to the problem.

Women slaves brought the highest price. Relatively few ever reached the more distant markets of Egypt or Arabia, however, as most were appropriated as concubines by the Egyptian troops in the Sudan. Even if a slave was freed en route, her only practical solution was to become a soldier's wife or mistress. Learning this saddened Gordon, and when a captured chief's daughter was brought to camp, he, on an impulse of compassion, took the young girl to the primitive store in Gondokoro to outfit her with new clothes.

Nor were Egyptian administrators to be trusted. The officer whom Gordon had entrusted with the command at Sobat connived with a slaver and let a cargo of sixteen hundred slaves slip by. The boat was intercepted downriver at Fashoda, but Gordon was furious. The real culprits, he realized, were the Egyptian officials as well as the Khartoum slave merchants. They worked in tandem, the Egyptian officials growing fat in the transaction.

Gordon also began to realize that there was a basic fallacy in concentrating his efforts and resources along the Nile. Most of the traffic was moving freely overland in the west from Bahr al-Ghazal, a region long controlled by the great Zubair slaving family. Equatoria Province, in fact, had had relatively little slaving since Baker put Abu Sa'ud out of business.

While the slave baron Rahma Mansur al-Zubair controlled Bahr al-Ghazal, Equatoria had been the empire of Abu Sa'ud's father, the infamous slaver Ahmad al-Aqqad. In 1868 al-Aqqad had in fact been sold a contract by the Egyptian government providing exclusive four-year trading rights in a region of about ninety thousand square miles. But in 1871 the business had been taken over by his son, Abu Sa'ud, who fought in the Bunyoro uprising and otherwise made so many problems for Baker that he was captured and sent to Cairo for trial.

Gordon was determined to open a new station just upriver from the Sudd where the first habitable land emerged from the swamplands. This spot, Gaba Shambe, was assigned to Romolo Gessi and Willy Anson, Gordon's nephew, sent there to plant the local grain, *dhoora*. Gordon stopped by on his way to Gondokoro only to discover that Anson had just died of malaria and that Gessi seemed on the verge of death. Gessi returned with Gordon to

Gondokoro, but this marked the beginning of the sickness and death which would plague Gordon's mission.

Back in Gondokoro on September 3, 1874, Gordon faced another kind of staff problem. As Baker had predicted, Abu Sa'ud had reverted to type. He was overbearing in his manner and, worse, he was totally dishonest. Gordon caught him extorting ivory from the local chieftains and secretly inciting them against the mission, even after Gordon had given him a second chance. The former slaver had been useful. He had arranged for the submission of the neighboring native chiefs, something that Ra'uf Bey had not accomplished in six years, but his disloyalty was inexcusable. Gordon had no choice but to send him back to Cairo in disgrace. In a stinging letter of dismissal, Gordon wrote: "When I took you up to Cairo, there was not an Arab or foreigner who would have thought of employing you, but I trusted to your protestation, and did so. Soon, however, I came little by little to repent my action and to find out my fair treatment was thrown away. . . . You are an ambitious man, grasping man, and unworthy of the authority I gave you."

It is likely that Abu Sa'ud's intrigues and agitations were responsible for an attempt made on Gordon's life. The would-be assassin, a dissident chief called Larco, stalked into Gordon's tent after first surrounding it with a hundred of his warriors. The stolid Gordon wrote: "I watched his movements and then got up, took up my two guns, and put them down—ready. I then told him to walk off, which he did; I feel sure he meditated hitting me on the head with one of his knob sticks."

Casualties from illness grew steadily more numerous. By September, deWitt had died. Engineer Kemp was so ill that he had to be sent home. Russell, Campbell and Auguste Linant de Bellefonds would also have been evacuated but were too sick to travel; then before long de Bellefonds succumbed to fever. Campbell and Russell, barely alive, were sent to Khartoum. Shortly after arrival there, they too died.

Chaille-Long had successfully reached the Buganda Kingdom but ended up spending much of his time in King Mutesa's capital, Rubaga, convalescing from illness. When he returned to Gondokoro in October, he was still so sick that Gordon had him invalided to Khartoum for treatment. Except for periodic malaria attacks, Gessi managed to stay relatively healthy. The problem was mosquitoes, and there was not much that could be done about them. "Never let your mosquito curtain out of sight," Gordon told his men, "it is more valuable . . . than your revolver."

Despite frequent scorpion stings and recurring bouts of malaria, Gordon managed at first to stay in good health. He attributed this to Faith: "The intense comfort of no fear, no uneasiness about being ill is very great and more than half the cause of good health." But the other half of the credit he gave to a newfound nostrum. "I have been studying medicine a good deal, and found out a great thing, i.e. that 1 1/2 gram of ginger, 1/2 gram of Ipecucuanha and 3 grams of rhubarb make a splendid daily pill and can be taken without hurt for a lifetime." Another favorite was Werburgh's Tincture, which Gordon swore could cause a sack of sawdust to break out in a sweat.

Gordon received scant sympathy from Cairo when he complained of his casualty rate. The chief of the Egyptian General Staff, the American General C. P. Stone, only muttered, "The chief has no right to be ill," and that presumably went for his staff as well.

To avoid the dolorous, pest-infected atmosphere of Gondokoro, Gordon shifted his operations to two new stations on the west bank of the Nile. The principal one was Lado, just north of Gondokoro, and this became Gordon's provincial capital. The other was Rejaf, to the south, built in the shadow of an incongruous conical mountain piercing its flat surroundings.

The spells of melancholia which bedeviled Gordon occurred with greater intensity in Equatoria—exacerbated by his loneliness, the dreadful climate, harassment by the tribes and the inevitable frustrations of his mission. His therapy for the "doles" was to place a hatchet and a flag outside his door indicating his wish not to be disturbed. Thus secluded, he read the Bible until his depression passed. When he emerged from his room a few hours later, he was ready again to face the problems of the day.

Chaille-Long, in his memoir, described that on one occasion Gordon's lonely retreat could not even be interrupted by an assault on the stockade. The garrison troops were having difficulty "in repelling the savage hordes," as Gordon remained in his hut. Chaille-Long entered despite the hatchet and flag and found Gordon "seated calmly at a table on which were an open Bible and bottles of cognac and sherry." Chaille-Long tried to explain their jeopardy, but Gordon only answered abruptly: "You are commander of the camp." Chaille-Long retreated from the room and attended to the business at hand: "The savages were driven away by a vigorous sortie."[5] In *Eminent Victorians*,[6] Lytton Strachey repeated this story, going beyond Chaille-Long's reportage to suggest that Gordon was a drunkard. Strachey's catty innuendo went this way: ". . . the Holy Bible was not his only solace. For now, under the parching African sun we catch glimpses for the first time of Gordon's hand stretching out towards stimulant of a more material quality."[7] Strachey's unfortunate comments tainted Gordon's reputation for many years, though for Gordon to enjoy his brandy from time to time would seem quite normal—even making allowances for Victorian rectitude. Gordon's record of long hours, inexhaustible energy and total devotion to work should be a convincing rebuttal to Strachey's dubious insinuations.

Chaille-Long's implication that Gordon's oft-recurring depression immobilized him at desperate moments of danger is also suspect, even as Gordon's long record of bravery under fire speaks for itself. According to Bernard M. Allen, in *Gordon and the Sudan*,[8] no attack such as Chaille-Long reported took place. Chaille-Long's 1876 book on his Equatoria experiences, *Central Africa*, devoted nine pages to the period in question at Lado without making any reference to hostile actions by the natives—whom he described as friendly. Not until 1884 did Chaille-Long use the vignette in his self-serving *The Three Prophets*[9] and again in 1912 in *My Life in Four Continents*.

Gordon himself made no reference to the attack, even in letters to his sister Augusta, with whom he shared his closest confidences. Nor did Ernest Marno, an Austrian who was visiting Lado at the time, mention any such incident in his detailed diary or in two letters he wrote to the Austrian Geographical Society at that time.[10]

Gordon was eager to make progress in opening the territory to the south, a step necessary to block slave trading. When Chaille-Long returned from his mission to Mutesa in October 1874, nothing had changed. A treaty offered to Mutesa by Gordon earlier, in August, acknowledging Buganda's independence under Egyptian suzerainty, had been ignored by the African chieftain. But Chaille-Long had at last made an important geographic discovery: a major lake that existed between Lake Victoria and Lake Albert, interrupting the course of the Nile. The explorers John Hanning Speke and James Grant had earlier speculated that this was so, but Chaille-Long was the first actually to find it. Known today as Lake Kyoga, the American named it Lake Ibrahim in honor of Khedive Ismail's father.

Grant responded to Chaille-Long's discovery by stirring up opposition in the Royal Geographical Society to the Khedive's attempts to annex Buganda. In a letter to the *Times* of January 30, 1876, Grant wrote: "The English flag was the first to be planted there." Trade with the Kingdom of Buganda had never been conducted via the Nile and Egypt, but had moved eastward through Zanzibar. Moreover, he claimed acidly, Mutesa was in reality "more civilized than the Government [of Egypt] which is attempting their civilization. The nobel endeavours being made by Christian societies are ripening for the good of the races in Central Africa, and would be thwarted and opposed by the Mohammedan element."[11]

It was typical that Gordon should give exclusive credit to Chaille-Long for the historic discovery of Lake Ibrahim (Kyoga) without trying to attribute the accomplishment to his sponsoring mission. But there were still gaps of knowledge about the course of both the Victoria Nile and the Albert Nile before it could be determined that water communication between Gondokoro and Lake Albert and between Lake Albert and Lake Victoria was possible.

On his return from Buganda on October 18, 1874, Chaille-Long reported that Mutesa's capital had been moved to a site on Lake Victoria called Rubaga (near present-day Entebbe), where an astonishingly large army of some 150,000 well-armed warriors was garrisoned. Included in his entourage was his harem of two hundred rotund wives, whom he force-fed on milk to make them fatter; some were so large that they could no longer walk—only roll about. The African chief doubtless felt pleased that in addition to the gifts which had been showered on him by the Sultan of Zanzibar—including firearms—he could now boast that the Egyptians were courting him as well.

But Gordon's arrival in Equatoria had, in fact, greatly upset Mutesa. Chaille-Long reported that the African chieftain had urgently sought advice from court magicians, surrounding himself with assorted charms. While Mutesa had tried Islam and Christianity from time to time, this new threat from Egypt caused him to seek solace from more familiar, pagan gods. The gods were propitiated by daily executions of a dozen subjects as Mutesa watched from his leopard-skin throne, dressed in a gold-embroidered gown and an enormous white turban and holding a silver-mounted sword in one hand and an ornately carved scepter in the other. Accordingly, Chaille-Long might have felt encouraged, as well as horrified, that Mutesa had welcomed him in a macabre ceremony in which thirty people were sacrificed—

presumably the equivalent of a gun salute. But there had been no political progress.

Gordon's satisfaction with Chaille-Long's mission was qualified. Contact with the Mutesa had been amicable, but there had been trouble near Foweira, where Kabarega's tribesmen attacked Chaille-Long's party and harassed it all the way to Mrooli. Apparently Baker's old enemy the Kingdom of Bunyoro was still a menace. And now the American was ailing, adding to an already swollen sick bay. In a letter to Augusta, Gordon wrote: "I was made ill by the utter feebleness of my staff; my friend [Chaille-Long] came back sick; took possession of me as servant, and of my things as his; lost his own bed, took mine. I got wet and caught a chill." Chaille-Long was, in fact, very ill, and further friction with him was avoided when Gordon sent him off to Khartoum to recover.

Gordon's strategy was to extend his influence southward to the great lakes by establishing a string of small garrisons. These not only would serve a police function but would encourage legitimate trade which, he hoped, would eventually supplant the slave trade. The Nile was central to this plan as the safest and easiest way to travel, but what had still to be determined was where steamer travel would be interrupted by rapids or waterfalls. Above the new post of Rejaf, along the 130-mile stretch to Dufile, there was talk of unnavigable white water. Beyond Dufile to Lake Albert might be safe, but there was need for proof.

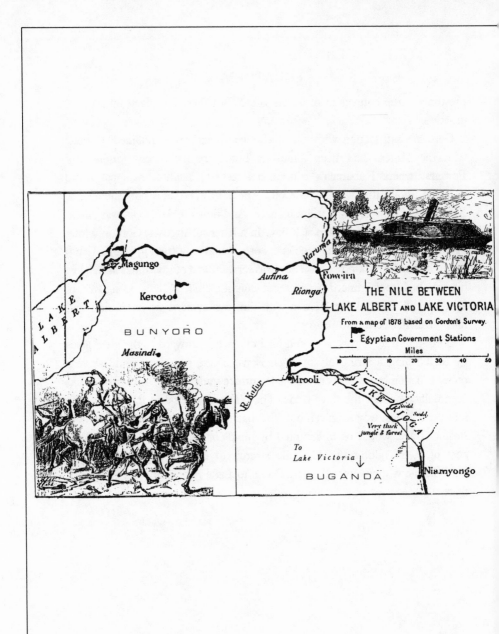

Gordon's stations on the Victoria Nile between Lake Albert and Lake Victoria

16

KINGDOM OF BUGANDA

It was years in time and has worn me very much. I shall never be fit for anything again.
—Charles Gordon on Equatoria and the Victoria Nile expedition

Gordon's plan was to carry the thirty-eight-ton steamer *Nyanza* and two smaller ten-ton sailing vessels in manageable pieces from Gondokoro to Dufile, above the rapids, where the boats would be reassembled. The problem was to find porters to do the job. The suspicious natives, whose hostility had been stirred up by Abu Sa'ud before Gordon fired him, could not be relied upon. Gordon disciplined a cantankerous chief named Bedden, south of Rejaf, by seizing his cattle, and this made even more difficult the recruitment of porters in the area.

Gradually Gordon won the confidence of the native chiefs, but then had to deal with another problem. If the friendship of the tribes was to be preserved, their grain could no longer be confiscated as the Egyptian army had done in the past. Grain now had to be imported all the way from Khartoum, but this would put Gordon at the mercy of lazy or venal Egyptian officials who could not be relied upon to make timely deliveries. The situation was further complicated by the Governor General's diverting grain to the southwestern province of Darfur, where government troops were closing in on the rebellious Sultan Ibrahim. The best solution seemed to be to send the dependable Gessi to Khartoum to oversee the operation, although that left Gordon shorthanded for his push to the south.

The most powerful slave trader in the Sudan was Rahma Mansur al-Zubair—known more commonly as Zubair. He was from the proud Ja'aliyin tribe in the north and traced his ancestry to the Abbasid caliphs of earliest Islam. (Abbas had been the uncle of the Prophet Mohammed.) As a twenty-six-year-old petty trader, he had pioneered the Bahr al-Ghazal region, where a network of tributary rivers rising in the west seeped through the Sudd to join the White Nile just south of Fashoda. His fortunes improved when he married the daughter of the important Azande chief Tikima, and soon his flourishing slave trade required him to build a vast *zeriba*, or stockade, to hold the slaves pending shipment. Strategically placed astride the main south-north overland slave route near the border of present-day Chad, Zubari's *zeriba* grew into the town called Deim Zubair ("Zubair's Town").

The Baltic German naturalist Dr. Georg Schweinfurth, the first European to discover the African pygmy, once visited Zubair at his estate—an establishment he described as "a king's court." The slave baron's large compound was filled with square huts surrounded by tall hedges. Schweinfurth wrote: "There were various state apartments before which armed sentries kept guard day and night. Special rooms, provided with carpeted divans, were reserved as ante-chambers, and into these all visitors were conducted by richly-dressed slaves who served them with coffee and sherbet." A special touch was given to the ambiance by chained lions which lolled about like house cats.

After reaching an alliance in 1866 with the Rizayqat tribe of the cattle-grazing Baggara people in southern Darfur Province, Zubair controlled the trade routes from Bahr al-Ghazal through Shaka in Kordofan to the north. He was reputed to have exported some eighteen hundred slaves yearly. By 1869 Zubair was in fact an independent ruler of Bahr al-Ghazal, having refused to pay taxes to the Egyptian Khedive and having fended off efforts by Khartoum to tame him.

Since the 1850s Bahr al-Ghazal had been nominally an autonomous vassal of the King of Darfur. Toward the end of 1869, however, an Egyptian army from Khartoum arrived to assume control of the area. Zubair opposed this interference, defeated the Egyptians in battle and killed their commander.

Faced with Zubair's presence and power, the Khedive in December 1873 annexed the Bahr al-Ghazal region as a province of the Egyptian Sudan but made Zubair its governor with the rank of bey. He was provided with regular troops but obliged to pay yearly tribute of £15,000 in ivory. Zubair no longer had to stoop to trafficking in slaves himself, but could control and profit from the trade of others through his territory. He not only had attained a certain respectability but was looked upon as a local benefactor by many slaves, who vied to work for him and enjoy his "generosity."

While Sir Samuel Baker had struggled to control the river traffic and subdue the tribes south of Gondokoro, Zubair grandly ran his western empire unmolested. Within a few months of Gordon's arrival in Gondokoro, the ambitious Zubair had marched into Darfur with his army of seven thousand men, and on November 3, 1874, he seized its capital, El Fasher. He had killed Darfur's Sultan Ibrahim in the advance, so he was effectively in charge by the time he claimed the kingdom for Egypt.

Zubair's motives were anything but nationalistic. He was simply enlarging his personal sphere of power. But to legitimize his move and forestall opposition, he sent word to the Sudan's Governor General, Ismail Ayyub Pasha, that his Darfur campaign had been launched for Egypt's benefit. Ismail Ayyub saw through Zubair's sham and rushed his government forces quickly to Darfur, but the wily slaver was already there, savoring his triumph.

Finessed by Zubair, Ismail Ayyub had no choice but to acknowledge the slaver's strength and to reward him with the coveted Egyptian rank of pasha. Inevitably the two men jockeyed for power. With good reason the Governor General feared that Zubair intended to consolidate his power and combine Bahr el-Ghazal with Darfur into an Egyptian province independent of Khartoum and coequal with the Sudan. At stake were not only the Governor General's power and prestige, but the commercial advantages of this vast area, equal in size to France. It was strategically located at the hub of overland slave traffic; along its southern borders were the coveted copper mines of Hofra el-Nahas. The Governor General ordered Zubair to retire to Bahr al-Ghazal in August 1875, but that had little effect on the slaver, whose enterprises continued to flourish.

As Gordon attempted to eliminate the Nile as an avenue for slave traders, the Zubair slaving empire to the west not only controlled Bahr al-Ghazal but dominated Kordofan and Darfur as well. Zubair was a law unto himself and was, in effect, challenging the Governor General's authority. Gordon privately reported to British Consul Stanton in Cairo on November 18, 1874, his dispute with the Governor General over Bahr al-Ghazal, pointing out the lie behind Ismail Ayyub's assertion that the government now exercised authority over the old slaver's domains. Gordon was granted authority in Bahr al-Ghazal, although it would be some time before his writ would become effective.

Gordon's perception of the Darfur drama was colored by his contempt for the Governor General. "News has come that the Darfur war is over. Darfur with Kordofan will be made a *hokumdircat*—a Governor General–ruled area reporting directly to Cairo and separated from the Sudan, which I am glad of. This conquest will have a great effect on these countries." Gordon did not realize that the fox had gotten into the chicken coop, with Zubair now threatening to become independent of the Sudan. This would put Gordon's own mission in certain jeopardy, but at this point Gordon only dimly perceived the danger. He was having his own more pressing problems in Equatoria.

Gordon's staff, almost totally depleted by illness, welcomed reinforcements in November 1874. The steamer *Tell Hewein* arrived in Gondokoro with two young officers from Gordon's own service, the Royal Engineers. The assignment of Lieutenant C. M. Watson and Lieutenant W. H. Chippendall had been in response to a request made by Gordon nine months before, and their arrival at this moment was timely. The new officers could lead the projected expedition to Lake Albert.

Arriving with the Englishmen was a young Frenchman, Ernest Linant de Bellefonds, brother of the dead Auguste. An adventurous spirit and a mastery of Arabic made him a welcome addition. Gordon immediately marked him to replace Chaille-Long at Mutesa's court.

Gondokoro's malarial environment was unendurable, and sickness continued to plague Gordon's staff. It was hoped that the more salubrious climate of Lado, where the mission would be moved at the end of December, would improve health, but the damage had been done. Engineer Kemp and newly arrived Watson had to be invalided to Cairo. Chippendall and Ernest Linant de Bellefonds were also stricken but fortunately recovered.

After six weeks of convalescence in Khartoum, Chaille-Long returned, bringing four hundred new troops to augment the garrison. Gordon was dismayed to learn that the American had been given Egyptians rather than the better-suited black Equatorial troops, and wrote home testily: "They were Arab!!! Now, out of 250 Arabs I brought here, I should say half were dead and 100 invalided; so you may imagine my horror. . . . This reinforcement was worse than useless." In fact, eighty-four came down with the fever the day after they arrived.

Making matters worse, Chaille-Long was backsliding into his old bad habits. A few weeks before, Gordon had written Stanton, asking him to thank the Khedive for promoting the American, "who has turned out first rate," but now "[Chaille-Long]* has tumbled back into procrastination and forgetfulness which annoys me."

Soon after the new year 1875 arrived, a party of five hundred laborers carrying ivory suddenly arrived in Lado from Fatiko under their leader, Wad el-Mek. This provided a welcome addition to Gordon's planned expeditions. To further augment the force, Chaille-Long was to march westward from Lado to Makraka country to find porters and to raise a new body of native troops. The American would be accompanied by the young Austrian Ernest Marno, newly arrived from Khartoum. Manpower was always the problem in mounting an expedition, but Gordon was nearing sufficiency.

With the launching of three new expeditions, one to Lake Albert under Chippendall, one to King Mutesa led by Ernest Linant de Bellefonds, and one to Makraka under Chaille-Long, Gordon was kept very busy. There were the inevitable problems of administration, and he could not easily break away and indulge himself in new exploration without letting things slip at home base. In early February, trouble broke out at the Sobat station when a dozen freed slaves stole some guns and attacked the garrison soldiers. Gordon had to rush to the outpost by steamer to get matters under control.

By chance, Gessi had arrived at Sobat escorting a London *Times* correspondent, Captain Frederick Burnaby, who had taken leave from the Royal Horse Guards to report on the Upper Nile. Burnaby enjoyed considerable prominence in England for earlier acts of derring-do. He would become well known for an intrepid ride by horseback to Khiva in Central Asia.[1] He would also fight in two military campaigns in the Sudan and forfeit his life by the Nile. But at the moment, the strapping guardsman was looking in on Gordon's antislaving crusade for the *Times*, and had arrived just in time to see Gordon at his best.

A flying visit from the "Great Pasha," as Gordon was fondly known in Equatoria, was always an event. Burnaby captured the atmosphere: "Nearer and nearer came the steamer—the one bugler nearly burst his lungs in ringing out the clear strains of a General's salute—the black captain lowered his sword and the 17 men composing the garrison brought their arms to the

---

* In Gordon's letter the name was omitted for purposes of discretion and a blank inserted, but the identity was obvious.

'Present,' as a short, thick-set man, who appeared to be in the picture of health and was attired in the undress uniform of a Colonel of Engineers, hastened down the ship's side and, approaching the officer and his small force, rapidly inspected the men and their accoutrements." If one did not look closely, it could have been Wellington inspecting his legions at Waterloo!

Gordon rounded up the former slaves who challenged the garrison and had them soundly flogged first, then, reported Burnaby, "the Colonel went steadily ahead, giving out one order after another, administering justice to the natives, censuring or praising officials, ordering punishment here and reward there."

In the southern expedition, Ernest Linant de Bellefonds and his small force easily covered the four hundred miles to Mutesa's village, Rabaga, near Lake Victoria. His mission, as explained by Gordon, was to make friends with Mutesa on behalf of Egypt and to convince the chief to give up trafficking in slaves. The Frenchman had also to persuade Mutesa of the advantages of legitimate trade between Egypt and the Kingdom of Buganda—a subtle way of inducing Mutesa to become a tributary of the Khedive.

An astonished Linant de Bellefonds soon found he was not the only white man at court. Henry Stanley was there, busy exploring Lake Victoria in an effort to prove beyond doubt that the huge lake was the source of the White Nile. Also intent on Christianizing Buganda, Stanley was there to lobby for the admission of missionaries as well as to convert Mutesa himself to the "true Faith." Stanley and Linant, a good French Protestant, joined forces, impressing the King with such biblical accounts as the Creation and the Flood, the story of Christ, and the nature of angels.

By the time Stanley left, he was satisfied that he had made a convert who would welcome British Protestant missionaries. Linant was similarly optimistic, if naive. Not comprehending the greater implications of a growing British presence on the Khedive's objectives in Central Africa, he volunteered to carry back with him an article which Stanley had written for the London *Daily Telegraph* calling for an early dispatch of missionaries to Buganda.

Linant could not be expected to conclude that English missionaries might be forerunners of British rule—for that matter, London's African policy had not yet crystallized. Nor did the Frenchman realize that while Stanley was attempting to win over Mutesa to Christianity, the shrewd chieftain was exploiting the explorer's presence to deflect Gordon's efforts to bring Buganda into the Khedive's orbit. Mutesa was, moreover, close to the Sultan of Zanzibar, who was a friend of the British. Close alignment with Egypt was therefore imprudent. Besides, Mutesa refused to believe that an Egyptian presence could be helpful to him when Linant denied his request to attack Buganda's Bunyoro rival, Kabarega. However well-meaning Gordon's policy of peace may have appeared, it did not satisfy Mutesa's need to remove Kabarega as a threat to his power in the lake region, and his resentment poisoned the negotiations with Linant. The hidden currents of African politics were not understood by Linant, however, and when he left on June 15 without any firm agreement—with only Stanley's article for the *Telegraph* in his pocket—he believed naively that his mission had been a success.

As this was going on, Chippendall's mission at Dufile was to stockpile stores so that a strong advance base for lake exploration could be maintained. That was accomplished. But the next stage, in which Chippendall was to explore a stretch of the Nile between Dufile and Lake Albert to determine whether it was navigable, was less successful. He had traveled only fifty miles upriver to Wadelai when he encountered a raging smallpox epidemic. Beating a hasty retreat, Chippendall returned to Dufile. Native reports had it that the Nile, southward from Dufile, was navigable all the way to Lake Albert, but the English engineer had not verified that with his own eyes.

Chaille-Long returned from his mission in Makraka in early March and briefed Gordon at Rejaf on the situation there.[2] Two days later the American was on his way to Cairo, never to return. Gordon had discussed with Chaille-Long an ambitious plan to advance on Buganda by way of East Africa. The distance between Cairo and Gondokoro was 2,700 miles, and travel was difficult, particularly through the Sudd. Mombas Bay on the Indian Ocean was only two hundred to four hundred miles from Egyptian ports, and the East African overland route from Mombas Bay to Buganda and the lake country was more salubrious than the Nile route from Gondokoro. Gordon proposed to the Khedive[3] that Chaille-Long lead such an expedition because of his experience in Rabaga, but it was obvious as well that Gordon, who now thoroughly disliked the man, was glad to have him leave Equatoria. Gordon insisted on complete secrecy surrounding the project for political reasons.

Chaille-Long in his memoir related his reservations regarding Great Britain's agreement on the "extension of the Khedive's authority to the Indian Ocean." He wondered if there was an *entente* between the Khedive Ismail and Gordon, acting on behalf of the British. "Was it possible that the British Government would wink at the enterprise if under Gordon's authority?" Adding to his suspicions, Chaille-Long noted that Gordon in his letter to him had specified that "the proposed expedition should be considered as belonging to his government." What did Gordon mean by "his government"?[4] Was it the Egyptian government for which he worked, or was it the British government to which he owed his basic loyalties? But Chaille-Long was eager to be off, and he left the next day on the mail steamer from Lado.

Turning his attention to the task at hand, Gordon was determined to put a steamer on Lake Albert. Without command of the lake, he could not establish the kind of permanent presence which the Khedive wanted and which would be needed if the tribes were to be controlled. The solution, however difficult, required transporting to a navigable portion of the river the materials necessary to assemble or build a boat. His plan was, first, to place a station on the Nile, a day's march away, where the necessary materials would first be transported. Another station, a day's march beyond, would then receive the materials, and so on, station by station, until they reached the head of the falls.

The Nile held other hazards. Herds of hippopotamuses, which churned the river, were powerfully dangerous. They resented Gordon's nuggers and did not hesitate to attack. "We were afraid every minute of being swamped by them. Sometimes they are very fierce and bite the boats in two! . . . Their strength is terrible."

Gordon had made a reconnaissance upriver from Rejaf during the first week of April. The more he studied the Nile, the more he began to believe that his steamer, the *Khedive*, might safely pass through the cataracts after all, provided the river was high. If he could navigate the river, he could establish posts along the banks, which would be preferable to inland on the trail where his men would be vulnerable to native attack.

Three nuggers made it successfully through the Bedden rapids. Then with the help of ropes the *Khedive* was guided through as well and was able to reach Kerri. But farther on it became more difficult. Gordon described a torturous day's efforts: "agony, . . . really quite painful—ropes breaking and nuggers going down a six-knot current. I am really quite exhausted." At the next rapids, Yerborah, one boat sank and the other two got stuck on the rocks.

Making matters worse, the Bari tribesmen could be seen creeping through the grass around the edges of the camp, making menacing little attacks. Gordon had high respect for the fighting spirit and skill of the Bari warriors: "brave fellows, [who] know that our soldiers cannot hit them in most cases when they fire, and so in they rush and it is over." Fortunately no attack had yet occurred.

It was not until August 20 that Gordon learned that the steamer *Khedive* was about to arrive from Kerri. As days passed and the boat failed to arrive, he feared that it might have fallen victim to hostile Bari tribesmen downstream. Ernest Linant de Bellefonds, now back from Buganda, volunteered to mount a commando raid against the Bari and burn their huts. This, Gordon hoped, might distract them and prevent them from attacking the *Khedive*, if they had not already done so.

Linant and his small party, most of whom were the elite guard—Baker's Forty Thieves—were last seen by Gordon on a hill across the Nile. Suddenly, as Gordon watched through his glasses, they vanished from view. Only one soldier escaped and staggered back to tell the tale; a Bari ambush had killed all but the bearer of the grim news. Ernest Linant de Bellefonds, like his brother and so many others, had given his life for Gordon's mission. In his pocket was found, and duly forwarded, Stanley's letter to the *Daily Telegraph* asking that missionaries be sent to Buganda. Making the disaster even sadder was the realization that the *Khedive* had not been in jeopardy and the mission had been in vain.

Disaster struck again when the *Khedive* was dashed against the rocks as Gordon tried to get it through the rapids. That would mean more delay while the vessel was unstuck and repaired. As workers struggled to free the *Khedive*, a Bari native stood on a bluff with his arms uplifted as though invoking the wrath of his gods, screaming curses at the wounded *Khedive*. The boat would not be budged, although it was Nile rocks, not Bari curses, that impeded progress. In desperation Gordon sent word to Gessi in Khartoum to come to his rescue.

Gordon began to despair. From August 1 to September 23, he had fought the river. "It was years in time, and has worn me very much. I shall never be fit for anything again." His new troops were showing signs of desertion. "The whole affair is like walking on rotten ice, you know not when a break may occur." A cow let loose among the troops as a *coojoor*, or hex, was making the superstitious troops very nervous.

Bad food and lack of cleanliness were nearly as depressing. Gordon did not want to appear to be "fastidious," but he admitted that "cockroach nests in your sugar, rice, etc., do not tempt one to eat." He dreamed of bananas, which he would find in the higher lands of Buganda. And there was tremendous loneliness: "I can talk to no one so I write a great deal."

It was October when the real blow fell.

It is all over! I started from Dufile this morning and, keeping on a higher level to avoid the wet edges of the river, came out about five miles from here. I fancied for some time I heard a noise like thunder, which increased as we approached the river. At least we stood above it on a rock bank covered with vegetation, which descended abruptly to the stream, and there it was appalling to look at, far less to think of getting anything up or down except in splinters. Of course, the idea is all over of taking up the screw steamer or the nuggers or indeed anything.

What Gordon saw was Fola Falls, which he called Makade.

Disappointment, tribal harassment and Equatoria's rotten weather plunged Gordon into another attack of the doles. "What a climate it is! The only thing (except God's keeping) to keep well is to keep employed at anything; never be idle or you will mope and succumb." Typical of Gordon were his pointed barbs as he shared his innermost thoughts in letters to his sister Augusta. While fighting depression and bad health at Fola Falls, he found strength at least to castigate Egyptian soldiery: "I have garrisons small on purpose to make them keep awake; and it has its effect, for they are in a frightful fright along the line. I cannot help feeling somewhat of a malicious enjoyment at their sufferings. I never, in the course of my life, saw such wretched creatures dignified by the name of soldier."

By the time Gordon had returned to Dufile, his liver was paining him gravely, with the climate more insufferable than usual. Then, when he reached Moogie post, his sergeant died of fever. This provoked an outpouring of anguish: "I am very low, I feel my servant's death . . . not that it is not better for him in all the miseries of this wretched land. God will make it up for him . . . it is all God's will and I hope I shall be able to bear it."

With the setbacks and disappointments, Gordon fell into a vile temper. He found fault with the Khedive for not answering his letters. When a letter did arrive, castigating him for drawing funds from the Khartoum government, Gordon, as he had done on more than one occasion in China, fired off an angry telegram tendering his resignation. But before it was sent, a flattering letter arrived from Egypt's ruler, telling Gordon that he was in overall command of a new expeditionary force being transported by sea to Mombas Bay in East Africa by (British) Admiral McKillop. So the Khedive had accepted his plan to approach Buganda from the east. Mollified, Gordon wrote his sister: "I could not, therefore, leave him; so the telegrams telling him I would be in Cairo were destroyed and I stay."

Gordon met Gessi at Kerri and put him in command of the Lake Albert project. With a thousand men, the Italian began his march past Fola Falls to Dufile, where he would reassemble his boat and explore Lake Albert. Just after Christmas, Gessi arrived safely in Dufile; Gordon could now turn his attention toward Lake Victoria and the vital reconnaissance mission up the Victoria Nile, which sickness had forced Chippendall to abandon. New stations had to be established along this stretch of the Nile if Egypt was to challenge Mutesa's control of Buganda.

Walking southward from Dufile, Gordon reached Fatiko, which had figured so prominently in Baker's day. After leaving a contingent of soldiers to man a small garrison there, he pushed on to Foweira, where he established another post. This was a desolate trek; Gordon found the uninhabited "vast, undulating prairie of jungle grass and scrub trees" very tedious. Thirty miles farther, past insect-ridden marshes looking like "muddy beer," the party reached Mrooli on Lake Kyoga (Lake Ibrahim), where still another station was established. This was ten miles from Masindi, where Baker had fought Chief Kabarega, but now Gordon found that the old enemy had suddenly decamped, permitting uncontested occupation of this strategic spot. The recalcitrant chieftain had vanished into the jungle with his "magic stool," an ancestral symbol of power which was supposed to guarantee the rule of whoever had it in his possession.

Gordon seized the opportunity to send soldiers to the vacated Bunyoro capital of Masindi and to Magungo on the western limits of Bunyoro to stake the Khedive's claim. When Gordon reached Mrooli district, seventy-three miles upriver from Foweira on the Nile, he established another station. Mutesa could begin to feel the Khedive's encroachment.

Gordon's plan had called for the expedition to proceed to Ripon Falls, where the Nile roars out of Lake Victoria to begin its long journey to the Mediterranean. But Gordon declined to lead the last advance in person, preferring to retrace his steps to Dufile. His health was now precarious. In his stead he sent a native officer, Nuehr Agha, with 120 men to set up two bases in Buganda, one at Cositza (Ripon Falls) near Mutesa's capital on Lake Victoria and one at Urondogani (Murchison Falls) near Lake Albert. In a dispirited letter to Augusta, Gordon wrote: "Everything seems to go wrong. It may be my liver which makes me think this. . . . Oh! how I wish I had finished this work. I have yet two months of weariness—shall I get through it? You will understand my grief at not having surveyed the gaps in the Victoria Nile. . . . If I were well I would do it, but I keep day by day feeling my liver more."

There was another reason for delegating command of the march to Victoria: fear of lionization back to England. Most Nile explorers gloried in this, but Agag needed to be leashed. In August he wrote his sister: "Now do not be angry with your brother, but he will not go on to the Lake, even if he gets the steamer up. . . . I do not care for wretched pinchbeck honours of this sort—perishable and useless."

When Gordon returned to Dufile on February 8, 1875, he found that the damaged *Khedive* had been floated off the rocks and patched, but it had been sent downstream for further repairs. The thirty-eight-ton *Nyanza* was still being reassembled above Fola Falls. Two nuggers were immediately available, however, so Gordon in early March sent Romolo Gessi and a new addition to his staff, Carlo Piaggi, to proceed with the reconnaissance of Lake Albert, while he himself returned to headquarters at Lado.

Then came the news that the expedition sent by the Khedive to East Africa under Chaille-Long to march on Buganda had foundered. Word had sped up and down the coast that the Egyptian invasion heralded a revival of the once-flourishing slave traffic through Zanzibar. British Consul John Kirk was predictably infuriated, and hovered offshore on board Her Majesty's warship

Thetis while London pondered the problem of the Khedive's embarrassing initiative.

Conscious of the antislavery sentiment in England as well as the strategic advantage of keeping a friendly Sultan of Zanzibar in power, free of Egyptian dominance, the British convinced the Khedive to stop McKillop and Chaille-Long's expedition. This news provoked Gordon to write wistfully on March 9, 1876; "The Khedive withdrew his troops from Juba [East Africa] by the command of the British Government." However disappointed he was to have his strategy scrapped, Gordon now realized how impractical the scheme had been and was honest enough to admit it in an apology to Consul Kirk.

So preoccupied was Gordon with forcing passage through the inhospitable Albert and Victoria Niles, with their terrible marshes, impassable cataracts, and surly natives, that he gave scant attention to larger British strategic considerations. In January 1875 he had analyzed the matter from his vantage point only: "The center of Africa would be much more effectually opened out, as the only valuable parts of the country are the high lands near Mutesa, while all south of this and Khartoum is wretched marsh." But Gordon's proposed course of action would also have disturbed the Abyssinians, already quarreling with Egypt, as well as Sultan Barghash of Zanzibar, a valuable client whose East African coastal territories would be violated. British Consul Kirk, charged with keeping a British perspective about events in East Africa, had blown the whistle.[5]

Gordon's liver revived and he was soon back at work surveying the Nile near Fola Falls. His quick recovery came as a happy surprise: "Is it not odd that since I left Foweira, where I was so unwell, I have been quite well—in fact, as well as ever?" Improving his spirits even more was the fact that Gessi's expedition to Lake Albert had been wonderfully successful. Gordon met his Italian friend at Kerri as he triumphantly returned full of stories of his adventures. In a report to Cairo, Gordon crowed: "The Egyptian flag was raised on Albert Nyanza [Lake Albert] on 10 April, 1876, and henceforward the navigation of that lake is vested in the Government."[6]

Gessi had circumnavigated Lake Albert in nine days and found it to be 140 miles long and 50 miles wide—very much smaller than Gordon had estimated. The party had been menaced by Kabarega's soldiers, whom they had had to fire on, but far more dangerous had been a fearful storm on the lake. "The rain was in drops the size of a dollar," and the Arab sailors could only huddle in terror and pray as their small boat was tossed on the waves.

Gessi's intrusion was terrifying to Kabarega. It was a harbinger of worse to come and spelled the eventual downfall of his supremacy along the eastern shores of Lake Albert. The distraught chief sought help from his neighbor Mutesa, who, he reasoned, was also at risk from Egyptian advances. Unlike Kabarega's hostile approach, Mutesa's tactics all along had been conciliatory, but on this occasion he gave Gordon frank counsel:

To Sir Canell Gorlden. February 6th, 1876
My dear friend Gorden hear this my word—be not angry with Kaverega Sultan of [B]unyoro. I been heard that you been brought two manwar ships but I pray you fight not with those Wanyoro. . . . I am, Mtesa king of [B]uganda for it you fight with governour [Kabarega] you fight with the king. I want to go to Bommbey [suggesting he would turn to the British for help against Egypt]. If the governour of Bommbey refuse me . . . will I not find another road.[7]

Gessi had become the first European to circumnavigate Lake Albert—an important step in proving that it was the Victoria Nile which gave birth to the White Nile, not some other major river entering Lake Albert from the south. Again, Gordon had given a subordinate, and in this case a close friend, the glory of making a new discovery, and Gessi, like Chaille-Long after his discovery of Lake Kyoga, could take pride in the accomplishment. Gordon may have had brief pangs of envy. In a letter written a month later, he harked back philosophically to Gessi's work: "How should I feel if Gessi said 'I put the steamer on the Lake' . . . I do not think I should care a bit now, but in old times it would have annoyed me."

On June 7, Piaggi returned from his exploration up the Victoria Nile, an offshoot of Gessi's Lake Albert exploration, confirming Chaille-Long's description of Lake Kyoga. There had been doubt that Kyoga was a real lake—perhaps it was a seasonal flood plain—but another piece of puzzle now fitted in. Piaggi, however, reported a river flowing northward out of Lake Kyoga which might be the true Nile; natives had told him that the river "goes an immense way." Gessi, too, claimed that there was evidence to suggest that a river exited the Victoria Nile above Lake Albert and flowed westward. Could either of these be the true route of the Victoria Nile?

KINGDOM OF BUGANDA

It was commonly believed that the Victoria Nile flowed through the northern end of Lake Albert before leaving it as the Albert Nile. There were explorers who had taken exception, such as the learned Dr. Schweinfurth, who contended that the main stream of the Victoria Nile joined the Albert Nile well below Lake Albert, bypassing the lake altogether, so Gessi's and Piaggi's reports, while inconclusive, had to be taken seriously. Gordon himself would have to settle the matter once and for all.

17

TRACKING THE NILE

I am tired, tired and no earthly rest will give me quiet.
—Charles Gordon after exploring the Victoria Nile, January 1877

G ordon was not interested in pleasing geographers; this was not exploration for exploration's sake.[1] His reasons for determining whether the river was navigable or whether boats could be transported overland to Lake Victoria were strategic. Without ability to patrol the great lake, Egyptian control of Buganda and Bunyoro would be impossible.

Gordon steamed southward from Dufile aboard the *Nyanza* on July 20, 1876, accompanied by two steel sailboards. The stretch of the Nile from Dufile to Lake Albert was quite navigable, as Romolo Gessi had earlier discovered, despite large masses of papyrus clogging its shoreline. The *Nyanza* was able to reach the lake within eight days.

While resting at Magungo, where the Victoria Nile empties into Lake Albert, Gordon received disturbing news from Nuehr Agha—the first since the officer and his detachment had been sent to Buganda. The shrewd Mutesa had forced Nuehr Agha to build his stockade at Rubega, the capital, rather than a safe distance from it at Urondogani★ as Gordon instructed him. Because of this, his Egyptian troops found themselves virtual prisoners.

Heading up the Victoria Nile from Lake Albert, the *Nyanza* was soon stopped by Murchison Falls, a spectacular 130-foot plunge of the river through a gorge no more than twenty feet wide. The Gordon party had to disembark and proceed by foot to Lake Kyoga. To permit accurate surveying of the river, Gordon was forced to keep close to its edge, which made the march through the tall, tangled grasses almost unendurable. Gordon's journal was filled with phrases of desperation such as "I am nearly dead" and "I am quite sure no one will ever do it again." Each day there was some other

---

★ Ripon Falls, where Lake Victoria's waters spill out to begin the Victoria Nile.

misery to undergo: August 2—"A dead, mournful spot this is with a heavy damp dew penetrating everywhere—it is as if the Angel Azrael had spread his wings over this land"; August 6—"To map the river for eight or ten miles I have to walk in pouring rain, through jungle some 18 miles"; August 8—"I have never had such fatigue. It has utterly prostrated me—a deadly coldness and emptiness at the stomach makes you feel inclined to drop . . . what misery! and what for?"

Gordon finally reached Foweira in mid-August and there learned more about Nuehr Agha's predicament. The officer dejectedly reported to Gordon that annexation of Buganda was out of the question. The Egyptian garrison which he had established was in effect held hostage by the Buganda King. Gordon summed it up starkly: "Mutesa has annexed my soldiers; he has not been annexed, himself." Gordon discovered, furthermore, that Mutesa was buying large quantities of powder in Zanzibar and was "evidently meditating something." His boastful letters to Gordon, claiming to be the "greatest king in Africa," bespoke an ominous aggressiveness.

Gordon wearily considered going to Rubega himself to get his men "out of the mess," but he soon gave up the idea. To do so would arouse Mutesa's suspicions and convey a sense of hostility which Gordon wanted to avoid. Moreover, there were indications that his troops would not be stopped if they attempted to leave Rubega peacefully. Negotiations seemed to be the best course to follow.

The only realistic option which would advance the Khedive's plans was to offer Mutesa a treaty of friendship recognizing his independence. This, Gordon hoped, would have some appeal to the African chief as a counterbalance to growing British influence radiating from Zanzibar; as a result of Stanley's efforts, there now was a British Christian mission with Mutesa. Gordon analyzed it this way: "The Egyptians are beginning not to like the English at all; and we may depend on it they will not put up much longer with our [British] dictations. Every little thing helps to deepen this dislike. Our interference in Zanzibar, in Abyssinia, and now this mission, which as composed is more secular than spiritual." On September 2, Gordon wrote the British missionaries in Buganda from Mrooli advising them to stick to spiritual matters. "They that take the sword shall perish with the sword." These were strong words, even from a Bible-toting soldier.

To negotiate with Mutesa, Gordon chose a new member of his staff whom he had hired unseen as physician. Gordon knew little about Dr. Edouard Karl Oskar Theodor Schnitzer other than that he was an apostate German Jew (and Gordon was not fond of either apostates or Jews) who had embraced Islam and now called himself Emin Pasha. He was unaware of much of Schnitzer's/Emin's curious career but knew he had not been born a Moslem.

Although Schnitzer had been graduated as a qualified physician in Germany, he was for unclear reasons denied a license to practice. This apparently drove him to seek his fortune abroad, although his sudden departure from Germany hinted at other reasons. Rejected by the Turkish Imperial Service, by the British for an assignment in East Africa, and by Emperor Maximilian's expeditionary force preparing to occupy Mexico, Schnitzer nonetheless made his way to Turkey, where he found medical employment at Antivari with the Port Quarantine Officer. In 1871 he entered the personal service of a wealthy Turkish official, Ismail Hakki Pasha, which took him to several exotic Near Eastern cities. To avoid the inconvenience of being a foreigner and infidel, Schnitzer adopted his Turkish name, Emin, and became—at least outwardly—a Moslem. He also appeared to have developed a relationship with his employer's wife, which, when Ismail Hakki died, evolved into "marriage." At least that is what he claimed when he returned to Germany to visit his apprehensive bourgeois family with Madame Ismail Hakki, her four children, and a collection of Circassian slave girls in tow.

By September 1873 Emin found tension with his own family combined with the burden of his adopted Turkish assemblage more than he could handle; he suddenly decamped, leaving no forwarding address. Emin next appeared in Khartoum as an indigent trader on December 3, 1875. Thanks to the small Austrian colony, he was saved from starvation. In return he played the piano for his benefactors and amused them with his superb chess playing. Giegler Pasha, an Austrian in the Khedive's service in Khartoum, wrote Gordon about Emin's talents. As Gordon was desperate for a doctor, his last having died in the south, he invited Emin to join the Equatorial mission as medical officer. Emin accepted with alacrity and left for Lado by steamer. Shortly after joining Gordon, Emin was sent on to Rubega to negotiate an amicable agreement with Mutesa.

Gordon recounted Emin's reception: "He was ushered into a large shed, on each side of which the Viziers were ranged, ten in number, and all seated at the end in a sort of alcove having an exit (for Mutesa to escape by)." The King sat on a dais wearing a huge white turban and dressed in gold-embroidered clothes. For ten minutes there was utter silence, but after the doctor said that he had brought presents, His Majesty warmed considerably and entered into a lively conversation about the biblical Revelations. The meeting ended pleasantly after Emin allowed that Mutesa was "a wonderful sultan of great power and magnificence."

For all his brave posturing, Mutesa seemed in somewhat of a panic about Gordon's presence in Central Africa. As a gesture of goodwill, the King gave Emin a letter for Gordon which extolled Christians and accused "Mussulmans" of being "bad." Presumably Mutesa thought that he could deal with Gordon as an Englishman rather than as an Egyptian official, but this proved the wrong tack to take with Emin, who professed to be a good Moslem—or with Gordon, who did not appreciate this slight to his Moslem master. A thoroughly confused Mutesa, who had assumed all white men were Christians, tried to set things straight. Emin had been deeply offended, but recognizing that his task was to establish good relations with the King on behalf of the Khedive, the German overcame his pique and presented his host with all his dress shirts. Relations were now on a firm footing, and Emin was treated cordially for the remainder of his stay at court. The enigmatic German turned out to be a skillful negotiator, and his mission was as successful as one could expect under the circumstances.

Having sorted things out reasonably well, Gordon now began to dream of returning to England. His fantasy was "to lie in bed till eleven everyday; to walk not further than the docks; and not to undertake those terrible railway journeys, or to get exposed to the questioning of people and their inevitable dinners." He added wistfully, "I want oysters for lunch."

It was August 28, 1876, in Mrooli when Gordon first heard the news that Sultan Abdul Aziz of Turkey had been forced from his throne on May 29 as a result of European pressure. The Khedive Ismail had only a tenuous connection with his suzerain power, so this development did not seem particularly significant to Gordon. In his journal he noted: "Great excitement among the troops about the new Sultan and deposition of Abdul Aziz."

Emin Pasha, through astute flattery of Mutesa in addition to his gift of English dress shirts, successfully extricated the garrison from Rubega and rejoined Gordon. Mutesa, however, did not sign a treaty, nor was any

191

mention of it made in the letter to Gordon. He replied to Gordon's message raising the issue with only "bits of prayers and requests for guns." Gordon concluded, "I have given him as good letter, and have, D.V. [God willing] done with him."

The march back brought new reminders that danger lurked in the tall grasses. Gordon suddenly heard a shout and a crash of loads thrown down, and then a volley about twenty yards in the rear. "About 10 or 12 of those irrepressible vermin had made an attack on the porters. There was no way to defend oneself from the spear-throwers hiding in the grass. This sort of work is much more dangerous for me . . . than regular war would be." The attack brought on pain in Gordon's heart, one of several angina episodes in his life.

As they approached Masindi, Gordon discovered that the garrison he had ordered established there was instead two days away at Keroto, apparently because it would be less vulnerable to tribal attack. Kabarega had in the meantime reoccupied Masindi, and Gordon's troops would have been in serious trouble if the chief had chosen to attack as they passed by. It had been a close call, and Gordon was understandably annoyed with the detachment's commander for having failed to carry out his strict instructions to take Masindi.

Gordon's mission was drawing to a close—none too soon as far as the weary Governor was concerned. For all his disappointment at not annexing Buganda, he had accomplished much. Certainly the contributions to exploration and discovery made by his mission had been prodigious. Chaille-Long had discovered Lake Kyoga, Chippendall had made the first probe of the Albert Nile, and Romolo Gessi had been the first to circumnavigate Lake Albert. Gordon himself had explored and mapped for the first time the Victoria Nile from Magungo, where the Victoria Nile debouched into Lake Albert, to Foweira north of Lake Kyoga. Chaille-Long's and Gordon's efforts had finally proved that the Nile's course passed through the northeastern end of Lake Albert to descend through the Sudan to Egypt; it did not have a separate channel bypassing Lake Albert.[2] This finding, beyond its geographic importance, gave the Egyptian Khedive a better claim to the lands surrounding the lake.

Gordon had succeeded in establishing a string of outposts south of Lado and Gondokoro as far upriver as Mrooli on the Victoria Nile near Lake Kyoga, deep in Bunyoro—Kabarega's domain. But he had not annexed

Buganda for the Khedive nor reached firm agreement with King Mutesa, who annoyingly delighted in waving the Union Jack given him by Stanley. Lake Victoria and its shores were still beyond Egypt's reach.

Gordon had succeeded in ending the slave traffic on the Nile, but would this accomplishment survive his departure? Little progress had been made in stopping Zubair and the slavers of the Bahr al-Ghazal; their *razzias*, or slaving commandos, still raided with impunity as they plied the remote desert tracks. That had been beyond his effective writ, of course, but it was discouraging for Gordon to accept that, overall, the Sudan slave traffic continued unsuppressed.

At least, Zubair was no longer on the scene in the Sudan. The slaver had appealed directly to the Khedive in his power struggle with Sudan's Governor General for control of Darfur. Confident of his power, Zubair in June had traveled to Cairo to make his case in person. This, however, proved a major mistake in judgment, as Zubair found himself indefinitely detained—and, as it turned out, in dignified exile from his country for many years to come.

For the Khedive, this detainment was also containment. Zubair was a threat to the entire Sudan, perhaps even Upper Egypt. Let alone his large-scale slave trading, he was capable of marshaling the ingrained hatred the Sudanese felt for Egyptians. The resulting power vacuum in Bahr al-Ghazal did not, however, mean the end of Zubair's slaving empire—his son, Suleiman Zubair, took control—nor did it mean the end of Zubair as a political factor in the Sudan equation.

Gordon had made a deep impression on Equatoria, and his reputation had spread along the caravan routes. But until the provinces of Bahr al-Ghazal and Darfur could be administered by incorruptible officials willing to suppress slaving, the situation he had sought to arrange would remain as it was.

Gordon left Lado by steamer on October 6, 1876, on the first leg of his journey home. He was seen off by a shower of arrows shot at his steamer by hostile tribesmen. No one was hurt, but it was a reminder that as long as slaving persisted there could be no progress in civilizing the natives and making them useful citizens.

Gordon had survived a host of enemies no less troublesome than hostile natives. "I have been terribly attacked here by cavalry (sand flies), infantry (tortoises), and artillery (opal-colored insects) and have suffered a good deal, especially from the artillery whose attacks are something fearful," he wrote in mock-military parlance. He could also have complained about other assaults on his person, and the "wild vines, convolvuli and other creepers" which bound him hand and foot as he tried to hack his way through scrub jungles and fetid marshlands. There had been angina attacks, ague, malaria, unidentifiable fevers and questionable food to savage his liver. He had even been struck by lightning. Worst of all had been the depression which descended on him from time to time.

On his way back to Khartoum, Gordon received word that the Khedive had honored him with one of Egypt's highest decorations. This horrified Gordon. "A terrible thing has happened, you know I wrote and said . . . that we had occupied Dubaga [Rubaga]; I telegraphed this to H. H. [the Khedive], and you know afterward that it was all humbug, and that I had to withdraw my men from Mutesa." When the Khedive responded to Gordon's premature message of success with congratulations, conferring on him the Medjidieh, First Class, he shuddered that he had obtained the accolade under false pretenses.

In Khartoum, Gordon found Romolo Gessi nursing his disappointment that he had received only the Medjidieh, Third Class, for his accomplishments. According to Gessi's son, who edited his father's memoir posthumously, Gordon had ungraciously said to his old friend, "What a pity you are not an Englishman," the implication being that Cairo favored the English over an Italian mercenary. It is unlikely that Gordon meant anything untoward by his remark, but Gessi's son took it as an expression of Gordon's annoyance that " . . . the exploration had not been accomplished by his countrymen, Watson and Chippendall, who had failed to advance beyond Wadelai." As the son's account went, "Gessi, who was hot-tempered and independent, and who moreover was an ardent lover of his own country, took off his cap and, throwing it at Gordon's feet, immediately gave in his resignation."[3]

The relationship between Gordon and Gessi must have survived this incident, however, as they traveled amicably together on to Cairo. While there was a period of coolness and Gordon from time to time made disparaging remarks about Gessi in his correspondence, they would once again work and fight together in the Sudan some years later.

Gordon's hair had turned gray during his three years in Equatoria, and he had aged considerably. Yet to Edwin DeLeon, an American who happened to meet Gordon in Cairo, Gordon still looked fit as though "he had just come from promenading on the shady side of Pall Mall, [but] he seems to be swept away by the rushing flood of feelings and thoughts long pent up in his own breast."[4] Gordon, in fact, was contemplating quitting the Sudan for good, but he did not want to make the final decision until he reached Cairo. The argument went on within himself: "Comfort-of-body—a very strong gentleman—says 'you are well; you have done enough; go home, go home and be quiet and risk no more.' . . . Mr. Reason says: 'What is the use of opening up more country to such a government? There is more now under their power than they will ever manage. . . . Retire now and avoid troubles with Mutesa.' . . . Mr. Something—I do not know what—who says: 'Shut your eyes to what may happen in the future, leave that to God, and do what you think will open the country thoroughly to both lakes. Do this, not for H.H. or for his government, but do it blindly and in faith.' "[5]

Yet Gordon wanted to be certain of the Khedive's attitude: "If he desires you to stay, then stay, if he seems indifferent, then do not hesitate, but go away for good." Gordon need not have worried about the Khedive, as Egypt's ruler valued his services and trusted him completely. Trust and honesty were rare commodities in Egypt. The Khedive knew this well, having just dismissed his powerful Finance Minister, Ismail Sadiq Pasha, for breach of trust. By chance, Gordon on his way to Cairo had passed the broken man in Korosko as he was being transported to Wadi Halfa. Gordon assumed Ismail Sadiq had been guilty as charged when he was executed soon after. The incident reminded Gordon of the twin devils of hopeless corruption and arbitrary justice in Egypt. "How God works! When I was going up to the Sudan he [Ismail Sadiq] was all-powerful; when I am coming down few would envy his lot—poor man!" In the next breath Gordon leaped to his all-important decision. As though it were his only option when faced with such venality and such cruelty, he would resign from the Khedive's service. "I have, D.V. [God willing], made up my mind to serve H. H. no more."

In Cairo, Gordon reported his intention to resign—much to the disappointment of the Khedive, who urged him to take a vacation, but to stay on in the job. Gordon, at first, was not to be dissuaded. With his usual raw frankness he made the point that antislaving operations in Equatoria were useless unless the rest of the Sudan stopped wallowing in official corruption and encouraging the slavers. At that very moment, in fact, Governor General Ismail Ayyub of the Sudan was in Cairo arguing for the release of Zubair, which, if it occurred, would mean that the infamous slaver could resume his insidious operations in the Sudan. Gordon was tired, discouraged and not in good health. As he had written to a friend, Miss Dykes, the Sudan was "a land of silence and death."

The Khedive, whose charm and power of persuasion were famous, promised Gordon that reforms would be made. Gordon succumbed and agreed tentatively to return, but he continued to agonize over the decision after reaching England. He discussed it with close friends and with Lord Derby, the British Secretary of State for Foreign Affairs. By mid-January 1877, Gordon had again made up his mind. He sent a wire to the Khedive that he did not intend to return.

"I am tired," he wrote, "tired, and no earthly rest will give me quiet."

18

GOVERNOR GENERAL
OF THE SUDAN

I feel a great contentment. A star, when it makes its highest point, is
said to have culminated; and I feel I have culminated.
—Charles Gordon on his assignment
as Governor General of the Sudan

ordon's homecoming stirred up the press in England. The *Times*
extravagantly lauded his pacification of the Central African "savages" and suggested he now be sent as governor to Bulgaria, where
Christians were demanding relief from Turkish oppression. The paper
suggested that the popular colonel, who had a knack for taming the unruly,
could make that strife-ridden corner of the Balkans "as peaceful as an English
county." The idea appealed to Gordon, who discussed the position with Lord
Derby on January 11, 1877. Big-power politics in the Balkans killed the idea,
however, and Gordon turned his attention once again to East Africa.

Gordon had long been interested in East Africa. He believed it held the key
to Central African commerce, profitable to the European and uplifting to the
African. Encouraged by William Mackinnon, shipping magnate and later
promoter of the British East African Company, Gordon envisioned a
concession from the Sultan of Zanzibar that permitted an expedition to the
African interior—led by himself and his friend Romolo Gessi.

The Khedive, however, would not be put off so easily. Reminding him
that they had parted in Cairo with the words "*au revoir*," promising reunion,
Ismail shamed him in a letter saying: "I refuse to believe that when Gordon
has once given his word as a gentleman, anything will ever induce him to go
back on it."

The point was made, and Gordon returned to Cairo, holding out for
command of the entire Sudan, not just Equatoria. Only with that kind of
power could he hope to beat the slave traffickers and control Khartoum's
corrupt administration, which so often abetted the culprits. General Gerald

Graham had suggested he insist on the governor generalship, and somewhat to Gordon's surprise, the Khedive readily agreed. Gordon would be ruler of more than a million square miles of territory.

"I am astounded at the power he [the Khedive] has placed in my hand."[1] Gordon was pleased, but he knew well the difficulty of the task. Ismail's instructions concerned the suppression of slavery and the improvement of the means of communications. But in fact, Gordon's first order of business as Governor General concerned Abyssinia. Since Lord Napier's defeat of King Theodore in 1868 and that mad ruler's death while defending his mountain bastion at Magdala, much had occurred. With help from the British, the Abyssinian chieftain of Tigre Province, Prince Kassai, emerged as victor in the power struggle following Theodore's death. According to custom, he was crowned by an *abouna,* or Coptic Metropolitan, sent by the Coptic Patriarch of Alexandria, and retitled Johannes, King of Abyssinia. The new King put out the eyes of the legitimate heir, Goobasie, who had contested the succession, but was unable to gain control of the northern province of Bogos (roughly the Eritrea of today), west of the Egyptian-held Red Sea port of Massawa.

In 1874 Bogos was seized by the Governor of Massawa, a Swiss named Werner Munzinger, in the name of the Khedive. The Swiss adventurer, driven by personal ambitions, convinced the Khedive to annex the neighboring province of Hamaçem as well. With £4 million in his pocket from sale of his shares in the Suez Canal to the British, the Khedive leaped at the proposal and sent an expedition to seize the two provinces.

The Egyptians proved no match for the rugged Abyssinian mountaineers. In the crucial battle on March 18, 1876, near Gura in the highlands south of Massawa, the Egyptian expedition lost nine thousand men, many more as prisoners, a vast amount of arms, and a rich treasury of English gold. To the survivors, the Abyssinians were hideously cruel. They mutilated forty Sudanese soldiers, whom Johannes sent back to the Egyptian lines with the message that if the Khedive wanted eunuchs, he could have them. When two thousand Egyptian prisoners, starved for three days to the point of desperation, refused to march any farther, the Abyssinians ordered them to lie naked on the rocks to be shot at as target practice. Johannes, who had ably led his troops in victory, missed an opportunity to cut off the retreating Egyptians, however.

In Cairo, Johannes's envoy was confined for weeks by the heavy-handed Egyptians before the British Consul secured his release. The Abyssinian King was furious at this treatment of his representative, but more troubling was the Egyptian-encouraged insurrection led by the maverick prince Walid el-Michael in Bogos and Hamaçem; it would not be so easy for Johannes to regain these border provinces. The Khedive, for his part, had grown weary of the costly, inconclusive war between Egypt and Abyssinia. Knowing that Egypt could never win, he turned to Gordon, as Governor General of the Sudan and its Red Sea appendages, to find grounds for agreement between the Khedive and Johannes.

Gordon wrote Johannes, offering the King a frontier which, although it excluded the province of Bogos, came with the guarantee of the good behavior of Walid el-Michael. The pitifully weak Egyptian garrison in Bogos, however, provided little leverage with which to influence Michael to be party to the bargain he wanted to strike. Moreover, Michael cared little for the Egyptians. It was a situation made complex by competing interests and personalities. In his usual colorful fashion Gordon reported his views in a letter home:

> There were two courses open to me with respect to this Abyssinian question; the one, to stay at Massawa and negotiate peace with Johannes and to ignore Walid el Michael, and if afterwards Walid el Michael turned rusty, to arrange with Johannes to come in and catch him. . . . Johannes would have been delighted, and we would be rid of Walid; but it would first of all be very poor encouragement to any future *secessions*, and would debase Egyptian repute. The process of turning in the polecat [Johannes] to work out the weasel [Walid el-Michael] would play havoc with the farmyard [the country] . . . and it might be that the polecat Johannes, having caught the Weasel Walid, might choose to turn on the hens (which we are). . . . For to tell the truth we, the hens, in the days of our prosperity, stole the farmyard from the polecats, when they were fighting among themselves and before they knew we were hens. The other course open to me was to give Walid el Michael a government separated from Johannes, which I have done, and I think that was the best course . . . though in consequence we are like a fat nut between the nutcrackers.

Massawa on the Red Sea and Harrar on the Gulf of Aden were claimed by Egypt, so were Gordon's to administer. They were large, strategically important tracts, although Egypt's ability to control them was minimal. Besides, they were an economic liability—but perhaps the same could be said for the Sudan. Gordon felt a little overwhelmed by his diverse and far-flung empire with its many problems.

He was more amused than impressed by the trappings of power. Certainly they did not compensate for the trials and tribulations of his responsibility. As Marshal of the Egyptian Army, he could wear a gold-encrusted uniform which fairly dripped with braid and piping. With tongue in cheek he wrote his sister Augusta: ". . . so I and the Duke of Cambridge [Commander in Chief of the British Army] are equals!" But trying not to betray too much vanity, he quickly added: "God must undertake the work, and I am for the moment used as His instrument." The fatalism which consoled Gordon in so many moments of difficulty was expressed in the same thoughtful letter: "The events of the future are all written, and are mapped out in all their detail for each one of us; the Negro, the Arab and the Bedouin's course— their meeting with me—is decreed."

Marching through the gorges of the Abyssinian highlands, Gordon was spied upon by dog-faced baboons who, "as among us, quarrelled constantly." He grew to love riding by camel, that unlovable beast of the desert, and by May 1877 he would predict: "I expect to ride 5,000 miles this year, if I am spared. . . . on one goes, stalking along—the camel's foot makes no noise, and you learn yourself!"

As Gordon approached the town of Keren, capital city of Bogos, he was met in a high pass by two hundred cavalry and infantry, who escorted him the rest of the way. "I am most carefully guarded," he noted. Six or eight sentries surrounded him whenever he stopped—"irksome beyond measure." Even worse was the ritual in which eight or ten men insisted on helping him off his camel as though he were a cripple.

In Keren a group of Abyssinians from the Egyptian garrison danced for Gordon while "three horsemen with kettle drums rode before them, beating their little drums." As Gordon inspected the black garrison troops, one white face suddenly appeared, shrouded in the usual Abyssinian white sheet. To Gordon's astonishment, the man announced himself as an Irishman named Macilvrey who had lived in Abyssinia for sixteen years. As a young boy he had accompanied Cameron to Theodore's court on the mission when the British Consul was taken hostage by the Abyssinian King. Like Cameron, Macilvrey was held prisoner for four years along with the other Europeans seized by the mad ruler. But unlike Cameron, the boy remained in the

200

country after he was freed, only to be taken prisoner once again, this time by Walid el-Michael on one of the brigand's raids into Johannes's territory. Gordon set the wretched man free to return to his wife and two children.

With an escort of two hundred infantry and sixty prancing horsemen, Walid el-Michael arrived pompously in Keren for his meeting with Gordon. Gordon explained the Egyptian offer to him: Michael would be given either a provincial government under King Johannes or one within Egyptian-controlled territory. The offer was committed to paper, much like a treaty. Ally or not, Michael had to be handled as carefully as Johannes if peace was to be achieved.

The old Prince was advised by a priest whose Christianity was so twisted that he believed Christ to have been "killed by accident." Gordon noted that the priest "was a great deal too humble," and was always stooping to kiss his feet. Walid el-Michael, however, had to be considered a strong enemy, and Gordon wrote: "As long as he remains quiet, I cannot do anything against him."[2]

If Michael and his entourage were playing a charade with Gordon, Johannes was more forthright in his lack of enthusiasm. To Gordon's letter he replied bluntly: "You are a Christian. I write to you. You must speak of the frontier of Abyssinia. The whole world knows the ancient frontier!"[3] Gordon never felt satisfied unless he could beard an adversary face to face, so this negotiating by correspondence left him somewhat frustrated. When they did meet, though, Gordon would have had to deal from weakness. Gordon at least had the feeling that the King was "opposed to the idea of war."[4]

Before the Abyssinian question could be resolved, problems called Gordon to Khartoum. On his journey there, Gordon paused in the Sudanese border town of Kassala long enough to write up an account of his mission for Sherif Pasha,* Egypt's Foreign Minister. The report was sent to Olagnier, a Frenchman in the Egyptian bureaucracy on whom Gordon relied for support, expedition, and sometimes inside information. As an assistant to Sherif Pasha, Olagnier enjoyed high rank in the Foreign Office, with responsibilities concerning the administration of the Sudan. Gordon came to depend on Olagnier's support, in return for which Gordon looked after the welfare of him and his family. But more than that, Olagnier also seemed to be

---

* Gordon used the transliteration "Cherif Pasha," rather than "Sherif Pasha."

Gordon's confidential informant on developments in Cairo, and some of their correspondence suggests a relationship unknown to Sherif.[5]

While traveling between Kassala and Qadarif, Gordon found himself suddenly transported back to another time and place. There before him, materializing out of the dust, "were a number of men in regular chain shirts of links with a gorget. The men seemed to have walked out of the pages of old crusader chronicles with helmets of iron, nose pieces and fringes of chain armor. They rode on horses which had the head and cheek defense and were covered with a sort of quilt of different colours." They even carried two-handed, cross-hilted swords. Indeed, the costumes were authentic, passed on, as treasured relics, from days of the Crusaders in the Holy Land many centuries before.

Loping along by camel, covering up to forty-five miles per day despite such vexations as biting beetles, Gordon reached Khartoum in the early days of May. On May 5 he was formally installed in office with a royal salute and a speech of welcome by the cadi, or chief justice. Less hospitable was the sister of his predecessor, Ismail Ayyub Pasha, who, to demonstrate her displeasure at being displaced, smashed every window in the official residency—130 in all—and ripped up the upholstery!

Gordon's inaugural address endeared him to his people by its brevity and sincerity. His words were simple: "With the help of God I will hold the balance level." But there was no settling into the job. Awaiting Gordon was the immediate problem posed by some six thousand Turkish Bashi-Bazouks, mercenary frontier guards whose arrogance and brutality made life miserable for townspeople and passing caravans. The Bashi-Bazouks were also in league with the slavers. Gordon knew he must disband them, but it had to be accomplished "neatly" to circumvent mutiny.

Gordon quickly instituted a series of reforms. Flogging with the dreaded rhino whip was banned, the influential *ulema*, or clergy, had privileges restored to them, and symbolic of his wish to be accessible to all people, he had a box prominently displayed outside his office where complaints could be deposited for his personal attention. From his own pocket he distributed alms to the town poor.

While Gordon attended to matters in Khartoum, problems in the provinces persisted—particularly as regarded Zubair's slaving empire in Bahr al-Ghazal. After Zubair's seizure of Darfur Province "in the name of the

Khedive" and his scarcely disguised challenge to Ismail Ayyub Pasha's power as Governor General of the Sudan, the slaver had wanted to rule Darfur and Bahr al-Ghazal provinces as autonomous states under direct Egyptian suzerainty. When his request to the Khedive was rejected and he was "detained" in Cairo by the Khedive, Zubair nonetheless arranged to keep his slaving enterprise alive through his son, Suleiman. From his exile Zubair regularly corresponded with Suleiman and guided him in the operations. But shortly before his detainment in Cairo, Zubair had met with his chiefs under a large tree on the road between El Obeid and Shaka. There they swore everlasting loyalty to him.

In Cairo Zubair tried every possible maneuver to gain his freedom. It was rumored that he had passed out lavish bribes to ministers in the government—but to no avail. When Gordon passed through Cairo to take up his new position in Khartoum, Zubair even appealed to him for help in gaining release. When he was rebuffed by the new Governor General, Zubair secretly sent word to his chiefs: "Obey the orders given *under the tree.*" This was, in fact, a code to signal an uprising in Darfur.

As agitation in Darfur commenced, Gordon came up with a plan to end slavery in twelve years. The plan called for the immediate registration of every slave, by his master, up until January 1, 1878. After that date, no new registrations could be made, thus no new slaves could be legally acquired. The existing law which returned runaway slaves to their owners would be enforced as well. European slaveholders were subject to special attention; their slaves would either have to be freed or their masters would face stiff taxes from which they had heretofore been exempt.

Gordon noted in his journal: "I do believe the people rejoice at my being here." Slave traders, on the other hand, had no reason to rejoice, and they prepared to defy Khartoum rather than lose their fortunes.

The next four months would find Gordon rushing southwest on camelback to battle with slavers and recalcitrant tribesmen who had flourished under the old system. The situation had become ominous as news was received that Zubair's son, Suleiman, and other slave dealers, in response to Zubair's signal to revolt, had raised a large army at Shaka, the slaving capital three hundred miles to the south. Making matters worse, Haroun el-Rashid, nephew of the late Sultan of the province, had attracted a considerable following of people tired of Egyptian rule and outraged by the excesses of

Egyptian garrisons placed in the province by Gordon's predecessor, and in February the rebel chieftain led an uprising which cut off some sixteen thousand Egyptian troops in Darfur's capital of El Fasher and in the lesser garrisons in Dara and Kolkol.

It was typical of Gordon to set out to suppress an uprising of major proportions and to rescue thousands of trapped Egyptian soldiers with a flying squad of only three hundred not particularly brave soldiers. He did not think of the Darfur people as enemies and had a certain amount of sympathy for the insurgents; he thought "the poor people have been driven into it and Haroun has only taken advantage of their discontent." It never occurred to him that he had set himself an unreasonable task. "I feel I shall succeed. . . . this feeling . . . has accompanied me when in China and the Lake District. . . . The Gordons and the camels are of the same race; let them take an idea into their heads and nothing will take it out."

Gordon was convinced that the "matter of Darfur has been exaggerated" and that its problems flowed only from "the continuation of this bad government and the exactations [sic] of Halid Pasha," the Governor. Gordon also had a strategic sense about Darfur. In his confidential correspondence with Olagnier in Cairo, he wanted Sherif Pasha to be reminded that the peoples west of El Fasher, living in Waden Baghesin and Bumiera (near the borders of present-day Chad), spoke Arabic and were Moslem. They could be "bound to the Sudan." If they were dealt with properly, they could be encouraged to trade via the Nile rather than through the pitiless desert south from Tripoli. "A treaty will be enough. We will have a secure road toward Lake Tchad, which is only 12 miles from the border." Besides, this would be a convenient way to check French imperial incursions toward the Nile from the west.[6]

Recognizing that the longer-term solution for Darfur was good government, Gordon wrote Richard Burton on June 21, 1877, offering him the governorship of the province. At the time, Burton was languishing in a dull Foreign Office assignment in Trieste, and Gordon thought he could be lured by the challenge. "Now is the time for you to make your indelible mark in the world," he wrote the erratic explorer. But despite a good salary offer, Burton refused: "You and I are too much alike. I could not serve under you nor you under me. I have a wife and you have not."[7]

Gordon now appreciated that old Zubair Pasha had been "forced to retire" in Cairo not a moment too soon, as he would surely have set himself up as independent ruler of Darfur. Gordon confided to Olagnier, "I am telling you all this because I trust you. You may talk to Cherif Pasha."[8] The subject of Zubair was still a very delicate matter, even though the old slaver was under detention because he had much influence in high places and was capable of great mischief. (Such was his prestige that the next year he was given command of a contingent of Egyptian troops and sent off to fight in the Russo-Turkish War.) Gordon's confidential letter to Olagnier revealed exasperation: "I cannot work any longer with Halid Pasha." The Governor is "just impossible, and so rude and brutal with anyone dealing with him. . . . It is either he or me who leaves this place."[9]

Gordon came galloping alone on his magnificent racing camel into the Egyptian outpost of Foggia, resplendent in his golden marshal's uniform. He suddenly found himself in the midst of the garrison "before the men had time to unpile their arms." This tickled Gordon, who guessed that it must have been "fearful to see the Governor General arrayed in gold cloths flying along like a madman with only a guide, as if pursued." The Egyptian Mudir, or Governor, had no time to collect his wits before his Khartoum master appeared before him.

Gordon's next stop was Oomchanga, as miserable a place as could be imagined. What nature had not done to make this waterless spot uninhabitable, the Bashi-Bazouks and other "scum of Cairo and Stamboul" had accomplished with their brutality. The only product in these parts besides slaves was ostrich feathers. (It had taken an enterprising Syrian merchant to buy up all the black ostrich feathers there, foreseeing many mourning widows in Egypt as a result of the Russo-Turkish War.)

The long journey by camel to western Sudan gave Gordon a view of slaving along the desert routes that he had not seen from his Nile stations in Equatoria. As his caravan ended one long march near El Obeid, his camel nearly ran over a small boy who had been abandoned by a slave caravan. The terrified little lad led Gordon to a small group of other children chained together. They had been left to die in the desert by the slavers, who fled when they heard that Gordon was approaching. The boy, about seven years old, "like a spider with legs like a fly," begged Gordon to buy him as his slave for one dollar.

Gordon took pity on the boy and arranged for a missionary lady in El

Obeid, Miss Felkin, to care for him. The boy was renamed Capsune and later sent to England for his education. Gordon saw to his continued support and kept in touch with him for the rest of his life. This story had a happy ending, but what of the thousands of others who found no respite from the cruelties of the slavers as they were dragged across the desert to market and an uncertain future? The question worried Gordon deeply.

Gordon's military strategy was to use the soldiers from isolated and vulnerable outposts to form a more self-sufficient force of about four thousand to hold the main road and move against Haroun el-Rashid in El Fasher. For the moment, however, Gordon had collected only five hundred nondescript troops, so his plan was to negotiate a peace in Darfur without having to fire a shot.

Fortunately, the mere threat of Gordon's advance was enough to send Haroun el-Rashid scurrying to the Mara Mountains (Jebel Mara). With this, many of his troops abandoned him and came over to the government. Gordon had won another round, but the victory was due to his bluff and courage, not to the valor of his soldiers. He was bitter: "Now what I want to impress on you is the position I have been in over and over again. . . . that is, being with troops in whom one has not the least confidence; you feel sure that, should the enemy attack you, you will be utterly destroyed. . . . We were threatened by an attack from thousands of determined blacks. It gave me a pain in the heart like I had when surrounded at Masindi." The pattern of his angina attacks was becoming clear: They usually occurred when he was faced with great fatigue or great stress.

Dara was the next stop, and Gordon appeared without warning—in the terrible heat of midday on July 13. The atmosphere of the garrison was like "the relief of Lucknow" during the Indian Mutiny; the eighteen hundred troops there had been cut off without news for six months, and food was selling "at famine prices." Some of the soldiers were dressed in medieval armor, carrying flat swords that dated from the Crusades. This was the second time he had seen this phenomenon. Gordon attributed it to the migration of Bedouins southward from the Holy Land after the Crusaders withdrew.

Gordon became restless in Dara as he awaited reinforcements, but the monotony was broken when six hundred Rizayqat tribal refugees straggled in from Shaka. They told horror stories of how their once-powerful tribe had been pillaged by Suleiman Zubair and his slave army. Reports of this army gave him pause: "There are too many to disarm and it would be dangerous to keep them together anywhere after being accustomed to hear treason spoken and to despise the Government as they have for so many years." Then it occurred to Gordon: What if the entire Rizayqat tribe came over to him to escape harassment by Zubair? How could he feed them?

Gordon's thoughts were then interrupted by another crisis; seven hundred warriors of the nearby Leopard tribe had threatened Dara and had to be driven off. Gordon's forces proved worthless, cowering in the stockade, as he led a few brave tribesmen into the fray. Gordon frothed with contempt: "The wretched Bashi-Bazouks, who prance up to me, are a set of errant cowards." The Leopards were finally defeated, not by clash of arms, but by being isolated from their water holes and left to die a terrible death of thirst unless they surrendered. In an act of mercy, Gordon permitted them to save themselves by swearing allegiance to the government on the Koran.

Gordon relieved the beleaguered provincial capital, El Fasher, and its eight thousand defenders with only 150 men. His success raised the obvious question: How could this large garrison, backed by an even larger force only three days away, have allowed itself to be hemmed in by Haroun el-Rashid? This sorry performance was more than matched by that of an expeditionary force Gordon had sent from Dara to attack another threatening tribe. In this case, the commanding officer had accepted a bribe from the enemy—£200 in money, £50 worth of ostrich feathers and ten camel loads of *dhoora* (grain)—and spent nineteen days doing nothing. Gordon's disgusted reaction was "I will have him shot"—which he didn't. To cap his woes, Gordon discovered a plot to raise the pious townfolk against him by blaming him, unjustly, for stopping the *muezzin* call to prayer from the mosque.

Gordon's problems grew daily more complicated: "The whole country is suffering from famine and it will get worse. . . . The smell of the putrefying dead is fearful." Then news arrived that Zubair's son, with his hordes, was only two days from Dara, "plundering right and left," driving the victimized tribesmen to take refuge in the city. The slaver's lieutenants, it was reported, had met while Gordon was in El Fasher and had sworn on the Koran to fight to the death against government forces. Gordon summed up the situation: "Haroun is ravaging the country to the north, and I am placed between two forces. The whole of the tribes around Zubair's son are hostile to him, and partially hostile to me, and in favor of Haroun—but asking me to help them against the armed forces of Zubair's son—a triangular duel."

The strain on Gordon was beginning to tell. In the midst of his trials "there came down a terrific storm of dust and rain and wind," the fearful *haboob*, flattening his tent. Day became night, and nothing escaped the fine dust which covered everything. When rain followed, the dust became a thin gruel of mud. Even the scorpions sought shelter from the storm—in Gordon's case, by hiding in his shoes. In vile humor, Gordon railed against the Egyptians: "I hate (there is no other word for it) these Arabs; and I like the blacks—patient, enduring and friendly, as much as the Arab is cowardly, cruel and effeminate. . . . I would not stay a day here for these wretched creatures, but I would give my life for these poor blacks."

The good news that Haroun el-Rashid had fled to the hills was matched by the bad news that Suleiman Zubair's six thousand men had moved closer to Dara. In the company of only one aide, Gordon set off for Dara at a fast gallop. The only obstacle to their course was a swarm of flies that formed a virtual hood over their faces. Nor did the swarm discriminate when it came to the camels, spurring the poor beasts to run even faster. Reaching Dara at 4:00 in the afternoon, Gordon entered the town "like a thunderbolt." The people "were paralyzed and could not believe their eyes." He had ridden eighty-five miles in thirty-six hours!

At dawn the next day, September 2, 1877, before going "on stage," Gordon donned his costume of "golden armor," the Egyptian marshal's uniform, and with a small escort of Bashi-Bazouks who had caught up with him, rode three miles to Suleiman Zubair's menacing encampment. After coolly riding amid some three thousand astonished cutthroats and staring them down, he strode into Suleiman's tent. "The whole body of chiefs were dumbfounded." Gordon accepted a cup of water—a protocol ritual practiced in the desert even among enemies—and ordered the young slave prince to appear before him with his family on the morrow. Would Suleiman attack or submit? Gordon had to wait for the answer.

At least Suleiman was willing to talk. Gordon's meeting with the "nice-looking lad of 22 years," dressed incongruously in a blue velvet riding jacket, was charged with tension. Suleiman Zubair's troops were "like antelopes, fierce, inspiring, the terror of Central Africa." They outnumbered Gordon's miserable levies ten to one. Facing the slaver and his heavily armed family, Gordon was brief: "I gave them in choice Arabic [Gordon's command of Arabic was limited] my ideas: that they meditated revolt; that I knew it, and that they should now have my ultimatum, viz., that I would disarm them and break them up."

Suleiman listened in silence, rose sullenly with his family and left to consider.

Before the day was out Suleiman had sent a letter of submission—much to Gordon's relief. Whether this was genuine or only a cover to mask an intention to attack, Gordon could not yet know. Much later in the campaign he learned from the interrogation of some of Zubair's chiefs that the young man had received almost unanimous advice to attack Gordon. Only one, a black officer named Nur Angara, opposed the idea. He warned Suleiman that Gordon was an Englishman and that the English never forgave those who hurt one of their own. As had been the case in Abyssinia when Consul Cameron was taken hostage by the Negus, England would not stop until vengeance was theirs. Sincere in this conviction, Nur Angara took his own troops—amounting to half of Zubair's force—over to join Gordon. Suleiman Zubair had lost the round.

Suleiman, at least, wanted consolation prizes. He asked to be given the ceremonial robes which signified official approbation and a command position as Governor in Bahr al-Ghazal. In other words, he wanted to save both his face and his foothold. Gordon flatly refused, demanding more evidence of Suleiman's loyalty. Suleiman "had been very rude," while he, the Governor General, had "gone out of the way to be civil." He had done his best for Suleiman with no reciprocation. Gordon had given a schoolmaster's lecture to a "bad little boy," and Zubair, insulted, sulked all the way back to Shaka. With only half his troops and none of his face, he had been defeated and humiliated by one Englishman with ice-blue eyes. He had been out-maneuvered and resented it.

Gordon knew he would have to go to Shaka himself. Otherwise he could not be sure that Suleiman was abiding by his promise to put down his arms. Under the circumstances, the Governor General was remarkably charitable in his opinion of Suleiman: "The terror in which he has kept the mightiest of these freebooters is something wonderful. He is a thorough young ruffian . . . but I like him, though he hates me; I hope God will change his heart toward me when I get to Shaka." Gordon's relationship with Suleiman was not unlike his relationship with Burgevine in China: Both men were charming rascals, brave, and able, and despite the fact they were his adversaries, Gordon found himself attracted to them.

In fact, Gordon had a certain admiration for many of the slavers. They were a hardy breed whom he had found to be worthy opponents, though he hated what they stood for. "I like these slave-dealers; they are a brave lot, and putting aside their propensity to take slaves, are much finer people than those of Lower Egypt—they are far more enterprising."

With the risks very much on his mind, Gordon entered Suleiman's slaving den in Shaka—almost the first Westerner to do so—with only four companies of lackluster troops. His band played "Salaam Effendina" ("Vive le Khedive"), an act akin to playing "Marching Through Georgia" in Atlanta after the Civil War. But somehow he survived. He was even given a cordial reception. "The cub is now very friendly and comes to sit by me," Gordon wrote. Nonetheless, he ordered Suleiman to return to Bahr al-Ghazal, and again refused to make the slaver Chief of the Zeribas, a position of provincial prominence—despite Suleiman's obsequious acts such as fondling Gordon's naked feet and offering to bribe him with "a wedge of gold." Gordon liked the "cub," but could not trust him.

Gordon did not realize how near death he was. He would discover two years later how the scheming young slaver had lolled about the veranda with him, at the same time contemplating seriously Gordon's murder. Events would indeed prove that the cub was not yet tamed.

Gordon left Shaka intact but uncertain. "I hope that the Shaka business is satisfactorily disposed of, but looking at the mass of slaves there, it will be a long time ere that work is ended." As Gordon's caravan began the long journey back to El Obeid, the group was accompanied by various "wives" and "children" whom Gordon suspected of actually being slaves on their way to the marketplace. "When you have the ink which has soaked into blotting-paper out of it, then slavery will cease in these lands."

From El Obeid, Gordon wrote to Olagnier that he was exhausted. Since they last met, Gordon had traveled 2,300 miles. Even so, another battle had been won: Johannes in Abyssinia had accepted the proffered peace terms.

Back in Khartoum in October, Gordon was greeted by six elephants which bowed dutifully before him—Gordon had requested the beasts in February, with the plan of using them in building the railroad. Otherwise, in Gordon's long absence, things had not gone well. There were petty crises and widespread crime. His secretary had absconded with some money, and because the man's concubine knew where the money was hidden, his family strangled her and threw her down a well to prevent her from talking. To stem the growing tide of violence, Gordon summarily hanged an infamous murderer. He hoped the example would "tend to keep the town quiet for some months." Gordon described his managerial style to his sister: "Your brother is much feared and, I think, respected, but not over much liked. . . . 'Never' is the answer to many requests, shouted with a loud voice and followed with 'Do you understand?' " Gordon could be amazingly objective about himself, and rarely shrank from being his own critic.

Of more relevance to the Governor General's principal mission in the Sudan was the Slave Convention, between Great Britain and Egypt, which equated slave trading with murder as a capital crime. This proclamation, which Gordon posted, would not deter big traders like the Zubairs, but it at least broadcast the government's stand. This was a step forward.

Gordon was no desk man, and by October 23, 1877, he was off again to inspect the provinces. This time he visited the areas north of Khartoum, Berber, Merowe, Dongola, and Wadi Halfa, along the border with Egypt where a new railroad link had been finished. The trip was meant to be a relief from the stresses of Darfur and the worries of Khartoum, but there was still the telegraph line which bound him to his responsibilities. No sooner had he left Khartoum than a message arrived informing him about two Russian agents "egging on Johannes of Abyssinia to attack Egypt." In a letter to General Stanton, now British chargé d'affaires in Munich, Gordon could not resist a whimsical comment about the Russians to the effect that their plot made him like them more than ever.

While coasting down the Nile, Gordon did manage to relax and reflect immodestly on his position. He wrote his sister Augusta: "The quiet of today on board the steamer . . . is quite delightful. . . . I feel a great contentment. A star, when it makes its highest point, is said to have culminated; and I feel I have culminated. He has made me succeed, not in any very glorious way, but in a substantial and lasting manner. I entirely take that prophecy of Isaiah as my own and work toward it as far as I can."

That passage read: "And it shall be for a sign, and for a witness unto the Lord of hosts in the land of Egypt, for they shall cry unto the Lord because of the oppressors, and He shall send them a Saviour and a great one, and he shall deliver them."

Gordon's reverie would not last long. It was interrupted by news of problems along the Abyssinian border. The irrepressible Walid el-Michael was again harassing King Johannes's territory, despite Gordon's bribes to keep him quiet. Gordon felt that he was being stretched too thinly and needed help. From Suakin, he appealed to Sherif Pasha, asking for more foreign officers. He had grown tired from trying to cover the Sudan and Egypt's Red Sea appendages by himself, and he wanted specific men from the Cairo pool of foreign advisers: the Americans Colonel William Dye and Lieutenant Colonel Charles F. Loesch, veterans of the Union Army; as well as Colonel R. E. Colston and Colonel H. C. Derrick, Virginians from the Confederate Army. He promised Sherif that the Americans would "not be mixed up with the *mudirs* or the Egyptian soldiers, so would not interfere with the current ruling structure." Gordon asked Sherif Pasha "not to mention this matter to His Highness [the Khedive]. If you have reason to think His Highness will be against hiring them," he added in a footnote, "you are to destroy this letter." (In fact, Gordon later canceled the draft of new officers.)

So it was off to Abyssinia to bring the brigand-prince Walid el-Michael to heel. As in Darfur, Gordon had supreme confidence in his ability to solve the situation through his own powers of will and persuasion. Friends and advisers warned him against an encounter with Walid, but he would not be dissuaded and went on to the brigand's camp, pitched on a high plateau, six hours away.

As Gordon arrived in camp, seven thousand heavily armed men, looking none too friendly, were drawn up to receive him. Walid el-Michael did not greet Gordon right away on the excuse he was ill, but his son and a covey of priests waving sacred pictures did the honors. The Governor General and his ten-man escort were taken to their quarters, a tightly clustered group of huts imprisoned by a stockade. It made Gordon feel that he was "in the lion's den," fleas and all. A chorus of priests chanted hymns in the early morning—"I suppose to exorcise me," he wrote.

Gordon was somewhat Machiavellian in strategy. He recommended that Walid el-Michael seek Johannes's pardon for his marauding soldiers. This was predicated on Gordon's belief that if Sudanese soldiers were to attack the

Prince's forces at some later date, they could retreat into the Abyssinian wilds. But if King Johannes closed his border to them, they would have no choice but to "fight desperately," making the inferior Sudanese army's task even more difficult. When Walid el-Michael found the plan unacceptable, Gordon had no choice but to buy him off again. A subvention of £1,000 per month was agreed upon.

Gordon had gained time, but nothing else. The arena of trouble now shifted unexpectedly to Cairo, and Gordon, back in "civilization," would find himself quite out of his depth.

19

FROM CAMEL TO CAIRO
AND BACK

When one depends on one man, a bit of cheese or fig will cause
perhaps a change in that man's digestion and temper.
—Charles Gordon, referring to Egypt's Khedive Ismail

As 1878 began, Gordon found himself suddenly wrenched from his camel-riding, trouble-shooting life in remote lairs of iniquity and made to brave the even more fearsome salons of "civilized" Cairo. Fighting tribal conspiracies or unscrupulous slavers was nothing compared to facing international bureaucrats and Egyptian high society. The Khedive had summoned him to help with Egypt's now serious financial problems. This was indicative of Ismail's confidence in Gordon, unwarranted though it was in terms of any skills which the Governor General possessed. Gordon dreaded the assignment. "I have now been one year Governor General and I have lived a very rough sort of life, so much so that I have lost all my civilized tastes; the idea of dinners at Cairo makes me quail."

Indeed, Gordon's first obligation upon arrival in Cairo was to dine in style with the Khedive himself. He was lodged handsomely in a palace, which had recently accommodated General Ulysses S. Grant, "full of light, mirrors and gentlemen to wait on you." He was flattered but confessed, "I wish for my camel."

Khedive Ismail, like his predecessors, was shockingly profligate. His concept of fiscal policy did not go beyond squeezing the peasantry for taxes to an unendurable extent and borrowing recklessly from European creditors, thereby incurring obligations which Egypt could never hope to meet. The Suez Canal was perhaps the Khedive's only good investment, but his perilous economic position had forced him to sell his shares to the British in November 1875, during Disraeli's government, for £4 million. When the British government thus became the most influential stockholder in the Suez,

214

not only did it gain vital strategic advantage but its stake in the Egyptian economy rose accordingly. And Great Britain's grip on political power in Egypt was tightened.

Steps were taken to put Egyptain finances on a sounder basis after the British Paymaster General, Stephen Cave, M.P., found that Egypt's debt had risen to an appalling £81 million.[1] *The Cave Report,* which described a variety of other abuses, resulted in the imposition on Egypt in 1876 of four "Debt Commissioners," of English, French, Austrian and Italian nationalities, to oversee collections so that European bondholders could be assured of full payment. English and French Comptrollers General were also appointed to supervise Egyptian expenditures and collections.

Adding to the Khedive's problems was the Russo-Turkish War, which erupted in April 1877, and Turkey's demand that its vassal, Egypt, contribute thirty thousand soldiers to the cause. Not only would this be costly and require raising taxes, but the conscription of soldiers would also deplete Egypt's agricultural labor force. Even nature was unhelpful: The Nile in 1877 was lower than it had ever been. This created a food shortage, raised prices of foodstuffs, and brought on starvation. It was ruinous to the *fellahin,* Egypt's peasant farmers, who could not make enough to live on, much less pay the crushing taxes levied on them.

When the two major creditor nations, England and France, finally insisted that a "Commission of Inquiry" be appointed, the Khedive refused to agree on the scope of inquiry. For the board to have full details about Egypt's financial status would, in the Khedive's view, be an infringement on his sovereignty. If he had to accept such a commission, it would have to include an Egyptian representative, and the four members of the Debt Commission, whom the Khedive considered adversarial, should be excluded. For the time being his conditions were accepted, but the British would get their way.

The British member of the Debt Commission was a Captain Evelyn Baring—later to be made Earl of Cromer—scion of a prominent British banking family. In this capacity, Baring did not represent the British government, nor did he report formally to London, but he was a loyal British civil servant and it was clear where his true loyalties were. Baring was the principal architect of the concept of the Committee of Inquiry and thus earned the Khedive's lasting animosity. He questioned the accuracy of the statistics on the Egyptain economy drawn up by the English Comptroller

General, Romaine, and proposed that the true facts be gathered by on-the-spot investigators in the provinces. For the Khedive, this was getting too close for comfort.

Under this pressure from his European creditors, the Khedive sent for his friend Gordon, whom he trusted to defend his interests and whose Englishness might prove useful. To the astonishment of the British and French, he appointed Gordon the Egyptian representative and president of the Commission of Inquiry. As vice president of the commission, Ismail named another old friend, Ferdinand de Lesseps, builder of the Suez Canal, whose French nationality, he hoped, would be helpful in dealing with the French.

Gordon, who had nothing in his background to suit him for this assignment, was caught in a riptide. He knew he was not technically qualified, but his role was not as expert but as loyal servant of the Khedive, who could be relied upon to stand up to the Europeans and support the Khedive's positions. Here was the boy at military school butting authority in the solar plexus. He would not have disagreed with Baring's accusation that he was a "useful instrument" of the Khedive—in fact, he took pride in his loyalty to his employer. The point was that he feared Europe's unwillingness to soften the terms of Egypt's debt would be intolerable to the Egyptian people whose taxes paid the interest.

Baring, for that matter, came to this view as well, blaming the hard line on the French, particularly the French representative in Cairo, Baron Des Michels. Baring considered the French bondholders far less reasonable than the English, believing that "it was impossible for any one of ordinary humanity and common sense to ignore the pitiable condition in which the people of Egypt were then placed. The British Government thus became in a certain degree responsible for the oppression which necessarily accompanied the collection of taxes."[2] It would not be the last time that Gordon and Baring found themselves in agreement; their differences often arose from contrasting styles and conflicting personalities rather than substance.

Because he refused to support their position, Gordon immediately became a target of European attack. Goschen and Joubert, as staunch defenders of British and French bondholders, questioned Gordon's qualifications. H. C. Vivian, British Consul General in Cairo, warned that Gordon's acceptance of the role as Egyptian representative might well lead to the downfall of the

Khedive. And Baring felt it necessary to state his opposition to Gordon's appointment as well.

Baring and Gordon had few things in common, but one was that they had both gone to Woolwich Academy. Baring was several years Gordon's junior and had been commissioned in the Royal Artillery, while Gordon was in the Engineers. As Gordon condescendingly noted, "He was in the nursery when I was in the Crimea." They were also destined six years later to have lead parts in trying to save the Sudan from the Mahdi. Each would fight that epic battle with different weapons: Baring with bureaucratic expertise, Gordon with stubborn physical resistance.

In March 1878, Gordon and Baring met face to face as adversaries in Cairo. Gordon, loyal to the Khedive, rejected the concept of including the four European Commissioners of the Debt (including Baring) in the Commission of Inquiry. Baring, intent on protecting England's bondholders, found that position untenable. Gordon's short account of their meeting summed it up:

> When downstairs, in one of the many ante-chambers of the palace His Highness gave me, I found Baring. He has a pretentious, grand, patronizing way about him. We had a few words together. I said, "I would do what his Highness asked me." He said, "it was unfair to the creditors," and in a few moments all was over. . . . When oil mixes with water, we will mix together.

In his memoir, *Modern Egypt*, Baring chose to overlook this meeting, and he dismissed Gordon casually: "The negotiation with General Gordon, however, soon broke down and he left Egypt. The sole reason why the negotiations broke down was that it was evident to everyone concerned, including Gordon himself, that he was not fitted to conduct any financial inquiry."[3]

Gordon had very little good to say about any of the Europeans engaged in the financial drama in Cairo. He did not like one of the British negotiators, Walker, because the man parted his hair in the middle. Another, whose name was Pasquali, provoked Gordon to say that he had no time for people whose name ended in "i," whom he fully expected "to break into song at any moment."

While Gordon stuck by the Khedive in the face of European pressure, the Khedive in the end sacrificed him. Ismail no longer supported Gordon's dogged stand on excluding the Debt Commissioners from the Board of Inquiry, or his sensible proposal to relieve Egypt of its impossible burden by lowering the interest on the debt, even though that had been his own position. Sherif Pasha, who by then was Egyptian Minister of Finance, presided over a final meeting in which a disgusted Gordon watched helplessly as de Lesseps buckled under on the issue, leaving Gordon alone in his stand. The pressure on the Khedive by European representatives had been intense, and Egypt's ruler realized that if he continued to oppose European vested interests, he would be forced from power.

Gordon was furious, even if he pretended otherwise when he wrote home: "H. H. threw me over completely at the last minute; but far from being angry, I was very glad, for it relieved me of a deal of trouble. . . . I laughed at all this farce." His laughter was unconvincing, particularly when he discovered that he would have to personally finance the whole unhappy excursion to Cairo. More important, it hurt him to learn that the Khedive "was bored" with him for his performance.

Gordon was less harsh in his judgment of de Lesseps, who he thought had slavishly followed the Khedive's lead in almost everything. As an aside he found it remarkable that the Frenchman, in his seventies, had just become father of a child. Gordon thought this extraordinary, though on reflection he thought all the credit should go to de Lesseps's "pretty young wife" of only twenty-two years.

Gordon blamed the failure of his Cairo mission on the weakness of the Khedive. "When one depends on one man, a bit of cheese or fig will cause perhaps a change in that man's digestion and temper." But the Khedive's problem was caused neither by cheese nor fig. Realist that he was, Ismail knew he was outpowered by England and France. He saw no point in playing Sancho Panza to Gordon's Don Quixote. While Khedive Ismail's tenure of power was, as it turned out, not significantly prolonged by this submission, he had shown more wisdom than weakness—certainly more than had Gordon—in bowing to the inevitable. Gordon admitted later: "I was too outspoken at Cairo."

While Cairo had opened Gordon's eyes to the realities of big-power politics in Egypt, his nomadic existence in the Sudan and his preoccupation with problems of slavery had kept him remote from the big issues in Europe. When Disraeli became Prime Minister in 1874, a change in imperial attitude was bound to affect British policy toward Egypt. The Prime Minister's master stroke in quickly buying up the 44 percent bloc of Suez Canal shares, put on the market in Paris in 1875 by the near-bankrupt Khedive, set the tone. A vital lifeline in India was now under British control, and Egypt's strategic importance became all the more apparent. Turkey's nominal role as Egypt's suzerain increased Britain's stake in the survival of the Ottoman Empire, as well.

When Russia took advantage of France's preoccupation with the Franco-Prussian War to repudiate clauses in the 1856 Treaty of Paris neutralizing the Black Sea, Britain could only protest. With only Turkey, "the sick man," as an ally, war against Russia seemed unwise, though Gladstone's government was nonetheless accused by many in England of being too soft toward Russia. When Disraeli became Prime Minister, however, things changed.

Parliament's action in 1876 of bestowing on Queen Victoria the new title "Empress of India" was a signal to St. Petersburg: Russia's steady advance across the Central Asian steppes toward Afghanistan and India would not go unresisted. Disraeli was no less concerned with Russian designs on the Balkans, although Turkey's mistreatment of Balkan Christians made defending the Sultan against Russian advances more difficult to justify.

The Turkish provinces of Bosnia and Herzegovina rose in revolt during the summer of 1875. The next year saw Bulgaria, Serbia, and Montenegro revolt, with Russian instigation, against the Sultan's rule. Russia intervened to prevent Turkish troops from seizing Belgrade. With support from Austria and Germany, the Czar formally insisted that Turkey adopt sweeping reforms as regards the Balkan peoples. Disraeli rejected this request, accusing Russia of "asking us to sanction them in putting a knife to the throat of Turkey." To punctuate Britain's refusal and to impress upon the Sultan that Britain would remain faithful to its treaty obligations, Disraeli stationed the Mediterranean fleet off the Dardanelles.

Faced with Turkey's rejection of Russia's demands, Czar Alexander II declared war on the Ottoman Empire. In April 1877 one Russian army, led by Alexander himself, marched through Rumania and Bulgaria, while another harassed Turkey in the Caucasus.

Gladstone called for England to join the Russians against the Sultan, but

Queen Victoria threatened to abdicate rather than "kiss the feet of [Russian] barbarians." As Russian troops neared Constantinople, Disraeli dismissed the offers of Russian armistice as "a comedy" and sent five warships into the Sea of Marmara to protect British lives. Parliament, now thoroughly alarmed at the prospects of Russian control over the Dardanelles, voted funds to place the army on a war footing.

The passions of the British public were aroused, as exemplified by this popular ditty of the day:

> We don't want to fight,
> But by jingo, if we do,
> We've got the men, we've got the ships
> And we've got the money too.

This was how the term "jingoism" came into being.

The Russian threat to Constantinople occurred at precisely the time that Gordon found himself outmaneuvered in Cairo. These developments made it difficult for the Khedive to oppose British demands, and on March 30, 1877, he signed the document establishing a Commission of Inquiry.

It was less than a month after Russia forced Turkey to the bargaining table at San Stefano that the Ottoman Empire in Europe seemed doomed. But Russia had overstepped. The San Stefano agreement was undone by British and other European powers in the Treaty of Berlin. Turkey had been given a reprieve, and in a separate Turko-British Convention, Great Britain was rewarded with the strategic island of Cyprus in return for a promise to defend Turkey's territorial integrity against future Russian aggression. Disraeli had avoided war and achieved "peace with honour," but at a price. Bismarck, who emerged with more power, would rattle Europe in the future, and Balkan nationalism now aggravated the "Eastern Question" more than ever.

Two years later Gordon would privately publish an essay in which he set down his reflections on the Eastern Question.* It was his belief that the Treaty of Berlin, which was supposed to be beneficial to Turkey, caused the Sublime Porte to lose Bulgaria and Rumelia as well as Bosnia and Herzegovina. Turkey had gained the dubious advantage of occupying a hostile Balkans. The result was bad for Turkey and worse for Europe.

---

* *Memorandum on the Treaties of San Stephano and Berlin* (London: Edward Stanford, March 1880).

A better solution would have been for England to buy Cyprus and for Bulgaria and Rumelia to be reunified. Greece should be enlarged. And as far as the Near East and Red Sea area were concerned, Britain should annex Egypt, either directly or by assuming total authority; France should annex Syria, which would give Paris as much motive as London to stop Russian advances toward Turkey; and Italy should extend its control in the Abyssinian Red Sea coastal areas.

Moreover, according to Gordon in his essay, Russia, in the great power equation, need not be so worrisome. "I believe, it would be quite possible to come to terms with Russia on these questions; I do not think she has sailed under false colours when her acts and words are generally considered. [Russia] was an avowed enemy of Turkey, while England by its policies has more subtly harmed that country: What did we do to press Turkey to carry out reforms?—absolutely nothing!"

But Gordon's thoughts on the Eastern Question, whatever their worth, were still in the future when Gordon beat a retreat from Cairo in February 1878. He traveled first to the Gulf of Aden coastline, through Zeila near Djibouti, then Berbera, farther along the coast in what is today Somalia, finally to Harrar, now in eastern Ethiopia.

Slave traffic was rampant in this area, but Gordon's humiliating experience in Cairo had sapped his crusading ardor for the moment. "I feel quite different to what I did before. I have no hope whatever in any change for the better in headquarters." He had read the handwriting on the wall, quite accurately as it would turn out: "H. H. will be curbed in and will no longer be absolute sovereign. H. H. does not a bit like me, but fears me and feels—or rather thinks—I am necessary. This thought makes me act very differently: I now look only to benefit the peoples. . . . I am on an incline and down it I must go: there is no stopping."

Harrar was a remote, walled citadel, a "forbidden city" denied to European eyes until Richard Burton made exploration history by visiting there in 1855. Gordon had gone to Harrar despite a stern warning from the British Consul in Aden as to the danger there: "The human head, once struck off, does not regrow like the rose."[4] At the entrance to the city, Gordon was greeted by two dying cows whose throats had been slit as a sacrifice in his honor. At the Governor's mansion, "there was another cow sobbing out her life, with streams of blood flowing over the threshold."

221

SLAVERS AND BRIGANDS

The Governor of Harrar was none other than Mohammed Ra'uf—now elevated to the rank of pasha—whom Gordon had fired for incompetence in Equatoria four years before. Now Gordon fired him again for the crimes of misgovernment and tyranny. Among other outrages, Ra'uf Pasha had capriciously strangled the local Emir and imprisoned the chief of the important Gala tribe.

On his return journey, Gordon discovered in Massawa that Walid el-Michael, who had wheedled extra ammunition out of the Egyptian administrator, had attacked Johannes's troops and killed their commander, Ras Bariou. Gordon was irritated: "It is inconceivable what owls these Egyptians are."

But if Michael posed the greatest obstacle to making peace with King Johannes in Abyssinia, Suleiman Zubair was still the *bête noir* of the Sudan. There was intelligence that the unruly young scoundrel had driven out the old chief of Bahr al-Ghazal Province and otherwise ignored his pledge of good behavior. For Gordon, this meant a punitive expedition in order to keep some semblance of peace in the south.

First, however, there was the matter of the Sudan's finances. His brief fiasco in Cairo had impressed upon him the need to balance the Sudan's chronically unbalanced budget. Making matters worse was an effort by Sir Rivers Wilson, the British head of the Commission of Inquiry in Cairo, to have the Sudan increase its tribute payments to Egypt. Only by appealing to the British Foreign Office over Wilson's head was Gordon able to stop this raid on the Sudan's meager resources.

Gordon proposed other savings by cutting off from the Sudan the province of Harrar. This remote appendage had long been a drain on the Sudan's resources without providing anything useful in return. The Governor General also saw savings to be made by curtailing the scope of the Khedive's pet railway project, which was meant to link Egypt with the Sudan and give Cairo better control of this troublesome colony. Steamships on those navigable parts of the Nile would be both cheaper and better.

Because of limited resources, the Sudan could no longer afford the Khedive's dream of extending Egypt's territory deep into Equatorial Africa. Mrooli, some hundred miles north of Lake Victoria, would mark the southern border of Egypt's claim. It was disheartening to have his efforts in Uganda go for naught. Dr. Emin had performed magnificently in the south;

at the same time as Gordon was trying to tame Suleiman Zubáir in Darfur, Emin had courageously visited the old enemy, Chief Kabarega of Bunyoro, and succeeded in patching up some of their differences. And Emin had made a second visit to Mutesa to maintain relations with Buganda. Nonetheless, Gordon could not see how the great lake region in Equatoria would pay for the cost of maintaining an Egyptian presence there, particularly since it would likely find itself in competition with European powers now scrambling for Africa. The future of the Khedive Ismail was, in any case, uncertain.

Khartoum in July 1878 was depressing. The heat was enervating, and pestilence rife. A record-breaking flood brought on a malaria epidemic so bad that the year was long remembered as "the mosquito year." But worst of all, things were at a standstill: "When I find, in spite of all I do, no real progress is made, I feel sickened and wish I were at rest." While flying through the lonely desert on his favorite racing camel he could be content, but in the Governor General's palace, he only felt immured by bureaucratic frustrations.

Malaria in Khartoum was almost endemic. Though he suffered, he never felt afraid: "It is a very great comfort to me never to have the least fear of death when I am ill." To keep himself diverted, Gordon made a small zoo on the palace grounds. His pet ostrich disgraced itself, however, by kicking a man's nose off. To raise money as reparation for the unhappy victim, Gordon had the ostrich's feathers plucked yearly and sold. But Gordon's favorite animal was a strolling hippo that was "loveable."

Amid the heat and sickness came the news that Khedive Ismail had offered to abdicate. "I am stronger than ever in my belief that if H. H. had taken my advice, he would have fallen with dignity," Gordon contended, even as he realized that with Ismail gone, his own future was uncertain.

In the meantime, Gordon continued at his tasks, but to do his job thoroughly, he needed to find honest and efficient administrators. Though it was not easy to attract them to the Sudan, he attempted to recruit more Europeans. For one, Emin Pasha had proved himself in the south, and Gordon rewarded him by making him Governor of Equatoria Province.

Romolo Gessi, who had left in December 1876, had petitioned Gordon repeatedly to be rehired. Gordon refused. He advised Gessi, then in Cairo, not to leave his family, but what really may have been the issue was, as

Gordon complained in a letter, that the Italian had become "very much too grand" and may have indulged in "peculation." Gessi was so angry with Gordon for rejecting him that in a fit of pique he threatened to publish their correspondence, some 250 letters, presumably to embarrass the Governor General. Gordon dismissed the threat: "For what interest would anyone have in reading them?—Fancy his keeping the letters, one by one."

Despite this tiff, Gessi turned up again in Khartoum in early 1878. He needed Gordon's permission to explore the headwaters of the Sobat River, which, flowing from the southeast, joins the White Nile near present-day Malakal. Gessi was apprehensive; Gordon was not predisposed to geographical exploration, he knew, and had in fact notified the foreign consuls in Khartoum that policy on this matter would be strictly enforced. Gessi, moreover, feared that Gordon might wrongly suspect him of instigating an article in the Italian magazine *Exploratore* [5] which accused the Governor General of banning explorers to keep them from seeing firsthand the rampant "collaboration between the authorities and the slavers."

The Italian's fears were unfounded. Gordon greeted Gessi warmly and even encouraged him to extend the Sobat expedition by crossing the watershed and following the Juba River, rising in the Abyssinian highlands, to its mouth on the Indian Ocean. Gordon hoped this would reveal a new route linking the southern Sudan with East Africa. He offered Gessi arms and a government steamer to transport him to the south. The old friendship was reestablished.

Gordon, in conversation with some missionaries passing through Khartoum en route to Buganda, learned of an English merchant marine officer named Frank Lupton who had been plying the Red Sea in the Khedive's service. Without knowing much more about him, except that he never drank, Gordon hired Lupton and earmarked him to administer the troubled Bahr al-Ghazal Province.

In Khartoum, the German telegraph engineer Carl Christian Giegler was made Gordon's deputy, while the Austrian adventurer Ernest Marno, who had served briefly in Lado three years earlier, was also given a government post. For Governor of Darfur, Gordon picked an Italian engineer named Messedaglia who would be aided by an Austrian naval officer of Venetian descent named Emiliani Danziger. It was a motley collection of expatriates who now formed Gordon's foreign legion.

FROM CAMEL TO CAIRO AND BACK

One of the most fateful appointments made by Gordon was a young Austrian adventurer named Rudolf C. Slatin, whose Sudan career would prove to be the longest and most harrowing of all. The origins of this extraordinary man, destined to survive eleven years in cruel detention, were commonplace. Growing up in Vienna in a family which teetered between bourgeois respectability and lower middle class, Slatin learned to live by his wits. His father and mother, both Jewish, had become Roman Catholic—an advantage in Austrian society. Rudolf's father died early, making it imperative that Rudolf become self-supporting at a young age.[6] At seventeen, the adventurous Rudolf chose to seek his fortune in Africa.

In Cairo, the first stop in his odyssey, Rudolf Slatin found work in a bookstore. He was befriended by a German explorer named Heuglin who invited him to join a scientific expedition to the Red Sea coast. These plans went awry, but Slatin struck out on his own for the Sudan anyway. He wandered about from autumn 1874 to the end of 1875, finding work where he could. He stayed for a while with the Austrian missionaries at Delen, but his efforts to go on to Darfur's capital, El Fasher, were blocked when Zubair invaded that province.

In Khartoum's tightly knit European community, Slatin came to know Dr. Emin. Both applied to Gordon for employment in Equatoria, although Slatin had first to return to Austria to perform his military duty. In July 1878, while Slatin was completing his service with the Austrian army on the Bosnian frontier, Gordon wrote to offer him a job. The young Austrian hastened to Khartoum.

In the interim Suleiman Zubair, smarting under his banishment to Bahr al-Ghazal, had risen in revolt. The slaver's forces fell upon the government station at Dem Idris and massacred the entire garrison of two hundred soldiers, butchering many of the women and children as well. Governor Idris barely managed to escape, but all his supplies fell into Suleiman's hands. Gordon feared that the steamer *Ismailia*, stuck in the Sudd's papyrus marshes, might also be seized.

It became clear that this was not simply an isolated act of revenge by Suleiman—it was a serious bid for power. More ominously, evidence of complicity on the part of Suleiman's illustrious father in Cairo gave the revolt a dangerous dimension. When Gordon seized Zubair Pasha's house in Khartoum, lived in by relatives since the great slaver had been exiled to

225

Egypt, he found forty valuable hand-tooled saddles sent by Zubair for shipment to Darfur. Here was evidence to suggest that the horse-proud chiefs of Darfur might have been recruited to join in the revolt.

Gordon suddenly realized that Gessi, fortunately at hand, was precisely the man he needed to lead a compaign against the rebellious Suleiman. He canceled the Italian's Sobat River expedition and appealed to him for help. Gessi was not enthusiastic, but finally agreed. In his memoir, Gessi wrote: "As a European, I thought it my duty to sacrifice my own plans and . . . I accepted the command."[7] He had, in fact, succumbed to Gordon's blandishments as most people did.

20

DARFUR CAMPAIGN

There is no need for a guide, as it is only necessary to follow . . .
the track of the skeletons of negroes scattered along the way.
—Romolo Gessi on Darfur

R omolo Gessi sailed on the steamer *Bordein* from Khartoum at 4:00 in the afternoon on July 15, 1878. From his balcony Gordon waved him farewell, while most of the townfolk saw him off from the shore. Additional troops were to be collected along the way. The Italian hoped he would make his final advance with 7,656 men in all, but even this optimum force would be none too large to dislodge Suleiman and his six thousand crack fighters from their two strongholds, Dem Suleiman and Dem Idris, deep within Bahr al-Ghazal.

Zubair's slave dynasty had been built on the power and wealth which came to those who traded in human beings on a large scale, but young Suleiman's defiance of Khartoum sounded a political note as well. Since leaving the Sudan, his father had never ceased his efforts to return, complaining constantly that the corrupt Egyptian officials in Khartoum and Cairo had no right to interfere with his slaving kingdom, fairly won by the sword and gun. In the old slaver's opinion, Egyptian officials who decried the morals of slave trading were hypocrites, and Gordon, a European, had no right to interfere with the established order and custom of the land. In fact, neither the Egyptian nor the Sudanese establishment really wanted him to upset the system. Gordon's mandate had come from Khedive Ismail; with the Khedive's humiliation at the hands of European bondholders and his removal altogether under European pressure, whatever personal backing was given Gordon's efforts by the deposed ruler was no longer a factor.

The rebellion raised by Suleiman was profound in its implications. At the core was the issue of who would run the Sudan: slave barons like the Zubairs, who meant to gain the country by force and run it by terror; Egyptians, who were interested only in exploitation and territorial aggrandizement; or

227

Europeans, who may have been sincere as far as slaving was concerned but were distracted by more pressing problems elsewhere.

Gordon made a frantic appeal to Egypt's Chief Minister Nubar Pasha for more troops to put down Suleiman's rebellion. Back came an incredible response—an offer to send Suleiman's father, Zubair Pasha! The Governor General was appalled. What cynicism! How could Cairo suggest putting the old fox in with the chickens? The time would come when Gordon would recommend precisely the same thing, but now he huffily declined the Minister's offer. He wanted no help from Cairo "in any way."

It was clear that if the Sudan was going to remain more or less unified and free from slaving, it would be because of Gordon and Gessi and no one else. The battle lines had been drawn: Gordon against the Zubair family. Gessi, however, felt no particular loyalty to Egypt, which had never adequately appreciated his work in Equatoria anyway; he was willing to fight Suleiman only because of his loyalty to Gordon and because he was a soldier at heart.

Gessi landed his troops at Chambe on the Nile to make the long march westward. His scouting report told him that when crossing the county "not a village was to be found; nothing was to be met with but the ruins of huts. There is no need for a guide, as it is only necessary to follow . . . the track of the skeletons of negroes scattered along the way."[1] As the men proceeded, they encountered flood waters which slowed up the campaign; for three hours one day they struggled through water up to their necks. The tribes they met along the way were reserved, unimpressed as they were with the chances of defeating Zubair. Things were not helped when some of Gessi's Egyptian officers took advantage of the young tribal girls.

It was not until mid-November 1878 that Gessi felt ready. By capturing and then doubling a spy sent by Suleiman, he deceived the slaver into believing that Dem Suleiman would be his first target, when in fact he planned to attack Dem Idris. With Suleiman thus deceived, Dem Idris was taken on December 27 without a shot being fired. Gessi had the whole night to increase its fortifications before Suleiman discovered the ruse and could bring his main force to bear.

Dem Idris had been held by Abul Ghassem, one of Suleiman's lieutenants, who flaunted a special pennant of revolt celebrating the massacre of the once-Egyptian garrison. When a stiff wind blew the pennant down, it was said that Abul Ghassem had four oxen and a small boy killed to appease an angry heaven. A new flag which had been dipped in the boy's blood was raised again on the ramparts, only to be ripped down—this time by Gessi's attacking troops. The heavens had not been appeased.

Shortly after dawn the next day, six thousand of Suleiman's troops swept down on Gessi's hastily built fortifications—defended by less than 2,500 men. With almost suicidal bravery, waves of Suleiman's warriors flung themselves at the stockade, but Gessi's new artillery pieces, supported by withering rifle fire, beat them off. Suleiman's army retreated after two and a half hours; four thousand were left dead in the field. While Gessi's force had clearly won the round, fever and fatigue were the new enemy, one not so easily driven off. In addition, the inability to resupply the beleaguered outpost with needed ammunition, because of the water-sodden countryside, was particularly worrisome.

Two weeks later Suleiman returned with reinforcements and attacked in full force. Before going into battle, the slaver's officers had sworn on the Koran to succeed or die in the effort; they then drove their black slave troops forward, literally lopping off the heads of any who faltered. Two attacks were repulsed by Gessi's men. A third attack was made the next morning, the fighting going on for seven hours before Suleiman's men broke and fled to the forest. It was a measure of Suleiman's bravery that he dismounted and refused to retreat with the others. If his lieutenants had not bodily removed him from the field of battle, he would surely have been killed.

Gessi's stockade was spared attack for another two weeks. With ammunition dangerously low, the men collected spent shells and refilled them. The wounded and sick were cared for, though no stocks of medicine remained. When the next blow fell on January 28, 1879, the little garrison was in bad shape, although morale was high. Suleiman's force attacked viciously for two days, but Gessi's men held out—even after the stockade burned down and they had to defend themselves in the tall grass outside. Suleiman's troops finally wearied and withdrew to new positions above the charred stockade; they dug in behind hastily felled trees.

A small shipment of powder, enough to sustain one more attack, finally arrived. Going on the offense, Gessi bombarded Suleiman's log enclosure with Congreve rockets, burning the barricades to a crisp. He attacked with a now-or-never resolve. After hours of fighting and heavy losses, Suleiman's men fled in defeat, leaving hundreds of charred dead bodies behind. As they retreated along a waterlogged road, even more died by sinking horribly in quicksand.

Gessi's victorious but tired force was then struck by smallpox. As the men convalesced, they were invaded by some twelve thousand camp followers, women, children and hawkers hungry for food already in pitifully short supply. But then came some good news: A relief column was advancing from the north. More immediately helpful, an ammunition caravan finally arrived from Bahr al-Ghazal.

Badly weakened by his unsuccessful campaign against Gessi, Suleiman appealed to the slave traders of Shaka for reinforcements, and appealed to the renegade Sultan Haroun el-Rashid of Darfur to join him.

Back in Khartoum, Gordon had to deal with the larger picture. While there was the news of Gessi's successes, delayed intelligence reported the possibility that Haroun and Suleiman would join forces. Trouble was brewing also in Kordofan Province, where a former lieutenant of Zubair's named Sabahi had murdered Gordon's administrator in Edowa. The rebellion was beginning to look like a widespread revolution.

Gordon himself set out from Khartoum in the hope of bringing relief to the still-outnumbered Gessi. Specifically he wanted to prevent Suleiman from getting support either from Kordofan or from Haroun in Darfur. Gordon's plan was to pick up soldiers along the way and to get close to Gessi so as to relieve the pressure. His target city was Shaka, the slaver's den, where he hoped "to make a clean sweep, a death blow to the slave dealers."[2]

Nature, as usual in the Sudan, posed a greater hazard than hostile man. When Gordon and his fifteen-man escort reached the Darfur border, they found the wells dry. "I have never, in China or elsewhere, felt such heat," he despaired.The closest wells were a day and a half away, but the tired and thirsty little band had no choice. They straggled on despite the risk of attack by Sabahi and his rebels. Taking advantage of the relative coolness of the night and the cover it provided, they made it safely.

Unknown to Gordon, Gessi had prepared to strike what would have to be a crippling, fatal blow to Suleiman's revolt. With fresh ammunition supplies and a trickle of reinforcements, the Italian was now deep within enemy territory, but he could not remain much longer. Early in March 1879, Gessi marched his troops out of the battered, burned-out stockade which had been their home for four months and made their way to Dem Suleiman for a final showdown with the slave chief. This would be Gessi's test; everything hung on its outcome.

After three days of travel, Gessi approached within four miles of Suleiman's heavily fortified town, surprising a large force in a ravine gathering water from a stream. By seizing this water source, Gessi knew he would have a valuable advantage over his adversary. He quickly overwhelmed Suleiman's men and cut them off from their fort. The Italian then turned his attention to the stockade. His preliminary bombardment ignited the flimsy straw huts, turning the compound into a raging inferno.

Suleiman's army fought Gessi's until nightfall, when they retired to their smoldering fort. Deprived of water and secure defenses, what remained of Suleiman's army fled under cover of darkness. As Gessi surveyed the scene in the morning, he saw the town totally deserted except for one lone, brooding figure sitting near the gate. It was Suleiman. Gessi's troops rushed down the hill but arrived too late; the slaver had escaped. Nonetheless, a great victory had been won. Gessi had broken the back of the slaver's rebellion.

In the meantime, Gordon was making his way toward Shaka. He encountered ragged groups of slaves being transported by the *jellabas*, those donkey-mounted slave merchants who acted as middlemen between the powerful slave raiders and the marketplace. He was sickened. He wanted to release the slaves, but legally he was caught in between. Cairo had decreed draconian punishment for slave traders, but had ruled, inconsistently, that "the sale and purchase of slaves in Egypt is legal."[3] As a practical solution he would usually enlist the men and boys in the army, while the freed women were encouraged to become wives of the soldiers. "What else can I do?" he complained.

Two slave dealers and seventeen miserable slaves, including women who "were quite nude," were brought into the camp. Gordon noted that slaves when freed never showed any joy; perhaps they had been drained of all emotion by their brutalization, or they had nowhere to go. "These captives," he noted, "make the total of captured caravans since June 1878 sixty three."

"I appeal to my countrymen who have wives and families, and who can realize to some degree the bitterness of parting with them—to God—what it must be for those poor black peoples to have their happy households rent asunder for an effete, alien set like the pashas of Egypt and Turkey," Gordon wrote in an article which appeared in the London *Times*.[4] The Darfur

231

experience had affected Gordon deeply; he wrote to his friend Watson: "The gate of mercy is shut and locked and the key lost."[5]

Then in a long letter to his sister from Edowa, dated March 31, 1879, he agonized again about his decision to leave the Khedive's service: "To die quickly would be to me nothing, but the long crucifixion that a residence in these horrid countries entails appalls me." Gordon thought about remaining, not as Governor General of the entire Sudan, but simply as Governor of the western and southern provinces, to complete his dream of crushing the slave dealers. "Many will say it is a worthy cause to die in. But, oh! it is a long and weary one, and for the moment I cannot face it."

On April 7, 1879, Gordon arrived in Shaka, much to the consternation of a town devoted to the slave trade. He was pleased with "the grief of the slave dealers, of whom there are some hundred, on hearing that they were to clear out. . . . We must have caught 2,000 [slaves] in less than nine months, and I expect we did not catch one fifth of the caravans. . . . how many died en route? . . . The Government of Egypt . . . is nothing else but one of brigandage of the very worst description. It is so bad that all hope of ameliorating it is hopeless; so I do the only thing possible, that is, vacate them."

Gordon was in a foul mood. Shaka may have been cleaned out, but Suleiman Zubair was still at large, having escaped to Darfur. And Haroun el-Rashid with his Darfur rebels was still holed up in the mountains waiting for an opportunity to strike. Gordon and Gessi were in sporadic correspondence by courier and hoped for a rendezvous soon to plot their mop-up strategy. In the meantime Gordon wondered: "The 25,000 black troops I have here [throughout the Sudan] are either captured slaves or bought slaves. How are we to recruit if the slave trade ceases?"

While waiting in Shaka, Gordon received four of Suleiman's men, including his chief secretary, who had been sent to plead the slaver's case—an indication that he knew Gordon was closing in on him. They tried to convince the Governor General that Suleiman had really been loyal to the Khedive all along. Unconvinced, Gordon ordered them shot. "Had Sepehr's [Zubair's] son not massacred the unfortunate soldiers in the Bahr al-Ghazal, I might have pardoned them, but no, I shall not do so."

During his long hours in Shaka, Gordon had time to read newspapers from home when they caught up with him; it was a rare pleasure. He learned of

British reverses in Afghanistan: "It is just as well we have these lessons taught us *en petit*. We are a great deal too confident in ourselves and despise ordinary precautions. . . . Men now risk dangers in the hope of paper distinction. However savage or despicable your enemy may be, you never should despise precautions which you would take against a European foe. . . . " Paraphrasing a motto he learned from Richard Burton, Gordon regretted: "Now the race is for honours, not honour."[6]

Gordon and Gessi were not able to consult, face to face, until June 25, 1879, in Taweisha, some eighty miles north of Shaka. Gessi was war-weary but cheered at the news that he had been awarded the Egyptian rank of pasha and given the coveted Osmanli, Second Class, citation for his campaign. After the plotting strategy, Gessi set out once again on Suleiman's trail. With only a 250-man escort—his main force remaining three hundred miles to the south—he was vulnerable to attack, but it was important to stop Suleiman before he reached Haroun's camp. Suleiman, with ten times the number of troops, had left Shaka, proceeding unwittingly toward Gessi, intent on joining Haroun.

While still traveling in the west, Gordon received a telegram from Cairo announcing the removal of Khedive Ismail from office by the Turkish Sultan and his replacement by Ismail's son, Tewfik Pasha. Gordon was ordered to proclaim the news throughout the Sudan. The inevitable fall of his patron was now formally decreed.

With Ismail out, Gordon felt more than ever that he should leave the Sudan, but he had much to do before going to Cairo and tendering his resignation. First, he had to meet the young Austrian Rudolf Slatin, whom he had appointed Mudir of Dara in Darfur Province, at a rendezvous on the Nile. Slatin would soon find himself in charge of the campaign against Haroun el-Rashid, so it was important that he have the benefit of Gordon's briefing.

Slatin's first position after arriving in the Sudan in January 1879 had been Inspector of Finances. This had required him to travel in the provinces, examining the tax system. It gave him an opportunity to see at close range the inequity and corruption which dominated provincial governments—a disillusioning introduction to the realities of the Sudan. The distribution of the tax load was grossly unjust, he discovered, and the tax collectors, mostly from the hated Bashi-Bazouks and the pro-Egyptian Shaigiya tribe, were cruel in their methods. The experience had been traumatic. Years later he recalled: "Feeling my utter inability under the circumstances to effect any reform and having at the time little or no financial experience, I felt it was useless to continue, and therefore sent in my resignation."[7] It was then that Gordon reassigned him to Darfur.

As arranged, Slatin and Gordon met along the Nile, east of El Obeid. In his memoir, *Fire and Sword in the Sudan*, the Austrian reported coming upon his commander sprawling under a large tree, "evidently very tired and exhausted after his long ride, and suffering from sores on his legs."[8] With him were Hassan el-Juwaizer, former Governor of Kordofan and Darfur, and Yusef es-Shellali, one of Gessi's officers, who had quarreled with the Italian and was returning to Khartoum. Slatin produced a bottle of brandy to revive them, and then they set out by camel for Tura el-Hadra, where Gordon's steamers waited for him.

"Gordon shot far ahead of us," recalled Slatin, "and we found it impossible to keep up with his rapid pace." On arrival Gordon and Slatin boarded the *Ismailia*, where they discussed the Darfur situation and the campaign against Haroun. "It was past 10:00 when he bade me goodbye, and, as I stepped over the side, he said in French, 'Goodby, my dear Slatin and God bless you; I am sure you will do your best under any circumstances.'" Gordon told Slatin that he would probably be returning to England and expressed the hope they would meet there. While the two men would, in fact, never meet again, both were destined to find their lives enmeshed in the drama which would later unfold in the Sudan.

Upon arriving in Khartoum, Gordon described himself as a "wreck, like the portion of the *Victory* towed into Gibraltar after Trafalgar." He could find satisfaction in his recent Darfur campaign, but Suleiman was still at large, though Gessi was on his heels.

Suleiman had a force of about eight hundred with him, while another contingent of his army traveled separately. A third group of about eight hundred had abandoned Suleiman and fled westward rather than risk defeat by Gessi. Taking advantage of this dispersal, Gessi, with his 250 men, pursued the slaver and surrounded the village where he was staying. Gessi's own account of the ambush describes the slaver's capture: "At 6:00 A.M. in a violent shower of rain, we arrived at Gara. Everyone there was asleep. There was neither sentinel nor scout to give the alarm. . . . I went forward some 20 paces and sent a message to Suleiman [saying] 'I give you five minutes to surrender.' "[9]

Suleiman and most of his men did surrender. The young slaver was furious to the point of tears when he discovered how few men Gessi had. He turned to one of his chiefs and ranted, "They have not more than 300 men, and you told me that there were 3,000 among them; if only my father had been here to take command we should never have been beaten."[10]

Intelligence reached Gessi that Suleiman and his men would try to escape, and he decided to act decisively. The information had been fabricated, unbeknownst to Gessi, by members of Suleiman's entourage who were conspiring to inherit the large store of loot collected by the slaving army, but it made no difference to Gessi, who concluded he could no longer put up with Suleiman's intrigues. The Italian commander spared the common soldiers on the understanding they would return to their villages; the petty slave dealers, 157 in all, were packed off to Khartoum in chains; and Suleiman and his principal officers were sentenced to death. Gessi gave the order for execution, and they were summarily shot.

Gessi telegraphed the news to Gordon at Foggia as the Governor General was making his way back to Khartoum. Gordon took full responsibility for Suleiman's execution, which predictably aroused criticism in Cairo, where Zubair Pasha still had considerable influence. Gordon wrote home at the time: "Gessi only obeyed my orders in shooting him [Suleiman]; I have no compunction about his death."

While a compassionate man, capable of crying over the deaths of his Chinese troops in the Ever Victorious Army, he was a soldier who understood the cruel realities of war. He had written Gessi on June 13, 1879: "I am not going to leave Darfur till I hear of Suleiman's *entire* collapse."[11] He had confidence in Gessi's judgment; rather than burden his friend with requests for explanation, he backed him completely. He even found time to add a friendly touch, in a letter sent him from El Obeid, joshing him for probably having "taken nearly all the women of the country from their husbands!!!"[12]

When Gordon left Khartoum on July 29, 1879, for Cairo he had the satisfaction of knowing that the Zubair slave empire was no longer. Not long afterward, Haroun el-Rashid's Darfur revolt collapsed as well, although it was March 1880 when Slatin finally caught up with Haroun. Slatin surprised him in his camp and shot him dead as he tried to flee. Haroun's head was cut off and sent to El Fasher as proof of victory.

21

BEARDING THE NEGUS

I am neither a Napoleon nor a Colbert; I do not profess to have been either a great ruler or a great financier; but I can say this: I have cut off the slave dealers in their strongholds and I made all my people love me.

—Charles Gordon after leaving the Sudan, 1880

W hen Gordon finally did reach Cairo at the end of August 1879, he was in a better position to discover just how Ismail had been forced out. The Commission of Inquiry's first report, released a year before, had recommended three main actions: Egypt's ruler would relinquish his own landed estates, some 900,000 acres; this land would serve as security for a new loan of £8.5 million to meet payments on the debt; and a new ministry would be formed headed by a European to control finances. Realizing that he had no choice, the Khedive grudgingly accepted these "recommendations" even though it meant a loss of sovereign power.

The man chosen to be Minister of Finance, the English administrator Rivers Wilson, worked out the details of a loan with the banking house of Rothschild—always in the forefront of Egyptian financing—so that the dividends due the European creditors in November could be met. But complications arose when claims by individual bondholders upset the formula agreed upon by the Rothschilds. Another problem arose when disaffected military officers angrily demonstrated in front of the Khedive's palace to protest a 50 percent cut in pay. When their pay demands were met, this semimutinous act by the officers seemed to be rewarded, and the Khedive's unpopular Chief Minister, Nubar Pasha, was forced from power. The crisis eventually blew over, but the sweet fruits of insubordination were apparent to the army, the incident doubtless setting a precedent which would later contribute to a major military upheaval.

Inspired by the rash of nationalist sentiment in Egypt, Khedive Ismail thought he saw an opportunity to regain some of his lost powers. In a spasm

237

of independent action he summarily fired Rivers Wilson as Minister of Finance and also de Blignières, a Frenchman who headed the Ministry of Works. When Gordon first heard of these events, he bet on the Khedive—" the perfect type of his people, thoroughly consistent to all their principles—a splendid leopard! . . . the numberless cages out of which [Ismail] had broken his way when it seemed quite impossible for him to do so." Gordon also applauded Ismail's efforts to have the interest rate on Egypt's debt reduced from 7 to 5 percent.

Gordon, however, underestimated the power of the leopard's keepers, England and France, and probably was taken by surprise, as were most, by Bismarck's role in the affair. The German "Iron Chancellor," eager to enter the race for African empire, saw this as an opportunity to intervene under the guise of protecting German creditors, even though they were few in number and held only £100,000 worth of Egyptian bonds. On May 17, 1879, the German Consul General in Cairo accused Ismail of illegal conduct toward his German creditors and demanded that the Khedive's decree be rescinded. England and France could demand no less and joined in the demarche. When the Sultan of Turkey under European pressure refused to back the Khedive, in fact deposed him, Ismail had no choice but to accept exile in Europe. As the royal yacht steamed out of Alexandria's harbor, English and French warships added a final touch to the affair by firing a salute to the departing *Khedive*.

Gordon's first duty as Governor General in February 1877 had been to find a formula for peace between Egypt and Abyssinia, and so was his last. Though exhausted and eager to leave for England, Gordon could not leave the new Khedive with the matter unresolved. This time Gordon intended to see the Negus, "King of Kings" Johannes, in person.

In December 1878, the troublemaker Walid el-Michael had finally made his submission to Johannes. Soon afterward in January Gordon had received a letter, purportedly from the Negus, saying that while he could not make peace with the Khedive, he might with "the Sultan of the Sudan," as he referred to Gordon, and wanted to send an envoy to talk.

Before setting out on his Darfur campaign Gordon had, in fact, gone to the border town of Gedarif to meet with Johannes's representative. As he did not have explicit authority, the Governor General had been hard put to satisfy the King's request that he prove his right to negotiate on behalf of the Khedive;

but as he discovered later, neither did the Abyssinian emissary. The episode gave Gordon hope that King Johannes had no intention of going to war with Egypt, whether or not formal agreement could be reached. The only way to discover Johannes's true attitude was to meet with him, and this is what Gordon was determined to do, despite warnings from his advisers that he would be risking his life. Gordon set out armed only with a letter of accreditation and letter from the new Khedive, Tewfik, announcing his accession to power and embroidered with carried letters from the British and French governments signifying their hopes for peace.[1]

Gordon wrote the British and French Consuls General before he left, pleading that they use their influence to stop Abyssinian attacks near Massawa. He argued that because France and England had "meddled" in the Egyptian government and had pressured it to "save money," the Egyptians themselves did not have adequate military strength to meet the Abyssinian challenge. The least the two powers could do was restrain Johannes.

To the Italian Consul, Gordon took a different line. He claimed that "King Johannes has been well disposed toward Egypt until the arrival of . . . Mr. Mattiucchi [head of an Italian trading company]. I am disturbed by his lack of courtesy in this matter so important to Egypt, and since I heard that he will be back here [in Massawa] in three months, I am very concerned about the idea of a repetition of this same situation which occurred after his first visit to the King."[2] On the basis of such incidents, Gordon was convinced that the Italians and Johannes were in league together, explaining in part the Negus's increased hostility.

It was September 1879 before Gordon arrived in Massawa. By then the Abyssinians effectively held Bogos, so it could no longer be a point of bargaining—unless Egypt was prepared to go to war over it. Yet as he was about to march inland from Massawa, Gordon received a telegram from Khedive Tewfik telling him to cede nothing but to avoid war. This instruction left very little room to maneuver.

Gordon reported his alarm by letter to Olagnier in Cairo, indicating that he had telegraphed "the Caisse," or Egyptian Treasury: "You must be aware of the threatening attitude of Abyssinia, and I am warning you *secretly* that Egypt will be forced to arm in order to defend herself. It is possible we shall need money and therefore we will have to draw about £300,000 from National Debt Administration if we don't interfere in order to prevent any hostile action from Johannes." Gordon informed Olagnier of his "rude letter" to the Italian Consul General about Mattiucchi's machinations; he reminded Cairo that had there been no "officious pressure from Europe" forcing the Khedive to abandon its war with Abyssinia in 1876, "Egypt would have ended up by deterring Johannes by pitting him against his various tribal enemies."[3]

The French Consul in Massawa was also worried by the Italian intrigues, confirming that Mattiucchi's visit to the King had caused him "to beat the drums and declare war against the French, the British and the Egyptians." According to the Consul, Mattiucchi made no secret of his goal "to have an Italian seaport in Abyssinia." Gordon at least felt relieved that France, Britain's great rival, for once was not contributing to the problem: "The authority given the Consul is very limited and he has been told very clearly that he must remain neutral." The Consul had been instructed by Paris to give Gordon "moral support," however, but warned him to be careful since "we don't want to be involved in anything."[4]

While traveling inland from Massawa, Gordon received news that Walid el-Michael and his officers had been imprisoned at Debra Tabor, and that the troublemaker's son, Mefti, had been killed. This put Gordon in jeopardy, as the brigand's partisans in the area, enraged at the news, might vent their anger by killing him. This pending threat, like others before in Masindi and Darfur, may have been what triggered in Gordon another attack of angina, although he chose to blame it on the rough road.

As he approached the mountaintop garrison of Johannes's Commander in Chief, Ras Aloula, Gordon put on his impressive marshal's uniform. This did nothing to improve the ambience. The Commander, reclining on a couch and so thoroughly swathed in white sheeting that only his nose could be seen, saluted Gordon unenthusiastically and beckoned him to sit on a silk-covered stool. The meeting, attended by Ras Aloula's senior officers and a group of priests, who glared menacingly, was disconcerting for its silence. Gordon was given permission to smoke even though the custom had been banned by the King, who often had the lips of smokers cut off and the noses of those caught taking snuff bobbed. "How little worth any alliance with such a meddling king would be to Egypt," thought Gordon; "he will end in forbidding other things and so lose his crown."

The interpreter was so completely dressed in Abyssinian clothes that it was not apparent he was a European—a German who had somehow wandered far afield. As Gordon talked, Aloula unlimbered a bit—even unshrouded himself enough to reveal "a good looking young man of about 30 or 35." At least Gordon was treated to "wildly melodic" priestly chanting from the Psalms of David every morning at 3:00 to start the day agreeably.

Ras Aloula agreed that Gordon must see the King in person if anything was to be settled, so the Governor General left on September 19 for the royal encampment at Debra Tabor. It was a long journey—thirty-eight days—up the steepest of mountains and over the worst brigand-infested roads imaginable.

In his first audience with Johannes, Gordon found the Negus seated on a raised dais, flanked on the left by the chief priest and his uncle, Ras Arya. Gordon sat on a stool to the King's right while a gun salute was fired.

Gordon moved his stool to a spot closer to the throne where he could talk with the monarch on the same level. This breach of etiquette provoked Johannes to bark: "Do you know, Gordon Pasha, that I could kill you on the spot if I liked?" Gordon retorted: "Do so at once, if it is your royal pleasure; I am ready. You would confer a favour on me by so doing, for you would be doing for me that which I am precluded by my religious scruples from doing for myself." "Then my power has no terror for you?" Johannes asked. "None whatsoever," replied Gordon. Gordon was dismissed and sent to his quarters, a "half-finished, wretched hut."

The next meeting took place at daybreak after Gordon had been serenaded by the priests. It was substantive but futile. The tone was set by Johannes's chill greeting: "What did you come for?"[5] The Negus claimed not to have seen the new Khedive's letters announcing his accession and accrediting Gordon as his envoy. When the missing letters were finally found in a pile of other unread correspondence, including a letter from the British and one from the French warning against an attack on Egypt, Johannes had his clerk given forty lashes for his negligence.

King Johannes was "a man of some 45 years, a sour, ill-favored looking being. He never looks you in the face. When you look away he glares at you like a tiger." The King got drunk every night, but was up at dawn, "reading the Psalms."

Johannes stated his demands: In return for his promise of peace, he wanted Metemmeh, Changallas, and Bogos returned to him, and the ports of

Zeila and Amphilla ceded to Abyssinia; in addition, he wanted a reparation of £2 million. If his demands were not met, the Negus warned bluntly, "I shall fight you. Will Egypt fight me?" The Governor General, bemused by this simplistic exchange, replied that such decisions were the Khedive's to make; privately, he felt confident the demands would not be met.

In response, the King asked Gordon how many troops he could produce if war came to pass. Sensing Johannes's apprehension, Gordon replied: "With London soldiers, we can bring fourteen thousand against you." Memories of Napier's campaign had not died, and this gave the Negus pause. He hinted that after taking his baths he might modify his demands, but Gordon, concluding the futility of further negotiations, saw tactical advantage in discouraging even that. It was "no use," Gordon later wrote Gessi on a bleak Christmas day; "I saw plainly that anything I could give up would surely never come up to what . . . the King's pride would require and thus it was better he should keep to his absurd demands."[6] On that solid note of disagreement, the King went off to "take the baths" at a natural hot spring two days' journey away.

The royal court seethed with intrigue. It did not seem coincidental that Mitzilia, the Greek Consul at Suez, and Bianchi, an Italian of Mattiucchi's company, were visiting Johannes when Gordon arrived. Two other Italians, including a mysterious man calling himself Neretti who had been at the primitive, remote court for eight years, appeared, expressing sentiments hostile to Egyptian interests. Gordon, with good reason, suspected they were poisoning the King's mind against him and the concessions Egypt was willing to offer. The Greek's mission seemed to have been to convince the King that the Coptic metropolitan, traditionally supplied by the Egyptian Coptic Church, should be replaced by a Greek Orthodox prelate. Gordon liked Bianchi personally and conceded justification for Italian ambitions in Abyssinia, but Bianchi's influence at the Negus's court was contrary to Egyptian interests. Johannes appealed to Gordon as an Englishman and a Christian in an effort to gain more generous terms, while the Greek Consul, in collusion with the King, hinted that valuable gifts might be Gordon's if he cooperated.

Johannes returned from the baths on November 6. Two days later, he had his final audience with Gordon. When the Governor General took the opportunity to ask for the release of twenty-three captured Sudanese and Egyptian soldiers, Johannes erupted in fury. All Gordon emerged with was a letter of twelve spare lines for the Khedive, written in a style reserved for servants and rudely stating: "I have received the letters you sent me by that man [Gordon]. I will not make a secret peace with you. If you want peace, ask the Sultans of Europe."[7] A large bribe was attached to the letter; Gordon returned it haughtily.

The mission had not been successful, and Gordon departed. The Khedive, ruling out concessions of any kind, gave Gordon no leeway for negotiations; nor was Johannes in any mood to compromise. He was bitter about Egypt's seizure of Abyssinia's traditional territory and confident of victory if forced to go to war. But as Gordon was about to reenter Sudanese territory, two hundred of the King's soldiers suddenly seized the small party and mysteriously took them to a village belonging to Ras Arya, the King's uncle.

It was the King's idea, Ras Arya said, contending that Johannes was thoroughly bad and on the verge of madness. The disaffected uncle had been told that the Governor General must return to the Sudan through Massawa, rather than more directly by way of Galabat and Gedarif. On being finally allowed to proceed, Gordon was asked by his venal host, "Have you a watch to spare?"[8]

Unsure of his safety, fearing the King's playing cat and mouse with him, Gordon destroyed all his notes. He telegraphed the Khedive asking that a regiment of Egyptian troops and an armed steamer meet him at Massawa. It was entirely possible that the mad monarch might seize the occasion to attack Massawa, and Gordon wanted to be prepared.

At Axum the party was mobbed by hostile tribesmen, but £1,400 of gold saw them through the crisis. Finally on December 8, Gordon reached the safety of Massawa, where the British warship *Seagull* met him, but no effort had been made by the Khedive to assure Massawa's safety as urged by Gordon. Annoyed by this lack of regard for his or the city's safety, Gordon telegraphed his displeasure to Tewfik. But Gordon was at least safe.

In a letter home Gordon described Johannes: "The King is rapidly going mad. [He] is hated more than Theodore was. Cruel to a degree, he does not, however, take life. He cuts off the feet and hands of people who offend him. He puts out their eyes by pouring hot tallow into their ears! . . . [The Abyssinian people] is a race of warriors, hardy and, though undisciplined, religious fanatics; their weakest point is greed."

Gordon's health was not good. The rigors of the Darfur campaign followed by the stress and hardship of his Abyssinian mission had weakened him. When the British consulate doctor examined him in Alexandria, his diagnosis was "nervous exhaustion" and "alterations of the blood, giving rise to haemorrhagic spots on the skin." The doctor urged Gordon to abstain "from all exciting work"—a tall order.[9] Gordon's own idea of therapy was to lie in bed until noon and have oysters every day for lunch—or so he dreamed as he came to an end of his trials in the Sudan and Abyssinia.

Gordon's send-off by the Egyptians was not gracious. Khedive Tewfik, who did not like Gordon and was glad to see him go, had been unnerved by the rumor that Gordon was plotting to take advantage of succession turmoil, in the wake of Ismail's removal, to set himself up as king of an independent Sudan. In addition, a confidential telegram from Gordon to Tewfik from Massawa had been leaked to the British press. In the ciphered telegram was the suggestion that Gordon had tried to detach Egypt from its territories along the Red Sea and give them to Italy and Abyssinia. Gordon was angry. "It was my duty in this affair to give my straightforward opinion to the Khedive. . . . If the councillors of the Khedive and his courtiers pretend that I have betrayed their land in the matter of taking from them a foot[hold] on the Red Sea, then they lie."[10] Gordon's advice had been made in the interest of peace, but it had only aroused Nubar Pasha's ire.[11] When the story was leaked to the press, Egyptian hard-liners were predictably upset, and of couse so were the British.

Gordon was disheartened by the complacent attitude of the British government on the matter of the Sudan. In a meeting with Evelyn Baring, who had resigned his place on the Debt Commission to take the more prestigious job of English Comptroller General, the two men found no meeting of the minds. Gordon argued strenuously that his antislaving crusade must be carried on after his departure, while Baring seemed only concerned with the state of Egypt's finances. By now, Gordon's outspoken comments and general lack of tact had alienated everyone in Cairo, and he was dismissed as a peevish zealot without adequate balance. He was, in fact, in an angry mood, particularly after learning that Ra'uf Pasha, twice fired by him for maladministration, had been named as his successor.

Gordon's last few days in Cairo were trying. Only with the greatest difficulty was the British Consul General, Edward Malet, able to prevent Gordon from engaging Prime Minister Nubar Pasha in a duel! When Nubar

Pasha made a derogatory remark about Malet's predecessor, Vivian, Gordon bristled with indignation. He announced to Malet: "I will not permit anyone to speak in such a way of a man who belongs to the same order of knighthood as I do; Nubar Pasha shall apologise to me or fight." Gordon had never taken his Companion of the Bath order so seriously before; his challenge may have been a strangely archaic way to vent long-festering resentments toward Nubar for lack of official support, or it may have been symptomatic of the fatigue and frustration he felt on the eve of his departure. Whatever the case, Malet finally calmed the irascible Gordon before a duel with the Egyptian Prime Minister could take place.

On leaving Egypt, Gordon summed up his accomplishments in the Sudan in an interview with the *Times* correspondent in Alexandria: "I am neither a Napoleon nor a Colbert; I do not profess to have been either a great ruler or a great financier; but I can say this—I have cut off the slave dealers in their strongholds and I made all my people love me."[12]

That he had cut off the slavers, no one could deny. In his battles to stop the slave trade in the years 1875–79, sixteen thousand Egyptians and some fifty thousand natives of Darfur had died. The loss of life in Bahr al-Ghazal he guessed to have been about eight thousand and some 470 slave dealers had been driven out of business.

But that Gordon made the people of the Sudan love him was another matter. Certainly those who depended on the slave trade for a livelihood found him inimical. And there were others who resented an administration in Khartoum headed by a Christian infidel. Some of the tribes felt antagonistic toward a regime in Khartoum which had tried to collect taxes from them and otherwise interfere with an autonomy they had long enjoyed.

But if Gordon was not universally loved in the Sudan, he was respected. His extraordinary magnetism and reputation for scrupulous honesty made him a leader who commanded obedience and respect. When he departed the Sudan, he left a dangerous leadership vacuum.

PART V

Odd Jobs and Reflection

INDIA

Men at times, owing to the mysteries of Providence, form judgments which they afterwards repent of.
—Charles Gordon after resigning as
private secretary to the Viceroy of India

ordon left behind a caldron of intrigue in Cairo as Tewfik struggled to consolidate his position as the new Khedive. En route to Italy, Gordon wrote to Olagnier, his contact in Sherif Pasha's office, that Nubar Pasha was "completely finished" as far as France was concerned, Premier Gambetta having lost faith in him. Great Britain concurred that the Egyptian Prime Minister had to go. De Blignières, the French Commissioner of Debt, Gordon predicted, would be outmaneuvered and undercut by Baring and the British. Gordon advised Olagnier to steer clear of the infighting between the French and English, and warned him about too freely "expressing his opinions," lest he compromise himself so badly that Gordon would not be able to "undo the damage."[1] Gordon urged Olagnier to leave Egypt. "It is necessary that you make a move," he advised, and in the meantime "be careful not to be a partisan of anyone."[2]

Gordon hinted at some plan of action he intended to pursue when he was back in England: "I can arrange the division of Syria, Egypt and Abyssinia." This seemed to refer to Gordon's favorite thesis that as long as Great Britain ruled the oceans and controlled Egypt, it should have fear of neither French dominance of the Levant nor Italian possession of Abyssinia's Red Sea coast—a division of power which eventually worked out, in fact, but at the time was not a welcome thought in Whitehall.

Gordon's mind was still on Africa when he stopped in Naples to pay respects to the deposed Khedive Ismail. The Khedive was in a similar frame of mind, and all talk at lunch was about past glory. The physical pleasantness of life—the luxurious villa near gently smoking Vesuvius, the Mediterranean perfectly framing a colorful countryside—was inadequate distraction for

249

Ismail. Gordon, like Ismail, was a ruler out of work, but he at least had a future to look forward to.

Gordon was accompanied to lunch by a French liberal named Joseph Reinach, formerly Gambetta's secretary, with whom he had struck up a friendship on shipboard. Later the two men passed their time in Naples seeing the sights and going to the ballet. *Sardanapalus*, with its chorus of scantily clad maidens, annoyed Gordon; his comment after the performance was: "And you call that civilization."

Reinach, as Chaille-Long had in Equatoria, found Gordon one night sipping liquor in his room as he read the Bible. Reinach noted that the colonel seemed to consume a great deal of brandy, though this was a time which coincided with an attack of depression. It was typical for Gordon's bouts of the "doles" to occur at moments of inactivity, and this trip home after such intense activity in the Sudan was clearly a letdown.

Reinach, in later years, was generally critical of Gordon. "Like many heroes, [Gordon] was but a hero in the short run . . . a mystic who liked the sound of his own voice." Notwithstanding, Reinach found Gordon greatly interesting and entertaining; and this "extraordinary man" had, moreover, "mastered the art of speaking English and French at the same time." His thoughts inundated Reinach as they cascaded forth, "often profound, sometimes super-heated," never dull.[3] However critical of Gordon, Reinach was much taken with him, and they corresponded for years—as did many others who met Gordon.

In Rome Gordon became even more listless with depression. He stopped at St. Peter's, but in his present mood he found nothing there to interest him. He wrote Olagnier that he intended calling on the Pope while in Rome. He was concerned about the prospect of Jews flooding Jerusalem, and he hoped to get from His Holiness a brief to mount a crusade and preach against these people.[4]

It was apparent that Gordon was in ill temper and on edge with fatigue. Nor did his temper improve when he arrived in Paris. He called on the British Ambassador, Lord Lyons, to complain that Her Majesty's government had done nothing to oppose Egypt's unfortunate choice of Ra'uf Pasha to succeed him in the Sudan. As Lord Lyons recoiled with shock, Gordon uttered the blasphemy that it would be better if the French appointed the next Governor General in the Sudan if the British were so apathetic. He threatened to ask the French to do so himself.

In February Gordon wrote Olagnier from London a reassuring but enigmatic note: "Remain calm, the 'entente cordiale' cannot exist forever and you would be far too useful to be put aside"[5]—in a reference perhaps to Olagnier's function as a British agent in the Khedive's court. Gordon, now no longer involved with Egypt, curiously continued to ask Olagnier for intelligence. From the United Service Club in Pall Mall, Gordon wrote on April 30, 1880: "Through Cherif Pasha or the others, can you give me a short history of each Pasha who is part of the Egyptian ministry. I will not betray you. . . . also the nationality of each Pasha is very important."[6] Why would Gordon, who had written Olagnier, "I have come back to my regiment and I leave Egypt," now want such information?

Upon arriving in England, Gordon, once again something of a celebrity, devoted much of his time to avoiding social lionization. Everyone wanted to meet "the uncrowned King of the Sudan," as some newspapers delighted in calling him. Happily, he could find refuge with his good friends the Freeses, at Chislehurst.

Gordon regaled the Freese children with endless stories of his Sudan adventures. This was the one kind of audience which Gordon truly enjoyed. "My boys hung upon his words," recalled Mrs. Freese. "He told them he had seen strong men on the march cry like children at the miseries of their positions when, as sometimes happened in marching, there was no place for shelter when darkness came on and they had to lie down to sleep in the road, almost in pools of water. . . ."[7]

Octavia Freese remembered Gordon as "looking very thin and older." She had been startled to learn that he had sent in his resignation from the Army, although it had not been accepted. For all the warmth of their reunion, Gordon sensed that he and Octavia Freese had grown apart on religious matters, and he complained in a letter to his sister that his "dear friend was now over-ready to use her tusk." Gordon always found it difficult to accept criticism, even from those close to him. The Freeses were never to see Gordon again after this visit.

Gordon's happiest moments of relaxation came when he played with his two young nieces at his brother's home in Chelsea. Like all children, they adored him, and with them he was able to emerge from the inhibited citadel of himself. But eager callers would wrench him back to the adult world of socialization, where he felt ill at ease; if he saw them coming, he would find a hiding place. The picture of England's intrepid hero scurrying for cover under the dining-room table must have been a curious sight. Gordon also visited his sister Augusta, of course, whose kitchen (the only place in her home where she permitted Gordon to smoke) provided him another haven from London society.

At the few social functions that Gordon was virtually compelled by etiquette to attend, he was always ill at ease. Once engaged in conversation, however, he seemed to enjoy himself. If a recluse by habit, Gordon could be stimulated by interesting people, but he rarely made the initial effort to meet them. He liked people in their natural habitat, not as ornaments collected by aggressive hostesses. To confidantes like Mrs. Freese, he would disdainfully dismiss the Prime Minister and other distinguished persons—even royalty—as "a mass of glitter to be worms in 30 years time."

An often-told story about Gordon described his rejection of an invitation to dinner sent by the Prince of Wales—a command appearance by all standards of court etiquette. When the Prince's equerry protested, "But you cannot refuse the Prince," Gordon is supposed to have replied: "Why not? I refused King Johannes . . . and he might have cut off my head for refusing. I am sure HRH will not do that." The flustered equerry pleaded: "Well then, let me say you are ill." Gordon would have none of that, assuring the Prince's messenger that he was not ill. He finally permitted the equerry to give the Prince of Wales the excuse: "I always go to bed at half-past nine."[8]

An understanding Prince of Wales (later King Edward VII) let Gordon off with a luncheon invitation that was graciously accepted. At this intimate gathering the Prince and the Duke of Cambridge both protested Gordon's intention to resign his commission. The Duke, as Commander in Chief of the Army, offered generously instead to grant him a year's leave—or more—so that Gordon could have the rest he wanted.

Gordon may have been a popular legend and a public hero, but his exploits in the Sudan did not bring official accolades. Not only had he served a foreign master, the Khedive of Egypt, but he had publicly disapproved of many of his own country's actions in Egypt. While it could be argued that he had served humanity in suppressing the slave traffic in the Sudan, the British government was not convinced he had served British national interests. He was seen more as a loose cannon rolling about the deck than as a team player of the empire.

Gordon repaired to the continent in early 1880, but Africa was still on his mind. He again discussed with the British shipping magnate William Mackinnon his old dream of penetrating Central Africa from Zanzibar. And he wrote Gessi, "I hope (this is a secret) to go to Zanzibar in two months but the scheme's not yet evolved."[9] Then a new possibility of action presented itself when Gordon, while in Lausanne, received an offer from Cape Colony to take command of its military forces, which were faced by disturbances among the Basuto tribesmen. But Gordon was still undecided as to what to do, and assignments from the War Office were conspicuously lacking.

In Lausanne Gordon chanced to meet a Reverend R. H. Barnes, Vicar of Heavetree near Exeter. The two men found mutual interest in religious discussion and quickly struck up a friendship. Not until a few days later when Barnes happened to call on Gordon in his hotel and found him signing Sudanese death warrants—a residual chore remaining from his Governor General duties in the Sudan—did he realize that his new friend was "Chinese Gordon" recently of Khartoum fame. They would remain good friends for the rest of Gordon's life and write to each other regularly on all manner of subjects.

While passing through Brussels, Gordon called on H. C. Vivian, now British Minister to Belgium—the man whose honor he had rashly offered to defend in a duel with Nubar Pasha. Gordon, who had remembered H. C. Vivian from academy days in Woolwich as "a pretty blue-eyed boy," considered the mature Vivian in Cairo a "stuck-up donkey." Now he decided he liked Vivian. Mrs. Vivian, who was occupied with eight-month-old twins and a two-and-a-half-year-old son, took a sisterly interest in Gordon and urged him to marry. Gordon recoiled at the idea.

It was Gordon's talk with King Leopold in Brussels about the Congo that held the most promise for the future. Despite the loss of his luggage in transit and thus a lack of appropriate clothes for a royal audience, Gordon spent nearly two hours with Leopold on March 2, 1880. The Belgian monarch was concerned about developments in the Congo and wanted Gordon's advice. The two men got along well, and groundwork was established for Gordon's ultimate acceptance of an assignment from the King as administrator of the

Congo. The idea appealed to Gordon, although he did not yet feel free to make any firm commitment.

When two legendary people meet, it does not, of course, follow that they will like each other. But when Gordon and Florence Nightingale saw each other after his return to London from the Continent, they became friends immediately. They had hardly known each other during the Crimean War, but now they discovered they shared very similar religious beliefs.

Gordon sought Florence Nightingale's help in convincing the War Office of abuses in military hospitals. Gordon's cousin Mrs. Hawthorne had found terrible mistreatment of patients, but could make no headway against the entrenched bureaucracy. While the military establishment proved too much even for Florence Nightingale, she and Gordon remained good friends and corresponded regularly.

Another interesting lady of the day whose company Gordon enjoyed was Richard Burton's wife, Isobel. She had once appealed to Gordon to intervene with the Foreign Office in behalf of her illustrious but temperamental husband, who was paying the price of official disapprobation for some real or imagined outrage. Gordon, who had his own problems with the Foreign Office, could only reply helplessly, "I have written letters to the F.O. that would raise a corpse; it is no good." When he reached London he called on Lady Burton and spent a pleasant afternoon with her. Distressed to learn that she did not know the origin of the Union Jack's design, he sat on the floor cutting out the crosses of St. George, St. Andrew and St. Patrick and fashioning a flag out of them.

As Gordon was casting about trying to find a new project, Disraeli's government fell in April 1880 and was replaced by Gladstone and the Liberals. Gordon was elated by "Dizzy's" defeat; it would set in motion developments that would jar Gordon out of his quandaries. In late April the Marquis of Ripon was appointed Viceroy to India and soon thereafter invited Gordon to become his private secretary. If Ripon's offer of the position to Gordon was mystifying, Gordon's ready acceptance was even more so. The job did not fit him.

India was in a disturbed state. A financial scandal had rocked the Military Accounts Department, and Indian harvests had been bad, many blaming the Army, which had requisitioned draft animals needed in the fields. Russian advances in Central Asia continued to be worrisome, and Disraeli's "forward policy" had been discredited by problems with Afghanistan, not least of which was the massacre of the overbearing British Resident, Cavagnari, and his military escort by an angry mob in Kabul in September 1879. General Frederick Roberts's swift retribution, characterized by public hangings and village burnings, only kept the frontier in turmoil. Moreover, the Kabul throne was taken by Abdur Rahman, who had just arrived from a long exile in Russia and could be expected to favor that hospitable neighbor.

Lord Ripon was going to India with a mandate for reform, and it seemed that he hoped Gordon, who had a reputation for equitable handling of "natives," would help the mission's image. There were those in Parliament who even felt that Gordon's appointment lent more prestige and character to the mission than did Ripon's own appointment as Viceroy.

Some speculated that Gordon's appointment was somehow motivated by the need for the right man to deal with the Russians as the two empires veered toward collision in Central Asia. Moreover, in a book which appeared at this time, *Merv, the Queen of the World*, Charles Marvin wrote: "To select the border line between the English and Russian empires in Asia, there should be no appointment of committees or commissions; the task should be given to a single man."[10] After much florid hyperbole Marvin identified the "Atlas" he had in mind for the job as "Chinese Gordon," a name which he claimed "sprang spontaneously to his readers' lips."[11] Others thought the appointment was a terrible mistake. But whatever the reaction, Gordon's new assignment attracted public discussion.

Gordon should have known better than to accept a post so unsuitable to his temperament. He later admitted: "Men at times, owing to the mysteries of Providence, form judgments which they afterwards repent of."

Lord Ripon had a disconcerting preview of Gordon's unpredictability when at the farewell banquet his new private secretary shocked the distinguished guests by insisting that all courses be served on the same plate. "We shall have to rough it out in India, so I may as well begin now." Whether this was his way of making a statement in protest against British India's stilted and structured society or whether it was just another example of his eccentric sense of humor is difficult to know.

As Gordon prepared for his assignment he had to see much of Reginald Baliol Brett, 2nd Viscount Esher, who was secretary to Lord Hartington, Secretary of State with responsibility for Indian affairs. In the midst of many critics, Brett was a staunch supporter of Gordon, and later became a good friend. Then on board ship, en route to India, Gordon struck up a friendship with Brett's brother, Lord Ripon's aide-de-camp, so Gordon's relationship with the Brett family became even stronger.

Passing through Cairo on his voyage to India with Lord Ripon, Gordon had the opportunity to renew his acquaintanceship with British Consul General Malet. During Gordon's last visit with Malet, there had been an embarrassing moment when Gordon tried to press upon him a filigree cigarette box as a memento. The Consul, rigorously opposed to accepting gifts, had awkwardly offered to buy the box instead, and Gordon, even more awkwardly, agreed to sell it to him. At this meeting, Gordon insisted that Malet accept an ivory pocket knife which had been carried through the Indian Mutiny by Lord Clide. Malet accepted the present graciously, to the delight of Gordon, who cheered: "Ah! Now I am satisfied; you have got something from me."

By the time the viceregal party had reached Aden, Gordon was feeling pangs of regret about the India assignment. "I have been an idiot, and took this place with Lord Ripon, who is a kind and considerate master; but I hate India and how I ever could have taken the post is past my comprehension." Gordon went on to complain about the endless quarrels which seemed to be going on in the Indian bureaucracy, and vowed he would get out of the assignment as soon as he could.

What Gordon found in India after his arrival only confirmed his worst fears. Consistent with his longstanding scorn of what he considered overpaid bureaucrats, he was aghast at the high salaries enjoyed by British officials in India. He wrote Augusta: "The way Europeans live there is absurd in its luxury. . . . All the salaries are too high by half, above the rank of captain. . . . It is a house of charity for a lot of idle, useless fellows."

Gordon's arrival in India in 1880 was on the eve of restless stirrings by the Indians for greater reform and greater autonomy. The wounds of the mutiny and the nationalist sentiments awakened by it were festering quietly, ultimately to break out in a less violent but in the long run more profound independence movement. In the meantime, "reform" was the watchword, and within three years Calcutta would be the site of an Indian National Conference to discuss such matters.

In 1885 the Indian National Congress, destined to be the vehicle for total independence, was founded in Bombay by a British Indian civil servant named A. O. Hume for "moral, social and political revival." The Viceroy, then Lord Dufferin, professed to be pleased with this development and told Hume that "he found the greatest difficulty in ascertaining the real wishes of the people and that it would be a public benefit if there existed some responsible organization through which the Government might be kept informed regarding the best Indian national opinion."[12] (Lord Dufferin would later frown on Congress as a "microscopic minority" with no claim to represent Indian opinion.)

It was clear to Gordon that the British administration had little concern for Indian sensibilities. He wrote Florence Nightingale: " . . . the element of all government is absent, i.e. the putting of the governors into the skin of the governed." Petty points of protocol and the rituals of viceregal rule irritated him. He refused to tell the little white lies required by etiquette. Knowing, for example, that Lord Ripon would never have time to read a transcript of an address sent to him by some group or other, he refused on one occasion to promise that the Viceroy would.

More important were the basically different outlooks which the two men had. The issue of Afghanistan particularly troubled Gordon, who claimed later that his disagreement with official policy toward that consistently difficult country had much to do with his decision to leave India.

The Treaty of Gandamak, signed with the British on May 26, 1879, by Mohammed Yaqub Khan, new Emir of Afghanistan, had been an effort to halt their advance into the country. But the Second Anglo-Afghan War, as this campaign became known—like the First Afghan War, a half century earlier—was an ill-advised reaction to Russian initiatives in Central Asia that seemed to threaten India. When, according to the terms of the treaty, the British placed Sir Louis Cavagnari in Kabul as Resident in July 1879, they were courting trouble. And, indeed, mutinous Afghan soldiers and street mobs rose up, murdering Cavagnari and massacring his small military escort. This had provoked the British to send a harsh, retributive campaign into Afghanistan led by General Frederick Roberts to force Yaqub Khan off his throne and into exile.

Having been asked by Lord Ripon to review the evidence which had been raised during the inquiry into Yaqub Khan's part in Cavagnari's murder, Gordon concluded that the deposed Afghan leader had not been responsible for the incident, as accused. Moreover, three out of five viceregal council members at the inquiry had come to that conclusion.

Gordon's efforts to reopen the question, however, met with strong opposition in the Indian government, particularly on the part of the Viceroy's Military Secretary, White, for whom the thought of a rehearing was traumatic. Lord Ripon in the end agreed with White, rejecting Gordon's suggestion to reinstate Yaqub Khan in Kabul. "Take him back, yourself, My Lord. You can easily do it with 3,000 cavalry. If you succeed, you will be looked upon as the greatest Governor General India ever had, and if you fail and are killed, you will have a splendid marble monument put up to you."[13] By expressing his disdain for the British policy, Gordon made no friends in the Indian government establishment either.

Gordon's resignation caused a stir in India as well as England. The abruptness of Gordon's departure so soon after his arrival made tongues wag.

Lord Ripon and Gordon parted amicably, both realizing that the arrangement would not work. Gordon's resignation on June 2, 1880, was an embarrassment to Lord Ripon, even though Gordon did his best to shoulder all the blame. In his announcement Gordon admitted that he had "repented" of accepting the appointment without sufficient contemplation, but he "had not the moral courage to say so at that time."

Gordon found Reginald Brett a great help when he arrived back in England in November. It was an awkward time for Gordon, but he could relax at the Brett household. Brett remembered: "He would generally come in the morning, a queer figure, with a loose comforter round his throat and a hat—by no means a good one—tilted back on his head; the eternal cigarette between his lips. . . . He would lounge into the library and stand—for he hardly ever cared to sit—for hours at a time, leaning against the mantelpiece, or walking up and down the room."[14] One of the most penetrating descriptions of Gordon's personality was written by Brett (Lord Esher): "His talk was as fresh as a spring morning, full of humour, and his language as simple as the book of Genesis. . . . He saw with wonderful clearness, perhaps sometimes not very far."[15]

Gordon has often been accused of having bad judgment as regard to people. Brett's explanation for this trait in such an otherwise perceptive person is as good as any: "His charity knew no bounds. Repentance made up, in his eyes, for every crime. . . . His religion was never obtruded, but it was as much a part of his daily life as smoking cigarettes. He literally walked with God."[16]

In the Brett household Gordon felt free at last to express his frankly held views. He had, for example, a simple remedy for the Russian threat to Afghanistan: "I think of great importance [is] to have a Russian envoy with the Court of the Viceroy [in India], and an English envoy with Kaufman [the Russian proconsul in Afghanistan]. A great many misunderstandings would then be avoided."[17]

Soon Gordon's thoughts would be wrenched away from Afghanistan and India. China was about to intrude once more.

CHINA, IRELAND, MAURITIUS

> . . . he is a fine, noble, knightly gentleman, such as is found but once in many generations.
> —*Vanity Fair* magazine on Charles Gordon, February 19, 1881

Two days after his resignation from Lord Ripon's service in India was announced, Gordon received a telegram from his old friend Sir Robert Hart in China. Hart was still serving as Inspector General of the Imperial Customs, an extremely powerful position in the Chinese government. "I am directed to invite you here," he wrote on June 6, 1880. "Please come and see for yourself. The opportunity of doing really useful work on a large scale ought not to be lost; work, position, conditions can all be arranged with yourself to your satisfaction."

Although details were conspicuously lacking, Gordon read the message in the context of a crisis which had blown up between China and Russia. Imperial Russia in its inexorable march toward the east had reached China's borderlands. In pursuit of its "Eastern Destiny," it was inevitable that Russia would clash with the Celestial Empire. Between 1870 and 1880, Nicholas Mikhailovich Prjevalski, the famous Russian explorer and outrider of empire, traveled widely in eastern Turkestan and northern Tibet, making both the British in India and the Chinese nervous about the Czar's intentions. But when the Russians occupied the town of Ili and the rich, strategically located valley leading into western Chinese Turkestan, relations between the two empires became tense. By 1880 China was, in fact, on the verge of going to war. Against this background, Gordon was intrigued by the invitation—the "well-broken horse" was again ready for anything. Within forty-eight hours Hart had his reply: "Gordon will leave for Shanghai first available opportunity. As for conditions, Gordon indifferent."

Rumors that Gordon might soon appear again in China set off alarm bells in St. Petersburg. Visions of an "Ever *More* Victorious Army" with well-trained mercenaries filibustering in the Ili Valley under command of the

Englishman was not a pleasing prospect for the Czar. Nor did it appeal to the British government, which reacted almost instantaneously with a message to Gordon vetoing his plans: "Your going to China is not approved." Despite Gordon's promise not to involve the British government, it was no time for the loose cannon again to roll about the China deck.

Gordon would not be put off so easily. He telegraphed the Adjutant General: "Arrange retirement, commutation or resignation of service. My counsel, if asked, would be peace, not war." After issuing a public statement reiterating that his aim was to prevent war, he boarded a cargo ship at Bombay bound for China. Gordon's public comments, originally phrased as ever, may have been mollifying, but his penchant for talking directly to the public was annoying to the Army, particularly when he announced gratuitously that he preferred promoting peace to gaining "any paltry honours in a wretched war." By the time he reached Ceylon another telegram from London awaited him reversing the government's position: "Leave granted on your engaging to take no military service in China."

If London was tolerant, the British Minister in Peking, Sir Thomas Wade, was not. He ordered Gordon to reside at the British legation and have no contacts without first obtaining official permission. Wade was not simply being pompous; as much as he wanted to control the colonel's freewheeling, he wanted to protect Gordon from any untoward incident in the highly charged atmosphere of Peking. True to form, Gordon ignored Wade; he refused to enter, much less stay at, the legation.

The China which Gordon saw this time was awash with intrigue, and he braced himself to be on his guard. Seeing old friends again was pleasant, however. Quincey, the lad he had saved from the rubble of battle at Quinsan, met him in Hong Kong. Thanks to Gordon's early help, he was a prosperous government official with a wife and three children. The murdered Lar Wang's son, handsome in his youth, had risen to the rank of mandarin and with age had grown coarse of feature—"like an ox," as Gorden commented. Gordon also had a reunion in Shanghai with some of his old bodyguard, the young men he captured from the Taipings and converted to his service.

In Hong Kong, Gordon stayed with Sir John Hennessy at Government House, but soon moved on to see his old friend and patron Li Hung-chang, with whom he was anxious to talk about the China situation. Li had risen in rank since Gordon fought with the Ever Victorious Army and was now

"Senior Guardian" to the Heir Apparent, wearing the coveted Yellow Jacket and peacock feather in his hat.

When Gordon first received Hart's message, he assumed that the invitation had originated with Li. This proved not to be the case, but Li, as leader of the faction favoring peace, was very much involved in a bitter struggle for power with the war party which had gained ascendancy in Peking behind the Machiavellian Dowager Empress. It also soon became clear to Gordon that Li was being importuned by "friends"—foreign and Chinese—to overthrow the puppet boy Emperor in order to prevent the hard-liners from declaring war against Russia. Gordon himself, in fact, was approached by the German Minister, who darkly suggested that he should help Li seize power from the irresponsible, bellicose Manchus. Gordon saw the folly in any such adventures. "Li is worth giving one's life for," he wrote, "but he must not rebel and lose his good name."

When Gordon and Li met in Tientsin their reunion was a warm one. As Gordon saw the situation and defined his own role, he must bolster his old friend in efforts to seek peace with Russia, but dissuade him, if necessary, from doing anything foolish—such as using his provincial strength to rise in revolt against the Emperor. The dimensions of the crisis, Gordon feared, could involve him more dramatically than he had anticipated. Wanting to be free to act, he telegraphed the War Office, resigning his commission in the Army: He could not "desert China in her present crisis."

After consultation with Li, Gordon saw his next move as dissuading the war faction in China, which dominated policy, from taking up arms against Russia. He would be a knight errant whose mission was to save China from its impulsiveness. Gordon appeared before the Imperial Council and listened impatiently to the mandarins as they talked pompously of the strength of the empire. Mired in the past, they were oblivious to the realities of the modern world. They talked confidently about the wooden forts of Taku as adequate for Peking's defense. Gordon spoke his mind with utter candor, accusing the council of "idiocy." When the interpreter became alarmed by the stridency of language and refused to utter the Chinese equivalents of such rude phrases, Gordon grabbed an English-Chinese dictionary and pointed to the word for "idiocy." The mandarins were then under no illusion as to what he meant. This was an affront to their dignity and they could have called for his head, but it was somehow accepted that the fiery British soldier was bound by no conventions—English or Chinese. Such fervor, coming from a warrior revered in China, had its effect.

Gordon suggested a five-point peace plan and no less than a blueprint for China's development. He also made a plea for the reorganization of the Chinese army along lines which would establish a guerrilla-warfare capability. Having spoken his mind, he returned to Tientsin amid well-meaning warnings from the diplomatic colony that his bull-in-the-china-shop performance could result in his assassination. Warnings of death had never frightened Gordon, but he knew it was time to go home. He had spoken his mind. The rest was up to China. By August 16, 1880, Gordon was in Shanghai ready to sail for England.

In fact, the Imperial Council had been surprisingly receptive to Gordon's presentation despite its jagged edge. Whether Gordon can be credited with keeping China out of war with Russia is debatable, but surely his influence was significant in the mandarins' decision. Even Minister Wade, who had watched apprehensively from the sidelines, thought so. The treaty of St. Petersburg (or Ili, as it is sometimes known) was negotiated and ratified in 1881.

On the eve of Gordon's departure from China, a message from the Military Secretary of the Horse Guards was thrust in his hands. It read: "Leave cancelled, resignation not accepted, return England forthwith." Gordon himself had realized that his continued presence in China served no useful purpose; he did not need War Office prodding. When he reached Aden, he answered with a short message: "You might have trusted me."

Without assignment again, Gordon grew restless. He was tired of being treated by the Army as a mischievous truant, but if the service found his nonconformity irksome, the public loved it. Kindred individualists also admired Gordon. Sir William Mackinnon, now empire-building in East Africa in earnest, was delighted by Gordon's activities and offered him free passage to Zanzibar if Gordon would throw in his lot with him.

At this time Dr. George Birkbeck Hill was rushing to publish a collection of Gordon's letters from the Sudan, which inevitably would become a best-seller.[1] Gordon refused to be a part of the enterprise, although he finally cooperated to the extent of making his letters available and reading the proofs. Rather than hurt anyone's feelings, he insisted that whenever

263

unflattering remarks were made the name of his subject would be blanked out. And he insisted that he not be praised in the book.

Hill's book was based on some three hundred to four hundred letters written by Gordon in which "he poured forth his thoughts." While Gordon did not want to be praised, Hill could not resist a few adulatory lines in the preface to the second edition as Gordon was about to begin his epic defense of Khartoum: "A thoughtful foreigner might well have felt some contempt for a land which, in time of need, was suffering one of its greatest men thus to wear his life uselessly away. . . . For the time everyone talks of Gordon, thinks of Gordon. The long neglect has come to an end and his name is now a household word. . . ."[2]

Vanity Fair, the popular British magazine, wanted to publish a profile of Gordon which would be illustrated by the well-known caricaturist Pelligrini, who signed himself "Ape." At first Gordon refused, saying, "*I do not like* to be put before the world in any way." But he finally gave in, rationalizing that whether one "poses as a personage" or "avoids society," one "still gets abused."

The cartoon was neither typical nor flattering. Pelligrini, like almost everyone, was entranced by his eyes and exclaimed, "He is all eyes!" Gordon was portrayed in a top hat, which detracted from his exotic image. Better would have been for the Victorian hero to be wearing a mandarin's hat or tarboosh or his gold-encrusted Egyptian marshal's uniform.

The brief profile written by Jehu Junior was more perceptive:

Chinese Gordon is the most notable of living Englishmen. . . . Colonel Gordon is the most conscientious, simple-minded and honest of men. He has a complete contempt for money, and after again and again rejecting opportunities of becoming rich beyond the dreams of avarice, he remains a poor man with nothing in the world but his sword and his honor. . . . And as it is found that besides being utterly without greed, he is also entirely without vanity or self-assertion, he is set down by the officials as being "cracky" and unsafe to employ in comparison with such great men as Lord Chelmsford, Sir Garnet Wolseley and Sir George Colley. He is very modest and very gentle, yet full of enthusiasm for what he holds to be right. . . . This enthusiasm often leads him to interfere in matters which he does not understand, and to make in haste statements he has to correct at leisure. But he is a fine, noble knightly Gentleman, such as is found but once in many generations.[3]

's School, Taunton, England, Gordon's childhood
From Fulland's School's prospectus, 1878

Charles George Gordon, age eleven, with his uncle, William Augustus Gordon. Daguerreotype photo

Gordon's battery, Crimean War

Charles Gordon as subaltern after returning from the Crimean War

Taiping rebels, the "Long-hairs." *From The Illustrated London News, March 4, 1857*

The Ever Victorious Army commanded by Gordon forming a square. *From The Illustrated London News, March 12, 1864*

Li Hung-chang, Governor of Kiangsu Province, China, to whom Gordon, as commander of the Ever Victorious Army, reported.

Soochow Stockade, where the Taiping rebel commander, Ching Wang, was beheaded by Li Hung-chang. *From The Illustrated London News, March 12, 1864*

The Mosque El Mooristan, Cairo. Watercolor by David Roberts

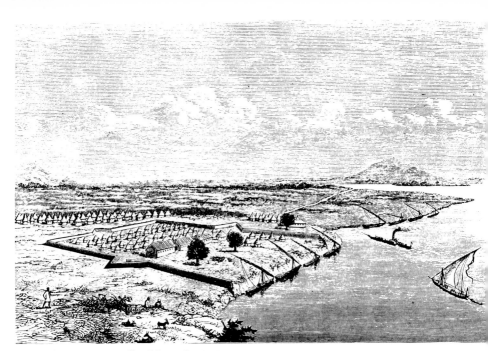

Gondokoro, Gordon's first station in Equatoria Province

Romolo Gessi, Gordon's old friend and comrade-in-arms. *From Seven Years in The Sudan, ed., Felix Gessi, London: Samson Low, Marston & Co., 1892*

Zubair Pasha, Sudanese slaver and antagonist Gordon

Murchison Falls on the Victoria Nile. *From Sir Samuel Baker, The Albert N'yanza, London: 1866*

Colonel Charles Chaille-Long, American assistant to Gordon in Equatoria

King Mutesa of Buganda. Painting by Mrs. Henry M. Stanley as photographed by her explorer husband

General Gordon in Egyptian uniform as Governor General of the Sudan. Photo by Buchta, 1878. *Printed by permission of the National Portrait Gallery, London.*

King Johannes of Abyssinia, Gordon's adversary

Evelyn Baring, Earl of Cromer, British Consul General, Egypt. *From Earl of Cromer, Modern Egypt, London: Macmillan & Co., 1908*

Chief Masupha's Basuto stronghold on Thapa Bosiu Mountain, South Africa. *From The Illustrated London News, December 4, 1880*

Chief Masupha of the Basuto Tribe, South Africa

Charles Gordon in the uniform of the Royal Engineers. Portrait by Lady Abercromby. *Printed by permission of the National Portrait Gallery, London.*

The Mahdi of Allah

Charles Gordon. Cartoon by "Spy"
(Carlo Pellegrini). *From Vanity Fair,
1881. Printed by permission of the
National Portrait Gallery, London.*

General Charles G. Gordon, 1880. Photo by Adams Stilliard. *Printed by permission of the National Portrait Gallery, London.*

Gordon's sketch map of the Seychelle Islands showing the area he believed to have been the Garden of Eden. *Printed by permission of The Gordon Boys' School Museum Trust, West End, Woking, England*

Gordon leaving London for the Sudan, 1884, shaking hands with the Duke of Cambridge

Gordon's triumphal entrance to Khartoum, 1884, to rescue the city as the Mahdi approached. *From Pictorial Records of the English in Egypt, James Sangster & Co.*

A buzzard's eye view of Khartoum, January 1885. *From The Graphic, London, February 1885*. A The Austrian Mission Convent; B Garden of the Austrian Mission; C The Palace; Gordon's Headquarters; D Government Buildings; E Army Barracks; F Tutti Village on Tutti Islands; G Omdurman; H Fortified Camp, Omdurman; JJ The White Nile; KK The Blue Nile

Night attack by British Sikh troops against Mahdist Hadendowa soldiers at Suakin, Sudan. Engraving of R. Caton Woodville's painting. *From The Illustrated London News, April 4, 1885*

Gladstone Cabinet, 1880–1885. *Seated left to right:* The Marquis of Hartington, Minister of War; Lord Granville, Foreign Minister; *standing:* Prime Minister Gladstone.

Canadian whalers transporting the First Division of the Camel Corps up the Nile for the relief of Gordon. *From The Illustrated London News, November 20, 1884*

General Sir Garnet Wolseley, Commander in Chief, Gordon Relief Expedition, on his Nile steamer. Sketch by Villiers. *From The Graphic, London, November 15, 1884*

Ansar warrior of the Mahdi

Gordon's steamers shelling Ansar warriors along the Nile banks. *From The Illustrated London News*

Breaking of the British square, Battle of Abu Klea. *From The Illustrated London News*

Pencil sketch of General Gordon by E. Clifford, 1882. *Printed by permission of the National Portrait Gallery, London.*

neral Gordon scanning the hori-
ı for a relief steamer. Cartoon cap-
ned "Mirage." *From Punch, April
34*

Gordon's head being shown to Slatin in the Mahdi's camp. *From
Rudolf C. Slatin, Fire and Sword in The Sudan, London: Edward
Arnold, 1896*

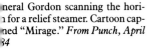

AT LAST!

Punch cartoon, "Too Late" (*below*), published as correction for previous cartoon,
"At Last," prematurely printed on the basis
of false reports of Gordon's rescue.

Mahdi's tomb, Khartoum, rebuilt after the Battle of Omdurman, 1898, when it was shelled by the British Army. Photo by author

Memorial statue of Gordon erected in Khartoum but moved to England after Sudan's independence. Photo by Dan Wages

CHINA, IRELAND, MAURITIUS

But in mid-November 1880, with time on his hands, Gordon paid a visit to troubled Ireland. With sporting guns in hand, he set out to shoot game and find some solution for Ireland's agony.

A series of poor crops had worsened the grinding poverty of the people and encouraged a continuing exodus to a better life in America. The land tenure system kept relations raw between landlord and tenant. And as English rule weighed heavily on their backs, Irish activists waged underground warfare: sometimes this broke out in public riots.

Gordon was shocked by what he saw as he tramped through the Irish countryside. "Poor wretches of Irish! I think they are more to be pitied than coerced," he wrote home. He thought their condition, at least in west Ireland, was more pitiable "than any people of Turkey, China or Africa." He wrote to a friend: "Tell the people of England that within twelve hours of their capital there exists a deeper misery and more unnatural justice than seen in China or Central Africa."

Gordon shot off a memorandum to a friend in the Royal Engineers, Colonel Donnelly—with copies to Prime Minister Gladstone and First Lord of the Admiralty Lord Northbrook—which called for the English government to buy out the landlords in the south, west and midlands and rent the lands out to Irish farmers. Donnelly could not resist sending the memo to the *Times,* so Gordon's hastily conceived plan burst upon the nation to freshen the controversy anew.

> I believe that these people are patient beyond belief, loyal, but at the same time, broken-spirited and desperate, living on the verge of starvation in places in which we would not keep our cattle. . . . the priests alone have any sympathy with their suffering. . . . In common justice, if we endow a Protestant, why should we not endow a Catholic university in a Catholic country. . . ."[4]

As could be expected, Gordon's visit to Ireland pleased the Irish common man and most of the Irish press. The *Freeman's Journal* of Dublin called Gordon "one of the most remarkable men of our own or any time," an extravagant accolade even if his views agreed with the Irish Land League.

Gordon's article caused howls of anguish from the government, which resented Gordon lending his prestige and voice to causes outside his ken.

This was not what a disciplined Army officer should do. His friend Watson did not hesitate to criticize Gordon for this, nor did others. Idleness, in Gordon's case, was always a dangerous state, a time when Agag could break loose.

In December 1881 Gordon was glad enough to escape from the public eye and relax with his good friend the Reverend Horace Waller and his family in Northamptonshire. Gordon, having first met Waller at Chatham, had kept in touch with him during the African experience. One of the leading activists in the antislavery movement, Waller had had much to write about while Gordon was in the Sudan, although they often disagreed about the best means of eradicating slavery. Sometimes Waller's views, like those of the Anti-Slavery Society, struck Gordon as unrealistic. At one point Gordon was so annoyed that he considered dropping his good friend from his long list of correspondents. But he persevered in trying to bring Waller around to his way of thinking.

Conversely, Waller persevered in trying to shake Gordon from his religious unorthodoxy. As they endlessly argued doctrine at Waller's rectory at Twywell, Gordon steadfastly stood by such favorite personal beliefs as predestination and fatalism. He complained to his sister Augusta that Waller was "wrapped up in Church dogmas." But Waller did succeed in convincing Gordon to participate in Holy Communion, a sacrament from which he had drifted since his conversion at Pembroke Dock. Gordon now wholeheartedly embraced the "Comm," as he called it, and thereafter found much comfort in it. He wrote Mrs. Freese enthusiastically about this new development and exhorted her to remember that Communion "is the tree of life." Communion is "love philtre for one's enemies, . . . a deadly weapon against envy, malice and all uncharitableness."

Not only had Gordon made progress toward Christian orthodoxy during his stay in England, but he edged a little closer to social orthodoxy. On one occasion he sallied forth from his small flat at 114 Beaufort Street to dine with the Duke of Sutherland at Stafford House in London (now the Oriental Club), although it had taken three invitations to get him there. Then there was a dinner party given by Baroness Burdett-Coutts. The Baroness, a collector of famous friends, was a generous patroness of various charities— which perhaps helped Gordon to rationalize this sortie into "frivolous" high society. Gordon and the Baroness got on famously, and a new friendship was born. After that evening, he was certain always to carry with him a letter case she had given him.

Gordon's professional idleness was becoming irksome to him. It was pleasant enough to visit old friends—he made the rounds at Gravesend, of course—and he frequently called on such old friends as Reginald Brett in London, but he was eager to return to action. He saw Florence Nightingale occasionally and implored her in a note: "My dear Miss Nightingale, what am I to do?"

A solution appeared suddenly as fate intervened. Quite by chance Gordon met a friend and fellow engineering officer, Colonel Sir Howard Elphinstone, at the War Office. Elphinstone was complaining about his new assignment as Engineering Officer at Mauritius, a remote way station on the route to India by way of the Cape. Since the Suez Canal had been built, it was well off the beaten track and offered little military challenge, much less glory. Aside from its natural beauty there was nothing to commend it.

Gordon impulsively offered to take Elphinstone's place. "Mauritius is as good for me as anywhere else," he thought—anything to escape England and to return to work! At that time, the British Army permitted an officer to find his own replacement if a particular assignment did not suit him. Ordinarily the substitute would receive compensation, but Gordon would not accept money from Elphinstone. By early May 1881, Gordon was at Le Havre awaiting a ship for Mauritius.

In Le Havre, Gordon received news of Romolo Gessi's death. The loss of an old friend was saddening, but the circumstances of his death made the tragedy even more difficult to bear. The valiant Italian's last months in the Sudan had been unhappy ones. As Governor of Equatoria, he had quarreled frequently with Mohammed Ra'uf Pasha, Gordon's replacement. By September 1880 Gessi resigned rather than suffer further harassment from Ra'uf. As Gessi was traveling downstream through the Bahr al-Ghazal on the steamship *Saphia*, it became hopelessly mired in the choking tall grass of the Sudd. There it remained during the worst two months of the year, November and December, as the sun beat down mercilessly on six hundred passengers. Food stocks were rapidly exhausted, leading survivors in desperation to eat those who died of starvation or fever. By the time rising waters freed the *Saphia* and the *Bordein* coming from the other direction could rescue it, 430 of those aboard had died.

267

Gessi survived, but wracked with fever and tortured by the acts of cannibalism, he was in awful shape. An Austrian friend, Ernest Marno, aboard the *Bordein* nursed him until they reached Khartoum in January. Housed at the Italian consulate and cared for by sisters of the Italian Christian Mission, Gessi struggled for life. Even then, Ra'uf Pasha and his other enemies in Khartoum made life difficult for the poor man. Finally Gessi tried to return home, taking ship at Berber, but he died at Suez.

"Gessi, Gessi, Gessi!" Gordon moaned in a letter home. "How I warned him to leave with me." He recalled a conversation between them in far-off Taweisha when they were pursuing the slaver Suleiman Zubair: "Whether you like it or not, or whether I like it, your life is bound up with mine."

Passing through Egypt on his way to Mauritius, Gordon wrote Reginald Brett about the Sudan situation: "It is quite hopeless to expect any aegis of protection to be placed over the poor people of the Soudan. It only needs a word from Tewfik in order to stop the outrages on these people. That our Government can be so ignorant, or else so *insouciant*, is astonishing."

When he arrived in Port Louis, Mauritius, Gordon was dismayed. The social setting consisted of endless garden parties, lawn tennis and the other kinds of social sacraments he so abhorred. He refused to live in the stylish hills, insisting on staying at first in a "piggery of a hotel" in the heart of Port Louis.

Gordon summed up his impression of Mauritius in a lighthearted letter to Colonel Elphinstone: "My dear Elphin, it is only fair to let you know what you escaped." Gordon referred to his commanding officer as "an old Major General," age seventy. The Procurer General "died the other day of abscess of the liver; while the Paymaster-General died yesterday, both taken ill just as I came here." The latter's funeral was "all higgledy-piggledy—General with cocked hat on backwards, etc., etc." Referring to his own job, he wrote, "A Colonel RE [Royal Engineers] is a farce, there is only three quarters of a battery, three Coys. of the 58th Regt. and five sappers!"

Gordon's arrival was, as he put it, "sort of a thunderbolt" among the members of the garrison community—even more so as he persisted in staying at a hotel. "The General's wife," he shuddered, "is a dragon. . . . They say that HRH in one of his furies with someone, said to the Adjutant General, 'send him to hell.' When the Adjutant General protested, 'We have no station there,' His Royal Highness said, oh well, 'Send him to Mauritius.' If you want to find a place where things have been let go to sleep, I recommend you to try Mauritius."[5]

It was at this time that Gordon vowed to master his body and fight his self-indulgences with renewed vigor. "Ever since the realization of the sacrament," he wrote Augusta, "I have been turned upside down; the process dates from the time I was at Twywell [with the Wallers]. I have today smitten that immense serpent, a yellow-brindled one, and for six months no spirits at all and only 15 cigarettes a day."

Gordon's vows of abstinence became more burdensome as time passed, and he warred with his conscience. He regularly reported on the state of battle to Augusta. By Christmas he could proudly proclaim that he had faithfully served his six-month sentence and had extended his vow to abstain from liquor for another six months. "I was always open to attack on the flank, and kept on praying for strength against it." A week later he added smoking to the new vow: "I do this because I think anything is cheap to give up if one can have more communion with God." By March he could report: "I am so glad God gave me freedom from bondage."

While on his binge of asceticism, Gordon banned still another indulgence: newspapers. He had always loved reading the papers, particularly when he was abroad, but in a letter to Mrs. Freese he reasoned: "As long as we prefer the paper of today to the Bible, things are wrong with us, yet I greet the paper with greater joy than my Bible." To his sister Augusta, he confided that newspapers stimulated him to proclaim his own opinions. This, he admitted, was a disease that he must cure.

Gordon's temptation to write letters to the press about political issues was in reality a form of Agag, ego gratification, against which he now struggled. His Christian conscience made him retreat from public recognition because he craved it too much. Too often had he succumbed and nibbled at this forbidden fruit.

Gordon restrained himself from addressing political issues publicly, but he continued to air his views for the benefit of his friends. Being in Mauritius understandably caused him to wonder about its military significance. What was the point of a garrison of four thousand soldiers with two 6½-inch guns? Half as many could defend the island as well. He wrote Reginald Brett that the money spent on the Mauritius garrison would be better spent on two torpedo launches and four Alphabet gunboats armed with thirty-eight-ton guns, which could defend the island from hostile landings far better than sea forts at Port Louis.

Mauritius gave Gordon time to think about strategic issues. He was, for example, ahead of his time in recognizing the liability of colonists who offended the sensibilities of the natives. "Taking Mauritius with its large French population, the Cape with its ever-conflicting elements, Hong Kong with its vast population of Chinese, Singapore and Penang ditto," he asked Brett, "does it not strike you that if at suitable spots we can establish fortified coaling-stations, without the detrimental accompaniment of population, who may be with us or against us, but who at any time are a nuisance, we should do well?" Consistent with this, he suggested taking an island in the Chagos group, strategically located vis-à-vis India, Suez and Singapore, and making it a maritime fortress with all the advantages of providing "no temptation to colonists."[6]

As regards the Mediterranean: "The occupation of Bizerte [Tunisia] or of any other place in the Mediterranean signifies not a jot, *as long as we have command of the sea.*" Without command of the Mediterranean, Malta and the Suez Canal could not be held. "Depend on it, it is very much better to let France and Italy take Tunis, Tripoli and Syria and for us to keep a firm, distant hold on Egypt, than it would be to oppose them."[7]

India, of course, epitomized British land commitments. "Look at India, it dictates our policy entirely and, whatever advantages it gives us, it certainly hampers us." Gordon, however, was never much of an economist, and he glided over India's economic benefit to England as a source of raw materials for its mills and a large market for its products.

Gordon spoke more like a blue-water sailor than a soldier. French and Italian colonies would "present vulnerable points of attack, *if we keep command of the sea.* My idea would be to make strong naval depots in each of the great seas. These points, once fixed ought to be supplied with a flotilla of fast, heavily armed, light-draft gunboats, so that when the fleet was away these gunboats could meet a hostile squadron in shallow waters and prevent the land being captured by land forces."

In Mauritius Gordon also developed theories about land warfare. South Africa had been consistently in the headlines with the disasters at Ulundi, Laing's Nek and Majuba. "Mounted men" was the answer, he wrote Brett.

Large forces of infantry were a mistake and artillery "was useless, would always be useless, and was a cause of delay and danger. . . ."[8]

Then there was Egypt. If "Absalom stole the hearts of the people from David, how did it all happen? By sympathy with them. [The Control and Consuls Department in Egypt] worked too much for the bondholders and for the Egyptian Ministers and not for the people. To govern men . . . 'to get into their skins,' that is, try and realize their feelings and do to others as you would they should do to you. This is the true secret," declared Gordon—a secret England would never learn. Whether it be China, Ireland, Egypt, the Sudan or anywhere else, Gordon championed the common man, and this did not make him popular with the British establishment.

Gordon lectured Brett on how he should use his influence: "Why do you not, with those of the rising generation, the successors of Gladstone, etc., form some sort of community and acquaint yourselves with all the ins and outs of our relations with the Colonies and Foreign Powers, and thus prepare yourselves for the mantles of those now in office? [Abandon] your dinner parties, etc. you could come to some definite platform. . . . Six united men, with honest intentions would carry enormous weight."[9] Here was Don Quixote; Gordon seemed to believe that the exercise of one man's will to dominate the natives of the Sudan was a technique which could be applied in England.

Gordon propounded his strategic theories more formally in a "Memorandum on Colonial Defenses" which he submitted to the Royal Commission on Empire Defense headed by Lord Carnavon in August 1881. He had only been asked about the role of Mauritius, but he let the commission have the benefit of his views on wide-ranging strategic concepts.

Contrary to conventional wisdom at the time, Gordon saw the vulnerability of the Suez Canal in time of conflict and preached the strategic importance of the Cape as key in the alternative sea route to India. "In the event of war we could not without incurring complications with and hostility of other nations close the canal to those neutral nations whose vessels would have free traffic through it. Any nation with which England found itself at War could close the canal to British use by scuttling in it a vessel or two."

Another theory of Gordon's expressed at that time is not without present-day relevance: "The defense of India from a Russian advance is by raising the tribes near the Persian Gulf and supplying them with money, arms and a few adventurous officers (no troops) and leading them on to the Russian flank from the Persian Gulf and keeping good friends with Afghanistan." For this purpose, he believed Aden should be made a crown colony having supervision of the Persian Gulf and the Red Sea.[10] Gordon would surely have appreciated Leon Trotsky's dictum: "The road to Paris and London lies via the towns of Afghanistan, the Punjab and Bengal."

The somnambulant life in Mauritius gave Gordon time not only to address himself to the contemporary problems of the empire, but to set straight biblical geography as well. Since his experiences in Armenia after the Crimean War, he had been interested in establishing the true sites of biblical events, and had he not been assigned to Mauritius he probably would have taken leave to search for them in Syria and Palestine. His devotion to the Bible and his mapmaking proclivities had combined to lead him to some interesting, if not scientifically sound, geographic theories.

Gordon visited the Seychelle Islands from Mauritius, ostensibly on official business, but actually to explore a thesis he had arrived at that the biblical Eden lay beneath the sea nearby. This was to obsess him. The Bible stated that the Eden River, prior to the Flood, branched into four different rivers, but Gordon knew of no such instance in geography. (River deltas, in which a single river often split into many parts before debouching into a sea, were a different matter altogether.) To the contrary, smaller rivers often joined to form one major river in draining the lands. What then were the four rivers referred to in the Bible which Gordon believed joined to form the River Eden? Two were clearly the Euphrates and the Tigris (Hiddekel), both of which flowed into the Persian Gulf.

While most biblical cartographers identified the Gihon (encompassing the Land of Kush, or the Sudan) with the Nile, and the Pishon with the Indus, Gordon reasoned that the Pishon rather than the Gihon was the Nile's predecessor in the time before the Flood, but it then emptied into the Red Sea instead of the Mediterranean. The biblical Gihon, in his calculations, had been a large river rising in Turkey and flowing southward through the Jordan Valley and what is now the Dead Sea, then through the Gulf of Aqaba into the Red Sea near the coast of the Sudan, or Kush. The Pishon and Gihon, therefore, flowed out from the Red Sea through the Bab el Mandeb—Gate of the World—into the Gulf of Aden, or as Gordon would have it, "Gulf of

Eden," and on to the Land of Eden itself before all was submerged and inundated by the Great Flood.

The Tigris and Euphrates flowed into the Gulf of Aden—or Eden—via the Persian Gulf, according to Gordon. Within the great district known as Eden, which existed as dry land before the Flood and extended as far south as the area now defined by the Seychelle Islands, was the original Garden of Eden. Gordon pinpointed the small island of Praslin in the Seychelles as the surviving remnant of that hallowed place of man's creation.

The granite islands of the Seychelles are unique in that they were not formed by volcanic eruptions but broke away from the mainland with the continental shifts. Some of their plant and animal species, such as the fabled coco-de-mer tree (*Lodoicea seychellarum*), some as old as a thousand years, are found nowhere else on earth. A local legend which developed after Gordon's visit has it that the male coco-de-mer at night stalks the female tree to fertilize it. Anyone who has seen the phallic protuberance coming from the male tree and the pudendum-shaped fruit of the female tree can understand how the legend arose. Spared this erotic fable, Gordon had his own theory. He was convinced that the coco-de-mer tree was the biblical Tree of Knowledge, while its aphrodisiacal nut was the Forbidden Fruit given to a hungry Adam by a curious Eve. He also spotted a breadfruit tree on the island, which he dubbed the Tree of Life. A reenactment of the Fall seemed at hand—except that no Eve was about—as he suddenly spied a snake winding about a coco-de-mer tree. Taking his revenge on the biblical troublemaker, he shot it dead.

Gordon's idyll in the Seychelles was brief, but he was convinced that he had found the Garden of Eden. He asked Colonel Donnelly to pass the news of his discovery on to the illustrious T. H. Huxley, new president of the Royal Geographical Society. An admirer of Gordon as a person, Huxley restrained himself from offering any scientific judgment on this unorthodox thesis.[11]

Gordon received his promotion to major general on March 24, 1882, at the age of forty-nine. Despite his lack of regimental soldiering, he had made good military progress. The promotion meant, however, that he had too much rank for his position as Engineering Officer in Mauritius and had to be transferred. This was a welcome development. Having heard nothing from an earlier offer to help out the Cape government in its Basuto tribal crisis,

Gordon was delighted to receive, only days before he was scheduled to be transferred, an invitation from Capetown to become Commandant General of Colonial Forces. Within two days, on April 4, 1882, Gordon was aboard the three-hundred-ton trading schooner *Scotia*, bound for South Africa.[12]

SOUTH AFRICA

> A grub like myself, who can put himself into other people's skins
> and find out their feelings, is better adapted than a bigger man for
> the solution of such questions.
> —Charles Gordon while engaged with the Basuto problem, 1882

When in March 1880 Prime Minister Gordon Sprigg of the Cape government first felt out Gordon on accepting the position of Commandant General of the colony's armed forces, the tribal problem was still festering. The powerful Zulus had been finally defeated by the British at Ulundi in 1879, and in the aftermath public agitation for tribal disarmament had become strong. The Peace Preservation Act passed in 1880 decreed that not only guns but the tribesmen's assegais, or spears, be turned in.

This act was particularly resented by the Basuto tribes. Although less formidable than the Zulus, the Basutos, whose secluded homelands were wedged between the Orange Free State and Natal in the Drakensberg mountain range, made the neighboring Boer settlers uneasy. The Boers had defeated the Basutos in 1868, but the Basutos were still armed and mounted. They had worked in the mines and bought arms with their earnings; they were loath to part with their rifles, which they considered almost divine.

Paramount Chief Letsie, who had inherited at least titular Basuto leadership from the revered old Chief Mshweshwe, ordered his people to comply with the new law. But many of the subchiefs, particularly his more militant half brother Chief Masupha, ignored his word and defied the government. The few who agreed to surrender their weapons were contemptuously known as "loyals" by the others.

Gordon knew that to accept Sprigg's offer meant leading the Cape Colony army in forcibly disarming the Basutos. With this he did not agree, and so he declined the offer. His acerbic telegram of refusal read out in the Cape Legislative Assembly in May went this way: "To act as Mr. Sprigg supposes would be to bring on hostilities [with the Basutos] which the Colony cannot possibly desire. Kindly read this to the House, if not irregular, and ask Mr. Sprigg to believe, if only for a moment, that I should not act as a madman for the sake of making a clap-trap reputation."[1]

Gordon's friend General Wolseley, now serving as High Commissioner for Southeast Africa and Commander of the Forces, also opposed disarming the Basutos. After all, "the Basutos and other quiet and orderly native tribes had cheerfully assisted Britain" in the Zulu War.[2] Finally, a new Governor of Cape Colony, Sir Hercules Robinson, proposed a formula which at first seemed agreeable to the Basutos—even to the firebrand Masupha. "Robinson's Award," as it was known, called for disarmament but made provision for returning weapons to their owners on license.

Gordon had been following events in Basutoland from Mauritius, and in the spring of 1881, when fighting broke out between the Basutos and government forces, he volunteered his services as Basuto administrator. The Basutos interested Gordon; while he had been opposed to a policy of coercion, the idea of his being their mentor and architect of peace appealed to him. His application was ignored, however, probably because the precarious Spriggs administration was about to fall.

In August the newly appointed Acting Governor's Agent for the Basutos, Joseph Orpen, met with the "loyal" chiefs, who doubted that Masupha and other Basuto hard-liners would abide by Robinson's formula. Nor did they believe that the Cape government could protect the loyals from extremists like Masupha. To make their point, a spokesman related an old Basuto story about a lion whose presence in the grass near a village terrified the people. One day when a child pelted the lion with stones, the townsfolk were astonished to see a frightened rabbit hop out from beneath the lion. Finally it was known that the lion, which had so frightened them, had long been dead and its empty skin was being used by the rabbit as its burrow. This story was, of course, meant to convey the loyals' conviction that the British lion was but an empty skin, and Mr. Orpen was left to conclude that he was the rabbit.

As the Basuto problem worsened in 1882, the frustration felt by the new administration mounted. In desperation Thomas Scanlan, by then Prime Minister, sought Gordon's services. Governor Sir Hercules Robinson accordingly telegraphed Lord Kimberley, Secretary of State for the Colonies: "Ministers request me to enquire whether H.M.'s Government would permit them to obtain services of Colonel Charles Gordon to come to this Colony for the purpose of consultation as to the best measures to be adopted with reference to Basutoland in the event of Parliament sanctioning their proposals as to that territory, and to engage his services, should he be willing to renew the offer made to their predecessors in April 1881, to assist to terminating the war and administering Basutoland."[3] Permission was received, and Gordon was queried. It was a measure of Gordon's eagerness to have the position that he accepted with alacrity and took the next boat to Capetown.

Socially, Gordon got off to a bad start in Capetown, but that was to be expected. Welcomed at a formal dinner given in his honor at the Governor's mansion, Gordon tripped on Lady Robinson's train as the guests went in to dinner. Then in his confusion he addressed his hostess as Lady Barker, a woman whom Lady Robinson detested.

If Gordon felt unsure of himself in social situations, he was the soul of self-confidence in his judgments on the Basuto problem. Soon after his arrival in Capetown he produced a memorandum containing his recommendations. There was something in it to annoy almost everyone. He criticized the carelessness with which the British government had transferred Basuto administration to the Cape government and chastised the colony for not permitting Basuto representation in the colonial Parliament. Gordon recommended that a *pitso*, or conclave, be held in which the Basutos could express their own preferences in the matter.

In such a conclave the Basutos would doubtless choose the Queen as their ruler, not the Cape government, and this would be embarrassing to the British government, which did not want any change in the status quo. After due deliberation, Lord Kimberley made it clear that the colony should not expect the crown to relieve it of its responsibilities for the Basutos.

Gordon also recommended generous compensation to those Basutos who had suffered because of their loyalty to the Cape government. In a constructive vein, he submitted a new plan for administrating the Basutos. His blueprint, which called for withdrawal of colonial military forces and the formation of a governing body to consist only of a Resident and two assistants appointed by the Cape government, was tantamount to Basuto self-government. Not surprisingly, this found no favor in Capetown.

The Cape government now had second thoughts about using Gordon as its troubleshooter in Basutoland. Orpen was well entrenched in that position and seemed to be doing well. Gordon, for that matter, agreed that he should not replace Orpen. As an alternative assignment, the Cape government offered the general the position of Commandant General of the Colonial Forces—the same job it had originally offered him in 1880. Gordon accepted the position and left for the Eastern Province to command and revitalize the Cape's forces.

John Merriman, Commissioner of Crown Lands and Public Works, assured Gordon that the health of the armed forces had a distinct bearing on the tribal problem, and that a moment might come when Gordon's particular genius with tribal peoples could be used. Gordon always found it difficult to resist the prospect of action in out-of-the-way places where he could be his own master. But as he jolted along by train through the vastness of South Africa toward his headquarters at King Williams Town, his instincts warned him that he was "going into a regular hornet's nest." The last half of Gordon's seven-hundred-mile journey had to be made by cart over rutted roads and through empty hills where an occasional homestead gave evidence of the pioneering spirit of the *Voortrekkers*.

As in the Sudan, Gordon traveled incessantly in his job. The forces under his command, whether regulars from England, Boer volunteers, tribal levies or native irregulars recruited locally, felt his presence. So did the government in Capetown, which Gordon bombarded with memoranda. Typically, his observations and recommendations were puzzling. He contradicted himself, was undiplomatic in his criticism, and changed courses abruptly, and broached revolutionary suggestions which often rode roughshod over the realities of politics. His style was disconcerting. He took the Cape Mounted Rifles by surprise by reviewing them in a frock coat and top hat, an idiosyncrasy which had begun when he led the Ever Victorious Army. He was firm and consistent in one conclusion, however: The Cape forces suffered from idleness, incompetence and insubordination.

British recruits in Gordon's opinion were generally unsuitable. They were poor horsemen, bad marksmen and uninterested in learning the ways of the country. Local people, he was convinced, would make better soldiers. The young white men of South Africa were born in the saddle and from earliest age hunted with firearms. A properly led native militia, Gordon believed, could best maintain local security. He also raised the hackles of the commander of the Cape Mounted Rifles when he suggested that Her

Majesty's officers were not above gaining "the suffrages of the men and using them as a collective body in refusing to carry out any order that they may dislike."[4] Gordon, moreover, did not hesitate to criticize and make observations on subjects beyond his proper jurisdiction. In a memorandum on the Transkeian Provinces, for example, he blamed the civil administration of the Cape government six hundred miles away for many of the military deficiencies, and recommended that the provinces be administered by a lieutenant governor stationed on the spot.

Even though the government had by this time canceled the Peace Preservation Act as unworkable, Gordon found it natural that the tribes resented the substitution of their traditional tribal structure with a superimposed white man's rule that they did not understand. "A grub like myself," he wrote his sister Augusta, "who can put himself into other people's skins and find out their feelings, is better adapted than a bigger man for the solution of such questions."

Gordon could not resist giving his opinions publicly about the Basuto problem—so much so that the press began speculating that Gordon's writ went beyond the Colonial Forces and that he had a secret political mission related to the tribal problem. In fact, not only was Gordon now left out of Basuto affairs, but he found his rightful authority in the military rapidly eroding. His recommendations were refused, ignored or politely deferred by Capetown. Even Orpen, closer at hand, resisted his recommendations about troop management in Basutoland. Privately, Gordon complained bitterly that he had less authority than he had had in the Sudan. "Though I have great influence," he wrote, " I have to explain everything and discuss it." Gordon never liked explaining his actions.

Gordon was by now thoroughly frustrated. The general's master plan for reorganizing the military had not been accepted, and his freely given advice on Basutoland was consistently disregarded. In conversation with Scanlan, Gordon betrayed his restlessness. King Leopold still wanted him for the Congo, he told the Prime Minister, implying that he did not want to stay in the colony if he had outlived his usefulness. He also explained to a puzzled Scanlan that the Congo attracted him because "it is a climate which precludes any hope of old age; there is a good chance then of ending one's pilgrimage, which I incessantly long for."

Just as Gordon was on the verge of resigning in July 1882, Merriman,

Commissioner of Crown Lands, talked him into remaining—at least until the next session of Parliament. To keep Gordon's energies usefully channeled in the meantime, he suggested that Gordon visit Basutoland with J. W. Sauer, Secretary of Native Affairs. It was made clear to Gordon, however, that he would not be on a negotiating mission and had no authority to make promises. He was to confine himself to discovering whether Masupha was prepared to accept government authority as exercised by a magistrate. At last the general would be involved in the Basuto problem, the reason he had come to Cape Colony in the first place. This was cheering, but it was a prelude to a fiasco.

Merriman, a most able official, admired Gordon and seemed to be one of the few who now thought he could be useful in the Basuto situation. He admitted that Gordon was "a queer fellow," but assured Prime Minister Scanlan that "he liked him as much as ever. . . ."[5] Perhaps because Gordon was so pleased with Merriman's proposal, he did not fully grasp government policy as it was explained to him—or he simply was not listening.

Merriman had been frank in describing the government's strategy as "divide and rule." One chieftain should be pitted against another, and intertribal frictions and jealousies should be exploited. This ran directly contrary to Gordon's previously expressed views and was alien to his conviction that honest personal diplomacy with the chieftains could bring them around to a more cooperative attitude. That was his style, one which had worked in China and the Sudan. Merriman, nonetheless, thought he had clearly conveyed the government's point of view and wrote Sauer confidently: "You will find Gordon ready to fall in with your wishes."[6] He did not, however, take into consideration Gordon's tendency to interpret official policy as he thought best and his predilection for improvising new policy on the spot.

Gordon set out with Sauer in high spirits, armed only with confidence in God's benevolence, his own disdain for death and a bundle of religious tracts ordered from London. He had no doubt that he could bring peace—even salvation—to the Basutos.

At Marija, an outpost of the Paris-based Evangelical Missionary Society, Gordon, Sauer, Orpen and the Inspector General, Arthur Garcia, joined by the local magistrate, Major Hook, prepared for the meeting with Chief Letsie at Letsie's nearby camp. While waiting for Letsie, Gordon readily agreed to talk to the Reverend Adolphe Mabille's Sunday-school class. In this curious episode Gordon again exhibited a deeply emotional side of his character. As he stood before the sea of children's faces, he suddenly bolted for the door. Mabille found him sitting dejectedly nearby, head in hands, and had to talk him into returning to his young audience. In a letter home Gordon explained his behavior: "When I looked into the faces of those dear black lambs of the Savior and recalled all that the black race has suffered from our own, I could not go on."[7]

Sauer opened the discussion by taking Chief Letsie to task for not being able to control his half-brother rival, Masupha—or even his sons, for that matter. Gordon, off-key as usual, explained that he had come in friendship and, just as he had refused to take up arms against the Basuto when the previous Cape government had asked for his help, he now sought peace. Sauer, intent on getting Letsie to attack Masupha, must have squirmed on his stool as he listened to Gordon's plea for peace.

Letsie on his part had no illusions. He accused the white man—English and Boer alike—of trying to sow discord between him and Masupha. The old chief had shrewdly guessed the government's divide-and-rule strategy and estimated quite accurately that London was looking for an opportunity to withdraw from the problem, leaving the Basutos to their own devices. White man's rule was onerous at best to the fiercely independent Basutos, but to be abandoned to the harassment of the Boer settlers would be intolerable. Old Letsie, with a tribal fondness for metaphors, explained how living in a cave was not without peril—for one thing the roof could fall in—but to be forced to abandon the cave and live exposed to the elements would be worse.

The talks ended with Letsie promising to raise an army to attack Masupha. Gordon was convinced that Letsie would do no more than make a token attack, a charade to please the government; in the last analysis the Basutos would not permit themselves to be divided. War was not a solution.

Gordon's peace formula called for the removal of government troops from Basuto territory, leaving the enforcement of law and order to a Basuto police force. In this way the rebellious Masupha could be isolated. Eventually, when the weak Letsie died, a united Basuto people might live in peace.

Gordon stopped off at the Church of England mission in Thlotsie Heights and by coincidence met Cecil Rhodes there. Rhodes was then serving on a commission to settle claims by the "loyals" who had suffered because of their allegiance to the government. The two men, much alike in their strong will and individualism, also agreed on how to deal with the Basutos. Both believed the Cape government had proved incapable of handling the problem and should relinquish control of the Basuto territory to the British, to be ruled directly as a colony through a Crown Resident.

Gordon by now had become so engrossed with the Basutos that he considered volunteering to spend the next two years as administrator of these unhappy people. This would mean a demotion, but rank was of little concern to Gordon. In his enthusiasm for the idea Gordon asked Cecil Rhodes if he would be willing to work with him in restoring peace to the Basutos. "There are very few men in the world to whom I would make such an offer," he told his new friend. Rhodes turned him down, recognizing that each of them was too strong-willed to work easily together and realizing perhaps that the Cape government would never agree to the assignment of the uncontrollable Gordon to so volatile a place. Rhodes, moreover, had his own dreams to be fulfilled.

Gordon made a lasting impression on Rhodes, and Gordon sensed in the younger man an exceptional power and ability. (The general would once again try to lure Rhodes to his service as he set out on his last and fateful adventure in the Sudan, but the dynamic entrepreneur was by then too busy pursuing his own destiny.) Among Rhodes's papers was found a record of a conversation about Gordon which took place between the great empire-builder and one of his colleagues, E. A. Maund, just before Gordon's death: "It is curious, but somehow he [Gordon] exercised a strange influence on me. He united spiritual ideas or sentiment with tremendous activity, and had such a belief in his own way of doing things as to amount to obstinacy. . . . We got on, however, capitally together for we both believed in moral suasion rather than force in dealing with native chiefs."[8] It appears that Rhodes's handling of the Matebele tribal crisis fourteen years later may indeed have been inspired by Gordon's approach to the Basutos.

Rhodes was fascinated by Gordon's faith and how it could survive so strongly in an age of science and reason, particularly since his own early religious upbringing had not. Maund, who coincidentally had lived near Gordon's sister Augusta, recalled that Gordon often talked of science and did not see science and Christian faith as incompatible. Religion, rather, was a force to "confound priestcraft." Rhodes summed Gordon up as "a fanatical enigma."[9]

Rhodes gave helpful advice to Gordon as they talked together at Thlotsie Heights. He warned that Sauer, as superior officer, must not be upstaged during their discussions with the Basuto chiefs. Taking Rhodes's advice to heart, Gordon stayed in the background and made it clear in the discussions with the tribesmen that Sauer was "the great man of the Whites" and that he, Gordon, was but his servant.[10]

Gordon's ego could not be suppressed for long, however. All his life in difficult situations he had met the crisis by facing down his opponents. Alone, he had imposed his will on the slaver Suleiman Zubair and his warriors. Alone, he had sought out King Johannes of Abyssinia in his mountain citadel and scoffed at his threats. Alone, he was now determined to take on Masupha, and win him over by force of his will.

Gordon's plan to see Masupha was acceptable to the government on condition that the visit would be in the general's private capacity. In a note to Sauer, Gordon expressed his understanding of the government's position and acknowledged that he had no authority to reach agreements in the government's behalf. This would be only an informal sounding.

Masupha's kraal was perched on a flat-topped mountain called Thaba Bosiu, "Mountain of Night," which commanded 150 acres of rich pastureland in a secluded valley below. The four-hundred-foot plateau was accessible only by three steep trails. A pile of boulders at the top of each trail stood ready to be rolled down on hostile intruders. Basuto folklore attributed magical qualities to Thaba Bosiu; it rose to great heights during the night, making attack under cover of darkness impossible, then subsided to its normal height at dawn.

Accompanied only by Arthur Garcia, Captain Nettleton, Resident Magistrate of Mafeteng, and the Reverend Mr. Keck from the nearby French church mission to act as interpreter, Gordon climbed the steep hill and was received by Masupha. Some two hundred Basuto warriors, brandishing their assegais, crowded around their chief to hear what Gordon had to say. The general stressed his private role in this matter but impressed upon the suspicious chief his opinion that failure to reach agreement with the government would place him at the mercy of the neighboring Boers, and the Boers would ultimately push Masupha's people southward to less desirable land in the Transkei.

As Gordon waited for Masupha's response, completely at his mercy, Sauer was meeting with rival Chief Letsie in Marija. To Sauer's astonishment, the feeble Letsie had actually gathered a large army under his son Lerothodi and was preparing to march on Masupha. This was a development the government wanted but never really believed would occur. When news of the impending invasion by Letsie reached Masupha, it not only placed Gordon in a hopeless position as far as his mission of peace was concerned, but exposed him to physical danger as well.

Gordon had exceeded his instructions and had, in fact, assumed a negotiating role. Even though he described his mission as a "personal" one, the distinction was a fine one. As far as the chief was concerned, Gordon had promised that no attempt would be made by the government to coerce him. With Letsie's forces about to attack, Masupha could only conclude that he had been betrayed. Gordon was more furious than frightened, convinced that Sauer had purposely deceived him. In fact, Sauer had simply been taken by surprise by Letsie's unexpected action and determination.

When Masupha angrily demanded an explanation, Gordon could only deny knowledge of the government's role in encouraging Letsie's bellicosity and otherwise distance himself from official policy.

Before leaving the kraal in humiliation, Gordon sent a cryptic message to the Prime Minister: "As I am in a completely false position up here and can do more harm than good, I am leaving for the Colony, whence I propose coming to Cape Town, when I trust the Government will accept my resignation." Masupha fortunately believed Gordon's protestations of innocence and in the end made no effort to harm or hold him. People had always believed Gordon; he was a symbol of probity and honor. It was Sauer whom the Cape Colony public blamed for the general's predicament, and there were even those who suspected that he had deliberately placed Gordon in danger. Gordon was so angry with Sauer that when he met him at the train, he refused to sit in the same carriage with him.

Sauer was in double jeopardy as it became obvious that Letsie's posturing force would, in fact, never subdue Masupha. Already blamed for wrecking Gordon's peace initiative, Sauer was soon blamed by the public for encouraging a war which could not be won. Sauer could only try to extricate himself from his untenable position in this matter by publicly blaming Gordon for the mix-up which had occurred and claiming that the general well knew the dangers he was walking into.

While in South Africa, Gordon had renewed his acquaintance with the Governor's aide-de-camp, an officer who had served with him in China.* Gordon called on him on the eve of his departure, giving him for temporary safekeeping the whole of his correspondence on the South African problem; only a designated few were to see it. As a gesture of gratitude, Gordon offered to put in a good word for his friend with General Wolseley. Then on the very morning of his departure, as the young aide recalled, Gordon asked "whether it was consonant with the dignity of a Major General in H. M.'s army to be going home with less than a sovereign in his pocket." The aide graciously offered to be Gordon's banker, prompting the general to explain that he "could not ask the Colonial authorities for any money, as perhaps he had rather disappointed them."†

A thoroughly disillusioned and angry Gordon sailed for England aboard the *Kinfauns Castle* on October 14, 1882. In a farewell note to Prime Minister Scanlan, he apologized for putting the government "in a fix," but expressed the belief that what he had said to Masupha "will ventilate the question and be the best for the Colony." Gordon wrote his sister Augusta: "What a queer life mine has been with these fearful rows continually occurring."

The Basuto affair contributed to the fall of Scanlan's government in the early summer of 1884. It was a government which would not be missed, certainly not by Gordon, who referred to it as "a feeble invertebrate for-mation." Sauer could never quite shed public blame for placing Gordon in mortal danger. The whole affair led to the British government's again taking

---

* A. Egmont Hake, who wrote *Events in the Taeping Rebellion* (London: W. H. Allen, 1891), included in his book an appendix entitled "Reminiscences by One Who Served with Gordon in China." The author of the reminiscences, not identified by Hake, became the Cape Colony Governor General's aide-de-camp.

† Two of Gordon's nephews serving at the Cape then also saw their uncle off and later remarked to the Governor's ADC that Gordon had been very generous to them. The ADC later wrote: "I had then and still have a very strong suspicion how he [Gordon] disposed of my loan of a few hours before."

direct responsibility for the Basutos, the solution which Gordon had favored all along. The *Cape Times* described the Cape government's decision to give Basutoland back to the crown as "Gordon's policy without Gordon." In the long run the winners in this unfortunate saga were the Basutos; that would have pleased Gordon.

THE HOLY LAND

We can only keep alive the light within us, we cannot kill the evil
things.
—Charles Gordon during his sojourn in Palestine, 1883

While still nursing his grievance over the way things had turned
out in Cape Colony, Gordon's thoughts returned to his long-
cherished dream to visit Palestine. He had much to resolve
about his faith, and the Holy Land seemed the right place in which to do it.
In addition, he wanted to test out various theories about the true whereabouts
of certain hallowed sites. Thanks to his shipping magnate friend Sir William
Mackinnon, he could get cheap passage to Jaffa, and he knew living there
would be inexpensive.

Still in the offing was King Leopold's invitation to administer the Congo.
Mackinnon, who had recently visited the Belgian King, assured Gordon that
His Majesty wanted his services more than ever, but the time was not yet
right. Gordon was willing, but believed that his employment should be under
some sort of international auspices. All in all, now seemed an ideal time to
take several months off to reflect in Palestine while the Congo proposition
ripened.

Gordon landed in Jaffa on January 16, 1883, in company with Herbert
Drake, a friend from Gravesend days. Drake unfortunately proved to be
neurotic and an awful nuisance. The two men got on each other's nerves as
they discovered how unlike their views were on almost everything, particularly religious matters, about which Gordon had never been tolerant. Gordon
wrote Augusta in exasperation that Drake was not a "converted man," and
"appears to consider it possible to know God of his own reason. One can
scarcely like companionship with one who, as far as I can see, doubts the
many treasures of my existence. I think Drake will join the American list as
he is going to join them [American missionaries] in their home. . . . I am

very glad of it . . . he was a burden to me . . . he was very selfish and 'Herbertish,' indeed."[1]

Gordon started off badly in Palestine, having one of his attacks of depression. It was, he wrote Augusta, "the feeling we have that we have lost the world and not gained Him, leaving a gap in us." Gordon was not finding it easy to relax in contemplation, missing, as usual, the world of active challenge. Gordon's friend Wilfrid Scawen Blunt referred to the year in Palestine as "a complete religious debauch which left him more than ever the prey of his own visions, a puppet in the hands of his imagined duty to do this or that for God. . . . He was waiting for a call."[2]

This call, which Gordon was awaiting, might have been the call of active military service as much as a call to serve God. He was still a man of two worlds: the one in which he lived and the one to which he longed to ascend. A. Egmont Hake, in his biography *The Story of Chinese Gordon*, published in 1884, wrote: "And now that we ourselves are face to face with new difficulties in Egypt and the Sudan, there are thousands who feel and say that if we were wise, to him [Gordon] only should we look for deliverance. . . . He has gone to the Holy Land to be forgotten."[3]

Gordon could not escape the turmoil of the world even if he had wanted to. After he arrived in Jaffa, he discovered that French intelligence agents were keeping him under surveillance. While his own government considered his religious retreat in the Holy Land but another mark of his eccentricity, the French were convinced he had some hidden political mission. Since the British occupation of Egypt, Anglo-French relations had been strained as the two countries jockeyed for position in the Near East. The French wasted their time in keeping track of him, but could not be blamed for wondering if this prominent "tourist" was now up to some mischief in an area so close to what they considered their sphere of interest.[4]

In Palestine, Gordon visited an old acquaintance from the Crimean War, Laurence Oliphant, whom he had also known in China. Oliphant was prominent in London society; he was one of those Victorian gadabouts who knew everybody. Now he was living in Haifa, having become a mystic, but in earlier days he had popped up in such diverse places as Italy, where he worked in Garibaldi's movement in the early 1860s,[5] Schleswig-Holstein, Denmark, and the Orient on secret missions for British intelligence. His career as a secret agent ended in 1864, however, when in an indiscreet article for *Blackwood's Magazine* he divulged his mission to spy on Danish defenses and criticized the Foreign Office for interfering with European national strivings.[6]

Oliphant's meeting with Gordon in Haifa was memorable. The general expounded on the folly of British policy in Egypt and the Sudan, favoring Sudanese independence under native rulers and decrying the placement of English officers in command of Egyptian troops. The Mahdi, that self-styled "Messiah of Allah," had been still an obscure preacher in Aba Island when Gordon was Governor General, but had since risen meteorically to prominence, and now ruled much of southwest Sudan. Gordon, ill informed about these developments, believed that the conflict could be settled by a civil commissioner sent by England to negotiate with the Mahdi. Perhaps some formula of independence could be worked out. If this did not work, Gordon believed that the Mahdi could be "threatened with a rebellion of the local Sudanese chiefs, whom he felt could easily be induced to combine against him."[7] Gordon also favored building a railroad from Suakin to Berber, though he feared that the Egyptians would not be pleased by the diversion of trade to Suakin.

With the Bible and Concordance as his only guides, Gordon then turned his thoughts away from the world of politics and went in search of holy sites. His archaeological theories, based on subjectively interpreted biblical passages and his own logic, were not endorsed by more orthodox scholars and geographers, but they nonetheless attracted a certain following. Later, "Gordon's Calvary" would even be considered reasonable by various biblical scholars. Gordon one day gazed up at a spot known as Skull Hill, which indeed resembled a human skull. This, he was sure, was the biblical Golgotha, the "place of the skull," where the crucifixion of Christ had taken place. In a slim volume entitled *Reflections in Palestine, 1883,*[8] he expressed the not completely original thought that "the cross stood on the tip of Skull Hill in the center of it, and not where the slaughter house stands" as conventional scholarship had it. Gordon imagined that "if the Cross were in the center of Skull Hill, the whole city and even the Mount of Olives would be embraced by those stretched out arms . . . unto 'a disobedient and gainsaying people.' "[9] Gordon also concluded that the sepulcher where Christ was placed after being taken down from the Cross was an old tomb in a garden near Skull Hill. Most experts dispute this, but "Gordon's Tomb," as it is still called, attracted enough attention so that it was purchased in 1893 by public subscription, endorsed by the Archbishop of Canterbury and preserved for many years as a Christian holy place.

Gordon also firmly believed that he had discovered the true boundary between the tribes of Benjamin and Judah, and claimed to have located the place where Noah built the Ark out of gopher wood. Gordon believed that with the subsiding of the Flood, the Ark came to rest on Mount Moriah, not Mount Ararat. Whether his evidence was sufficient or his conclusions valid, Gordon at least applied the same diligence as when scouting the vulnerable points of Taiping fortresses in China. His military background may also have given rise to a random thought, more worthy of a soldier than a servant of God, in which he noted: "The Russian Convent commanded the whole city, and was in itself a strong fortress, capable of holding a formidable garrison which Russia could despatch in the guise of priests without anyone being the wiser."

Gordon, by some mathematical calculation, predicted the date when Christ would descend to earth again. The general—always the consummate engineer—warned facetiously that on Judgment Day Jerusalem would have a terrible traffic jam.

As Gordon ranged beyond the topography of the Holy Land, his notions became less plausible. He hypothesized that when the Devil fled from the throne of God at the Creation to seek refuge in the farthest corner of the hemisphere of darkness, he in fact went to the antipodes of Jerusalem—more precisely, the Bass Isles in the vicinity of Pitcairn Island in mid-Pacific.

In a strange letter to the worldly explorer Richard Burton, Gordon described with great assurance some of his theories: The Rock of Harrar in Abyssinia was the platform on which Adam had been molded out of clay from the potter's field; one of the Seychelle Islands was the site of Eden; after the Fall, Adam was brought to Mount Moriah to till the ground; Noah fashioned the Ark twelve miles from Jaffa on Ain Judeh. Gordon's friend Wilfrid Blunt commented on the letter to Burton, so fantastic in its detailed thesis: "Was ever such a serious letter written to so mocking a reader?"[10] Even Octavia Freese criticized some of his letters from Palestine as fantasy; this "rent him," as Gordon put it, and their friendship grew apart.

Gordon's personal theology found renewed expression during his stay in the Holy Land as well. While professing belief in the literal meanings of the

Bible, Gordon himself was guilty of groundless embellishments no less egregious than the doctrinal elaborations of which he accused the clergy: "Isolated passages of the Bible and detached portions may be made to support almost any opinion." He compared such presumption with the simple purity of God's word, believing firmly, "He alone can reveal His own words."

Throughout his life Gordon was troubled by the temptations of the flesh as well as his love of cigars and brandy. On principle he considered any pleasure of the body sinful indulgence—although he could never quite give up smoking. From a very early age, he seemed to look upon sex as an evil to be suppressed, and from Palestine he wrote the Reverend R. H. Barnes how he had wished he was a eunuch at age fourteen. Mortification of the flesh permeated his views on baptism, as he described them in *Reflections in Palestine*: "True baptism . . . is virtually the acknowledgement of the flesh being able to do no good thing. The adult who wishes to be free of his carnal nature and who believes in Jesus and is baptized does receive the Holy Ghost in his body." Faith, he was convinced, was impossible without an indwelling of the Holy Ghost. Man's carnal nature began when Satan insinuated himself "as a traitor" into man's bodies. "Carnal man has a dormant soul, therefore, he has Satan usurping the dormant soul's functions and using the body as he wills."

Gordon's attitude toward sex has been variously explained by his biographers, whose theories range from its being a psychological consequence of his obsession with death to the likelihood that he was, in fact, a repressed homosexual. It is always difficult to diagnose sexual aberrations from the written, historical record alone—even by experts—but it is next to impossible to do so after a century or so has elapsed and attitudes have changed radically. But if Gordon had repressed homosexual tendencies, there has never been evidence that he ever considered giving in to them or even admitting them to himself. Homosexuality was a forbidden subject in Victorian times; people did not talk about it. There must have been some experience in his youth to cause Gordon to wish he were a eunuch, but whatever it was, it has never surfaced. What seems certain is that Gordon justified his sexual dormancy on a religious conviction that the flesh is the dominion of the Devil.

Gordon's remarks on the Fall, sin and Satan placed a heavy burden of blame on Eve. His interpretation of these subjects in Genesis is very ornate. "Had Eve never eaten what was forbidden, she never could have been worked in by the spirit of disobedience—Satan. There can be no doubt that there was a real spiritual entry of Satan into Eve's body by the fact of her eating."

He explained that when referring to Eve he meant Adam as well, yet he continued to dwell on her original sin to the exclusion of his. "In eating of the forbidden tree, Eve *trusted in herself, distrusted God and communed with Satan*" (Gordon's underlining suggests much fervor on this point), and he continued to blame her for the "moral poisoning" that forever beset mankind. The fruit which Eve ate—the coco-de-mer nut—"out of animal desire" and unquenchable curiosity were "the *vehicles* of the virus of evil." The Genesis account, in which God placed blame in equal shares on the serpent, Eve and Adam, was more evenhanded than Gordon's. It seems likely that these deeply felt views of the sinfulness of Eve were somehow central to Gordon's lifelong celibacy.

Gordon found solace in the Eucharist, the Christ-given antidote to this virus of evil. The sacrament of Holy Communion now featured prominently in Gordon's mind as the defense against the evil which had infected mankind ever since Eve had flouted God's command to resist temptation. Once he had dismissed that sacrament as unacceptable Church dogma, but now he believed that Communion was "the tree of life," as he wrote Mrs. Freese: "The Comm is a deadly weapon against envy, malice and all uncharitableness; it is a love philtre for one's enemies."

In the village of Ain Karim, three miles from Jerusalem, Gordon lived in the house of an American missionary, Dr. Spoffard, but he took Communion at a nearby Greek-Russian church. He liked the little chapel there and appreciated that the communicants did not question one's Christian credentials before sharing the bread and wine. With sly humor he wrote Augusta: "It is odd that no queries were asked when we poisoned ourselves in Eden; but that when we wish to take the antidote, queries are asked."

In *Reflections in Palestine*, Gordon oddly devoted much space to "human ingestion" in formulating his personal Christian doctrine. He thought it "appropriate that the tongue, which first touched the forbidden fruit and acquired evil, should be the first member to take the bidden fruit, the bread and wine." Gordon quoted liberally from the Apostle James, but his own emphasis was impassioned. "In eating, the first member of sensation of the body is the tongue. 'The tongue is a fire, a world of iniquity!' 'The tongue defileth the whole body, and setteth on fire the whole of nature, and it is set on fire by hell.' 'Everything has been tamed, but the tongue no man can tame; it is an unruly evil, full of deadly poison with which we bless God and curse men who are His image, thereby implying it is used by God and also by Satan. . . .' [James 3:6–9]"

Gordon shared James's concern that the tongue can betray unchristian thoughts and was convinced it had the capacity to do much harm through uncontrolled speech. An ancient Egyptian proverb went: "The tongue is the best and the worst thing in the world"; but to Gordon it was only the worst. It "is the instrument of lies, of treachery, of slander, of blasphemy, of spite, of malice, of unclean speaking, in fact of all iniquity, to the Satanic and carnal. . . . The tongue is glib, serpent-like, and it is odd that women have it in such perfection. . . . It is their defense. Yet, when women speak good, how well they speak out."

Gordon's preoccupation with death as a release from worldly trials and as a longed-for passage to the kingdom of God frequently intruded in his correspondence with family and friends. From Palestine he wrote Augusta: "Death would be a blessing at any moment." Reflecting Ephesians 6:11, he believed that through death the "wiles of the Devil" could be destroyed. In May he confessed in a letter: "I have a very great desire for death."

Such was Gordon's paradox: his will to die was no less strong than his will to live. When under full steam, fighting Taipings or chasing slavers in the Sudan, he seemed to glory in life. When not faced with dragons to slay, he could become depressed, and then final release and the joys of the next world beckoned him. Certainly he was not consciously suicidal; the taking of one's own life was a sacrilege. If he courted danger as an acceptable way of finding death, as he sometimes suggested, it seems at odds with his long-held belief in predestination, and in fact Gordon found a way out of that doctrinal corner when he abandoned rigid predestination and accepted a measure of free will.

Gordon had never been very comfortable with the idea that man should passively await his fate without taking positive actions to determine it. He was by nature a man of action; how could this ever have been squared with his belief in predestination? While he had earlier written his sister, Augusta,

"We have nothing further to do when the scroll of events is unrolled than to accept them as being for the best," he did not now believe in just waiting for it to be unrolled. "You could not say I sat still and let things happen. . . . It is a delightful thing to be a fatalist, not as that word is generally employed, but to accept that *when things happen* and *not* before. God has for some wise reason so ordained them to happen."

Gordon's reflections on death also seem to have led him to greater orthodoxy, at least in the matter of rewards and punishment after death. From being convinced that all of man's actions were predetermined by God, he had been forced to conclude that God would hardly punish man for his earthly transgressions. Man would, therefore, find bliss after death regardless of unworthy actions in life. But while in Palestine, seeds of orthodoxy planted by Waller two years before seemed to have grown. In a letter dated October 9, 1883, to his friend Barnes, he admitted contritely: "I had the heresy of no free will and no eternal punishment. I have come back to the fold."

Reflections in Palestine, 1883 was a compendium of doctrinal agonizing, personal soul searching and biblical geography based on a reckless mix of clues from the Bible, pragmatic engineering, personal intuition and sheer fantasy. Richard Burton referred to it as "a silly little book," and Lord Northbrook, First Lord of the Admiralty, called it "the book of a madman."[11] However this product of his Palestine sojourn struck others, Gordon felt unfulfilled. He wrote his sister Augusta: "I am trying the experiment of giving up all hindrances to a holy life, and though rid of those hindrances (which were pleasures to me), I am yet empty of any increase of spiritual joy."

In Palestine Gordon found it difficult to shed all such hindrances; his mind sometimes strayed back to politics and Africa despite his claim that affairs in Egypt or the Cape no longer troubled him.

Although he reminded himself that he must "avoid going down into Egypt, i.e. 'the world,'" he could not resist commenting on the situation in Cairo and Alexandria, which he saw as fomented by an obscure army colonel named Arabi. In February he was moved to give his opinions about the rise of the Mahdi in the Sudan: "He [God] has permitted this revolt which will end, I believe, in the suppression of the slave trade." As for Egypt and the Arabi movement against the Khedive, Gordon was pleased that God had "upset the Egyptian people thoroughly," and was convinced that they would "get their liberty from the oppressing Pashas."

Gordon found his Palestine retreat an emotionally maturing experience. Insightful flashes seemed to occur in a process of self-analysis rather than during his more objective efforts to refine Christian doctrine. He referred to the self as a cavern "wherein things of darkness did once luxuriate" until the light of the Christ's spirit "illuminated" it. But he concluded gloomily, "We can only keep alive the light within us, we cannot kill the evil things."

In a thoughtful and reflective letter to his friend Barnes, Gordon wrote:

> I went to the Crimea hoping, without having a hand in it, to be killed. I survived and lived, but not wishing to be too closely acquainted with God, nor yet to leave Him. I used to pray as my men went up the breaches in China for their success; thank Him if they succeeded; never wanted to know Him any closer. Swung as a pendulum in wide sweeps. Came home from China, saw my father die. Saw, if Jesus did really die, He must have died for some greater result than that seen in the Christian world. Went to every sect, found no good. Slaved at prayer; up in November at 4:00 A.M.; and one night at Ranger's House something broke in my heart, a palpable feeling, and I knew God lived in me. . . .

Nothing as profound as that experience took place in Palestine. Despite its biblical environment, the Holy Land had not been as spiritually fulfilling. Moreover his experiment in contemplation had come to an end; the world would not allow him his indulgence any longer. Mackinnon passed on to him more urgent inducements from Leopold. The Belgian King urged Gordon to accept the Congo post as soon as possible and tried to press on him an immediate retainer. On October 15, 1883, when Leopold telegraphed him a firm offer, Gordon replied in the affirmative.

As his stay in the Holy Land drew to a close, Gordon unexpectedly found himself again visiting Oliphant. Port Said in Egypt was closed to regular steamer traffic because of a quarantine, so he had to take passage from Jaffa in a small native sailing craft bound for Gaza. Because of a storm the boat had put into port in Haifa, so he took advantage of the delay to spend a few days with his friend.

The long arm of French intelligence had reached him even in a small storm-tossed sailing smack. Suddenly as he was boarding, a strange

Frenchman with no evident purpose, who had been staying at the same hotel as Gordon in Jaffa, asked if he could accompany him on his voyage. The suggestion of surveillance was obvious but Gordon graciously agreed.[12]

Oliphant and his houseguest, Valentine Chirol, were fascinated by Gordon as they came to know him better during this unexpected visit. The general delightfully reminisced about China days, revealing things that Oliphant had never heard of when he was there at the same time serving as Lord Elgin's secretary. Gordon also discussed people in high places in England with rare candor—although he always left them nameless. His strong criticisms were more in pity than anger; however scurrilous his remarks, he would quickly add, "But I pray for him regularly." By now Gordon's prayer list must have been lengthy. He asked Oliphant how to spell Valentine Chirol's name, explaining that he wanted to add his houseguest to the list.

Chirol, then a peripatetic British journalist, had gotten on splendidly with Gordon. He listened "with rapt interest to the flood of reminiscence" exchanged by Gordon and Oliphant about China. But Gordon's mind, he remembered vividly, was strangely erratic. Starting with an uncompromising denunciation of the selfishness and greed of Western policy in China, Gordon asserted that there "could be no salvation for the Chinese until they had thrown off the incubus of foreign traders and diplomats." Within a hour he argued just the opposite, declaring that some foreign power, preferably British, was needed to cleanse China of its "dens of corruption and oppression sucking the life blood out of the people." Chirol concluded that Gordon was "incapable of seeing more than one question at a time." As Oliphant later said to Chirol, laughing, "That is a man after my own heart, for he is not afraid of contradicting himself, and whatever he says always rings true."[13]

Gordon and Oliphant spent long hours discussing the Sudan. Since the general's previous visit, the situation had greatly deteriorated, and Gordon felt that the time for negotiations with the Mahdi had passed. El Obeid had fallen, and the Mahdi's increasingly militant following, the Ansar, was preparing to march on Khartoum. "If it were not for the Sudanese, whom I love," Gordon said, "the easy way out of it for the English Government would be to invite the Turks to go [into the Sudan]. It is not probable that they have the sense to make the proposition, or that the Turks would be such fools as to accept it."[14]

The thought that Whitehall might try to send Gordon back to Khartoum at this critical time was raised, but, recalled Oliphant, "he refused altogether to anticipate the possibility . . . partly because he felt bound in honour to go to the Congo for the King of the Belgians, and partly because he had already had too many differences with the heads of departments under which he had served, and was regarded with too little favour on account of his refusal to look at every question through official spectacles to be *persona grata* to the English Government."[15]

Gordon left Haifa on foot in mid-December to reach Acre, twelve miles away, where he could find a ship bound for Marseilles. His parting words to Oliphant and Chirol were foreboding: He insisted that they would never meet him again, saying that he had "no more work to do for God on this earth" and would "never return from the Congo."

PART VI

The Moslem Messiah
and the Christian Martyr

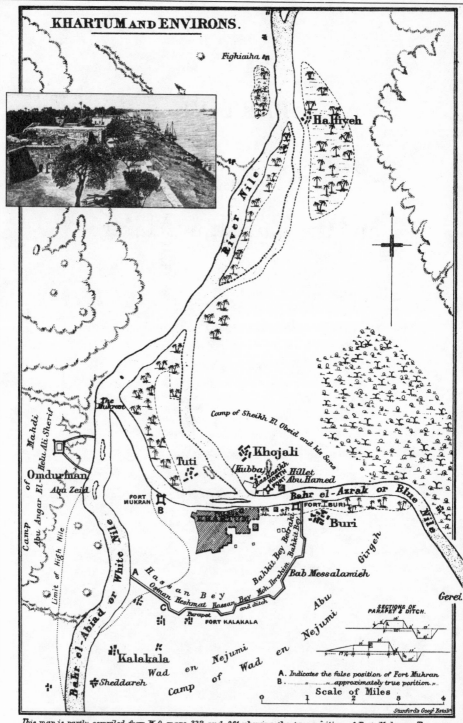

KHARTUM AND ENVIRONS.

Fighiaiha

Halfiyeh

River Nile

Camp of Sheikh El Obeid and his Sons

The Mukran

Tuti

Khojali

(Kubba)

Hillet Abu.Hamed

Ras Hamik

FORT NORTH

Bahr el-Azrak or Blue Nile

Omdurman

Camp of Mahdi Abu Angar El-Helu Ali Sherif

Aba Zeid

FORT MUKRAN

B

FORT BURI

Buri

Girgeh

Limit of High Nile

Bahr el-Abiad or White Nile

Hassan Bey Osman Heshmat Hassan Bey and ditch

Bakhit Bey Bey akit

Moh.Ibrahim Bakhit Bey

Bab Messalamieh

Gerei

A

C Parapet FORT KALAKALA

Abu

Nejumi

SECTIONS OF PARAPET & DITCH.

Kalakala

Wad en Nejumi Wad en Nejumi

Camp of

Sheddareh

A. Indicates the false position of Fort Mukran.
B. " " approximately true position "

Scale of Miles

0   1   2   3   4

Stanford's Geog.l Estab.t

This map is partly compiled from W.O. maps 332 and 381, showing the true position of Fort Mukran. The space between A. & C. indicates the broken down parapet which the Arabs crossed in the assault on Khartum.

Khartoum defenses and Ansar emplacements

THE MAHDI

Death to the "Turks," those dogs and swine.
—Ibrahim Wad Abdullah,
Ansar commander at the siege of El Obeid

Unnoticed by the world, Mohammed Ahmad ibn Abdullah was born in about 1844 on Lehab, a small island in the Nile near the town of Dongola. His father, a boat builder, had been an ordinary artisan, but claimed descent from the Prophet Mohammed. Like the young Jesus Christ, the boy had become a carpenter, but rather than follow his father's profession, as did his three brothers, he decided to devote his life to Islam. From this path he never swerved. He attended the *khalwa*, or school, of a revered religious teacher, Sheikh Mohammed al-Khair, in the Nile town of Berber. Then in 1861 he sought more advanced theology under Sheikh Mohammed al-Sharif Nur al-Da'im, a leader of a Moslem sect called Sammaniya near Khartoum.

As Mohammed Ahmad fell more and more under the spell of Moslem mysticism, he sought a retreat for meditation. Isolated Aba Island, located in the middle of the White Nile about 160 miles south of Khartoum, appealed to him; it was quiet and wooded, perfect for contemplation. While riverboats sometimes stopped to pick up wood for their boilers, Aba had few visitors. Mohammed Ahmad moved there with his brothers, who continued to ply their craft of boat building while he lived a hermit's life of contemplation in a cave near the Nile.

Mohammed Ahmad's asceticism and piety gradually attracted disciples, who clustered at his feet as he spoke. They would listen to him attentively until he seemed to drift off into a religious trance. Word began to spread that he could perform miracles. In the Sudan, where dervish mendicants with their begging bowls were commonplace and where there was a surfeit of "saints," Mohammed Ahmad somehow seemed different. Certainly his heritage was appropriate for a holy man. He claimed that his forebears had

301

come from holy Medina and were of the Prophet's family descended through Fatima, the Prophet's daughter. He had also been blessed with a birthmark on his right cheek and a slight V-shaped gap between his two main front teeth, physical characteristics of the Prophet himself. The young man was tall and handsome with his dark compelling eyes, aquiline nose and captivating smile. Most important of all, he was charismatic and inspiring, qualities necessary for a religious leader.

Young Mohammed Ahmad's piety almost proved his undoing. On one occasion when visiting his teacher Sheikh Mohammed al-Sharif in Khartoum to reaffirm his devotion, he was dismayed at what he saw. His master had obviously spared no expense in planning a lavish celebration of his son's circumcision, a special occasion among the Sudanese. Heedless of the constraints of piety, there would be popular music, dancing girls and a grand feast. When the disillusioned ascetic criticized his master for such an exhibition of public debauchery, he was peremptorily expelled from the sect.

Mortified by his sudden fall from grace, Mohammed Ahmad sought forgiveness. As a symbol of repentance, the young man bound himself in the *sheba*, a kind of yoke used for unruly slaves. The *sheba* was a wooden fork configured so that it pressed on the wearer's Adam's apple. One end was tied with tight thongs to the right arm, which had to be kept stiffly outstretched to prevent the fork from piercing the throat. As the guests, led by the town barber, who had performed the circumcision, left the mosque, Mohammed Ahmad in this pitiful state could be seen by all, crying out for forgiveness. As local lore had it, Sheikh al-Sharif was so embarrassed and enraged by this spectacle that he shouted epithets at Mohammed Ahmad and banished him "forever."

Reports of this incident reached a rival leader of the Sammaniya sect, Sheikh al-Qureishi Wad al-Zain, who preached at Mesellamiya on the Blue Nile. The sheikh was much impressed with Mohammed Ahmad's religious zeal and invited him to join his *tarika*, or branch of the sect. The Aba Island hermit with such prominent patronage began to attract a growing following—so much so that Sheikh al-Sharif tried to make peace with Mohammed Ahmad and lure him back. But by now the young zealot had become a teacher in his own right and preferred to remain loyal to Sheikh al-Qureishi, whom he genuinely loved. When Sheikh al-Qureishi died, the pious Mohammed Ahmad grieved deeply, resolving to build a tomb in commemoration of him. He rallied the other disciples of Qureishi and set about this labor of love.

At this time there appeared in Mesellamiya a young man of the Ta'aisha tribe, one of the cattle-raising Baggara peoples of southwestern Darfur, who called himself Abdullahi ibn Mohammed. Abdullahi sought out Mohammed Ahmad and asked if he could join his *tarika*.

According to the lore which sprang up about Abdullahi, Abdullahi's father, a *figi*, or pious soothsayer, had tried to make the pilgrimage to Mecca with his family but had died along the way in Kordofan Province. On his deathbed the old *figi* told Abdullahi that a great future awaited him as disciple of a great reformer soon to appear. The intense young man, anxious to fulfill his father's prophecy, struck out on his own to find the man he was destined to serve. Like many Sudanese distressed by the corruption of their religion at the hands of the "Turk," as they referred to anyone in the Egyptian administration, Abdullahi was convinced that the day of judgment was at hand. A Mahdi, or Messiah, would soon appear to purify the faith and offer salvation to the faithful. Ironically, Abdullahi had first sought out Zubair as the Mahdi for whom he was searching—such was the great slaver's prestige in southern Sudan. A bemused Zubair protested that he was not the Mahdi and turned the young man away. It was sometime later that Abdullahi turned his attentions to Mohammed Ahmad.

Abdullahi and Mohammed Ahmad took an almost immediate liking to each other. Abdullahi the stern activist complemented the visionary Mohammed Ahmad. Abdullahi was made Mohammed Ahmad's loyal lieutenant, soon to be declared a Khalifa, or Prince of the Church, and ultimately to become the Mahdi's powerful successor.

The circumstances in which Mohammed Ahmad became convinced that he was the Mahdi and the inspiration for this momentous decision may be debated, but the revelation seems to have taken place in the early summer of 1881. At least it was June 1881 when on Aba Island he publicly declared himself to be the Mahdi and set in motion one of the most astounding religious movements in history.

Gordon by now was in Mauritius, long gone from the Sudan. But even if he had been in Khartoum it is unlikely that he would have taken seriously

Mohammed Ahmad's declaration. Certainly he would not have imagined the proportions that the Mahdiya movement would soon assume. Few Europeans were even aware of the Mahdi tradition in Islam or how it began.

According to some Islamic traditions, Mohammed prophesied that there would one day appear a descendant al-Mahdi, one who was guided aright by Allah. The Mahdi would bring justice to the world and restore religious purity to Islam. Among the various Moslem sects, there are differences of interpretation, however. The Sunni sect of Islam continues in its belief that the Mahdi has not yet come, although there have been many claimants to the dignity throughout history. Coincidentally, as Mohammed Ahmad asserted his right to the title, so had the head of the powerful North African Senussi sect, whose seat of power was in Libya. The Shia sect of Islam more specifically holds that Mohammed Abd' al-Gasim, recognized as the twelfth and last Imam in the lineage of Ali—husband of Mohammed's daughter, Fatima—and remembered for his mysterious disappearance in 1879, will reappear one day as the Mahdi to restore righteousness to a corrupt world. The inspiration for Mohammed Ahmad may have been in part influenced by Mohammed ibn Abd' al-Wahhab, the great Arabian reformer and founder of the still-powerful Wahhabi sect of the Arabian Peninsula—although Wahhab never claimed such holiness.

Mohammed Ahmad's ascent to sainthood is believed to have occurred after a great vision, the details of which vary with the chronicler. Some say the Prophet gave Mohammed Ahmad his sword. Whatever miracles appeared to Mohammed Ahmad, he now believed he was the Expected Mahdi, sanctified and mandated to go forth as Allah's Imam on earth.

Mohammed Ahmad not only claimed to be the Mahdi, but canonized himself Imam and Successor to the Apostle of God as well. As the Successor, he believed he must replay the role of the Prophet and unify Islam once again. As Imam, he saw himself as leader of all Moslems, a role which the Sultan of the Turkish Empire, the Wahhabi leaders in Arabia and the Senussis of North Africa, among others, could never accept. As Mahdi, Mohammed Ahmad would preside at the Day of Judgment when the end of the world approached.

Accepted theology did not inhibit Mohammed Ahmad. He was a fundamentalist who preached a simple message: Trust in God, be faithful in the observance of Islam, be humble, and adhere to a rigid code of ethics. A place in heaven would await the faithful who accepted this.

The similarity of the Mahdi's beliefs and Gordon's is striking; both had stripped away superfluous doctrine from their respective creeds. Intolerant of structured dogma, both believed in the simple word of God as each knew it. Both believed in a hereafter and had no fear of death. Both believed in predestination, and both saw the sword as a weapon with which to serve God. Both were really Old Testament men, but both had great capacity for compassion and forgiveness.

In addition, Gordon and the Mahdi were spontaneously inclined toward religious faith early in their lives. Faith seemed to well up within them rather than to be imposed upon them. And in each case there were early tutors who, rather than inspire them, proved to be sources of troubling disillusionment. Just as Gordon at an impressionable age found his headmaster at Fulland's school, the Reverend Rogers, to be insensitive, the young Mohammed Ahmad discovered to his dismay that his theological mentor Sheikh Mohammed al-Sharif had strayed from the ascetic piety he preached.

Neither man was ever awed by the established order; they dared to be different and follow their own destinies. Both had a reclusive side, yet both were natural leaders of men and were possessed of some indefinable charisma that attracted people to them. Each was conscious of the Devil's existence as a dark angel of temptation, although Gordon was more rigorous in refusing his visitations than was the indulgent Mahdi.

News of the self-styled Mahdi reached Khartoum through none other than Mohammed Ahmad's teacher, Mohammed al-Sharif, who had so offended the young man's religious sensibilities. The Governor General, Mohammed Ra'uf, whom Gordon had only contempt for—as did Mohammed Ahmad—could not imagine this dervish as a threat. But Mohammed Ahmad's declaration had been, if not insane, seditious, and punishment was in order.

The Governor General sent to Aba Island his assistant Abu Sa'ud (the very same former slaver whom Gordon had unwisely hired when he went to Equatoria as governor, then fired for corruption and disloyalty) with a deputation of clerics to reason with the "fanatic." Mohammed Ahmad's response was one of disdain. He rejected their overtures, asserting that henceforward he would be the one to guide the Sudan, not the Governor

General. For this presumption, Mohammed Ra'uf sent two companies of soldiers to seize the impostor by force. The result was a tragic fiasco. Through bad leadership, the well-armed Egyptian soldiers became hopelessly confused in the tall marsh grass. They were killed, almost to a man, by enraged followers of the Mahdi wielding only heavy sticks.

The Mahdi of Allah had proved his resistance to bullets; his followers thought he must indeed be divine! And with this knowledge, on August 12, 1881, Mohammed Ahmad, the Mahdi, declared a *jihad*, or holy war, against the Sudan's Egyptian rulers and their supporters. This was the beginning of a long march to power.

After the massacre of the Egyptian column, Aba Island was unsafe for the Mahdi. Soon a punitive expedition could be expected, and the Mahdi, confined to the island, would be vulnerable to capture. In fact, Assistant Governor General Giegler Pasha, formerly Gordon's telegraph officer, ordered a column to be sent from El Obeid to prevent the so-called Mahdi from leaving the island, but it had been unable to do so. In a strategic retreat, reminiscent of the Hegira, the Prophet's flight from Mecca to Medina, the Mahdi with his followers escaped to a remote place in the Nuba Mountains of southern Kordofan called Jebel Qadir. Here he established a camp where he could build his army, which he called the Ansar, "Helpers," just as the Prophet had referred to his own militant followers.[1]

The Mahdi attracted different groups for different reasons. The religious zealots, the core of his movement, followed him in the conviction that he was in fact the Messiah sent by God to purge Islam. He also won over certain tribal groups, such as the Ja'aliyin and Danaqla, whose people flocked to his banner more in opposition to Egyptian rule than religious conviction. Gordon, in fact, had been unwittingly the architect of their dissidence with his antislavery campaign that disrupted their traditional way of life. The cattle-raising Baggara nomads, noted for their fighting abilities, provided an important source of Ansar warriors. The Baggaras were not religious zealots, but as nomads they resented government efforts to extract taxes from them or control their freedom to roam from one grazing land to another.

Rashid Bey, the Mudir, or Governor, of Fashoda, on his own initiative sent a small force to surprise and seize the Mahdi. But on December 9, 1881, it too was lured into an ambush and wiped out. People began to talk of the

Mahdi's invincibility—he could turn Egyptian bullets into water! More flocked to his banner.

In March 1882, Ra'uf was removed as Governor General of the Sudan, in part because of his incompetence in dealing with the man who called himself the Mahdi. When Giegler Pasha became Acting Governor General, he was determined to rid Kordofan of this growing menace. He organized a new army, this time a formidable force of six thousand under the command of Yusuf al-Shallali. After a grueling sixteen-day march from Fashoda, Shallali's force was surprised at dawn on June 7, 1882, by howling Ansar spearmen, who easily broke through the flimsy thornbush *zeriba*. Terrified by the unexpected attack, the Egyptians offered little resistance and were soon slaughtered. This was the third miraculous victory by the Ansar in which an army with modern rifles had been proved impotent.

With each victory the Mahdi seized more precious arms and supplies with which to equip his rapidly growing force, but more significant, with each victory his prestige increased. To make the best use of the captured arms, the Mahdi shrewdly formed a special unit of sharpshooters, called the Jihadiya, or Holy Warriors, and encadred them with some of Zubair's Bazingers—black slave troop veterans—who now pledged themselves to the holy cause. For the rank-and-file Ansar soldiers, the Mahdi extolled their spears as a symbol of the uprising and endowed with almost holy attributes. And indeed, except for a government victory over Mahdist rebels at Sennar on the Blue Nile south of Khartoum, the Egyptians had proved no match for the Ansar zealots. (It was, in fact, argued by the faithful that at Sennar the Mahdi had not been present to invoke his divine blessing.) The Mahdi now decided that he was strong enough to go on the offensive. He would attack El Obeid, capital of Kordofan and queen city of the south.

As the Mahdist movement gained startling momentum in the Sudan, the Egyptian Khedive faced a more immediate threat at home. Ahmad Arabi, a disaffected army colonel of humble *fellahin*, or peasant, origins, had managed to stir up deep resentments within the army against foreign influences in Egypt. With very little warning Khedive Tewfik on September 8, 1881, found himself in Abdin Palace surrounded by hostile army units demanding a new government.

Tewfik capitulated almost immediately and formed a new "national government" with Arabi as Secretary of State for War. British and French reaction was swift. The British Mediterranean fleet under Admiral Sir Beauchamp Seymour was rushed to Alexandria harbor, and the French joined the British in presenting a joint demarche demanding the dissolution of the new regime and the resignation of Arabi. On May 27, 1882, the government under pressure did resign, but a popular upwelling of Egyptian nationalist sentiment, particularly in Cairo, where mobs took to the street, forced the Khedive to reinstate Arabi and reconstitute the national government.

The British later admitted that they had underestimated Arabi and his movement. The army had long resented the Turkish officer corps, which was corrupt as well as alien, but this was more than a military coup d'état. The *fellahin* were being crushed by intolerable taxes extracted from them to finance the profligacy of the court. Food prices rose accordingly. Even the elite pasha class was unhappy with Egypt's subservience to the British and French influence exerted by the two powerful proconsuls, Evelyn Baring for England and de Blignières for France.

Egypt had to endure layered foreign domination: It was a satrapy of Turkey but was essentially controlled by the British and French, while foreign bondholders—principally British and French—in effect held the mortgage on the country. European influence brought with it a Christian presence which the Moslem *ulema*, or clergy, found offensive, particularly since it gave heart to the Christian Copts, long resented by Moslems. European pressures on the Khedive to eradicate slavery and slaving threatened to upset a whole way of life for many in Egypt. Egypt was ripe for revolution, and Arabi had become the champion of the Egyptians, whatever the source of their unhappiness.

By early June the situation in Egypt had become so alarming to the European community that there was a mass exodus. Twenty-five Western warships were in Alexandria harbor boarding Europeans fleeing the country. More than half of the European population had already left, but some six thousand were still waiting their turn and were forced to endure the violence and indignity of angry Egyptian crowds.

On June 11, 1882, serious rioting broke out in Alexandria, killing some fifty Europeans. The riots, in which careering crowds wielding *naboots*, or large sticks, clubbed their victims to death, were suspected of being carefully organized by Arabi partisans. But if there were any doubts about Arabi's intentions, they were dispelled when soldiers began placing cannon along the harbor, pointing menacingly at the British and French ships.

Gladstone had long resisted British involvement in Egypt. Aside from an ingrained aversion to imperial aggressiveness with the moral and economic burden it imposed, he feared that it would put British-French relations on a collision course. But when Disraeli's government bought controlling interest in the Suez Canal, Great Britain's course had been irrevocably set: The British could not extricate themselves from Egypt even if they wanted to. The Suez Canal, critical gateway to India, had to be defended. Now of immediate concern were the lives of Englishmen in jeopardy.

Faced suddenly with Egyptian batteries pointed at his ships, Admiral Seymour sent an ultimatum to the Egyptian army threatening to fire if the guns were not removed. At 7:00 in the morning on July 11, 1882, British naval bombardment began. Alexandria was shelled for the rest of the day, while Royal Marines were sent ashore to quell the worsening rioting in the streets. Arabi narrowly escaped capture and fled to Cairo on horseback, from where he lit a fuse destined to demolish any remnant of real Egyptian sovereignty when he threatened to blow up the Suez Canal and cancel Egypt's foreign debt if the foreign presence was not withdrawn.

Faced with this kind of provocation, the British took the final plunge and prepared to occupy Egypt. The French were invited to join in the action but chose not to participate in a move which they interpreted as a British bid for domination of Egypt.

"I would hang or shoot Arabi without the least hesitation," Sir Samuel Baker publicly announced.[2] Writing from King Williams Town in Cape Colony on July 21, 1882, Gordon expressed a very different and, for then, heretical point of view: ". . . under the pretence of benefiting the people under the real object of securing the bondholders, our Government usurped the role over Egypt and suffered the consequences. Pity it is, our Government always goes against liberty of peoples, and favoring of autocrats. You may argue now, it is not a natural movement—that is said of all movements, even that made against Charles I, James II, etc., and it is the fashion to say it is only agitators. Agitators are fruits of existing seeds; does not Parnell represent Irish national feelings?"[3]

When he wrote Baker, Gordon did not know of Seymour's bombardment of Alexandria. Obviously, Gordon was at odds with British policy. And this was but the beginning. On September 13, 1882, Gordon's old friend General Wolseley led twenty thousand British troops in an invasion of Egypt. The expeditionary force landed in the canal area near Ismailia and marched inland to engage Arabi's forces at Tel-el-Kebir, some sixty miles from Cairo. It was a set-piece battle, with the British quickly, totally routing the Egyptians. Arabi was taken into custody, to be exiled later to Ceylon, and the British occupied Cairo on September 14. As Gladstone feared, France was no longer a partner in Egypt but a jealous rival and would remain so for twenty-two years. Egypt was now Britain's responsibility, as was the Sudan, though Gladstone vowed to exclude the Sudan and let it dangle ambiguously as the forces of the Mahdi grew ever stronger.

Gordon was one of the several experts consulted in London—and not the most welcome one. Out of step with official thinking as usual, the general expressed sympathy for Arabi and for the Egyptian *fellahin* who had to bear the real burden imposed by English and European creditors. Ever since Khedive Ismail had enlisted his help in standing up to European economic pressures, Gordon had sided with the Egyptians in their efforts to resist mortgaging their country to foreign bondholders. After Tel-el-Kebir, Gordon wrote ruefully to Baker: " . . . it seems that the Government have taken up a policy to reinstate those parasite pashas."

As for events in the Sudan, Gordon was not alarmed. The Mahdi, now preparing to march on the Sudan's second city, El Obeid, was but part of God's "intricate scheme." With the grace of God, the Sudanese would at last gain their freedom from Egyptian oppression. Gordon complained: "I foresaw the Egyptian and Sudan affair and was not listened to." The general still favored negotiations with the Mahdi. Before the attack on El Obeid, it might have been useful, but few would believe that Kordofan's well-defended capital could be reduced by the spear-carrying Ansar.

El Obeid, some 250 miles southwest of Khartoum and the seat of Egyptian provincial government, had long been a prosperous trading center. Its 100,000 people lived well by Sudanese standards. Greek, Syrian and Egyptian merchants had become rich by exporting Kordofan gum and importing merchandise for El Obeid itself as well as distant Darfur. Kordofan was a cattle- and camel-raising province that boasted rich harvests in corn, sesame and watermelon as well. After Khartoum, El Obeid was the

THE MAHDI

Sudan's most important city, and as a trading post it had attracted a polyglot population made up of various tribal peoples, whose rivalries, born in antiquity, stubbornly persisted. Until the summer of 1882, there had been as satisfactory an equilibrium of life as could be expected under the corrupt and repressive Egyptian administration.

By early September, El Obeid, an important objective, found itself besieged by the Mahdi's hordes, which had already invested most of Kordofan. Before long, most of the Sudanese inhabitants—who were either genuinely attracted to the movement or feared the Mahdi's fury when the city was taken (few doubted it would be)—abandoned the city to join the advancing holy army.

As the Mahdi's force marched on El Obeid, it numbered about thirty thousand warriors, who had been convinced by their leader that their sticks and spears would triumph over the guns of the city's garrison. "Anointed by God," the Mahdi was believed invincible, his cause righteous. If any of the faithful were killed in battle, martyrdom and a place in Paradise would be their reward. But more concretely, El Obeid's garrison protected a treasury of awesome proportion, which would be theirs when the town fell.

The Egyptian Governor of the city, Said Pasha, whose garrison numbered only three thousand men after the defection to the Mahdi of some key units, prepared the defenses as best he could. A ditch was dug and a parapet erected around the entire town, but the real defense core consisting of brick government buildings was barricaded to form a more compact and defensible citadel. The foreign merchants and a small group of Austrian missionaries, whose evangelist efforts in Kordofan were an anathema to the Moslem zealots of the Mahdi, took shelter in the inner defense zone.

What next occurred in El Obeid was described more than a decade later by Father Joseph Ohrwalder, in *Ten Years Captivity in the Mahdi's Camp*, a book of notes compiled by Major General F. R. Wingate. Father Ohrwalder was a Catholic missionary at the Austrian mission at Delen, west of El Obeid in the Nuba hills, and had been captured by the advancing Mahdi army. An unwilling witness to the siege of El Obeid, Father Ohrwalder, describing the agonies of the siege, told of the dawn of September 8, 1882, as the Mahdi's army came upon the city. The clouds of dust churned up by the approaching horde at first hid it from sight, but the defenders of El Obeid could hear the roar of voices, "sounding like approaching thunder," as the Ansar prepared to attack. Soon the "myriads of flags and banners became visible." About ten thousand men led by a commander named Fikki Minneh approached from the east while the Mahdi with the main force of twenty thousand Ansar warriors came out of the dust to attack the southwest corner of the town. Ohrwalder's account described "masses of wild fanatics," rolling "like waves through the deserted streets." When the Ansar reached the fortified government buildings, they erupted "like a torrent suddenly let loose, with wild shouts dashed up the ramparts, from which the din of a thousand rifles and the booming of the guns suddenly burst forth."

Ohrwalder had been amazed at the fearlessness of the Ansar, who "cared neither for the deadly Remingtons, nor the thunder of the guns." They just kept coming and by sheer force of numbers drove the defenders to the rooftops. In a frenzy to save their own lives the cornered garrison troops continued to pour fire on the mob below. The rifles of the defenders, now cherry-red with heat, fired continuously until the streets "became literally choked with the bodies of those who had fallen." Screaming "Death to the Turks, those dogs and swine!" Ibrahim Wad Abdullah, one of the Ansar commanders, "attacked again and again, hoping that the bodies of those who fell would soon fill up the ditch and make a passage which he could cross."

The tide of battle turned by afternoon and the Egyptian garrison troops sallied forth, "dashing over the heaps of the slain," to drive the invaders from the town. Despite the horror with which he called up memories of the Ansar on that terrible day, Father Ohrwalder conceded their reckless bravery: "These fanatics, dancing and shouting, rushed up to the very muzzles of the rifles with nothing but a knotty stick in their hands, only to fall dead, one over the other."[4] The price for bravery, however, was high. When the Ansar army retired to the nearby village of Kaba, they left ten thousand dead in the streets of El Obeid.

The first round his, El Obeid's Mudir, Said Pasha, then made a critical mistake. Instead of pursuing the Ansar and inflicting on them total defeat, he withdrew his troops back to the garrison. As it would develop, the government lost its last chance to stop the Mahdi movement. The Mahdi's army dug in a short distance from the town and mounted a siege that would last for four terrible months. From that day on, El Obeid was totally cut off from the rest of the Sudan.

THE MAHDI

According to the Mahdi's chronicler Ismail ibn Abd al-Qadir, the Prophet had visited the Mahdi and explained why the Ansar had failed in its hard-fought "Friday Battle" in El Obeid: The Ansar had been disobedient— they had not entered the city in an orderly fashion from the east as instructed, and they had been diverted by the abundance of booty which they seized.[5] Victory would otherwise have been attained.

As regarding the Mahdi, Father Ohrwalder wrote: "Mohammed Ahmad was a powerfully built man of dark brown complexion and carefully kept skin; he had a pleasant smile which showed to advantge the curious slit between his front teeth. . . . He wore a *jibbeh* on which parti-colored strips of cotton had been sewn; on his head the white skull cap or *takid*, around which a broad white turban was bound; he also wore a pair of loose drawers and sandals."[6]

The Mahdi sent Father Ohrwalder to his deputy, the Khalifa Abdullahi. Not sharing the "gentle manner" of the Mahdi, the Khalifa was bombastic and full of threats, warning Ohrwalder that he must obey or die. Either he embraced Islam or be prepared for death. As Ohrwalder, with no intention of renouncing Christianty, awaited his end a large comet appeared in the east. The great comet of 1882, known seventy years before as the comet Pons in Europe, became known in the Sudan as Nigmet el-Mahdi, "Star of the Guided One." For the Sudanese, a comet was a harbinger of catastrophe, and indeed the father's predicament was almost enough to make him believe this superstition. Paraded before forty thousand soldiers and a howling mob of onlookers, Ohrwalder along with other infidels were told to bow their heads for decapitation. Suddenly the Mahdi himself appeared and in an act of mercy dramatically gave them reprieve. The missionary prisoners were released to the custody of a Greek merchant named George Stambuli, who had ingratiated himself with the Mahdi. Thus spared, Father Ohrwalder could continue as witness to the events which led to the fall of El Obeid.

Life in the Mahdi's camp was not easy for foreign prisoners. Despite the Mahdi's mercy, Ohrwalder and the other captured missionaries were in daily danger of being killed by zealots or religiously incited mobs. The chaos caused by thousands of devotees, their war drums constantly beating, their horses neighing, made an extraordinary spectacle; but the stench of death and the filth from humans and beasts strewn haphazardly about was almost

313

unendurable. Conditions within El Obeid's beleaguered garrison were even worse.

The blockade was soon felt by El Obeid's defenders. Necessities grew scarce, and prices skyrocketed. As camel meat and beef were exhausted, donkeys were slaughtered for food. Dogs and mice were eaten as well, and finally the garrison was reduced to foraging for cockroaches and white ants. Others meticulously searched the excrement of animals for undigested grain particles to eat. Sickness added to malnutrition, and scurvy, dysentery and various gastric illnesses brought death. Father Ohrwalder's description of the conditions, based on reports of missionaries who had found refuge in the garrison, was appalling: "The dead and dying filled the streets; the space within the fortifications being so limited, there was not room for all of the people, and in consequence many lay about in the streets and open spaces." Hanging over the town was a smell of mortifying corpses and the sky "was black with . . . carrion-kites which feasted on the dead bodies." These grotesque vultures "became so distended by constant gorging that they could not even fly away, and were killed in numbers by the soldiers, who devoured them. . . ."[7]

Dara, the other major town in Kordofan, about fifty miles north of El Obeid, was under siege by the Ansar as well. With its food exhausted and hopes of rescue gone, that garrison surrendered on January 5, 1883. Despair deepened in El Obeid at the news of Dara's capitulation; on January 19, Said Pasha also surrendered the garrison at El Obeid.

With the fall of Dara and El Obeid, the Mahdi for the first time had ample supplies, including badly needed firearms. Now the Mahdi could increase his cadre of armed regulars, the Jihadiya, to bolster the less disciplined tribal volunteers.

El Obeid allowed the Mahdi command of western Sudan, effectively cutting off Darfur Province, but it also provided him a closer base from which to launch an assault on Khartoum itself.

As seen by Khartoum, the scope and nature of the Mahdi's movement had changed. No longer could it be dismissed as a tribal uprising—it was a religious crusade of civil war proportions. Foreign merchants in Khartoum, always attuned to developments which affected their lives or their livelihood, began their exodus. Whatever complacency still lingered in Sudan's capital was fast disappearing.

SEEDS OF
MISUNDERSTANDING

Why this was *not* done long ago and why the right thing is never
done till it is absolutely extorted from those who are in authority, is
inexplicable to the Queen.
                    —Queen Victoria on Gordon's assignment to the Sudan

D espite all that was happening in the Sudan, Gordon's mind was
elsewhere. The Congo assignment now concerned him. Henry
Stanley had been used by King Leopold to tame the Congo,
principally for the monarch's own profit, notwithstanding the great
explorer's idealized rationale "to spread what blessings arise from amiable
and just intercourse with people who hitherto have been strangers to
them."[1] Since 1879, Stanley's prodigious efforts had built the "Congo
Free State" from a chain of trading stations along the upper Congo River.
This was ostensibly Belgium's entry in the imperial contest for Africa, but
in reality the Free State was Leopold's private preserve. The Belgian
monarch had envisioned Gordon as an effective administrator of his
sprawling fiefdom and would now at last have the general there.

For Gordon, the Congo promised new action, providing an opportunity
to fight the slave traffic at one of its important sources, although Leopold's
record in exploiting the Congo was hardly one to suggest that he was
interested in promoting good works. There were, however, other compelling reasons at work deep in Gordon's psyche. Once again Gordon seemed
driven by an obsession to gain release from the burden of life and join his
Maker: ". . . if by the keeping of my promise [to King Leopold] I would
get a free and speedy passage to it [death], I would be very glad; and it
seems that the Congo is the route which is quickest to it." Such morbidity
may have been expressed in a fit of the "doles," that "wailing place in
the ruins of the body," but Gordon's other face, Agag, pride and the

315

gratification of ego, was not without influence in his enthusiasm for the Congo. With all its frustrations and hardship, ruling the Sudan had given him great contentment; like a star when "it makes its highest point," he had "culminated." Perhaps in the Congo he could renew this contentment.

King Leopold's overtures had been conveyed by Sir William Mackinnon, with whom Gordon had earlier discussed plans for an expedition to Central Africa by way of Zanzibar. The King of Belgium seemed so insistent in the telegram forwarded by Mackinnon on October 15, 1883, that Gordon immediately sought War Office approval to accept. The Foreign Office, however, did not like the idea and immediately placed obstacles in his way. Gordon's presence in the Congo, Whitehall feared, would alarm the French, who were already sensitive about British competition for Central African preeminence. In addition, events in the Sudan were reminders that the southern rebellion would not go away, and despite War Office reluctance to use the unpredictable Gordon in sensitive posts, his knowledge of the Sudan might prove necessary and valuable.

The reply Gordon received from the War Office had been garbled in transmission so that it conveyed a meaning exactly contrary to that intended. Instead of "The Secretary of State has *declined to sanction* your employment on the Congo," the garbled message read, "The Secretary of State *decides to sangdon* your employment on the Congo."[2] By mid-November this communication was unscrambled, but Gordon was nonetheless determined to go, being willing to resign his commission and lose his major general's pension if need be. Gordon's eagerness to serve the Belgian King seemed also to derive from a conviction that his own government would find no appropriate assignment for him.

As the fateful year 1884 began, Gordon arrived in Brussels to be launched on a new adventure. He had a successful audience with King Leopold, that "very tall man with a black beard," who generously agreed to provide £7,000 insurance benefits in the event of death to compensate for his loss of an Army pension. It was perhaps characteristic of Gordon that he wrote Stanley from Brussels, assuring him that he had no intention of trying to replace him as top man. But it is difficult to imagine how two such individualists, each with a well-developed ego, could ever have worked in harmony. Agag still lurked within Gordon, as evidenced by a letter he sent to the Anti-Slavery Society on January 5, 1884, in which he enclosed a suggested press release, "without attribution," heralding the end of slaving in the Congo "now that General Gordon is going out as second in command to Stanley." Then he caught himself and added to his letter: "Above all things, put in no gilt for me; you can do so for King Leopold and Stanley."

News traveled quickly in London. On the same day Gordon wrote to the Anti-Slavery Society, the *Times* broke the news that he was bound for the Congo, and expressed regret that the British Army would lose "one of its brightest ornaments." This premature announcement must have been as disturbing to the War Office as it was embarrassing for Gordon, since by that date the general had not yet submitted his resignation (it was not posted until August 7) and the Secretary of State had already decided against permitting Gordon's accepting the Congo assignment.

But before the War Office could tighten its harness on Gordon, ominous developments in the Sudan caused a shift in British policy and changed the situation dramatically. A signal disaster had occurred in which an Egyptian army under British General William Hicks was totally annihilated near El Obeid by the Mahdi.

General Hicks, a respected veteran of the Indian Army, had arrived in Khartoum in March 1883 to assume command of Sudanese forces. The British government, trying to distance itself from the Sudan problem and the Mahdi's rebellion, left him to his own devices, refusing to provide him with counsel or even allow him to use British communication channels in pleading his needs with the Egyptians. Foreign Minister Granville had tartly telegraphed Cairo: "Her Majesty's Government are in no way responsible for the operations in the Sudan which have been taken under the authority of the Egyptian Government, or for the appointment of actions of General Hicks."[3]

Against his better judgment, Hicks had proceeded to attack the Mahdi deep within the Kordofan desert with a ragtag army made up of dispirited veterans of the Arabi revolt, many of whom had to be forcibly transported to the Sudan in chains. The campaign had been a disaster from beginning to end. While the Mahdi, husbanding his strength, shadowed the Egyptian army, Hicks plunged on into the trap set for him, outstripping his supply line and stretching his ill-trained men to the breaking point.

The officers bickered among themselves, poorly attended camels wandered off into the desert to die, and native guides, secretly in the pay of the Mahdi, led the army astray through waterless terrain.

Finally, battle was joined on November 3, 1883, when the Ansar ambushed Hicks's disorganized force. The end came quickly on the following day at Shaykan, near El Obeid. The crumpled pages of a diary kept by one of Hicks's officers, Major Herlith, which eventually reached Khartoum, told the pathetic story:

> These are bad times; we are in a forest and everyone is depressed. The General [Hicks] orders the band to play, hoping that the music may liven us a little; but the band soon stops for the bullets are flying from all directions, and camels, mules and men keep dropping down; we are all cramped up together, so the bullets cannot fail to strike. We are faint and weary, and have no idea what to do. . . . It is Sunday and my dear brother's birthday. Would to God that I could sit down and talk to him for an hour! The bullets are falling thicker. . . .[4]

The diary entry was never finished, as one of the bullets reached Herlith.

According to Ansar accounts, revealed years later, the European officers, led by Hicks, fought bravely to the end. Hicks was the last officer to die, slashing at the enemy with his sword until he was killed by a shower of spears. The bodies of the Egyptian dead were ignited so it could be said they were burned by hellfire.

The Mahdi's victory at Shaykan was a triumph. He had led his Ansar against a large, relatively modern, well-equipped army commanded by a British general and had defeated it soundly. He had outgeneraled Hicks, and his Ansar had outfought the Egyptians. As the Ansar returned jubilantly to El Obeid, the Austrian prisoner Ohrwalder heard an eerie sound like a rushing stream; it was the Ansar host chanting *La Illaha îl 'lallah*—in praise of God. People kissed the ground the Mahdi walked on and fought to get a sip of the Great One's bathwater from obliging eunuch attendants.

The news of Hicks's defeat and the destruction of an Egyptian army reached Cairo on November 22, 1883, stunning both the British and the Egyptians. Shock waves reverberated within the Gladstone government when the news reached London. Government policy, formally enunciated on October 25, had called for a withdrawal of British troops from Cairo to Alexandria, where a caretaker garrison of two thousand to three thousand would be maintained for a while. And in November—only days before the word of the Hicks debacle arrived—Gladstone at the Lord Mayor's Banquet had stated that British troops would be withdrawn from Egypt altogether. The new jeopardy in which Khartoum found itself and the threat this posed for Egypt itself, however, dictated urgent reconsideration of this policy.

Consul General Malet in Cairo privately took much of the blame for the Hicks fiasco—he even blamed himself for not having dissuaded the Egyptians from their folly—but he was publicly exonerated for reasons of politics. While it was true that Malet bore the brunt of responsibility, London was not blameless for its ostrichlike posture on the Sudan. Baring, in his memoir, described as a "sin of omission" the government's failure "to stop the departure of the Hicks expedition."[5]

Sir Charles Dilke, president of the Local Government Board and an influential Cabinet officer,[6] reflected the new urgency in a journal entry: "On December 12 there was a meeting at the War Office about the Soudan, Lord Granville [Foreign Minister], Hartington [Minister of War], Northbrook [First Lord of the Admiralty, and cousin of Evelyn Baring], Carlingford and myself being present, with Wolseley [Adjutant General of the Army] in the next room but one. We again told the Egyptians that they had better leave the Soudan and defend Egypt at Wadi Halfa [the Egyptian-Sudanese border town]. . . . Lord Granville told Hartington, who was starting for Windsor, what to tell the Queen, and I noted that the old stagers like Granville and Mr. Gladstone waste a great deal of time on concocting stories for the Queen, who is much too clever to be taken in by them, and always ends by finding out what they are doing."[7]

Colonel de Coetlogon, the British officer who succeeded Hicks as Commander of the Egyptian Army in the Sudan, reported to Cairo that Khartoum could not hold out for more than two months if the Mahdi continued to advance on it, a statement that *Times* correspondent Frank Power in Khartoum corroborated alarmingly in his dispatches to London. Evelyn Baring, now in Cairo as Malet's replacement, had also become convinced that Khartoum could not be held; the Egyptians, he suggested, must be made to fall back to the border at Wadi Halfa.

In the meantime, Egypt was having difficulties on still another front. On November 4, 1884, its garrison near Suakin on the Red Sea had been badly mauled by Hadendowa tribesmen—Kipling's "Fuzzy-wuzzies," part of the

Beja tribal group led by an able old slaver named Osman Digna (or 'Uthman Diqna). When Osman Digna pledged his allegiance to the Mahdi, he brought most of the tribes along the Red Sea into the rebellion with him. The Egyptian government proposed to deal with this threat to its strategic Red Sea coast by sending an expedition led by British General Valentine Baker, Commandant of the Egyptian Gendarmerie. Besides the Gendarmerie, the force would include six thousand black Sudanese troops whom Cairo proposed he led by the infamous slaver Zubair, still in Egyptian exile.

Opposition to Zubair flared from several quarters. Frank Power reported for the *Times* from Khartoum that Zubair's appointment "will nullify Gordon's and [Sir Samuel] Baker's work" in suppressing the slave traffic. Britain's antislavery groups were predictably aghast at the idea. But Baring telegraphed on December 9 an entirely logical but unpalatable view from Cairo: "As Her Majesty's Government have hitherto left all responsibility to the Egyptian Government, it appeared to me it would not have been just to object."[8]

No sooner had Baring sent this message than news of fresh disaster reached Cairo. Osman Digna's tribesmen had inflicted a new defeat on the Egyptians and threatened the critically important port of Suakin itself. Nearly a thousand troops had been killed. This debacle caused Baring to reverse his stand against British involvement. On December 10 he telegraphed Granville that the Egyptians were "drifting without any very definite or practical plan of action, and will continue to do so *until* they are told what course to pursue."

By this time the Austrian, Rudolf Slatin, now Governor of Darfur, had been forced to surrender that province to the Mahdi. Despite his feigned conversion to Islam, he had become unacceptable to his troops, who were rapidly being won over to the Mahdi's side. Slatin's opponent, Ansar Commander Modibbo, with whom he had fought several bloody engagements before giving up, graciously accepted the surrender. Modibbo magnanimously greeted his defeated adversary with the statement: "Let anger depart from the heart. Be patient; it is written 'God is with the patient.' " Slatin had need of patience; soon he would be handed over to the Mahdi and given the patched *jibba* dress of the Ansar to wear. As Abdel Kader, the Moslem name given him, he would begin twelve years as a prisoner of the Mahdi.

As a result of the rash of setbacks in the Sudan, the Egyptians were panic-stricken. The Khedive and his ministers could not handle the problem alone. Use of British forces would only fan religious fanaticism, but they needed the British to arrange for Turkish troops to come to their aid. Baring reported that the Egyptians "had resolved to place themselves absolutely in the hands of Her Majesty's Government."

On December 13, Baring was sent a reply based on a Cabinet decision. While British or Indian troops were out of the question, London had no objection to Turkish troops being sent to the Red Sea ports of the Sudan, provided they were paid by the Turkish government and would not be a burden on Egypt's precarious finances. The same message stated that the proposed use of Zubair Pasha was "inexpedient," both politically and as regards the slave trade. The message was explicit in calling on Egypt to "abandon all territory south of Assuan [Aswan], or at least Wadi Halfa," in return for which the British would assist in maintaining order in Egypt proper and in helping to defend the Sudan's Red Sea ports.

Sherif Pasha's reply, however, reminded the British that the Sultan's *firman* of August 7, 1879, appointing Tewfik as Khedive, forbade the cession of territory. In addition, to abandon eastern Sudan would place Egypt itself in jeopardy. Sherif, at least, was not prepared to cave in to the British and preside over the dismemberment of greater Egypt.

In a December 22 dispatch, Baring warned that if neither British nor Turkish help was forthcoming, the Sudan would be lost, and if that was the case, Her Majesty's government would have to exert more direct control over the Egyptian government in Cairo. "If the abandonment policy is carried out . . . it will be necessary to send an English officer of high authority to Khartoum with full powers to withdraw the garrisons and to make the best arrangements he can for the future government of the country."

Determined not to lose all of the Sudan, Sherif Pasha proposed a formula to force the Turkish hand: Egypt would return the eastern Sudan and Red Sea coast to Turkey, transferring all Egyptian troops stationed in those areas to Khartoum, where they could defend at least the Nile Valley.

London's final position was telegraphed back to Baring on January 4, 1884. It reiterated approval for sending Turkish troops to the eastern Sudan provided the Sultan paid for them, but disagreed with Sherif's plan to defend Khartoum. By secret message, Baring was informed that if the Egyptian government did not follow British advice, it must resign. If anyone doubted that the Egyptian government was now only a facade for British power and presence, the wording of the telegram received by Baring would have quickly dispelled such doubts: ". . . the advice of Her Majesty's Government should be followed [by Egypt] as long as the provisional occupation continues." Granville added: "Ministers . . . must carry out this advice or forfeit their offices."[9]

And forfeit their offices they did as the Cabinet resigned *en masse* rather than bear the stigma of giving up the Sudan. Moreover, it was patent sophistry for Gladstone to claim that the Sudan was an Egyptian problem, not a British one, since Egypt ceased to exist as a fully sovereign entity after the British occupation. The more flexible Nubar Pasha was brought back to replace Sherif Pasha as Prime Minister, and on January 8, Baring reported that the new government, obviously under British pressure, "entirely concurred in the wisdom of abandoning the Sudan, retaining possession only of Suakin."

In the meantime Gordon had arrived back in England from Palestine. He stayed as usual with his sister Augusta at 5 Rockstone Place, Southampton, as he prepared himself for the Congo. Suddenly on January 8 he had a caller who would change his life.

The bearded man who appeared at the door introduced himself as Mr. W. T. Stead, editor of the *Pall Mall Gazette*, one of the more strident critics of government policy toward the Sudan. As Gordon listened, his unexpected visitor perched on Augusta's leopard-skin divan and recounted the government's decision to pressure Egypt to withdraw from Khartoum. Stunned by the news, the general succumbed to an attack of "Agag" and permitted himself to give Stead two hours of unvarnished opinion, even though he had promised himself to stay out of the debate on the Sudan. Gordon predicted that the abandonment of the Sudan would have fatal consequences—the peace of the East would be jeopardized. "The danger to be feared is not that the Mahdi will march through to Wadi Halfa, [but that it] arises from the influence which the spectacle of conquering Muhammedan power established close to your frontier will exercise upon the population you govern." He predicted: "Every man will go over to the Mahdi, in all the cities of Egypt it will be felt that what the Mahdi has done they may do."[10]

Gordon was appalled at the prospect of giving up the Sudan, where he had given so much to stamp out slaving and bring order out of chaos. Furthermore, from a practical point of view there were not enough boats or camels in the Sudan to evacuate the 10,000 Egyptian and other foreign civilians, not to mention the 24,000 soldiers who found themselves in jeopardy throughout the Sudan. Even if there were, the evacuees would be "plundered to the skin and even their lives will not be spared." But looking at the political implications of such a cataclysmic event, Gordon firmly believed that the British "must either surrender absolutely to the Mahdi or defend Khartoum at all hazards."[11]

During this fateful interview, Gordon found that he shared many opinions with Stead. Gordon had recognized him as a kindred religious soul as well. When the *Pall Mall Gazette* editor left with his pile of notes, Gordon pressed upon him a copy of *The Imitation of Christ*.

The next day, January 9, 1885, the *Pall Mall Gazette* headlines blared: "Gordon for the Sudan." The lead article attacked the government for its policy, using Gordon's arguments as ammunition. In his turgid outpouring, Stead wrote: "We cannot send a regiment to Khartoum, but we can send a man who on more than one occasion has proved himself more valuable in similar circumstances than an entire army. Why not send Chinese Gordon? . . . to do what he can to save what can be saved from the wreck of the Sudan."

Two days later, Gordon with his friend Barnes visited Sir Samuel Baker at Sandford Orleigh. When the old explorer urged Gordon to return to the Sudan, "Gordon was silent, but his eyes flashed and an eager expression passed over his face as he looked at his host." Barnes recalled that late in the evening, after they had retired, Gordon came to his room and said in a soft voice, "You saw me today?—that was *myself*—the self I want to get rid of."[12] Agag had broken loose from his cage.

The *Times* and other leading papers picked up the *Pall Mall Gazette* story, the the *Morning Advertiser* on January 12 asserted confidently: ". . . all England has been looking for the employment of General Gordon in the present crisis in Egypt." Overnight England cried out for Chinese Gordon's return to the Sudan. He was the man of the hour. Lord Cairns, quite swept along by popular emotion, referred to him in the House of Lords as "one of our national treasures."

Privately other opinions were expressed. Gladstone's secretary probably echoed the Prime Minister's opinion when he accused the general of not being "clothed in the rightest of minds." Sir Charles Dilke thought Gordon "insane." The grand old imperialist Disraeli used the word "lunatic." Foreign Minister Granville was more charitable and confined himself to the observation that Gordon had "a small bee in his bonnet." In the corridors of power, General Wolseley, Adjutant General in the War Office, was one of the few who had complete confidence in Gordon. Old comrades in the Crimean War, Gordon and Wolseley had remained friends through the years even though their careers had taken very different directions. It was said that they prayed daily for each other.

Politics prevailed. Gladstone could not ignore public opinion that the jingoistic press had aroused. The situation in the Sudan may have seemed hopeless to the Liberal government, but Hicks's death brought such a public outcry that the Liberals could not ignore it. The word of General Wolseley, hero of Tel-el-Kebir, was crucial as well: Great Britain had an imperial destiny that ought not to retreat before spear-throwing dervishes. And Minister of War Lord Hartington, who represented the Whig faction within the Cabinet, also believed in a more aggressive approach toward the Sudan problem.*

As private secretary to Secretary of War Hartington, Gordon's good friend Reginald Brett had much influence. He also had large financial holdings in both the *Times* and the *Pall Mall Gazette*, which gave him leverage on editorial content. Reginald Brocklehurst, another of Gordon's close friends, also had influence in the War Office, and it was considered significant by some that he encouraged Stead to visit Southampton for the latter's memorable interview with Gordon on the Sudan which exploded with such force in the *Pall Mall Gazette*'s headlines the next day.

Wilfrid Blunt, well known as a sympathizer of the Arab "natives" and opponent of colonialism, saw these friends of Gordon as characters in a backstage intrigue. Their strategy was to use Gordon to undercut Gladstone's policy of withdrawal and force on the government a forward-thrusting policy

---

* Wilfrid Scawen Blunt in his biography of Gordon, *Gordon at Khartoum* (London: Jonathan Swift, 1912), pp. 162–164, expressed the opinion that Stead may have been an agent of the Hartington faction in the Cabinet and had interviewed Gordon on its behalf. The claim has never been substantiated.

calculated to attach Egypt and the Sudan to the empire. Blunt speculated that a letter to the *Times* sent by Sir Samuel Baker, recommending that Gordon retain Khartoum and the eastern Sudan, may have been inspired by the Rothschilds, who held £9 million in Egyptian debt. Baker's letter, featured on the first page of the *Times*, and Stead's interview with Gordon were, in Blunt's Machiavellian mind, part of the imperialists' campaign. While Blunt was well informed, he was something of a gossip and an eccentric. Moreover, he was so opposed to British expansion that he was prone to see imperialist plots where none existed.[13] Conspiracy theories are always tantalizing, and backroom maneuver surely had its place in British politics, just as in most other countries; but whether or not there was any secret alliance between an imperialist clique within the War Office and the press, the latter's influence on the public was to be critical in what soon would occur.

Queen Victoria, too, felt strongly about the situation. "Half measures were not enough."[14] She pressed Granville on Baring's idea to send a British officer to the Sudan.

The germ of the idea to use Gordon's strange genius again in the Sudan had been originally planted by Lord Dufferin, British Ambassador to Turkey, as early as 1882, soon after Gordon returned from South Africa. Dufferin in a dispatch to the Foreign Minister suggested that "some person like Gordon" should be found to administer the Sudan fairly; "good government could be maintained there without drawing upon Egypt either for men or money." Without first speaking with Gordon, Granville tried the idea out on Edward Malet, Consul General in Cairo, but the Egyptian government wanted nothing to do with the former Governor General of the Sudan—who had clashed with Khedive Tewfik.

The idea was revived from a different quarter. Before the *Pall Mall Gazette* took up the cry, Bevin Edwards, a British engineering colonel who had served with Gordon in China, wrote Sir Andrew Clarke, Inspector General of Fortifications, that Gordon was the man for the Sudan. Clarke passed the suggestion to Chancellor of the Exchequer Erskin Childers, who sent it to the Foreign Minister. Then Granville wrote Prime Minister Gladstone suggesting that Baring in Cairo be sounded out as to whether it was possible "to use Gordon in some way." The Foreign Minister reminded Gladstone that Gordon "is popular at home, and a sensible opponent of slavery." No one in the government seemed to have a better idea.

Baring was no admirer of Gordon. Their previous clash over Egypt's debt crisis and Gordon's staunch backing of the Khedive Ismail had upset him, and he suspected the mental balance of this "man who sought guidance in the words of the Prophet Isaiah."

When on December 1, 1883, Baring received Granville's suggestion that Gordon be used, he tried it out on the Egyptians once again. The Consul reported the strong objections of the Prime Minister: "The movement in the Sudan being religious, the appointment of a Christian in high command would probably alienate the tribes who remain faithful." Baring himself believed Gordon was "personally unfit" for the job but preferred to put the onus of rejection on the Egyptians.[15]

Gordon had not left Cairo without burning a few bridges, and there was still a lingering resentment on the part of Khedive Tewfik and several Egyptian pashas over Gordon's outspoken criticism of them. Unless there was pressure to the contrary, the consensus was against Gordon's return.

Baring, aside from his personal feelings toward Gordon, believed that Great Britain should not involve itself in Egypt's Sudan problem. To send Gordon to the Sudan in any capacity would be inconsistent with this policy. On December 3, 1883, Baring wired back to Granville his "hope that H. M. Government will adhere steadfastly to the policy of non-interference in the affairs of the Sudan."[16]

With public interest aroused by the *Pall Mall Gazette*, and with Nubar Pasha installed as Egyptian Prime Minister, Granville on January 7, 1884, again asked Baring: "Could General Charles Gordon be of assistance?" Baring demurred and suggested instead that the new Egyptian Minister of War, Abdul Kader Pasha, arrange the Egyptian evacuation of the Sudan from Khartoum.

Events moved rapidly. Granville on January 14 wrote Gladstone that he had confidence that Gordon could organize the tribes to escort the Khartoum garrison safety to Suakin, but "a little pressure on Baring might be advisable."[17] Gladstone agreed, with the following caveat: "While his [Gordon's] opinion on the Sudan may be of great value, must we not be very careful in any instructions we give, that he does not shift the centre of gravity as to political and military responsibility for that country? . . . if he reports what should be done, he should not be the judge *who* should do it, nor ought he to commit us on that point of advice officially given."[18]

SEEDS OF MISUNDERSTANDING

Since the Hicks debacle, British public opinion was fast rising against Gladstone. Gordon's appointment was born of expediency. The government simply saw a usefulness in exploiting his prestige and popularity; if Gordon could extricate Egypt from the Sudan that would be an extra benefit. Gordon's mission was meant to be a quick and easy fix. If Gordon was sent to Equatoria by Khedive Ismail in 1873 to assuage British antislavery sentiment, he was now being used by his own government to assuage political opinion.

Armed with Gladstone's permission, Granville pressed Baring once again on Gordon, outlining a vague plan in which he specified that Gordon from Suakin would only "report to Her Majesty's Government on the military situation of the Sudan."[19] Baring realized that public pressure was behind Granville's insistence and graciously acquiesced: "Gordon would be the best man if he will pledge himself to carry out the policy of withdrawal from the Sudan as quickly as it is possible consistent with saving lives. He must also fully understand that he must take his instructions from the British representative in Egypt [i.e. Baring himself]."[20] In a private letter to Baring, Granville revealed quite frankly his motives for promoting Gordon's appointment: "He may possibly be of great use, and the appointment will be popular with many classes in this country."[21]

When Gordon presented himself at the War Office on the afternoon of the 15th, his old friend Wolseley explained that the ban on his going to the Congo had been lifted and he need not resign his commission; however, Great Britain had an assignment for him which would take precedence over the Congo. Specifically, Wolseley asked if he would go to Suakin "to inquire into the conditions of the Sudan."[22]

Gordon seemed willing—even enthusiastic. In drawing up a plan of action on the spot as requested by Wolseley, Gordon included the phrase "proceed to Suakin and report . . . on the military situation and return." "Inquire" had now become "report," though both words still indicated an observer's role; Foreign Minister Granville, on the other hand, was beginning to think in terms of an executive role for Gordon when he wrote the Prime Minister of the general's mission to "organize the tribes to escort the Khartoum garrison safety to Suakin."

Baring, it should be noted, telegraphed Granville on January 16 stating that because the Egyptian War Minister, Abdul Kader, had refused to go to

Khartoum (believing it physically not practical to evacuate the troops), the Egyptian government had asked for a well-qualified British officer to *conduct* the retreat. Baring's final acceptance of Gordon as the well-qualified British officer was on the condition he *"carry out** the policy of withdrawal as soon as possible." The role of Gordon had been raised several notches.

Gordon paid a visit to Reginald Brett, then with friends Horace Waller and Captain Brocklehurst took the boat train to Dover on January 16, 1884. Gordon broke the news of the aborted Congo mission to Leopold, then was summoned back to London the next day for an urgent meeting at the War Office. Gordon was exhilarated that his government, long neglectful of him, finally had urgent need of him. "Government and authorities have been exceedingly kind," he wrote, "and I have every reason to be grateful to them for I have often worried them, and they have decided to let me stay in Her Majesty's service."[23]

The historic meeting on January 18, 1884, was convened at 3:00 P.M. with Foreign Minister Granville, War Minister Hartington, Sir Charles Dilke, and the Earl of Northbrook, First Lord of the Admiralty, present. Before being presented to them Gordon was briefed by Wolseley: "HMG want you to understand this Government are determined to evacuate the Sudan. . . . Will you go and do it?" Gordon's reply was quick and unequivocal: "Yes."

In Gordon's cryptic account, his meeting went as follows: They—"Did Wolseley tell you our ideas?" He—"Yes, he said you will not guarantee further government of Sudan and you wish me to go and evacuate it. They said yes and the meeting was over. I left at 8:00 P.M. for Calais."

Dilke's record of the meeting was somewhat more detailed: "Gordon said that he believed that the danger at Khartoum had been 'grossly exaggerated' and that the two Englishmen there [Colonel de Coetlogon, Commander of the Egyptian Army in the Sudan, and *Times* correspondent Frank Power] 'lost their heads'; he would be able to bring away the garrisons without difficulty."[24] (This, of course, was at variance with Gordon's explosive first interview in the *Pall Mall Gazette* when he declared an evacuation to be impossible.)

Lord Northbrook, in writing to Baring on the meeting, stated that Gordon was "to report on the best way of withdrawing garrisons," but he added more

---

* Author's italics.

accurately than had Dilke that Gordon could "perform such *other duties*★ as may be entrusted to him by the Khedive's Government through you [Baring]."[25] Lord Hartington's report to Gladstone omitted the important enabling words "other duties" and instead transmitted Gordon's notes made at the earlier January 15 meeting in which the general's role was described as only advisory.

Gladstone was thus left with the impression that Gordon's role would be purely advisory, a critical source of misunderstanding, as it would turn out. When the Prime Minister approved Gordon's assignment, he was in effect concurring in the terms of the mission as contained in the letter sent him by Lord Hartington, which lacked the more activist flavor of Granville's correspondence with Baring on the subject.

The official, formal instruction to Gordon was further confusing; in bureaucratic jargon, it ordered the general to "pay especial consideration to the question of the steps that may be usefully taken." Gordon was told: "You will consider yourself authorized and instructed to perform such other duties as the Egyptian Government may desire to entrust to you, and as may be communicated to you by Sir E. Baring."

This was buck-passing in the best bureaucratic tradition. It would cover the government and shift the blame to Baring and the Egyptians if things went awry, but it would permit the government to share in the credit if things went right—or so Granville perhaps deluded himself. The Foreign Minister slyly provided Baring with even more implied authority when in the transmitted instructions, he rephrased the key line to read "other duties *beyond those specified in my dispatch.*"

After the whirlwind day at the War Office, Gordon set a few personal matters in order and dashed off farewell notes to Augusta and his friend the Reverend Mr. Barnes, then had a hasty dinner at the Knightsbridge mess with Captain Reginald Brocklehurst of the Horse Guards. He dashed to the Charing Cross station for an 8:00 P.M. boat train to Calais. Were it not for his brother, who packed his uniform case, or his nephew, who delivered it to him at the train, he would have left with only the clothes on his back.

Gordon was accompanied by Colonel John Donald Hamill Stewart of the

---

★ Author's italics.

11th Hussars. The Anglo-Irish cavalry officer had seen service in the Sudan and had been the author of dispatches from Khartoum predicting the present state of affairs. Eminently well qualified to be Gordon's Chief of Staff, he was a brilliant officer from his school days, having passed out first at Sandhurst, and had been sent to the Sudan to collect intelligence in December 1882.

Stewart's assessment of the Mahdi movement and his realistic plan for southern Egypt's defense in the event the Mahdi's advance threatened the frontier were encyclopedic in detail. He came to the conclusion that the Mahdi's success was in large part a result of Egyptian misrule in the Sudan and inept military action. He saw, as Gordon did, that efforts to stamp out the slave trade, however morally good, caused serious dislocations in the country's economy. His recommendation was that Egypt abandon all territory south and west of Khartoum.

Stewart was to prove a stalwart and loyal assistant until he met a tragic death, but at the time of their departure, Gordon had suspicions that he was Baring's confidential informant. He referred to Stewart as "my wet nurse." Baring admitted in his memoir that he had been glad that Stewart went along to provide a leavening influence on the mercurial Gordon.

Gordon and Stewart were seen off at the station by an impressive panoply of brass. The Duke of Cambridge, Chief of Staff of the British Army, was there with Foreign Minister Granville, along with Gordon's old friend General Wolseley. Wolseley had hastily made the rounds of London's better clubs to collect money for Gordon, who typically had neglected to take care of his banking and had not a shilling in his pocket. While the Foreign Minister bought Gordon his ticket, the Duke of Cambridge with the aplomb of a good butler ushered the general to his compartment and held the door for him. Fearing he had not collected enough money, Wolseley at the last moment gave Gordon his gold watch, which presumably could be converted to cash if need be.

The august statesmen who saw Gordon off at Charing Cross met the next day and wondered aloud whether they had committed "a giant folly" in sending Gordon off. Queen Victoria had no such doubts, however. Referring to Gordon's mission, she wrote a sharp note to Major General Sir Evelyn Wood, Sirdar, or Commander, of the Egyptian army: "Why this was *not* done long ago and why the right thing is never done till it is absolutely extorted from those who are in authority, is inexplicable to the Queen."* [26]

---

* An ominous note was sounded by the *Manchester Evening Mail* when an article at this time appeared stating: "We learn on unquestionable authority that General Gordon told a Devonshire friend before leaving for the Sudan that he had all his life been affected by presentiment, and never in the worst times in China had he the least expectation of being killed; but on this occasion, he had a distinct presentiment that he would never return from Khartoum; and he actually distributed a few trinkets as memorials."

CAIRO CONSULTATION

A comet of no uncommon magnitude had been launched on the
political firmament of the Soudan.
    —Evelyn Baring on Gordon's assignment to the Sudan

As he sat in the train watching the French countryside race by,
Gordon finally had time to contemplate the awesome task before
him. He saw no reason to stop at Cairo on his way to Khartoum, so
he planned to enter the Sudan by way of Suakin on the Red Sea. In this way
he would be spared having to meet with Evelyn Baring and Nubar Pasha,
both of whom he had come to dislike from his earlier association with them.
Consul General Baring was one of the "humbugs" who Gordon believed
inhabited the British diplomatic service, and Prime Minister Nubar Pasha
epitomized all that was wrong with the Egyptian pasha class. Furthermore,
Gordon could justify taking the Red Sea route on the grounds that he wanted
to negotiate with some of the important tribal leaders between Suakin and
Berber, whose cooperation would be crucial to a successful evacuation.

Gordon's strategy, conceived in London and developed as he traveled
across Europe between Calais and Brindisi, called for returning the Sudan to
its hereditary sultans—for the most part, tribal chieftains—who had ruled
their traditional areas without interference before Egyptian administration
had been imposed. If the former tribal structure of the country was revived,
the Mahdi's influence might be restricted to religious matters. Safe evacuation of the Egyptian garrisons in the Sudan was possible, in addition, only if
the tribes along the routes of egress permitted it. Without the lure of
autonomy, they would surely throw in their lot with the Mahdi and join the
holy war against Egypt.

En route, from Lyons, Gordon sent Granville specific recommendations
for approval, one of which called for his being made Governor General. Such
authority was necessary if he was to implement his strategy. In anticipation of
Granville's acceptance of his ideas, he worked up draft announcements for

Khedive Tewfik to issue, one promising independence to the traditional tribal leaders in the Sudan and appealing to them to refrain from further hostilities, the other naming him Governor General. The most sensitive part of the first decree had reference in it to "the evacuation of the country and the withdrawal of the troops,"[1] which if prematurely known in the Sudan could compromise the operation.

A report on the Hadendowa tribe given Gordon upon his arrival in Port Said by his old officer Ali Bey Tuhain described how the critical eastern Sudan tribes, which straddled the evacuation route between Berber and Suakin, had split into two factions after the death of their leader, Sheikh Mohammed Mousa. Only one faction—albeit the larger one under Osman Digna—sided with the Mahdi.[2] Gordon reasoned that there was still room to maneuver.

Gordon proposed that he himself issue an appeal to the troublesome Hadendowa and Bishareen tribes in the Red Sea area, asking them to permit the Egyptian troops beleaguered by Osman Digna's forces to return safely to their Suakin garrison. He promised to visit these tribes within a fortnight to discuss a future government based on their own tribal leadership.

The fall of El Obeid, the massacre of Hicks's army by the Mahdi and Osman Digna's marauding in eastern Sudan should have made Gordon realize that he was not dealing with a collection of tribes whose peace could be bought by promises of local autonomy or which could be neutralized by playing one against another. The Sudan was faced with a religious movement whose momentum would only be quickened when it became known that the Egyptians intended to flee the country. Gordon persisted in believing that the Mahdi's revolt, while cloaked in religious inspiration, was at its root an uprising in protest against Egyptian rule—one in which the tribes sought to regain the fruits of slaving, if permitted to rule themselves.

However wrong he was, it was only natural for Gordon to underestimate the Mahdi—who had been so insignificant when Gordon served in the Sudan as Governor General that he had never heard of him. He dismissed this would-be Messiah's remarkable victories as the product of Egyptian military bungling and ignored the Mahdi's intrinsic appeal.

The British Cabinet, when it met on January 22, 1884, was willing to have Gordon made Governor General—even Gladstone did not object so long as Gordon used his new powers only to evacuate the Egyptians—but other points in Gordon's plan were referred to Baring for decision. Foreign Minister Granville's communication to the Consul General simply dodged responsibility: "We have not local knowledge sufficient to judge; you may settle the terms and act upon them at once as time presses or after consultation with him [Gordon]."[3]

Queen Victoria, usually canny in her insights, feared that evacuation would be very difficult, perhaps impossible. In her journal entry of January 23, 1884, she noted that Lord Northbrook, Baring's cousin, had described Gordon to her as "an extraordinary man with an enormous power over uncivilized people." Nonetheless, she added cautiously, "His attempt is a very dangerous one."[4] Unlike Gladstone, whom she disliked, the Queen could view the stark reality of the situation without being blinded by the need to appease the public. But, of course, she was not running for office.

The unquestioning confidence the British public placed in Gordon, its conviction that he would somehow fix everything, was touching and understandable. If Gordon could single-handedly defeat the slavers in the Sudan, why couldn't he defeat the dervishes? But it was puzzling why Gordon allowed himself to be swept along on this tide of goodwill after declaring so categorically that evacuation was impossible.

It seems probable that, with his fine record of success, Gordon believed that his strategy here would work as well. If it did not prove feasible to marshal tribal power against the Mahdi on the promise of Egyptian evacuation, British forces could be relied upon to step in—Gladstone's policy of noninvolvement notwithstanding. There were intimations to that effect in Gordon's memorandum outlining his proposed plan: ". . . seeing the difficulty of asking Her Majesty's Government to give a decision or direction as what should be done in certain cases . . . I can therefore only say that I will carry out the evacuation as far as possible . . . to the best of my ability and with avoidance, as far as possible, of all fighting. I would, however, hope that Her Majesty's Government *will give me their support and consideration should I be unable to fulfill all their expectations.*"*

Gordon's reason for hope was based on at least one piece of solid evidence. On November 23, 1883, Admiral Hewett had been ordered, in view of the growing menace posed by Osman Digna's Hadendowa tribesmen, to patrol

---

* Author's italics.

the Red Sea off Suakin to "maintain Egyptian authority" over the Red Sea ports.[5]

When Baring received Gordon's proposals from the Cabinet, he responded uncritically: "All Gordon's suggestions are excellent."[6] But the Consul General had never wanted any Englishman, much less Gordon, sent to the Sudan. Aside from seeing the hopelessness of the situation, Baring had had the wit to recognize that if a British officer became beleaguered, "the British Government might be obliged to send an expedition to relieve him." Baring had bowed to the government's wishes just as the government had bowed to public opinion. He did, however, insist that Gordon meet with him and the Egyptian leaders in Cairo before going on to Khartoum so that a meeting of the minds could be reached and the chain of command understood.

Baring recalled his position frankly in his memoir, *Modern Egypt:* "I mistrusted General Gordon's judgment and I was in reality averse to his employment. . . ." But faced with three requests from Granville for Gordon's services, based on "public opinion in England calling loudly for his employment" and the urgings of Prime Minister Nubar Pasha, Sir Evelyn Wood as Sirdar of the Egyptian Army, and Colonel Watson, a Sudan expert on Wood's staff, Baring gave in. "With this array of opinion against me I mistrusted my own judgment . . . and [thought I] might be unconsciously prejudiced against General Gordon."[7]

Colonel Watson, Gordon's friend from Equatoria service, and Major General Gerald Graham, his comrade-in-arms since Woolwich school days, met him in Port Said to escort him to Cairo. Graham knew Gordon well enough to understand how he felt about the Consul General and urged his old friend to put his differences aside. In any case, the desert track from Suakin to Berber was unsafe because of Osman Digna's forays in that region. Gordon had no alternative but to go to Cairo and endure once again the oppressive influence of British Foreign Office bureaucracy and the depressing spectacle of Egyptian perfidy.

Social amenities were a chore which Gordon dreaded, and, as usual, he came without proper costumes for the formality of Cairo dining. For the inevitable formal dinner in his honor at the British residency, he had to send out for the right dress clothes at the last minute. When he later tried to sell his dinner jacket and have the proceeds sent to the Boys' Club at Gravesend, the housekeeper informed him that it had been borrowed, not bought.

THE MOSLEM MESSIAH AND THE CHRISTIAN MARTYR

On January 25, 1884, the day after he arrived in Cairo, Gordon paid his respects to Khedive Tewfik. He apologized for the harsh language he had used when last in Egypt. Most of Gordon's forty-eight-hour stop in Cairo was devoted to working out with Baring a mutually understood set of instructions. The general had brought with him Granville's instructions, the heart of which stated: "You are also desired to consider and report upon the best mode of effecting the evacuation of the interior of the Soudan and upon the manner in which the safety and the good administration of the Egyptian Government of the parts on the seacoast can best be secured."[8] Then came the critical phrase giving Baring wide latitude: "You will consider yourself authorized and instructed to perform such other duties as the Egyptian Government may desire to intrust to you and as may be communicated to you by Sir Evelyn Baring."[9]

Gordon arrived also with his own memorandum which he had composed between Port Said and Cairo, setting forth the strategy he had conceived. "My idea is that the restoration of the country should be made to the different petty sultans who existed at the time of Mohammed Ali's [Egyptian] conquest and whose families still exist; that the Mahdi should be left altogether out of the calculations." This was a new dimension. Gordon had become so fascinated with the role of architect of a new Sudan that evacuation seemed to be relegated to second place.

His priorities were not so farfetched: A peaceful evacuation would be possible only if the tribes could be placated with promises of autonomy. Nevertheless, critics of Gordon like Dilkes and Gladstone himself would soon come to believe that Gordon had deceived them and had never had any intention of evacuating the Egyptian garrisons—contrary to policy, he had all along harbored schemes to save the Sudan.

At least, the experts on the spot found Gordon's ideas sensible. Colonel Stewart, perhaps one of the wisest of Sudan hands, expressed his "cordial agreement" with Gordon's plan—even extolled it as "an act of justice" and a "politic act by raising a rival power to that of the Mahdi." Baring also admitted that it seemed "wise and politic," although much later, with benefit of hindsight, he concluded that "everyone had underestimated the Mahdi and overrated the sultans."[10]

At a meeting on January 25, Baring, Gordon, Nubar Pasha, Colonel Stewart and Sir Evelyn Wood worked on new instructions, combining those

336

of Granville with the new provisions of Gordon's plan. Evacuation, in this document, came first in the rhetoric, but Gordon was permitted great latitude "as regards the most opportune time and the best method for effecting the retreat" and was assured that it was "neither necessary nor desirable" to be given "detailed instructions."[11] In fact, the new instructions specified that Gordon might have to take "a few months" to carry out the evacuation safely. This was a virtual blank check. Another passage in the instructions was significant for establishing Baring and Egyptian Prime Minister Nubar Pasha as Gordon's point of control. The Khedive would not be able to communicate directly with Gordon as had been the case during the general's previous assignment in the Sudan.

In these final instructions, Gordon's strategy of restoring the country to its component tribal parts and endeavoring "to form a confederation of those sultans" was stipulated. The forging of a confederation represented still another dimension to Gordon's sultan-making authority, and the instructions provided Gordon with "full discretionary power to retain the troops for such reasonable period as [he] may think necessary in order that the abandonment of the country may be accomplished with the least possible risk to life and property." Baring, Wood and Nubar all seemed to have been taken into Gordon's camp; evacuation, *per se*, had been subordinated to restructuring the Sudan.

Baring blandly reported to Granville that instructions didn't matter much anyway, since Gordon, "a man who habitually consults the Prophet Isaiah when he is in difficulty, is not apt to obey the orders of any one." He nonetheless had to suffer stern criticism from the government for substantially changing Gordon's instructions. In his memoir, Baring conceded this but denied that he had gone beyond the guidelines established by London: ". . . on the day [January 18] on which General Gordon received his instructions in London, Lord Granville telegraphed to me: 'Gordon suggests that it may be announced in Egypt that he is on his way to Khartoum to arrange for the future settlement of the Soudan for the best advantage of the people.' If General Gordon was to arrange for 'the future settlement of the Soudan,' I fail to see how he could do so without exercising some executive authority."[12]

What would have been the purpose of giving Gordon the rank of Governor General, Baring reasoned, if he was not to exercise executive authority? Even

Gladstone had announced publicly that Gordon's mission to the Sudan was "for the double purpose of evacuating the country by extricating the Egyptian garrisons and reconstituting it by giving back to those sultans their ancestral powers."

This, then, was the genesis of Gordon's instructions, its metamorphosis from a mere reporting function to a dynamic executive role charged with restructuring the Sudan as prerequisite to Egyptian evacuation. The confusion and misunderstanding that led to the tragic end of Gordon's mission may be traced to this uncertainty.

Following the instruction-drafting meeting, Baring wrote Granville on February 1, 1884, giving the Foreign Minister assurances that Gordon "fully understands that he is going to Khartoum for the purpose of carrying out the policy of evacuation."[13] This was less than candid, though Baring did confess that the "widest discretionary powers" had been given Gordon "as regards the manner of carrying out the policy and as to the best time and mode of announcing it at Khartoum." That there was new emphasis placed on restructuring the Sudan government went unmentioned.

With charm, persuasion, and logic on his side, Gordon had his way in Cairo. Gordon may have seemed to exceed his original instruction, but it had been Baring who stretched his own instructions. But responsibility belonged, more than anywhere else, with the government. The Cabinet had, first of all, been unrealistic in its assessment of the Sudan; it was unduly influenced by public pressure and politics; and it acted cynically in sending Gordon to the Sudan. From this witches' brew of policy it was perhaps inevitable that the Cabinet would soon ladle out contradictory and confusing instructions to the men on the spot, would be dilatory in making decisions and unfair in burdening Baring and Gordon with broad responsibility and then faulting them when they took it.

Evelyn Baring's role would be crucial to Gordon as a guide, or at least as interpreter of London's instructions. Equally important, Baring would be necessary to make sense out of Gordon's sometimes unclear correspondence. The Cairo meetings, brief as they were, at least gave Baring a chance to know Gordon better, and vice versa, although no meeting of the minds occurred. Even as Baring was writing to Granville, "What a curious creature he is," Gordon was writing home, "They think me very queer—and I am." Nubar Pasha, whom Gordon had previously challenged to a duel in an archaic act of honor, was given even more reason to be perplexed by this eccentric British officer. In the way of many Mediterraneans, Nubar greeted his old sparring partner with a forgiving bear hug, but such an un-British show of familiarity simply offended Gordon, who did little to hide his contempt.

Committed to winning over the hereditary sultans at the Mahdi's expense, Gordon now dropped a bombshell. If he was to be sultan-maker, he needed a sultan in fact if not in title. He proposed enlisting his archenemy and antagonist Zubair Pasha, descendant of the Abbasid dynasty of Khalifs, most powerful "sultan" of them all and the one Sudanese whose influence among the tribes might approach that of the Mahdi. This was a radical suggestion but one consistent with Gordon's strategy. The idea was inspired and typical of his ingenuity.

Ironically, Zubair's presence in Cairo had first worried Gordon—so much so that en route he had telegraphed the Cabinet asking that it arrange for the old slaver to be deported to Cyprus, where he could be kept under better control. This had not been legally possible, so Zubair was still living a lordly existence in Cairo when Gordon arrived. They met coincidentally at the just-resigned Prime Minister Sharif's house, where their mutual rancor encased them like ice. But the general, already nursing his embryonic idea of using Zubair, had Baring arrange another meeting.

In the presence of Baring, Nubar Pasha, Stewart, Watson and Giegler (Gordon's previous aide in the Sudan and later Governor General), the two antagonists soon squared off against each other. The old enmity flared anew, accentuated by the fact that both were performing before such a distinguished gallery and a record of the meeting was being made. According to young Reginald Wingate, who was also present and who was much later to win prominence as Governor General of the Sudan, Gordon extended his hand to Zubair. The slaver put his hand behind his back and growled, "I cannot touch the hand that is soiled with the blood of my son."[14] Despite Gordon's protest that it had been his duty to eliminate the man who had raised such a serious rebellion—a rebellion which Gordon accused Zubair of engineering—the great slaver was not ready to let bygones be bygones.

Despite the atmosphere of this highly charged meeting, Gordon told Baring that "he had a mystic feeling toward Zubair" and would be willing to take him to the Sudan. To flesh out this astonishing idea, Gordon gave Baring a well-reasoned memorandum in which he documented Zubair's influence over most of the Mahdi's chiefs who formerly owed allegiance to him. The main flaw to Gordon's strategy of returning power to the sultans was that many of them were weak, and Khartoum, an artificial city founded by the Egyptians, did not even have a traditional sultan to whom autonomy could be restored—nor did Dongola or Kassala. Zubair would be able to compensate for this problem.

Nubar Pasha, Watson and Stewart were all against the idea, and Baring himself doubted that the slaver would ever forgive Gordon enough to work with him. More important, Baring knew that England would never forgive Zubair or permit the infamous slaver to be reinstated. The Anti-Slavery Society and the Conservatives, among others, would raise such a cry as to make the move politically unthinkable. Still fresh in his mind was the furor caused when Valentine Baker had wanted to use Zubair for the Suakin campaign.

Baring, moreover, had "no confidence in opinions based on mystic feelings." One moment Gordon wanted Zubair exiled (this communication did not, by coincidence, reach Baring until Gordon expressed his interest in using Zubair), the next moment he wanted him as the keystone of his policy. Baring wondered if Gordon's mercurial judgment could thus be trusted and vetoed his request for Zubair—the first request made of him since he had pledged himself to support the General.

Gordon and Stewart prepared to leave Cairo for Khartoum on January 26, 1884. To quote the apprehensive British proconsul, "A comet of no common magnitude had been launched on the political firmament of the Soudan!"

CAIRO TO KHARTOUM

. . . Gordon has taken his leap in the dark. . . . the deed is done
and we must now abide by the result and hope for the best.
—Colonel Stewart, February 13, 1884, after Gordon issued the
Khedive's *firman* revealing Egypt's intention to abandon the Sudan

It was a curious-looking party that boarded the Cairo-Assiut train at 10:00 P.M. on the evening of January 26, 1884. With General Gordon and Colonel Stewart was the Emir 'Abd al-Shakour, grandson of the late Sultan of Darfur and heir-pretender to that princely tribal throne. The Emir was the first of the traditional sultans tapped by Gordon to retrieve his hereditary lands from the Mahdi. But the vision of 'Abd al-Shakour, bedecked in a magnificent, if ill-fitting, gold-studded uniform festooned with decorations cascading down his chest, provoked Gordon to say that "if he started off on his journey in his guise, he would certainly be murdered en route."[1] The trip had to be made unostentatiously.

The Emir's twenty-three wives and concubines, a bevy of brothers and mountains of luggage required several extra carriages to be attached to the train, delaying its departure. Sadly, 'Abd al-Shakour would soon begin a drinking binge, forcing Gordon to jettison him and his harem at Korosko. The Emir made his own way to Dongola before giving up and returning to the comforts of Cairo. The strategy of restoring the hereditary princes had not begun auspiciously.

Gordon and Stewart were occupied with the pressing logistics of the moment, but nagging at them were worries about what awaited them in Khartoum. Major General Sir Gerald Graham, soon to be swept into his own adventures at Suakin, prepared to board the train with Gordon, since he intended to travel with his old friend as far as the Sudan border.

Sir Evelyn Baring, of course, was on hand to say goodbye to Gordon and Stewart, although a bad sore throat prevented him from talking much. The Consul General had upset Gordon by refusing to accept Zubair as centerpiece of the Sudan strategy. That evening Gordon in pique had refused to attend a farewell dinner given in his honor by his host in Cairo, General Evelyn Wood, Commander in Chief of the Egyptian Army. Sir Evelyn, it seemed, had also opposed his Zubair proposal. According to Reginald Wingate, in attendance, Gordon accosted Sir Evelyn just before dinner and in impetuous anger said: "You were one of those who voted against Zubair; I won't sit down to table with you. I'll have a plate of soup in my rooms."[2]

Baring tried his best to cheer up the general at the station, saying: "Well Gordon, I see you are very upset about this Zobeir [Zubair] business; let us have a compromise. If, when you get to Khartoum, you find that Zobeir is really vitally important for your purpose, I will give you a promise that I will do my best with the home Government to arrange for him to join you."[3] In fact, Baring was beginning to see merit in the idea, believing that the old slaver might well prove "a valuable instrument in the execution of General Gordon's policy."

Gordon had rejected the idea of taking a military escort to Khartoum, as this would sound a militant rather than peaceful note. He had with him only one aide, Ibrahim Fawzi, whom he had fired five years before in Equatoria. Gordon was venturing virtually alone into a land he had once ruled, but which was now rapidly turning hostile. If the British public was confident that its miracle-maker would succeed, the rest of the Western world watched with skeptical wonder. After leaving Cairo, Gordon telegraphed to the Sudan government a curious message of good cheer: "Do not be panic-stricken. You are men, not women; I am coming." He wrote his sister Augusta a more humble note: "May He be glorified, the world and the people of the Soudan be blessed and may I be the dust under His feet."

On the train ride to Khartoum, Gerald Graham, a friend of Gordon's since the Crimean War, proffered advice. Graham warned Gordon against underestimating the Mahdi. This was good advice, but Gordon unfortunately did not listen. He wrote his sister from Cairo regarding the Mahdi: "I am not—thanks to God—moved even a little." This was not whistling in the dark; Gordon really could not believe that the Mahdi's power extended very far beyond Kordofan.

To Graham, Gordon explained his plan to detach the southern, "negro-inhabited" provinces of Equatoria and Bahr al-Ghazal, and cede them to Leopold's Congo, where antislaving measures would be undertaken with more resolve—by himself, he still hoped. And he clung to his plan for a federation of sultans in the rest of the Sudan and, given hope by Baring's parting words, still saw Zubair as the key to this plan.

The rail trip to Assiut took five days through Egypt's dusty countryside. From Assiut the party progressed by Nile steamer to Korosko, south of Aswan. Three hundred miles, much of it by camel, still lay ahead before Gordon and Stewart would reach Khartoum. Pleased to be on camelback again, Gordon was oblivious to the dangers of crossing the arid Nubian desert—sometimes called "the Waterless Sea"—through territory whose tribes were of questionable loyalty. Graham bid Gordon goodbye near Korosko with a hearty "God bless you."

On February 7, 1884, Gordon reached the village of Abu Hamed on the Nile. He had successfully crossed the sea of sand, where survival depended on unerringly reaching the next water hole in time, a feat of navigation which even the best Arab guides had difficulty in performing. Gordon was fine, although he narrowly avoided being thrown by an unruly camel at Abu Hamed. To be unseated from one's camel is a bad omen in the Sudan, and Gordon could be grateful that his skill in handling these uncongenial beasts saved him from an inauspicious beginning to his mission—if not a broken neck as well.

Impressed with the warm reception he received in Abu Hamed, Gordon impulsively sent off a telegram to Baring recommending a reversal of the agreed-upon policy. Perhaps evacuation would not be necessary after all; since the Mahdi's influence did not seem to have seriously infected the natives, there was perhaps no need to abandon the Khedive's rule in the Sudan. While Gordon would soon be disabused of this notion, it was this kind of erratic message-sending that perturbed Baring. The Consul General quickly learned to read Stewart's more measured views before accepting Gordon's impulsive telegraphic outpourings.

Two days before arriving in Berber on the next leg of his journey, Gordon sent a letter to the Mahdi. The communication, the first with his adversary, was ill conceived in substance and poorly prepared in style. Only Gordon's ignorance and underestimation of the Mahdi could account for his clumsy gesture of goodwill, offering an Egyptian tarboosh and scarlet robe of honor, customarily given by the Khedive to subordinates. It was the message itself, however, that was certain to infuriate the Mahdi; Gordon proposed that the

Ansar's leader, who had conquered all before him, satisfy himself with the sultanship of Kordofan. With dreams of religious leadership over all Islam and with the ranks of his followers daily swelling as he repulsed Khartoum's feeble efforts to stem the tide of rebellion, the Mahdi could scarcely be bought off with promises of a province he already ruled.

Gordon's posture as a generous ruler tossing crumbs of favor to a rebellious chieftain was, moreover, inconsistent with his January 30 effort to ransom Slatin and his troops captured in Darfur for £10,000—an obvious admission of impotence. Why Stewart, who knew better, did not restrain Gordon in this matter is something of a mystery, unless one assumes he was unable to do so. Stewart's concern with the Mahdi's growing power was clearly revealed in his journal entry of January 31, but dutifully he recorded the thoughts of General Gordon: "It is possible the danger of an attack by the Mahdi had been greatly exaggerated." The colonel added his own more ominous view: "I would, however, like to point out that the Blue Nile is at present closed by the rebels and that Khartoum gets all its food supply by the Blue Nile." Stewart went on to point out that while Khartoum was believed to have a three-month stockpile of food, the Mahdi's plan was probably "to allow matters to ripen and to wait until Khartoum is forced through hunger to submit," as had been the strategy in the case of El Obeid.[4] How right he was.

As Gordon was making his way to Khartoum to effect a peaceful evacuation of the Egyptian garrisons, events along the Sudan's Red Sea coast were anything but peaceful. Osman Digna had organized his Hadendowa tribal people into a potent fighting force for the Mahdi. Notorious as a slaver, the tribal leader had joined the Mahdi's cause when he was put out of business by the British naval patrols in the Red Sea. He soon proved himself a formidable guerrilla fighter, and by mid-October 1883, he had completely routed an Egyptian force. Then on November 5, the very day that Hicks's army was being fatally attacked near El Obeid, he intercepted and roundly defeated a column of five hundred Egyptian troops marching to relieve a beleaguered garrison at Tokar, forty-five miles south of Suakin.

The inexperienced Egyptian troops, having been surprised by an ambush, did not have time to form their squares and fled in panic. More than a third of the Egyptians were killed, and Captain Moncrief, the British Consul in Jidda, who happened to be accompanying the column as an observer, was killed in the fighting as well. Shortly afterward a regiment of Sudanese troops, hurriedly sent from Massawa, also met disaster at the hands of Osman Digna. Only two officers and thirty-three men survived the massacre to return to Suakin with their doleful account of what had befallen them.

The threat posed by Osman Digna to the eastern Sudan, particularly the strategic seaport of Suakin, provoked the Egyptian government in late October to organize an expeditionary force to protect Suakin. The aim was to open a route to Berber on the Nile, which would permit the evacuation of the Khartoum garrison. The Egyptian Gendarmerie, under the command of General Valentine Baker, had been selected for the mission, as the Egyptian army was still being reorganized after the Arabi uprising.

Valentine Baker, the younger brother of the great Nile explorer Sir Samuel Baker, was a valiant and able officer who had hoped to become Commander in Chief of the Egyptian Army, but was frustrated in this ambition in 1882 when Queen Victoria herself vetoed the appointment. He had, it seemed, been accused of assaulting a young lady in a railway carriage some years before. While there had been doubt as to his guilt, he became the center of scandal and was drummed out of the 10th Hussars in disgrace. He joined the Turkish Army as a mercenary and saw duty in the Russo-Turkish War, rising to the rank of major general.

Baker leaped at the chance to lead his Gendarmerie against Osman Digna in the hope that he could distinguish himself in battle and rehabilitate his tarnished reputation. So eager was he that Baring feared that he "would be led into the committal of some rash act."[5] The British Consul General went so far as to warn Baker before he set out for Suakin that in the event he did not feel confident of his troops he should "remain and defend Suakin, however painful the consequences might be as regards the garrisons of Sinkat and Tokar."[6]

Baker and his force of 3,715 had no sooner landed at Suakin on December 27, 1883, than he received a change of orders from Sir Evelyn Wood. The Sirdar, nominally in behalf of the Khedive but really of the British who had just installed Nubar Pasha as their more malleable Prime Minister, conveyed a more conservative approach to the eastern Sudan. Baker's new instructions, of vital consequence to Gordon's mission, canceled the plan to open the Suakin-Berber escape route. Baker was permitted to relieve the Sinkat and

Tokar garrisons only if he could guarantee success. His orders read: ". . . sacrifice [of these garrisons] is better than you and your troops should attempt a task which you cannot fairly reckon to be within your power."[7]

In actuality this was the voice of Baring, who had grown very uneasy about this whole operation. Baker was subjected to new, watered-down instructions which exuded lack of confidence in his force. In fact, the Gendarmerie was not an effective fighting force, but Baker had confidence in himself and was fiercely determined to accomplish his original mission to relieve Tokar and Sinkat.

On February 2, 1884, Baker's men marched out from Trinkitat toward Tokar. Two days later at an oasis called El Teb, a thousand Hadendowas led by Osman Digna swept down upon the unprepared Egyptians. Baker's cavalry bolted out of control, running down some of their own infantrymen. Before the panic-stricken Egyptians could regroup, the Hadendowas were upon them, cutting them up with their spears and knives. The British War Office official report later described the battle as "a scene of butchery which has probably never been rivalled." More than two thousand Egyptians were killed, while the rest ran for their lives back to Trinkitat. Baker reported disdainfully: ". . . only threatened by a small force of the enemy, certainly less than 1,000-strong, the Egyptian troops threw down their arms and ran, carrying away the black troops [southern Sudanese] with them and allowing themselves to be killed without the slightest resistance."[8]

London hastened to dissociate itself from this debacle, which had followed closely on the heels of Hicks's disaster. Lord Derby for the government announced: "It is a misfortune, but it is a misfortune for which we, sitting in London, can hardly hold ourselves responsible." In the House of Commons, Prime Minister Gladstone himself observed: "Baker Pasha was under no military necessity to undertake this expedition."[9] But if the politicians in London persisted in pretending that the Egyptian government had a will of its own and could thus be made to bear the blame for El Teb, Baring in Cairo was honest enough to shoulder the blame himself. "Manifestly, they [the Egyptians] could form no independent opinion of the military value of General Baker's force. The main responsibility, therefore, rests on the [British] authorities in Cairo, and notably on myself."[10]

Baring now second-guessed himself. After the sad news of Baker's defeat reached him he realized that he should have followed his instincts that either the general "should not have been sent to Suakin or, if sent, should have received no discretionary power to advance."[11]

To save Suakin from its own panic, if not from Osman Digna's Hadendowa warriors, Admiral Hewett, standing offshore, was ordered to land his Royal Marines to defend Suakin by force if necessary. For all Gladstone's opposition to involvement, in the Sudan, British troops now patrolled Suakin!

The strategic importance of Suakin on the Red Sea route to India placed it in a different category from the rest of the Sudan. The policy which bound Gordon was not applicable to Suakin, although this was difficult to explain to the Sudanese—nor could Gordon understand it either. The El Teb disaster and Osman Digna's control of the eastern Sudan called for prompt remedial measures. Hewett's five hundred marines could hold Suakin for the moment, but sterner action would be required.

London hurried to prepare a British force with which to relieve Tokar and avenge Baker's defeat. Lieutenant General Sir Frederick Stephenson, now Commander in Chief of British forces in Egypt, was placed in charge of the operation, while Gordon's old friend Major General Sir Gerald Graham was chosen to command the expeditionary force. Herbert Stewart would lead the cavalry and Colonel Sir Redvers Buller would command the infantry. In all, four thousand men would establish a base in Trinkitat from which to launch the campaign.

News of the El Teb defeat caused an uproar in England. First Hicks, now this! Gladstone's opponents leaped at the opportunity to attack the great Liberal. The government was no longer able to shift the blame to Egypt. Some newspapers suggested that "conniving at a slaughter of Egyptian troops" ranked with the Bulgarian atrocities. The *Times* quoted an unnamed but "prominent" person as saying, "I am ashamed to call myself an Englishman,"[12] and a mass meeting was held at Mansion House to condemn the government's Sudan policy. The influential Anti-Slavery Society saw Gladstone's passive policy as encouraging the revival of slavery. The Prime Minister, who at times seemed to be an apologist for the Mahdi, referring to his followers as "a people rightly struggling to be free," offended opponents of slavery who realized that a Mahdi victory would result in a resumption of unrestricted slaving.

Gordon did not hear the bad news of El Teb until he arrived in Berber on

February 11. Awaiting him there was a telegram from Lord Granville asking if El Teb affected his judgment about proceeding to Khartoum. Gordon's reply was prompt: "I must say it would reflect discredit on our name to recall me. . . ." He also expressed confidence that "God will bless our efforts."[13]

Gladstone personally drafted a second message to Gordon describing the plan to land a British force in Suakin: "Would such a step injure or assist your mission?" Gordon was opposed to such a military operation and replied: "As to sending forces to Suakin to assist withdrawal, I would care more for rumours of such intervention than for forces."[14] Gladstone, however, was once again forced to bow to public pressure, and efforts were begun to organize a British expeditionary force.

Still another blow fell. On February 12 the imperiled Sinkat garrison tried to break out, only to be massacred by Osman Digna's tribes. This news triggered more criticism of Gladstone and provoked a formal debate in Parliament on a Vote of Censure. To save itself, the government moved rapidly forward and ordered General Graham to proceed to Suakin. The *Times* put its finger on the apparent contradiction inherent in this policy: "At Khartoum General Gordon is offering peace and liberty in the name of England to the population akin to those which General Graham at Trinkitat, also in the name of England, must put to the sword."[15]

Even before arriving in Khartoum, Gordon realized this inconsistency. As he met with the local notables in Berber, he worried over it. As he viewed the situation, El Teb had hurt British and Egyptian prestige while Graham's invasion reduced his credibility as a man of peace. In order to restore his credibility, he now played his lone card: an offer of tribal autonomy.

After "pondering all night," Gordon made up his mind to "open Pandora's box." Colonel Stewart noted in his journal of February 12 that he had been called by Gordon at 5:00 A.M. and told of the decision to proclaim openly "the divorce of the Sudan from Egypt." Stewart argued against it, fearing the Sudanese, left "to stew in their own juice," would flock to the Mahdi's banner. Ignoring his assistant's warning, Gordon within hours called before him Hussein Pasha Khalifa, Mudir of Berber, and Mohammed Tahir, judge of the Civil Court, and showed them the Khedive's secret *firmans*. Shortly afterward he read the proclamation in public in nearby Metemmeh, announcing the Khedive's decision to evacuate Egyptians from the Sudan.

Gordon felt strongly at the time that the announcement turning the Sudan over to the Sudanese would help improve Egyptian prestige. The prospect of self-rule and the benefits to be derived from it would distract the Sudanese from the Egyptian failure at El Teb, he hoped; it would make an orderly evacuation possible without further massacres. While Gordon would be proved wrong, he had not acted illogically. Without an announcement spelling out Egyptian intentions, the moment evacuation operations actually began in Khartoum the Sudanese would know that the Egyptians were leaving the country. By linking the evacuation with the "gift" of self-rule rather than having it appear as a stark retreat under pressure, Gordon could at least hope that the withdrawal might be peaceful.

The sheikhs of Berber were excited by the prospects of "getting luscious governmental plums." A deputation of notables came immediately to ask about the benefits to be expected. But Stewart was dubious about the wisdom of Gordon's act and described it in his journal as "a leap in the dark." He wrote Baring apprehensively that he could only "hope for the best."[16] Baring, too, had his doubts, believing that the situation after El Teb was too unclear to rush into this gamble.

Not until many years later could it be learned from European prisoners of the Mahdi how the Ansar greeted Gordon's important pronouncement. They were jubilant; in the face of the Mahdi's invincibility the Egyptians and their British masters had capitulated! The Mudir of Berber's own decision to join the Mahdi had been directly triggered by what Gordon had told him about Egyptian intentions to withdraw. The Mudir in conversation with Slatin in the Mahdi's camp later claimed to have warned Gordon in Berber against publicly announcing the contents of the *firman* and could not understand "what induced him to disregard [this] advice almost immediately afterward at Metemmeh."[17]

The Mudir viewed Gordon's announcement as a tragic mistake which later led to the fall of Berber, thus dooming Khartoum by cutting it completely off from Egypt. Slatin at the time wondered that Gordon did not seem to understand the force of the Mahdi, and in his memoir asked rhetorically: ". . . how could he expect them [the tribes] to help him when in the words of that fatal proclamation, it was decreed that they were to be abandoned to their fate. . . ."[18]

From his vantage point within the Mahdi's camp, Ohrwalder saw the nature of the Mahdi's movement with such clarity that it was difficult to understand how Gordon's presence in Khartoum could accomplish anything. The Mahdi's revolt was not political, in Father Ohrwalder's opinion, and therefore it was not susceptible to a negotiated truce. It was a religious movement, a militantly religious movement. "Had Gordon only known before how boundless was the wild fanaticism and how completely the Mahdi's followers were intoxicated by it, he would not have accepted the mission."[19]

If Gordon misjudged the psychology of the Sudanese, he also misjudged the fervor with which the British would react to issues of slavery—else, typically, he did not care. The problem arose when a delegation of Berber's leading citizens asked the new Governor General the question uppermost in their minds: Would the 1877 landmark edict freeing the slaves in 1889 be nullified by the Egyptian withdrawal from the Sudan? Bowing to the hard reality, Gordon assured them that the slaves would not have to be freed, and immediately issued a proclamation announcing: ". . . none shall interfere with your property; whoever has slaves shall have full right to their services." While this was greeted with joy in the Sudan, it caused outrage and anger in England. Gordon, who had crushed Zubair's slaving empire, was now a traitor to the antislavery cause.

Parliament rang with voices of condemnation. Sir Stafford Northcote was cheered when he asked accusingly if "General Gordon's powers extended to the issue of such a proclamation." Baring defended Gordon and telegraphed Granville on February 21 that the general's announcement was "of very little practical importance"; obviously the 1877 edict could not be enforced once Egyptian troops were withdrawn. The British Consul General pointed out that it was "easy enough to understand his reasons for making it."[20] Gordon's champion the *Pall Mall Gazette* loyally editorialized: "The Government stood by their agent with commendable courage and, as is usual when responsible authorities well informed as to the facts resist the clamors of ill-informed public opinion, the cry subsided."[21]

Gordon, who had promulgated the 1877 edict banning slavery, though he even then had doubts as to its workability, felt it would be impossible to overturn a social and economic institution with deep roots in the Sudan by simple fiat. His contention was that if the slave traffic could be stamped out, then slavery would in time die a natural death. Issuing the edict now in a bid for Sudanese tribal support did not seem to Gordon a great sacrifice, but opinion in London was otherwise.

Stewart agreed with Gordon on this issue, writing in his journal on February 15: ". . . it would really seem as if this proposed liberation of the slaves in 1889 was one of the important cause of the present revolt."[22] Baring likewise agreed with Gordon—perhaps influenced by Stewart's judgment. Since Mahdi rule in the Sudan would surely see the revival of the slave trade, Baring thought the Anti-Slavery Society should welcome any act which lessened the Mahdi's power. Unfortunately, "The Society failed to see this"; engrossed in detail, "they forgot the main principle."[23]

Gordon entered Khartoum in triumph. The Sudanese crowded the docking area to welcome the steamer *Tewfikieh*, which brought him from Berber. As he walked through the narrow streets to the Governor's mansion where he had spent many lonely hours, the townfolk surged around him, those who could get close enough kissing his hands and feet, and the crowds adoringly called him "Father." He delivered a short speech, saying: "I come without soldiers but with God on my side to redress the evils of the Sudan. I will not fight with any weapons but justice." In the enthusiasm of the moment, the ecstatic townspeople did not think about the implications of Gordon's not bringing soldiers, particularly British soldiers, to defend the city, or the inconsistency of his peaceful professions while British marines were being landed in Suakin.

As *Times* correspondent Power jubilantly reported: "The Government books, recording from time immemorial the outstanding debts of the overtaxed people, were publicly burned in front of the Palace. The *kourbashes*, whips and other instruments used for administering the bastinado in Government House were all placed on the burning pile. The evidence of debts and the emblems of oppression perished together."[24]

Colonel Stewart was less exuberant in his private reports to Baring and could see the difficulties looming. On February 17, he wrote: "I must confess, the more one looks at it, the more difficult it becomes."[25] From Father Ohrwalder's vantage point in the Mahdi's camp, the public rejoicing at Gordon's arrival in Khartoum in February did not bespeak any particular confidence in Gordon's own efforts. The significance of Gordon was, in his opinion, that he was a precursor of an English expedition to take possession of the Sudan for England. Ohrwalder later commented: "Had the people of Khartoum realized that this was not the case, not a soul would have remained in Khartoum [and] the evacuation originally ordered could have been carried out without difficulty."[26]

Gordon's arrival in Khartoum was heralded in London as well. While the British were jubilant, Gladstone and the Liberals were relieved. The timing was fortunate, and they basked in the general euphoria. News of Gordon's safe landing at Khartoum reached London on the eve of the concluding day of debate on censure. The public celebration along with the announced resolve to send an expeditionary force to secure Suakin saved Gladstone's government.

The debate on censure ended on an ominous note as far as the Sudan's fate was concerned. On February 19, Lord Hartington articulated government policy when he flatly said, ". . . we are not responsible for the rescue or relief of the garrisons in the western or southern or the eastern Sudan."[27] Suakin, because of its strategic position astride the Red Sea route to India, was a special case, but the Minister of War's statement signaled an abrupt departure from Gladstone's policy enunciated at Albert Hall on January 25. At that time, referring to the relief of the Egyptian garrisons in the Sudan, Gladstone's son Herbert, speaking for his father, had said: "The Government would bear that responsibility without resigning it to others." Now a few weeks later, England had no such responsibility. But this crucial shift in policy was not transmitted to Gordon.

British policy problems with regard to the Sudan flowed from the clash between Gladstone's fundamental aversion to British involvement in the Sudan and the public's jingoistic urges, which found focus in Gordon's daring Khartoum mission. The issue was complicated by the several factions in Gladstone's government, one faction of which was led by Minister of War Hartington and favored a more forward policy. The Queen as well was opposed to Gladstone's isolationism and caution. But if there was a discordant chorus in London, the cacophony which issued from Gordon's one-man band in Khartoum was no less confusing. Caught between them was Baring, who had his own ideas but tried valiantly to reconcile London's shifting positions with Gordon's erratic and contradictory messages.

What neither Baring nor London understood or made allowances for was Gordon's stream-of-consciousness style of communication. The general had a fertile and imaginative mind, but from a bureaucratic point of view he had an unfortunate habit of sharing his fast-changing perceptions with Cairo and London as they occurred to him in a torrent of telegrams and dispatches. Each message was meant not as a definitive statement, simply as another shutter opening to reveal his thoughts of the moment. Gordon himself once warned the readers of his messages: "Do not put any confidence in what I will do, for long before you get my letter, circumstances may have altered. My letters are the impressions of the moment and I cannot be bound by them."

This style confused his readers, and for those who thought Gordon was an eccentric anyway, his erratic reporting confirmed such opinion. Compounding the confusion was the primitive communication link on which Gordon had to rely. The sequence of messages was often shuffled and the content garbled. Baring, as a way station for messages between Khartoum and London, tried to bring order out of confusion, but the task was not easy.

Baring and Gordon did not have either a congenial or a compatible relationship, but Baring was supportive of Gordon's efforts. Baring realized that he, much less London, could not keep up with the fast-breaking events in the Sudan, and thus counseled the Foreign Office to give Gordon his head. But this obvious wisdom was lost on a government prone to meddle. In some ways London's reservations about Gordon's judgments were justified. The general may have been on the scene and was thoroughly versed in Sudan lore, but he was woefully wrong in his estimation of the Mahdi.

Critics of Gordon who pointed to his confusing messages as evidence that he lacked good judgment failed to take into account that he had to adjust repeatedly not only to shifts or ambiguities in London but to changes in the situation within the Sudan. With every week that passed, as more tribes flocked to his banner, the Mahdi grew more powerful. With every battle won, the Mahdi's Ansar warriors became better equipped and better able to win the next one.

In one regard, at least, Gordon's instincts were sound; he believed that the British government must be prepared to introduce troops to stop the Mahdi—or hold him at bay until an evacuation of the Egyptians could be accomplished—if his strategy of winning over the tribes north and east of Khartoum failed to work.[28] When Gladstone made it clear he opposed such military intervention—except in Suakin—he doomed Gordon's mission in Khartoum.

30

TROUBLE IN SUAKIN

So 'ere's to you, Fuzzy-Wuzzy, at your 'ome in the Sowdan;
You're a pore benighted 'eathen but a first class fightin' man.
An' 'ere's to you, Fuzzy-Wuzzy, with your 'ayrick 'ead of hair—
You big black boundin' beggar—for you bruk a British square.
—Rudyard Kipling, "Fuzzy-Wuzzy"

ebruary was a critical month for the Sudan. It opened with the
surprising recommendation from Gordon that the Egyptians continue to play a role in the Sudan after all. While he had little respect
for Egypt, if self-rule was to work, there had to be some power behind it.

Even before arriving in Khartoum, Gordon wrote Baring on February 8,
from the Nile village of Abu Hamed, that the Egyptians could usefully
exercise a loose suzerain role with only advisory powers over the autonomous
tribes. Zubair, in Gordon's opinion, was still "the only man who
is fit for Governor General." Baring, however, had received contrary
opinions from Colonel Stewart. It was clear that Stewart with Gordon's
knowledge served as Baring's eyes in Khartoum, and it was his view which
had the most impact on the Consul General. The "nursemaid," as Gordon
referred to Stewart, kept the parent advised of the precocious child's
progress.

Stewart did not think Egypt's prestige was very high in the Sudan, and he
considered the sending of Zubair "a dangerous experiment."[1] In another
letter dated February 13, Stewart characterized Gordon as being "so full of
sympathy for the people that he is inclined to use every effort to mitigate the
effort of our withdrawal."[2] Baring perceived that Gordon's views were at this
time indeed undergoing a change. He believed that Gordon was becoming
emotionally involved, and concern for the Sudanese was competing with
expediency in his thinking.

As Gordon arrived in Khartoum, he shifted his position once again.
Because of the inevitable chaos following an Egyptian withdrawal, the

loose Egyptian suzerainty would not suffice, he feared, and the more he thought about the perfidious Egyptians, even in a modest role as advisers, the more he realized that the Sudanese would not—and should not—put up with them. His new formula called for Her Majesty's government to step in and exercise the suzerain responsibility. Gordon favored the "Afghan" model in which Zubair, like the Emir of Afghanistan, would be installed within the framework of general British "moral" support, without British soldiers or subsidy. In this scenario Egypt would be totally out of the picture.

Colonel Stewart's views were also changing. While still cautious about Zubair, he wrote Baring, admitting that Gordon's ideas "would greatly facilitate our retirement from the country."[3] As Stewart came over to Gordon's way of thinking, so did Baring, and the Consul General telegraphed the Foreign Minister on February 19: "I believe Zubair Pasha to be the only possible man. He undoubtedly possesses energy and ability, and has great local influence." As for the fear that the old slaver would permit or encourage a revival of the slave trade, Baring endorsed Gordon's opinion that Zubair's presence would make little difference since slaving was bound to return anyway without a European enforcer. Gordon's solution to cut the Sudan off from the source of slaves by ceding the southern provinces of Equatoria and Bahr al-Ghazal to the Congo, to be administered by himself under King Leopold's authority, was an ingenious one. Baring, however, with higher imperial policy considerations in mind, could not go that far and consistently vetoed suggestions from Gordon that he go to the south and arrange this scheme of things.

In general, Baring's thinking was now in concert with Gordon's, except that he did not believe that Gordon and Zubair could peacefully coexist in Khartoum. As Gordon's old friend Watson had warned in Cairo, Zubair would probably kill Gordon to avenge the execution of his son, Suleiman. Nor did Baring agree with Gordon's idea that Zubair be given British moral support, on the grounds that such support would be meaningless. But the Consul General did agree that Zubair's appointment should have the "approbation of Her Majesty's Government"; it was a fine point of distinction which only diplomats could make.

In the meantime, in Khartoum Gordon pursued a strategy of conciliation and peace. He stopped movements of Egyptian troops which could be construed as threatening to the Mahdi. He invited Sheikh el-Obeid, leader of the Mahdist tribes along the Blue Nile, to discuss peace, and opened Khartoum to normal trade with the surrounding areas.

Atmospherics were important if a peaceful evacuation was to take place. Gordon, for example, ordered Khartoum's Egyptian troops to Omdurman, across the Nile from Khartoum, to await transport by steamer to Berber as a demonstration of his intention to evacuate them, leaving Khartoum guarded only by Sudanese troops. Egyptian and other foreign women and children had also prepared for movement north to Egypt. These were concrete and highly visible actions in fulfillment of his mission. Before events stopped him, he had successfully evacuated more than two thousand persons—a feat which the Cabinet could not recognize in its growing conviction that Gordon never seriously intended to evacuate the Egyptians.

Times correspondent Power reported enthusiastically on Gordon: "It is wonderful that one man could have such influence on twenty thousand people."[4] The general did everything he could to raise Khartoum's morale and calm public fear. Over his desk—or "throne," as he facetiously called it—he mounted a large plaque bearing a message in Arabic: "God rules the hearts of all men." But not everyone was pleased by Gordon's gestures of peace. Gordon's reliance on God alone was met by skepticism, and the town Council of Notables complained that it was premature to strip Khartoum of any of its defenses.

While uneasiness increased in Khartoum as more Egyptian troops prepared to go, General Graham and a four-thousand-man British expeditionary force was about to reach Suakin. Hearing this, the Mahdi's followers began to distrust Gordon's peace protestations, and on February 24, Khartoum received word that Mahdist tribes had surrounded an Egyptian force up the Blue Nile. The tribes around Khartoum grew nervous. They asked themselves what advantage there could be to remain with Gordon, who, incredibly, was emptying out his garrison in Khartoum just as British troops were about to land in Suakin. Joining the Mahdi was becoming a more attractive alternative.

Gordon received another blow when Admiral Hewett on February 19 refused to issue a proclamation calling on Suakin sheikhs to meet Gordon in

Khartoum to talk peace. Hewett considered it an act of deceit on the British part to encourage gestures of peace when "English troops are about to be sent against the people in question."[5]

London, similarly, was skeptical of Gordon's plans. Lord Granville vetoed Gordon's and Baring's request for Zubair when in a message of February 22 he stated: " . . . public opinion of this country would not tolerate the appointment of Zubeir [Zubair] Pasha."[6] Although Gordon had given some consideration to Hussein Pasha Khalifa, Mudir of Berber, as an alternative candidate for Governor General, he had dismissed the thought on the grounds that the Mudir's power was too local. While dejected at Granville's rejection of Zubair, Gordon tried to think of other strategies.

As Granville was blocking Gordon on a policy level, Khartoum's officials were spoiling his peace policy on a tactical level. When ominous reports began to drift in that the Mahdi was distributing rifles to the tribes around Khartoum, even tribes traditionally friendly with the government threatened to join the Mahdi. Gordon's peace initiatives, discredited by news of the imminent British invasion of Suakin, disintegrated altogether when Khartoum's Council of Notables insisted that a column be sent to relieve the Egyptian commander, Saleh Bey, who was still surrounded by hostile tribes farther up the Blue Nile.

To salvage some personal credibility, Gordon sent word to Sheikh el-Obeid, who controlled most of the east bank of the White Nile north of Khartoum as far as Shendi, that military measures had been imposed upon him by the Council of Notables. Gordon, in fact, was only putting on a show of force and had no intention of involving his troops in serious combat at this time. To emphasize this, Gordon sent Colonel Stewart by steamer down the White Nile with a military escort to distribute proclamations promising peace if the tribes would remain loyal. Stewart noted in the February 18 entry in his journal that the people received the pamphlets he distributed "with joy . . . especially the ones cancelling the Slave Liberty Treaty."[7]

Back in London, however, the injudicious language of Gordon's telegram caused a minor scandal. The message, which read, "Expedition starts at once to attack rebels," provoked Sir Charles Dilke to rant that Gordon's message "frightened us out of our senses."[8] But Sir Charles was even more aroused by another Gordon telegram stating that he had issued a proclamation announcing: "British troops are now on their way and in a few days will reach

Khartoum."[9] Dilke branded this an "amazing lie," but his wrath knew no bounds when on the next day Gordon referred to "smashing up the Mahdi" and asked for £100,000 and two hundred Indian troops to be garrisoned in Wadi Halfa. Dilke growled: "We were evidently dealing with a wild man under the influence of the climate of Central Africa which acts even upon the sanest men like strong drink."[10]

Baring at this point was more confused than perturbed. Since leaving London, Gordon had proposed a bewildering array of actions, most requiring a policy change. On January 18, he talked only of reporting on the feasibility of evacuation. On January 24, he insisted on being made Governor General with executive powers, and charted a strategy to turn the Sudan over to the traditional sultans. On February 8 he recommended "evacuation but not abandonment," with Egypt remaining suzerain. By February 18 Gordon had changed the suzerain formula so that Great Britain itself, according to the Afghan model, would hover over the country giving "moral support," while Zubair as Governor General ruled a federation of hereditary sultans. On February 26, after London had rejected the Zubair plan and the Mahdi had shown no sign of reaching an agreement, Gordon suggested "smashing up the Mahdi" with the help of two hundred crack Indian troops.

Then three days later a sixth idea—one that made more military sense—called for Indian troops in Suakin to open the Suakin-Berber desert route to Khartoum. This latter idea seemed so logical that it probably was what inspired Gordon's proclamation announcing the imminent arrival of British troops in Khartoum. While Gordon's announcement was not based on fact and may have been meant as a psychological warfare gambit, he must at least have hoped that the gambit would give rise to fact.

Prime Minister Gladstone complained to the House of Commons that Gordon seemed to have forgotten the stipulation, made before he left England, that no British force would be used to aid him in his mission. Of course, before Gordon arrived in the Sudan he could not have foreseen that a full-fledged British fighting force would be launched in Suakin within striking distance of Khartoum, thus spoiling any chance of peaceful evacuation of the Egyptian garrisons. Nor did he anticipate that his strategy to use Zubair—the alternative to British troops—would be vetoed by London despite Baring's endorsement, especially as Gordon's instructions gave Baring virtually total authority.

Baring, trying to be objective in his memoir, believed that there had been an "underlying vein of common sense" in Gordon's apparent inconsistencies. Certainly at the time, he persisted in arguing the case for using Zubair as leader of a federation of autonomous sultans. The Consul General, probably prompted by Stewart, who now staunchly backed Gordon's plan, realized that some kind of viable buffer state had to be left in the Sudan so that the Mahdi would not be tempted to proselytize or conquer the tribes of southern Egypt as well.

Baring pleaded his case with Lord Granville in a message dated February 28: "From every point of view, whether political, military or financial, it will be a most serious matter if complete anarchy is allowed to reign south of Wadi Halfa."[11] Refusing to give even lip service to the myth of Egyptian autonomy in such matters, Baring pointedly added: "Her Majesty's Government must in reality be responsible for any arrangements which are now devised for the Sudan and I do not think it is possible to shake off that responsibility." The only alternative, in Baring's opinion, was to let Gordon and the Khedive do what seemed best, and that meant sending Zubair to succeed Gordon. English public opinion was violently against using the infamous slaver, but Baring argued that "any attempt to settle Egyptian questions by the light of English popular feeling is sure to be productive of harm. . . ."[12]

It is significant that while Gladstone himself was ill in bed when Whitehall reviewed the Zubair proposal, he was known to favor it. He favored almost any solution that would not require a British presence. Without Gladstone's strong personal intervention, the House of Commons would not approve the Zubair plan, and the Cabinet opposed the idea rather than arouse the antislavery lobby. Still in bed, he gave in to the Cabinet.

There had also been a theory bruited about within the Cabinet that Zubair might secretly have had a hand in inciting the tribes to join the Mahdi. Even Gordon, when asked about this, admitted the possibility that Zubair had stirred up the tribes to revolt "in hopes that he would be sent to quell it." But that only confirmed Gordon's insistence that Zubair had the necessary power to control the situation in the Sudan.

When the Zubair plan seemed doomed, Gordon rashly decided to take his case to the British public, whose clamor had been responsible for his going to the Sudan in the first place. Using Power in his *Times* capacity, he issued a press statement regarding the use of Zubair. On his own initiative, Power had in fact sent a dispatch to the *Times* describing the Zubair plan a few days before, so Gordon was not the first to leak the story as he had been accused. But to lend his name to the idea gave it added prominence. Baring was furious, particularly when Gordon threatened to resign if his proposals were not accepted. To bypass Baring, moreover, when the Consul General was still doing his best to plead the case was foolhardy on the part of Gordon.

When the story, directly quoting Gordon, broke in the London press on March 9, the antislavery forces rose in righteous wrath and attacked him bitterly. This made it impossible for Gladstone to reverse his Cabinet's position, even if he had been willing to do so. Mr. Sturge, chairman of the Anti-Slavery Society, informed Lord Granville that the society was "unanimous in the feeling that to countenance any . . . such an individual [Zubair] by the British Government would be a degradation for England and a scandal for Europe."[13] Public exposure of the plan also made Zubair realize his importance in the Sudan solution, and if the plan was implemented, he surely would take full advantage of the bargaining position it gave him.

Gordon, who was chastised by Baring for his press indiscretions, rationalized his act in a later journal entry, explaining that he went to the press "on purpose to save Her Majesty's Government the odium of such a step." This was contrived reasoning. Not only was the episode an example of Gordon's flagrant lack of discipline, but it revealed a woeful lack of understanding of public sentiment on the issue of slavery. Only Gordon's frustration and desperation could explain his action. If the Zubair plan was not already beyond resuscitation—which it probably was—Gordon had finished it.

Baring now was reluctant to back Gordon in his recommendation to use British force in Khartoum. The Consul General believed that Gordon's "combative spirit completely got the better of him. . . . As a soldier, he could not brook the idea of retiring before the Mahdi."[14] The specter of British forces evacuating Egyptian garrisons in the face of the Mahdi's power was not a pleasant one; there was fear that Hicks's humiliating defeat would be reenacted. In another scenario, the use of force could lead to the British conquering the Mahdi and occupying the Sudan indefinitely, a step against which Gladstone's government recoiled. Lord Northbrook put his finger on the problem by criticizing Gordon for "hankering after the *ignis fatuus* of arranging for a settled government of a country which could not be settled excepting by a lengthened and possibly a permanent occupation in force."[15]

That Great Britain thirteen years later decided that it must conquer and indefinitely occupy the Sudan for reasons of empire—principally to protect its critical Red Sea route to India—suggests that Gordon's insistence on finding some alternative to the Mahdi's rule, even if it required British force, was more wise than the negative views of the Cabinet. How London had been willing to plan a dynamic military action in Suakin and not plan to use the same expeditionary force to evacuate at least the Khartoum garrison strains comprehension. Under the circumstances, Gordon could be forgiven for believing that British forces would, if necessary, help to keep open the Suakin-Berber corridor of escape—and for encouraging the Sudanese to believe it as well.

Major General Graham's army was assembled at the Trinkitat base near Suakin on February 28. Sent from the British garrison in Cairo were the 19th Hussars, 1st Black Watch, 1st Gordon Highlanders, and 3rd King's Royal Rifle Corps. These units were joined by the 10th Hussars, 1st York and Lancaster, and the 2nd Royal Irish Fusiliers, diverted to Trinkitat while en route home from India. Already in the area were Admiral Hewett's Royal Marines. Some four thousand troops in all were poised to strike; they must break Osman Digna's power hold in the eastern Sudan.

Graham gave due warning by issuing a proclamation calling on Osman Digna to disband his forces. The Hadendowa leader predictably ignored the order, and the British force advanced toward his encampment at El Teb on February 29. The square was formed, anchored at all four corners by 7-pounders, and advanced steadily toward Osman Digna's left flank. The Hadendowas, estimated at six thousand men, soon lost their guns to British fire, the same guns taken from Baker's fleeing Egyptians, and were forced to charge the British with only their cunning, bravery and spears. The Black Watch Regiment was in the lead. Faced with trenches filled with Hadendowa spearmen, the Highlanders resorted to mass slaughter to clear the way, causing Graham later to chastise them for excessive firing, and stimulating considerable criticism in England for their brutality.

The 10th and 19th Hussars were surprised by a large group of tribesmen concealed in the low scrub. The Hussars charged several times while the tribesmen, lying prone in the brush, thrust their spears upward to pierce the bellies of the British mounts. Only when the Hussars finally dismounted and fired their carbines from a standing position could they rout their attackers; they did so only after suffering twenty dead and forty-eight wounded. The battle was won by the British, but it was testimony nonetheless to the courage of the Hadendowas, most of whom stubbornly refused to yield ground until killed. Total British casualties in the three-hour battle were thirty-four dead and 155 wounded, while Hadendowa casualties numbered more than two thousand dead. Osman Digna, however, was not defeated.

A second engagement took place at the wells of Tamai on March 13. This time the British were pressed more dangerously, and only with difficulty avoided disaster. Graham's troops advanced in two brigade-sized squares. In the front square were the 1st Black Watch, again positioned in the lead, a naval contingent, and the 1st York and Lancaster, followed at one thousand yards by the rest of the infantry in a second square. The lead brigade was surprised by a horde of frenzied Hadendowa warriors who erupted from a ravine where they had lain in wait—essentially the same tactic they had used before. The British square, overcome with smoke and fumes from their own guns and confused by a misguided order to charge shouted out by Graham, faltered, then broke when a critically placed machine gun jammed and let the tribesmen pour through the gap. As the Hadendowas cut and slashed, they took a terrible toll, terrifying the British with their savage fervor.

It was this engagement that inspired Kipling's famous poem in Cockney accent memorializing the "Fuzzy-Wuzzies," as he called the bushy-haired, "hayrack" Hadendowas, and earning them the distinction of having been the first to break the vaunted British square. Its final stanza:

> 'E rushes at the smoke when we let drive,
>> An', before we know, 'e's 'ackin' at our 'ead;
> 'E's all 'ot sand an' ginger when alive,
>> An' 'e's generally shammin' when 'e's dead.
> 'E's a daisy, 'e's a ducky, 'e's a lamb!
>> 'E's a injia-rubber idiot on the spree,
> 'E's the on'y thing that doesn't give a damn
>> For the Regiment o' British Infantree.
>>> So 'ere's *to* you, Fuzzy-Wuzzy, at your 'ome in the
>>> Sowdan;
>>> You're a pore benighted 'eathen but a first-class fightin'
>>> man.

THE MOSLEM MESSIAH AND THE CHRISTIAN MARTYR

An' 'ere's *to* you, Fuzzy-Wuzzy, with your 'ayrick
'ead of hair—
You big black boundin' beggar—for you bruk a British
square.

Redvers Buller drew up with the 1st Gordons, 2nd Royal Irish Fusiliers, and 3rd King's Royal Rifle Corps just in time to avert disaster. The beleaguered square was able to restore order; fierce hand-to-hand fighting and withering British fire finally pushed the Hadendowas back. The brave tribesmen left another two thousand dead and countless wounded on the battlefield. Despite bad generalship, British arms had again triumphed over native spears, but neither side was wanting in valor.

"Osman the Ugly," as the British press referred to Digna, and his Hadendowas had taken heavy losses, but they still remained a formidable fighting force. Nothing had been settled by the British action. The historian Charles Royle described the campaign as "a pointless concession to ill-constructed public opinion." Its usefulness, if any, would depend on whether or not it could assist in the evacuation of Egyptian troops from Khartoum.

On March 9, Gordon telegraphed Baring: "I shall await your decision [about Zubair]; if the wire is cut, I shall consider your silence is consent to my propositions, and shall hold on to Khartoum and await Zubair and British diversion at Berber." The general still hoped to send the Khartoum garrison to Berber, from where it could be escorted to Suakin by a British flying force. Baring, however, knew what Gordon did not yet know: The Cabinet had no intention of permitting Graham to advance to Berber.

While the Cabinet did not formally decide against sending British troops to Berber until March 25, Baring could see its position with enough clarity by March 9 to cable Gordon not to expect relief—even from the Turks, which had been another idea. Despite Baring's recommendation and Sir Evelyn Wood's endorsement that a relief force be sent from Suakin to Berber, Granville decided otherwise on the grounds of the "extraordinary risk" from a military point of view. Instead he instructed Graham to prepare his troops for rapid embarkation.

Without Zubair or British military help, Gordon found his position precarious. Most of the tribes around Khartoum, particularly those led by

Sheikh el-Obeid, were on the verge of joining with the Mahdi. Gordon's plan to return the Sudan to the hereditary sultans had been discredited by the Suakin invasion and the heavy casualties suffered by the Hadendowas. Moreover, the slender strand of telegraph wire keeping Khartoum in communications with Cairo was in imminent danger of being cut.

Gordon's last hope of conducting evacuation was to have Stewart try to take the Khartoum Egyptian garrison and non-Sudanese civilians to Berber anyway; Gordon would escape up the Nile to Equatoria and join Emin Pasha in defending the southern provinces, in the name of King Leopold of Belgium, against the Mahdi. After corresponding with London, Baring on March 12 ordered Gordon to hold Khartoum until he could sort things out with Granville (Baring had not yet given up on Zubair despite Gordon's disastrous interview in the *Times*). He forbade Gordon from proceeding to the south. This message never reached Gordon.

Baring warned Granville in late March that only two alternatives remained: He could hope Gordon would survive until the cooler weather of autumn, when a rescue campaign could be mounted, or he could immediately send a small detachment from General Graham's forces to open the road between Suakin and Berber, giving heart to the Khartoum garrison. Granville was adamant, however: "The distance, the nature of the country . . . and, above all, the climate render the march of a British force to Berber at the present season . . . impracticable."

On March 12 more than six thousand tribesmen swept into the area called Halfaya, only nine miles downstream from Khartoum, and cut the telegraph line. In a hurried letter to his sister Gordon wrote: "We hear the [enemy's] drums from the palace. . . . I have a great deal to do so you should not expect long letters." Two days later came the fateful news that Sheikh el-Obeid and all the tribes between Berber and Shendi had joined the Mahdi's revolt. Thereafter only messages sent by steamer to Berber through hostile territory or cryptic notes smuggled by spies would link Gordon with the outside world.

Halfaya and the rest of the area between Khartoum and Shendi were traditionally inhabited by Shaigiya tribesmen, noted for their military service to the government. When the Halfaya region was taken by the Ansar, a garrison of eight hundred loyal Shaigiyas was surrounded. However committed to a peaceful approach, Gordon was now forced to defend Khartoum from hostile encroachments. He was able to rescue the Shaigiyas with only three armed steamers, but a more serious challenge faced him two days later.

As tribesmen began menacing Khartoum at closer range, Gordon felt retaliation was in order if he was to defend the capital. A force of one thousand Egyptian and Sudanese troops, led by two Egyptian officers, Said Pasha and Hassan Pasha Ibrahim Eshellali, sallied forth to attack the nearby enemy within sight of Gordon's residency. In mid-battle, to the horror of the troops, the two commanding officers brandished their swords and decapitated the bugler, who was sounding the attack, and the gunner, who was directing artillery fire. Both officers then replaced their Egyptian fezes with Ansar turbans and ordered retreat. The betrayed troops broke and ran, barely making it back to Khartoum and safety behind the city walls.

The two turncoat officers were captured, court-martialed and executed for treason. Loyalty was a fragile thing, a discouraged Gordon learned. This defeat was demoralizing for the whole city. Gordon brooded over the episode, particularly over the execution, which was done Turkish-style—dismemberment and mutilation, culminating in decapitation.

Unaware of what had befallen Khartoum, Granville on March 13 sent a message to Baring stating that Gordon could remain in Khartoum to establish a settled government there, or he could save the garrison by taking it north to Berber without delay. Baring was aghast and quickly pointed out by return telegram the policy implications of permitting Gordon to stay indefinitely in Khartoum; it would "lead either to the Egyptian Government endeavoring to govern the Sudan unaided, or to a succession of English governors which must ultimately involve the English Government in becoming virtually responsible for the government of the Sudan."[16]

In another vain attempt to support Gordon's plan, Baring concluded: "His [Gordon's] main contentions appear to me to be perfectly clear and reasonable. They are, first, that the two questions of withdrawing the garrisons and of arranging for the future government of the country cannot be separated. Secondly that it is most undesirable, even if it be possible, for him to withdraw without leaving some permanent man to take his place. . . . no one but Zubair . . . to succeed Gordon."[17] But by now the issue of evacuating Khartoum was academic unless British troops were provided. It was too late for any other solution.

TROUBLE IN SUAKIN

With other avenues exhausted, Gordon turned his thoughts to personal diplomacy. His magnetism and force of will, when combined, had met through the years with remarkable success. Why not a meeting with the Mahdi? He had, in fact, discussed the possibility of visiting the Mahdi in a conversation with a Colonel Rhodes on the boat from Brindisi to Port Said. According to Gordon's brother Henry, the comments were casual and never intended to be taken seriously,[18] but they found their way to Cairo, where they horrified Baring. By the time the Consul General heard about it, Gordon had left Cairo for Khartoum; all Baring could do was fire off a frantic telegram to him saying: "I hope you will give me positive assurances that you will on no account put yourself voluntarily in the power of the Mahdi." Gordon, who was surprised by the message and its note of urgency, had quickly assured Baring that he had no intention of bearding the Mahdi in El Obeid. But now?

The only time Gordon had even written the Holy One was from Berber on February 11, when he presumptuously offered to name him Sultan of Kordofan if he would return power to the traditional chieftains elsewhere. According to Father Ohrwalder, the Mahdi had "laughed at Gordon's proposal," concluding that the General was "attempting to delude him with vain promises merely to gain time."[19] The messenger who had taken Gordon's letter to El Obeid reported that the Mahdi had written several drafts in reply, influenced each time perhaps by the events and his changing fortunes along the Red Sea coast. The Mahdi was puzzled that Gordon had arrived in Khartoum without troops, further convincing him that Gordon's letter was intended only as a tactic.

The Mahdi's reaction to Gordon's letter—after Admiral Hewett's landing in Suakin, reports of a British army en route to Trinkitat, and Osman Digna's defeats at El Teb and Tamai Wells—had been cautious. But when Graham's army withdrew leaving Osman Digna still in undisputed possession of the eastern Sudan (except Suakin), he could conclude that the British did not intend to use force to stop him. This may have accounted for the stern position he took in his reply to Gordon's letter.

The Mahdi's answer did not reach Gordon until March 27, when it was delivered by three Ansar envoys ("The demeanour of the emissaries was exceedingly cheeky") under a white flag of truce. The message read by one of the emissaries was uncompromising: "The Prophet cares not for those . . .

who worship other Gods and who forget that God is over all. The Prophet has informed me that those who declare enmity against me shall fail, and be conquered by the power of God." Gordon, however, was offered the hand of salvation if he would deliver himself up and "become a follower of the true religion," thereby gaining "honour in this world and in the world to come."[20] Otherwise, he warned, Gordon would perish.

In the event Gordon would accept his offer, the Mahdi had sent him appropriate clothing in which to appear before him: a patched *jibba*, the uniform of the faithful, and a turban. Gordon was, of course, incensed and hurled the bundle of clothes away in contempt. As retaliation, he sent to the Mahdi a red Egyptian tarboosh, a waistcoat, a pair of boots and a few coins. In a written reply to his adversary, Gordon rejected his claim as "The Mahdi of Allah" and forswore future negotiations or communications of any kind with him. He ordered the envoys to warn the Mahdi that the Ansar would be surrounded by the army of the Khedive and of Her Majesty the Queen.

The Mahdi's message and Gordon's reply ended any hope of peace. Gordon's peace policy had failed, if indeed it ever had any chance of succeeding. Hostilities were now inevitable. But it was Gordon who was surrounded, not the Mahdi. Sheikh el-Obeid controlled the Blue Nile in the Gezira region and was preparing to advance on Khartoum from the south. Saleh Wad el-Mek and his fourteen hundred men had surrendered at Fedasi to the Ansar Emir, Haji Mohammed Abu Girgeh, clearing the way for an attack on Buri at the south edge of Khartoum, while north of Khartoum the Ja'aliyin and Ababdeh tribes of Metemmeh were in position to attack the strategic town of Berber.

On March 25, Baring tried again to alert Lord Granville to the gravity of the situation. The government's negative stand on Zubair and its unwillingness to send British troops had made a bad situation worse. Khartoum was surrounded and out of effective communication. Steamers could not pass on the Nile if the rebels held both banks above the sixth cataract. And because of hostile tribes, Gordon could no longer lead the garrison overland to the north or by boat south to Equatoria. Baring pleaded once again for British or Indian forces: ". . . having sent Gordon to Khartoum, it appears to me that it is our bounden duty, both as a matter of humanity and policy, not to abandon him."[21] But Granville would not budge.

An outraged Queen Victoria made her views known at this point. She telegraphed the Minister of War, Lord Hartington, "Gordon is in danger. You are bound to try and save him. Surely, Indian troops might go from Aden: they could bear the climate. You have incurred great responsibility."[22] On the basis of the Queen's exhortation and Baring's "heavy cannon ball" message, as the Queen described it, Lord Hartington and Lord Granville spoke with Gladstone. Still the Prime Minister's response was that "imperfect knowledge" prevented the government from forming conclusions on a "remote and half-barbarous region."[23]

As March came to a close, Graham's force was withdrawn from the eastern Sudan except for a small defensive garrison left to hold Suakin. Denied the opportunity to save Gordon and the Khartoum garrison, General Graham ruefully observed later that his old friend "was appointed Moses of a new Exodus, but with the Red Sea closed against him."

Gordon, denied military relief, without telegraphic communications and completely surrounded by hostile tribesmen, could now only await the Mahdi with his grand army of Baggara horsemen and Dongolowi zealots. The siege had begun.

31

INDELIBLE DISGRACE

General Gordon and the others who have been faithful to the
Government are thrown over.
—*Times* correspondent Frank Power, Khartoum, March 23, 1884

A s spring came to Khartoum in 1884, suffocating dry heat descended on the parched land, bringing with it ink-black clouds
of dust, the dreaded *haboob*. No relief in the weather could
be expected until the light rains of July. No relief from the siege could be
expected until much later, if at all.

Gordon was near his wit's end. The Cabinet fumed about his messages
suggesting military aggression, but Gordon could see no alternative to
violence. The Mahdi had spurned his peace proposals, and London had
spoiled his strategy of peace by invading Suakin and attacking Osman Digna.
Fight or submit was his only real choice now. He and Stewart might be able
to escape from the beleaguered city by steamer, but this was unthinkable.
Gordon was not one to cut and run while the rest of the city was left to reap
the terrible whirlwind of the Mahdi's retribution. Nor would such an act do
credit to Britain's national honor. J. L. Garvin put it well in his biography of
Joseph Chamberlain: "If you send out a soldier to run away from those at
whose head you have placed him, you must not sent Gordon."[1]

At the end of March, Gordon revived the earlier proposal calling for a
Turkish relief force as a means to avoid direct British entanglement. On
February 11, Gordon had recommended sending a Turkish rather than
British army to Suakin to avenge Osman Digna's defeat of Baker at El Teb,
but now he suggested that the British finance three thousand Turkish
infantry and one thousand Turkish cavalry by public subscription to crush
the Mahdi himself. He realized "the time had gone by when Zubair almost
alone would suffice," so he pressed Baring to consider a Turkish expeditionary force as the best solution under the circumstances. "I get out of all

my troubles if the Turks come, for I shunt them [the Egyptians in the Sudan] on the Turks."

Baring thought Gordon's Turkish formula reflected the general's unwarranted personal commitment to save the Sudan from the Mahdi, an objective which he seemed to put before his mission to evacuate the Egyptians from Khartoum. In London the priorities were just the opposite; evacuation should first be accomplished.

Baring also believed—rightly so—that Gordon underestimated the power of the Mahdi. The Consul General doubted if the Turks with four thousand men could stop the momentum of this strange Messiah's movement which had already engulfed the Sudan. Gordon's glib comment ascribing to the revolt a "truly trumpery nature" and claiming that "500 determined men could put it down" was either wild hyperbole or an indication that he did not understand the true dimensions of the movement.

Receiving no response from London, Gordon on April 8 wrote Sir Samuel Baker, then in Cairo, suggesting he raise a Turkish army by public subscription or by tapping rich Americans. "We are hemmed in by . . . some 2,000 rag-bag Arbas," he said. Gordon even appealed directly to the Sultan of Turkey. Various schemes for privately mounted projects to rescue Gordon were also being bandied about.

Gordon joked with a disapproving Baring about this grim subject, writing that he could not see himself being forced "to walk about the streets for years as a dervish with sandaled feet." He overstepped the bounds of discipline, however, when in April he sent a message directly to Zubair appointing him Deputy Governor of the Sudan. Baring caught the message in time so it never reached the old slaver. Even if it had, it is unlikely that Zubair would have accepted Gordon's offer without demanding impossible terms, including relief from monumental debts which he had incurred.

The Turkish solution was politically unpalatable to the Cabinet and probably too late anyway in view of the Mahdi's power. Lord Granville concluded that the use of a Turkish expeditionary force "would involve a reversal of the original policy of Her Majesty's Government which was to detach the Soudan from Egypt, and restore to its inhabitants their former independence. . . ." This message, sent to Cairo but not seen by Gordon, accused the general of asking for Turkish troops "with a view to offensive operations . . . beyond the scope of his mission."[2]

THE MOSLEM MESSIAH AND THE CHRISTIAN MARTYR

Not having heard anything definite from London or Cairo, Gordon in exasperation sent Baring a strong message which reached him on April 17. The frustrated general lashed out at the Consul General, not knowing if the message would ever reach him. "You state your intentions of not sending any relief force up here or to Berber, and you refuse me Zubair. I consider myself free to act according to circumstances. I shall hold on here as long as I can; if I can suppress the rebellion, I shall do so. If I cannot, I shall retire to the Equator and leave you the indelible disgrace of abandoning the garrisons of Sennar, Kassala, Berber and Dongola with the certainty that you will eventually be forced to smash up the Mahdi under great difficulties if you would retain peace in Egypt."[3]

Gladstone, now recovered from his illness, had a short-lived triumph in Parliament. In his first appearance before the House, he brought cheers from friendly benches when he defended the government's handling of the Gordon situation. In reply to critical questions about Gordon, sparked by Frank Power's *Times* dispatch of March 23 implying government "abandonment" of Gordon, Gladstone claimed that Her Majesty's government had authorized the general only to advise and report. In a blatant example of buck-passing, the Prime Minister contended that the Egyptian government, not the British, had given Gordon executive powers to carry out the evacuation. Ignoring Gordon's obvious executive role as Governor General, Gladstone persisted in believing that the general had exceeded his instructions. Sir William Harcourt later commented on the Prime Minister's stellar performance that day: "With unparalleled eloquence, he withered them with the blast of his scornful indignation. . . . it was a rout."[4]

The general public, however, was not so easily convinced. Gordon was their popular hero, and the *Times* had just published a dispatch from Frank Power with disturbing news: "Khartoum is at present the center of an enormous rebel camp. The rebels' tents are within sight and their bullets often strike or go over the palace. . . . The situation is critical." Power's words bit deeply when he expressed his regret that General Gordon had been "abandoned" by the government. "Today," he wrote, "there arrived an unciphered telegram, sent by Sir Evelyn Baring, saying that no English troops will be sent to that place. In a word, General Gordon and the others who have been faithful to the Government are thrown over."[5]

Gladstone, who had assured Parliament that Gordon was only "hemmed

372

in," not "surrounded," and was in no danger, sent Gordon a fatuous message through Baring on April 23, ordering him to keep the government advised as to "immediate and prospective" danger at Khartoum and "to be prepared for such danger." Gordon was to advise the government "as to the force necessary in order to secure his removal," but no Turkish or other force would be sent "for the purpose of undertaking military expeditions."[6]

As a pall of apprehension blanketed Khartoum, Gordon busied himself with the defenses of the city. He had a force of 2,316 black Sudanese regulars, 1,421 Egyptian troops, 1,906 Bashi-Bazouks, or mercenaries from various Turkish subject peoples, 2,330 Shaigiya tribal irregulars and 692 volunteer townfolk—8,665 in all—to protect a population of some 34,000. Probably the most reliable were the southern blacks, a large number of ex-slaves, recruited by Gordon. These were excellent fighters, "the only troops we can depend upon," wrote Power. The Shaigiya force, on the other hand, was an uncertain ally at best, with a high rate of desertion. The tribe whose stronghold was Halfaya, just north of Khartoum, had been kept loyal only by the exertions of two exceptional sisters of the chief, Fatmeh and Nafiseh, who browbeat the tribal elders into supporting Gordon.

Gordon issued a local currency, redeemable in Cairo or Khartoum within six months, to keep the city's fragile economy going, and he devised a system of awards and decorations to keep morale up. But Khartoum's physical defenses were most important. As an engineer, Gordon understood fortifications. He erected deep trenches and crude earthwork barriers, festooned with barbed wire, along the four miles of the city's land perimeter. A few Krupp field pieces were also mounted along the entrenchments. Gordon relied mainly on homemade land mines that were made from spent artillery shells; they exploded with a frightening bang and filled the Ansar with terror. They usually worked splendidly, although Gordon wrote of one happy failure which occurred when "a donkey quietly grazing near the north fort, exploded one of the mines," but "walked off unhurt," only "angry and surprised."

The defense line was anchored at the extreme east by Fort Buri on the Blue Nile. Across the Blue Nile, in what today is Khartoum North, was the North Fort. Fort Mogren anchored the western end of the defense line, while opposite Khartoum was the important fortification at Omdurman village. Between Khartoum and Omdurman flowed the Nile, now a broad and even more powerful river formed by the confluence of the White and Blue. The summer high-water period of the Nile was approaching, and the fast-flowing currents provided natural defenses on the river flanks of Khartoum.

Gordon's only European officers were Colonel Stewart and Colonel de Coetlogon. The latter, who had commanded the Khartoum garrisons before Gordon's arrival, did not work well either with his new chief or with his native troops, and was soon transferred to Cairo. With his departure Gordon was spared the interminable complaining of a prophet of doom.

Since his successful use of boats in the Taiping campaigns, Gordon understood their military value in certain kinds of situations. With boats he could command the Nile, vital to supplying Khartoum. They brought foodstuffs from upriver and provided a viable though hazardous means of troop transport for those stretches of river free of cataracts. The wood-burning paddle wheelers were a maintenance nightmare with their temperamental machinery, but most of them could somehow be kept going most of the time. Rough armor plate protected them from shore fire, and two 9-pounder howitzers provided them with retaliatory fire power. Below deck were the women and children, squatting over primitive stoves, cooking for their sailors and gossiping among themselves. Goats and chickens wandered about as they awaited their turn in the cooking pot. Gordon complained that the boats had the "stink of badgers," but he knew his "navy" of seven steamers were his lifeline.

The Austrian Catholic Mission compound, nestled next to the Governor General's palace, was used by Gordon as an arsenal and ammunition dump. Food was conserved by rationing. Gordon estimated that the city's supply of maize would last through August, although there were indications already that merchants were hoarding this staple in anticipation of higher prices. While people were steadily dribbling out of Khartoum for fear of the Mahdi, an influx of womenfolk and children of the Ansar helped to consume much of the scarce food stocks. Gordon was advised to expel these people as the enemy in their midst, but he could not bring himself to drive them out into the desert.

For a full picture of Gordon as the siege of Khartoum wore on, the letters of Frank Power are most informative and revealing. The *Times* correspondent, who lived in the Governor General's palace, had chambers near enough to Gordon's that he could hear Gordon pacing up and down his room all night. Yet despite his lack of sleep, the general was always cheerful at breakfast. Power was amazed at his stamina: ". . . one day of his work and bother would kill another man." The correspondent concluded in wonderment that only Gordon's piety carried him through.

A natural leader of men, Gordon understood what his role must be if the fragile morale in Khartoum was to be sustained. His presence was more important to the city's defense than the hastily built ramparts. "I conclude no commander of forces ought to live closely in relation with his subordinates, who watch him like lynxes, for there is no contagion equal to that of fear." When anxiety deprived him of his appetite, he noticed with dismay that those at his mess would not eat either.

Gordon attended daily to his religious devotions. He read Thomas à Kempis's *The Imitation of Christ*. "It is not fear of death," Gordon wrote, "but I fear defeat and its consequences." As survival became more precarious, his struggle to survive became more intense. He was also beset by the conflict between predestination and free will. "I am torn in two with the thought of my impotence and God's omnipotence. If He is Almighty, He will work His will . . . so why should I trouble? Yet trouble I do, and am worn in the fight."

Concern for Gordon in England was mounting, but Parliament was divided. Not fully aware of what had occurred in the Sudan, the grumblers blamed Gordon for his own predicament. Lord Edmond Fitzmaurice excoriated Gordon for carrying out a policy of his own: "British blood and treasure were not to be poured out like water in order to rescue a soldier, however distinguished, from the consequences of deliberate disobedience to the orders he had received."[7] Foreign Minister Granville impractically suggested that Gordon be recalled. John Morley, with astonishing callousness and remarkable insensitivity to public opinion, thought the British people had tired of Gordon and that his death, while causing a row, "would soon blow over."

There were corollary matters distracting the government and Parliament from the Sudan problem. Egypt's finances were a major worry. Consideration was given to calling a conference of the great powers on this matter which affected the security of the Suez Canal as well as Egyptian stability. France was growing increasingly annoyed by the prominent British presence

375

in Egypt, while Bismarck was working to undermine Britain's colonial position in Central Africa. But most ominous of all was Russia's imperial expansion in Central Asia, which seemed to threaten India.

Pro-Gordon forces in government began to press for a relief expedition, even if it meant a prolonged occupation of the Sudan. Some wanted to leave Gordon to his fate. Charles Dilke led a third group, reconciled to the need for a relief expedition, but determined that there would be no occupation thereafter. A majority of six members of the Cabinet—Hartington, Northbrook, Derby, Selborne, Chamberlain and Dilke—could now at least agree on the need for a military expedition. The five members opposed included Gladstone himself and Foreign Minister Granville. Baring, who was in England for what would be a three-month conference to address Egypt's financial problems, was asked to give his views. He favored a "small and early" relief effort as proposed by Dilke.[8]

Beyond the fringes of the issues were the unorthodox: James O'Kelly, an Irish member of Parliament with a romantic bent, wanted to join the Mahdi! Randolph Churchill, distinguished member of Parliament and father of Winston, devoted his energies to attacking Khedive Tewfik—as though Egypt's leader had any independence amid the British-controlled events there. Two adventurous army officers, Colonel John Sterling and Colonel Frederick Burnaby (who had fought in the Suakin campaign), wanted to recruit two thousand British volunteers to rescue Gordon by dashing on camels across the desert to Khartoum from Suakin. Sir Redvers Buller, who had also served in the Suakin campaign, replied uncharitably: "Gordon is not worth the camels."

One of the more sophisticated plans was put forward by Wilfrid Blunt, who called for serious negotiations with the Mahdi. With his instinctive sympathy with the "natives," Blunt was convinced that the Mahdi could be reasoned with. He proposed either going to Khartoum himself to present his proposition or, if that proved impractical, working through a third party. Blunt specifically had in mind using Jemal ed-Din Afghani, a Moslem reformer living in exile in Paris. The proposal, reduced to its essentials, called for raising by public subscription a "Khartoum Fund" which, in return for the release of Gordon and the garrison, would be divided among the tribal chieftains in the Khartoum area. The amount given each chief would be determined by the extent of territory through which safe passage would be guaranteed. Blunt discussed the idea with Gordon's close friend Captain Brocklehurst, who seemed to think it had merit. But the government was not interested—Blunt believed that it was Baring who killed the idea.[9]

Prime Minister Gladstone tried to shut off the debate by announcing to the House of Commons on May 1 that there was "no military danger at the moment besetting Khartoum," and that the government awaited more information from Gordon (who, he failed to note, was out of communication).

May 1 would be more vividly remembered for a statement that appeared in an official "Blue Book" chronicling the exchange of messages between Gordon and the government. Gordon's last telegram, now surfaced, electrified the public by its accusation that government inaction was an "indelible disgrace." Just as Gordon's reckless use of such emotion-charged phrases as "smashing up the Mahdi" had upset officialdom in London, his choice of words "indelible disgrace" now aroused even greater public sympathy for the hero of Khartoum and ignited a firestorm of criticism aimed at Gladstone.

Gladstone was attacked in an epidemic of public protests. The Patriotic Association held a mass meeting in St. James Great Hall, Piccadilly, on May 8 protesting Gordon's abandonment. Earl Cadogan, who chaired the emotion-charged rally, accused the government of being "devoid of all principles, of all moral courage and all statesmanship." Preachers throughout England exhorted their parishioners to pray for Gordon, and the *Times* commented on the strength of public feeling in behalf of saving him. Most humiliating for Gladstone was a spontaneous round of hissing by the audience when he appeared at the inauguration of the Health Exhibit at Earl's Court. So intense was the audience's feeling that the shocked Prime Minister had to slip out by another entrance when the formalities were over.

Sir Samuel Baker, still highly respected as an elder statesman on Africa, spoke out on the need for a British expedition to the Sudan, although his main argument was the need to protect Egypt's vital Nile water supply. The loss of Khartoum, he pointed out, would deprive Egypt of an important monitoring point for estimating the rate of Nile flow, which was important to Egypt's existence. He claimed that a hostile power could divert the Blue Nile and the Atbara rivers from their courses, depriving Egypt of their waters. The great explorer hinted that the French, working hand in hand with the "dervishes," would not be beyond such trickery.[10]

377

Parliament as well as the public reacted to the Blue Book. The opposition again tabled a motion of censure. Gladstone, who had won many a battle in Parliament with his golden, if prolix, oratory, rose to the challenge. He cowed the House with ringing but misleading accusations that Gordon had only himself to blame by exceeding his instructions simply to "report," and had disobeyed orders by turning "the words 'support and consideration' into a license to conduct open war and bloodshed."[11] Ignoring the fact that four thousand British soldiers had just taken a startling toll of life in attacking Osman Digna's Ansar warriors at El Teb, the Prime Minister then uttered the astonishing statement that to send a relief army to Khartoum would be "a war of conquest against a people struggling to be free. Yes, these are people struggling to be free and rightly struggling to be free!"[12]

Baring firmly believed that Gordon "threw his [instructions] to the wind," and accused him of having "fighting instincts . . . too strong to admit of his working heartily in the interests of peace."[13] This unfairly ignored the fact that the Mahdi was the attacker, not Gordon, and that the British invasion of Suakin was the real act of aggression.

War Minister Hartington rose to defend the Prime Minister, but took a reasoned line. As head of the Whig faction of the government, he had often found cause to differ with Gladstone. Most significant on this occasion, however, was his acceptance of the principle of British responsibility for Khartoum and the concept of an expedition "to save the life and honour of General Gordon." It was this assurance that caused several members to abstain from voting against the government, thus saving Gladstone.

Although Hartington had committed the government to the principle of a relief expedition, Gladstone and his diehards still groped for some easier solution. On May 17 a dispatch was sent suggesting that Gordon bribe the tribes around Khartoum to permit the evacuation of the Egyptian troops. When Gordon finally received the message three months later, he did not realize it had originated in the Cabinet but instead blamed Edwin Egerton, who was temporarily acting for Baring in Cairo. An entry in Gordon's journal described "Egerton's" offer as "too generous to believe!" With undisguised sarcasm he added: "Egerton's chivalrous nature must have got the better of his diplomatic training when he wrote it!"

Then, on May 26, 1884, the fall of Berber and the massacre of the garrison and some five thousand townfolk occurred. London was now painfully aware of Khartoum's peril and the need for quick action. Berber, strategically located on the Nile north of Khartoum, commanded the route to Egypt and to the Red Sea as well. With this important crossroads in the Mahdi's hands, a rescue mission from either direction would be infinitely more difficult. Khartoum was now thoroughly cut off. Time had passed for any realistic solution other than a major relief force. But time, even for this, was fast running out.

With normal communication with Khartoum cut, the importance of intelligence both to and from Gordon was dramatically increased. The man responsible for maintaining a network of native spies to collect information and run messages to the besieged Gordon during these trying days was young Major Horatio Herbert Kitchener, seconded to the Egyptian army from the Royal Engineers. He had gained early recognition in Egypt and the Sudan for his intelligence activities. More than a decade later he would lead a British expeditionary force against the Mahdi's successor, the Khalifa Abdullahi, and become a public hero as Lord Kitchener of Khartoum. Still later he would become Great Britain's ranking soldier, Field Marshal Kitchener, Secretary of State for War, and lead British forces into World War I.

By the time General Sir Evelyn Wood was made Commander in Chief of Egyptian Forces, charged with creating a new army out of the shambles left in the wake of Arabi's defeat, Kitchener, because of his command of Arabic, had been assigned as one of twenty-six British training officers in Egypt. Made an Egyptian army major in early 1883, he was then only a newly promoted captain in the British Army. As the situation in the Sudan deteriorated after Hicks's disaster, Kitchener was sent south toward the border in February 1884. His intelligence reconnaissance mission was to scout out the road from Qena on the Nile to Queseir, the shortest span of land between the Nile and the Red Sea along the great river.

Gordon's efforts to find a way to evacuate Egyptian troops from Khartoum had suddenly made the border area critical. When Khartoum was cut off by the Mahdi's siege in March, Kitchener was assigned to Berber to open communication with Gordon and keep the route open between Berber and Suakin. He was instructed to support Gordon in any way possible and to report on the tribes in the Khartoum, Dongola, Suakin triangle, particularly as regards their loyalties toward the Mahdi.

Because Berber surrendered to the Mahdi in May, Kitchener and his assistant, Major Leslie Rundle, never arrived there. Instead they remained in Aswan, where an intelligence and courier communication network was organized. Kitchener raised a fifteen-hundred-man camel corps called the Ababda Frontier Force, named for the tribal group that provided the recruits, whom he hoped could be deployed against hostile tribes. He had wanted to use the force to recapture Abu Hamed for use as a more advanced base, but Cairo rejected his request. By June, Kitchener and Rundle were, however, able to inch southward to the border at Korosko, where their derring-do brought them into combat with one of the Mahdi's emirs.

Although longing for action, Kitchener wisely rejected a proposal from Cairo that the Kabbabish tribe, encouraged by a handsome subvention, be sent to rescue Gordon. He did not think the tribe could do it; but if it was not possible to take such dynamic action, at least it was worth trying to keep the border tribes neutral.

In native disguise, Kitchener set out on camelback with only a small Ababda tribal escort to negotiate with Mustapha Yawer, the Mudir of Dongola, and to prevent him from joining the rebellion. Kitchener reported that the Mudir was an untrustworthy rascal but did, in fact, keep him under control; this saved Dongola from falling to the Mahdi, a valuable contribution in light of later events.

For all the support Kitchener gave Gordon, the frustrations of the siege kept Gordon from fully appreciating his intelligence. Gordon complained that it was invariably his spies from Khartoum, not Kitchener's, whom he could depend on. One cryptic message in Arabic, intended for the Mudir of Dongola, was perhaps typical of the small scraps of paper Gordon would secrete on his agents:

> Khartoum and Sennar are well kept. Mohammed Ahmed furnishing information. Give him full details, where the troops are located, number. We have 8,000 troops in Khartoum. The Nile is in high flood. When messenger arrives give him 100 "Majidi Riyals" from the government funds.[14]

Gordon accused Kitchener of not spending "a sou in spies to give me information." In fact, Kitchener worked hard to get messages through to Gordon. Gordon's brother Henry, who later examined the record of the

Khartoum drama, was gracious enough to conclude: "Kitchener did all in his power to get messages into Khartoum and kept us acquainted with the position of affairs at Khartoum in a manner most reliable."[15]

Gordon resented some of the questions asked of him. On one occasion, for example, Kitchener passed on a message from Cairo asking exactly when the garrison would be in trouble as far as provisions and ammunition were concerned. Gordon sourly commented in his journal: "It is as if a man on the bank, having seen his friend in the river already bobbed down two or three times, hails, 'I say, old fellow, let me know when we are to throw you the life-buoy.'"

As the Ansar noose slowly closed around the doomed city, food supplies dwindled. The steamers went forth almost daily from Khartoum on foraging expeditions, but this became increasingly dangerous. Communications also became more difficult. Gordon managed to smuggle out a message on July 13: "We are all well and can hold out for four months." But this did not arrive in Cairo until the end of August.

Because of the long delivery time, messages from Cairo and London were often maddeningly *non sequitur*. Gladstone's message of April 23 seeking information—or as Dilke put it, asking "silly questions"—did not arrive in Khartoum until July 29, by which time Gordon and Khartoum were hungering for news of government intentions.

In communications to Gordon, Baring insinuated that Gordon's plea for troops was motivated by his ambitions to launch offensive operations. What was Gordon's "cause and intention in staying in Khartoum, knowing Government means to abandon Sudan"? Gordon tartly replied: "I stay at Khartoum because Arabs have shut us up and will not let us out! . . . hostilities are far from being sought for, but we have no option, for retreat is impossible unless we abandon civil employees and their families." And then Gordon reminded his critics that he had managed to send out six hundred soldiers and two thousand civilians before the siege began.

On July 31, Gordon tried to smuggle out another long letter to Cairo explaining his plight, but the letter was never received. The letter was not found until September 1888, when it was discovered blowing about the streets in a small Australian town near Wallaroo. Speculating that it had reached Australia through Arab peddlers in the region, perhaps as wrapping for trinkets, the London *Times* published the letter on November 5, 1888, by then a ghostlike voice from the grave. The letter ended with a postscript which read: "I also say that even if the road was open, the people would not let me go unless I gave them some government or took them with me, which I could not do. No one would leave more willingly than I would if it was possible."

Gordon devised a daring plan in which Stewart and a force of two thousand men would attack Berber by steamer, then burn the town to the ground and return to Khartoum. In this way he could loosen the Mahdi's stranglehold on this strategic junction, yet not risk disaster by trying to hold it.

A garbled and sensationalized version of Gordon's plan appeared in the *Dundee Advertiser*. Reading it while vacationing at Brechin Castle in Scotland as guest of the Earl of Dalhousie, Gladstone erupted in anger and accused Gordon of running amok. It was said that Gladstone's "face hardened and whitened, his eyes burned with a deep fire" when he read that Gordon was "careering up and down the Nile, crying for the blood of the Mahdi." Immediately the Prime Minister had Granville telegraph Cairo ordering Gordon's demotion to Governor and his subordination to British military command. Fortunately the message did not reach Gordon until late November, by which time it made little sense.

In the meantime Sheikh el-Obeid's encampment, twenty-five miles from Khartoum on the Blue Nile, had to be incapacitated before an expedition could be sent to Berber. In a mismanaged attack on el-Obeid, Gordon's commander Mohammed Ali suffered a disastrous defeat in which one thousand men were killed. This debacle, the sad consequences of a risky gamble, now made the Berber campaign impossible. Gordon had lost his last chance to break out; all he could now do was to pray for a relieving army.

Gordon now made the decision to send Stewart by steamer past hostile Berber to Dongola, where contact with the British could be made. He gave his assistant a letter for Baring which painted a picture of deepening despair and bitterness. It was the general's last message to the Consul General— destined to be long delayed in delivery. "While you are eating and drinking and resting on good beds," Gordon wrote, "we and those with us, both soldiers and servants, are watching by night and day, endeavouring to quell the movement of this false Mahdi." He explained that it was because of the silence from Cairo that he was sending off Stewart, and he begged Baring (who actually was still in London on consultation) to listen to Stewart "and send troops . . . without any delay."

Frank Power and French Consular Agent Herbin left with Stewart by steamer during the night of September 10. Now Gordon was alone.

GLADSTONE DELAYS; THE
MAHDI CLOSES IN

> With God's help, I shall defeat my enemies through my brave
> Ansar, and the hosts of angels sent to me by the Prophet.
> —The Mahdi as he moved on Khartoum from El Obeid

All hope of evacuating the Khartoum garrison without help from the British had died on May 26 when Berber fell. When hostile tribes surrounding Khartoum cut the town's fragile telegraph wire, the chance of retreating to Berber was probably nil; but with Berber lost, Gladstone could no longer pretend that Khartoum was safe or evacuation possible. Despite Lord Hartington's speech in Parliament on May 13, 1884, accepting for the government an obligation to rescue Gordon with a British expeditionary force, Gladstone still searched for an easier way out. The debate in the House of Commons, while finally culminating in a budget authorization for an expeditionary army, would surely have seemed as ominous to Gordon as the inexorable advance of the Mahdi's hordes. It was fortunate for his morale that he learned that a British army was on the way without having to watch the tortuous political process which led up to it.

As early as April 14, Baring had urged the government to prepare a relief expedition, and two weeks thereafter General Stephenson, as a result of Lord Wolseley's prodding, had orders to prepare a contingency plan for the rescue of Gordon—should such action become "necessary." The operational level, therefore, was diligent, but what of the policymakers who would finally have to issue the orders to march?

In mid-June, Stephenson had been ordered to take preliminary steps to build a railway from Suakin to Berber as a possible evacuation route, but by July 4 he was told that the government did not intend to launch an expedition "unless it should appear to be absolutely necessary for ensuring the safe withdrawal of Gordon from Khartoum."[1] Gladstone's excuse for stalling on this issue was that he was awaiting more information from Gordon, ignoring the fact that the beleaguered general could no longer communicate. Gordon, whose position was obviously very precarious, never received the absurd message asking if "danger had arisen" or "was likely to arise."

By July 25 there were nine ministers who favored an expedition and only three opposed, including Gladstone. Foreign Minister Granville characteristically refused to declare himself. The Prime Minister still called the tune, however, and would not yet agree to such a major step despite the strong consensus in favor of it. Lord Selborne, the Lord Chancellor, represented the majority in the Cabinet when on July 29 he submitted a memorandum attacking Gladstone for his dilatory position. But the most telling criticism of the Prime Minister's policy came from Lord Hartington, who, mindful he had committed the government to rescuing Gordon, felt betrayed by Gladstone, and felt personally guilty that nothing had been done. To Hartington, it was a matter of personal honor and good faith, so on July 31 he gave the Prime Minister what was tantamount to an ultimatum: approve a budget for a military expedition or accept his resignation.

Faced with the defection of the leading Whig statesman, which could bring down the government, Gladstone rapidly capitulated. On August 5 he recommended to the House a budget of £300,000 as an authorization for a relief expedition. Dilke quickly saw through the Prime Minister's stratagem of approving a sum so inadequate that no meaningful action could take place: Gladstone was trying to find a way out of his difficulty by limiting the government to an inadequate budget, "which we were to use *or not*,* as he thought right later."[2] He even tried to revive the Zubair formula at this late date, as it might provide him with an excuse to renege later on the commitment. In addition, the Prime Minister took advantage of the summer holiday season, which found many of the ministers out of town, to avoid holding Cabinet meetings.

On August 19 the Prime Minister alarmed Hartington by backtracking; Gladstone questioned the wisdom of taking precipitate action and complained that the Cabinet might have become "the slaves of Gordon's ideas."[3]

Although worried by Gladstone's attitude, Hartington as War Minister had his own weapon. Once his ministry began preparations for the campaign,

---

* Author's italics.

the project gathered momentum of its own. While Gladstone dithered, the military forged ahead. Hartington confided to Dilke that the War Department had already spent £750,000—£450,000 more than had been allocated in the budget. But all was not smooth in the military either. The practitioners of war had differing theories as to command and tactics. These had to be resolved before the Army marched, and this used up more precious time.

One issue was who should command the expedition. Lord Hartington, normally considered a lackluster minister, had shown unexpected power in forcing Gladstone to approve the campaign. Now he insisted that Sir Garnet Wolseley, Adjutant General of the Army, be its commander. Wolseley had built a brilliant reputation; his very name had become synonymous with efficiency. The phrase "all Sir Garnet" had entered the English vocabulary to mean "all is in perfect order." After leading the 1874 Ashanti campaign in West Africa, he had been rushed to South Africa as High Commissioner in the wake of the Zulu War in 1879; later in Egypt he had led British troops in that "tidy little war" against Ahmad Arabi Pasha to become the hero of Tel-el-Kebir. He had played an integral role in sending Gordon off to Khartoum, and he remained thereafter one of the general's staunchest protectors in the political jungles of London. There had been suspicious souls among the Liberals who suspected Wolseley of engineering Gordon's assignment as part of a Machiavellian plot to confound Gladstone's anti-imperial policies toward Egypt and the Sudan. Wolseley was, in any case, enormously popular in England, and was immortalized in caricature as "the very model of a modern Major General" in Gilbert and Sullivan's *Pirates of Penzance*.

There were those, however, who were unimpressed with Wolseley, and those who heartily disliked him. The Duke of Cambridge, Commander in Chief of the British Army, for one, could not abide him. (Nor did Wolseley like the Duke; he referred to him in private as that "clown" with a "great, square bottom.")

Of humble Irish origins, Wolseley was intensely ambitious and became known for his clique of officers, men fiercely loyal to him, who had hitched their wagons to his rapidly accumulating stars. Wolseley annoyed some in the Army by reassembling these favorites whenever he marched off to a new war.

General Sir Frederick Stephenson, as Commander in Chief of British Forces in Egypt, was Wolseley's major competitor for command of the

Sudan expedition, but the job went to Wolseley. He was appointed to the command on August 26, and arrived in Cairo two weeks later. Baring, guardian of British policy in Egypt and all-powerful proconsul, returned from England with him. The reluctant British military juggernaut was at last beginning to roll.

It was not until October 8, however, that Baring was authorized to give Wolseley his marching orders, setting forth a very limited objective for the expedition. The instructions read: "The primary object of the expedition up the valley of the Nile is to bring away General Gordon and Colonel Stewart from Khartoum. When the object has been secured, no further offensive operations of any kind are to be undertaken."[4] Nothing was mentioned about evacuating the Egyptian garrison in Khartoum; presumably they were to be left to their fate. Nor was the problem of Gordon's certain refusal of rescue under these circumstances addressed. Would he be forcibly taken, or would the expedition look the fool for turning around and leaving Khartoum empty-handed?

Launching the expedition was delayed by "the battle of the routes," a bitter argument between those such as General Stephenson and the "Cairo clique," who favored the shorter, 480-mile, overland route from Suakin, and those led by Wolseley, who insisted on an approach upriver on the Nile from Egypt. While the Nile route was much longer—1,650 miles—its proponents cited the logistical and tactical advantages of using boats to transport the troops, and the more easily available drinking water provided by the river. As early as May, Naval Commander Hamill had surveyed the river route from Cairo to Dongola. With strong backing from Hartington, this route was finally chosen. Still, the decision was not enough to restore harmony between the Stephenson and the Wolseley factions.

Wolseley, who had used small boats with considerable success in his Canadian (Manitoba) Red River campaign of 1870 against rebellious back-woodsmen, was eager to use the same kind of craft on the Nile. These flat-bottomed "whalers," he argued, could best navigate the cataracts. Stephenson, however, had already contracted with the Mudir of Dongola to provide a force of five thousand loyal tribesmen to drag native boats through the cataracts. He objected to Wolseley's elaborate plan, which included the recruitment and importation of some four hundred Canadian *voyageurs* to man the boats on the grounds that it would take too long.

His own simpler concept of native boats would enable the expedition to go forward in September before the Nile began to fall, exposing treacherous rock shoals. In late August, Egerton, acting for Baring, grumbled that the boat expedition was taking too much time, saying that "if it hadn't been for the infernal plan of these 'Red River men' [as he called Wolseley's clique], we would in a day or two have a brigade or two at Dongola . . . for everything was ready for it—stores up the river and men handy."[5]

Stephenson's and Egerton's fears, as it turned out, were all too justified. Because a fleet of Canadian whalers had to be constructed especially for the expedition, critical time was lost. Stephenson was passed over by Wolseley, who chose Colonel William Butler, with whom he had served in Canada, to prepare the strange armada. The "unofficial" and privately recruited *voyageurs*, incidentally, would be Canada's only contribution to the Nile campaign; John Macdonald, the country's first Prime Minister, refused to send regular Canadian troops.[6]

The relief expedition promised excitement and glory, and so attracted volunteers from among the elite of the British officer corps. When finally constituted, Wolseley's roster of officers, laden with nobility and aristocracy, read like Debrett's *Peerage*. Even the Prince of Wales volunteered to go, but Queen Victoria would not allow it. Making the whole affair even more romantic was Wolseley's scheme to form a camel corps which would dash across the Bayuda desert from Korti to Berber and Metemmeh, a shortcut avoiding a large loop in the Nile, then upstream to Khartoum. Wolseley's plan was to take men in groups ranging from fifty to one hundred from the Household Guards and other crack units to make up the corps. In all, an elite force of some sixteen hundred men and sixty-eight officers, divided into Heavy, Light, Guards and Mounted Infantry, would compose this exotic unit.

The concept of a camel corps fascinated the London press, which referred to it as a "social circus" because of its socially prominent officer corps. A Grenadier Guardsman of distinguished lineage, Lieutenant Count Gleichen, in his popular book *With the Camel Corps up the Nile*,[7] described the corps' distinctive uniform: red serge tunics, yellow ocher breeches, dark blue puttees and snow-white pith helmets—a throwback to an earlier era of military sartorial splendor in marked contrast to the plain khaki battle uniforms of the other units in the campaign.

GLADSTONE DELAYS; THE MAHDI CLOSES IN

The Duke of Cambridge, who felt that as Commander in Chief of the British Army he had not been adequately consulted, was furious when he heard about Wolseley's colorful but unorthodox corps. He called it "outrageous," an affront to Army tradition and a blow to regimental morale, but he finally dropped his objections and reconciled himself to what he nonetheless considered Wolseley's folly. The whole campaign command structure irritated Cambridge, who found fault with most of the officer selections although the Duke managed to have a friend of the Prince of Wales, Commander Lord Charles Beresford of the Royal Navy, given command of the Nile flotilla.

Cambridge did not approve of Wolseley's appointment of Colonel Frederick Burnaby, a swashbuckling member of the Royal Horse Guards whom, it will be recalled, Gordon had first met briefly in Equatoria and who more recently had tried to organize a private expedition to rescue Gordon when it looked as though Gladstone would take no action. A Tissot portrait showing Burnaby, a giant of a man, sprawling on a divan and languidly smoking a cigarette belied his reckless courage.[8] Wolseley finally had his way about Burnaby in the strange, bazaar-type personnel bargaining with the Commander in Chief, but only by a ruse in which Burnaby, feigning leave in South Africa, dropped off in Egypt and "unofficially" joined the expedition.

Sir Evelyn Wood, Sirdar of the Egyptian Army, felt slighted after the campaign command plums were passed out, and he had to be satisfied with the backwater command of communications and logistics for the area south of Assiut. His knack for logistics was demonstrated by his own personal baggage train, which consisted of countless cases of fine wine and delectables. He believed in traveling comfortably. But matters were complicated by jealousy between Wood, now of the "Cairo clique," and Redvers Buller of the Wolseley gang. (Buller, in fact, had served under Wood in the Zulu War of 1879.) The two officers argued fiercely and loudly—Wood was deaf and Buller lisped—over shipping priorities until Wolseley stepped in to mediate.

The touchy problem of General Stephenson's command relationship with the expedition also had to be worked out. Despite his position as commander of the British army of occupation in Egypt, Stephenson was not included among those accompanying the expedition up the Nile. He was left to manage things in Cairo and the Delta. Perhaps it was inevitable that he would not be part of Wolseley's team, the two men having quarreled over the route to be taken. But as an experienced Egyptian hand, Stephenson found it a bitter pill to swallow.

It was an oddity of the campaign that the British Army contracted with Thomas Cook & Sons, the famous travel agency, to transport the eleven thousand or so British troops and all equipment needed for the campaign from Cairo to Wadi Halfa. Never before had military logistics for a major British Army campaign been entrusted to a private company. Having built a reputation by carrying thousands of tourists up the Nile to see the archaeological delights of Thebes, Luxor and Aswan, Cook was not an illogical choice. But problems would arise from this unorthodox arrangement.

If things were not completely "all Sir Garnet," the expedition was nonetheless poised on the border at Wadi Halfa ready to invade the Sudan on October 5, 1884, as the Nile began to fall.

Crowds flocking to the Mahdi's banner in El Obeid became so large that the city's water supply was overtaxed. The Mahdi had to move his followers to Rahad, a day's journey away, where a "sea of straw huts" suddenly sprang up, "stretching as far as the eye could reach."[9] This became staging area for an army quite different from Wolseley's, one which was prepared to imprison Khartoum, not to free it. An advance force under Mohammed Abu Girgeh was sent to the Gezira just south of Khartoum to reinforce the faithful already encamped along Khartoum's southern flank.

The Austrian prisoner Rudolf Slatin accompanied the Ansar camp to Rahad and again was made to appear before the Mahdi to pledge his allegiance. The Messiah once again impressed Slatin by his large head and sparkling black eyes. On each cheek the Mahdi had three parallel scars identifying his tribal origin. He always seemed to be smiling. His white teeth often flashed, revealing the V-shaped aperture between the two front ones—the *falja*. This traditional sign of good luck in the Sudan seemed to have an irresistible attraction for Sudanese women, and for all his piety the Mahdi never wanted for the choicest female companionship. Women, too, may have been attracted by a perfume he customarily used; made from musk, sandalwood and attar of roses, it came to be known as *rihat el-Mahdi*, "the odor of the Mahdi." It was said in awe that the Holy One smelled better than the dwellers in Paradise.

GLADSTONE DELAYS; THE MAHDI CLOSES IN

Still assigned to the Khalifa Abdullahi's entourage, Slatin met the former Mudir of Berber, who had just surrendered to the Mahdi. It was only then Slatin realized that the important town had fallen. Hussein Khalifa, one of the Sudan's most powerful tribal leaders—the person who had warned Gordon against issuing the Khedive's announcement calling for Egyptian evacuation—presented himself to the Mahdi covered with ashes of humility and wearing the *sheba* neck yoke symbolizing slavery, to ask forgiveness for not submitting sooner.

Slatin was incredulous when he heard from Hussein Khalifa that Gordon planned to reinstate the Sudan's tribal leaders. How could they "oppose the Mahdi with his 40,000 rifles and his hosts of wild fanatics panting for blood and plunder"?

News also reached Slatin that Haji Mohammed Abu Girgeh had been attacked by Gordon at Buri and been defeated. There was momentary gloom in the camp, but the Khalifa Abdullahi growled to Slatin that the general would reap "God's vengeance." Because of Abu Girgeh's defeat, the Mahdi sent Abdu Rahman Wad en-Nejumi to reinforce Khartoum's besiegers in the Gezira area, while Sheikh el-Obeid held the region of Halfaya across the Nile, north of Khartoum.

The Mahdi's main forces at Rahad, poised to march on Khartoum, were divided into three units, each commanded by a leader of khalifa rank. Khalifa Abdullahi, as number two and heir to the Mahdi's power, was Commander in Chief and led the Blue Flag Division. The Green Flag Division was under the command of the Khalifa Ali Wad Helu, and the Red Flag under Khalifa Mohammed Sherif. Every Friday on the Moslem sabbath, the Mahdi reviewed his troops in an immense square. The faithful swore that the Prophet himself rode by his side and voices from Heaven wafted down to bless him. Some claimed that passing clouds were caused by a host of angels' wings that blocked the sun and provided shade for the Ansar.

Joseph Cuzzi, the government's representative captured at Berber, was dispatched by the Mahdi to Khartoum with a letter demanding Gordon's surrender. Gordon had no intention of giving himself up and had only contempt for those who had. Cuzzi and Slatin, moreover, had offended the general by embracing Islam. Gordon would not receive Cuzzi, but sent a letter to the Mahdi refusing to surrender. He also warned: "If you have letters to send me again, do not send a European."

Undaunted, the Mahdi sent Cuzzi back to Gordon with another demand to submit and repent. This time a Greek prisoner, George Calamatino, accompanied him, but Gordon would see neither of them. Slatin had secretly given the Greek a letter of his own for Gordon which explained the circumstances of his surrender and apostasy, but the general would not be budged and refused to reply. He justified his actions in a journal entry: ". . . it is not a small thing for a European, for fear of death, to deny our Faith; it should not be regarded as if it was taking off one coat and putting on another. It is perhaps as well to omit this if this journal is published, for no man has a right to judge another. . . . It is better to fall with clean hands than to be mixed up with dubious acts and dubious men."

As soon as the holy fasting of Ramadan was over, the Mahdi announced that he had been ordered by the Prophet, Mohammed, to march on Khartoum. The massed Ansar, fired by religious zeal, responded with jubilation. The great holy war was nearing its climax; heaven was near. Any tribesman disposed to shirk his sacred duty was warned that he would suffer for his lack of faith.

Slatin was awed at the size of the crusade: "The Mahdi's summons brought about a wholesale migration of the entire population such as had never been seen before in the Sudan."[10] It was August 22 when the Ansar host began its two-hundred-mile march from Rahad. The horde proceeded along three routes. The northern route was followed by the camel-driving tribes, while the southern route with its more abundant water supply was given to the cattle-grazing Baggaras and their hard-driving cavalrymen. In between, the route via Duem, was taken by the Mahdi himself, the Khalifa Abdullahi, and most of the other emirs leading their armies. This was the route Hicks had taken in the opposite direction on his ill-fated expedition to humble the Mahdi. Father Ohrwalder estimated that some 200,000 in all took part in the grand march. It was an awesome sight, the banners fluttering over a sea of white-robed humanity marching to the beat of war drums.

As the march proceeded, a Frenchman mysteriously appeared from the desert, insisting that he meet with the Mahdi. Wild rumors accompanied his arrival. Some thought the stranger was the Emperor of France; others believed him to be an infidel spy or an assassin commissioned by the British to kill the Mahdi. Gordon, whose agents brought news of the Frenchman's presence, had no less fantastic a theory; he speculated that he might be the

French author Ernest Renan, known for his book *Life of Jesus*, who had disappeared in the wilds of Africa years before.

The Frenchman, who identified himself as Olivier Pain, claimed to be a Moslem on a secret mission from the government of France. The Khalifa received Pain first but made it clear the Mahdi did not need France's help. Imperial rivalry between England and France was of no interest to the Mahdi, if indeed he was fully aware of it, nor had the quarrels of infidels any place in a holy war. When the Mahdi finally received the uninvited stranger he was not cordial; the only allies he wanted were God and His Prophet, Mohammed. Certainly he would never ally himself with a nation of "unbelievers." The Mahdi, who conducted the audience in the midst of his multitudes, received thunderous acclaim when he boasted: "With God's help, I shall defeat my enemies through my brave Ansar and the hosts of angels sent to me by the Prophet."[11]

Later, to his fellow European Slatin, Olivier Pain confided that his mission had no official sanction; he was a radical journalist on the staff of Henri de Rochefort's publication *Intransigéant*. But, he hinted, he would be rewarded by a royal stipend if he succeeded in this journalistic coup. The state of Franco-British friction was such that French intelligence would take great interest in his story. It soon dawned on the adventurous Frenchman, however, that he was now a prisoner like Slatin, with little hope of ever being allowed to leave.

Soon afterward, Slatin learned that Pain had fallen deathly ill with typhus. When the Austrian reported this to the Khalifa, the imperious leader simply pointed out: "If he dies here, he is a happy man; God in His goodness and omnipotence has converted him from an unbeliever to a believer."[12] Pain died a quick death.

At Duem the Mahdi reviewed his army and addressed his followers massed beside the Nile. At the climax of his oration, he cried out: "God had created this river; he will give you its waters to drink and you shall become the possessors of all the lands along the bank."[13] This, of course, included Egypt, and the crowds howled thunderously with joy.

At Tura el-Hadra, about one hundred miles from Khartoum, the Mahdi's legions celebrated the Moslem feast of Kurban Bairam on September 30. The Mahdi delivered moving prayers, weeping copiously as he spoke. Crying was calculated, Slatin knew, to lift his followers to new heights of zeal. It was whispered about the camp that the Mahdi packed pepper under his fingernails so he could induce tears on demand by waving his hands over his eyes.

When the Mahdi announced the ambush of Gordon's two-thousand-man force, led by Mohammed Ali, who had disobeyed orders by venturing too far inland from the river, there were more cheers. Slatin understood, sadly, what this meant for Khartoum.

Gordon later attributed Mohammed Ali's defeat to Divine retribution when he learned that his commander had shot a twelve-year-old boy for calling him a "dog." The general also believed that the confusion caused by Khartoum peddlers swarming over the battlefield in search of loot may have contributed to the debacle. Whether the defeat was Divinely intended or not, Gordon was never able to mount another offensive after this grievous loss.

As the Ansar force came within a day's march of Khartoum, the Mahdi sent for Slatin and asked him once more to write Gordon and urge him "to save himself and his soul" by surrendering. A dejected Slatin agonized over what he should say as he perched on his rough string bed under the stars and wrote by the light of a crude lantern.

Slatin secretly included a private letter to Gordon with a long apologia for his own actions since his own surrender of Darfur and asked Gordon to accept him if he could escape. He was ready to share "either victory or death" with Gordon. Slatin's letter, sent off by courier on October 15, did not impress Gordon, who mentioned it without comment in his journal entry of October 16.

THE JOURNAL

Yea, the stork in the heavens knows her appointed time. . . .
—Jeremiah 8 : 7

W ith Stewart having left on September 10, 1884, taking Gordon's journal with him for delivery to Cairo, Gordon was alone. Contemplating the situation, he jotted down random thoughts which would provide the world a record of his last days in Khartoum.

How times had changed—once he had been the Governor General of the Sudan, now he was a prisoner in Khartoum. "When I left, no man could lift his hand or foot in the land of Sudan without me, and now, we cannot calculate our existence over 24 hours."[1] Khartoum was terribly vulnerable. The Ansar did not have to attack; it could simply block grain sales to the city and starve the occupants into submission—as it had done in the siege of El Obeid. Wryly, Gordon observed: "The stomach governs the world. . . . It was the stomach which caused our misery from the beginning [a reference to Eve's hunger for the forbidden fruit]. It is wonderful that the ventral tube of man governs the world, in small and great things."

Gordon's journal was criticized by some as a disorganized grab bag of miscellany rather than a disciplined chronicle of events. Gordon himself recognized the journal's lack of organization, with its haphazard inclusion of candid personal observations; to his writing, he appended the caveat: "This journal will want pruning out if thought necessary to publish."

By the time the journal was published, however, the public was hungry for every word, every thought, jotted down by the hero of Khartoum, personal or professional, germane or not. It was his ramblings in the journal that told most poignantly the story of Khartoum's human tragedy. Gordon's stream-of-consciousness style provided insights which no biography or history of the time has been able to equal.

One moment Gordon would comment: "One is drawn toward the children

395

of this country, both browns and blacks"; his next thoughts would turn to how soldiers reacted to their wounds. He included a sketch of the human heart, showing how a bullet had lodged in the wall of the ventricle, causing an agonizing death eleven days later. Next, he railed against apostasy: "You ask me to become a Mussulman to save my life," he argued rhetorically with Ansar leaders who urged him to surrender, "while you, yourself, acknowledge Mohammed Achmet [Ahmad] as the Mahdi to save your life. Why, if we go on this principle, we will be adopting every religion whose adherents threaten our existence. . . ." Recalling Chapter 16 of the Koran, which permits Moslems to apostasize if forced to do so, Gordon continued, "So the Muslims here are well off in this respect vis-à-vis the Mahdi."

Gordon mused on a turkey cock and his harem of five hens: "I am sorry to say that one of his wives, having sat with patience for three weeks on eggs, and brought forth two chicks, *he killed them*." He then embarked on a long religious treatise on the "fore and future existence of what we call animals." Without so much as a change of paragraph, Gordon moved on to God's preference for man over other animals by having breathed life into him. Then to the juggernaut of militant Islam: "I do not believe that fanaticism exists as it used to do in the world, judging from what I have seen in this so-called fanatic land. It is far more a question of property, and is more like communism under the fiat of religion which seems to excite and to give colour to acts which men would otherwise condemn."

Suddenly, Gordon lashed out: "One cannot help feeling vicious against Sir Auckland Colvin, Sir Edward Malet and Sir Charles Dilke, for it is on account of those three, whose advice was taken by Her Majesty's Government, that all [Sudan's] sorrows are due." This trio, he contended, had protected European bondholders at the expense of the Sudanese people. "We are an honest nation, but our diplomatists are cronies and not *officially* honest." And the *Times* correspondents in Cairo and Alexandria had encouraged their misdeeds.

On the local front, Gordon saw most of the European expatriates as turncoats or opportunists who could not be trusted. He was convinced that Cuzzi had betrayed Berber to the Mahdi and turned the official ciphers over to the Ansar. For his services, Gordon noted, the Italian received two horses, a wife, a slave, $60, and most useful of all, an ointment to preserve "an odor of sanctity."

Gordon thought about many things and jotted down his observations as they occurred to him. It was as though his journal took the place of Stewart or Power as a companion. He worried about his own leadership and expressed unending remorse for having executed the two Egyptian officers Said Pasha and Ibrahim Hassan Pasha for treason. Over and over, he harked back to this "juridical murder," especially after he learned that the two men might have been innocent after all. "I shall send for their families and give each of them £1,000, which is all I can do."

"I have led the officers and officials the lives of dogs while I have been up here. It is spurs in their flanks every day. . . . The near approach of the Mahdi has not troubled me, for if he fails he is lost and there will be no necessity for an expedition to Kordofan [his base]; if he succeeds, he may by his presence prevent any massacre." Yet, Gordon admitted to his "dire anxiety"—not that he might die but that he might be beaten.

One moment Gordon's words suggested resignation: "I have always felt we were doomed to come face to face ere the matter ended." The next moment he imagined a grand finish: "I toss up in my mind whether, if the place is taken, to blow up the palace and all in it, or else to be taken and with God's help to maintain the Faith, and if necessary to suffer for it (which is most probable). The blowing up of the palace is the simplest, while the other means long and wearing suffering and humiliation of all sorts. I think I shall elect for the last, not from fear of death, but because the former has more or less the taint of suicide, as it can do no good to anyone and is, in a way, taking things out of God's hands." A few days later he wrote: "D. V. [God willing], I will not give up the place except with my life."

After a mid-September visit from the Greek courier for the Mahdi, George Calamatino, Gordon heard the story that the Mahdi invoked tears by packing his fingernails with pepper. "I must confess that the pepper business has sickened me. I had hitherto hoped I had to do with a regular fanatic who believed in his mission, but when one comes to pepper in the fingernails, it is rather humiliating to have to succumb to him. . . . I would recommend the Mahdi's recipe to Cabinet Ministers justifying some job." Suddenly a new mood, balanced enigmatically between humor and pathos, intruded:

397

"Haunting the palace are a lot of splendid hawks; I often wonder whether they are destined to pick my eyes, for fear I was not the best of sons."*

Gordon satirized his bureaucratic superiors. They did not know the difference between the town El Obeid and the Sheikh el-Obeid. He sketched irreverent cartoons, one showing Baring and Egerton sputtering at Gordon's reference to them as "arrant humbugs." But a few paragraphs later Gordon admitted, almost contritely: "I owe it is not right to scoff at one's superiors. I do not do it in malice, and I hope those who are remarked upon will not be offended. . . . Life is a very leaden business and if anyone can lighten it, so much the better." (Baring, of course, could not see why life's leadenness had to be lightened at his expense. He felt that Gordon held him up to "odium and ridicule" in a strange compulsion to pour forth "the vials of wrath on the official classes.")[2]

On September 20 a smuggled note from Kitchener brought the electrifying news that a relief expedition was on the way. Gordon had written earlier: "I have the strongest suspicion that these tales of [British] troops at Dongola and Merowe are all gas works. If you want to find Her Majesty's forces you would have to go to Shepheard's Hotel in Cairo." His skepticism was now justified, as troops had not yet reached Dongola. But Gordon admitted to satisfaction that at least Kitchener had set up an advanced intelligence bivouac at Debbe near Dongola from where the courier had come.

Kitchener's momentous information was stated most casually; in a sort of "oh-by-the-way" manner. He wrote: "The relief expedition is evidently coming up this way. . . ." Kitchener was, of course, unaware at the time of writing that Gordon had sent off his ciphers with Stewart and could not read Egerton's telegram, which broke the news more formally. Nor could Gordon read that the British relief column had a very limited mission: to rescue only himself and Stewart, not necessarily the garrison. Kitchener's note included an encouraging line to the effect that the Mahdi had abandoned Darfur and was without adequate reinforcements to send to Khartoum.

Gordon blanketed Khartoum with pamphlets spreading the news and ordered gun salutes that afternoon as a morale booster for the city—and to

---

* Gordon here alludes to Proverbs 30:17: "The eye that mocketh at his father and despiseth to obey his mother, the ravens of the valley shall pick it out, and the young eagles shall eat it."

impress upon the nearby Ansar enemy that the British were indeed coming. Yet Book I of the journal ended on September 23 with no jubilation. Instead, Gordon promised only that he would not "rat out" on Khartoum, adding: "The troops had better not come beyond Berber till the question of what will be done [with the garrison and other foreigners] is settled."

The second book of Gordon's journal was sprinkled liberally with tactical advice. The general recommended that a "fighting column," about a quarter of the force's strength, move quickly overland from Dongola to Metemmeh, leaving troops to guard the precious water wells along the arid Bayuda desert track so that the Ansar could not fill them in, thereby cutting off the route of withdrawal. Half the expeditionary force should remain in Dongola to protect river communications with Egypt. Gordon, in the meantime, would send three steamers with two guns each down the Nile to link up with the column at Metemmeh. Together they would seize the strategic town of Berber. With Berber secure, a quarter of the force would remain there as an advance base while the fighting column dashed on to Khartoum.

Gordon also envisioned luring the "Arabs" down to Giraffe, on the Blue Nile, where he would destroy them, "then coax them to El-Eilafun," from where he would push up to evacuate the Sennar garrison, defeating the "Arabs" there. At the same time, steamers would move up the White Nile in an effort to rescue the Equatoria garrison, which was still under Emin Pasha's command, and the Bahr al-Ghazal garrison, which unknown to Gordon had already been taken by the Mahdi.

This was ambitious enough, but to Gordon it was minimal—even inadequate. However operationally successful this might be, evacuation of the Sudan would be a grievous blow to British prestige. How much better it would be, he wrote, to install a Turkish or Zubair regime in the Sudan, and use British troops to strike at the heart of the Mahdi's power base in Kordofan, where he imagined the Mahdi would likely retreat as the British neared Khartoum. The Ansar must be soundly "smashed up" for once and for all.

As a master of guerrilla warfare and an expert on Arab tribal warriors, Gordon warned against using "heavy lumbering columns." He favored "parties of 40 to 60 men, swiftly moving about," aided by native allies. Sudan "is the country of the irregular, not of the regular. I do hope you will not drag on the artillery: it can only produce delay and do little good."

THE MOSLEM MESSIAH AND THE CHRISTIAN MARTYR

Having no way of knowing if his advice would reach the relief army in time or, if it did, be heeded at all, Gordon went on: "The time to attack is the dawn, or rather before it. . . . 60 men would put these Arabs to flight just before dawn, which one thousand would not accomplish in daylight." Arab fighting strength, Gordon explained, was in their horsemen, who dared not act in the dark.

Having received from Kitchener a sketchy roster of senior officers named to command the expedition, Gordon thought Redvers Buller (who had denigrated Gordon as not worth the camels needed to rescue him) should "have full swing" in mounting little "biting" raids against the Arabs. "I believe he is well off (and I think not married) which is an enormous advantage. . . . It is the very same warfare we will have to exercise if ever we would oppose Russia in her advance in Afghanistan."

He praised the bravery of the Sudanese: "The wretched peasant, with that filthy cloth . . . is a determined warrior, who can undergo thirst and privation."

Hearing the laugh of Danubian cranes, which had marked his way up the Nile at the beginning of his Sudan odyssey, and now flew overhead, he reflected on Schiller's "cranes of Ibycus."

Addressing an escaped Ansar soldier, who was "dreadfully itchy" and could give no useful intelligence, Gordon smiled at how the unkempt soldier "saw himself in the mirror and asked who it was." Gordon philosophized: "Where there are no mirrors everyone must be a complete stranger to himself. . . ."

Back to the matters at hand, Gordon on September 27 recorded the dispatch of three steamers upriver to Shendi, where they were to collaborate with tribesmen under the Mudir of Dongola, as well as raise the Shaigiyas, north of Khartoum astride the route to Shendi. The Shaigiyas, traditionally friendly with the Egyptians, nonetheless were a worry to Gordon: Would they turn hostile as the Mahdi gathered momentum and the plight of Khartoum worsened? Their friendship would be important to the advancing British force; yet living where they did made them vulnerable to the Mahdi.

Gordon dwelled again on the need to evacuate all the Egyptian garrisons in the Sudan. "I altogether *decline* the imputation that the projected expedition has come to *relieve me*. It has come to SAVE OUR NATIONAL HONOUR in extricating the garrisons from a position our action in Egypt has placed these garrisons." Gordon pointed out that in his own rescue mission—albeit a one-man mission—he had failed; the British military expedition must thus evacuate the Egyptians, not simply rescue him. "As for myself, I could make good my escape at any moment if I wished. I am not the *rescued lamb*, and will not be."

Gordon had never seen the actual instructions given Wolseley, which explicitly called for rescuing Gordon and Stewart, ruling out further offensive operations of any kind. Despite Gladstone's suspicions that Gordon was hanging on expressly for the purpose of making an expedition necessary, the Prime Minister had never specifically given the beleaguered general orders to flee Khartoum and abandon the city to its fate. Just before the telegraph line was cut, Baring had in fact passed on Granville's hope that Gordon would remain. A later communication from the Foreign Minister "suggesting" but not "ordering" him to depart was never received by Gordon.

However much Gordon felt impelled to remain with his charges, he had at least not been insubordinate in staying on. Whether he intentionally tried to force government action by remaining is a different matter. In a letter of November 5 to his sister Augusta, he wrote: "I expect Her Majesty's Government are in a precious rate with me for holding out and forcing their hand." Tactics surely placed some part in Gordon's actions, but it was a sense of honor and duty which basically drove him. That he had placed his own life in jeopardy for what he felt right is evidence enough that he was not simply trying to manipulate policy for some baser motive such as ego or stubbornness.

Gladstone, by trying to retain the support of the Radicals while not alienating other Liberals, was the one principally responsible for both Gordon's and the government's predicament. Lord Hartington's biographer B. H. Holland phrased it accurately when he wrote: "If, for political reasons, he dared not openly and explicitly recall Gordon, what right had Gladstone to believe that it was Gordon's duty to desert his post?"[3]

Would Wolseley, upon arriving in Khartoum, order his close friend to withdraw with his forces? Would Gordon obey his order? And, if not, would Wolseley have him forcibly removed? (Gordon claimed this would have been impossible in view of his popular support in Khartoum.) These were questions which never had to be answered, but they loomed as urgent at the moment.

Gordon had his own ideas worked out, however out of step with official policy they were. Once the British force reached Khartoum it should, in Gordon's opinion, give the country to the Sultan (who would send Turkish troops to hold it) or establish Zubair in power. Kordofan must next be taken to break the back of the Mahdi's movement. Having left the country in suitable other hands, Gordon would go south to Equatoria and Bahr al-Ghazal to detach these provinces from the Sudan so that slave trading could not be revived, and administer them as part of Leopold's Congo. All this, however, was far removed from British intentions.

Gordon's motives for remaining in Khartoum have long been argued by historians and biographers, but the general's own remarks on this subject should not be ignored. In a telegram received by Foreign Minister Granville as early as March 11, Gordon stated: "You must see that you could not recall me *nor could I possibly obey* until the Cairo employees get out from all the places. . . . It may have been a mistake to send me up, but having been done, I have no option but to see evacuation through, for even if I was mean enough to escape, I have no power to do so."

As Wolseley prepared to invade the Sudan, Gordon realized the consequences of his stand. He could not let Wolseley advance beyond Dongola without Wolseley fully knowing his intentions, so he jotted them down in his journal on September 29, hoping they would reach the relief column:

My idea is to induce Her Majesty's Government to undertake the extrication of all peoples or garrisons . . . and that if this is not their programme, then to resign my commission and do what I can to attain it. As long as a man remains in Her Majesty's service, he is bound to obey the orders of his superiors, but if he resigns, he cannot be held as insubordinate if he disobeys. . . . Therefore, if her Majesty's forces are not prepared to relieve the whole of the garrisons, the General [Wolseley] should consider whether it is worth coming up—in his place I would not do so.[4]

As the Mahdi marched north to seize Khartoum and Wolseley marched south to save Gordon from the Mahdi, Gordon's situation became more muddled. Summing it up: Gordon, as a point of honor, refused to save only himself by escaping, even if he could, while Gladstone for political reasons would not order him to leave. A virtual captive of the Mahdi, Gordon had thus become a *cause célèbre*. Gladstone, under political and popular pressure, had been forced to authorize an expeditionary army to rescue him—after the Prime Minister had passed up a logical opportunity to do so less expensively and less dramatically when British forces had been engaged in a pointless punitive operation against Osman Digna near Suakin. While Wolseley, in fact, planned to evacuate the Khartoum garrison as well as rescue Gordon himself, his orders expressly forbade him from extricating the other garrisons throughout the country—such operations were probably beyond the force's capability anyway. And Gordon would not allow himself to be saved if these garrisons were not saved as well; the captain would go down with the ship. This all added up to a very awkward situation.

Gordon in a last, feeble effort to come up with a way out of the problem wrote in his journal: "Let [Khedive] Tewfik Pasha send up Abd el-Kader Pasha [Egypt's Minister of War] as Governor General to replace me at once. Lord Wolseley can then do what he thinks fit . . . the abandonment, etc., and I am free of all responsibility. . . . Of course, I should have the privilege of laughing in my sleeve if, after all, Her Majesty's Government found they could not get out without the establishment of Turks or Zobeir [Zubair], or the retention of the Sudan under Egypt." Gordon must have known that Gladstone realistically could not replace him without creating a public and political storm in England, and the very suggestion that he would be replaced by an Egyptian would cause all resistance to the Mahdi to dissolve instantly in Khartoum. He admitted: ". . . the proposition I made is in some degree a trap, for I feel confident that there will be no end of trouble, in placing Abd el-Kader Pasha in my place and trying to evacuate. . . ."

As Khartoum's future became bleaker, signs of treachery began to appear. Gordon reported in his journal that his secretary, Ibrahim Rushti Bey, had been caught stealing from the precious food stocks. Another official, Ahmad el-Awaan, whom Colonel Stewart had thought highly of, was discovered to be a secret agent of the Mahdi. In a one-man campaign, Ahmad el-Awaan spread the word around town that Gordon had invented the news about the British advance. His next step would have been to set fire to the ordnance depot within the Austrian Catholic Mission compound. Awaan was court-martialed and executed for his treason. In reflection, Gordon wrote in his journal: "Although man is the essence of treachery, I believe every man wishes to be honest; his interests prevent him."

Gordon continued to underestimate both the Mahdi's strength and his motives. Gordon's spies were strangely wrong in reporting the Mahdi's whereabouts, and they badly misreported the size of his army—consistently estimating three thousand to four thousand men, while later Slatin's memoir indicated there had been some 200,000 spear-carrying zealots "creeping forward like a great tortoise."[5] Saleh Bey, a friend of Gordon's held captive by the Mahdi, sent word secretly that the Ansar also had forty thousand rifle-bearing soldiers. Gordon, however, refused to believe this and had his messenger jailed for dissembling.

"Cambyses, son of Cyrus of Isaiah, lost his army B.C. 525 in these deserts . . ." Gordon suddenly remembered, jotting down in his journal this depressing thought for Wolseley to contemplate.

Gordon continued to find fault with Kitchener's intelligence, and delighted in imagining comical scenarios to enliven his journal. In one, Kitchener is chatting with Colonel Chermside, British commander in Suakin. Chermside asks if there is any news of Gordon; Kitchener replies: "Nothing particular . . . steamers at Metemmeh. Abuse, as usual, of Intelligence Department. . . . He finds it more difficult to get his letters through, and will have time to get over his liver complaint. . . ." In another, Kitchener is reporting to Chermside: "Hurrah! capital news! The Mahdi has *him* [Gordon] on the hip! . . . bottled *him* up now. We will have no more impertinent remarks about the Intelligence Department."

Gordon had a sixth sense about conspiracy. He could smell it. On October 12 he staged lightning raids throughout the city to break up a dissident underground; sixteen ringleaders in a plot to seize and surrender Khartoum to the Mahdi were jailed. Among those arrested were the Mudir of Khartoum, the leading mullah, and one of the chief judges—three of the most important people in town. "I confess," he noted in his journal, "I am more perplexed about these arrests than I like. . . ." Where did the people stand now? "I declare if I thought the town wanted the Mahdi, I would give it up, but, as far as I can judge, the mass of the people approve of the arrests."

THE MAHDI FACES GORDON

Reliance for succour on others than God . . . will bring you
nothing but destruction.
—The Mahdi, in a message to Gordon
as Khartoum waited for a British relief column

Ansar horsemen galloped into the Mahdi's camp from Berber
bringing word that the steamship *Abbas* had foundered on the
rocks, and Colonel Stewart, Frank Power and French Consul
Herbin had all been murdered. Slatin, shocked by the news, had to translate
documents found in the wreckage. It was a chilling experience for the
Austrian to find suddenly in his hands Gordon's papers, particularly the
general's military report which Stewart was carrying to the British relief
expedition. And it was saddening for Slatin to write for the Mahdi a letter to
Gordon informing him of the latest developments.

The Mahdi's letter, which reached Gordon on October 22, 1884, gloated
over Stewart's death. In addition, it reported that Bahr al-Ghazal had been
taken and Governor Lupton captured. The Mahdi took particular delight in
citing Gordon's own messages which had been retrieved from the ill-fated
Abbas and which carefully inventoried the dwindling supplies of food and
ammunition. He taunted Gordon for expecting reinforcements.[1] In a final
exhortation to surrender, the Mahdi wrote: "If you return to the Most High
God and become a Moslem and surrender to His order and that of His
Prophet and believe in us as the Mahdi, send us a message from there . . .
after laying down your arms."[2]

The Mahdi's summons fell on deaf ears. Gordon told his commander at
Omdurman Fort, "I am here like iron and hope to see the newly arrived
English. . . . It is impossible for me to have any more words with
Mohammed Achmed, only lead."[3]

The Mahdi had gained an intelligence windfall from Stewart's demise.
Although Slatin in his translations had tried to gloss over items damaging to

Khartoum's defense, there were enough letters in Arabic to provide the Mahdi with an accurate picture of the beleaguered capital. The Mahdi hoped that such documentary evidence of Stewart's misadventure would convince Gordon of the hopelessness of Khartoum's plight and the wisdom of his surrender. Stewart, Herbin and Power, the Mahdi intoned, had died "by the will of God," and their infidel souls were "condemned to the fire and to eternal misery."

Many years later, Father Ohrwalder described the circumstances surrounding the deaths of Stewart and his companions. The *Abbas* had successfully passed Abu Hamed when it came to grief on cataract rocks near the village of Hebbeh. After waiting two days on a small island in midstream, Stewart sent a messenger to the local sheikhs of the Monasir tribe asking for camels with which to continue their journey. Sheikh Suleiman Wad Naaman, who responded, professed to be pro-government and offered to help. Exuding hospitality, he invited the Europeans into his house while the camels were being rounded up. As they feasted on dates, the old sheikh lifted his water bottle as a signal to the Arabs squatting nearby, who then rushed to attack the defenseless Europeans. "French Consul Herbin, standing near the door, was the first to fall, his head was chopped off with an ax."[4] Power and Stewart were similarly dispatched. The tribesmen then rushed down to the stranded boat and killed the other passengers. Only two artillerymen, who jumped into the river, escaped the slaughter.

Together with the Mahdi's official message, Slatin discreetly enclosed a letter in which he once again pleaded his case to Gordon. Once again Gordon refused to reply. Gordon explained in his journal: "I shall have nothing to do with Slatin's coming in here to stay unless he has the Mahdi's positive leave; . . . his doing so would be breaking of his parole, which should be as sacred when given to the Mahdi as to any other power, and it would jeopardize the safety of all those Egyptian prisoners with the Mahdi."

Hansal, the Austrian Consul, however, did answer Slatin, if enigmatically. He asked Slatin to meet him at Omdurman Fort to speak about "steps to be taken for our rescue." Slatin was puzzled, although he shrewdly guessed that the Consul wanted to defect and join the Mahdi's camp. There had, in fact, been rumors about Hansal to that effect. Gordon, too, had heard these rumors: "I hear Hansal . . . is disposed to go with *his seven female attendants* to the Arabs; I hope he will do so."

THE MAHDI FACES GORDON

When Slatin glimpsed the Englishman Frank Lupton being dragged into camp in shackles, he knew that hope was running out. Even though Emin Pasha still resisted in Equatoria, the formation of a government redoubt in the south was now unlikely. Nor could the Upper Nile now reliably serve as an escape corridor for the Khartoum garrison.

Before Slatin could leave to meet Hansal in Omdurman, his fortunes changed abruptly for the worse. He found himself accused of being unfaithful to the Mahdi, a most serious crime. He was shackled hand and foot, with an iron ring around his neck, making it almost impossible to move his head, and dragged before the Khalifa. Slatin's furtive letters to Gordon had apparently been intercepted by the Mahdi and interpreted as subversive.

Suddenly the sprawling encampment was packed up in a flurry of activity, and the Mahdiya host began the last leg of its crusade. Immobilized by his chains, Slatin had to be strapped on a donkey to make the journey. On the afternoon of October 21, 1884, the first day of the Arab new year 1302, he was able to glimpse the palm trees of Khartoum from across the White Nile.

To the accompaniment of booming war drums and blaring elephant-tusk trumpets, the Mahdi set up main camp along the southern and western edges of Omdurman Fort. The Khalifa Abdullahi's own troops flew a dark blue flag, while Khalifa Ali Wad Helu's tribesmen assembled under a green flag. The third division under Mohammed Sherif could be identified by its red banner. Other Ansar units were deployed to various segments of Khartoum's perimeter to augment the besiegers already in place. Several emirs were sent to reinforce Wad en-Nejumi, whose camp extended to the White Nile south of Khartoum's earthwork defenses, and Abu Girgeh's host encamped between Wad en-Nejumi and the Blue Nile east of the city. Some ten thousand Ansar faced Khartoum's southern land defenses, which stretched between Buri Fort on the Blue Nile and Mogren Fort on the White Nile. Completing the noose drawn around the city was the Mahdi's main encampment in Omdurman across the White Nile, and the encampment north of Khartoum of Sheikh el-Obeid's tribesmen at Khojali across the Blue Nile.

Slatin was elated when the Greek, George Calamatino, brought news that Wolseley was advancing up the Nile with an English army. But with the Mahdi's vast host already surrounding Khartoum, could the British arrive in time if they were now only in Dongola? Bound by heavy chains, eighty-three links in all, Slatin could only while away the hours full of hopes and fears. Because of the weight of the chains, he was obliged to remain lying down, but could hear the incessant "crack of the rifles and the booming of the guns" on both sides.[5]

Toward the end of December, "just as blessed sleep, which makes one forget all one's troubles," was stealing over him, he was awakened by the sentry. A servant of the Khalifa thrust before him a note to translate. It was written on a small scrap of paper and signed by Gordon but not addressed to anyone. The language was French, its wording was enigmatic:

> I have about 10,000 men; can hold Khartoum at the outside till the end of January. Elias Pasha wrote to me; he was forced to do so. He is old and incapable; I forgive him. Try Hajji Mohammed Abu Girga, or sing another song.[6]

The Khalifa demanded to know the meaning of the message. He was particularly interested in the reference to Abu Girgeh. Slatin, who genuinely could not understand the cryptic references to one of the Mahdi's top lieutenants, infuriated the Khalifa by his inability to decipher the note. He could, however, understand Gordon's estimate that Khartoum must be relieved by the end of January. It was now almost the end of December; it would be close.

Slatin got the latest news about the British advance from one of the Greeks in the camp. The Camel Corps had reached Debbeh, near Dongola, on December 28 and was preparing to cross the Bayuda desert to Metemmeh. Spies had kept the Mahdi well informed about British movements, so he could take timely countermeasures. The Mahdi gave no evidence of fearing the British; if anything, he seemed insulted that they would send so small an army against his mighty hordes. Hadn't he destroyed Hicks's army? And hadn't Hicks been British? In light of the news, he ordered the Ja'aliyin and Barabra tribes of the area to converge at Metemmeh and engage the British when they arrived.

Slatin also learned that some of the emirs belonging to Khalifa Ali Wad Helu's flag would soon lead their forces in a dash to Metemmeh. They would serve as reinforcements for the Ja'aliyins in the battle to prevent the British from reaching the Nile and going on to relieve Khartoum. "There was something in the wind," realized Slatin. The decisive moment was near.

DEATH THROES OF A CITY

Better a ball in the brain than to flicker out unheeded.
—Charles Gordon during the siege of Khartoum, 1884

The Moslem year 1302, which began on October 21, 1884, did not begin auspiciously. As the Mahdi with his grand army of the Ansar had encamped at Omdurman, Gordon sent a flotilla of steamers downriver to await the British expedition's arrival at Metemmeh. But then came the letter from Slatin with the sickening news of the capture of the *Abbas* and the murder of Stewart and the rest of his party. The same letter, in deliberate juxtaposition, enclosed the Mahdi's third demand that Gordon surrender.

An eclipse of the sun two days before had been considered a harbinger of evil tidings by Gordon's men in Khartoum. Gordon now had reason to agree, but he was slow to accept the report of Stewart's death as true. Spies, after all, had reported the safe passage of the *Abbas*. As for the captured military report, included by the Mahdi as proof of Stewart's fate, it could have been copied and slipped to the enemy by the treacherous Awaan. This explanation was farfetched and did not stand up to simple analysis, but Gordon did not want to accept the obvious.

Not until November 3 when Kitchener smuggled a message to Gordon with confirmation of the tragedy did the general completely believe it. He brooded for days, blaming the British for not having informed him sooner of the expedition which would have made Stewart's mission less urgent, and blaming himself. "I look on it as being a nemesis on the death of the two pashas," he wrote in reference to his execution of the two Egyptian officers. Fatalism was his only solace. "It is sad but being ordained, we must not murmur."

For all his grief, Gordon indirectly replied to the Mahdi's letter with a defiant note to one of the Ansar officers: "Whether he [the Mahdi] has captured 20,000 steamers like the *Abbas,* or 20,000 officers like Stewart, or not, it is all one to me. I am here like iron and hope to see the newly arrived English. It is impossible for me to have any more words to Mohammed Achmad [Mohammed Ahmad, the Mahdi]—only lead."

Even as he privately agonized, Gordon tried to convince himself that he had done the right thing to send Stewart and Power off. "I was glad they went (1) because I thought it was quite safe; (2) because I knew if Europe knew the state of affairs, the Government would be shamed into action."

Gordon wrote in some detail the circumstances surrounding Stewart's departure from Khartoum. "A long conversation took place between me and Stewart in which Stewart wished me to 'order him' to leave. I declined to do so on account of eventualities which might arise." But he did write an "official letter" saying that Stewart would be performing a "service" by going and providing Wolseley and Baring with a true picture of the gravity of Khartoum's situation.[1]

A few days after Kitchener's letter arrived with the news of Stewart's death, Gordon was given an English newspaper dated September 15. It had been thrown out with the trash and found blowing about the palace grounds by a servant. The crumpled pages had been used by Kitchener to wrap his dispatches, and in them was contained a wealth of news. "Pure gold" for Gordon, it was the first real news from home to reach him since February 24. He learned that Lord Wolseley had been seen off at Victoria Station to take command of the "Gordon Relief Expedition." ("NO," an exasperated Gordon corrected in his journal, "not for Gordon's relief but the relief of the Sudan garrisons.") He also learned that Lord Northbrook, as Special Commissioner to Egypt, had had an audience with the Khedive, and learned that Abd el-Kader, previous Governor General of the Sudan, had been made Egyptian Minister of Interior.

From the scanty information received from Kitchener about the progress of the expedition, Gordon hoped that he might expect relief as early as November 10. This estimate would prove very wide of the mark, but it stirred Gordon to think about several problems that would arise if the British insisted on a "rapid retreat" once the Khartoum garrison was rescued. Should government stores be destroyed as the garrison was evacuated? Should the unreliable Shaigiya tribesmen be disarmed before the Egyptians left? Should there be negotiations with the Mahdi? And what should be done about the Sennar and Kassala garrisons?

DEATH THROES OF A CITY

Suddenly at 5:30 in the morning on November 12, 1884, Gordon was awakened by a violent fusillade at Omdurman. News of the attack had reached Khartoum the night before, but a lazy telegraph clerk had failed to notify Gordon. Because of this mischance the steamers had not had time to get steam up and move out of range. The steamer *Ismailia* was soon struck by three shells, killing one man and wounding fifteen, while the *Husseinyeh* ran aground while dodging enemy fire.

By noon the firing had stopped. Gordon wrote of six hours of anxiety: "I have lived *years* in these last *hours!* Had I lost the *Ismailia*, I should have lost the *Husseinyeh* and then Omdurman and the North fort! And then the town!"

Gordon boxed the ears of the errant telegraph clerk, then, typically, the general's conscience pricked him and he gave the terrified young man a bonus of money. "I know all this is brutal but what is one to do? if you cut their pay, you hurt their families."

The attack on Omdurman gave Gordon a new appreciation of his adversary. A few lines in the journal convey the general's feelings of shameless fear and apprehension:

One tumbles at 3:00 A.M. into a troubled sleep; a drum beats—tup! tup! tup! It comes into a dream, but after a few moments one becomes more awake and it is revealed to the brain that *one is in Khartoum.* . . . Where is this tup, tupping going on? A hope arises it will die away. No, it goes on and increases in intensity. . . .

. . . up one must get and go on the roof of the palace; then telegrams, orders, swearing and cursing goes on till about 9:00 A.M. . . . Men may say what they like about glorious war, but to me it is a horrid nuisance.[2]

Adding to Gordon's gloom, the steamer *Husseinyeh* ran aground in a vulnerable location. The *Ismailia*, despite five shell holes, steamed by Arab guns more than twenty times to divert attention from the grounded *Husseinyeh*. In thus trying to save the *Husseinyeh*, the *Ismailia* was knocked out of action by two hits. Her gun was removed and set up on the bank of the Nile to cover the approach to the *Husseinyeh*. Gordon admitted that his poor opinion of Egyptian soldiers was not justified by the brave performance of the crews of both boats during this engagement.

Omdurman Fort survived the attacks on it although the garrison lost four dead and sixteen wounded. The North Fort, across the Blue Nile from

411

Khartoum and manned by the Shaigiyas, was also coming under increased attack by the Ansar. Gordon feared that the Shaigiyas, if threatened, might collapse. "It is really absurd that one should have to pay and keep such troops."

A caravan from Berber arrived in the Mahdi's camp on November 20. According to Gordon's spies, it brought word of clashes between the tribes and the British expeditionary force. Though these reports were not true—the first British clash with the Ansar was still nearly two months away and the Camel Corps would not even reach Korti until mid-December—such rumors suggested a growing nervousness about the British advance among the tribes to the north. But Gordon was surprised at the Mahdi's own apparent lack of concern. "They are uncommonly confident or ignorant."

The gun duels continued. The Ansar's Nordenfeldt machine gun kept on "grunting all day at intervals of half seconds." Gordon's Mogren Fort responded with its Krupp gun. No damage was done by either side, but the valiant *Husseinyeh* was finally sunk inadvertently when the Ansar tried to shove it off the shoal that held it in its grip.

At last there was a moment of joy in Khartoum as the steamer *Bordein* came into view. There was the hopeful anticipation of a show of British red-coated soldiers on board—the redder and more conspicuous the better. Even a token force might unnerve the Mahdi. But no, after furious cannonading by the Ansar from the shore, the unscathed *Bordein* put into dock with nothing to show for its valiance except a pouch of letters and seven wounded Arabs. Even the news it brought was disappointing. The expeditionary force had only reached Ambukol near Korti, 185 miles farther away than Gordon had calculated.

The *Bordein* brought an official Foreign Office message, but having been enciphered in the codes lost when Stewart was murdered, it was unreadable. But new and highly puzzling instructions from Khedive Tewfik were *en clair* and unfortunately could be read by Gordon. Under British instructions, the Khedive informed Gordon that he had been demoted from Governor General of the Sudan to Governor of Khartoum. Gordon had no way of knowing that this gratuitous and by now meaningless gesture had been the result of Gladstone's temper tantrum in Scotland, ignited by a garbled news story in the local press that had Gordon rampaging up and down the Nile, "smashing up" the Mahdi. The general instead interpreted the message to mean that the policy of evacuation had been abandoned, and that the Sudan's provincial administration would be parceled out to British officers. Why couldn't Kitchener tell him that?[3] Gordon did, however, hear that Kitchener had been given authority to pay the Mahdi up to £20,000 as ransom for his release. He would never agree to that—nor, in his opinion, would the Mahdi.

Stores of food in Khartoum were rapidly dwindling. Gordon had been reduced to itemizing what was left. On November 28, 174,000 *okes* of biscuit and 1,165 *ardebs* of *dhoora* remained. But with despair and disgust, he knew there were officers in his garrison who waylaid the women to whom Gordon had issued biscuits and robbed them of their precious supply.

Omdurman Fort was in an even worse position. Gordon's journal entries now frequently began with the assuring comment "Fort Omdurman all right." To relieve the tension, Gordon indulged himself by inventing more little charades. Whimsically, he imagined Baring writing Egerton from Metemmeh: "Metemmeh! At last, after the most fearful sufferings, every bone in my body dislocated with those beastly camels." As the charade went on, Baring discovers Gordon's journal: ". . . it appears that that duffer, the Mahdi has at last roused himself . . . fear it is too late." But more shocking to Baring still featured in the charade is the tone of the journal and the disrespect shown to the Prime Minister: ". . . it is *simply deplorable* and (do not mention it, please) he has actually made a sketch (brace yourself up to hear it) of our high priest."

In December, Omdurman Fort was still "all right." Gordon brooded more about Tewfik's *firman* removing him as Governor General: "When Wolseley and Baring arrived [Gordon still believed the rumor that Baring would accompany Wolseley], they had better have a *firman* from him [the Khedive], giving them authority." With evident whimsy Gordon suggested he might appoint Baring Governor General, then "bolt."

Gordon ruminated about Zubair again. What if he simply "found" Zubair in the city and appointed the old slaver ruler just as the British rescue troops arrived? The Anti-Slavery Society would, of course, "empty their vials of wrath," Gordon mused, and the Cairo officials would wring their collective hands. But the problem would be solved. "I might clear out of the country in disgrace to prevent any appearance of connivance on the part of —— in this arrangement . . . which he will or ought officially to deplore."

With whose name would Gordon fill in the blank? Gordon's imagination ran riot as he spun out the fevered scenario: Gordon, as an Egyptian official, would be entirely responsible for the appointment of Zubair; "The Government will chuckle over it all and will preserve the fiction that they have nought to do with the Sudan or Egypt." The distraught general added pathetically: "I am not going to England again . . . I shall not much mind the abuse."

Reality interrupted reverie when at 5:00 P.M., an artillery duel began. "Arab shells from Goba fall just about 200 yards short of the palace." At 7:30 P.M.: "Battle begun again because the buglers played 'Salaam Effendina' [Egyptian martial tune]."

December 4: "Omdurman fort all right." Reports circulated that the rescue steamers were near. "The buglers are bugling now 'come to us, come to us.' In the French tradition of conversing by bugle calls, one of the Dervish buglers replies 'come to us, come to us.' "

December 6: "I have given up all ideas of landing at Omdurman; we have not the force to do it."

December 7: "The 270th day of our imprisonment." He chronicled the exact number of shells which exploded, some very near. As absolute ruler of this crumbling domain, nothing escaped his vigilance, certainly not murder: "The cock turkey has killed one of his companions; reasons not known— (supposed to be correspondence with Mahdi or some harem infidelity)." Then a sudden insight: ". . . the Mahdi business will be the end of slavery in the Sudan. The Arabs have invariably put their slaves in the front . . . and the slaves have seen that they were plucky while their masters shirked: is it likely that those slaves will ever yield obediently to those masters as heretofore?"

December 8: "Omdurman fort reports 'all right.' " Gordon noted that the dervishes had two gun batteries with regular embrasures and wondered if such European sophistication could be of Slatin's design. (It wasn't.) Reports told of the advance of the expeditionary force. A letter arrived from Wadji Barra, the Mahdi's Emir in command of the north bank of the Blue Nile, demanding Gordon's surrender and claiming that news of the expeditionary force was lies. Gordon replied, "Go to . . . etc."

December 9: "The siege of Sevastopol lasted 326 days, while we are at our 271st day." At least at Sevastopol, Gordon noted, the English and their allies dealt with an enemy "who would recognize the rights of war." Human glory "composed of 9/10 twaddle."

December 10: "Fort Omdurman is all right." Insurrections in Kordofan had cut off the Mahdi's return to that province, so "we and he are like two rats in a box." News arrived that the expeditionary force was near, but Gordon believed it had been concocted, like the Kordofan report, to make him smile kindly on the informants.

December 11: An extra month's pay to garrison troops to retain their loyalty. 3:30 P.M.: The Arabs fired three shells at the palace. "This always irritates me, for it is so personal."

December 12: Gordon traced the overoptimistic reports of the approaching expeditionary force to a leading mullah who was trying to keep his parishioners' spirits up. More tedious chronicling of dervish shelling, hoping that the Mahdi would run out of ammunition before Khartoum ran out of food.* ". . . the Arabs have fired over 2,000 shells at us which, however, have accounted for only three lives."

December 13: Gordon was fast losing hope. *If some effort is not made before ten days time the town will fall.* One hundred men are all we require, just to show themselves." In the next breath Gordon modified his plea. "All that is absolutely necessary is for fifty of the Expeditionary Force to get on board a steamer and come up to Halfaya [a few miles north of Khartoum] and thus let their presence be felt; this is not asking much, but it must happen *at once;* or it will (as usual) be too late. I send this journal for I have little hopes of saving it if the town falls," he wrote in despair as he readied the *Bordein* for a downriver run two days thence.

December 14: Last entry before the journal was sent off with the *Bordein.* "NOW MARK THIS, if the Expeditionary Force—and I ask for no more than two hundred men—does not come in ten days, *the town may fall;* and I have done my best for the honour of our country. Good Bye."

These words, a martyr's valediction, are saved from sounding theatrical by a very human footnote—the last words in the journal: "You send me no information though you have lots of money."

---

* Gordon's calculations were based on known supplies of ammunition taken by the Ansar from Hicks's army after its defeat. This was essentially the Mahdi's only significant source of supply.

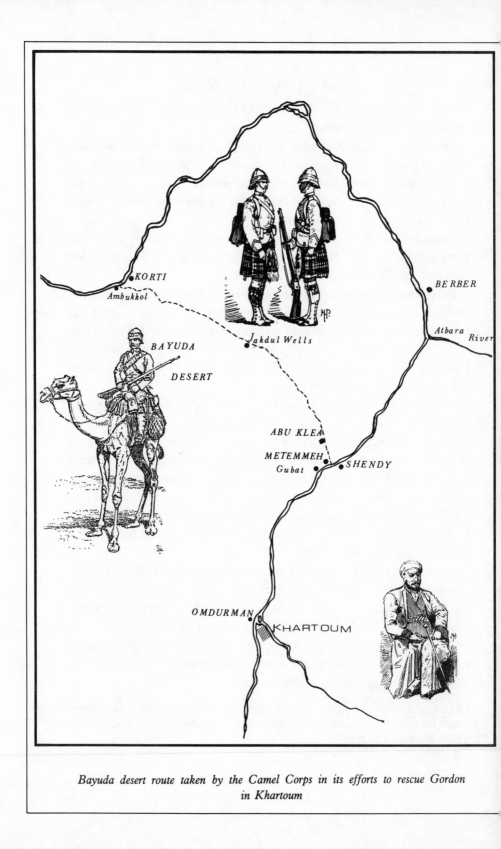

Bayuda desert route taken by the Camel Corps in its efforts to rescue Gordon in Khartoum

THE BATTLE OF ABU KLEA

It was a beautiful and striking sight, such a one as Fitzjames must
have seen when Roderick Dhu's men rose out of the heather.
—Colonel Sir Charles Wilson as the Battle of Abu Klea began,
January 17, 1884

All was definitely not "Sir Garnet." An accumulation of problems plagued the British expeditionary force and could be blamed for an agonizingly long three months of preparation before the advance into the Sudan could actually begin. Coal, of course, was vital to the operation of the steamers moving supplies up the Nile, so it was with dismay that Wolseley saw the supply line of this vital fuel suddenly dry up in late October 1884. Thomas Cook & Sons, contractors responsible for shipping the coal from England to Alexandria, were not at fault; Chief of Staff Sir Redvers Buller simply had not adequately monitored the requisitions. By the time the problem was corrected, thirteen more critical days had been lost. Wolseley was understandably upset about this and annoyed with Buller. He wrote in his journal: "I should not have relied upon my trust in him on such a vital question, and ought personally to have gone into it."[1]

Other logistical failings added to the confusion. When Thomas Cook & Sons landed the whalers, built hurriedly in England, they had somehow become separated from their oars, causing further delay before they could be launched on the Nile. There was a serious rate of spoilage among food stocks. Bad packing ruined half the tea, vital to British fighting men, and much of the biscuit supply was similarly ruined. Medical supplies were pilfered by the natives. Perhaps as much as half of the critically needed supplies disappeared in this way, although medical alcohol seemed to find its way to thirsty British rankers who resented Wolseley's decision to ban the customary rum issue. Tinned meat, decomposed by the desert heat, was inedible; much of it exploded before reaching the commissaries. And an estimated quarter of the sugar was lost by spillage or theft.

Boots issued to the troops did not stand up to the hard wear given them in the desert. From the outset, other clothing shortages developed; one unit found itself without enough trousers. Perhaps the most serious problem was caused by the shoddily made water skins, which leaked so badly that the parched troops often ran out of water in the desert before the next well could be reached.

Camels presented new logistical problems never before encountered by the British Army. Members of the Camel Corps had to be taught the intricacies of controlling these adaptable but temperamental beasts. The troops also had to get used to the body filth characteristic of camels, and such other unattractive traits as belching and biting. Conversely, the camels had to get used to their inexperienced and largely unsympathetic riders. Enormous quantities of grain were required for the ravenous beasts, which could not forage on the barren desert, and this further taxed the long supply line.

More serious was a miscalculation resulting in a shortage of camels. The army purchased eight thousand when twelve thousand were needed. Camel saddles were in short supply, and among those that did arrive, padding was insufficient, causing debilitating saddle sores for the animals. The quality of the camels was substandard as well. In a sellers' market the sudden demand caused prices to jump wildly, and camel dealers seized this golden opportunity to unload their old and sick creatures on the British.

Because of the camel shortage, the flying force, whose success depended upon crossing the 180 miles of the Bayuda desert before the enemy could rally its defenses and prevent it from linking up with Gordon's steamers at Metemmeh, had to shuttle men and supplies across the arid expanse. The delay would prove critical. General Wolseley, who had described the expedition as "the biggest operation the English Army has ever undertaken," had on this occasion fallen short of this reputation as meticulous logistician.

A serious source of concern was Mustafa Yawer, Mudir of Dongola, who consistently cheated the British on camel transactions and otherwise interfered with their progress. Kitchener, who knew the area better than any other Englishman and had largely been responsible for keeping him from going over to the Mahdi, believed the Mudir not only was lining his pockets at British expense, but was in secret an avowed enemy as well. Sir Charles Wilson, chief intelligence officer, also distrusted the Mudir. Wilson blamed the Mudir's obstructions for a good part of the army's four-month delay on the border.

Leadership of the expedition, dominated by the "Wolseley ring," consisted of interesting and in some cases talented officers, but not particularly compatible ones. General Sir Redvers Buller, Wolseley's Chief of Staff, had led an active life and distinguished career, earning the Victoria Cross for an act of valor while commanding irregular cavalry in the Zulu War. More recently, he had fought in the Suakin campaign. While brave and popular with his men, he was prone to bicker with his officers and suffered from a surfeit of caution when making critical field decisions.[2]

Sir Herbert Stewart, as commander of the "flying" camel column, was an inspired selection, eminently worthy of the honor paid him by this coveted assignment. He had dash and daring—just the sort of officer to lead this new and unorthodox unit. Wolseley thought so highly of Stewart that he would have preferred him to Buller as Chief of Staff, but he needed the able Scot to lead the advance.

Colonel Sir Charles Wilson accompanied Stewart and the Camel Corps as Intelligence Officer. His judgments were usually sound. Unlike Wolseley, who refused to believe "absurd rumors that the desert is occupied by large, hostile armies," Wilson correctly estimated the strength of the Mahdi's considerable forces. He had also accurately predicted the venal propensities of the Mudir of Dongola. Intelligence was the right place for the methodical Wilson. Combat command was not.

Lieutenant Colonel Sir William Butler, commander of the whaler fleet, was a Wolseley man who had served with him in the Red River campaign. An engaging Irishman with a romantic streak, he gloried in "sails and oars flashing in the sunlight" to save "the noblest knight among us all."[3] Butler envied Stewart's role with the Camel Corps but consoled himself by disparaging the "swells" on camelback, "too precious to trust themselves in boats."[4]

Lord Charles Beresford, Wolseley's aide, commanded the fifty-seven-man naval contingent whose function would be to take over the steamers at Metemmeh. He tended to gravitate toward the center of action where glory could be found. An Irishman of noble birth and well married, he knew everyone of note, including members of the Royal Family. He moved in the most stylish sporting circles of England. Even in Egypt he revealed himself as an incurable gentleman sportsman when, on the way south to Wadi Halfa, he bought three racing camels, which he named Bimbashi, Ballyhooly and Beelzebub. Queen Victoria considered him "a trifle cracky," but that did not prevent him from rising quickly to the rank of admiral.

Colonel Henry Brackenbury, one of the "Wolseley ring," was Deputy Adjutant and Quartermaster General. For all his brilliance and efficiency, he was an irritating and unattractive man. He reminded Wolseley of his camel. While the Commander in Chief recognized Brackenbury's worth, he was less than flattering in his personal comments about him. Wolseley wrote his wife: "Brack . . . had become yellower and certainly much uglier than ever. As he grows older his legs seem to become shorter." Brackenbury, once an officer in the Intelligence Bureau, was never popular in the Army; he was particularly disliked by the Commander in Chief, the Duke of Cambridge himself, who distrusted his vaunting ambition and referred to him once as "a very dangerous man."[5]

Wolseley's campaign plan was not complicated. A strong force of infantry would be boated up the Nile from the railhead at Sarass, south of Wadi Halfa, by the Canadian *voyageurs* in the thirty-foot whalers, twelve men to a boat. The army would then assemble in Dongola for the assault on Khartoum. The Camel Corps would try to reach Gordon more quickly overland by short-cutting the loop in the Nile between Korti and Metemmeh and crossing the Bayuda desert. Simple in concept, the operation proved more complex in practice.

Navigating four cataracts in the river slowed the advance, the more so because the river was falling and exposing more rocks. It was not until November 6 that the first battalion to travel by whaler, the 1st South Staffordshire, embarked from the railhead. Because of the coal shortage, the last infantry battalion was not able to leave until December 19. It was backbreaking labor in ninety-degree heat to drag the whalers through some twenty miles of angry rapids, and it took its toll of soldiers who capsized or lost their footing on the rocks and were drowned. The twelve miles of fast, foaming rapids between Ambigol and Mangal were particularly dangerous.

Thanks to a letter of advice which finally got through from Gordon on November 17, after fifteen days in transit, Wolseley made the decision to stage the forces at Korti instead of Dongola, cutting the distance the Camel Corps would have to travel across the barren Bayuda Desert. In the letter was the news that Gordon had sent the steamer flotilla downstream to meet the expedition at Metemmeh.

Gordon predicted he could hold out for forty days—twenty-seven days from the arrival of his letter. This spurred Wolseley to speed up troop movements, which had been maddeningly slow. He rode back to Wadi Halfa from Dongola to look for the causes of delay. Frustrated by the problem, he even offered a £100 prize from his own purse to the battalion which moved south with most dispatch (the prize was won by the 1st Royal Irish).★

Wolseley was now intent on using the Camel Corps as a flying column with some chance of reaching Khartoum before it was too late, while the infantry proceeded more deliberately upriver in whalers supported by steamers under the command of General Earle. The Camel Corps consisted of four regiments, sixteen hundred men in all, and was ready to ride south from Wadi Halfa on November 12. The Guards regiment, with a company of Royal Marines attached, led off. The other regiments soon followed.† The Guards and the mounted infantry arrived at Korti on December 14, exactly the date beyond which Gordon could not guarantee Khartoum's survival.

The rest of the Camel Corps soon arrived, as did the 19th Hussars mounted more traditionally on horseback. But aside from the Staffordshires in Korti as advance guard, the rest of the infantry could not be expected until mid-January because of the difficult river journey and tremendous logistical burden involved. If Gordon and the Khartoum garrison were to be rescued in time, it would have to be the Camel Corps to do so. Wolseley's flying column concept was proving out.

On December 30 a spy brought in another message from Gordon. Perhaps fearing interception, the crumpled slip of paper dated December 14 stated blandly: "Khartoum all right," but the spy verbally passed the real message that was less encouraging:

★ Queen Victoria, who was following this drama attentively, wrote Wolseley an angry letter when she heard of this, berating him for "bribing" British soldiers for doing what duty required of them.[6]

† The heavy regiment included the Household Cavalry, Dragoons and Lancers. The light regiment was made up of Hussars. The mounted infantry regiment included detachments from various regiments in Egypt.

> We are besieged on three sides. Fighting goes on day and night. Enemy
> cannot take us except by starving us out. Do not scatter your troops. Enemy
> are numerous. Bring plenty of troops if you can.[7]

In still another message memorized by the spy, Gordon made it clear that the
city was suffering from lack of food. "We want you to come quickly."

Wolseley referred to these messages when he spoke with Baring in Cairo:

> Gordon's message compels measures that will postpone my arrival in
> Khartoum. He wants me not to leave Berber in my rear, so I must move by
> water and take it before I march on Khartoum. Meanwhile I shall have
> established a post at Metemmeh by men and stores sent across the
> desert. . . . if he is *in extremis* before infantry arrive by river [I shall] push
> forward Camel Corps to help him at all hazard.[8]

Only hours after Gordon's message arrived, a thousand men on camelback
left Korti as a band played "The Campbells Are Coming."

The Corps' first objective was Metemmeh, 170 miles away, where it would
meet the steamers sent by Gordon. This advance unit was led by Kitchener,
whose months of intelligence activities had made him an expert on this
inhospitable stretch of desert. He knew that the Mahdi's forces would stalk
them and somewhere between Korti and Metemmeh would probably attack.
He knew also that it would be fatal to leave unguarded the vital water wells
along the way which, if denied them by the Ansar, would leave the force
stranded in the desert without a lifeline to the rear—at their enemy's mercy.

It was now that the camel shortage told. Relays of camels had to be sent
back to Korti to bring up supplies, preventing an unbroken dash to
Metemmeh. In all, nine days were lost this way, and the Ansar, which lurked
in the vicinity, had that much more time to muster their attack. It was not
until January 8, 1885, that Stewart himself could leave Korti with the rest of
his corps and assume command at a bleak water hole in the desert called
Gakdol. Much to his disappointment Kitchener had to leave the scene of
action there when he was sent back to Korti as escort for one of the camel
trains needed to bring up more supplies.

The full Camel Corps, now numbering eighteen hundred, assembled on
January 13 for the march to Metemmeh. The intrepid Colonel Burnaby,
reveling in his "unofficial" adventure, dashed up to join the corps at Gakdol.
Wolseley had personally picked Burnaby to accompany Stewart, realizing

that if anything should happen to the able Scot, a combat-blooded replacement would have to carry on.* Wilson, while next in rank to Stewart, would never do. He had had no battlefront experience. Wolseley had earlier written his wife that as long as Stewart was safe, he didn't mind, "but a stray bullet might any moment rob me of all confidence in the success of the operation he is now entrusted with."

The forward force now consisted of the Camel Corps, a few infantrymen of the Royal Sussex Regiment to guard the wells and a small naval "brigade," fifty-seven men in all, under Lord Charles Beresford, to man the steamers at Metemmeh.

It was late afternoon on January 16, 1885, when advance pickets of the Camel Corps came over a rise to see the water wells of Abu Klea in the distance. There, blocking their way, was an awesome sight: some ten thousand Ansar warriors brandishing their spears, massed about two miles away. This startling tableau revealed the unfortunate and dangerous wages of delay; the Ansar had taken full advantage of two weeks to prepare their reception of the British force. They were anticipating the encounter with all the religious fervor their leaders could muster. Mohammed al-Khair, Emir of Berber, had posted an inspirational notice exhorting the faithful to prepare quickly for battle: " . . . you are not to fight the enemies of God with ammunition, but with spears and swords." The sabers of Islam with God's blessing were presumed to be more powerful than the guns of the infidel. "It behooves you . . . to carry on the Holy War against the enemies of the faith and to fight against the heathen. Great victory and much plenty await you, for God has promised it to you."[10]

The Camel Corps bivouacked for the night behind a quickly erected *zariba*. Darkness would soon fall, so it was too late to fight that day, but morning would bring the inevitable clash. It was Friday, the Moslem sabbath, and the white-robed tribesmen prepared for their prayers at sundown. Darkness fell, and the frequent whine of bullets told the British they could expect a restless night as the few Ansar sharpshooters who did

---

* Burnaby was a fast-rising star in the British Army and the toast of London society. Jenny Churchill, Winston's American mother, referred to him as a "gentle-voiced, amiable man, notwithstanding an enormous frame and gigantic strength" whom she "had occasion to see a great deal of."[9]

have ammunition, the elite Jehadiya, picked at them blindly simply to keep them awake.

The right wing of the Ansar was commanded by the Emir of Metemmeh, Abu Saleh, while the left, consisting of Berber tribesmen, was led by their Emir, Mohammed al-Khair. Ansar pennants drooped listlessly in the dying breezes of the evening, and battle drums throbbed in the distance. During the night the drums would sometimes seem to grow louder, causing the tired troops to stand to in expectation of an attack.

At about 7:00 in the morning the main body of the Arabs, some five thousand Ansar, advanced to within twelve hundred yards of the British square, but then inexplicably stopped. Captain Willoughby Verner described the scene in his diary: "Thousands of spearheads sparkled in the sun and many bright banners were visible along the dusky line of savages."[11]

Stewart now took the initiative. The British marched forward to engage the enemy at 9:00. As the square moved down the slope the riderless camels (camels did not like going downhill) lagged to the rear of the square. Part of the rifle company skirmished in front while the mounted infantry, now dismounted, began to fire at the enemy five hundred to seven hundred yards away. At the instant before the battle was joined Wilson remembered the scene almost with ecstasy: "It was a beautiful and striking sight, such a one as Fitzjames must have seen when Roderick Dhu's men rose out of the heather."[12] The Ansar, who had cleverly concealed their horses in a ravine until they rose to attack, "advanced at a quick step even pace as if on parade." Wilson was struck with "a feeling of pity mixed with admiration" as they advanced in close formation over bare ground in the face of withering Martini-Henry fire.[13]

Captain Verner, whose diary captured the battle scene at point-blank range, noted that at the next moment the "savages were up to the bayonets of the Heavy Camel Regiment, hurling in spears and cutting and stabbing on all sides." Then a large mass "swept round still more to their right and enveloped the rear corner of the square." Great confusion followed when "the savages, who had broken into the square, crept under the camels and attacked the rear rank of the opposite side."[14]

Colonel Burnaby, whose sector of the square bore the brunt of attack, was among those killed in this first rush. He had ordered his men to make way for the forward skirmishing riflemen so they could reenter the square as they fell back, but this had only provided the Ansar with an opening through which they poured. Typical of his reckless courage, Burnaby had dashed forward to help the riflemen regain the square when an Ansar spear pierced his jugular.

When news of Burnaby's death reached Wolseley, he was saddened and worried. The general feared that if Stewart was now to be killed, he had no worthy replacement on the spot to lead the column in its crucial dash to Khartoum. The trauma of Burnaby's death provoked Wolseley to vent his dislike for the Royal Family in his journal: "How delighted the Prince of Wales and the Duke of Cambridge will be that poor Burnaby is killed. His high military spirit, energy, zeal and remarkable personal courage were not sufficient in the eyes of those Royal tailors to cover up the fact that socially Burnaby was distasteful to them and their set."[15]

To return to the vivid chronicler of the battle, Verner narrowly escaped being impaled on an Ansar spear by shooting his attacker just in time. He then spotted another Arab hurling a long spear at him. It missed, killing Major Carmichael instead, but in the next instant Verner was hit and fell to the ground. In a dizzying scene of carnage, he watched the rush of enemy pass over him and saw their spears "hard at work stabbing our men who were down." He could now see with relief that the mounted infantry were rallying: "They poured such a heavy fire into the flank of the stream of Arabs coming up the hill that they wavered and halted—and then fell back."[16]

The worst was over, but Verner was dumbfounded to watch an Ansar sheikh, still within the square, plant his standard and pause in his bloody work long enough to read aloud from the Koran. Wilson was witness to this act too, and recognized the man as Sheikh Musa, Emir of the Duguaim tribe of Kordofan. "If any man deserved a place in the Moslem paradise, he did," Wilson later said. In the next moment, the pious sheikh was shot dead in midsentence by a British rifleman.

Wilson saw Stewart's horse shot; as the commander fell off, three Arabs rushed at him. Wilson shot one while fire from the mounted infantry accounted for the others, saving Stewart's life by a frighteningly small margin. Colonel Talbot, another officer present at the carnage, referred to the Battle of Abu Klea as "an Inkerman on a small scale"—a soldier's battle in which "strength, determination, steadiness and unflinching courage" won the day.[17]

★　★　★

The British may have won the round but they sustained very heavy casualties. Winston Churchill was later to describe Abu Klea as the "most savage and bloody action ever fought in the Sudan by British troops."[18] The British square had been broken and 10 percent of the British force lay dead or wounded.

Wolseley noted in his journal of January 22 receipt of a tepid message of congratulations from the Queen—and "another from the Khedive, much more cordial."[19]

Abu Klea revealed some serious weaknesses in British arms which later became the subject of outraged inquiry in Parliament. The Gardner machine gun, while devastating when working properly, was prone to jam. At Abu Klea, the Gardners often froze after firing only a few rounds (just as they had during the Battle of Tamai), permitting the Ansar to plunge through an opening in the square. The standard British rifle, the Martini-Henry, also frequently jammed and proved to be no match for the "obsolete" but reliable Remingtons taken by the Ansar from Hicks's Egyptian army and used to good effect by the Jehadiya snipers. Beresford estimated that half of the Martinis failed at Abu Klea that day.

Wilson blamed the cartridges, which dented easily and jammed in the breeches. In his memoir of the battle he wrote: "Can you imagine a more dreadful position than that of being face to face with an Arab and your only arm a rifle that will not go off?"[20] The bayonets, too, were faulty and sometimes bent upon impact, not something to be desired in hand-to-hand combat. Kipling suggested he was one of the few who forgave the Martini when he wrote: "When 'arf of your bullets fly wide in the ditch/Don't call your Martini a crosseyed old bitch."

Beside a failure of arms, the square was ruptured as a result of human failings as well. Wilson felt that cavalry simply could not be turned into infantry. Trained to break the enemy's square, dismounted cavalry troops instinctively stepped back after firing rather than standing firm. They were unused to fighting defensively on the ground, as the Camel Corps had to do. The troops, too, were from different units and had not had time to train together and develop the cohesiveness of an established regiment.

While camels could not be used for cavalry charges as horses could, they nonetheless had their usefulness at Abu Klea. Milling around within the square, their sheer mass blocked the attacking Arabs. Captain Verner, in fact, owed his life to a camel which, after Verner had fallen wounded, toppled over him, protecting him from enemy spears.

However costly, Abu Klea cleared the way to Metemmeh. The Ansar suffered at least a thousand dead. But the ordeal was not yet over; another round was yet to be fought.

It was important for the British to reach the Nile without delay. Water supplies were nearly exhausted, and a beachhead on the river was essential if they were to link up with the steamers. Stewart left part of the corps to guard the baggage while he led some thousand men in an all-night forced march through scrub and brambles toward the river. As the column advanced, the grass became thicker and the prickly acacia scrub more dense. Men and camels floundered about in the dark, utterly confused, making enough noise to alert the Ansar to their progress—or lack of it. They finally reached open ground six miles from the river.

Scouts reported a massing of hostile tribesmen near a village called Abu Kru, but the warning time was short. The first Ansar attack came at 8:00 A.M., January 19, 1885, and caught the men exhausted from their all-night march. They had not slept for forty-eight hours. Verner described the engagement: "All at once, over the hill on our left front, a white-coated host appeared and, urged on by their chiefs on horseback, came charging down toward us." The tired men managed "a tremendous cheer and then opened a terrific firing. . . . Masses of the enemy . . . appeared to fall in lines under the deadly Martini fire."[21]

British casualties were modest under the circumstances—twenty-three killed and ninety-eight wounded—but one consequence of the brief engagement was serious: Stewart was mortally wounded in the groin and lay dying. With Burnaby already dead, command devolved upon Sir Charles Wilson as senior officer. Precisely what Wolseley had feared now occurred.

Wilson met his first crisis well. As he led some twelve hundred men toward the river, several thousand Ansar warriors in crescent formation swept down on the column. Eight hundred zealots in the van rushed the square but this time failed to break it. The front line of the Arab attackers, including five emirs, was cut down by continuous British fire. The brief contest was soon over as the Ansar scuttled off to nearby Metemmeh, permitting the British to set about fortifying the village of Gubat on the Nile to serve as advance base for the dash to Khartoum.

THE MOSLEM MESSIAH AND THE CHRISTIAN MARTYR

On January 21, as Wilson marched toward the key Arab-held village of Metemmeh, suddenly the British troops spontaneously erupted in cheers. They saw Gordon's four steamers coming into view. Wilson read a brief note from Gordon, dated December 29, brought by Khasm el-Mus, captain of the flotilla. It said: "Khartoum all right and can hold out for years." Intelligence told another story. Omdurman Fort had fallen shortly before the Battle of Abu Klea, and the foodstock situation in Khartoum was desperate. Spies reported that the people had been reduced to eating gum and hides. Gordon's oddly hopeful message may have been meant sarcastically, but more likely it was written with the possibility of interception in mind. Certainly the steamer crews did not express much optimism about Khartoum. Whatever the case, Wilson was unsure of himself in his new command and wary of dangers lurking upriver. He made the fateful decision to conduct preliminary reconnaissance before sending a rescue party to Khartoum.

FORFEIT DAYS

> What I have gone through I cannot describe. The Almighty God
> will help me.
> —Charles Gordon, while awaiting the Mahdi's attack on Khartoum

When Gordon sent off the *Bordein* on December 14, it carried not only his last journal but also final farewells to friends and loved ones. Despite a remaining glimmer of hope that relief would arrive in time, he sensed the end. To his beloved Augusta he wrote: "This may be the last letter you will receive from me, for we are on our last legs owing to the delay of the expedition." Resigned to his fate, he looked forward to joining his God—the deep-seated longing he had had for most of his life. He reminded his sister, whom he owed much for his Faith, "God rules all and as He will rule to His glory and our welfare, may His will be done." At the bottom of his letter he scrawled a postscript, a last rendering unto Caesar: "I am quite happy, thank God, and like Lawrence* I have tried to do my duty."

Gordon penned a last note to his old friend Wolseley. However much Gordon was frustrated by the slow progress of the expedition force, his dispatches and letters never placed blame on the Chief of Staff himself. Gordon's final report was brief; he described his situation as "extremely critical, almost desperate," and estimated that Khartoum would fall within a week. Anticipating the grief and self-recrimination that this would cause Wolseley, he assured his friend that he felt no "bitterness to Her Majesty's Government." Gordon also wrote Watson, his friend since Equatoria days, predicting that Khartoum would fall by Christmas Day. Gordon left his letters to fellow officers unsealed so that the advance force which would forward them could benefit from the information they contained.

---

* Brigadier General Sir Henry Lawrence was killed defending Lucknow in the Indian Mutiny, 1857.

In Khartoum, however, Gordon kept up a brave front in an effort to sustain public morale. He reminded the townfolk repeatedly that British troops were on their way, and to lend credence to this, be ostentatiously commandeered several houses in town in which to billet British officers upon their arrival. If hope of British relief was not enough, he promised that God was watching over them. For the deserving, he struck distinctive medals which he designed himself and presented with touching ceremony. But he was a one-man band in a hall of despair. Evidence of his crumbling cause was everywhere.

As had been the situation at El Obeid, an acute shortage of food was the crippling consequence of the Mahdi's blockade. Since it had become too dangerous for the troops to forage along the banks of the Nile, Khartoum had to live off its fast-dwindling stocks. In early January, a last crop of *dhoora* was harvested on Tuti Island before it had ripened. Food distributions were drastically curtailed to preserve what little grain remained. A search of merchants' houses was rewarded with a few more bags of grain which had been hoarded, but this did not significantly improve the situation.

What few donkeys and horses remained were soon butchered for meat. Rats, cats, and dogs were chased down for food; even leather was soaked and eaten. Gum and date-palm fiber were pounded into cakes, although a diet of such invariably led to an enervating dysentery. By now, corpses littered the streets, victims of starvation and flux. Garrison soldiers, many too weak to function, stood listlessly at their posts waiting to die.

Regretfully, Gordon finally encouraged those starving and frightened townspeople who wanted to do so to join the Mahdi. Many took advantage of the offer—perhaps half the town's population. Gordon wrote the Mahdi asking that they be well treated. The people of Khartoum "are the same as yourself. I have supported them for eleven months and now it is necessary to send them to you."

In his last letter to Watson he wrote bitterly: "I will never set foot in England again. . . ." He felt that he had been let down by both the British and the Turks. He looked upon the Prime Minister as his nemesis and vowed to accept nothing whatever from the Gladstone government.

As January arrived and his daily rooftop vigils produced no signs of the expeditionary force on the distant horizon, Gordon sent messages to Queen Victoria and the Sultan of Turkey by secret courier. To judge by the tone of these smuggled messages—the only word to reach the British since his dispatches of December 14—there had been a sad degeneration of Gordon's spirit. "During the twelve months that I have been here, these two powers [Great Britain and Turkey], the one remarkable for her wealth, the other for her military force, have remained unaffected by my situation. Although I am personally too insignificant to be taken into account, the powers were bound nonetheless to fulfill the engagement upon which my appointment was based, so as to shield the honour of the governments. What I have gone through I cannot describe. The Almighty God will help me."

Omdurman's plight was worse than Khartoum's. A feeble effort mounted by Gordon to relieve the garrison had failed; its commander, Faraj Bey Allah, had signaled Gordon that food and ammunition were completely exhausted. The garrison, under close and continuous fire, was helpless. Sometime during the second week of January—accounts differ—Gordon ordered Faraj Allah to surrender, and the pitiful survivors of Omdurman Fort marched to the Mahdi's lines under a white flag. Not only had an important and staunchly defended garrison been lost, but the Mahdi's guns could now move within closer range of Khartoum.

Gordon received a last appeal from the Mahdi—his final terms: "We have written to you to go back to your country. . . . I repeat to you the words of God, 'Do not destroy yourselves. God, Himself is merciful unto you.' " This was the kind of message that Gordon himself might have sent if their positions had been reversed. Each man recognized the other as a brave soldier and a man of God. Neither wanted to destroy the person of the other.

The Mahdi was fighting to rid the Sudan ot the corrupt "Turk," and to purify the soul of all Islam. Gordon was fighting to save the Egyptian garrisons from extinction as a matter of personal honor and the honor of England—even if England's government did not want him to. England was fighting to save Gordon alone and thus for political motives appease an incensed public—even if Gordon did not want it to. Perhaps no stranger mix of motives for high drama ever existed.

The Mahdi's message to Gordon was remarkable for its reasonableness: "I understand that the English are willing to ransom you alone from us for £20,000. . . . If you agree to join us, it will be a blessing to you. But if you wish to rejoin the English, we will send you back to them without asking for so much as a farthing."[1] In retrospect, there were those who felt that Gordon should have accepted the Mahdi's offer and allowed himself to be repatriated.* But aside from a strong sense of duty and honor that would not permit Gordon to abandon his garrisons, it made little military sense to surrender Khartoum just as a British relief army was approaching.

On January 20, 1885, the Ansar army in Omdurman fired a 101-gun salute signifying victory, but this did not square with what Gordon spied from his roof. He could see women of the Mahdi's camp keening in little groups and huddles. Their wails of grief betrayed a catastrophe which the Mahdi was trying to mask with jubilant artillery fire. A spy soon confirmed to Gordon that only three days previously the British had badly defeated the Ansar in the fiercely fought battle at Abu Klea.

Gordon took full advantage of the welcome news, posting it throughout the city. There was general jubilation as the townfolk took new heart. They could not know that the news of Abu Klea would, in fact, seal Khartoum's fate.

When the British did not appear in the days just after the news of Abu Klea, joy turned to disillusionment. Mahdi agents spread rumors in town that the reports of Abu Klea were not true, alleging that Gordon had fabricated the news simply to keep up public morale. Disillusionment turned to fear as the falling Nile brought the day nearer when the Ansar could safely flank Khartoum's defensive fortifications and attack.

Khartoum's Council of Notables, led by the half-Italian, half-Egyptian Bordeini Bey, counseled Gordon to surrender, but the general would have none of it. While people were free to leave and throw themselves on the Mahdi's mercy, those who stayed would defend the town to the end. In a gloomy conversation with Bordeini Bey, a frazzled Gordon complained bitterly: "The people no longer believe me. I have told them over and over again that help is coming . . . so they condemn me as a liar." Gordon vented his frustration and anger on his discouraged Commander in Chief, Faragh Pasha, and in a stormy meeting slapped his face for also daring to suggest surrender.

---

* A former French Ambassador to Egypt, M. de Billing, claimed that an agent of the Mahdi in Paris had come to him with a proposal to ransom Gordon for fifty thousand francs. De Billing passed this offer on to the British, but Lord Granville rejected the offer. This is not necessarily incompatible with the Mahdi's letter to Gordon with more generous terms which was sent later. (London *Times*, July 13, 1885.)

Gordon was particularly alarmed by the unmined mud flats exposed by the falling Nile, which would permit a flanking attack. At this critical time, a high-ranking officer in command of this vulnerable sector of the defense line defected to the Mahdi; it had to be assumed that he passed intelligence of this problem to his new master.

Khartoum's small Greek colony, influential in business matters, felt themselves in special jeopardy as Christians. While usually sturdy survivors in political winds of change, their future now seemed undeniably grim. Gordon was grateful for their loyalty, feeling responsible that because of their confidence in him, they had stayed on. Therefore, he kept the *Ismailia* docked off the palace grounds and secretly urged the Greeks, if an attack seemed imminent, to make their way northward on it to meet the British. Greek Consul Leontides unfortunately counseled his community to hold off flight in the hopes the British would arrive in time. In truth, the Greek community feared the fate of exile from their adopted country almost as much as the Mahdi.

On Sunday, January 25, Gordon as usual searched the horizons from the palace roof for signs of steamers. Because of rumors that the Ansar would attack, he was particularly anxious. He looked in vain for the telltale puffs of smoke that always heralded a boat's approach. The British had had a week to make the trip after their victory at Abu Klea, but he saw nothing downriver.

Suddenly Gordon noticed through his glass an increase of activity in the Mahdi's lines west of town, across the White Nile. He also saw small boats laden with white-robed Ansar crossing the Nile to reinforce Wad en-Nejumi's camp near the village of Kalakala, south of Khartoum. Sensing that attack was at hand, Gordon ordered all able-bodied men capable of holding a rifle to join the defenders at the city walls. As the sun plunged over the horizon bringing instant night, Gordon made his rounds, exhorting his troops to remain alert. He then retired, probably to smoke and read his Bible before he sank into an uneasy sleep.

As Khartoum's populace waited anxiously for British redcoats to appear as their saviors, Wilson's forces on January 21 maneuvered for attack on Metemmeh village, where the battered but still-strong Ansar tribes were holed up. Wilson was faced with his first difficult decision: Should he attack the well-defended town, possibly gaining a morale advantage but risking a repulse with heavy casualties, or should he bypass it? Reasoning that even if he won Metemmeh he could probably not hold it once Ansar reinforcements arrived, the cautious commander chose not to attack.

To have assaulted Metemmeh and failed would surely have caused a further delay in reaching Khartoum, and if reports of additional Ansar collecting at Sayal and moving upriver toward Metemmeh were true, Wilson would have to risk defeat. He could not take that risk. His initial indecision, however, caused some grumbling among his officers. Wilson himself admitted much later that "the morale effect was bad . . . and our withdrawal gave the enemy fresh heart."[2] One officer wrote in his diary: "Nothing could have been more disgraceful than the dispositions made for the attack. We were actually marched up in square to within 800 yards of a loopholed town wall with guns, and kept paraded in front of it without advancing for over three hours, and then we retired. We [presented] to the enemy the largest target possible."[3]

While Gordon's steamers were in good repair and were immediately available to carry an assault force upriver to Khartoum, Wilson delayed the mission so that he could conduct reconnaissance patrols along the Nile. Wilson was subjected to much criticism for losing three crucial days in this way, particularly since the reported Ansar buildup did not materialize, but in his memoir of the campaign, *Korti to Khartoum*, Wilson went to some pains to defend his decision: "I had every reason to believe that forces of the enemy were advancing against us from the north and south, and I could not leave the small force in its position on the Nile without ascertaining whether it was likely to be attacked."

Wilson described his rationale: "I knew that Khartoum was still holding out, and I hoped that the pressure upon the town could be relieved by the large number of men sent down by the Mahdi to meet us, and that news of our victories would have gotten into Khartoum and given Gordon and his garrison fresh heart." Realizing that Khartoum still held out despite predictions that it would fall by Christmas, Wilson could not believe "that a delay of a couple of days would make much difference."

Wilson, in his first combat command, saw his first duty to be to his soldiers who "had been so roughly handled" by the Mahdi at Abu Klea. "It was these considerations that made me undertake a reconnaissance down the river before starting for Khartoum."[4]

FORFEIT DAYS

The plan called for Beresford to command the steamers, but at this crucial moment he was afflicted with a painful rash of boils and could not walk without assistance—nor could he sit. Unkind gossip in England later insinuated that Beresford encouraged Wilson in his procrastination, hoping to recover so that he would not miss out on the action and glory of the rescue operation, but such stories, later spread in an atmosphere of recrimination, were probably untrue. Wilson's own frank description seems the most accurate. While an officer such as Burnaby might have realized the urgency and taken the dare, as Wolseley had anticipated, Wilson placed the lives of all his men ahead of Gordon's single British life and the lives of the Egyptian garrison.

On January 22, Wilson reconnoitered the Nile downriver in three steamers while another steamer did the same southward. The next day was spent fitting out the boats for the assault. The naval brigade had been so decimated in the fighting and Beresford so afflicted by his painful rash of boils that crew arrangements had to be changed. It was not until the morning of January 24 that the force could start. Wilson with 240 Sudanese soldiers and Captain Trafford with twenty men of the Royal Sussex Regiment, dressed in bright red coats (which drooped on them because they had to be borrowed from outsized Guardsmen) for maximum visibility and effect as Gordon recommended, boarded the steamers *Bordein* and *Telahawiya,* for the last and crucial lap of the race.

TOO LATE

A brave soldier who fell at his post; happy is he to have fallen; his
sufferings are over.
—Rudolf Slatin Pasha, January 26, 1885,
upon learning of Gordon's death

In the Mahdi's Omdurman camp there was as much indecision as there
was in Wilson's headquarters at Gubat. After the defeats at Abu Klea and
Abu Kru, the Mahdi summoned his emirs for what promised to be a
critical council of war on January 24, 1885, the day Wilson sailed toward
Khartoum.

Rudolf Slatin, still confined by chains and only imperfectly aware of what
was going on, was nonetheless one of the few reliable European sources on
the climactic events of late January. The Mahdi had to reach a decision on
attacking Khartoum before the British arrived, but why had the British
delayed after Abu Kru? "Did their commanders not know that Khartoum
and the lives of all in it were hanging by a thread? In vain I and thousands of
others wait for the shrill whistle of the steamer and for the booming of the
guns announcing the English had arrived, the delay was inexplicable; what
could it mean?"[1]

The Mahdi, as seen in El Obeid, disliked attacking a defended, fortified
town. It was better to let the inhabitants starve to death or surrender and beg
for mercy. But now, with the British approaching, he did not have time to
wait.

As night fell on the Nile, the Mahdi and his khalifas and emirs met under a
solitary tree on the desert to make the crucial decision. The Mahdi's instincts
were to withdraw, or more histrionically phrased, make a second *hejira*
and go back to Kordofan. He claimed to have had a dream in which the
Prophet advised him to return immediately to El Obeid. But his influential
uncle, Mohammed Abd al-Karim, alone among the khalifas, begged him to
attack immediately and seize Khartoum before the British arrived. Moham-

436

med Abd al-Karim knew the Baggara tribesmen were eager to avenge the humiliation of Abu Klea.

Intelligence reaching the Mahdi that Khartoum's flanks were exposed by unmined mud flats and that the town was demoralized to the point of treachery and apathy made victory seem certain. With Khartoum and its forts under Ansar control, the British expeditionary force would be at a military disadvantage, but should the British pose a threat, the Ansar would still have time to retire after wiping out Khartoum's forts. The British would be left an empty prize.

Mohammed Abd al-Karim's military logic swung sentiment in favor of attack, and the Mahdi made the critical decision to strike. With inspirational flourishes and divine blessing he exhorted his leaders to prepare for battle. Death would be rewarded with Paradise, but victory would be theirs. Consistent with the strategy to deny Khartoum to the British, no quarter would be given; the time for mercy was over, although it was said that the Mahdi wanted to capture Gordon alive as a showpiece. Wad en-Nejumi would lead the assault in the early hours before dawn on Monday, January 26, 1885.

Slatin remembered the night as "the most excitingly anxious one" in his life. "If only the attack were repulsed, Khartoum would be saved; otherwise all would be lost."[2]

Father Ohrwalder, also an apprehensive observer of the fast-approaching climax, remembered when the moon had set leaving the scene in inky darkness: ". . . the Dervishes stealthily advanced in perfect silence toward that portion of the defense which had been destroyed during the high Nile, and which, as the river receded, had left an open space in which ditch and parapet had almost disappeared." Then the dervishes, breaking their silence and "shouting their wild battle-cry, dashed in wild disorder over this open ground."[3]

On the basis of what Ansar warriors returning from Khartoum reported, Father Ohrwalder pieced together this chilling picture of the attack: "On coming through the open spaces, the Dervishes broke up into two parties. One party dashed along the parapet, breaking all resistance and slaughtering the soldiers in all directions; the other party made for town."

According to Ohrwalder's account: "The inhabitants, roused from their sleep by the shouts of the Arabs and the din of rifle shots, hurried out, anticipating what had occurred. Like a pent-up stream suddenly released, over 50,000 wild Dervishes with hideous yells, rushed upon the 40,000 inhabitants of Khartoum. . . ."[4] Ohrwalder recalled vividly that the fanatical hordes cried "Lil Kenisa! Lil Saraya! [To the church!* To the palace!]" as they searched for treasure.[5]

It would long be argued later whether or not Faragh Bey, commanding Khartoum's defenses, betrayed the town and admitted the enemy. He might genuinely have felt that resistance was hopeless—he had recommended surrender earlier—or he might have been angry at Gordon for having slapped his face. Father Ohrwalder, however, did not think he had been a traitor, on the evidence that he was soon killed by the Mahdi. The town defenders might simply have been taken by surprise or have been too weak and dispirited to fight. Some of the soldiers had, in fact, left their posts to go into town and forage for food.

The image of that fearful night was also seared into Slatin's memory. "I was just dropping off to sleep at early dawn," he wrote in his memoir, "when I was startled by the deafening discharge of thousands of rifles and guns. . . . It was scarcely light and I could barely distinguish objects. Could this possibly be the great attack on Khartoum? A wild discharge of firearms and cannon, and in a few minutes complete stillness."[6]

As daylight began to flood the land, Slatin was gripped with fear. "The sun was now rising red over the horizon." Soon, to his horror, his worst fears were realized as shouts of rejoicing could be heard in the distance. In a few minutes his guards were excitedly telling him that Khartoum had been taken by storm.[7]

"I crawled out of my tent, and scanned the camp; a great crowd had collected before the quarters of the Mahdi and Khalifa." Suddenly people surged toward Slatin's tent. The Austrian prisoner feared that he, too, would be killed in what was obviously an orgy of bloodletting in Khartoum. The crowd was led by three black soldiers, one of whom he recognized as a man called Shatta. In Shatta's hands was "a bloody cloth in which something was wrapped up, and behind him followed a crowd of people weeping." The soldiers approached Slatin's tent and stood leering, making rude remarks.

---

* Austrian Roman Catholic Mission compound.

Slatin would never forget his shock when Shatta undid the cloth; it was the head of General Charles Gordon!

"The blood rushed to my head," recounted Slatin, "and my heart seemed to stop beating; but with a tremendous effort of self-control, I gazed silently at this ghastly spectacle. His blue eyes were half-opened; the mouth was perfectly natural; the hair of his head and his short whiskers were almost quite white."

The soldiers with their grisly trophy wanted Slatin to make positive identification of Gordon. "Is not this the head of your uncle, the unbeliever?" they asked. (The Ansar always referred to Gordon as "your uncle" when talking to Slatin.) With great effort, Slatin kept his composure. "What of it? a brave soldier who fell at his post; happy is he to have fallen; his sufferings are over."[8]

Gordon's head, for many days mounted on a tall pole in front of the Mahdi's tent, served as a macabre flagstaff to remind the "faithful" that Islam had triumphed over the hated Egyptians, the "Turk," and their infidel protectors.

The steamers *Bordein* and *Telahawiyeh* finally were cast off at 8:00 in the morning of January 24 for their dash to Khartoum. Wilson, while unaware that the Mahdi was about to make the decision to attack the city, knew that the rescue mission would be hazardous. He later reflected: "We were going to fight our way up the river and into Khartoum in two steamers of the size of 'penny' steamers on the Thames, which a single well-directed shell would send to the bottom; with crews and [native] soldiers absolutely without discipline; with twenty English soldiers. . . ."[9]

Bluff had always been a useful weapon in Great Britain's little wars against the "heathen," but British conceit in thinking that some 260 men, twenty of whom wore bright red coats, could reach Khartoum and return, much less hold at bay hordes of Ansar zealots until the main force of the expedition arrived, was monumental. Nonetheless, this token force as harbinger of the full fury of British strength had the potential of making the crucial difference in Khartoum's fate. It was the point Gordon made repeatedly; Baring himself reached the same conclusion, and both Slatin and Ohrwalder, who knew the Ansar at close range, agreed after the fact. This question would be debated for years, but whatever the truth, Wilson was committed to try as England and much of the world watched and waited.

The Sudanese steamer captains, Khasm el-Mus of the *Bordein* and Abd al-Hamid of the *Telahawiyeh*, aware that only twelve more days remained before the falling Nile would make the dangerous sixth cataract at Shablouka unnavigable, pushed onward. But with Omdurman in Ansar hands the fire from batteries on both shores was deadly. At the sixth cataract, the *Bordein* ran aground, causing a further twenty-four-hour delay. Wilson fervently hoped that Gordon would see the steamers fifteen to twenty miles off and create a diversion to permit the boats to get through safely.

But as the steamers drew close enough to see Khartoum in the distance, a Shaigiya tribesman on the shore shouted the news that the town had been captured. Reluctant to believe this, Wilson went on. Near Halfaya, Ansar batteries began firing at a distance of no more than seven hundred yards, as Wilson wrote, "tapping like hail against the ships' sides, whilst the shells went screaming overhead." After both boats had run the gauntlet, the Sudanese gunners on board "sent up a wild cry of delight . . . their blood up, quivering with excitement."[10]

Gordon's palace came into view above the trees, but there was no trace of an Egyptian flag flying. More shore artillery opened up, indicating that Tuti Island, off Khartoum, was no longer in Gordon's hands. Wilson heard "the roll of musketry from each side, and high above that could be heard the grunting of a Nordenfeldt and the loud rushing voice of the Krupp shells fired either from Khartoum, itself, or from the upper end of Tuti Island."

Hundreds of dervishes firing from the shore were determined to resist their landing. The women, brandishing sticks, shrieked, "Death to the English."[11] "It became plain to everyone that Khartoum had fallen into the Mahdi's hands."[12] The boats had no choice but to turn about and run full speed downriver. They were too late!

EPILOGUE

The greatest gift a hero leaves his race is to have been a hero.
—Lord Esher, 1910[1]

It would be several years before a coherent account of Khartoum's tragedy and its aftermath, told from a European perspective, would reach the Western world. Not until the end of 1891 when Father Ohrwalder escaped to Egypt would the drama of Khartoum's fall really begin to be known. More would be learned about the catastrophe when Rudolf Slatin escaped in 1895. With the Mahdi's seizure of Khartoum, a shutter slammed down, hiding the moil of a theocracy determined to purify Islam and rid itself of foreign influences.

The exact circumstances of Gordon's death will always remain something of a mystery. Kitchener immediately made an effort to reconstruct what happened on that fateful January 26, 1885, in Khartoum on the basis of very scanty testimony. A servant of Gordon's secretary was one of the few persons available to him.[2] The simple man had no apparent motive but to tell the truth, and his story was accepted at the time by both Kitchener and General Wilson. It was confirmed to some extent by one of the spy-messengers who also escaped the cataclysm in Khartoum and made his way to British lines. In this account, Gordon and a small group had reached the palace gate on their way to the Austrian Church Mission compound, long planned as a redoubt, when a marauding band of Ansar fired on them. Gordon was killed instantly by the volley and fell near the gate. His head was severed and taken to the Mahdi, where its identity briefly became confused as it lay among other similar grisly trophies piled in front of the Mahdi's tent. Slatin made the identification.[3]

Gordon's bodyguard, Khalil Agha Orphali, claimed that his master had died in hand-to-hand fighting on the palace stairs. But a more dramatic end is the one that every British schoolboy knows and the one told with

441

variations by many chroniclers, including Slatin, Father Ohrwalder, Baring and several latter-day biographers of Gordon.[4] This version originated with the town notable Ibrahim Bey Bordeini, who escaped from Omdurman in 1887; it was confirmed by one of the Mahdi's emirs, Sheikh Medawi. While neither Bordeini nor Medawi had been an eyewitness, both claimed to have heard the details from Ansar warriors who had taken part in the attack.[5] The stories of these two sources were obtained too late for inclusion in Kitchener's official report, but this version, dramatized in G. W. Joy's painting *Death of Gordon*,[6] more befits a martyr and is the one that has endured as the favorite.

In Joy's painting, Gordon, in his hastily donned uniform and red tarboosh, coolly glares down the palace stairs at several spear-flourishing attackers. His sword is still sheathed and in his right hand is an unaimed revolver.

According to the two sources, the cornered general demanded to see his attackers' master, but one of the Ansar—probably Sheikh Mohammed Nebawi[7]—rushed forward shouting, "O cursed one, your time has come!" and plunged his spear into Gordon's body. Gordon only had time to look disdainful and turn his back on the assassins before toppling down the stairs to his death.[8] The curtain falls; the play is over.

After Gordon's death it seemed somehow important to know whether he died passively as a martyr or fighting to the end as a soldier. Khalil Agha Orphali, when he was discovered to be still alive in Omdurman in 1898, testified that Gordon had aggressively defended himself until he fell. The old bodyguard claimed that Gordon was hit by a spear as he tried to fight his way out of the palace. The general struck at his assailant "but missed him and hit another." Then a dervish fired at Gordon, "hitting him in the chest and forcing him to lean on the wall; he received a spear thrust through his left side which threw him down."[9]

There were even those unable to accept the reality of Gordon's death in any form, and took refuge in an anonymously written tract claiming that their hero had escaped and was biding his time in the south as a legendary "White Pasha."[10]

The foreign community, as could be expected, suffered badly when Khartoum was taken. Nicola Leontides, the Greek Consul, who had missed an opportunity to escape on the *Ismailia*, had his hands chopped off before being beheaded. His body was doused with kerosene and burned in the street. Aser, the Honorary American Consul, cheated his assailants by dying of a heart attack after being forced to watch his brother beheaded. An Austrian tailor had his throat slit before the terrified eyes of his wife and children. His older son was killed on the spot, and his daughter taken away to augment some khalifa's harem. The dead tailor's Venetian wife, "worked up into a state of mad despair," seized her son of five with her right hand while she held her suckling babe to her breast with her left and "fought against these murderers like a tigress being robbed of her young."[11]

George Calamatino, the El Obeid Greek who had ingratiated himself with the Mahdi and served as a benevolent overseer for the European prisoners in the Mahdi's camp, tried to lead the Greek colony in Khartoum to safety, but his charges were intercepted and beheaded. "Pale, terror-stricken and trembling," Calamatino fled to Omdurman and "for some months he lay on the point of death, so great had been the shock of witnessing the massacre of his fellow countrymen."[12]

The Shaigiya tribesmen, whose allegiance had worried Gordon, proved loyal in this terrible test, but paid with their lives. They were ruthlessly hunted down and killed, giving new currency to an Ansar proverb: "The Shaigiya, the Egyptian and the dog shall find no rest in Mahdiya."

Young women and girls were spared death. The most comely were assigned to the Mahdi's harem, while the others, in order of their beauty, were parceled out to the khalifas and lesser Ansar chiefs. According to Father Ohrwalder, old women were "given a few rags with which to partially cover themselves" and sent to Wad en-Nejumi's camp, where they suffered "the agonies of hunger, thirst, heat, and cold." Ohrwalder was horrified to see "little babies, not yet weaned, left to die of hunger . . . and young widowed mothers wandering naked though the market of Omdurman, begging."[13]

Faragh, commander of Khartoum's garrison, who had been suspected of betraying the town on the fateful morning of attack,[14] was called before Ansar leaders and asked to produce the "hidden treasure" of Khartoum. If such treasure existed, Faragh did not know where it was. Just as he had obstinately stood up to Gordon, the hotheaded soldier defied his Ansar interrogators. Gordon had slapped his face for suggesting surrender, but the Ansar beheaded him on the spot for his defiance. Father Ohrwalder concluded: "If he was really a traitor, he richly deserved his fate; but if not, his death was that of a brave man."[15] He estimated that ten thousand lives had been forfeit to the "wild fury of these fanatical Arabs."[16] Headless corpses littered the streets for days while the victors feverishly collected plunder.

The return journey of the *Bordein* and the *Telahawiyeh* with Wilson and the rescue party met with disaster when both steamers foundered in the rapids. Fortunately, Lord Beresford, recovered enough from his boils to pilot the *Safieh*, came to Wilson's assistance before the stranded troops met Stewart's fate. On the afternoon of February 4, 1885, Wilson and his men arrived safely at the British advance camp at Gubat. They had failed in their mission, but they had survived.

In England the reaction to Khartoum's fall was one of profound grief, soon to change to anger and recrimination. Baring in Cairo was shocked. In his memoir, *Modern Egypt*, he stated: "Rarely has public opinion in England been so deeply moved as when the news arrived of the fall of Khartoum." When General Gordon's fate was made known, "a wail of sorrow and disappointment was heard throughout the land."[17]

Baring had disapproved of Gordon and had never wanted him to return to Khartoum, but in his memoir he produced a fair appraisal of the General's genius. "I have alluded to General Gordon's numerous inconsistencies, have pointed out errors of judgment with which he may justly be charged. But, when all this has been said, how grandly the character of the man comes out in the final scene of the Sudan tragedy. History has recorded few incidents more calculated to strike the imagination than that presented by this brave man who, strong in the Faith which sustained him, stood undismayed amidst dangers which might have appalled the stoutest hearts."[18] And: ". . . no soldier about to lead in forlorn hope, no Christian martyrs tied to the stake or thrown to the wild beasts of Ancient Rome, ever faced death with more unconcern than General Gordon."[19]

A catastrophe of this kind inevitably brings in its wake a search for scapegoats. For every martyr, there must be villains. The attachment of blame in national matters seems to be a catharsis; it rarely cures the problem but it provides relief and vents the helpless rage of the public. Tantalized by the catchphrase "too late," the British press focused on

Wilson's fatal three-day delay at Gubat. Leading the pack of baying press hounds was Charles Williams, a correspondent representing the Central News Agency. In a vicious article for the *Fortnightly Review* he accused Wilson of stalling at Abu Klea and charged him with military incompetence—"having no more notion of what could or should be done than a bugler."

The judicious Baring, no witch hunter, also concluded at length "after a careful examination of all the facts" that had the steamers left Gubat at the earliest opportunity—the afternoon of January 21—"they would probably have arrived at Khartoum in time to save the town."[20]

Wilson's own defense of his actions, which stressed his responsibility to the forces under his command in the face of reports that the Ansar were massing for a new attack, is not without merit. The issue, perhaps difficult to adjudicate in the heat of public emotion, contrasted two concerns: the rescue of Gordon and the Khartoum garrisons with all that meant for British prestige, and the safety of more than a thousand British troops whose units had already sustained heavy casualties at Abu Klea.

Wilson was not officially censured. In a report to War Minister Hartington dated April 13, 1885, Wolseley simply transmitted Wilson's explanation for the delay at Gubat without endorsing it. "The reasons given by Sir Charles Wilson must speak for themselves," he wrote, knowing how these words would be interpreted. Wilson never forgave Wolseley for this backhanded, implicit condemnation. Wolseley wrote to his wife: "I hate to see Sir C. Wilson because I cannot help remembering that he *might* have been at Khartoum easily the day before it was betrayed."

Kitchener exonerated Wilson in his official report,[21] and Reginald Wingate, an equally respected Sudan expert, later concluded after much study of the situation that Wilson could not have prudently started his steamer journey before he did. Wingate went so far as to assert that with both banks of the Nile in enemy hands and with the hazard presented by the sixth cataract, it had not been a justifiable military risk to send the two steamers at all.

Winston Churchill, whose interest in the Sudan was aroused by his service with the 21st Lancers during the Battle of Omdurman in 1898, ventured a judgment based on longer perspective in his classic account,

The River War. As Gordon himself had recorded in his journal, Churchill believed that Khartoum became defenseless by mid-December. The arrival, therefore, of twenty British soldiers could not have materially affected the situation.[22]

Slatin, however, who had observed the Mahdiya at closest range while a slave of the Khalifa Abdullahi, was of another mind: "How fatal had been the delay at Metemmeh!"[23] Father Ohrwalder, a veteran of the El Obeid siege and, like Slatin, held prisoner, also believed that a token British force, had it arrived sooner, could have saved the city. Ohrwalder was convinced that the Ansar defeat at Abu Klea had "struck terror into the Mahdists,"[24] and the puzzling delay of the British at Gubat was the basis of the decision to attack Khartoum.

Whatever one's opinion, more costly to the episode was the general military mismanagement which had much earlier, and for much longer, put the expedition so far behind schedule. If Wilson was to be blamed for anything, it should have been for his role in canceling further camel purchases on October 11 before enough had been rounded up to transport the Camel Corps across the Bayuda desert in one fast dash. But even before, the long arguments over which route to take and the snail's pace with which the expedition was organized had given the Mahdi time to besiege Khartoum and press the town's endurance to the breaking point.

More important than the delays caused by tactical miscalculation or military mismanagement was the infinitely longer delay caused by political misjudgment. These early, frustrating months of protracted government inaction can be solidly blamed on Prime Minister Gladstone. According to Baring: "In a word, the Nile Expedition was sanctioned too late, and the reason why it was sanctioned too late was that Mr. Gladstone would not accept evidence of a plain fact, which was patent to much less powerful intellects than his own."[25]

More fundamentally, Gladstone can be blamed for choosing, unrealistically, to ignore the Sudan problem as an intrinsic part of the Egyptian problem. He failed to see until too late that only British troops could accomplish the evacuation of the Egyptian presence in the Sudan. Gordon, alone, could not produce a miracle. While this should have been obvious, Gladstone wanted an easy solution to appeasing public emotions and did not anticipate the consequences of sending Gordon alone to Khartoum.

EPILOGUE

To think that Gordon or anyone else could single-handedly evacuate the Khartoum garrisons was to underestimate the Mahdi's power. Gordon's prestige in the Sudan was greatly exaggerated in England. In fact, he was widely blamed in the Sudan for ruining a lucrative way of life when he stopped slave trading and nationalized ivory exports. Gordon himself admitted that he had "laid the egg which hatched the insurrection in the Soudan."

At the news of Gordon's death, Wolseley was saddened and depressed. He had been unable to rescue a dear friend. In addition to the grief he felt, the Nile expedition was his first major command failure and he knew that it would damage his reputation. And, in fact, the Nile campaign was the watershed of his military glory.

Queen Victoria was shocked and sickened. She blamed Gladstone, whom she detested anyway, for refusing to send the expedition till it was too late.[26] She telegraphed her displeasure to the Prime Minister, making her views public. Then she sent her secretary, Sir Henry Ponsonby, off to London "to speak to Mr. Gladstone, Lord Hartington and others about the alarming state of affairs."[27]

She sent an emotional condolence to Gordon's sister Augusta, referring to "the stain left upon England" for Gordon's "cruel, though heroic fate. That the promises of support were not fulfilled—which I so frequently and so constantly pressed on those who asked him to go—is to me *grief inexpressible:* indeed, it has made me ill."[28]

General public reaction to Gordon's death was, first, grief, then profound unhappiness with how matters had been handled by the government. The tragedy of Khartoum was all the worse after having been dragged dramatically along through the months of climax-building melodrama. Britain's pride had been injured.

Once known amiably as G.O.M., "Grand Old Man," Gladstone now had to endure an epithet formed by a reversal of these initials to M.O.G., "Murderer of Gordon." When he insensitively attended the theater on the very night that Gordon's death was announced, he was hissed by an enraged crowd out front on the street. And for weeks he had to run the gauntlet of taunting crowds as he came and went to his Downing Street residence.

EPILOGUE

London music halls, where the common man's emotions were massaged, churned out new ditties to mark the Sudan catastrophe. In one, Gladstone was featured sitting in Hell on a red-hot burner between Pontius Pilate and Judas Iscariot; in another Gordon was eulogized in a jingoistic chorus: "His life was England's glory/ His death was England's pride."

The press kept up a drumbeat of outrage. *Punch*, embarrassed by premature printing of a cartoon celebrating the rescue of Khartoum, corrected the gaffe in its next issue with a grief-struck Britannia, shielding her eyes from a mob of dervishes bursting through Khartoum's gates. The cartoon's caption, "Too late," was rapidly becoming the theme of the Khartoum disaster.

Gordon spoke from the grave when his Khartoum journal was published. The public could now read the dreadful but fascinating account of his last days, made all the more endearing by his eccentric style. People reveled in his criticism of the government and in his scathing lampoons and satirical sketches.

The British wanted revenge for the long series of disasters in the Sudan beginning with Hicks's massacre. Humiliation had been heaped upon humiliation. Just as the public had forced Gladstone to send Gordon on an ill-conceived, impossible mission to Khartoum, it now clamored for a punitive expedition to "smash up the Mahdi"—that phrase which had so infuriated the Prime Minister when Gordon used it. Only because the Prime Minister under pressure agreed in principle to mount a new expedition against the Mahdi did he squeak by in the House of Commons by fourteen votes.

Although the shadow of Gordon's memory still hung darkly, Gladstone had other problems besides the Sudan. His passive handling of Russian provocation in Afghanistan and, domestically, his Land Act, which alienated many Englishmen without appeasing Irish Nationalists, contributed to his fall from public grace. When the Irish parliamentary figure Charles Parnell and his followers abandoned Gladstone in June 1885, the beleaguered Prime Minister was forced to step aside in favor of Lord Salisbury, new leader of the Conservative Party.

The duel between the "Great Christian Soldier," as Gladstone once referred to Gordon, and the "Great Christian Statesman" himself was over. Gordon lost his life and Gladstone lost his office, although Gladstone returned briefly to power again in January 1886 when the Irish Nationalists turned against Salisbury. He did not survive for long, however, as the Tories won power in the parliamentary elections of 1892.

Wolseley was surprised by the government's decision on February 6, 1885, to press the attack against the Mahdi and to try to crush Osman Digna in Suakin. The Red Sea coast still had strategic importance for Britain which transcended that of the endless deserts and swamps of the Sudan. While Wolseley agreed that the Sudan should be retrieved from the Mahdi, he realized that Gladstone had approved this ambitious plan only to save his government and appease public sentiment running strongly against him.

In the meantime the Commander in Chief had to worry about his troop disposition in the Sudan; the position was precarious as long as Berber remained in Ansar hands. Wilson's flight from Khartoum had been a close call, and it had to be assumed that the Mahdi would give chase. In fact, Wad en-Nejumi was sent northward with a large force, and Ohrwalder wrote, "Had not the English already retreated before he reached Metemmeh, they would not have escaped."

Major General Sir Redvers Buller, now in command of the desert column, had been ordered to attack Metemmeh and then join up with Major General Earle's river column to attack Berber. But Buller's camel strength was by now hopelessly depleted, and the force was in no condition to fight. The glamorous Camel Corps, which had entered the fray with such high spirits, now trudged back across the Bayuda on foot, harassed by Ansar sniping. The corps' few remaining mounts were used to carry the large number of sick and wounded. Walking on the desert was bad enough, but the misery of the soldiers was made worse by their shoddily made boots.

In late February, Wolseley was forced to recall both the desert column and the river column. The latter's commander, General Earle, had been killed in an engagement at Jebel Kirbekan. The offensive against the Mahdi would have to be postponed until cooler weather in the autumn. A new expeditionary force under General Sir Gerald Graham did land in Suakin in mid-March to tame the Hadendowas and begin construction of a railway to Berber so as better to control eastern Sudan and facilitate a campaign against the Mahdi. Osman Digna's tribes had lost none of their zeal, however, as Graham discovered while skirmishing with his old foe. In the Battle of Tofrek on March 22, sometimes called "McNeill's Zariba," the "Fuzzy Wuzzy" surprised the British and lunged at their hastily formed *zariba,* nearly breaking the square before being repulsed.

Events far away would completely change the British military position in the Sudan. In an obscure village named Penjdeh on Afghanistan's northern border, Russian troops suddenly attacked on March 30. This incident, as trivial as it may have been in the cooler light of history, seemed then to be in callous disregard of the efforts of an Anglo-Russian Commission to delineate a boundary between northern Afghanistan and Russian Central Asia. It was interpreted by the British, moreover, as a harbinger of further Russian advances into Afghanistan and a signal that the Czar had ambitions toward India itself.

The Penjdeh incident was useful in at least one way to Gladstone. It gave him an excuse to renege on his promise to crush the Mahdi. With the possibility of further clashes with Russia, perhaps even war, the defeat of the Mahdi would have to wait.

Gladstone's "policy of scuttle," as his critics referred to it, stimulated various alternative schemes to salvage the Sudan, or at least parts of it. Kitchener drew up a plan, and Wilson, smarting under continuing criticism, had his own ideas. Gladstone knew that Queen Victoria was opposed to British withdrawal but was unaware that she had tried to persuade Wolseley to ignore the government's decision, sending him secret messages through Lady Wolseley.

The undeniable fact was, however, that the Mahdi controlled most of the country. The Ansar was still on the offense, engaged now in a campaign against Abyssinia no less spirited than the one successfully concluded against the British. The Christian "infidel," King Johannes, Gordon's old nemesis, now bore the brunt of the Mahdi's efforts to regain irredentist territory along the Sudan's southeastern border.

On June 20, 1885, the Mahdi suddenly died. While he had enforced a spartan existence on his people in which "earthly pleasures" were forbidden and punishable by flogging, amputation of limbs or death, he had himself become overindulgent. He succumbed quickly to a typhus

450

fever which was sweeping Khartoum and Omdurman. The Mahdi's tomb was a simple conical edifice built in Omdurman which, among the low-lying mud huts of the town, nonetheless stood out.*

Before he died the Mahdi reiterated his will that Khalifa Abdullahi be his successor. Although there were other aspirants, particularly among members of the Mahdi's own family, the Khalifa was the anointed one and assumed the reins of power. He worked to fulfill the Mahdi's dream of conquering Egypt, and by December his army was on the Egyptian border, poised for invasion.

But on December 29, 1885, General Stephenson with a reinforced garrison attacked the Ansar at Ginniss, routing them so completely as to end officially the First Sudan War. A troubled Sudan languished under the Khalifa for thirteen years, penetrated only by the famous detective, Sherlock Holmes, who, incognito, made a "short but interesting" visit to the Khalifa in Arthur Conan Doyle's "The Adventure of the Empty House."

Was Gordon's life but a fascinating vignette in the grand sweep of Victorian history? Or did it have a more profound impact on imperial progress and the British people?

In an inscription on his monument in London's St. Paul's Cathedral, Gordon is praised for having "saved an Empire by his warlike genius." Though the sentiment may be sincere, the statement is hyperbolic. It stretches the case to say that he saved the empire, but Gordon did leave his mark. (Not until 1898 would Lord Kitchener march another British army up the Nile to conquer the country and avenge Gordon's murder, salvaging the strategically important Sudan.) He was an irregular soldier at heart who, ahead of his time, understood the role of the guerrilla in warfare and possessed the genius of leadership. Fearlessness, iron will, and supreme confidence in his alliance with God were his awesome attributes. Armed only with his "wand of victory" in China or alone astride his racing camel in the Sudan, he cast a spell over those he commanded and those he fought. His St. Paul's memorial also pays tribute to a man who "at all times and everywhere gave his strength to the weak, his substance to the poor, his sympathy to the suffering, his heart to God."

---

* A rebuilt Mahdi's tomb still dominates Omdurman's skyline to this day, the original having been badly damaged by the British when they invaded in 1898.

EPILOGUE

While it is easy to think of Gordon as an eccentric individualist, frequently at odds with the system, he was in many ways a product of nineteenth-century England. It was an age of Wilberforce, Booth and countless other reformers and soldiers of salvation. Modern England, the materialist, mercantile power, displayed its conscience in Africa, where human beings, emerging bewildered from the dark, were brutalized and sold into slavery. Slavery and slaving had to be abolished; the deprived people of Africa had to be given the advantages of Christianity and British civilization. But the century also saw England reach its imperial apogee; it was a time for soldiering as well. Gordon was a man of his times.

Perhaps this is why Charles Gordon fitted the mold of hero so well; perhaps this is his historical significance. By dying while defending Khartoum he became a Christian martyr, but he also entered Britain's pantheon of immortals. Heroes are necessary; they provide symbols of national pride and totems around which a people can rally in common cause; they are essential to folklore and national history. Charles Gordon's importance can be found in what he meant to his countrymen.

NOTES AND REFERENCES

Charles Gordon throughout his life was a prolific letter writer. During certain periods of his service he also kept journals in which he often shared his views on a variety of subjects, not always relevant to the record of events he was chronicling, but usually revealing of the man. Letters written by Gordon, unknown and uncatalogued because they languish in forgotten attics, will probably continue to appear from time to time. Such strays may not reveal any new facet to Gordon's personality but they will always delight history lovers and biographers interested in Gordon.

In an effort to capture Gordon's personality as faithfully as possible I have liberally quoted from his letters and journals. His sometimes stream-of-consciousness style of writing and his tendency to jot down his thoughts impulsively do indeed reveal insights as to his nature. As he once suggested, his journal-keeping style was sometimes intended to permit the reader to follow the peregrinations of his mind. I have not for the most part cited specific sources for these many quotations. To have done so in a nonacademic book would have been tedious, inappropriately cluttering the pages with distracting numerals. The quotations used have been taken from various published volumes containing his letters and from several unpublished manuscript collections, all listed in the bibliography.

PREFACE

1. Earl of Cromer (Evelyn Baring), *Modern Egypt*, 2 vols. (London: Macmillan, 1908).
2. Ibid., Vol. I, p. 430.
3. Wilfrid Scawen Blunt, *Gordon at Khartoum* (London: Jonathan Swift, 1912), p. 138.

4. John Morley, *The Life of William Ewart Gladstone* (London: Macmillan, 1903).

5. *Vanity Fair* (London), February 19, 1881.

6. Mary St. Leger Harrison, *The Fortnightly Review*, September 1885, xliv, pp. 395–412.

7. *Vanity Fair*, February 19, 1881.

8. *Academy*, July 11, 1885, xxvii, pp. 19, 20.

9. Lytton Strachey, *Eminent Victorians* (New York: Putnam, 1918), p. 203.

10. General Sir Gerald Graham, *Last Words with Gordon* (London: Chapman & Hall, 1887, from *The Fortnightly Review*, January 1887).

11. Winston Churchill, *The River War* (London: Eyre & Spottiswoode, 1951; originally published 1899), p. 67.

PROLOGUE

1. J. S. Gregory, *Great Britain and the Taipings* (London: Routledge & Kegan Paul, 1969), p. 60.

2. Sir Samuel Baker, *The Albert N'yanza*, 2 vols. (London: Sidgwick & Jackson, 1962; originally published 1886), Vol. II, p. 516.

3. Ibid.

4. Ibid., p. 277.

5. Olivia Manning, *The Remarkable Expedition* (New York: Atheneum, 1985; originally published by Doubleday, 1947), p. 69.

CHAPTER ONE

1. Charles George Gordon, *Gordon's Travels*, unpublished childhood journal, dated May 3, 1847. Collection, Gordon Boys' School, Woking, Surrey.

2. Ibid.

3. Ibid., pp. 14–15.

4. Ibid., p. 18.

5. Ibid., p. 20.

6. *Somerset and Dorset Notes and Queries;* quoted in Lt. Col. the Hon. Gerald French, *Gordon Pasha of the Sudan: The Life of an Ill-Requited Soldier* (Glasgow: William Maclellan, 1958).

7. Letter from Gordon to Barnes, dated Jaffa, October 13, 1886, Boston Public Library's Rare Books and Manuscripts Department.

8. Lord Godfrey Elton, *Gordon of Khartoum: The Life of Charles George Gordon* (New York: Knopf, 1955), p. 268.

9. Christopher Hibbert, *Queen Victoria in Her Letters and Journals* (New York: Viking, 1985), p. 76.

10. Lytton Strachey, *Queen Victoria* (London: Chatto & Windus, 1921), p. 211.

11. "One Who Knew Him Well" (Octavia Freese), *More About Gordon* (London: Richard Bently & Sons, 1894), p. 77.

12. Col. Sir William F. Butler, *Life of Charles George Gordon* (New York: Macmillan, 1891), p. 13.

13. Robert M'Cheyne was a Presbyterian minister, prominent in Scotland and known for his mission in Palestine.

14. Thomas Scott's *Commentaries* carefully analyzes the Bible in search of veiled meanings.

15. Hibbert, *Queen Victoria*, p. 123.

16. Ibid., p. 124.

CHAPTER TWO

1. Charles George Gordon, *Gordon's Travels*, unpublished childhood journal, dated May 3, 1847. Collection, Gordon Boys' School, Woking, Surrey.

2. Christopher Hibbert, *Queen Victoria in Her Letters and Journals* (New York: Viking, 1985), p. 125.

3. Norman Rich, *Why the Crimean War?: A Cautionary Tale* (Hanover: University Press of New England for Brown University, 1985), p. 208.

4. Demetrius C. Boulger, *General Gordon's Letters from the Crimea, the Danube and Armenia* (London: Chapman & Hall, 1884), pp. 16–17.

5. Rich, p. 136.

6. Lt. Col. Garnet J. Wolseley, *Narrative of the War with China in 1860* (London: Longman Green, Longman & Roberts, 1862), p. 33.

7. Ibid.

8. Ibid., p. 34.

9. H. E. Wortham, *Gordon: An Intimate Portrait* (London: George Harrap, 1933), p. 43.

10. A. Egmont Hake, *The Story of Chinese Gordon* (London: Remington, 1884), p. 21.

11. Hibbert, *Queen Victoria*, p. 135.

12. Hake, *Story of Chinese Gordon*, p. 27.

CHAPTER THREE

1. *Illustrated London News,* September 5, 1857.
2. Ibid., October 10, 1857.
3. Ibid.
4. Ibid., September 26, 1857.
5. Wilfrid Scawen Blunt, *Gordon at Khartoum* (London: Jonathan Swift, 1912), p. 92.
6. Ibid., p. 2.

CHAPTER FOUR

1. Pat Barr, *Foreign Devils* (Harmondsworth: Penguin Books, 1970), p. 54.
2. Ho Ping-ti, *Studies on the Population of China, 1938–1953* (Cambridge, Mass: Harvard University Press, 1969), pp. 237–38.
3. While the dynasty in later usage became known as the Ch'ing dynasty, "Manchu dynasty" was then the more common usage and will be used throughout.
4. The three elements of the Triad were Heaven, Earth and Mankind.
5. Franz Michael, with Chung-li Chang, *The Taiping Rebellion,* 3 vols. (Seattle: University of Washington Press, 1966). Documents contained in Vols. II and III provided much of the background for this chapter on the Taiping Rebellion.
6. Lt. Col. the Hon. Gerald French, *Gordon Pasha of the Sudan: The Life of an Ill-Requited Soldier* (Glasgow: William Maclellan, 1958), p. 43.
7. Nanking was then known by its official Chinese name, Chin-Ling.

CHAPTER FIVE

1. In addition to Harry Parkes, the delegation consisted of Lieutenants de Norman, Loch and Anderson and Captains Brabazon and Bowlby, accompanied by fourteen escorting troops.
2. Stanley Lane-Poole, *Life of Sir Harry Parkes.* 2 vols. (London), Vol. I, p. 398.
3. Lt. Col. Garnet J. Wolseley, *Narrative of the War with China in 1860* (London: Longman Green, Longman & Roberts, 1862), p. 279.
4. Bernard Meredith Allen, *Gordon in China* (London: Macmillan, 1933), p. 15.
5. Lt. Col. Wolseley, p. 279.
6. Col. Sir William F. Butler, *Life of Charles George Gordon* (New York: Macmillan, 1891), p. 44.

7. The Elgin Marbles are now in the British Museum, although they are claimed by the Greek government.
8. L. C. B. Seaman, *Victorian England* (London: Methuen, 1973), p. 102.
9. Lt. Col. Wolseley, pp. 323–28.
10. Thomas Meadows, *The Chinese and Their Rebellions* (London: 1847), pp. 193–97.

CHAPTER SIX

1. J. S. Gregory, *Great Britain and the Taipings* (London: Routledge & Kegan Paul, 1969), p. 133.
2. Ibid., p. 148.
3. Ibid., p. 149.
4. Ibid., p. 148.
5. Public Record Office, London, F.O. 17, No. 371.
6. Elliott Paul Carthage, *The Role of Frederick Townsend Ward in the Suppression of the Taiping Rebellion*, Ph.D. thesis, St. John's University, 1976 (Ann Arbor: University Microfilm International). This dissertation contains a wealth of information about Ward and the Taiping Rebellion not theretofore published.
7. Bernard Meredith Allen, *Gordon in China* (London: Macmillan, 1933), p. 47.
8. Field Marshal Viscount Garnet J. Wolseley, *The Story of a Soldier's Life*, 2 vols. (London: Archibald Constable, 1903).
9. Sir Frederick Bruce to Gen. Charles W. Staveley, October 11, 1862, Foreign Office General Correspondence between the Foreign Office and Its Representatives in China, 1850–1865, Public Record Office, London, F.O. 17, No. 374.
10. The agreement, signed in January 1863, was called "Agreement of Sixteen Articles." *Memorial of Li Hung-chang*, January 28, 1863, appearing in James C. Cheng, *Chinese Sources for the Taiping Rebellion,1850–1864* (Oxford: Oxford University Press for Hong Kong University Press, 1963), p. 109.

CHAPTER SEVEN

1. Public Record Office, London, F.O. 17, No. 391.
2. Bernard Meredith Allen, *Gordon in China* (London: Macmillan, 1933), p. 69, quoting *Memoirs of Li Hung-chang*.
3. The American Col. Chaille-Long, Gordon's deputy in Khedive Ismail's Sudan service in 1874, quoted Gordon in his memoir *My Life on Four Continents* as reporting that Kirkham "behaved well in China, stuck to me, and when I

returned, I left him at Aden with a strong letter to King Johannes (of Abyssinia), who might wish a faithful valet." To Gordon's astonishment, Johannes made Kirkham a general! Sometime later Kirkham, resplendent in an Abyssinian general's uniform, was arrested for disorderly conduct in the bar of Shepheard's Hotel in Cairo. Upon investigation, British Consul Stanton discovered that he was en route to England to deliver a proposal of marriage to Queen Victoria on behalf of King Johannes. The unfortunate Kirkham was sent back to Abyssinia to report failure to his unrequited monarch. When Chaille-Long told this story about Kirkham, "the Royal Matchmaker," Gordon was quoted as quipping: "Dear me, why did not Stanton let him execute his mission? What would the Queen have said?" Charles Chaille-Long, *My Life on Four Continents* (New York: Hutchison, 1912), pp. 75–76.

4. Samuel Mossman, *General Gordon's Private Diary of His Exploits in China* (London: 1885), p. 186.

5. H. E. Wortham, *Gordon: An Intimate Portrait* (London: George Harrap, 1933), p. 88, from Li Hung-chang's *Memoirs*.

6. Ibid.

CHAPTER EIGHT

1. Bernard Meredith Allen, *Gordon in China* (London: Macmillan, 1933), pp. 100–01.

2. H. E. Wortham, *Gordon: An Intimate Portrait* (London: George Harrap, 1933), p. 91.

3. Allen, *Gordon in China*, p. 115.

4. A. Egmont Hake, *Events in the Taeping Rebellion* (London: W. H. Allen, 1891), pp. 298–99.

5. Samuel Mossman, *General Gordon's Private Diary of His Exploits in China* (London: 1885), p. 211.

6. Allen, *Gordon in China*, p. 124.

7. Charles George Gordon, "Notes of the Operations Round Shanghai in 1862, 63, 64," annotated by L. N. Russell, *L'Art de la guerre* (Paris: 1874), pp. 120–21.

8. Ibid., p. 121.

9. Charles Chaille-Long, *My Life on Four Continents* (New York: Hutchison, 1912).

10. Lt. Col. the Hon. Gerald French, *Gordon Pasha of the Sudan: The Life of an Ill-Requited Soldier* (Glasgow: William Maclellan, 1958), p. 31, from Field Marshal Viscount Garnet J. Wolseley, *The Story of a Soldier's Life*, 2 vols. (London: Archibald Constable, 1903).

11. Hake, *Events in the Taeping Rebellion*, pp. 298 fn., 299.

12. Gordon, "Notes on the Operations Round Shanghai," p. 122.

13. Franz Michael, with Chung-li Chang, *The Taiping Rebellion*, 3 vols. (Seattle: University of Washington Press, 1966), Vol. III, p. 1195.

14. Ibid., pp. 1196–97.

15. Chaille-Long, *My Life on Four Continents*, p. 74.

16. Some scholars of the Taiping Rebellion have interpreted Gordon's arms transactions with the Taipings as evidence that he was guilty of trying to make a personal profit. Such authorities, however, do an injustice to Gordon by not putting the incidents in the context of Gordon's efforts to remove the threat of Burgevine's potent mercenary force at Soochow. Gordon wisely and in good faith sought (1) redefection by Burgevine and (2) surrender of the rebel garrison at Soochow. Gordon's furnishing arms to the Taipings was partly by way of paying a ransom for Burgevine and partly by way of replacing the arms stolen by Morton. There is no evidence to suggest that Gordon sought to make money; in fact, he refused monetary rewards offered to him by the Emperor on more than one occasion. His disregard for money was to be characteristic of him during the rest of his career.

17. Public Record Office, London, F.O. 17, No. 395.

CHAPTER NINE

1. H. E. Wortham, *Gordon: An Intimate Portrait* (London: George Harrap, 1933), pp. 102–03.

2. Bernard Meredith Allen, *Gordon in China* (London: Macmillan, 1933), pp. 174–75.

3. A. Egmont Hake, *Events in the Taeping Rebellion* (London: W. H. Allen, 1891), p. 498.

4. Andrew Wilson, *The Ever-Victorious Army: A History of the Chinese Campaign Under Lt. Colonel C. G. Gordon, CBRE, and of the Suppression of the Taiping Rebellion* (London and Edinburgh: 1868), p. 203.

5. Wortham, p. 112.

6. Ibid., pp. 112–13.

7. Lord Godfrey Elton, *Gordon of Khartoum: The Life of Charles George Gordon* (New York: Knopf, 1955), p. 67.

CHAPTER TEN

1. Andrew Wilson, *The Ever-Victorious Army: A History of the Chinese Campaign Under Lt. Colonel C. G. Gordon, CBRE, and of the Suppression of the Taiping Rebellion* (London and Edinburgh: 1868), p. 216.

NOTES AND REFERENCES

2. Ibid., p. 219.

3. Bernard Meredith Allen, *Gordon in China* (London: Macmillan, 1933), p. 209.

4. Transliterated as "Changzhou" in the current National Geographic Society map of China.

5. Franz Michael, with Chung-li Chang, *The Taiping Rebellion*, 3 vols. (Seattle: University of Washington Press, 1966), Vol. III, p. 1466.

6. Wilson, *The Ever-Victorious Army*, p. 248.

7. Allen, *Gordon in China*, p. 71.

8. Wilson, *The Ever-Victorious Army*, p. 253.

9. That the sword was, in fact, one belonging to the Chung Wang, and had been given him by the Heavenly King, became a subject of controversy a century later. A British authority on China, C. A. Curwen, who had bought the sword from a descendant of the Duke of Cambridge and presented it to the People's Republic of China in 1962, accepts Gordon's account of the sword's origins. The Chinese scholar Professor Luo Ergang, however, has disputed it for a variety of reasons. See Liu Jianyi, "Whose Sword Did 'Chinese Gordon' Take?" *China Reconstructs*, Vol. XXXV, No. 7 (July 1986).

CHAPTER ELEVEN

1. Wilfrid Scawen Blunt, *Gordon at Khartoum* (London: Jonathan Swift, 1912), p. 94.

2. A. Egmont Hake, *The Story of Chinese Gordon* (London: Remington, 1884), p. 7.

3. "One Who Knew Him Well" (Octavia Freese), *More About Gordon* (London: Richard Bently & Sons, 1894), p. 18.

4. "Gordon from a Medical Point of View," *The Lancet*, June 21, 1884, p. 1136.

5. Freese.

6. Ibid., p. 3.

7. Ibid., p. 5.

8. Ibid., p. 6.

9. Ibid., p. 38.

10. Ibid., p. 44.

11. Lord Godfrey Elton, *Gordon of Khartoum: The Life of Charles George Gordon* (New York: Knopf, 1955), p. 98.

12. W. E. Lilley, *The Life and Work of General Gordon* (London: Abraham Kingdon, 1885), p. 35.

13. Ibid., p. 56.

14. Ibid., pp. 97–99.

15. Freese, p. 16.
16. Ibid., pp. 36–37.
17. Ibid., pp. 61–62.
18. Elton, *Gordon of Khartoum*, pp. 105–06.
19. Lilley, pp. 93–94.
20. Freese, p. 73.
21. Ibid., p. 77.

CHAPTER TWELVE

1. "One Who Knew Him Well" (Octavia Freese), *More About Gordon* (London: Richard Bently & Sons, 1894), pp. 83–84.
2. Charles Chenevix Trench, *The Road to Khartoum* (New York: Norton, 1978), p. 65.
3. Freese, p. 8.
4. Ibid., p. 94.
5. Ibid., pp. 89–90.
6. Ibid., p. 95.
7. Ibid., p. 110.
8. Isaiah 35:

> The wilderness and the dry land shall be glad,
>   the desert shall rejoice and blossom;
>   like the crocus, it shall blossom abundantly
> And rejoice with joy and singing.
>
> The glory of Lebanon shall be given to it,
>   the majesty of Carmel and Sharon.
> They shall see the glory of the Lord,
>   the Majesty of our God.
>
> Strengthen the weak hands
>   and make firm the feeble knees.
> Say to those who are of a fearful heart,
>   "Be strong, fear not!
>   Behold, your God
>   will come with vengeance,
>   with the recompense of God.
>   He will come and save you."
>
> Then the eyes of the blind
>   shall be opened,
>   and the ears of the deaf unstopped;

Then shall the lame man leap like a hart,
  and the tongue of the dumb sing for joy.
For waters shall break forth in the wilderness,
  and streams in the desert,
The burning sand shall become a pool,
  and the thirsty ground springs of water;
The haunt of jackals shall become a swamp,
  the grass shall become reeds and rushes.

And a highway shall be there,
  and it shall be called the Holy Way;
The unclean shall not pass over it,
  and fools shall not err therein.
No lion shall be there
  nor shall any ravenous beast come up on it;
They shall not be found there,
  but the redeemed shall walk there.
And the ransomed of the Lord shall return,
  and come to Zion with singing;
Everlasting joy shall be upon their heads;
They shall obtain joy and gladness,
  and sorrow and sighing shall flee away.

CHAPTER THIRTEEN

1. Worries about Egypt's water source began early. Travelers in the twelfth century spoke of a great Christian prince called Prester John, who ruled Abyssinia. He was alleged to control the source of the Nile, since its water gushed forth from a cavern in his realm. The Sultan of Cairo, it was said, had to pay tribute to Prester John lest the Abyssinian ruler shut off the flow. (Henry Yule in *The Times* of London, October 15, 1888.) The Sultan's fear of a Christian conspiracy to deprive him of Egypt's lifeblood was so strong that he forbade Christian travelers to go to India by way of the Red Sea, where they might conspire with Prester John. (Malcolm Letts, "Prester John, a 14th Century Manuscript," *Transactions of the Royal Historical Society*, 4th Series, XXIX, London: Royal Historical Society, 1947, pp. 19–20.) In 1704 the King of Abyssinia allegedly wrote to the ruler of Egypt: "The Nile would be sufficient to punish you, since God has put into our power His fountain, His outlet and His increase, and that we can dispose of it to do you harm!" (*The Times* [London], October 17, 1888.)

2. Florence Baker was made of very stern stuff, having shared with Sir Samuel, step by step, his African adventures. Baker had found Florence in the Balkan village of Widdin, where she was up for auction in a Turkish slave market. He was

462

immediately struck by her beauty and was attracted to her. Rather than see her sold as a slave, he placed the highest bid and won her himself.

3. Sir Samuel Baker, *The Albert N'yanza*, 2 vols. (London: Sidgwick & Jackson, 1962; originally published 1886), Vol. 1, pp. 79, 80.

4. G. Douin, *Histoire du Règne de Khédive Ismail*, 3 vols. (Cairo: 1936–41).

5. T. D. Murray and A. S. White, *Sir Samuel Baker: A Memoir* (London: 1895), pp. 150–53.

6. "Unpublished Letters of Charles George Gordon," *Sudan Notes and Records*, Vol. 10, 1927, p. 2.

CHAPTER FOURTEEN

1. Richard Gray, *A History of the Southern Sudan, 1839–1889* (London: Oxford University Press, 1961), p. 105. From a letter from Gordon to the Reverend Horace Waller.

2. M. Augusta Gordon, ed., *Letters of General C. G. Gordon to His Sister* (London: Macmillan, 1888), p. 91.

3. Sir Samuel Baker, *The Albert N'yanza*, 2 vols. (London: Sidgwick & Jackson, 1962; originally published 1886), Vol. II, p. 157.

4. M. Augusta Gordon, p. 110.

5. Ibid., p. 148.

6. Pierre Crabites, *Gordon, the Sudan and Slavery* (New York: Negro Universities Press, 1969; originally published, London: George Routledge, 1933), pp. 28–30. From Egyptian Archives, No. 8047.

7. "Unpublished Letters," *Sudan Notes and Records*, Vol. 10, 1927, pp. 1–16.

8. Charles Chaille-Long, *My Life on Four Continents* (New York: Hutchison, 1912), pp. 65, 66.

9. Ibid., p. 68. Of French lineage, Chaille-Long had sympathy for the French in Egypt and antipathy for the British. In his writings he suggested that Gordon was more concerned with promoting British policy than carrying out the Khedive's instructions. In his 1912 memoir *My Life on Four Continents* (pp. 67–68), Chaille-Long claimed that the Khedive had ordered him: "Go to Gondokoro, but lose no time in making your way to Uganda; anticipate the London expedition, make a treaty with the King of Uganda. . . ." But history shows that at the time referred to, it was known in London and Cairo that Livingstone was dead. No expedition, therefore, was being launched from London, nor was Stanley even in London. And the fact that an earlier book by Chaille-Long, *Central Africa* (1876), which described in detail his journey to the court of Buganda, made no mention of the Khedive's secret instructions casts further doubts on this claim. It is unlikely

463

that Chaille-Long had a meeting such as he described with the Khedive before he left with Gordon for the Sudan.

10. Bernard Meredith Allen, *Gordon and the Sudan* (London: Macmillan, 1931), p. 16.

11. Ibid., p. 16, from *The Australian Geographical Journal*, 1874, p. 380.

12. Chaille-Long, *My Life on Four Continents*, pp. 82–83.

13. Ibid., pp. 85–86.

14. George Birkbeck Hill, ed., *Colonel Gordon in Central Africa 1874–1879, from Original Letters and Documents* (New York: Kraus Reprint, 1969; originally published, London: 1881), p. 13.

CHAPTER FIFTEEN

1. Charles Chaille-Long, *My Life on Four Continents* (New York: Hutchison, 1912), pp. 87–88.

2. Ibid., p. 88.

3. Pierre Crabites, *Gordon, the Sudan and Slavery* (New York: Negro Universities Press, 1969; originally published, London: George Routledge, 1933), pp. 29–30. From Egyptian Archives, No. 8047.

4. Sir Samuel Baker, *The Albert N'yanza*, 2 vols. (London: Sidgwick & Jackson, 1962; originally published 1886), Vol. II, p. 516.

5. Chaille-Long, *My Life on Four Continents*, p. 122.

6. Lytton Strachey, *Eminent Victorians* (New York: Putnam, 1918).

7. Ibid., p. 226.

8. Bernard Meredith Allen, *Gordon and the Sudan* (London: Macmillan, 1931).

9. Charles Chaille-Long, *The Three Prophets* (New York: Appleton, 1884); *Central Africa* (London: 1876).

10. Ernest Marno, *Aegyptischen Reise in der Aequatorial Provinz und in Kordofan, 1874–1876* (Vienna: 1878), pp. 52–67.

11. Chaille-Long, *My Life on Four Continents*, pp. 408–409.

CHAPTER SIXTEEN

1. Frederick Burnaby, *A Ride to Khiva* (New York: Harper, 1877); *On Horseback through Asia Minor* (Gloucester, Eng.: Alan Sutton, 1985; originally published 1898).

2. Chaille-Long's expedition to Makraka from January 31 to March 14, 1875, resulted in establishing a small garrison there of 117 men, helpful in inhibiting slaving west of the Nile and establishing communication with the Niam-niam people.

3. Charles Chaille-Long, *My Life on Four Continents* (New York: Hutchison, 1912), p. 147.

4. Ibid.

5. See M. F. Shukry, ed., *Equatoria Under Egyptian Rule: The Unpublished Correspondence of Col. C. G. Gordon with Ismail, Khedive of Egypt and the Sudan, 1874–1876* (Cairo: Cairo University Press, 1953), for details of this subject.

6. *Bulletin de la Societe Khedivale de Geographie du Caire*, ii serie A, June 7, 1886. Egyptian Archives.

7. George Birkbeck Hill, ed., *Colonel Gordon in Central Africa 1874–1879, from Original Letters and Documents* (New York: Kraus Reprint, 1969; originally published 1881), p. 159.

CHAPTER SEVENTEEN

1. While Gordon did not seek an explorer's glory, it was important for practical reasons to find the course of the Victoria Nile. The naturalist Dr. Georg Schweinfurth, whom Gordon once described as "rough, crusty and unapproachable," had just submitted a paper in London stating: "It may be that Lake Albert belongs to the Nile Basin, but it is not a settled fact; for there are seventy miles between Foweira and Lake Albert never explored." Gordon later commented: "This statement could not be positively denied, inasmuch as no one had actually gone along the river from Foweira to Manungo. So I went along with it much suffering, and settled the question." George Birkbeck Hill, ed., *Colonel Gordon in Central Africa 1874–1879, from Original Letters and Documents* (New York: Kraus Reprint, 1969; originally published, London: 1881), p. 177.

2. On December 6, 1909, Chaille-Long was awarded the "Daly Gold Medal" by the American Geographical Society with the citation: "Awarded in MCMIX to Charles Chaille-Long in recognition of valuable additions to geographical knowledge made by him in Africa. In 1874 he explored the unknown Nile north of Urondogani, discovered Lake Ibrahim (Lake Kyoga), and supplied the final evidence to prove that the river issuing from Victoria is the Nile."

Actually, the "final evidence" had been provided by Gordon. In accepting his medal, Chaille-Long damned Gordon with faint praise: "He has been misunderstood and misrepresented by his own countrymen. I had myself misunderstood some of his methods, which seemed to me illogical. . . . I have never subscribed to the attribution to him of what Burton called excessive 'religiosity.' I believe on the contrary, that he was actuated by all the legitimate aspirations of a soldier; in a word, Gordon was more a soldier than a saint." Charles Chaille-Long, *My Life on Four Continents* (New York: Hutchison, 1912), p. 542.

3. Romolo Gessi, *Seven Years in the Sudan*, ed. by Felix Gessi (London: Sampson Low, Marston, 1892), p. 139.

NOTES AND REFERENCES

4. Edwin De Leon, *The Khedive's Egypt* (New York: 1887), pp. 290–93.

5. Chaille-Long was convinced that Gordon was all along working primarily for British interests, not Egyptian. In an absurd conspiracy theory, described by the American in his book *The Three Prophets* (New York: Appleton, 1884), p. iv, he put forward the thesis that Gordon, the Mahdi and the Egyptian xenophobic revolutionary Arabi Pasha were all "automatons" through which the British secretly conspired to annex Egypt and the Sudan.

CHAPTER EIGHTEEN

1. *The Times* (London), March 1, 1877.

2. Letter from Gordon to Olagnier in Foreign Minister Sharif Pasha's office, Cairo, dated April 15, 1877, and sent from Kassala. Brinton Collection.

3. George Birkbeck Hill, ed., *Colonel Gordon in Central Africa 1874–1879 from Original Letters and Documents* (New York: Kraus Reprint, 1969; originally published, London: 1881), p. 208.

4. Letter from Gordon to Olagnier, dated April 15, 1877, from Kassala. Brinton Collection.

5. The Gordon-Olagnier correspondence in French was made available to the author through the kindness of John Brinton, Esq., a many-year American resident of Cairo now living in London, and his daughter, Ms. Alice Brinton. These documents in the Brinton Collection, to the best of the Brintons' and the author's knowledge, have never been published or catalogued. The author has been unable to find other references to Olagnier in the various Gordon archives which he examined. What is mentioned about Olagnier was gleaned from the letters themselves.

6. Letter from Gordon to Olagnier, dated June 7, 1877, from Foggia. Brinton Collection.

7. W. H. Wilkins, *The Romance of Isabel, Lady Burton* (London: 1897), Vol. II, p. 645.

8. Letter from Gordon to Olagnier, dated February 9, 1847, from Suez. Brinton Collection.

9. Letter from Gordon to Olagnier, dated January 11, 1878, from Suakin. Brinton Collection.

CHAPTER NINETEEN

1. Earl of Cromer (Evelyn Baring), *Modern Egypt*, 2 vols. (London: Macmillan, 1908), Vol. I, p. 30.

NOTES AND REFERENCES

2. Ibid., p. 37.

3. Ibid., p. 44.

4. Sir Richard Burton, *First Footsteps in East Africa*, ed. by Gordon Waterfield (New York: Praeger, 1966; originally published 1856), p. 1.

5. *Exploratore*, No. 11, p. 27, as quoted in Romolo Gessi, *Seven Years in the Sudan*, ed. by Felix Gessi (London: Sampson Low, Marston, 1892), p. 177.

6. Slatin's older brother first found work as a private tutor in the household of Austrian Prince Kinsky. The boy was later accepted as a clerk in the imperial court, where he prospered and achieved brief notoriety in 1889 as investigator of the mysterious double suicide of Archduke Rudolf, heir to the Hapsburg throne, and his loved one, Baroness Marie Vetsera.

7. Gessi, pp. 183–84.

CHAPTER TWENTY

1. Romolo Gessi, *Seven Years in the Sudan*, ed. by Felix Gessi (London: Sampson Low, Marston, 1892), p. 121.

2. George Birkbeck Hill, ed., *Colonel Gordon in Central Africa 1874–1879, from Original Letters and Documents* (New York: Kraus Reprint, 1969; originally published, London: 1881), pp. xi, xii.

3. Ibid., p. 345.

4. *The Times* (London), March 23, 1881.

5. Letter to Watson from Gordon, dated April 23, 1879, from Morrow article in the *National Review*, February 1927.

6. In Lesley Branch, *The Wilder Shores of Love* (New York: Carroll & Graf, 1954), p. 4: reference is made to Gordon's use of Burton's phrase.

7. Rudolf C. Slatin, C.B., *Fire and Sword in the Sudan*, trans. by Maj. F. R. Wingate (London: Edward Arnold, 1896), p. 5.

8. Ibid., p. 6.

9. Gessi, p. 322.

10. Ibid.

11. Letter from Gordon to Gessi. British Library, A. 54495, 5450.

12. A. 57486 B. British Library.

CHAPTER TWENTY-ONE

1. Letter from Gordon to Gessi, December 25, 1879. British Library, Add. 57486. B.

2. Memorandum written by Gordon, referring to his letters written to the English, French and Italian Consuls General in Cairo, August 29, 1879. Brinton Collection.

3. Letter from Gordon to Olagnier, dated September 2, 1879, "en route from Massaw." Brinton Collection.

4. Letter from Gordon to Olagnier, entries for September 6 and 9, 1879, from Massawa. Brinton Collection.

5. Letter from Gordon to Gessi, December 25, 1879. British Library, Add. 57486 B.

6. Ibid.

7. George Birkbeck Hill, ed., *Colonel Gordon in Central Africa 1874–1879, from Original Letters and Documents* (New York: Kraus Reprint, 1969; originally published, London: 1881), pp. 415–16.

8. Ibid., p. 423.

9. Ibid., p. 427.

10. Letter from Gordon to Gessi, December 25, 1879.

11. A. Egmont Hake, *The Story of Chinese Gordon* (London: Remington, 1884), p. 367.

12. *The Times* (London), January 22, 1880.

CHAPTER TWENTY-TWO

1. Letter from Gordon to Olagnier, January 16, 1880, from "viz a viz Messina." Brinton Collection.

2. Ibid.

3. British Library, Add. 43921 f. 186.

4. Letter from Gordon to Olagnier, January 16, 1880. Ibid.

5. Letter from Gordon to Olagnier, February 5, 1880, from London. Brinton Collection.

6. Letter from Gordon to Olagnier, April 30, 1880, from the United Service Club, London. Brinton Collection.

7. "One Who Knew Him Well" (Octavia Freese), *More About Gordon* (London: Richard Bently & Sons, 1894), pp. 197–98.

8. Bernard Meredith Allen, *Gordon and the Sudan* (London: Macmillan, 1931), pp. 167–68.

9. Letter from Gordon to Gessi, February 22, 1880. British Library, Add. 57486 B.

10. A. Egmont Hake, *The Story of Chinese Gordon* (London: Remington, 1884), pp. 371–72.

11. Ibid.

12. Michael Edwardes, *History of India* (London: Thames & Hudson, 1961), p. 321.

13. Wilfrid Scawen Blunt, *Gordon at Khartoum* (London: Jonathan Swift, 1912), Appendix A, "Colonel Donnelly's Conversation with Gordon, 30 October, 1880," pp. 509–11.

14. Viscount Esher (Reginald Baliol Brett), *Today and Tomorrow* (London: Macmillan, 1910), p. 163.

15. Ibid.

16. Ibid., pp. 163–64.

17. Ibid., p. 164.

CHAPTER TWENTY-THREE

1. George Birkbeck Hill, ed., *Colonel Gordon in Central Africa 1874–1879, from Original Letters and Documents* (New York: Kraus Reprint, 1969; originally published, London: 1881).

2. Ibid., pp. xi, xii.

3. *Vanity Fair* (London), February 19, 1881, pp. 107–08.

4. According to his old friend Lilley from Gravesend, Gordon was so moved by the conditions of poverty in Ireland that he gave away all the money he had with him and had to borrow his fare home. W. E. Lilley, *The Life and Work of General Gordon* (London: Abraham Kingdon, 1885), p. 44.

5. Letter from Gordon to Sir Charles Elphinstone, dated "May 1881," from Mauritius. Copy of letter made available to the author by the Hon. Robert Gordon, former United States Ambassador to Mauritius. The original letter is in the Corps of Royal Engineers Headquarters Museum, Chatham, England.

6. Viscount Esher (Reginald Baliol Brett), *Today and Tomorrow* (London: Macmillan, 1910), pp. 167–68. It is interesting to view Gordon's remarks in the context of today's use of the British island of Diego Garcia, in the Chagos group.

7. Ibid., p. 170.

8. Ibid., p. 172. Also see Maj. Gen. G. Tylden, "General Gordon in South Africa," *Journal of the Society for Army Historical Research*, Vol. 20 (1941), pp. 106–07.

9. Esher, p. 178.

10. Col. C. G. Gordon, "Empire Defense, 1879–1882," *Journal of the Society for Army Historical Research*, Vol. XLII, No. 170 (June 1964).

11. Lord Godfrey Elton, *Gordon of Khartoum: The Life of Charles George Gordon* (New York: Knopf, 1955), p. 251.

12. William Hurstwick Spence, "Recollections of a Voyage with General Gordon," *Contemporary Review*, February 1890, lvii, pp. 272–81.

NOTES AND REFERENCES
CHAPTER TWENTY-FOUR

1. British Library, Add. 51302, "Gordon Miscellaneous."
2. *Graphic*, December 4, 1880.
3. Lt. Col. the Hon. Gerald French, *Gordon Pasha of the Sudan: The Life of an Ill-Requited Soldier* (Glasgow: William Maclellan, 1958), p. 197.
4. Correspondence between Maj. Gen. Gordon C.B. and Mr. Scanlan, Prime Minister of the Cape of Good Hope, on the Subject of the Colonial Forces and the Affairs of Basutoland Between May and September 1882. From V.C. Malherbe, *Eminent Victorians in South Africa* (Capetown: Jut, 1972), p. 67.
5. Malherbe, p. 76.
6. P. Lewsen Van Riebeeck Society, ed., *Selections from the Correspondence of J. X. Merriman, 1870–1890* (Capetown: 1960), Vol. I, p. 111.
7. Edwin W. Smith, *The Mabilles of Basutoland* (London: Hodder & Stoughton, 1939), p. 310.
8. Lord Godfrey Elton, *Gordon of Khartoum: The Life of Charles George Gordon* (New York: Knopf, 1955), p. 257.
9. Ibid.
10. Malherbe, p. 81.

CHAPTER TWENTY-FIVE

1. Letter from Gordon to his sister Augusta, January 4, 1883. British Library, Moffitt Collection, Add. 51297. Boston Public Library's Rare Books and Manuscripts Department, Letter #78 in Barnes correspondence.
2. Wilfrid Scawen Blunt, *Gordon at Khartoum* (London: Jonathan Swift, 1912), p. 138.
3. A. Egmont Hake, *The Story of Chinese Gordon* (London: Remington, 1884), p. 407.
4. Letter from Gordon to his sister Augusta, January 4, 1883.
5. George Macaulay Trevelyan, *Garibaldi and the Thousand* (London: Longmans Green, 1909), p. 122.
6. Christopher Andrew, *Her Majesty's Secret Service* (New York: Viking, 1986), pp. 4–5.
7. Laurence Oliphant, *Haifa* (London: Blackwood, 1887), pp. 347–48.
8. Charles George Gordon, *Reflections in Palestine, 1883* (London: Macmillan, 1884).
9. Romans 10:21, Isaiah 65:2.
10. Blunt, pp. 137–38.

11. Sir Mountstuart Duff, *Notes from a Diary, 1896–1901* (London), Vol. II, p. 75.

12. Elizabeth Surtees-Allnat, *Gordon: A Woman's Memories of Him and His Letters to Her from the Holy Land* (London: Remington, 1885), p. 71.

13. Sir Valentine Chirol, *Fifty Years in a Changing World* (London: Jonathan Cape, 1927), pp. 43–44.

14. Oliphant, *Haifa*, p. 350.

15. Ibid.

CHAPTER TWENTY-SIX

1. F. R. Wingate, *Mahdiism and the Egyptian Sudan*, 2nd ed. (London: Frank Cass, 1968; first ed. 1891). On p. 48 is the text of a proclamation issued by the Mahdi, adopting the name Ansar for his followers. It was taken from the Mahdi's manuscript book captured at the Battle of Toski in 1889, containing letters and decrees of the Mahdi and the Khalifa. The document is entitled "A proclamation to abolish the name of 'Dervish' and adopt the name 'Ansar.'" It reads in part as follows: "In the name of God, etc.—From Mohammed el Mahdi to all the brethren. All the faithful have already been cautioned not to call themselves 'dervishes,' but 'ansar.' That is to say, those whose hearts are entirely consecrated to God and whose souls have become enlightened by a desire to possess the joys of the world to come, quitting the pleasures of this life, and having full faith in the power of the Almighty who has created Paradise for those who are truly faithful to Him. The joys of Paradise are such as eye hath not seen, nor ear heard, nor hath it entered into the heart of man to conceive. A man who is in hope of gaining such a reward should certainly cease to be called a dervish, that is to say a poor man. But, on the contrary, he should be called an intelligent far-seeing man, a defender of God's cause, a follower of God's will, and abstainer from all things which would displease Him. Any man who calls such a man a dervish deserves to be beaten seven times and receive many stripes."

2. T. D. Murray and A. S. White, *Sir Samuel Baker: A Memoir* (London: 1895), p. 287.

3. Letter from Charles Gordon to Sir Samuel Baker, 1882. Royal Commonwealth Society Library, London, Library Notes Series #159, MS-42.

4. Father Joseph Ohrwalder, *Ten Years Captivity in the Mahdi's Camp, 1882–1892*, ed. and trans. by Maj. F. R. Wingate (London: Sampson Low, Marston, 1893), pp. 43–45.

5. Haim Shaked, *The Life of the Sudanese Mahdi* (New Brunswick, N.J.: Transaction Books, 1978), p. 103. From the "Book of the Bliss of Him Who Seeks Guidance by the Life of Imam the Mahdi," by Ismail ibn 'Abd al-Qadir.

6. Ohrwalder, p. 49.
7. Ibid., p. 60.

CHAPTER TWENTY-SEVEN

1. Roger Jones, *The Rescue of Emin Pasha* (New York: St. Martin's, 1972), p. 22.

2. Lord Godfrey Elton, *Gordon of Khartoum: The Life of Charles George Gordon* (New York: Knopf, 1955), p. 269.

3. Earl of Cromer (Evelyn Baring), *Modern Egypt*, 2 vols. (London: Macmillan, 1908), Vol. I, pp. 364–65. Baring wrote: "On August 18, he [Sir Edward Malet] telegraphed to General Hicks: 'I am debarred by my instructions from giving advice with regard to action . . . the policy of Her Majesty's Government being to abstain as much as possible from interference with the action of the Egyptian government in the Sudan.'"

4. Father Joseph Ohrwalder, *Ten Years Captivity in the Mahdi's Camp, 1882–1892*, ed. and trans. by Maj. F. R. Wingate (London: Sampson Low, Marston, 1893), p. 100, quoting Major Herlith's diary.

5. Cromer, Vol. 1, p. 428.

6. Sir Charles Dilke had served as Under Secretary of Foreign Affairs early in the Gladstone government.

7. Stephen Gwynn and Gertrude M. Tuckwell, *The Life of the Rt. Hon. Sir Charles W. Dilke*, 2 vols. (New York: Macmillan, 1917), Vol. 1, p. 555.

8. Cromer, Vol. 1, pp. 376–78.

9. Ibid., p. 382.

10. *Pall Mall Gazette*, January 9, 1884.

11. Ibid.

12. Elton, *Gordon of Khartoum*, p. 280.

13. H. E. Wortham, *Gordon: An Intimate Portrait* (London: George Harrap, 1933), pp. 274–75.

14. Christopher Hibbert, ed., *Queen Victoria in Her Letters and Journals* (New York: Viking, 1985), p. 286.

15. Cromer, Vol. 1, p. 424.

16. British Government *Blue Book*, quoted in Bernard Meredith Allen, *Gordon and the Sudan* (London: Macmillan, 1931), p. 201 fn.

17. John Morley, *The Life of William Ewart Gladstone* (London: Macmillan, 1903), Vol. III, p. 149.

18. Ibid., p. 390.

19. Cromer, Vol. 1, p. 425.

20. Ibid., p. 426.

21. Ibid., p. 247.
22. Elton, *Gordon of Khartoum*, p. 281.
23. Wilfrid Scawen Blunt, *Gordon at Khartoum* (London: Jonathan Swift, 1912), pp. 173, 174.
24. Gwynn and Tuckwell, p. 29.
25. Cromer, p. 429 fn.
26. Hibbert, ed., p. 284.

CHAPTER TWENTY-EIGHT

1. British Public Record Office, F.O. 78, No. 3638.
2. Colonel Stewart's Journal, Papers of H. W. Gordon. British Library, Add. 52408.
3. Stephen Gwynn and Gertrude M. Tuckwell, *The Life of the Rt. Hon. Sir Charles W. Dilke*, 2 vols. (New York: Macmillan, 1917), Vol. II, p. 30.
4. British Public Record Office, *The Letters of Queen Victoria*, Second Series, Vol. III, p. 474.
5. Earl of Cromer (Evelyn Baring), *Modern Egypt*, 2 vols. (London: Macmillan, 1908), Vol. I, p. 408.
6. Ibid., p. 428.
7. Ibid., pp. 436–37.
8. Ibid., p. 444.
9. Ibid.
10. Ibid., p. 445.
11. Ibid., pp. 447–48.
12. Ibid., 448.
13. Ibid.
14. Sir Ronald Wingate, *Wingate of the Sudan* (London: John Murray, 1955), p. 48.

CHAPTER TWENTY-NINE

1. Colonel Stewart's Journal, Papers of H. W. Gordon. British Library, Add. 52408.
2. Sir Ronald Wingate, *Wingate of the Sudan* (London: John Murray, 1955), p. 47.
3. Ibid.
4. Colonel Stewart's Journal, entry dated January 31, 1884.

NOTES AND REFERENCES

5. Earl of Cromer (Evelyn Baring), *Modern Egypt*, 2 vols. (London: Macmillan, 1908), Vol. I, p. 400.

6. Ibid.

7. Ibid., p. 401.

8. Ibid., p. 404.

9. Ibid., pp. 405–06.

10. Ibid., p. 406.

11. Ibid.

12. Bernard Meredith Allen, *Gordon and the Sudan* (London: Macmillan, 1931), pp. 264–65.

13. Pierre Crabites, *Gordon, the Sudan and Slavery* (New York: Negro Universities Press, 1969; originally published London: George Routledge, 1933), p. 208.

14. Ibid., pp. 208–09.

15. *The Times* (London), February 12, 1884.

16. Cromer, Vol., I, p. 469.

17. Rudolf C. Slatin, C. B., *Fire and Sword in the Sudan*, trans. by Maj. F. R. Wingate (London: Edward Arnold, 1896), p. 298.

18. Ibid., p. 298.

19. Father Joseph Ohrwalder, *Ten Years Captivity in the Mahdi's Camp, 1882–1892*, ed. and trans. by Maj. F. R. Wingate (London: Sampson Low, Marston, 1893), p. 137.

20. Cromer, Vol. I, p. 474.

21. Ibid., p. 475.

22. Colonel Stewart's Journal, Papers of H. W. Gordon. British Library, Add. 52408.

23. Cromer, Vol. I, p. 403.

24. Ibid., p. 475.

25. Ibid.

26. Ohrwalder, p. 138.

27. Allen, *Gordon and the Sudan*, p. 271.

28. Gordon's biographer Bernard Meredith Allen (*Gordon and the Sudan*, p. 257) describes the general's meeting en route to Khartoum in Luxor with Professor A. H. Sayce, in which he said that he expected to be supported by troops if his single-handed peaceful efforts to evacuate the Egyptians from the Sudan failed. (Based on A. H. Sayce's memoir, *Reminiscences*, pp. 229, 230.) Then again in Berber, where Gordon talked to the Italian agent of the Khartoum government, Giuseppe Cuzzi, the general "gave him clearly to understand that he regarded himself as backed up in the last resort by the military power of England." (Based on Cuzzi's *Funfzehn Jahre Gefangener des Falschen Propheten*, p. 72.)

CHAPTER THIRTY

1. Earl of Cromer (Evelyn Baring), *Modern Egypt*, 2 vols. (London: Macmillan, 1908), Vol. I, p. 481.
2. Ibid., p. 482.
3. Ibid., p. 484.
4. British Public Record Office, F.O. 78, No. 3744.
5. Cromer, Vol. I, p. 486.
6. Stephen Gwynn and Gertrude M. Tuckwell, *The Life of the Rt. Hon. Sir Charles W. Dilke*, 2 vols. (New York: Macmillan, 1917), Vol. II, p. 38.
7. Colonel Stewart's Journal, Papers of H. W. Gordon. British Library, Add. 52408.
8. Gwynn and Tuckwell, Vol. II, p. 40.
9. Ibid.
10. Ibid., p. 41.
11. Cromer, Vol. I, p. 496.
12. Ibid., p. 497.
13. Ibid., p. 516.
14. Ibid., p. 493.
15. Ibid.
16. Ibid., p. 523.
17. Ibid., p. 624.
18. Sir Henry W. Gordon, *Events in the Life of Charles Gordon 1886–1887* (London: Kegan Paul), p. 342.
19. Father Joseph Ohrwalder, *Ten Years Captivity in the Mahdi's Camp, 1882–1892*, ed. and trans. by Maj. F. R. Wingate (London: Sampson Low, Marston, 1893), p. 98.
20. Bernard Meredith Allen, *Gordon and the Sudan* (London: Macmillan, 1931), p. 317.
21. Cromer, Vol. I, pp. 544, 545.
22. British Public Record Office, *The Letters of Queen Victoria*, Second Series, Vol. III, p. 485.
23. John Morley, *The Life of William Ewart Gladstone* (London: Macmillan, 1903), Vol. II, p. 402.

CHAPTER THIRTY-ONE

1. J. L. Garvin, *Life of Joseph Chamberlain*, 3 vols. (London: 1932–34), Vol. I., p. 512.

2. Earl of Cromer (Evelyn Baring), *Modern Egypt*, 2 vols. (London: Macmillan, 1908), Vol. I, p. 552.

3. Bernard Meredith Allen, *Gordon and the Sudan* (London: Macmillan, 1931), p. 331.

4. *The Times* (London), April 17, 1884.

5. Ibid., March 23, 1884.

6. Allen, *Gordon and the Sudan*, p. 333.

7. Lord Edmond G. Fitzmaurice, *Life of Granville George Leveson*, 2 vols. (London: Longmans, 1905), Vol. II, p. 386.

8. Stephen Gwynn and Gertrude M. Tuckwell, *The Life of the Rt. Hon. Sir Charles W. Dilke*, 2 vols. (New York: Macmillan, 1917), Vol. II, p. 48.

9. Wilfrid Scawen Blunt, *Gordon at Khartoum* (London: Jonathan Swift, 1912), pp. 225, 244 and Annex p. 535.

10. Sir Colin Scott Moncrieff, "The Nile," lecture at the Royal Institute, January 25, 1895. According to Moncrieff, Chief of Egypt's Irrigation Department, the Commander of British Military Forces in Egypt had asked him about the possibility that "dervishes" might divert the Nile. Moncrieff did not think so, but believed that "more civilized persons" were capable of building regulating sluices across the outlet of Victoria N'yanza (Ripon Falls). Sir Samuel Baker, in *The Times* (London) of October 17, 1898, stated that Atbara River, 230 miles upstream from its mouth, could be deflected to the Red Sea by native labor within four to five months provided they worked during the dry-bed period.

11. Allen, *Gordon and the Sudan*, p. 338.

12. Ibid.

13. Cromer, Vol. I, p. 563.

14. This unpublished "spy" message was kindly made available to the author by Mr. Archibald Roosevelt, former U.S. diplomat, from his private papers. It is believed to be a copy of the original, dated June 22, 1884, now in the Institution of Royal Engineers, Chatham.

15. Sir George Arthur, *Life of Lord Kitchener*, 3 vols. (New York: Macmillan, 1920), Vol. I, p. 103.

CHAPTER THIRTY-TWO

1. Earl of Cromer (Evelyn Baring), *Modern Egypt*, 2 vols. (London: Macmillan, 1908), Vol. I, p. 508.

2. Stephen Gwynn and Gertrude M. Tuckwell, *The Life of the Rt. Hon. Sir Charles W. Dilke,*, 2 vols. (New York: Macmillan, 1917), Vol. II, p. 61.

3. B. H. Holland, *The Life of Spencer Compton, 8th Duke of Devonshire*, 2 vols. (London: Longmans, 1911), Vol. I, p. 423.

4. Cromer, Vol. I, pp. 581–82.
5. Public Record Office Papers, F.O. 78, No. 3677.
6. *Canada Today*, Vol. 17, No. 3 (1986), p. 6.
7. Count Gleichen, *With the Camel Corps up the Nile* (London: Chapman & Hall, 1889).
8. Tissot's 1870 portrait of Burnaby now hangs in the British Portrait Gallery.
9. Rudolf C. Slatin, C.B., *Fire and Sword in the Sudan*, trans. by Maj. F. R. Wingate (London: Edward Arnold, 1896), p. 283.
10. Ibid., p. 305.
11. Ibid., p. 309.
12. Ibid., p. 318.
13. Ibid., p. 317.

CHAPTER THIRTY-THREE

1. Quotations from Gordon's journals are taken from A. Egmont Hake's compilation, published in the United States under the title *The Journals of Major-General C. G. Gordon, C.B., at Khartoum* (Boston: Houghton Mifflin, 1885).
2. Earl of Cromer (Evelyn Baring), *Modern Egypt*, 2 vols. (London: Macmillan, 1908), Vol. I, p. 431.
3. B. H. Holland, *The Life of Spencer Compton, 8th Duke of Devonshire*, 2 vols. (London: Longmans, 1911), Vol. I, p. 423. Lord Hartington's full name and title is Spencer Compton Cavendish, Marquess of Hartington.
4. Hake, *The Journals*, pp. 105–06.
5. Rudolf C. Slatin, C. B., *Fire and Sword in the Sudan*, trans. by Maj. F. R. Wingate (London: Edward Arnold, 1896), p. 317.

CHAPTER THIRTY-FOUR

1. A. Egmont Hake, *The Journals of Major-General C. G. Gordon, C.B., at Khartoum* (Boston: Houghton Mifflin, 1885), pp. 528–29.
2. Ibid.
3. Quotations from Gordon are from his journal, edited and annotated by Hake.
4. Father Joseph Ohrwalder, *Ten Years Captivity in the Mahdi's Camp, 1882–1892*, ed. and trans. by Maj. F. R. Wingate (London: Sampson Low, Marston, 1893), pp. 145–46.

5. Rudolf C. Slatin, C.B., *Fire and Sword in the Sudan*, trans. by Maj. F. R. Wingate (London: Edward Arnold, 1896), p. 334.

6. Ibid.

CHAPTER THIRTY-FIVE

1. Papers of H. W. Gordon. British Library, Add. 52208, item 58.

2. All quotations from Gordon's journals are from A. Egmont Hake, ed., *The Journals of Major-General C. G. Gordon, C.B., at Khartoum* (Boston: Houghton Mifflin, 1885).

3. For all his criticism, Gordon thought well of Kitchener. In his dark days at Khartoum, Gordon put in his journal a quote from a letter written by his old friend Samuel Baker, which struck a responsive chord in him: "The man whom I have always placed my hopes upon, Major Kitchener, R.E., who is one of the few *very superior* British officers with a cool and good head and a hard constitution combined with untiring energy, had now pushed up to Dongola."

CHAPTER THIRTY-SIX

1. Adrian Preston, ed., *In Relief of Gordon: Lord Wolseley's Campaign Journal of the Khartoum Relief Expedition, 1884–1885* (London: Hutchinson, 1967), p. 67.

2. Ibid., p. 112.

3. Peter Johnson, *Gordon of Khartoum* (Wellingborough: Patrick Stephens, 1985), p. 92.

4. Ibid., p. 94.

5. Christopher Andrew, *Her Majesty's Secret Service* (New York: Viking, 1986), p. 21.

6. Preston, p. 134.

7. Bernard Meredith Allen, *Gordon and the Sudan* (London: Macmillan, 1931), p. 414.

8. Ibid., p. 415.

9. *London Times, Fifty Years, 1882–1930* (London: Thornton Butterworth, 1932).

10. Sir Charles W. Wilson, *From Korti to Khartoum*, 4th ed. (London: Blackwood & Sons, 1886), pp. 298–99. The notice referred to was found by the British on the battlefield of Abu Klea.

11. Capt. Willoughby Verner, *Sketches in the Sudan* (London: R. H. Porter, 1885), no pagination.

12. Wilson, *From Korti to Khartoum*, p. 27.

13. Ibid.
14. Verner.
15. Preston, p. 122.
16. Verner.
17. *Nineteenth Century*, January 1886 edition.
18. Winston Churchill, *The River War* (London: Eyre & Spottiswoode, 1951; originally published 1889), p. 63.
19. Preston, pp. 122, 123.
20. Wilson, *From Korti to Khartoum*, p. 35.
21. Verner.

CHAPTER THIRTY-SEVEN

1. Anthony Nutting, *Gordon, Martyr and Misfit* (London: Constable, 1966), pp. 304–05.
2. Sir Charles W. Wilson, *From Korti to Khartoum*, 4th ed. (London: Blackwood & Sons, 1886), p. 109.
3. Diary of Captain Marling of the 60th Rifles, serving in the Mounted Infantry, quoted in Michael Barthorp, *War on the Nile* (Poole, Dorset: Blandford Press, 1984), p. 108.
4. Wilson, *From Korti to Khartoum*, p. 114.

CHAPTER THIRTY-EIGHT

1. Rudolf C. Slatin, C.B., *Fire and Sword in the Sudan*, trans. by Maj. F. R. Wingate (London: Edward Arnold, 1896), p. 339.
2. Ibid.
3. Father Joseph Ohrwalder, *Ten Years Captivity in the Mahdi's Camp, 1882–1892* (London: Sampson Low, Marston, 1893), p. 153.
4. There were more like 15,000 to 20,000 inhabitants in Khartoum (plus the garrison soldiers), since many people had left for the Mahdi's lines by that time.
5. Ohrwalder, p. 154.
6. Slatin, pp. 339–40.
7. Ibid., p. 340.
8. Ibid.
9. Sir Charles W. Wilson, *From Korti to Khartoum*, 4th ed. (London: Blackwood & Sons, 1886), pp. 129–30.
10. Ibid., p. 170.

11. Ohrwalder, p. 166.
12. Wilson, *From Korti to Khartoum*, p. 174.

EPILOGUE

1. Viscount Esher (Reginald Baliol Brett), *Today and Tomorrow* (London: Macmillan, 1910), p. 181.

2. On August 18, 1885, Kitchener completed a *Report on the Fall of Khartoum*, which was accepted as the official military account of Khartoum's seizure by the Mahdi and the death of General Gordon. It was reprinted for public consumption as Appendix 47 of H. E. Colville's *History of the Sudan Campaign*, 2 parts (London: Intelligence Department, War Office, 1899, 1900), the official record of Wolseley's campaign on the Nile and Graham's campaign in the Suakin area.

3. Sir George Arthur, *Life of Kitchener*, 3 vols. (New York: Macmillan, 1920), Vol. I, pp. 122–23.

4. Rudolf C. Slatin, C.B., *Fire and Sword in the Sudan*, trans. by Maj. F. R. Wingate (London: Edward Arnold, 1896), p. 343; Father Joseph Ohrwalder, *Ten Years Captivity in the Mahdi's Camp, 1882–1892*, ed. and trans. by Maj. F. R. Wingate (London: Sampson Low, Marston, 1893), p. 157; Earl of Cromer (Evelyn Baring), *Modern Egypt*, 2 vols. (London: Macmillan, 1908), Vol. II, p. 13; Bernard Meredith Allen, *Gordon and the Sudan* (London: Macmillan, 1931), p. 432.

5. F. Reginald Wingate, who became principal intelligence officer after Kitchener left the Sudan and ultimately rose to become Governor General of the Sudan, did extensive research on the death of Gordon and the fall of Khartoum. He acquired Bordeini's story from the town notable's journal and included the results of his research in his book *Mahdiism and the Egyptian Sudan* (London: Macmillan, 1891), pp. 163, 193–94. Wingate also acquired Medawi's story when he interrogated the Emir after he was forced to flee Khartoum following the Mahdi's death.

6. Now in the Leeds (England) Art Gallery, the painting is sometimes known as *General Gordon's Last Stand*.

7. In Medawi's version of Gordon's death, it is Sheikh Mohammed Nebawi; in Bordeini's version it is a Taha Hahin. See Cromer, Vol. II, p. 13 fn.

8. Another alleged eyewitness, a Syrian merchant named Ghalli, claimed that Gordon's last remark just before he was killed was: "You have entered the town at last just as the English are coming [but] you have outwitted them." This is probably a fanciful embellishment, which perhaps reflects Ghalli's somewhat pro-Mahdi sentiments. The remark does not sound like Gordon. For accounts of the death of Gordon and the fall of Khartoum the following sources are important: War Office 32/130/7700/2812, Correspondence No. 1884, Cairo, 22 June 1885, from General Wolseley to the Secretary of State of War.

NOTES AND REFERENCES

Sudan Notes and Records, Vol. 13, Part 1, p. 75.

Allen, *Gordon and the Sudan,* pp. 430–32.

Borelli Bey, *La Chute de Khartoum* (Paris, 1893), p. 95.

H. E. Colville, *History of the Sudan Campaign,* Appendix 47. Statement by Khalil Agha Orphali. University of Durham, Sudan Archive.

Ohrwalder, *Ten Years Captivity in the Mahdi's Camp, 1882–1892,* p. 157.

Slatin, *Fire and Sword in the Sudan,* p. 343.

Wingate, *Mahdiism and the Egyptian Sudan,* pp. 163, 193–94.

Statement by Khalil Agha Orphali.

9. University of Durham (England), Sudan Archive, Slatin Papers. Statement by Khalil Agha Ahmad (Orphali), typescript, 3 pp. (439/637/2).

10. Anonymous author, *The White Pasha,* 1889. This preposterous piece, taking advantage of the public obsession with the Gordon story, argued: "In the absence of any accurate or authentic evidence of his death, there is at least a strong presumption that General Gordon may have been miraculously saved by God, or escaped in the confusion of the fall of Khartoum." See Judith Prendergast, "G. W. Joy's 'The Death of Gordon': The Real Story," *Leeds Art Calendar,* No. 97, 1985.

11. Ohrwalder, p. 159.

12. Ibid.

13. Ibid., p. 169.

14. Sir Charles W. Wilson, *From Korti to Khartoum,* 4th ed. (London: Blackwood & Sons, 1886), p. 286. "Farag Pasha withdrew the soldiers from the gate near the White Nile and allowed the rebels to enter." Testimony of the servant of Ibrahim Rusht Bey, who had been Gordon's secretary in Khartoum.

15. Ohrwalder, p. 162.

16. Ibid.

17. Cromer, Vol. II, p. 15.

18. Ibid.

19. Ibid., p. 10.

20. Ibid., p. 8.

21. Arthur, Vol. I, p. 112 fn.

22. Winston Churchill, *The River War* (London: Eyre & Spottiswoode, 1951; originally published 1899), pp. 64, 67.

23. Slatin, p. 341.

24. Ohrwalder, p. 167.

25. Cromer, Vol. II, p. 17.

26. Philip Magnus, *Kitchener: Portrait of an Imperialist* (London: John Murray, 1958), p. 66.

27. Christopher Hibbert, ed., *Queen Victoria in Her Letters and Journals* (New York: Viking, 1985), p. 289.

28. Ibid.

BIBLIOGRAPHY

PUBLISHED MATERIAL CONTAINING
GORDON'S WRITINGS AND CORRESPONDENCE

Boulger, Demetrius C. *General Gordon's Letters from the Crimea, the Danube and Armenia.* London: Chapman and Hall, 1884.

Gordon, Charles George. *Memorandum on the Treaties of San Stephano and Berlin.* London: Edward Stanford, 1880. (Privately printed.)

———. "Notes on the Operations Round Shanghai in 1862, 63, 64." Annotated by L. N. Russell. *L'Art de la guerre.* Paris: 1874.

———. *Reflections in Palestine, 1883.* London: Macmillan, 1884. (This book is based in large measure on letters Gordon wrote to his friend the Reverend R. H. Barnes, who prepared it for publication.)

Gordon, M. Augusta, ed. *Letters of General C. G. Gordon to His Sister.* London: Macmillan, 1888.

Hake, A. Egmont. *Events in the Taeping Rebellion.* London: W. H. Allen, 1891.

———. *The Journals of Major-General C. G. Gordon, C.B., at Khartoum.* Boston: Houghton Mifflin, 1885; London: Kegan Paul & Trench, 1885.

———. *Private Diary of the Taiping Rebellion of C. G. Gordon.* London: Kegan Paul, 1890.

Hill, George Birkbeck. *Colonel Gordon in Central Africa 1874–1879, from Original Letters and Documents.* 4th ed. London: Thomas de La Rue, 1885. Facsimile reprint, New York: Kraus Reprint, 1969.

Mossman, Samuel. *General Gordon's Private Diary of His Exploits in China.* London: Low, 1885. (Mossman accompanied Gordon on many of his China campaigns against the Taiping rebels, reporting for the *China Herald.*)

Shukry, M. F., ed., introduction and notes, *Equatoria Under Egyptian Rule: The Unpublished Correspondence of Col. C. G. Gordon with Ismail, Khedive of Egypt and the Sudan, 1874–1876.* Cairo: Cairo University Press, 1953.

"Unpublished Letters of Charles George Gordon." *Sudan Notes and Records,* Vol. 10, 1927, pp. 1–59.

BIBLIOGRAPHY
UNPUBLISHED COLLECTIONS OF GORDON'S LETTERS AND JOURNALS

The voluminous collections of Gordon's letters in the British Library's Department of Manuscripts bear testimony to Gordon's prolific correspondence. Other archives in London and elsewhere in the United Kingdom, particularly those of the Royal Geographical Society, the Royal Commonwealth Society Library, the Royal Engineers Museum, Oxford University's Rhodes House Library, the Gordon Boys' School in Woking, Surrey, and the University of Durham's Oriental Section contain still more correspondence and other material relevant to Gordon. In the United States, the Boston Public Library's Rare Books and Manuscripts Department has a good collection of Gordon's correspondence with several of his good friends. Some private collections are noted in the British National Registry of Archives, but there must certainly be other personal holdings not registered.

I have drawn mainly on the following unpublished collections:

Boston Public Library: Rare Books and Manuscripts, Ms. ENG. 411, 450, Gordon correspondence with R. H. Barnes, Maj. Gen. J. F. D. Donnelly, Maj. Newsome, Col. Francis Howell Jenkins, Mrs. Dykes.

Brinton (John) Collection: A small, unregistered collection of letters written by Gordon to a correspondent within Egyptian Foreign Minister Sharif (Cherif) Pasha's office in Cairo during the years 1877–80, while Gordon was Governor General of the Sudan.

British Library (London): Department of Manuscripts.

Gordon Boys' School, Woking, Surrey: Collection. C. G. Gordon, *Gordon's Travels*, unpublished childhood journal, dated May 3, 1847.

Institute of Royal Engineers, Chatham: No. 150, Copy of Letter from Gordon in Mauritius to Col. Sir Howard C. Elphinstone, May 1881.

Royal Commonwealth Society Library.

GENERAL

Abd al-Qadir, Ismail ibn. *Kitab Sa'adat al-Mustahdi Bi-Sirat al-Imam al-Mahdi.* See: Shaked, Haim, *The Life of the Sudanese Mahdi.*

Allen, Bernard Meredith. *Gordon.* London: Duckworth, Great Lives Series, 1935.

———. *Gordon and the Sudan.* London: Macmillan, 1931.

———. *Gordon in China.* London: Macmillan, 1933.

Andrew, Christopher. *Her Majesty's Secret Service.* New York: Viking, 1986.

Arthur, Sir George. *The Letters of Lord and Lady Wolseley.* London: 1922.

———. *Life of Lord Kitchener.* 3 vols. New York: Macmillan, 1920.

BIBLIOGRAPHY

August, Thomas G. *The Selling of the Empire: British and French Imperialist Propaganda, 1890–1940*. Westport, Conn.: Greenwood Press, 1985.

Baddour, Abd el-Fattah. *Sudanese-Egyptian Relations*. The Hague: Martinus Nijhoff, 1960.

Baker, Sir Samuel. *The Albert N'yanza*. 2 vols. London: Sidgwick & Jackson, 1962. (Originally published 1886.)

Baring, Evelyn. See: Cromer, Earl of.

Barnes, Reginald Henry, and Brown, C. E. *Charles George Gordon: A Sketch*. London: Macmillan, 1885.

Barr, Pat. *Foreign Devils*. Harmondsworth: Penguin Books, 1970.

Barthorp, Michael. *War on the Nile*. Poole, Dorset: Blandford Press, 1984.

Beattie, John. *Understanding an African Kingdom: Bunyoro*. New York: Holt, Rinehart & Winston, 1965.

Berman, Richard A. *The Mahdi of Allah*. New York: Macmillan, 1932.

Besant, Annie. *Gordon: Judged out of His Own Mouth*. London: Theosophical Society, Free Thought Publishing Co., 1885.

Blunt, Wilfrid Scawen. *Gordon at Khartoum*. London: Jonathan Swift, 1912.

——. *Secret History of the English Occupation of Egypt*. New York: Alfred A. Knopf, 1922.

Boulger, Demetrius C. *General Gordon's Letters from the Crimea, the Danube and Armenia*. London: Chapman & Hall, 1884.

Bowle, John. *The Imperial Achievement*. Boston: Little, Brown, 1974.

Brook-Shepherd, Gordon. *Between Two Flags: The Life of Baron Sir Rudolf Von Slatin Pasha*. New York: Putnam, 1973.

Buchan, John. *Gordon at Khartoum*. London: Peter Davies, 1934.

Bulloch, John Malcolm. *Bibliography of the Gordons*. Aberdeen: Aberdeen University Press, 1924.

Burnaby, Frederick. *On Horseback through Asia Minor*. Gloucester (Eng.): Alan Sutton, 1985. (Originally published 1898.)

——. *A Ride to Khiva*. New York: Harper, 1877.

Burton, Sir Richard. *First Footsteps in East Africa*. Ed. by Gordon Waterfield. New York: Praeger, 1966. (Originally published 1856.)

——. *Personal Narrative of a Pilgrimage to Al-Madinah and Mecca*. 2 vols. New York: Dover, 1964.

Butler, Col. Sir William F. *The Campaign of the Cataracts, Being a Personal Narrative of the Great Nile Expedition of 1884–85*. London: Sampson, Low, Marston, Searle & Rivington, 1887.

——. *Life of Charles George Gordon*. New York: Macmillan, 1891.

Cameron, Nigel. *Barbarians and Mandarins*. New York: Walker-Weatherhill, 1970.

Carthage, Elliott Paul. *The Role of Frederick Townsend Ward in the Suppression of*

BIBLIOGRAPHY

the Taiping Rebellion. Ph.D. thesis, St. John's University, 1976. Ann Arbor: University Microfilm International.

Chaille-Long, Charles. *Central Africa.* London: 1876.

——. *My Life on Four Continents.* New York: Hutchison, 1912.

——. *The Three Prophets.* New York: Appleton, 1884.

Cheng, James C. *Chinese Sources for the Taiping Rebellion, 1850–1864.* Oxford: Oxford University Press for Hong Kong University Press, 1963.

Chirol, Sir Valentine. *Fifty Years in a Changing World.* London: Jonathan Cape, 1927.

Churchill, Lt. Col. Seton. *General Gordon: A Christian Hero.* London: James Nisbet, 1885.

Churchill, Winston. *The River War.* London: Eyre & Spottiswoode, 1951. (Originally published 1899.)

Cohen, Paul A. *Discovering History in China.* New York: Columbia University Press, 1984.

Colborne, Col. J. *With Hicks in the Soudan.* London: 1884.

Collins, Robert O. *The Southern Sudan 1883–1898.* New Haven: Yale University Press, 1962.

Colville, H. E. *History of the Sudan Campaign.* 2 parts. London: Intelligence Department, War Office, 1899, 1900.

Compton, Piers. *The Last Days of General Gordon.* London: Robert Hale, 1974.

Crabites, Pierre. *Gordon, the Sudan and Slavery.* New York: Negro Universities Press, 1969. (Originally published, London: George Routledge, 1933.)

Cromer, Earl of [Evelyn Baring]. *Modern Egypt.* 2 vols. London: Macmillan, 1908.

Curwen, C. A. *Taiping Rebel: The Deposition of Li Hsiu-Cheng.* Cambridge: Cambridge University Press, 1977.

Daly, M. W., compiler. *Bibliographical Series,* Vol. 40. Oxford: Clio Press, 1983.

Davis, David Brion. *Slavery and Human Progress.* New York: Oxford University Press, 1984.

De Leon, Edwin. *The Khedive's Egypt.* New York: 1887.

Douin, G. *Histoire du Règne de Khédive Ismail.* 3 vols. Cairo: 1936–41.

——. *Histoire du Soudan Egyptien.* Vol. I, *La Présentation 1820–1822.* Cairo: 1944.

Edwards, Amelia B. *A Thousand Miles up the Nile.* Los Angeles: Tarcher/ Houghton Mifflin, 1983. (Originally published 1891.)

Edwards, David L. *Christian England, from the 18th Century to the 1st World War.* Vol. 3. Grand Rapids, Mich.: William B. Erdmans, 1984.

El Nasri, Abdel Rahman. *A Bibliography of the Sudan, 1938–1958.* London: Oxford University Press for the University of Khartoum, 1962.

Elton, Lord Godfrey. *General Gordon's Khartoum Journal.* London: William Kimber, 1961.

BIBLIOGRAPHY

——. *Gordon of Khartoum: The Life of Charles George Gordon*, New York: Knopf, 1955.

English, G. B. *A Narrative of the Expedition to Dongola and Sennar*. London: Jack Murray, 1822.

Esher, Viscount [Reginald Baliol Brett]. *Today and Tomorrow*. London: Macmillan, 1910.

Fabuni, L. A. *The Sudan in Anglo-Egyptian Relations: A Case Study in Power Politics 1800–1956*. London: Longmans, 1960.

Fairbank, John King. *The Great Chinese Revolution 1800–1985*. New York: Harper & Row, 1986.

——. *The United States and China*, 4th ed. Cambridge, Mass.: Harvard University Press, 1981. (Originally published 1948.)

Farwell, Byron. *Eminent Victorian Soldiers, Seekers of Glory*. New York: Norton, 1985.

——. *The Great Anglo-Boer War*. New York: Harper & Row, 1976.

——. *Prisoners of the Mahdi*. New York: Harper & Row, 1967.

——. *Queen Victoria's Little Wars*. New York: Harper & Row, 1972.

Fitzmaurice, Lord Edmond G. *Life of Granville George Leveson*. 2 vols. London: Longmans, 1905.

Frazer, Peter. *Lord Esher: A Political Biography*. London, 1973.

Freese, Octavia. See "One Who Knew Him Well."

French, Lt. Col. the Hon. Gerald. *Gordon Pasha of the Sudan: The Life of an Ill-Requited Soldier*. Glasgow: William Maclellan, 1958.

General Gordon's Mission to the Sudan, 1885: A Summary of Events Prepared for the Cabinet. British Library, Miscellaneous Public Documents III, Victoria, 1885.

Gessi, Romolo. *Seven Years in the Sudan*. Ed. by Felix Gessi. London: Sampson Low, Marston, 1892.

Giegler, Carl C. *The Sudan Memoirs of Carl Christian Geigler Pasha, 1873–1883*. Ed. by Richard Hill. London: 1884.

Gleichen, Count. *With the Camel Corps up the Nile*. London: Chapman & Hall, 1889.

Gordon, Charles George. "Empire Defense, 1879–1882." Gordon memorandum to the Royal Commission on Colonial Defense. *Journal of the Society for Army Historical Research*, Vol. XLII, No. 170 (June 1964).

——. *Equatoria Under Egyptian Rule*. See: Shukry, M. F., ed.

——. *The Journals of Major-General C. G. Gordon, C.B., at Khartoum*. See: Hake, A. Egmont.

——. *Memorandum on the Treaties of San Stephano and Berlin*. London: Edward Stanford, 1880. Privately printed.

——. "Notes on the Operations Round Shanghai in 1862, 63, 64." Annotated by L. N. Russell. *L'Art de la guerre*. Paris: 1874.

BIBLIOGRAPHY

——. *Reflections in Palestine, 1883*. London: Macmillan, 1884.

——. "Unpublished Letters of Charles George Gordon." *Sudan Notes and Records*, Vol. 10 (1927), pp. 1–59.

Gordon, Sir Henry W. *Events in the Life of Charles Gordon*. London: Kegan Paul.

Gordon, M. Augusta, ed. *Letters of General C. G. Gordon to His Sister*. London: Macmillan, 1888.

Graham, Gen. Sir Gerald. *Last Words with Gordon*. London: Chapman & Hall, 1887. (From *The Fortnightly Review*, January 1887.)

Gray, Richard. *A History of the Southern Sudan, 1839–1889*. London: Oxford University Press, 1961.

Gray, Willy Todd. *The Agitation in Parliament and England Over Charles George "Chinese" Gordon and His Mission to the Soudan, January 1884 to February 1885*. Doctoral thesis, State University of Iowa, 1962. Ann Arbor: University Microfilm International, 1965.

Gregory, J. S. *Great Britain and the Taipings*. London: Routledge & Kegan Paul, 1969.

Gwynn, Stephen, and Tuckwell, Gertrude M. *The Life of the Rt. Hon. Sir Charles W. Dilke*. 2 vols. New York: Macmillan, 1917.

Hake, A. Egmont. *Events in the Taeping Rebellion*. London: W. H. Allen, 1891.

——. *The Journals of Major-General C. G. Gordon, C.B., at Khartoum*. Boston: Houghton Mifflin, 1885; London: Kegan Paul & Trench, 1885.

——. *The Story of Chinese Gordon*. London: Remington, 1884.

Halloway, Laura C., compiler. *Chinese Gordon, The Uncrowned King*, New York: Funk & Wagnalls, 1885.

Hallowell, J. H. *Did the Gladstone Government Abandon General Gordon?* London: 1885.

Hanson, Lawrence and Elizabeth. *Chinese Gordon: The Story of a Hero*. New York: Funk & Wagnalls, 1954.

Harris, John. *The Gallant Six Hundred*. New York: Mason & Lipscomb, 1973.

Hesseltine, William B., and Wolf, Hazel. *The Blue and the Gray on the Nile*. New York: 1961.

Hibbert, Christopher. *Africa Explored: Europeans in the Dark Continent, 1769–1889*. New York: Norton, 1982.

——, ed. *Queen Victoria in Her Letters and Journals*. New York: Viking, 1985.

Hill, George Birkbeck, ed. *Colonel Gordon in Central Africa 1874–1879, from Original Letters and Documents*. New York: Kraus Reprint, 1969. (Originally published London: 1881.) Fourth edition published 1885.

Hill, Richard Leslie. *A Bibliography of the Anglo-Egyptian Sudan from the Earliest Time to 1937*. London: Oxford University Press, 1939.

——. "The Gordon Literature." *University of Durham Journal*, Vol. 47, No. 3 (June 1955), pp. 97–101.

BIBLIOGRAPHY

Holland, B. H. *The Life of Spencer Compton, 8th Duke of Devonshire.* 2 vols. London: Longmans, 1911.

Holt, P. M. "The Archives of the Mahdi." *Sudan Notes and Records*, Vol. 36, No. 1 (1955), pp. 71–80.

———. *The History of the Sudan from the Coming of Islam to the Present Day.* London: Weidenfeld & Nicolson, 1980.

———. *The Mahdist State in the Sudan, 1881–1898.* Oxford: Oxford Clarendon Press, 1958.

———. *A Modern History of the Sudan.* London: Weidenfeld & Nicolson, 1961.

———. "The Source Materials of Sudanese Mahdia." *St. Anthony's Papers: Middle Eastern Affairs.* No. 1, London, 1958.

Jackson, H. C. *Black Ivory: The Story of El-Zubeir Pasha, Slaver and Sultan, as Told by Himself.* New York: Negro Universities Press, 1972.

———. *Osman Digna.* London: 1926.

———. *Sudan Days and Ways.* London: Macmillan, 1954.

James, Lawrence. *The Savage Wars: British Campaigns in Africa 1870–1920.* New York: St. Martin's, 1985.

Johnson, Peter. *Gordon of Khartoum.* Wellingborough: Patrick Stephens, 1985.

Jones, Roger. *The Rescue of Emin Pasha.* New York: St. Martin's, 1972.

Kapteijins, Lidwien. *Mahdist Faith and Sudan Tradition: The History of the Masalit Sultanate 1870–1930.* London: KPI, 1985.

Kinross, Lord. *The Ottoman Centuries.* New York: Morrow Quill Paperbacks, 1977.

Lane-Poole, Stanley. *Life of Sir Harry Parkes.* 2 vols. London.

Lilley, W. E. *The Life and Work of General Gordon.* London: Abraham Kingdon, 1885.

Macaulley, James. *Gordon Anecdotes.* London: Religious Tract Society, 1888.

Magnus, Philip. *Kitchener: Portrait of an Imperalist.* John Murray, 1985.

Malherbe, V. C. *Eminent Victorians in South Africa.* Capetown: Jut, 1972.

Manning, Olivia. *The Remarkable Expedition.* New York: Atheneum, 1985. (Originally published by Doubleday, 1947.)

Marlowe, John. *Mission to Khartoum: The Apotheosis of General Gordon.* London: Gollancz, 1969.

Marno, Ernest. *Aegyptischen Reise in der Aequatorial Provinz und in Kordofan, 1874–1876.* Vienna: 1878.

Martin, George. *Verdi: His Life and Times.* London: 1965.

Mathews, Noel, and Wainwright, M. Doreen, compilers, and J. D. Pearson, ed. *A Guide to Manuscripts and Documents in the British Isles Relating to the Middle East and North Africa.* Oxford: Oxford University Press, 1980.

McAleavy, Henry. *The Modern History of China.* New York: Praeger, 1967.

Meadows, Thomas. *The Chinese and Their Rebellions.* London: 1847.

BIBLIOGRAPHY

Michael, Franz, with Chung-li Chang. *The Taiping Rebellion.* 3 vols. Seattle: University of Washington Press, 1966.

Moorehead, Alan. *The Blue Nile.* New York: Harper & Row, 1962.

———. *The White Nile.* New York: Harper & Row, 1960.

Moorhouse, Geoffrey. *India Britannica.* New York: Harper & Row, 1983.

Morley, John. *The Life of William Ewart Gladstone.* London: Macmillan, 1903.

Morris, Donald R. *The Washing of the Spears.* New York: Simon & Schuster, 1965.

Morris, James. *Heaven's Command: An Imperial Progress.* New York: Harcourt Brace Jovanovich, 1973.

Morse, H. G. *In the Days of the Taipings.* Salem: Essex Institute, 1927.

Mossman, Samuel. *General Gordon's Private Diary of His Exploits in China.* London: 1885.

Murray, T. D., and White, A. S. *Sir Samuel Baker: A Memoir.* London: 1895.

Neufeld, Charles. *A Prisoner of the Khalifa.* New York: Putnam, 1899.

Newark, Peter. "More Than a Soldier." *Military History*, Vol. 3, No. 4 (February 1987).

Nutting, Anthony. *Gordon, Martyr and Misfit.* London: Constable, 1966.

Ohrwalder, Father Joseph. *Ten Years Captivity in the Mahdi's Camp, 1882–1892.* Ed. and trans. by Maj. F. R. Wingate. London: Sampson Low, Marston, 1893.

Oliphant, Laurence. *Haifa.* London: Blackwood, 1887.

———. *Narrative of the Earl of Elgin's Mission to China and Japan in the Years 1857, 58, 59.* London: 1858.

"One Who Knew Him Well" [Octavia Freese]. *More About Gordon.* London: Richard Bently & Sons, 1894.

Parliamentary Debates, 3rd Series, Vols. 284–294, 1884–1885.

Parliamentary Papers, Egypt, No. 11, 1883, C-3670, "Report on the Soudan" by Lt. Col. Donald Stewart.

Petherick, John. *Egypt, the Sudan and Central Africa.* Edinburgh: 1861.

Power, Frank. *Letters from Khartoum Written During the Siege.* London: Sampson, Low, 1885.

Prendergast, Judith. "G. W. Joy's 'The Death of Gordon.' The Real Story." *Leeds Art Calendar*, No. 97 (1985).

Preston, Adrian, ed. *In Relief of Gordon: Lord Wolseley's Campaign Journal of the Khartoum Relief Expedition, 1884–1885.* London: Hutchinson, 1967.

Rich, Norman. *Why the Crimean War?: A Cautionary Tale.* Hanover: University Press of New England for Brown University, 1985.

Richardson, Frank M. *Mars Without Venus.* Edinburgh: William Blackwood, 1981.

Santi, Paul, and Hill, Richard. *The Europeans in the Sudan 1834–1878: Some Manuscripts Mostly Unpublished, Written by Traders, Christian Missionaries, Officials and Others.* Oxford: Oxford Clarendon Press, 1980.

BIBLIOGRAPHY

Schell, Orville, and Shurman, Franz. *Imperial China*. New York: Vintage, 1967.

Seaman, L. C. B. *Victorian England*. London: Methuen, 1973.

Severin, Timothy. *The Oriental Adventure*. Boston: Little, Brown, 1976.

Shaked, Haim. *The Life of the Sudanese Mahdi*. New Brunswick, N.J.: Transaction Books, 1978.

Shibeika, Mekki. *The Independent Sudan*. New York: Robert Speller & Sons, 1959.

Shukry, M. F., ed., intro., notes. *Equatoria Under Egyptian Rule: The Unpublished Correspondence of Col. C. G. Gordon with Ismail, Khedive of Egypt and the Sudan, 1874–1876*. Cairo: Cairo University Press, 1953.

Slatin, Rudolf C., C.B. *Fire and Sword in the Sudan*. Trans. by Maj. F. R. Wingate. London: Edward Arnold, 1896.

Smith, Edwin W. *The Mabilles of Basutoland*. London: Hodder & Stoughton, 1939.

Sparrow, Gerald. *General Gordon, Mandarin and Pasha*. London: Jarrolds, 1962.

Speke, John Hanning. *Journal of the Discovery of the Nile*. New York: Greenwood Press, 1969. (Originally published 1863.)

Spence, William Hurstwick. "Recollections of a Voyage with General Gordon." *Contemporary Review*, Vol. LVII, February 1890.

Stanley, Henry M. *The Autobiography of Sir Henry Morton Stanley*. ed. by Dorothy Stanley. New York: Houghton Mifflin, 1909.

———. *In Darkest Africa*. 2 vols. London: Sampson Low, Marston, Searle & Rivington, 1890.

Stewart, Lt. Col. Donald. "Report on the Soudan." *Parliamentary Papers*, Egypt, No. 11, 1883, C-3670.

"Story of a Mahdist Emir." *Sudan Notes and Records*, Vol. 9 No. 2 (December 1926).

Strachey, Lytton. *Eminent Victorians*. New York: Putnam, 1918.

———. *Queen Victoria*. London: Chatto & Windus, 1921.

Surtees-Allnat, Elizabeth. *Gordon: A Woman's Memories of Him and His Letters to Her from the Holy Land*. London: Remington, 1885.

Symons, Julian. *England's Pride: The Story of the Gordon Relief Expedition*. London: White Lion Publishers, 1974. (First published by Hamish Hamilton, 1965.)

Tanes, Richard. *General Gordon, 1883–1885: An Illustrated Life of Charles Gordon*. London: 1970.

Theobald, A. B. *The Madiya: A History of the Anglo-Egyptian Sudan, 1881–1899*. London: Longmans, 1951.

Tibble, Anne. *With Gordon in the Sudan*. London: Frederick Muller, 1960.

Tingsten, Herb. *Victoria and the Victorians*, London: Allen & Unwin, 1972.

Trench, Charles Chevenix. *An Eminent Victorian Reassessed*. London: Allen Lane, 1978.

BIBLIOGRAPHY

——. *The Road to Khartoum*. New York: Norton, 1978.

Verner, Captain Willoughby. *Sketches in the Soudan*. London: R. H. Porter, 1885.

Wakeman, Frederick. *The Fall of Imperial China*. New York: Free Press, 1975.

Waley, Arthur. *The Opium War Through Chinese Eyes*. Stanford: Stanford University Press, 1985.

Warner, Philip. *Dervish: The Rise and Fall of an African Empire*. New York: Taplinger, 1975.

——. *Kitchener: The Man Behind the Legend*. New York: Atheneum, 1986.

Watson, C. M. "The Campaign of Gordon's Steamers." From *Royal Engineers Journal*, October 1, 1888. *Sudan Notes and Records*, Vol. 12, No. 2 (1929), pp. 119–41.

Watson, Sir Charles M. *The Life of Major General Sir Charles William Wilson*. London: 1909.

Wilson, Andrew. *The Ever-Victorious Army: A History of the Chinese Campaign Under Lt. Colonel C. G. Gordon, CBRE, and of the Suppression of the Taiping Rebellion*. London and Edinburgh: 1868.

Wilson, Sir Charles W. *From Korti to Khartoum*. 4th ed. London: Blackwood & Sons, 1886.

Wingate, F. R. *Mahdiism and the Egyptian Sudan*, 2nd ed. London: Frank Cass, 1968. (Original edition, London: Macmillan, 1891.)

Wingate, Major General Sir F. R. *Ten Years' Captivity in the Mahdi's Camp, 1882–1889*. Fron the Original Manuscripts of Father Joseph Ohrwalder, London: Sampson Low, Marston. 14th ed., 1893. Abbreviated version published under the title *Mahdiism and the Egyptian Sudan*. London: Macmillan, 1891.

Wingate, Sir Ronald. *Wingate of the Sudan*. London: John Murray, 1955.

Wolseley, Lt. Col. Garnet J. *Narrative of the War with China in 1860*. London: Longman Green, Longman & Roberts, 1862.

Wolseley, Field Marshal Viscount Garnet J. *The Story of a Soldier's Life*. 2 vols. London: Archibald Constable, 1903.

Woodcock, George. *The British in the Far East*. New York: Atheneum, 1969.

Woodham-Smith, Cecil. *The Reason Why*. New York: McGraw-Hill, 1953.

Wortham, H. E. *Gordon: An Intimate Portrait*. London: George Harrap, 1933.

Ziegler, Philip. *Omdurman*. New York: Knopf, 1973.

INDEX

INDEX

INDEX

INDEX

INDEX

INDEX

Mahdi (*cont.*)
  as Imam, 304
  jihad declared by, 306
  Khartoum taken by, 436–40
  Khartoum threatened by. *See* Khartoum
  letters exchanged with Gordon, 343–44,
    367–68, 370, 391–92, 394, 406,
    409–10, 431–32
  rise to power of, 289, 296, 306
Makade. *See* Fola Falls
Makraka country, 177
Malet, Edward, 244–45, 256, 319, 325,
  396
Malet, Lucas, xxii
Malta, 270
Manchester Evening Mail, 331n
Mao Tse-tung, 111
Marno, Ernest, 169, 177, 224, 268
Marvin, Charles, 255
Marx, Karl, 5
Masindi, 184, 192
Masindi, Battle of, 150, 183
Massawa, 198, 199, 239, 240, 243, 244
Masupha, Chief, 275, 276, 280, 281,
  283–84, 285
Matebele tribe, 282
Mattiucchi, Mr., 239, 240
Maund, E. A., 282
Mauritius, 267–73
Maximilian, Emperor, 190
M'Cheyne, Reverend Robert, 26
Meadows, Thomas, 63
Medawi, Sheikh, 442
Mediterranean Sea, 270
Mek, Saleh Wad el-, 368
"Memorandum on Colonial Defenses," 271
*Memorandum on the Treaties of San Stefano
  and Berlin* (Gordon), 220–21
Menges, Joseph, 155
Menskikov, General, 31
Merowe Province, 211, 398
Merriman, John, 278, 279–80
Merv, the Queen of the World (Marvin), 255
Messedaglia, Mr., 224
Metemmeh, 241, 368, 388, 399, 408, 409,
  418, 419, 420, 422, 423, 427, 428, 449
  Wilson's decision not to attack, 433–34
Methodists, xxv, 6
Michael, Walid el-, 199, 201, 212–13, 222,
  238, 240
  son Mefti, 240
Michel, Sir John, 61, 66
Mill, John Stuart, 6
Miller, Canon, 128
Minneh, Fikki, 312
Mitzilia (Greek Consul), 242
Modern Egypt (Baring), xxi–xxii, 217, 335,
  444
Modibbo, Commander, 320
Moffitt, Dr., 80, 120
Mogren Fort, 407, 412
Mohammed, Prophet, 173, 301, 302, 304,
  306

Mohammed Ahmad ibn Abdullah. *See*
  Mahdi
Mohammed Ali, Khedive, 6, 144, 148
Moh Wang. *See* T'an Shao-kuang
Mombas Bay, 179, 183
Monasir tribe, 406
Moncrief, Captain, 344–45
Montauban, Commissioner, 47
Montenegro, 219
More About Gordon (Freese), 124, 127
Moriah, Mount, 290
Morley, John, 375
Morton, Officer, 92, 93
Mossman, Samuel, 81
Mount Ararat, 38, 39, 290
Mount Moriah, 290
Mousa, Sheikh Mohammed, 333
Mrooli, 171, 183, 184, 189, 192, 222
Mshweshwe, Chief, 275
Munzinger, Werner, 198
Murchison Falls, 184, 188
Mus, Khasm el-, 428, 430
Musa, Sheikh, 425
Mutesa, King, 161, 163, 164, 167, 169,
  170–71, 176, 178–79, 183
  Egyptian troops held hostage by, 188,
    189, 191
  expedition to village of, 177, 178
  Gordon's negotiations with, 189–92, 193
  letters to Gordon, 186, 191, 192
  See also Buganda
My Life in Four Continents (Chaille-Long),
  159, 160, 168, 169

Naas, Lord, 68, 104
Nafiseh (Shaigiya), 373
Nanking, China, 50, 66, 69, 75, 105, 107
  fall of, to Imperial forces, 110, 111
Napier, Sir Robert, 125–27, 198, 242
Napoleon Bonaparte, 1, 2
Napoleon III, 2, 36, 136
Natal, 275
Nebawi, Sheikh Mohammed, 442
Negrelli, Luigi, 144
Neretti, Mr., 242
Nettleton, Captain, 283
Newman, Cardinal, 123
Nicholas I, Czar, 2, 24, 26, 36, 146
Nightingale, Florence, 29, 30, 34, 254,
  257, 267
Nigmet el-Mahdi, 313
Nile River, 5, 6, 138, 146, 152, 171, 272,
  377
  Baker expedition to conquer Upper,
    146–50, 151, 152, 157, 161, 165,
    174–75, 183
  as British rescue mission's route, 387,
    388, 389, 390, 407, 420, 427, 434, 435
  dangers of, 180–82, 188–89, 192,
    193–94
  defense of Khartoum and, 373–74
  determining navigability of, 179, 188

500

INDEX

501

INDEX

INDEX